Editorial material and organization © 2005 by Blackwell Publishing Ltd

BLACKWELL PUBLISHING
350 Main Street, Malden, MA 02148-5020, USA
108 Cowley Road, Oxford OX4 1JF, UK
550 Swanston Street, Carlton, Victoria 3053, Australia

First published 2005 by Blackwell Publishing Ltd

*Library of Congress Cataloging-in-Publication Data*

Sixteenth-century poetry : an annotated anthology / edited by Gordon Braden.
p. cm. — (Blackwell annotated anthologies)
Includes bibliographical references and index.
ISBN 1-4051-0115-6 (hardback : alk. paper) — ISBN 1-4051-0116-4 (pbk. : alk. paper)
English poetry — Early modern, 1500–1700.   2. England — Civilization — 16th century
— Sources.   I. Braden, Gordon, 1947–   II. Series.

PR1205.S589 2005
821′.308—dc22
2004008924

A catalogue record for this title is available from the British Library.

For further information on
Blackwell Publishing, visit our website:
www.blackwellpublishing.com

# Sixteenth-Century

*An Annotated Antho*

*Edited by*

## Gordon Braden

The

All
or t
othe

1

**Blackwell**
Publishing

*To the memory of Richard S. Sylvester*

# Contents

# Selected Contents by Theme

For the sake of simplicity, individual poems are listed here only once, under a single category; most of them could easily appear under several.

# Alphabetical List of Authors

# Chronology of Poems and Historical Events

The right-hand section below gives a chronology for the works included in this anthology. Unless otherwise specified, the date is that of the first appearance in print, which is sometimes much later than the date of composition. In most cases, the dating of poetry that did not move quickly to print is possible only within quite vague boundaries: for example, Wyatt's lyrics would have been written mostly in the 1520s and 1530s, Donne's from the mid-1590s on into the first decade of the next century. When more specific information or informed guesses are available, they are given here. Not every poem is this collection is covered by this list; some were not printed until the the nineteenth, or even the twentieth, century.

| *Historical and Cultural Events* | *Poems* |
|---|---|
| 1500 Epidemic in London, possibly the plague. | |
| 1502 Columbus begins his fourth and last voyage to the New World. | |
| 1503 Construction finished on Canterbury Cathedral. | |
| | 1505 Skelton, *Philip Sparrow* composed (?) |
| 1509 Henry VIII becomes king of England, marries Catherine of Aragon. | 1509 Skelton, "Addition" to *Philip Sparrow* composed |
| 1510 St. Paul's School, London, founded. | |
| 1512 College of Physicians founded. | |
| 1513 Henry campaigns with the Emperor Maximilian I against France; wins the battle of the Spurs. Battle of Flodden Field between England and Scotland, the latter allied with France; defeat and death of King James IV of Scotland, husband to Henry's sister Margaret. Their 18-month-old son becomes King James V. | |
| 1514 Peace with France and Scotland. | |
| 1515 Thomas Wolsey, favorite to Henry, becomes Cardinal and Lord Chancellor; Francis I becomes king of France. | |
| 1516 Birth of Mary, daughter to Henry and Catherine of Aragon. | |
| 1517 Martin Luther nails his ninety-five theses to a church door in Germany and initiates the Protestant Reformation. | |
| 1519 King Charles I of Spain, cousin to Catherine of Aragon, elected Emperor Charles V. | |
| 1520 Meeting between Henry and Francis I on the Field of the Cloth of Gold near Calais. | |
| 1521 Execution for treason of the Duke of Buckingham, grandfather to the Earl of Surrey. Henry writes *Assertion of the Seven Sacraments*, an attack on Luther, and receives the title "Defender of the Faith" from the Pope. War begins between Francis I and Charles V. | |
| | 1523 Skelton, *The Garland of Laurel* (with a passage from *Philip Sparrow*) |
| 1524 Extensive peasant revolt begins in Germany, under the leadership of Thomas Münzer. | |

| *Historical and Cultural Events* | *Poems* |
|---|---|
| 1525 Francis I taken prisoner after the battle of Pavia. German peasant revolt ends; execution of Münzer. | |
| 1526 Francis released after consenting to the Treaty of Madrid, but resumes hostilities against Charles. Publication in Germany of William Tyndale's translation of the New Testament. | |
| 1527 Henry, in love with Anne Boleyn, begins efforts to divorce his first wife. Rome sacked by imperial troops. | 1527 Skelton, *Against a Comely Custron* (?), *Divers Ballads and Ditties Solacious* (?) |
| 1529 After Wolsey's failure to obtain a papal nullification of his marriage to Catherine, Henry removes him as Lord Chancellor and appoints Thomas More. Peace of Cambrai between Francis I and Charles V. | |
| 1532 Submission of the Clergy acknowledges Henry's power over ecclesiastical legislation in England. More resigns as Lord Chancellor. | 1532 Wyatt, "Sometime I fled the fire that me brent" composed |
| 1533 Henry marries Anne Boleyn in secret; his marriage to Catherine is declared void by Thomas Cranmer, the new Archbishop of Canterbury; Henry is excommunicated by Pope Clement VII. Birth of Elizabeth, daughter of Henry and Anne Boleyn. | |
| 1534 Act of Supremacy makes the English monarch "protector and only supreme head of the church and clergy of England." Anabaptist kingdom proclaimed in Münster, under the leadership of Jan van Leiden; city besieged by episcopal forces. | |
| 1535 Execution of More. Publication of Miles Coverdale's Bible, the first complete translation into English. Storming of Münster and slaughter of Anabaptists. | 1535 More, *Louis, the Lost Lover* and *Davy, the Dicer* composed |
| 1536 Beginning of the dissolution of the monasteries in England and the transfer of their resources to the Crown. Fall and execution of Anne Boleyn; Elizabeth declared illegitimate by Parliament; Henry marries Jane Seymour. Thomas Cromwell becomes Lord Privy Seal and Henry's chief minister. In the north of England, Robert Aske leads a Catholic rebellion known as the Pilgrimage of Grace; believing himself to have won concessions from the Crown, Aske helps to dissolve the movement. Tyndale executed as a heretic by Charles V. | 1536 Wyatt, "Who list his wealth and ease retain" and "Mine own John Poins, since ye delight to know" composed (?) |
| 1537 Execution of Aske; birth of Edward, son to Henry and Jane Seymour, followed quickly by his mother's death. | 1537 Surrey, "When Windsor walls sustained my wearied arm" and "So cruel prison, how could betide, alas" composed |
| 1539 Statute of the Six Articles, authored by Stephen Gardiner, Bishop of Winchester, defining heresy in terms very close to those of Roman Catholicism. The Great Bible, | 1539 Wyatt, "Tagus, farewell, that westward with thy streams" composed |

| *Historical and Cultural Events* | *Poems* |
|---|---|
| based on Coverdale's translation, authorized for use in English churches. | |
| 1540 Henry marries and soon divorces Anne of Cleves; fall and execution of Thomas Cromwell, who had arranged the marriage. Henry marries Catherine Howard, cousin to Anne Boleyn and the Earl of Surrey. | 1540 Wyatt, "The pillar perished is whereto I leant" composed |
| 1541 Ireland proclaimed a kingdom. | 1541 Surrey, "From Tuscan came my lady's worthy race" composed<br>Wyatt, "Lucks, my fair falcon, and your fellows all" and "Sighs are my food, drink are my tears" composed (?) |
| 1542 English victory over Scotland at the battle of Solway Moss; death of King James V. His 6-day-old daughter Mary becomes queen of Scotland. Execution of Catherine Howard. | 1542 Surrey, "Divers thy death do diversely bemoan" composed |
| 1543 Henry marries Catherine Parr. | 1543 Surrey, "London, hast thou accusèd me" composed |
| 1545 Lending of money at interest legalized. First session of the Council of Trent, beginning the Catholic Counter-Reformation. | 1545 Surrey, "Wyatt resteth here, that quick could never rest" (?)<br>Skelton, *Philip Sparrow* |
| 1546 Execution of Askew. Ivan IV crowned as the first Tsar of Russia. | 1546 Askew, *Ballad* |
| 1547 Execution of Surrey; death of Henry, succeeded by his 10-year-old son, who becomes Edward VI, with the Duke of Somerset as Lord Protector. Repeal of the Six Articles; Gardiner imprisoned. Death of Francis I; Henry II becomes king of France. | |
| 1548 Mary Queen of Scots sent to France to be raised. | |
| | 1549 Wyatt, *Certain Psalms* |
| 1550 Fall of Somerset, replaced by the Duke of Northumberland. | |
| 1551 War resumes between France and Charles V. | |
| 1552 Execution of Somerset. Legalization of lending at interest revoked. | |
| 1553 Publication of the Forty-Two Articles of Religion, the basis for a more Protestant Anglican church. Death of Edward. Northumberland proclaims his daughter-in-law Jane Grey queen; both are soon arrested and Mary I becomes queen. Mary retains her Catholic allegiances, and makes Gardiner Lord Chancellor. Execution of Northumberland; brief imprisonment of Elizabeth. A rebellion headed by Sir Thomas Wyatt, son of the poet, is suppressed and Wyatt executed. Commercial relations established with Russia. | |
| 1554 Execution of Jane Grey; marriage of Mary to Prince Philip of Spain, son of the Emperor Charles V. Royal supremacy over the Church revoked. | |

## Historical and Cultural Events

1555   Act of Reconciliation re-establishes Catholicism in England. Extensive persecution of English Protestants begins; as many as 300 eventually executed. Muscovy Company chartered.

1556   Execution of Cranmer; Reginald Pole becomes Archbishop of Canterbury. Abdication of Charles V; Mary's husband becomes King Philip II of Spain.

1557   War with France, in alliance with Spain; France defeated at the battle of St. Quentin. Stationers' Company chartered.

1558   Loss of Calais, England's last remaining possession in France. Death of Mary and Pole; Elizabeth I becomes queen. Mary Queen of Scots marries the French dauphin.

1559   Acts of Uniformity and Supremacy revoke papal authority in England; Matthew Parker becomes Archbishop of Canterbury. A one-shilling fine is legislated for failure to attend Sunday services. Elizabeth declines a marriage proposal from Philip II. Shane O'Neill's rebellion in Ireland begins. Treaty of Cateau-Cambrésis ends the war between France and Spain. Henry II dies from wounds received in a tournament during the subsequent festivities; the dauphin becomes King Francis II, and his wife assumes the title Queen of England and Scotland.

1560   Treaty of Edinburgh secures the withdrawal of French troops from Scotland; Presbyterianism established in Scotland. Publication of Geneva Bible in Switzerland, with a dedication to Elizabeth. Death of Francis II; his brother becomes King Charles IX at the age of 10.

1561   The widowed Mary returns to Scotland, and comes into conflict with the Calvinists under John Knox. Merchant Taylors' School founded in London.

1562   Civil war begins in France; Elizabeth sends an occupation force to Le Havre in support of the Huguenots. Shane O'Neill comes to England and officially submits to Elizabeth, but on his return to Ireland continues his rebellion. Sir John Hawkins makes his first slave-trading voyage to the Caribbean.

1563   The Thirty-Nine Articles of Religion published; establishment of the independent Church of England completed. Potatoes introduced from America. Plague in London. Conclusion of the Council of Trent.

1564   Peace of Troyes with France; final renunciation of English claims to Calais.

## Poems

1557   Tottel, *Songs and Sonnets* (poetry of Wyatt, Vaux, and Surrey)
       More, *Works* (*Louis, the Lost Lover* and *Davy, the Dicer*)

1562   *The Whole Book of Psalms*

1563   *Mirror for Magistrates*, 2nd edn (Sackville, *Induction*)
       Googe, *Eclogues, Epitaphs, and Sonnets*

| *Historical and Cultural Events* | *Poems* |
|---|---|
| 1565 Sir Henry Sidney (father to Philip) made Lord Deputy in Ireland. Controversy over vestments marks the first clear dispute between the established Anglican Church and the Puritan movement. Probable first appearance of tobacco in England. | |
| 1567 Rebellion against Mary's rule in Scotland; she is defeated at the battle of Carbury Hill and abdicates in favor of her 1-year-old son, who becomes King James VI. Shane O'Neill killed and his rebellion ended. Sir Thomas Gresham's Exchange, modeled on the Antwerp Bourse, opens in London; Rugby School founded. Rebellion begins in the Netherlands against Spanish rule. | 1567 Turberville, *Epitaphs, Epigrams, Songs, and Sonnets* <br> Whitney, *The Copy of a Letter* |
| 1568 Mary flees from Scotland to England; placed in confinement. English College at Douai founded for the training of Jesuits. Publication of the Bishops' Bible as the authorized English Bible. | 1568 Elizabeth, "The doubt of future woes exiles my present joy" composed |
| 1569 Rebellion of the earls of Northumberland and Westmorland in support of Mary; on its failure, Westmorland flees to Spain and Northumberland to Scotland. Rebellion in Munster. | |
| 1570 Elizabeth excommunicated by Pope Pius V, an act which frees Catholics from loyalty to her. She visits Gresham's Exchange and names it the Royal Exchange. | |
| 1571 Discovery of a plot by the Italian banker Roberto di Ridolfi to free Mary and place her on the English throne leads to the arrest of the Duke of Norfolk (the Earl of Surrey's son). Henry Sidney resigns as Lord Deputy of Ireland. Lending of money at interest legalized again. Harrow School founded. Defeat of Turkish fleet by European forces in the battle of Lepanto. | |
| 1572 Execution of Norfolk, and of Northumberland, who had been returned to the English by the Scots. St. Bartholomew's Day Massacre of Protestants in France. | |
| | 1573 Gascoigne, *A Hundred Sundry Flowers* |
| 1574 Death of Charles IX; his brother becomes King Henry III. | |
| 1575 Death of Parker; Edmund Grindal becomes Archbishop of Canterbury. Henry Sidney reappointed Lord Deputy of Ireland. | 1575 Gascoigne, *The Posies* |
| 1576 The Theatre, the first London playhouse, built at Shoreditch. Grindal comes into conflict with Elizabeth for refusing to suppress Puritan prophesyings. | |
| 1577 Sir Francis Drake sent on an extended voyage to plunder Spanish shipping. | |
| 1578 Elizabeth begins serious negotiations to marry the French Duc d'Alençon, brother | |

| *Historical and Cultural Events* | *Poems* |
|---|---|
| to Charles IX. Henry Sidney recalled from Ireland. Plague in London. | |
| 1579  John Stubbs writes a pamphlet in opposition to Elizabeth's marriage with Alençon, and is punished by the amputation of his right hand. New rebellion in Munster begins. Union of Utrecht unites the northern Dutch provinces as a Protestant nation. | |
| 1580  Lord Grey de Wilton becomes Lord Deputy in Ireland. Drake returns to England after circumnavigating the globe. | |
| 1581  First execution of clandestine Jesuit missionaries in England. Levant Company chartered. | |
| 1582  Alençon's last visit with Elizabeth; despite the drafting of a tentative marriage treaty, their courtship ends. Lord Grey recalled from Ireland. Plague in London. Pope Gregory XIII promulgates the Gregorian calendar, at first accepted only in Catholic countries. | 1582  Elizabeth, *On Monsieur's Departure* composed Sidney, *Astrophil and Stella* composed |
| 1583  Death of Grindal; John Whitgift becomes Archbishop of Canterbury. Munster rebellion ends. University of Edinburgh founded. | |
| 1584  Discovery of a plot by Francis Throckmorton, working with the Spanish ambassador, to free Mary and place her on the English throne. Drake dispatched on an expedition against Spanish possessions in the Caribbean. | 1584  *A Handful of Pleasant Delights* (*Greensleeves*) |
| 1585  Execution of Throckmorton. The Earl of Leicester brings troops to the aid of the Dutch Republic, in rebellion against Spanish rule; Drake leads a naval expedition against Spanish possessions in the Caribbean. English colonists recruited by Sir Walter Ralegh settle on Roanoke Island in what is now North Carolina. | |
| 1586  Death of Philip Sidney from wounds received in battle in the Netherlands. Discovery of a plot by Anthony Babington and others to assassinate Elizabeth and free Mary; the conspirators (including Tichborne) are executed, and Mary convicted of treason for her participation. Roanoke colonists return to England with Drake. Censorship laws strengthened, to require prior licensing of all printed books. | 1586  *Tichborne's Lament* |
| 1587  Execution of Mary. Drake leads a raid against the Spanish fleet at Cadiz. A fresh group of colonists sent to Roanoke Island. | 1587  Ralegh, "Fortune hath taken thee away, my love" and Elizabeth, "Ah, silly pug, wert thou so sore afraid?" composed (?) |
| 1588  Spain sends an immense Armada against England; having suffered severely in a battle | 1588  *Six Idyllia* (*Adonis*) |

| *Historical and Cultural Events* | | *Poems* | |
|---|---|---|---|
| | with English ships in a battle off Gravelines and been driven into the North Sea by bad weather, it returns to Spain with heavy losses. Martin Marprelate tracts – anonymous Puritan attacks on Anglican clergy – begin to appear. | | |
| 1589 | Henry III assassinated; the Protestant Henry of Navarre claims the title of King Henry IV, but the civil war continues. | 1589 | George Puttenham, *The Art of English Poesy* (Elizabeth, "The doubt of future woes exiles my present joy," and quotations from Ralegh, "Fortune hath taken thee away, my love," and Elizabeth, "Ah, silly pug, wert thou so sore afraid?") Lodge, *Scylla's Metamorphosis* |
| 1590 | James VI personally involved in witchcraft trials in Scotland. | 1590 | Spenser, *The Faery Queen* Books I–III (with Ralegh, *A Vision upon this Conceit*) |
| 1591 | The Earl of Essex sent with English troops to support Henry IV in Normandy. Tea introduced in England. Trinity College, Dublin, founded. Roanoke Island colony found to have disappeared. | 1591 | Sidney, *Astrophil and Stella* |
| 1592 | Plague in London. | 1592 | Daniel, *Delia* Greene, *A Groatsworth of Wit* Nashe, *Summer's Last Will and Testament* composed Ralegh, *The Ocean's Love to Cynthia* composed (?) |
| 1593 | Failure to attend church services made punishable by banishment. Plague continues in London. Henry IV converts to Catholicism. | 1593 | Marlowe, *Hero and Leander* composed (?) *The Phoenix Nest* (Ralegh, "Would I were changed into that golden shower") *The Tears of Fancy* ("Those whose kind hearts sweet pity did attaint") Barnes, *Parthenophil and Parthenophe* |
| 1594 | Irish rebellion under Hugh O'Neill, Earl of Tyrone, begins. | 1594 | Drayton, *Idea's Mirror* |
| 1595 | A small Spanish force lands in Cornwall and burns several towns; rumors of a new Armada. Execution of Southwell. Ralegh leads an expedition to Guiana. | 1595 | Barnfield, *Cynthia* Chapman, *Ovid's Banquet of Sense* Spenser, *Amoretti* |
| 1596 | Second English raid against Cadiz. | 1596 | Spenser, *Faery Queen* Books I–VI |
| 1597 | Unsuccessful naval expedition against the Azores and other Spanish islands; a second Spanish Armada dispersed by bad weather on approaching England. | 1597 | John Dowland, *First Book of Airs* ("Come away, come, sweet love") |
| 1598 | Edict of Nantes, granting toleration to French Protestants and ending French civil war. The Theatre torn down, and its timbers used in building the Globe. Bodleian Library endowed. Death of Philip II. | 1598 | Marlowe, *Hero and Leander* Marston, *The Metamorphosis of Pygmalion's Image*, *The Scourge of Villainy* |
| 1599 | Earl of Essex sent to suppress the Irish rebellion; negotiates a truce and returns to England, where he is briefly imprisoned and permanently banished from the court. Whitgift orders the burning of satirical and other offensive books. | 1599 | Marlowe, *Ovid's Elegies*, with Davies, *Epigrams* (?) Mary Herbert, *To the Angel Spirit* composed (?) |
| 1600 | First East India Company chartered. | 1600 | *England's Helicon* (Marlowe, *The Passionate Shepherd*, and Ralegh, *The Nymph's Reply*) |

| *Historical and Cultural Events* | *Poems* |
|---|---|
| | Thomas Morley, *First Book of Airs* ("Absence, hear thou my protestation") Nashe, *Summer's Last Will and Testament* |
| 1601 Essex attempts to mount a rebellion against the government; convicted of treason and executed. Poor Law Act establishes the first uniform system of parish care for the poor. | |
| 1602 Bodleian Library opens. | 1602 Southwell, *Saint Peter's Complaint* (expanded edition, with *The Burning Babe*) |
| 1603 Death of Elizabeth; James VI of Scotland becomes King James I of England. O'Neill surrenders in Ireland. Plague in London. | |
| | 1604 Anthony Scoloker, *Diaphantus* (Ralegh, *The Passionate Man's Pilgrimage*) |
| | 1609 Spenser, *Two Cantos of Mutability* |
| | 1610 *A Poetical Rhapsody*, 2nd edn (Ralegh, *The Lie*) |
| | 1612 Orlando Gibbons, *First Set of Madrigals and Motets* (Ralegh, "What is our life? The play of passion") |
| | 1618 Richard Brathwait, *The Good Wife* (Ralegh, "Even such is time, which takes in trust") |
| | 1633 Donne, *Poems* Greville, *Caelica* |

# Introduction

In Shakespeare's *Much Ado about Nothing* the young Claudio, believing himself betrayed by Hero, denounces her and makes a threat: "Out on thee seeming! I will write against it." The moment tends to pass without emphasis in modern performance, or at least without the original stress on "write" as the dangerous word. Claudio certainly wants it to be a dangerous word, and he is reaching for a recognized weapon in the contemporary arsenal: those around him do not need to be told that he is threatening to broadcast his beloved's shame to a wider world by composing a satire against women (like the "sharp satires" that, according to Christopher Marlowe, disappointed lovers of another Hero compose). Claudio is, however briefly, contemplating the start of a literary career. He is disabused of his inspiration before he can follow through, but we find out later that two other members of the cast have taken steps in that direction. Friends of Benedick's produce "a halting sonnet of his own true brain," and a similar production by Beatrice is revealed; their piratical publication ("A miracle! Here's our own hands against our hearts") forces the happy ending from which the two budding poets had started to back away. The scene is supposed to be Sicily, but what shows through in these brief references is the literary world of London in the 1590s, in which both satires and sonnets were important currency. The development of that world over the course of the century is one of the stories inhabiting this anthology.

The roster of participants is by some criteria remarkably diverse. Two of them have since been canonized by the Catholic Church. Two ruling monarchs are here, Henry VIII for a probable attribution and Elizabeth I for three definite ones – the first English monarchs since Alfred the Great to qualify for such representation. Both Henry and Elizabeth headed courts in the Renaissance mold, where literary activity was an honored and – especially so in Elizabeth's time – expected component of graceful self-promotion; a fair amount of the material presented here is rooted in that milieu, written by people of high rank and privilege, intended primarily for one another's eyes, and circulating almost exclusively in manuscript. That milieu persisted and remained important into the next century, but it was gradually amplified by other possibilities. Part of the significance of George Gascoigne's career in the 1570s was the way in which he turned his very failure to make inroads into courtly circles into one of his great subjects, while directing his writerly ambitions to a larger reading public. The printing press had had an appetite for poetry in English as early as William Caxton's first edition of Chaucer in 1477; John Skelton published verses of his own devising during the 1520s, including a kind of Collected Poems in 1523. At key moments in the sixteenth century the sudden public dissemination of what had been coterie literature had a galvanic effect on a wider field of contestants. In 1557, some seventeen months before Elizabeth's accession, Richard Tottel's *Songs and Sonnets* made the poetry of her father's court generally available; reissued steadily over the next half century, his collection stimulated the production of a series of print anthologies (with names like *A Handful of Pleasant Delights* or *The Paradise of Dainty Devices*) that helped secure a broadly based taste for the kind of lyric poetry that has come to be thought of as Elizabethan. (One of Elizabeth's own poems appeared in print in 1589 to illustrate a point in a treatise on poetry-writing.) In 1591 the printing of Philip Sidney's *Astrophil and Stella*, five years after his own widely celebrated death, sparked the specific, intense craze for sonneteering that snags Benedick and Beatrice and was one of the leading edges of Elizabethan poetry in its self-consciously high style. More than half the poetry in this collection comes from the fabulously busy last ten years of the century; the literary scene which generated it was a messy business of overlapping centers, in which the court and the book trade shared territory with the Inns of Court – medieval law schools which had come to function as a kind of *de facto* urban university for young men of ambition – and of course the theater, which had been flourishing since the late 1580s.

At no point in the century did the practice of letters bring any particular safety with it. Six of the poets in this anthology were executed by the state, by beheading, burning, or drawing and quartering; another was stabbed to death in a tavern, and a number of others (including Elizabeth herself) found themselves in prison at one time or another. That record is without parallel in any other period of English literary history. The mid-century *Mirror for Magistrates*, a popular collection of cautionary tales about the downfall of the powerful, included in its roster the story of one William Collingbourne, executed in the late fifteenth century for authoring a satirical epigram about Richard III; his story resides between those of a duke and a king as a warning about the riskiness of being a poet: "I had forgot how newfound tyrannies / With right and freedom were at open war." There is a margin of professional self-glamorization in this; Collingbourne himself was a poet only for the duration of a tetrameter couplet, and we have no serious evidence that in the sixteenth century it was ever poetry as such which sent anyone to the block or the gallows. The mortality rate among poets is primarily testimony to the dangerousness of the period generally and the brutality of its politics, and to the fact that they were usually involved in courtly or public life in other ways than as writers. Yet the sense of something specially dangerous about poetry becomes real enough in the combativeness of the poets with one another; by the 1590s that combativeness reaches a sometimes parodic pitch, and the decade is marked by a succession of literary feuds, often pursued in open print. It is here that verse satire – "the cankered muse" – blooms into abundance, and was finally felt to be enough of a public nuisance that the Archbishop of Canterbury in 1599 ordered the collection and burning of as much of it as could be found and forbad the printing of any more (an act which terminated at least one significant literary career). The century ends with confirmation from one of the highest authorities in the realm that Claudio's threat to resort to satire was indeed not something to take lightly.

The tumult that conditions the production of poetry in the century, however, is not as visible in the poetry itself as we might perhaps expect. The pugnaciousness of writers as a guild is on view in poems such as the satire of John Marston's included here; four of the poets who died at the hands of the state left poems about their imprisonment and the prospect of execution, to the point that we can almost talk of an established genre (at least three more examples could be added to the ones in this collection). Yet the sixteenth century is not one of the great ages of political or religious poetry – not by the standard of, say, the century that follows. There are individual exceptions to this generalization, and the most distinguished one occupies more space in this anthology than any other single work; Edmund Spenser's *The Faery Queen* is a uniquely ambitious attempt to provide Tudor England with its summary epic, in which (among other things) the momentous and often violent public events of the time are represented and interpreted. That representation, though, is also an encryption into one of the most complicated allegorical structures ever mounted, and the reader has to work for it. A key element in the encryption, moreover, involves fitting the whole narrative within the armature of what is by a fair margin the dominant topic of sixteenth-century non-dramatic verse: poetry means, more than anything else, love poetry.

The profile of love among the topics for poetry is always high; in the sixteenth century it was made especially prominent by the extraordinary prestige and popularity of a particular species of love poetry: that marked by the formal and thematic imitation of the Italian poet Francesco Petrarca (1304–74), known in English as Petrarch. Beginning in the late fifteenth century, such imitation becomes a prominent feature of almost every vernacular literature in western Europe; when Sir Thomas Wyatt introduced both the sonnet and some of the characteristic sentiments and rhetoric of Petrarchism into English, he was making a move toward repairing his own country's belatedness in Renaissance high culture. His Petrarchan poems were among the most important works broadcast to a general readership by Tottel; *Astrophil and Stella* in turn achieves its great influence in part by giving English its first fully successful version not just of individual Petrarchan poems but of the Petrarchan lyric sequence, and inspiring a new round of imitation at that level. At every stage of this progress there are striking incongruities. In particular, the conventional Petrarchan situation of prolonged unsatisfied desire for an idealized woman – according to his own sequence, Petrarch loved the unattainable Laura for twenty-one years until her own death, and for another ten years after – can fit uneasily with the very different situation in which the new poet writes (as is the case with Wyatt), or can chafe painfully against some very un-Petrarchan impatience and lustfulness (as in Sidney's sequence). The whole business repeatedly opens itself up to mockery and abuse (a poem by Sir John Davies is perhaps the most economical example). Yet the abrasions themselves generate some memorable poetic energy – including the florid sensuality for which the 1590s have become notorious – and the enterprise takes the whole century to play itself out.

Petrarchism had a sufficiently tenacious hold on life in sixteenth-century Europe generally that special factors are not required to explain its durability in England; but England's experience does take special energy from the country's unparalleled historical accident of being ruled, successfully and for almost fifty years, by an unmarried woman. Elizabeth herself was no kind of feminist, except as far as her own case was concerned; her presence on the throne certainly did not do much to animate poetic ambition in other women. England sees nothing during her reign like the female Petrarchists active in sixteenth-century Italy, and must wait until Mary Wroth (Robert Sidney's daughter; 1587–ca. 1651/3) for someone to join their number. What Elizabeth's presence does do is instantiate at the summit of the political and social hierarchy an uncanny version of the classic Petrarchan situation, that of a charismatic woman simultaneously visible and unreachable, commanding in her chastity. Elizabeth seems to have recognized the coincidence and knowingly exploited it in various ways, especially in her careful dealings with the ambitious men who surrounded her at close range; for a half century the profession of courtier could be unusually hard to distinguish from the glamorous and maddening endeavor of Petrarchan courtship. In an even more intimate merger of the literature of private passion with the reality of political power, this courtship was at times conducted in verse; we do not know as much about the details as we would like to, but some evidence does survive. Included in this anthology is one reciprocal exchange of poems – they present themselves as love poems – between Elizabeth and the most talented poet among her favorites, Sir Walter Ralegh. We also have tantalizing information that Ralegh composed or meant to compose an epic poem about his relationship with the queen; its ruling conceit – the Ocean's longing devotion to the moon goddess Cynthia – seems to align a Petrarchan love narrative with England's early imperial ambitions. That alignment does not happen only in the inner circles; the love story that frames Spenser's big poem is itself a kind of Petrarchan idealization of the erotics of Elizabeth's court, with the absent title character meant to be recognized as an explicit figuration for the monarch to whom the poem is dedicated by one of her distant worshipers. Adoration from afar of a powerful woman could look like the key to understanding everything.

\* \* \*

This anthology inevitably trifles to some extent with its chronological boundaries. Several of the earlier poems, including some of Skelton's, may very well date from the late fifteenth century. At the other end I have reached into the seventeenth century when there seemed a compelling reason to do so (such as following Ralegh's story to its conclusion). English literary life does begin a significant change of mood around 1600, but there is no kind of clean break. A number of careers straddle the century mark; I have followed convention in, for instance, allotting Ben Jonson and Thomas Campion to the seventeenth century (they may indeed be found in Robert Cummings's anthology in this series). I thought it important, however, to provide a generous selection from John Donne, including poems that we are fairly confident date from 1602 and later; the story of English sixteenth-century love poetry looks very different with Donne at the end, and it seemed to me that that transformative event needed to be fully on view here. Perhaps disappointingly, I have not gone so far as to include any of Donne's religious poetry, which has less in the way of precedent in the sixteenth century but finds its natural company with the great devotional lyrics of the seventeenth. The most momentous literary career to bridge the two centuries is, for merely practical reasons, not represented at all: Shakespeare's poetry is widely accessible in numerous first-rate formats, and to do him justice would take up considerable space. It would be in the spirit of this anthology to read his *Venus and Adonis* and the entirety of his sonnets in conjunction with what is provided here.

In making my selection, I have followed the admirable (and unusual) precedent set by Richard S. Sylvester's *Anchor Anthology of Sixteenth Century Verse* (1974) of giving, as far as possible, complete works, or at least complete units from longer works. Doing so has meant reducing the number of worthy but more or less generic poets represented (no Thomas Churchyard, no Nicholas Breton) in favor of allowing the poetry that is here the proper elbow room to go about its business. To illustrate the growing fascination with the Petrarchan notion of a connected sequence of lyric poems, I include three such sequences in their entirety: Gascoigne's Green Knight poems, Sidney's *Astrophil and Stella*, and Samuel Daniel's *Delia*. (The last of these is given in what is to my knowledge its first reprinting in its most effective form, that of the second edition of 1592; if I had had more room, I would have followed it with the narrative poem to which Daniel always attached it.) Probably the most extreme choice has been to include the complete third book of *The Faery Queen*. I give the entire book because experience has taught me the folly of trying to trim Spenser's narrative sprawl from within; I give Book III, rather than the more traditional I or II, both for the sake of the thematic linkages with the other love poetry in the anthology and because its narrative diversity and lack of closure are I think truer to the experience of the poem as a whole. I have tried to give enough information for readers to pick up the relevant threads, but the difficulty of doing so is itself part of the point.

Spelling and punctuation have been modernized for all texts. Modernization can never be entirely complete or consistent; a few old spellings have been allowed to stand, usually for metrical reasons (though metrical intent can sometimes be difficult to determine; the question is a famously vexed one for Wyatt). When it appears that a vowel silent in modern pronunciation should be sounded, I have added a grave accent ("termèd"); I have preserved vowels that would disappear in modernization when it is clear that they indicate a separate syllable (i.e., "termes" is a two-syllable word, the equivalent of either "terms" or "term's"). Modernization has the advantage of helping the modern reader and reducing the number of glosses, and also of forcing the editor to come to some decision as to just what is supposed to be going on in a particular passage; but the modern reader should keep in mind that those decisions can of course be wrong, and that some momentous ambiguities (such as the popular quibbling on "fain" and "feign") can become almost invisible in the process. After some thought, I have decided not to insert quotation marks into the texts; in most cases it is not difficult to detect a change of speaker without them, but there are also occasions where some uncertainty on this score is a deliberate effect, and one worth preserving. I supply references to authoritative old-spelling editions, or to the nearest equivalent, when they exist. My own editorial choices do not always correspond to those in these editions. I cite variant readings when they are particularly credible or interesting, and also by way of continually reminding the reader of the indeterminate nature of most of these texts; these citations make no pretense at thoroughness.

# Anonymous

Western wind, when will thou blow,
The small rain down can rain.
Christ, if my love were in my arms
And I in my bed again.

From Royal MSS, Appendix 58 (British Library), 1503 or later; a collection of song lyrics, with musical settings, presumably for court use. (The setting for this poem was taken over by three Tudor composers for use in the Mass.) For a transcription of the texts, see Ewald Flügel, "Lieder-sammlungen des XVI. Jahrhunderts," *Anglia*, 12 (1889), 256–72.

2 The manuscript is unpunctuated; some editors end this line with a question mark.

In a goodly night, as in my bed I lay
Pleasantly sleeping, this dream I had.
To me there came a creature brighter than the day,
Which comforted my sprites that were afore full sad.
To behold her person, God knows my heart was glad,          5
For her sweet visage, like Venus' gold it shone.
To speak to her I was right sore afeared,
But when I wakèd, there was I alone.

Then when she saw that I lay so still,
Full softly she drew unto my bed's side.                    10
She bade me show her what was my will,
And my request, it should not be denied.
With that, she kissed me, but and I should have be dead,
I could not speak, my sprites were so far gone.
For very shame my face away I wried,                        15
But when I awoke, there was but I alone.

Then spake I, and goodly words to her said.
I beseech your nobleness on me to have some grace;
To approach to your presence I was somewhat afeared,
That caused me now to turn away my face.                    20
Nay, sir, quod she, as touching this case,
I pardon you, my own dear heart, anon.
With that I took her softly and sweetly did her bass,
But when I awoke, there was but I alone.

Then said she to me, O my dear heart,                       25
May I content in any wise your mind?
Yea, God knows, said I, through love's dart
My heart forever to have ye do me bind.
You be my comfort, I have you most in mind;

This poem and the next are from Rawlinson C.813 (Bodleian), a manuscript anthology, primarily of love poems, apparently compiled between 1522 and 1534, probably by one Humphrey Welles. Some of its entries (including passages from Chaucer) date from as early as the fourteenth century, though others refer unmistakably to current events. The whole collection has been edited by Sharon L. Jansen and Kathleen H. Jordan as *The Welles Anthology* (Binghamton, NY: MRTS, 1991).

6 *Venus' gold* Possibly "Venice gold."
13 *and* if (i.e., I could not have spoken to save my life).
23 *bass* kiss.

Have on me pity and let me not this moan.                               30
Leave, said she, this mourning, I will not be unkind.
But when I awoke, there was but I alone.

I prayed her heartily that she would come to bed.
She said she was content to do me pleasure.
I know not whether I was alive or dead,                                 35
So glad I was to have that goodly treasure.
I kissèd her, I bassed her out of all measure;
The more I kissed her, the more her beauty shone.
To serve her, to please her, that time I did me dever,
But when I awoke, there was but I alone.                                40

Such goodly sports all night endurèd I,
Unto the morrow that day gan to spring.
So glad I was of my dream verily
That in my sleep loud I began to sing,
And when I awoke by heaven king,                                        45
I went after her and she was gone;
I had no thing but my pillow in my arms lying,
For when I awoke, there was but I alone.

39    *dever* endeavor.

O lusty lily, the lantern of all gentleness,
O rose most ruddy, the root of all womanhead,
O gillyflower gentle, O primrose peerless,
Exceeding sugar in savor and sweetness,
O daisy delicious full many a fold,                                     5
When that ye be in your most gladness,
Amongs your new lovers remember your old.

Full filled with favor, the flower of all fairness,
It is no doubt when ye most jocund be;
Your prisoner is pained in piteous pensiveness,                        10
That when ye laugh full sore weepeth he.
It fareth by him as doth the sea
That never hath rest in hot nor cold.
Wherefore, fair mistress of mercy and pity,
Amongs your new lovers remember your old.                              15

The rhyme scheme implies that the first line of the poem is       5    *full many a fold* many times over.
missing.

# John Skelton (1460?–1529)

Little is known about Skelton's early years. In 1488 Oxford entitled him "laureate," a designation which he later received from Cambridge and Louvain as well. A modest postgraduate certificate in rhetoric, it had the aura of an ancient pedigree – the crown given to poets in ancient Rome and to Petrarch in the fourteenth century – and Skelton kept it close to his name for the rest of his life. He was at court around the turn of the century, writing poems on important personages and serving as tutor to the young Prince Henry. He was ordained a priest in 1498 and ca. 1503 became rector of Diss in Norfolk; he held that position for the rest of his life, though after 1512 he returned to London and received the title Orator Regius from his former pupil, now Henry VIII. In the early 1520s he published a series of fierce satires on Cardinal Wolsey, Henry's chief minister, but was subsequently reconciled with him. *A Garland of Laurel*, a lengthy poem of self-praise, incorporating numerous individual poems of Skelton's and listing and excerpting others, was published in 1523. Many of Skelton's poems have more or less ordinary prosody, but as a poet he is most famous for the antic meter that bears his name: Skeltonics. Lines of (usually) two or three beats, with great variation in syllable count, are rhymed successively for, it seems, as long as the poet can keep a particular rhyme going. The vehicle of some remarkable effects in Skelton's own work, the meter has found almost no use at the hands of any other writer.

The most consequential poem in Skeltonics is *Philip Sparrow*. It begins as the lament of a young girl for the death of a pet. The girl was real – Jane Scrope, living with her widowed mother, Lady Eleanor Wyndham, at Carrow Abbey in Norwich – and the occasion was presumably real as well, sometime before Lady Wyndham's own death in 1505. There is the germ of classical precedent, poems of Catullus (3) and Ovid (*Amores* 2.6) mourning in exaggerated terms the death of their mistress' birds, but Skelton quickly leaves any models behind. For about half the poem's length Jane proceeds with a kind of sophisticated childishness, interweaving her own hyperbolic lament with Latin phrases from the Office for the Dead and other liturgical texts – a mock elegy that is never really a joke. As the poem continues, it becomes a review of Jane's own reading, and in particular a survey of English vernacular literature and the state of English as a literary language at the beginning of the sixteenth century; Jane herself comes to stand for that language and its attractiveness, a mourning daughter tongue with an unknown future ahead. Then in the course of a Latin epitaph the speaker changes from Jane to Skelton the laureate, who goes on to praise Jane with an ardor that can alarm modern readers: a 40-year-old priest in love with the child for whom he has been pretending to speak. Contemporary readers seem to have been taken aback as well; Alexander Barclay attacked the poem for "wantonness" in his *Ship of Fools* (1509), and the "addition" which now ends Skelton's poem appears to be an aggrieved reply.

*Edition*: John Skelton, *The Complete English Poems*, ed. John Scattergood (Harmondsworth: Penguin, 1983).

## From *Against a Comely Custron*

Skelton laureate, upon a deadman's head that was sent to him from an honorable gentlewoman for a token, devised this ghostly meditation in English: convenable in sentence, commendable, lamentable, lacrimable, profitable for the soul.

> Your ugly token
> My mind hath broken
> From worldly lust,
> For I have discussed
> We are but dust     5
> And die we must.
>    It is general
> To be mortal;

---

*Custron* kitchen boy.
*ghostly* spiritual.

*convenable in sentence* suitable in meaning.
4 *discussed* decided.

I have well espied
No man may him hide                                           10
From Death hollow-eyed,
With sinews withered,
With bonès shidered,
With his worm-eaten maw
And his ghastly jaw                                            15
Gasping aside,
Naked of hide,
Neither flesh nor fell.
   Then by my counsel
Look that ye spell                                             20
Well this gospel;
For whereso we dwell,
Death will us quell
And with us mell.
   For all our pampered paunches,                         25
There may no fraunches
Nor worldly bliss
Redeem us from this.
Our days be dated
To be checkmated,                                             30
With draughts of death
Stopping our breath:
Our eyen sinking,
Our bodies stinking,
Our gummes grinning,                                          35
Our soules brenning!
To whom then shall we sue
For to have rescue
But to sweet Jesu
On us then for to rue?                                        40
   O goodly child
Of Mary mild,
Then be our shield,
That we be not exiled
To the dun dale                                               45
Of bootless bale,
Nor to the lake
Of fiendes black.
   But grant us grace
To see thy face                                               50
And to purchase
Thine heavenly place
And thy palace,
Full of solace,
Above the sky                                                 55
That is so high,

13   *shidered* shattered.
18   *fell* skin.
20   *spell* read.
24   *mell* meddle.
26   *fraunches* franchise, i.e., exemption.
31   *draughts* The word designates both the drawing of breath
and the moving of chessmen.

33   *eyen* eyes.
35   *gummes* gums.
36   *brenning* burning.
46   *bootless bale* pain without relief. An alternate text reads
"bottomless bale."

Eternally
To behold and see
The Trinity!
   Amen                                                         60
*Mirez vous y.*

*Mirez vous y* See yourselves there.


## From *Divers Ballads and Ditties Solacious*

With lullay, lullay, like a child,
Thou sleepst too long; thou art beguiled!

My darling dear, my daisy flower,
Let me, quod he, lie in your lap.
Lie still, quod she, my paramour;                                5
Lie still hardily, and take a nap.
His head was heavy, such was his hap,
All drowsy, dreaming, drowned in sleep,
That of his love he took no keep,

With hey, lullay, &c.                                            10

With ba, ba, ba, and bas, bas, bas,
She cherished him both cheek and chin,
That he wist never where he was;
He had forgotten all deadly sin.
He wanted wit her love to win;                                  15
He trusted her payment and lost all his prey.
She left him sleeping and stale away,

With hey, lullay, &c.

The rivers rowth, the waters wan;
She sparèd not to wet her feet.                                 20
She waded over, she found a man
That halsed her heartily and kissed her sweet:
Thus after her cold, she caught a heat.
My lief, she said, routeth in his bed;
I wis he hath an heavy head.                                    25

With hey, lullay, &c.

What dreamest thou, drunkard, drowsy pate?
Thy lust and liking is from thee gone.
Thou blinkered blow-bowl, thou wakest too late;
Behold, thou liest, luggard, alone!                             30

*Solacious* comforting.
1–2 The refrain mimics medieval carols in which Mary
sings to the Christ child.
6 *hardily* forcefully.
9 *keep* heed.
12 *cherished* fondled.
13 *wist* knew.

15 *wanted* lacked.
19 *rowth* rough. *wan* dark.
22 *halsed* embraced.
24 *lief* beloved. *routeth* snores.
29 *blow-bowl* drunkard.
30 *luggard* sluggard.

Well may thou sigh, well may thou groan,
To deal with her so cowardly;
I wis, pole-hatchet, she bleared thine eye.
Quod Skelton laureate.

33   *pole-hatchet* The insult is obscure: something to do with
a pole-ax, or possibly with ale-houses (which hung their signs
from a pole).   *bleared thine eye* made a fool of you.

The ancient acquaintance, madam, between us twain,
The familiarity, the former dalliance,
Causeth me that I cannot myself refrain
But that I must write for my pleasant pastance,
Remembering your passing goodly countenance,          5
Your goodly port, your beauteous visage;
Ye may be counted comfort of all courage.

Of all your features favorable to make true description,
I am insufficient to make such enterprise;
For thus dare I say, without tradition,               10
That dame Menalippe was never half so wise;
Yet so it is that a rumor beginneth for to rise
How in good horsemen ye set your whole delight
And have forgotten your old, true, loving knight.

With bound and rebound, bouncingly take up            15
His gentle curtal, and set nought by small nags!
Spur up at the hinder girth with, Gup, morel, gup!
With, Jast ye, jennet of Spain, for your tail wags!
Ye cast all your courage upon such courtly hags!
Have in sergeant-ferrer, mine horse behind is bare.    20
He rideth well the horse, but he rideth better the mare.

Ware, ware, the mare winceth with her wanton heel!
She kicketh with her calkins and killeth with a clench;
She goeth wide behind and heweth never a deal.
Ware galling in the withers, ware of that wrench!     25
It is parlous for a horseman to dig in the trench.
This grieveth your husband, that right gentle knight,
And so with your servants he fiercely doth fight.

4   *pastance* pastime.

6   *port* bearing.

7   *all courage* every heart.

10   *tradition* betrayal.

11   *Menalippe* Melanippe, an Amazon, in some accounts the
one whose girdle Hercules was ordered to steal.

16   *curtal* horse with a docked tail (with a pun on "kirtle").
*nags* slang term for testicles.

17   *Gup* go (as a command to a horse).   *morel* dark-colored
horse.

18   *Jast* jump.

19   *courage* heart.

20   Bring in the man who cares for the horses; my horse has
lost the shoes on the hind legs.

22   *Ware* beware.   *winceth* kicks.

23   *calkins* ends of a horseshoe.   *killeth with a clench* The
primary sense is "kills with the turned-down nail in her
horseshoe," though "clench" also carries the sense of "hard
embrace," and "killeth" may pun on "keeleth" in the sense of
"cools": she turns cold after a bout of passion.

24   *wide behind* with hind legs wide apart.   *heweth* strikes
one leg against the other.   *never a deal* not at all.

25   *wrench* sharp twisting motion.

So fiercely he fighteth, his mind is so fell,
That he driveth them down with dints on their day-watch.                    30
He breseth their brain-pans and maketh them to swell,
Their brows all to-broken, such clappes they catch,
Whose jealousy malicious maketh them to leap the hatch,
By their conusance knowing how they serve a wily pie.
Ask all your neighbors whether that I lie.                                  35

It can be no counsel that is cried at the cross.
For your gentle husband, sorrowful am I;
Howbeit, he is not first hath had a loss.
Advertising you, madam, to work more secretly,
Let not all the world make an outcry.                                      40
Play fair play, madam, and look ye play clean,
Or else with great shame your game will be seen.
    Quod Skelton laureate.

---

30 *dints* heavy blows. *on their day-watch* while they are at their daytime duties.
31 *breseth* bruises.
32 *clappes* blows.
33 *hatch* lower half of a double door.

34 *conusance* cognizance (their wounds are like a badge identifying them). *pie* magpie.
36 *counsel* private matter. *cried at the cross* proclaimed at the crossroads.
39 *Advertising* warning.

# Philip Sparrow

*Pla ce bo,*
Who is there, who?
*Di le xi,*
Dame Margery.
*Fa, re, mi, mi,*                                                           5
Wherefore and why, why?
For the soul of Philip Sparrow
That was late slain at Carrow
Among the nunnes black,
For that sweet soul's sake                                                10
And for all sparrows' souls
Set in our bead-rolls,
*Pater noster qui*
With an *Ave Mari*
And with the corner of a Creed,                                           15
The more shall be your meed.
    When I remember again
How my Philip was slain,
Never half the pain
Was between you twain,                                                    20
Pyramus and Thisbe,

---

1 I will please (Psalm 114.9, in the numbering of the Vulgate, from which Skelton is quoting; these numbers differ by one or two from those in most English bibles).
3 I have loved (Psalm 114.1).
4 *Dame Margery* Probably the senior nun at Carrow Abbey.
9 *nunnes* nuns.

12 *bead-rolls* list of souls to be prayed for.
13 Our father who.
14 *Ave Mari* Hail Mary.
15 *the corner of a Creed* a bit of the Nicene Creed.
21 *Pyramus and Thisbe* Babylonian lovers who killed themselves rather than live after one another's death.

As then befell to me.
I wept and I wailed,
The tears down hailed,
But nothing it availed                                        25
To call Philip again,
Whom Gib, our cat, hath slain.
    Gib, I say, our cat,
Worrowèd her on that
Which I lovèd best.                                           30
It cannot be expressed
My sorrowful heaviness,
But all without redress;
For within that stound,
Half slumbering, in a sound,                                  35
I fell down to the ground.
    Uneath I cast mine eyes
Toward the cloudy skies;
But when I did behold
My sparrow dead and cold,                                     40
No creature but that would
Have ruèd upon me
To behold and see
What heaviness did me pang,
Wherewith my hands I wrang                                    45
That my sinews cracked
As though I had been racked,
So painèd and so strainèd
That no life well nigh remainèd.
    I sighèd and I sobbed                                     50
For that I was robbed
Of my sparrow's life.
O, maiden, widow, and wife,
Of what estate ye be,
Of high or low degree,                                        55
Great sorrow then ye might see
And learn to weep at me!
Such paines did me fret
That my heart did beat,
My visage pale and dead,                                      60
Wan, and blue as lead;
The pangs of hateful death
Well nigh had stopped my breath.

*Heu, heu, me,*
That I am woe for thee!                                       65
*Ad dominum cum tribularer clamavi,*
Of God nothing else crave I
But Philip's soul to keep
From the mares deep

---

**29**  *Worrowèd* bit and pulled.
**34**  *stound* moment.
**35**  *sound* swoon.
**37**  *Uneath* with difficulty.

**64**  Alas, alas me (Psalm 119.5).
**66**  I have cried out to the Lord when I was troubled (Psalm 119.1).
**69**  *mares* marsh.

Of Acherontes well 70
That is a flood of hell;
And from the great Pluto,
The prince of endless woe;
And from foul Alecto
With visage black and blo; 75
And from Medusa, that mare
That like a fiend doth stare;
And from Megera's adders
For ruffling of Philip's feathers;
And from her fiery sparklings 80
For burning of his wings;
And from the smokès sour
Of Proserpina's bower;
And from the dennes dark
Where Cerberus doth bark, 85
Whom Theseus did affray,
Whom Hercules did outray,
As famous poets say:
From that hell-hound
That lieth in chaines bound, 90
With ghastly heades three,
To Jupiter pray we
That Philip preserved may be!
Amen, say ye with me!

*Do mi nus*, 95
Help now, sweet Jesus!
*Levavi oculos meos in montes*,
Would God I had Zenophontes
Or Socrates the wise
To show me their device 100
Moderately to take
This sorrow that I make
For Philip Sparrow's sake!
So fervently I shake,
I feel my body quake, 105
So urgently am I brought
Into careful thought.
   Like Andromach, Hector's wife,
Was weary of her life
When she had lost her joy, 110
Noble Hector of Troy;
In like manner also

72  *Pluto* god of the underworld.
74  *Alecto* one of the Furies.
75  *blo* blue.
76  *Medusa* Mythic creature whose sight turned viewers to stone.  *mare* goblin.
78  *Megera* Megaera, another Fury.
83  *Proserpina* Pluto's wife.
84  *dennes* dens.
85  *Cerberus* The three-headed guard-dog of Hades. Theseus confronted him during a trip to the underworld, and Hercules captured him as one of his twelve labors.

86  *affray* frighten.
87  *outray* defeat.
95  Lord (Psalm 120.5).
97  I have raised my eyes to the mountains (Psalm 120.1).
98  *Zenophontes* Xenophon (ca. 428–354 BC), prolific classical Greek author and member of Socrates' philosophic circle at Athens.
108  *Andromach* Andromache, wife of the greatest of the Trojan warriors, and a famous exemplar of misery after his death and that of their young son.

Increaseth my deadly woe,
For my sparrow is go.
It was so pretty a fool;                                          115
It would sit on a stool,
And learned after my school
For to keep his cut,
With, Philip, keep your cut!
    It had a velvet cap                                           120
And would sit upon my lap
And seek after small worms
And sometime white bread crumbs;
And many times and oft
Between my breastes soft                                          125
It would lie and rest:
It was proper and prest.
    Sometime he would gasp
When he saw a wasp;
A fly or a gnat,                                                  130
He would fly at that,
And prettily he would pant
When he saw an ant.
Lord, how he would pry
After the butterfly!                                              135
Lord, how he would hop
After the grasshop!
And when I said, Phip, Phip,
Then he would leap and skip
And take me by the lip.                                           140
Alas, it will me slo
That Philip is gone me fro!

*Si in i qui ta tes,*
Alas, I was evil at ease!
*De pro fun dis cla ma vi,*                                       145
When I saw my sparrow die!
    Now, after my doom,
Dame Sulpicia at Rome,
Whose name registered was
Forever in tables of brass                                        150
Because that she did pass
In poesy to indite
And eloquently to write,
Though she would pretend
My sparrow to commend,                                            155
I trow she could not amend
Reporting the virtues all
Of my sparrow royal.
    For it would come and go

117  *after my school* from my schooling.
118  *keep his cut* behave himself.
127  *prest* quick.
134  *pry* search.
141  *slo* slay.
143  If iniquities (Psalm 129.3).

145  From the depths I have cried out (Psalm 129.1).
147  *doom* judgment.
148  *Sulpicia* The name of two women poets of classical Rome.
151  *pass* excel.
156  *trow* swear.  *amend* do better.

And fly so to and fro, 160
And on me it would leap
When I was asleep
And his feathers shake,
Wherewith he would make
Me often for to wake 165
And for to take him in
Upon my naked skin.
God wot, we thought no sin;
What though he crept so low?
It was no hurt, I trow. 170
He did nothing, perdy,
But sit upon my knee.
Philip, though he were nice,
In him it was no vice.
Philip had leave to go 175
To pick my little toe;
Philip might be bold
And do what he would.
Philip would seek and take
All the fleas black 180
That he could there espy
With his wanton eye.

*O pe ra,*
*La, sol, fa, fa,*
*Confitebor tibi, Domine, in toto corde meo.* 185
Alas, I would ride and go
A thousand mile of ground!
If any such might be found,
It were worth an hundred pound
Of King Croesus' gold 190
Or of Attalus the old,
The rich Prince of Pergamy,
Whoso list the story to see.
    Cadmus, that his sister sought,
And he should be bought 195
For gold and fee,
He should over the sea
To weet if he could bring
Any of the offspring
Or any of the blood. 200
But whoso understood
Of Medea's art,
I would I had a part
Of her crafty magic!
My sparrow then should be quick 205

173  *nice* wanton.
183  Works (Psalm 137.8).
185  I will confess to you, Lord, with all my heart (Psalm 137.1).
190  *Croesus* king of Lydia (d. 546 BC), legendary for his wealth.
191  *Attalus* The original texts read "Artalus." There were three kings of Pergamum named Attalus (269–133 BC), all known to some degree as patrons of the arts.

194  *Cadmus* Brother to Europa; he was sent to locate her after her abduction by Jupiter.
195  *And* if.
198  *weet* learn.
202  *Medea* Witch who helped Jason retrieve the Golden Fleece; her skills included restoring the dead to life.

With a charm or twain,
And play with me again.
But all this is in vain
Thus for to complain.
   I took my sampler once                                               210
Of purpose, for the nonce,
To sew with stitches of silk
My sparrow white as milk,
That by representation
Of his image and fashion                                                            215
To me it might import
Some pleasure and comfort
For my solace and sport.
But when I was sewing his beak,
Me thought my sparrow did speak                                                     220
And opened his pretty bill,
Saying, Maid, ye are in will
Again me for to kill!
Ye prick me in the head!
With that my needle waxed red,                                                      225
Methought, of Philip's blood.
Mine hair right upstood
And was in such a fray
My speech was taken away.
I cast down that there was,                                                         230
And said, Alas, alas,
How cometh this to pass?
My fingers dead and cold
Could not my sampler hold;
My needle and thread                                                               235
I threw away for dread.
The best now that I may
Is for his soul to pray:

*A porta inferi*,
Good Lord, have mercy                                                              240
Upon my sparrow's soul,
Written in my bead-roll!
*Au di vi vo cem*,
Japhet, Cam, and Sem,
*Ma gni fi cat*,                                                                   245
Show me the right path
To the hills of Armony,
Wherefore the boards yet cry
Of your father's boat
That was sometime afloat,                                                          250
And now they lie and rot;
Let some poets write
Deucalion's flood it hight.

---

210–36  Cf. Wyatt, "Who hath heard of such cruelty before," which Skelton's passage may have inspired.

222  *are in will* intend.

228  *fray* fright.

239  From the gate of hell.

243  I heard a voice (Revelation 14:13).

244  *Japheth, Cam, and Sem* Japheth, Ham, and Shem, the sons of Noah (Genesis 5:32).

247  *Armony* Armenia, where Noah's ark came to rest.

248  *boards* Some sources of the text have "birds."

253  *Deucalion's flood* In classical mythology a great flood sent by Jupiter to end the Bronze Age.

But as verily as ye be
The natural sonnes three                                        255
Of Noah the patriarch
That made that great ark,
Wherein he had apes and owls,
Beastes, birds, and fowls,
That if ye can find                                            260
Any of my sparrow's kind
(God send the soul good rest!),
I would have yet a nest
As pretty and as prest
As my sparrow was.                                             265
But my sparrow did pass
All sparrows of the wood
That were since Noah's flood;
Was never none so good.
King Philip of Macedony                                        270
Had no such Philip as I,
No, no, sir, hardily!
    That vengeance I ask and cry
By way of exclamation
On all the whole nation                                        275
Of cattes wild and tame;
God send them sorrow and shame!
That cat specially
That slew so cruelly
My little pretty sparrow                                       280
That I brought up at Carrow.
    O cat of carlish kind,
The fiend was in thy mind
When thou my bird untwined!
I would thou hadest been blind!                                285
The leopardes savage,
The lions in their rage
Might catch thee in their paws
And gnaw thee in their jaws!
The serpents of Libany                                         290
Might sting thee venomously!
The dragons with their tongues
Might poison thy liver and lungs!
The manticores of the mountains
Might feed them on thy brains!                                 295
    Melanchates, that hound
That plucked Acteon to the ground,
Gave him his mortal wound,
Changèd to a deer,
The story doth appear,                                         300

264   *prest* neat.
270   *Philip of Macedony* King Philip of Macedon (d. 336 BC),
father of Alexander the Great.
276   *cattes* cats.
282   *carlish* churlish.
284   *untwined* undid.

290   *Libany* Libya, supposedly a site of particularly venom-
ous serpents.
294   *manticores* Legendary monsters part human, part lion,
part scorpion.
296   *Melanchates* Named by Ovid, *Metamorphoses* 1.232; the
hunter Acteon saw the goddess Diana bathing naked, was
changed by her into a stag and killed by his own dogs.

Was changèd to an hart;
So thou, foul cat that thou art,
The self-same hound
Might thee confound
That his own lord bote                                          305
Might bite asunder thy throat!
    Of Inde the greedy gripes
Might tear out all thy tripes!
Of Arcady the bears
Might pluck away thine ears!                                    310
The wild wolf Lycaon
Bite asunder thy backbone!
Of Etna, the brenning hill
That day and night brenneth still,
Set in thy tail a blaze                                         315
That all the world may gaze
And wonder upon thee,
From Ocean, the great sea,
Unto the isles of Orkady,
From Tilbury ferry                                              320
To the plain of Salisbury!
So traiterously my bird to kill
That never ought thee evil will!
    Was never bird in cage
So gentle of courage                                           325
In doing his homage
Unto his sovereign.
Alas, I say again,
Death hath departed us twain;
The false cat hath thee slain!                                 330
Farewell, Philip, adieu;
Our Lord thy soul rescue!
Farewell without restore,
Farewell forevermore!
    And it were a Jew,                                          335
It would make one rue
To see my sorrow new.
These villainous false cats
Were made for mice and rats,
And not for birdes small.                                       340
Alas, my face waxeth pale
Telling this piteous tale,
How my bird so fair,
That was wont to repair
And go in at my spare,                                          345
And creep in at my gore

305   *bote* bit.
307   *gripes* vultures.
308   *tripes* guts.
311   *Lycaon* king of Arcadia, changed by Jupiter into a wolf
because of his savagery.
313   *brenning* burning.
318   *Ocean* The great sea surrounding all the known world.
319   *isles of Orkady* the Orkneys.

320   *Tilbury ferry* about 20 miles east of London.
321   *Salisbury* about 80 miles west of London.
323   *ought thee* showed you.
325   *courage* heart.
329   *departed* parted.
335   *And* if.
345   *spare* a slit in a gown.
346   *creep* One of the original texts reads "gape."   *gore* slit.

Of my gown before,
Flickering with his wings:
Alas, my heart it stings,
Remembering pretty things! 350
Alas, mine heart it slayeth,
My Philip's doleful death,
When I remember it,
How prettily it would sit
Many times and oft 355
Upon my finger aloft!
I played with him tittle-tattle,
And fed him with my spattle,
With his bill between my lips;
It was my pretty Phips! 360
Many a pretty kuss
Had I of his sweet muss;
And now the cause is thus,
That he is slain me fro,
To my great pain and woe. 365
   Of fortune this the chance
Standeth on variance:
Ofttime after pleasance
Trouble and grievance.
No man can be sure 370
All way to have pleasure,
As well perceive ye may
How my disport and play
From me was taken away
By Gib, our cat savage, 375
That in a furious rage
Caught Philip by the head
And slew him there stark dead.
*Kyrie eleison,*
*Christe eleison,* 380
*Kyrie eleison.*
For Philip Sparrow's soul
Set in our bead-roll,
Let us now whisper
A *Pater noster.* 385

*Lauda, anima mea, Dominum!*
To weep with me, look that ye come,
All manner of birds in your kind,
So none be left behind.
To mourning look that ye fall 390
With dolorous songs funeral,
Some to sing and some to say,
Some to weep and some to pray,
Every bird in his lay:

358   *spattle* spittle.
361   *kuss* kiss.
362   *muss* mouth.
379–81   Lord have mercy, Christ have mercy, Lord have mercy (in Greek, but a part of the Latin liturgy).

385   *Pater noster* Our father.
386   Praise the Lord, my soul (Psalm 145.1).
392   *say* talk.

The goldfinch, the wagtail,                          395
The jangling jay to rail,
The fleckèd pie to chatter
Of this dolorous matter.
And robin redbreast,
He shall be the priest                               400
The requiem mass to sing,
Softly warbling,
With help of the red sparrow
And the chattering swallow,
This hearse for to hallow.                           405
The lark with his long toe,
The spink and the martinet also,
The shoveller with his broad beak,
The dotterel, that foolish peak,
And also the mad coot                                410
With a bald face to toot;
The feldefare and the snite,
The crow and the kite;
The raven called Rolfè
His plainsong to sol-fa;                             415
The partridge, the quail,
The plover with us to wail;
The woodhack that singeth *chur*,
Hoarsely, as he had the murr;
The lusty chanting nightingale.                      420
The popinjay to tell her tale,
That tooteth oft in a glass
Shall read the Gospel at Mass;
The mavis with her whistle
Shall read there the Pistle.                         425
   But with a large and a long
To keep just plainsong,
Our chanters shall be the cuckoo,
The culver, the stockdoo,
With Pewit the lapwing,                              430
The versicles shall sing.
   The bitter with his bump,
The crane with his trump,
The swan of Menander,
The goose and the gander,                            435
The duck and the drake
Shall watch at this wake;
The peacock so proud
Because his voice is loud

---

397   *pie* magpie.
407   *spink* finch.  *martinet* martin.
408   *shoveller* spoonbill.
409   *dotterel* plover.  *peak* silly creature.
411   *toot* peer.
412   *feldefare* fieldfare (a kind of thrush).  *snite* snipe.
415   *sol-fa* to sing a tune using the syllables *sol* and *fa*.
418   *woodhack* woodpecker.
419   *murr* catarrh.

422   *glass* mirror.
425   *Pistle* epistle.
426   *a large and a long* notes of different length, the large being equal to two or three longs.
429   *stockdoo* stockdove (wild pigeon).
432   *bitter* bittern (whose cry sounds like "bump").
433   *trump* trumpet.
434   *Menander* Greek comic playwright (d. ca. 290 BC); a malapropism for Maeander, a winding Greek river.

And hath a glorious tail, 440
He shall sing the Grail;
The owl that is so foul
Must help us to howl;
The heron so gaunce,
And the cormoraunce, 445
With the pheasant
And the gaggling gant,
And the churlish chough,
The knot and the ruff,
The barnacle, the buzzard, 450
With the wild mallard;
The divendop to sleep,
The water hen to weep;
The puffin and the teal,
Money they shall deal 455
To poor folk at large,
That shall be their charge;
The sea mew and the titmouse,
The woodcock with the long nose,
The threstle with her warbling, 460
The starling with her brabbling,
The rook, with the osprey
That putteth fishes to a fray,
And the dainty curlew,
With the turtle most true. 465
　At this *Placebo*
We may not well forgo
The countering of the co;
The stork also
That maketh his nest 470
In chimneys to rest;
Within those walls
No broken galls
May there abide
Of cuckoldry side, 475
Or else philosophy
Maketh a great lie.
　The estridge, that will eat
An horseshoe so great
In the stead of meat, 480
Such fervent heat
His stomach doth fret:
He cannot well fly
Nor sing tunably,
Yet at a braid 485

---

441　*Grail* Gradual, an antiphon sung between the Gospel
and the Epistle in the Mass.
444　*gaunce* gaunt.
447　*gant* gannet.
449　*The knot and the ruff* two kinds of sandpiper.
452　*divendop* didapper (a type of grebe).
460　*threstle* throstle.
463　*fray* fright.

465　*turtle* turtledove.
468　*countering* singing an accompaniment. *co* jackdaw.
469–77　The male stork was said to desert or kill an unfaithful
mate.
473　*galls* sores.
475　*side* haughty.
478　*estridge* ostrich.
485　*at a braid* on a sudden impulse.

He hath well assayed
To sol-fa above E-la.
*Fa*, lorel, *fa*, *fa*,
*Ne quando*
*Male cantando*,                                              490
The best that we can
To make him our bellman
And let him ring the bells,
He can do nothing else.
     Chanticleer, our cock,                                   495
Must tell what is of the clock
By the astrology
That he hath naturally
Conceivèd and caught,
And was never taught                                         500
By Albumazar
The astronomer,
Nor by Ptolemy,
Prince of astronomy,
Nor yet by Haly;                                             505
And yet he croweth daily
And nightly the tides
That no man abides,
With Partlot his hen,
Whom now and then                                            510
He plucketh by the head
When he doth her tread.
     The bird of Araby
That potentially
May never die,                                               515
And yet there is none
But one alone:
A phoenix it is
This hearse that must bliss
With armatic gums                                            520
That cost great sums,
The way of thurification
To make a fumigation,
Sweet of reflair
And redolent of air,                                         525
This corse for to cense
With great reverence
As partriarch or pope
In a black cope.
Whiles he censeth the hearse,                                530
He shall sing the verse

---

**487**   *E-la* The highest note on the musical scale.
**488**   *lorel* rogue.
**489–90**   Lest by singing badly.
**495**   *Chanticleer* The name, like Pertlot (Pertelote) below, is from Chaucer's *Nun's Priest's Tale*.
**501**   *Albumazar* Abu-Mashar (d. 885), Arab astronomer.
**503**   *Ptolemy* Greek astronomer of the mid-second century AD.

**505**   *Haly* Haly Aben Ragel (d. 1008), Arab astrologer.
**507**   *tides* periods of time.
**514**   *potentially* through its power.
**520**   *armatic* aromatic.
**522**   *thurification* burning of incense.
**524**   *reflair* scent.
**526**   *corse* corpse.
**529**   *cope* cape.

*Libe ra me*
In *de, la, sol, re,*
Softly be-mol
For my sparrow's soul.                                              535
Pliny showeth all
In his Story Natural,
What he doth find
Of this phoenix kind,
Of whose incineration                                              540
There riseth a new creation
Of the same fashion
Without alteration,
Saving that old age
Is turned into courage                                             545
Of fresh youth again;
This matter true and plain,
Plain matter indeed,
Whoso list to read.
   But for the eagle doth fly                           550
Highest in the sky,
He shall be the sudean
The choir to demean
As provost principal,
To teach them their ordinal;                                       555
Also the noble falcon,
With the gyrfalcon,
The tiercel gentle,
They shall mourn soft and still
In their amice of gray;                                            560
The saker with them shall say
*Dirige* for Philip's soul;
The goshawk shall have a role
The choristers to control;
The lanners and the merlins                                        565
Shall stand in their mourning gowns;
The hobby and the musket
The censers and the cross shall fet;
The kestrel in all this work
Shall be holy-water clerk.                                         570
   And now the dark cloudy night
Chaseth away Phoebus bright,
Taking his course toward the west;
God send my sparrow's soul good rest!
*Requiem eternam dona eis, Domine.*                                575
*Fa, fa, fa, mi, re,*
*A por ta in fe ri,*

---

**532** Free me.

**534** *Be-mol* sing in B [flat].

**536–7** Referring to the Latin *Natural History* of Pliny the Elder (d. 79 AD), a compendium of scientific and legendary facts about the natural world; the phoenix is discussed at 10.2.

**545** *courage* vigor.

**550** *for* because.

**552** *sudean* sub-dean.

**553** *demean* direct.

**561** *saker* large falcon.

**562** *Dirige* Direct (the opening of the service for the dead).

**567** *musket* sparrowhawk.

**572** *Phoebus* the sun.

**575** Lord, give them eternal rest.

**577** From the gate of hell.

*Fa, fa, fa, mi, mi.*
*Credo videre bona Domini,*
I pray God Philip to heaven may fly.                              580
*Domine, exaudi orationem meam,*
To heaven he shall, from heaven he came.
*Do mi nus vo bis cum,*
Of all good prayers God send him some!

*Oremus.*                                                        585
*Deus, cui proprium est miserere et parcere,*
On Philip's soul have pity!
    For he was a pretty cock,
And came of a gentle stock
And wrapped in a maiden's smock                                  590
And cherished full daintily,
Till cruel fate made him to die;
Alas, for doleful destiny!
But whereto should I
Longer mourn or cry?                                             595
To Jupiter I call,
Of heaven empyreal,
That Philip may fly
Above the starry sky
To tread the pretty wren                                         600
That is our Lady's hen:
Amen, amen, amen.
    Yet one thing is behind
That now cometh to mind:
An epitaph I would have                                          605
For Philip's grave.
But for I am a maid,
Timorous, half afraid,
That never yet assayed
Of Eliconis well                                                 610
Where the Muses dwell,
Though I can read and spell,
Recount, report, and tell
Of the Tales of Canterbury
Some sad stories, some merry,                                    615
As Palamon and Arcet,
Duke Theseus, and Partelet;
And of the Wife of Bath
That worketh much scathe
When her tale is told                                            620
Among the huswives bold,
How she controlled

---

579   I trust to see the good things of the Lord (Psalm 26.13).
581   Lord, hear my prayer (Psalm 101.2).
583   The Lord be with you.
585–6   Let us pray. Lord, who alone can pity and spare.
603   *behind* left.
610   *Eliconis* Helicon's.
612ff   Jane's reading list begins with some of the first English literature to become available during the early decades of print from the presses of William Caxton and Wynkyn de Worde, most importantly Chaucer's *Canterbury Tales* and Thomas Malory's *Le Morte d'Arthur* (which in addition to Arthurian material includes the story of Tristram and Isolde).
616–17   Characters from *The Knight's Tale* and *The Nun's Priest's Tale* in Chaucer's collection.
619   *scathe* harm.

Her husbands as she would,
And them to despise
In the homeliest wise,                                                                  625
Bring other wives in thought
Their husbands to set at nought.
    And though that read have I
Of Gawain and Sir Guy,
And tell can a great piece                                                            630
Of the Golden Fleece,
How Jason it wan
Like a valiant man;
Or Arthur's Round Table,
With his knights commendable,                                                     635
And dame Gaynor, his queen,
Was somewhat wanton, I wene;
How Sir Lancelot de Lake
Many a spear brake
For his lady's sake;                                                                     640
Of Tristram and King Mark
And all the whole work
Of Belle Isolde his wife,
For whom was much strife;
Some say she was light                                                                 645
And made her husband knight
Of the common hall
That cuckolds men call;
And of Sir Libius
Namèd Disconius;                                                                        650
Of Quater Filz Amund,
And how they were summoned
To Rome, to Charlemagne
Upon a great pain,
And how they rode each one                                                          655
On Bayard Montalbon;
Men see him now and then
In the forest of Arden.
What though I can frame
The stories by name                                                                     660
Of Judas Maccabeus
And of Caesar Julius;
And of the love between
Paris and Vienne;
And of the Duke Hannibal                                                             665
That made the Romans all
Fordread and to quake;

**632** *wan* won.

**636** *Gaynor* Guinevere.

**649–50** Sir Libius / Namèd Disconius *Libeaus Desconus*, a popular romance about the son of Gawain.

**651** Quater Filz Amund *The Four Sons of Aymon*, another popular romance, published in an English translation by Caxton and de Worde.

**656** *Bayard Montalbon* The names respectively of the horse and the castle of one of Aymon's sons.

**661** *Judas Maccabeus* Jewish leader who led a rebellion against the Seleucid empire (167–161 BC) and re-dedicated the Temple at Jerusalem; with Julius Caesar he appears on the medieval list of the Nine Worthies.

**664** *Paris and Vienne* Lovers in a French romance published in an English version by Caxton.

**665** *Hannibal* Carthaginian general who fought the Romans in the Second Punic War (218–201 BC).

How Scipion did wake
The city of Carthage,
Which by his merciful rage                              670
He beat down to the ground;
And though I can expound
Of Hector of Troy
That was all their joy,
Whom Achilles slew,                                    675
Wherefore all Troy did rue;
And of the love so hot
That made Troilus to dote
Upon fair Cressid,
And what they wrote and said;                          680
And of their wanton wills
Pandar bare the bills
From one to the other,
His master's love to further;
Sometime a precious thing,                             685
An ouch or else a ring,
From her to him again;
Sometime a pretty chain,
Or a bracelet of her hair,
Prayed Troilus for to wear                             690
That token for her sake;
How heartily he did it take
And much thereof did make;
And all that was in vain,
For she did but feign.                                 695
The story telleth plain
He could not obtain,
Though his father were a king,
Yet there was a thing
That made the male to wring.                           700
She made him to sing
The song of lovers' lay,
Musing night and day,
Mourning all alone,
Comfort had he none                                    705
For she was quite gone;
Thus in conclusion
She brought him in abusion.
In earnest and in game
She was much to blame;                                 710
Disparaged is her fame
And blemished is her name,
In manner half with shame.
Troilus also hath lost
On her much love and cost,                             715

668  *Scipion* Scipio, the name of two Roman generals who successfully fought against the Carthaginians; the second of them effected the final conquest and destruction of the city in 146 BC.
677–723  A sketch of the story of Chaucer's *Troilus and Criseyde*, set during the Trojan war.

682  *Pandar* Troilus's friend and Criseyde's uncle. *bills* letters.
686  *ouch* brooch.
700  *made the male to wring* caused trouble.
708  *brought him in abusion* deceived him.

And now must kiss the post.
Pandar, that went between
Hath won nothing, I wene,
But light for summer green;
Yet for a special laud                                      720
He is named Troilus' bawd;
Of that name he is sure
Whiles the world shall dure.
    Though I remember the fable
Of Penelope most stable,                                    725
To her husband most true,
Yet long time she ne knew
Whether he were on live or dead;
Her wit stood her in stead
That she was true and just                                  730
For any bodily lust
To Ulyxes her make,
And never would him forsake.
    Of Marcus Marcellus
A process I could tell us,                                  735
And of Antiochus,
And of Josephus
*De Antiquitatibus*;
And of Mardocheus,
And of great Assuerus,                                      740
And of Vesca his queen,
Whom he forsook with teen,
And of Hester his other wife,
With whom he led a pleasant life;
Of King Alexander,                                          745
And of King Evander,
And of Porsena the Great
That made the Romans to sweat.
    Though I have enrolled
A thousand new and old                                      750
Of these historious tales
To fill budgets and mails
With books that I have read,
Yet I am nothing sped,
And can but little skill                                    755
Of Ovid or Virgil

716  *kiss the post* have nothing to show for it.
719  *light for summer green* light clothing for summer (i.e., not much).
720  *laud* praise.
728  *on live* alive.
732  *make* mate.
734  *Marcus Marcellus* Roman consul who died (207 BC) fighting against Hannibal.
735  *process* story.
736  *Antiochus* Presumably Antiochus the Great (d. 187 BC), king of Syria, to whom Hannibal fled toward the end of his life for protection from Rome.

737  *Josephus* Flavius Josephus (first century AD), author of several works on Jewish history, including *Antiquitates Iudaicae* ("Jewish Antiquities").
739–44  The story of the biblical book of Esther (Hester), concerning Mordecai, Ahasuerus, and Vashti.
742  *teen* anger.
746  *Evander* Latin king allied with Aeneas in the second half of the *Aeneid*.
747  *Porsena the Great* Lars Porsena, legendary king said to have waged war against Rome in its earliest days.
752  *budgets and mails* pouches and bags.
754  *sped* skilled.
755  *skill* understand.

Or of Plutarch
Or Francis Petrarch,
Alceus or Sappho,
Or such other poets moe                                    760
As Linus and Homerus,
Euphorion amd Theocritus,
Anacreon and Arion,
Sophocles and Philemon,
Pindarus and Simonides,                                    765
Philistion and Phorocides;
These poets of ancienty,
They are too diffuse for me.
   For, as I tofore have said,
I am but a young maid,                                     770
And cannot in effect
My style as yet direct
With English words elect.
Our natural tongue is rude
And hard to be ennewed                                     775
With polishèd terms lusty;
Our language is so rusty,
So cankered and so full
Of frowards, and so dull,
That if I would apply                                      780
To write ornately,
I wot not where to find
Terms to serve my mind.
   Gower's English is old
And of no value told;                                      785
His matter is worth gold,
And worthy to be enrolled.
   In Chaucer I am sped,
His tales I have read.
His matter is delectable,                                  790
Solacious and commendable,
His English well allowed
So as it is enprowed.
For as it is enployed
There is no English void                                   795
At those days much commended;
And now men would have amended
His English, whereat they bark
And mar all they work.
Chaucer, that famous clerk,                                800
His terms were not dark,

---

757  *Plutarch* Prolific Greek biographer and philosopher from the late first and early second centuries AD.

759–66  A putative list of classical Greek poets and dramatists, with some possibly deliberate confusions. "Phorocides" is probably Pherecydes, an early writer of prose, Philistion the writer of mimes whom the epigrammatist Martial mentions. Of most writers on the list, very little survives; Linus and Arion are mythic figures with nothing extant to their name.

767  *ancienty* antiquity.
768  *diffuse* difficult.
775  *ennewed* renewed.
779  *frowards* ill-formed things.
784  *Gower* John Gower (d. 1408), English poet and friend of Chaucer, best known for his *Confessio Amantis*.
791  *solacious* pleasing.
793  *enprowed* put to good use.
801  *dark* obscure.

But pleasant, easy, and plain;
Ne word he wrote in vain.
　　Also John Lydgate
Writeth after an higher rate.　　　　　　　　　805
It is diffuse to find
The sentence of his mind,
Yet writeth he in his kind,
No man that can amend
Those matters that he hath penned;　　　　　810
Yet some men find a fault
And say he writeth too hault.
　　Wherefore hold me excused
If I have not well perused
Mine English half-abused;　　　　　　　　　815
Though it be refused,
In worth I shall it take
And fewer wordes make.
　　But for my sparrow's sake
Yet as a woman may　　　　　　　　　　　　820
My wit I shall assay
An epitaph to write
In Latin plain and light,
Whereof the elegy
Followeth by and by.　　　　　　　　　　　825

*Flos volucrum formose, vale!*
*Philippe, sub isto*
*Marmore iam recubas,*
*Qui mihi carus eras.*
*Semper erunt nitido*　　　　　　　　　　　830
*Radiantia sidera caelo,*
*Impressusque meo*
*Pectore semper eris.*
　　*Per me laurigerum*
*Britannum Skeltonida vatem*　　　　　　　835
*Haec cecinisse licet*
*Ficta sub imagine texta,*
*Cuius eris volucris,*
*Praestanti corpore virgo.*
*Candida Nais erat,*　　　　　　　　　　　840
*Formosior ista Joanna est;*
*Docta Corinna fuit,*
*Sed magis ista sapit.*
　　*Bien m'en souvient.*

804　*John Lydgate* Immensely prolific English poet of the early fifteenth century.
807　*sentence* meaning.
812　*too hault* in too high a style.
817　*In worth* in good part.
826–33　Fair flower of birds, farewell! Philip, you now lie under this marble, you who were dear to me. The shining stars will always be in the bright heaven, and you will always be imprinted on my heart.

834–44　Through me, the laureate British poet Skelton, these things could be sung, concealed under a fictitious image of her whose bird you will be, a virgin with an outstanding body. The naiad was fair, but this Jane is more beautiful; Corinna was learned, but this woman knows more.
842　*Corinna* Ovid's mistress in his *Amores*; the *docta puella*, "learned girl," was an ideal in Roman erotic elegy.
844　I remember it well (a posy used by Skelton in other poems as well).

THE COMMENDATIONS

*Beati im ma cu la ti in via,*                                845
*O gloriosa femina!*
Now mine whole imagination
And studious meditation
Is to take this commendation
In this consideration,                                       850
And under patient toleration
Of that most goodly maid
That *Placebo* hath said
And for her sparrow prayed
In lamentable wise.                                          855
    Now will I enterprise
Thorough the grace divine
Of the Muses nine
Her beauty to commend,
If Arethusa will send                                        860
Me influence to indite
And with my pen to write;
If Apollo will promise
Melodiously it to devise
His tunable harp strings                                     865
With armony that sings
Of princes and of kings
And of all pleasant things,
Of lust and of delight,
Thorough his godly might:                                    870
To whom be the laud ascribed
That my pen hath inbibed
With the aureate droppes,
As verily my hope is,
Of Tagus, that golden flood                                  875
That passeth all earthly good.
And as that flood doth pass
All floods that ever was
With his golden sands,
Who so that understands                                      880
Cosmography and the streams
And the floods in strange reams,
Right so she doth exceed
All other of whom we read,
Whose fame by me shall spread                                885
Into Perse and Mede,
From Britain's Albion
To the tower of Babylon.
    I trust it is no shame
And no man will me blame,                                    890
Though I register her name

845–6   Blessed are the immaculate in the way (Psalm 118.1),
O glorious woman!
860   *Arethusa* A nymph metamorphosed into a famous spring
in Sicily; Vergil invokes her as a Muse of pastoral poetry.
866   *armony* harmony.

875   *Tagus* A river in Portugal, whose sands were supposed
to contain gold.
882   *reams* realms.
886   *Perse and Mede* Persia and Media.

In the court of fame;
For this most goodly flower,
This blossom of fresh color,
So Jupiter me succor,                                              895
She flourisheth new and new
In beauty and virtue.
*Hac claritate gemina,*
*O gloriosa femina,*
*Retribue servo tuo, vivifica me!*                                 900
*Labia mea laudabunt te.*
  But enforced am I
Openly to ascry
And to make an outcry
Against odious Envy,                                               905
That evermore will lie
And say cursedly:
With his leather eye
And cheekes dry;
With visage wan                                                    910
As swart as tan;
His bonès crake,
Lean as a rake;
His gummes rusty
Are full unlusty;                                                  915
His heart withal
Bitter as gall;
His liver, his lung
With anger is wrung;
His serpent's tongue                                               920
That many one hath stung;
He frowneth ever,
He laugheth never
Even nor morrow,
But other men's sorrow                                             925
Causeth him to grin
And rejoice therein;
No sleep can him catch,
But ever doth watch,
He is so beat                                                      930
With malice, and fret
With anger and ire,
His foul desire
Will suffer no sleep
In his head to creep;                                              935
His foul semblant
All displeasant;
When other are glad,
Then is he sad,
Frantic and mad;                                                   940

---

**898–9** With this twin brightness, O glorious woman.
**900** Reward your servant, bring me back to life (Psalm 118.17).
**901** My lips will praise you (Psalm 62.4).

**903** *ascry* cry out.
**907** *say cursedly* pronounce curses.
**912** *crake* creak.
**936** *semblant* appearance.

His tongue never still
For to say ill,
Writhing and wringing,
Biting and stinging;
And thus this elf                                                    945
Consumeth himself,
Himself doth slo
With pain and woe.
   This false Envy
Saith that I                                                         950
Use great folly
For to indite
And for to write
And spend my time
In prose and rhyme                                                   955
For to express
The nobleness
Of my mistress
That causeth me
Studious to be                                                       960
To make a relation
Of her commendation;
And there again
Envy doth complain
And hath disdain,                                                    965
But yet certain
I will be plain
And my style dress
To this process.
   Now Phoebus me ken                                  970
To sharp my pen,
And lead my fist
As him best list,
That I may say
Honor alway                                                         975
Of womankind!
Truth doth me bind,
And loyalty
Ever to be
Their true bedell,                                                  980
To write and tell
How women excel
In nobleness;
As my mistress,
Of whom I think                                                     985
With pen and ink
For to compile
Some goodly style;
For this most goodly flower,
This blossom of fresh color,                                        990

---

947   *slo* slay.
969   *process* theme.
970   *ken* teach.

977   *Truth* Used here in the modern sense, but also as "troth," i.e., sworn fidelity – a near synonym for "loyalty" in the next line.
980   *bedell* beadle, herald.

So Jupiter me succor,
She flourisheth new and new
In beauty and virtue.
*Hac claritate gemina,*
*O gloriosa femina,*                                                995
*Legem pone mihi, domina, in viam iustificationum tuarum!*
*Quemadmodum desiderat cervus ad fontes aquarum.*
  How shall I report
All the goodly sort
Of her features clear                                              1000
That hath none earthly peer?
Her favor of her face,
Ennewèd all with grace,
Confort, pleasure, and solace,
Mine heart doth so enbrace                                         1005
And so hath ravished me
Her to behold and see,
That in wordes plain
I cannot me refrain
To look on her again.                                             1010
Alas, what should I feign?
It were a pleasant pain
With her aye to remain.
  Her eyen gray and steep
Causeth mine heart to leap;                                        1015
With her browes bent
She may well represent
Fair Lucrece, as I wene,
Or else fair Polyxene,
Or else Calliope,                                                 1020
Or else Penelope;
For this most goodly flower,
This blossom of fresh color,
So Jupiter me succor,
She flourisheth new and new                                       1025
In beauty and virtue.
*Hac claritate gemina,*
*O gloriosa femina,*
*Memor esto verbi tui servo tuo!*
*Servus tuus sum ego.*                                            1030
  The Indy sapphire blue
Her veins doth ennew;
The orient pearl so clear,
The whiteness of her leer;

---

**996** Lay down the law, lady, in the path of your justice (Psalm 118.33). The original sources here give the Vulgate reading *Domine*, "Lord," rather than *domina*, "lady," but in quotations from the Psalms at ll. 1061 and 1114 below *Domine* is changed to *domina*, and the failure to do so here is probably an oversight.
**997** In the way that a deer desires the fountains of water (Psalm 41.2).
**1003** *Ennewèd* renewed.
**1014** *eyen* eyes. *steep* brilliant.
**1018** *Lucrece* Lucretia, a traditional paragon of Roman female virtue; her rape in the late fifth century BC was said to have prompted her husband and others to depose the king and establish the Roman republic.
**1019** *Polyxene* A daughter of Priam, king of Troy; after the fall of the city, she was ritually sacrificed by the Greeks.
**1020** *Calliope* Muse of epic poetry, mother of Orpheus.
**1029** Be mindful of your word to your servant (Psalm 118.49).
**1030** I am your servant (Psalm 118.125).
**1031** *Indy* Indian.
**1034** *leer* cheek.

The lusty ruby ruds 1035
Resemble the rose buds;
Her lippes soft and merry
Embloomèd like the cherry;
It were an heavenly bliss
Her sugared mouth to kiss. 1040
    Her beauty to augment,
Dame Nature hath her lent
A wart upon her cheek,
Whoso list to seek
In her visage a scar 1045
That seemeth from afar
Like to the radiant star,
All with favor fret,
So properly it is set.
She is the violet, 1050
The daisy delectable,
The columbine commendable,
The jelofer amiable;
For this most goodly flower,
This blossom of fresh color, 1055
So Jupiter me succor,
She flourisheth new and new
In beauty and virtue.
*Hac claritate gemina,*
*O gloriosa femina,* 1060
*Bonitatem fecisti cum servo tuo, domina,*
*Et ex praecordiis sonant praeconia.*
    And when I perceived
Her wart and conceived,
It cannot be denayed 1065
But it was well conveyed,
And set so womanly,
And nothing wantonly,
But right conveniently
And full congruently 1070
As Nature could devise
In most goodly wise.
Whoso list behold,
It maketh lovers bold
To her to sue for grace, 1075
Her favor to purchase.
    The scar upon her chin
Enhached on her fair skin
Whiter than the swan,
It would make any man 1080
To forget deadly sin
Her favor to win;
For this most goodly flower,

---

1035  *ruds* red spots.
1048  *with favor fret* adorned with beauty.
1053  *jelofer* gillyflower.
1061  You have dealt well with your servant, lady (Psalm 118.65, with *Dominus* changed to *domina*).

1062  And from the heart the proclamations sound.
1065  *denayed* denied.
1078  *Enhached* inlaid.

This blossom of fresh color,
So Jupiter me succor,                                                    1085
She flourisheth new and new
In beauty and virtue.
*Hac claritate gemina,*
*O gloriosa femina,*
*Defecit in salutare tuum anima mea;*                                    1090
*Quid petis filio, mater dulcissima? Ba ba.*
    Soft, and make no din,
For now I will begin
To have in remembrance
Her goodly dalliance                                                     1095
And her goodly pastance:
So sad and so demure,
Behaving her so sure,
With wordes of pleasure
She would make to the lure                                              1100
And any man convert
To give her his whole heart.
She made me sore amazed
Upon her when I gazed,
Methought mine heart was crazed,                                        1105
My eyen were so dazed.
For this most goodly flower,
This blossom of fresh color,
So Jupiter me succor,
She flourisheth new and new                                             1110
In beauty and virtue.
*Hac claritate gemina,*
*O gloriosa femina,*
*Quomodo dilexi legem tuam, domina!*
*Recedant vetera, nova sint omnia.*                                     1115
    And to amend her tale
When she list to avail
And with her fingers smale
And handes soft as silk,
Whiter than the milk,                                                   1120
That are so quickly veined,
Wherewith my hand she strained,
Lord, how I was pained!
Uneath I me refrained;
How she me had reclaimed                                                1125
And me to her retained,
Embracing therewithal
Her goodly middle small
With sidès long and strait.

---

1090  My soul languishes for your salvation (Psalm 118.81).
1091  What do you seek for your son, sweetest mother?
Ba, ba.
1095  *dalliance* light conversation.
1096  *pastance* pastime.
1097  *sad* serious.
1100  *make to the lure* draw to her (the language of falconry).
1105  *crazed* shattered.

1114  How I loved your law, O lady (Psalm 118.97, with *Dominus* changed to *domina*).
1115  Let the old withdraw, let all be new (adapted from 2 Corinthians 5.17).
1117  *avail* achieve her purpose.
1118  *smale* small.
1121  *quickly* in a lifelike manner.
1125  *reclaimed* tamed (a term from falconry).

To tell you what conceit                                          1130
I had then in a trice,
The matter were too nice;
And yet there was no vice,
Nor yet no villainy,
But only fantasy;                                                1135
For this most goodly flower,
This blossom of fresh color,
So Jupiter me succor,
She flourisheth new and new
In beauty and virtue.                                            1140
*Hac claritate gemina,*
*O gloriosa femina,*
*Iniquos odio habui!*
*Non calumnientur me superbi.*
    But whereto should I note                                    1145
How often did I toot
Upon her pretty foot?
It raisèd mine heart-root
To see her tread the ground
With heeles short and round.                                     1150
She is plainly express
Egeria, the goddess,
And like to her image
Emportured with courage,
A lover's pilgrimage.                                            1155
There is no beast savage
Ne no tiger so wood
But she would change his mood,
Such relucent grace
Is formèd in her face;                                           1160
For this most goodly flower,
This blossom of fresh color,
So Jupiter me succor,
She flourisheth new and new
In beauty and virtue.                                            1165
*Hac claritate gemina,*
*O gloriosa femina,*
*Mirabilia testimonia tua!*
*Sicut novellae plantationes in iuventute sua.*
    So goodly as she dresses,                                    1170
So properly she presses
The bright golden tresses
Of her hair so fine,
Like Phoebus' beames shine.
Whereto should I disclose                                        1175

---

1132   *nice* delicate.
1143   I have held the unjust in hatred (Psalm 118.113).
1144   Let not the proud defame me (Psalm 118.122).
1146   *toot* peer.
1151   *express* to an exact likeness.
1152   *Egeria* Nymph said to have been adviser to and confidante of Numa, the second king of Rome.

1154   *Emportured* depicted (though the term is otherwise unattested, and may be a misprint for "importuned").   *courage* vigor.
1157   *wood* enraged.
1159   *relucent* refulgent.
1168   Your testimonies are miraculous (Psalm 118.129).
1169   Like young plantings in their youth (Psalm 143.12).
1174   *shine* brightness.

The gartering of her hose?
It is for to suppose
How that she can wear
Gorgeously her gear,
Her fresh habiliments                                        1180
With other implements
To serve for all intents
Like Dame Flora, queen
Of lusty summer green;
For this most goodly flower,                                 1185
This blossom of fresh color,
So Jupiter me succor,
She flourisheth new and new
In beauty and virtue.
*Hac claritate gemina,*                                      1190
*O gloriosa femina,*
*Clamavi in toto corde, exaudi me!*
*Misericordia tua magna est super me.*
    Her kirtle so goodly laced,
And under that is braced                                     1195
Such pleasures that I may
Neither write nor say;
Yet though I write not with ink,
No man can let me think,
For thought hath liberty,                                    1200
Thought is frank and free.
To think a merry thought,
It cost me little nor nought.
Would God mine homely style
Were polished with the file                                  1205
Of Cicero's eloquence
To praise her excellence!
For this most goodly flower,
This blossom of fresh color,
So Jupiter me succor,                                        1210
She flourisheth new and new
In beauty and virtue.
*Hac claritate gemina,*
*O gloriosa femina,*
*Principes persecuti sunt me gratis!*                        1215
*Omnibus consideratis,*
*Paradisus voluptatis*
*Haec virgo est dulcissima.*
    My pen it is unable,
My hand it is unstable,                                      1220
My reason rude and dull
To praise her at the full:
Goodly mistress Jane,

---

1177  One can only guess.
1180  *habiliments* clothes.
1192  I have cried out with all my heart; hear me (Psalm 118.145).
1193  Your compassion for me is great (Psalm 85.13).

1199  *let me think* keep me from thinking.
1215  Princes have persecuted me for no reason (Psalm 118.161).
1216–18  All things considered, this sweetest virgin is a paradise of pleasure.

Sober, demure Diane;
Jane this mistress hight,                                    1225
The lodestar of delight,
Dame Venus of all pleasure,
The well of worldly treasure;
She doth exceed and pass
In prudence Dame Pallas.                                     1230
For this most goodly flower,
This blossom of fresh color,
So Jupiter me succor,
She flourisheth new and new
In beauty and virtue.                                        1235
*Hac claritate gemina,*
*O gloriosa femina!*
  *Requiem eternam dona eis, Domine!*
With this psalm, *Domine, probasti me,*
Shall sail over the sea,                                     1240
With *Tibi, Domine, commendamus,*
On pilgrimage to Saint James,
For shrimps and for pranes
And for stalking cranes;
And where my pen hath offended,                             1245
I pray you it may be amended
By discreet consideration
Of your wise reformation.
I have not offended, I trust,
If it be sadly discussed.                                    1250
It were no gentle guise
This treatise to despise
Because I have written and said
Honor to this fair maid.
Wherefore should I be blamed                                 1255
That I Jane have named
And famously proclaimed?
She is worthy to be enrolled
With letters of gold.
  *Car elle vaut.*                                           1260
*Per me laurigerum Britonum Skeltonida vatem*
*Laudibus eximiis merito haec redimita puella est.*
*Formosam cecini, qua non formosior ulla est;*
*Formosam potius quam commendaret Homerus.*
*Sic iuvat interdum rigidos recreare labores,*              1265
*Nec minus hoc titulo tersa Minerva mea est:*
*Rien que plaisir.*

---

1224  *Diane* Diana, goddess of virginity.
1230  *Pallas* Pallas Athena, goddess of wisdom.
1238  Give them eternal rest, Lord.
1239  *Domine, probasti me* Lord, you have tested me (Psalm 138.1).
1241  *Tibi, Domine, commendamus* To you, Lord, we commend.
1242  *Saint James* Santiago de Compostela in Spain.
1243  *pranes* prawns.
1250  *sadly* seriously.

1251  *guise* behavior.
1260  For she is worthy.
1261–7  Through me, the laureate British poet Skelton, this girl is deservedly wreathed with extraordinary praise. I sang of this beautiful girl, than whom none is more beautiful; a beautiful girl preferable to any Homer would have commended. Thus at times it is pleasant to bring refreshment to hard labors, nor is my trim Minerva [i.e., wisdom] any less than this motto: Nothing but to please.

Thus endeth the book of Philip Sparrow, and here followeth an addition made by Master Skelton.

The guise nowadays
Of some jangling jays
Is to discommend                                1270
That they cannot amend,
Though they would spend
All the wits they have.
   What ail them to deprave
Philip Sparrow's grave?                          1275
His *Dirige*, her Commendation
Can be no derogation,
But mirth and consolation
Made by protestation,
No man to miscontent                             1280
With Philip's interement.
   Alas, that goodly maid,
Why should she be afraid?
Why should she take shame
That her goodly name,                            1285
Honorably reported,
Should be set and sorted
To be matriculate
With ladies of estate?
   I conjure thee, Philip Sparrow,      1290
By Hercules that hell did harrow
And with a venemous arrow
Slew of the Epidaures
One of the centaures
Or onocentaures                                  1295
Or hippocentaures;
By whose might and main
An hart was slain
With hornes twain
Of glittering gold;                              1300
And the apples of gold
Of Hesperides withhold
And with a dragon kept
That never more slept,
By martial strength                              1305
He wan at length;
And slew Geryon
With three bodies in one;
With mighty courage

1268  *guise* fashion.

1274  *deprave* desecrate.

1281  *interement* burial.

1291–1321  A series of references to the exploits of Hercules: the abduction of the hound Cerberus from the underworld; the battle with the centaurs; the capture of a deer sacred to Diana; the theft of the golden apples of the Hesperides; the killing of the three-bodied giant Geryon; the killing of the Nemean lion; the capture of the flesh-eating mares of Diomedes; and the fight with the river god Achelous, whose severed horn became the horn of plenty.

1293  *Epidaures* inhabitants of Epidaurus. The reason for the reference is obscure.

1295  *onocentaures* On etymological grounds these would seem to be creatures half-human and half-ass, but in Greek literature the term was used for something more apelike.

1296  *hippocentaures* The same thing as centaurs in the usual understanding: creatures half-human and half-horse.

Adaunted the rage　　　　　　　　　　　　　1310
Of a lion savage;
Of Diomedes' stable
He brought out a rabble
Of coursers and rounces
With leaps and bounces.　　　　　　　　　　1315
And with mighty lugging,
Wrestling and tugging,
He plucked the bull
By the hornèd skull
And offered to Cornucopia;　　　　　　　　1320
And so forth *per cetera*.
　　And also by Ecate's bower
In Pluto's ghastly tower;
By the ugly Eumenides
That never have rest nor ease;　　　　　　1325
By the venemous serpent
That in hell is never brent,
In Lerna, the Greeks' fen,
That was engendered then;
By Chimera's flames　　　　　　　　　　　　1330
And all the deadly names
Of infernal poustie
Where souls fry and rosty;
By the Stygial flood
And the streames wood　　　　　　　　　　1335
Of Cocytus' bottomless well;
By the ferryman of hell,
Charon with his beard hoar,
That roweth with a rude oar,
And with his frouncèd foretop　　　　　　1340
Guideth his boat with a prop:
　　I conjure, Philip, and call
In the name of King Saul;
*Primo Regum* express,
He bade the phytoness　　　　　　　　　　1345
To witchcraft her to dress,
And by her abusions,
And damnable illusions
Of marvelous conclusions,
And by her superstitions　　　　　　　　1350
And wonderful conditions,

---

**1310** *Adaunted* subdued. The original texts read "avaunted," i.e., "boasted of."
**1314** *rounces* rounciers (riding horses).
**1322** *Ecate* Hecate, goddess of magic and spells.
**1324** *Eumenides* the Furies, goddesses of retribution and spite.
**1326** *the venemous serpent* the multi-headed Hydra, slain by Hercules.
**1327** *brent* burnt.
**1330** *Chimera* a fire-breathing monster, part-goat and part-lion.
**1332** *poustie* power.
**1333** *rosty* roast.

**1334** *the Stygial flood* the river Styx, bordering the underworld.
**1336** *Cocytus* another river in the underworld.
**1340** *frouncèd foretop* furrowed forehead.
**1344** *Primo Regum* A biblical citation, from 1 Kings (now known as 1 Samuel); the story in question is told in chapter 28. *express* as stated.
**1345** *phytoness* Pythoness, a woman with magical powers; the term derives from the Greek myth of Python, but is applied in the Vulgate to the Witch of Endor (1 Samuel 28.7).
**1347** *abusions* perverse practices.
**1351** *conditions* qualities.

She raised up in that stead
Samuel that was dead;
But whether it were so
He were *idem in numero*                                    1355
The selfsame Samuel,
Howbeit to Saul did he tell
The Philistines should him ascry
And the next day he should die,
I will myself discharge                                     1360
To lettered men at large.
   But Philip, I conjure thee
Now by these names three,
Diana in the woods green,
Luna that so bright doth shine,                             1365
Proserpina in hell,
That thou shortly tell
And show now unto me
What the cause may be
Of this perplexity!                                         1370

*Inferias, Philippe, tuas Scroupe pulchra Ioanna*
*Instanter petiit: cur nostri carminis illam*
*Nunc pudet? Est sero; minor est infamia vero.*

Then such as have disdained
And of this work complained,                                1375
I pray God they be pained
No worse than is contained
In verses two or three
That follow as you may see:

*Luride, cur, livor, volucris pia funera damnas?*           1380
*Talia te rapiant rapiunt quae fata volucrem!*
   *Est tamen invidia mors tibi continua.*

1355 *idem in numero* one and the same.
1358 *ascry* challenge.
1360 *myself discharge* speak my mind.
1364–6 The three goddesses here are sometimes treated as manifestations of the same deity, though normally with Hecate in the place of Proserpina.

1371–3 Philip, the beautiful Jane Scrope urgently sought your funeral rites; why is she now ashamed of our song? It is too late; disgrace is less than truth.
1380–2 Why, ghastly Spite, do you condemn the pious funeral rites of a bird? May such fates as seized the bird seize you! Yet death is continuous for you because of envy.

## From *Garland or Chaplet of Laurel*

### To Mistress Margaret Hussey

Merry Margaret,
As midsummer flower,
Gentle as falcon
Or hawk of the tower.
   With solace and gladness,                  5

2 *midsummer flower* daisy (sometimes called "herb Margaret").
4 *hawk of the tower* a hawk that "towers," i.e., hovers at a great height.

Much mirth and no madness,
All good and no badness,
So joyously,
So maidenly,
So womanly                                                    10
Her demeaning
In everything,
Far, far passing
That I can indite
Or suffice to write                                           15
Of merry Margaret,
As midsummer flower,
Gentle as falcon
Or hawk of the tower.
  As patient and as still                             20
And as full of good will
As fair Isaphill;
Coliander,
Sweet pomander,
Good Cassander,                                               25
Steadfast of thought,
Well made, well wrought;
Far may be sought
Erst that ye can find
So courteous, so kind                                         30
As merry Margaret,
This midsummer flower,
Gentle as falcon,
Or hawk of the tower.

11   *demeaning* demeanor.
22   *Isaphill* Hypsipyle, queen of Lemnos, whose adventures earned her a particular reputation for devotion and endurance.
23   *Coliander* coriander.

25   *Cassander* Cassandra, Trojan prophetess who persisted in her accurate prophecies even though they were not believed.
29   *Erst* before.

# Sir Thomas More (1477–1535)

A lawyer and intellectual with an international reputation, More entered Henry VIII's service in 1517 as a Privy Councillor, and advanced to the post of Lord Chancellor in 1529. Unable to support the break with Roman Catholicism, More resigned in 1532, and in 1534 would not swear to support the Act of Succession; he was convicted of treason and beheaded. The Catholic Church canonized him in 1935. Over the course of his life More composed a large amount of Latin verse, and a smaller body of English poetry. The two poems given here were supposedly written in the Tower of London during his last days. According to his son-in-law William Roper, the first was written in response to an unctuously reassuring visit from Thomas Cromwell, who had actually been instrumental in More's downfall.

*Edition*: More's English poems are edited by Anthony S. G. Edwards in *The Yale Edition of the Complete Works of St. Thomas More*, vol. 1 (New Haven, CT: Yale University Press, 1997).

## Louis, the Lost Lover

Ay, flattering Fortune, look thou never so fair,
Nor never so pleasantly begin to smile,
As though thou wouldst my ruin all repair;
During my life thou shalt me not beguile.
Trust shall I God, to enter in a while          5
His haven of heaven ever sure and uniform;
Ever after thy calm, look I for a storm.

## Davy, the Dicer

Long was I, Lady Luck, your serving man,
And now have I lost again all that I gat.
Wherefore when I think on you now and then,
And in my mind remember this and that,
You may not blame me, though I beshrew your cat.          5
But in faith I bless you again a thousand times
For lending me now some leisure to make rhymes.

1 *Lady Luck* The earliest citation of this phrase in the *OED*.

5 *beshrew your cat* "To turn the cat" was a dicing term for making things appear the opposite of what they are; More's phrase probably means "curse whatever tricks you have planned."

# Henry VIII (1491–1547)

Several song lyrics, with musical settings, are attributed to King Henry VIII, most of them, including this one, in a manuscript (British Library Add. MS 31922), written not too long before 1515. (For a transcript of the texts in the manuscript, see Ewald Flügel, "Lieder-sammlungen des XVI. Jahrhunderts," *Anglia*, 12 (1889), 226–56.) There is no external confirmation of Henry's authorship, but there is no particular reason to doubt it either: virtuosity with poetry and music is certainly not a reputation he would have disowned. There does seem something authentically imperious in the doctrine expressed in the song given here: good times are the seminar of virtue, and therefore my festivities will go unopposed. The imperative of present pleasure does not, as it does in the classic *carpe diem* argument, rely on the anticipation of decay or death.

Pastime with good company
I love, and shall until I die.
Grudge who list, but none deny;
So God be pleased, thus live will I.
    For my pastance              5
    Hunt, sing, and dance,
    My heart is set.
    All goodly sport
    For my comfort,
    Who shall me let?            10

Youth must have some dalliance,
Of good or ill some pastance.
Company methinks there best
All thoughts and fancies to digest;
    For idleness              15
    Is chief mistress
    Of vices all.
    Then who can say
    But mirth and play
    Is best of all?            20

Company with honesty
Is virtue, vices to flee;
Company is good and ill,
But every man hath his free will.
    The best ensue,           25
    The worst eschew,
    My mind shall be.
    Virtue to use,
    Vice to refuse:
    Thus shall I use me.       30

5  *pastance* pastime.
10  *let* prevent.

14  *digest* disperse.
25  *ensue* follow.

# Sir Thomas Wyatt (1503–1542)

The son of a knight who had been imprisoned and tortured by Richard III and held several positions in the court of Henry VIII, Wyatt was born at Allington Castle in Kent and educated at Cambridge, and began his own court service as early as 1516; he seems at times to have been on terms of particular intimacy with Henry. By 1520 he was married to Elizabeth Brooke, but separated from her within a few years, accusing her of adultery. He had some measure of romantic involvement with Anne Boleyn before she became Henry's mistress: several of Wyatt's poems appear to refer to her, with varying degrees of explicitness. Sometime in his mid-thirties Wyatt formed a lasting attachment with Elizabeth Darrell, who had been a maid of honor to Catherine of Aragon, Henry's first queen; she bore Wyatt at least one child, and was remembered in his will. At the time of Anne Boleyn's fall in 1536, Wyatt was imprisoned in the Tower of London along with her accused lovers, and apparently witnessed her execution from his window (see below, "Who list his ease and wealth retain"). He was, however, released and eventually restored to favor, and in 1537–9 was Henry's ambassador to the emperor (and king of Spain) Charles V. In 1540 he witnessed the execution of his patron Thomas Cromwell (see below, "The pillar perished is whereto I leant"). Early the next year he was again imprisoned, on charges of treasonous activity brought by some of his long-standing enemies in the court. The speech he prepared for his own defense has survived, though the trial itself probably never occurred. Wyatt was pardoned and released at the intercession of Queen Catherine Howard, reportedly after confessing his guilt, and restored to royal service. He was on his way to Falmouth to greet the emperor's ambassador and escort him to court when he contracted a fatal fever.

Wyatt's repute as a poet was quite high in the elite circles within which his work circulated. Much of it was in a well-established tradition of song lyric that was central to the style of Henry's court; one of Henry's own productions in this line is given above. It is possible that Wyatt's songs were more literary in nature than their predecessors; despite the numerous musical references in them, there is no particular evidence that Wyatt himself had any expertise as a musician or composer, and only one of his poems ("Ah robin, jolly robin," not given here) comes down to us with a contemporary musical setting. Other efforts were quite clearly literary in their ambitions: the importation into English of prestigious forms of Continental poetry, notably the Petrarchan sonnet and the epistolary satire. Wyatt's sonnets appear to be the

first in English; several are translated or imitated from Petrarch and Continental Petrarchists, and Petrarchan themes and rhetoric irradiate his songs as well.

Wyatt's Petrarchism is selective, sometimes awkward, and almost always different in mood and situation from the classic Petrarchan ethos of endless, impossible desire and solitary reverie. Many of these differences are in keeping with the libidinous nature of Henry's court and Wyatt's experiences in it. The most common occasion in Wyatt's love poems is not the woman's chaste rejection of her hopeless lover but her desertion or betrayal of him; the male speaker in response characteristically insists on his own righteousness and deserving, sometimes explores the possibilities of appropriate revenge, and always stresses the importance of stability and trustworthiness. In some poems (notably "Each man me telleth I change most my device") it is not clear from Wyatt's phrasing whether he is talking about the vicissitudes of romantic love or the lethal shiftiness of life at court generally. Individual poems go against the usual pattern. In one ("There was never nothing more me pained") the male speaker must suffer in the awareness that he is the betrayer of the woman whose complaint fills most of the poem; in another ("It may be good, like it who list") he finds his own striving for rectitude disabled by the tumult around him: "For dread to fall, I stand not fast." The stand-out poem is "They flee from me that sometime did me seek," not quite like anything else we have from him. The righteousness is there, and a feint toward vindictiveness at the end; but the outrage and sarcasm are, in comparison with Wyatt's other poems, muted or baffled, dazed by the fleeting but overpowering sensuality of the first two stanzas (among the most erotic passages in English poetry) and by the speaker's memory of his own passivity in its presence. He does not know the answer to the question he poses in the last line.

One poem that may be by Wyatt was published in an anthology in the late 1530s, but for the most part his poems circulated in manuscript during his own lifetime. The textual situation is very complicated, though it is given ballast by the survival of the Egerton manuscript, Wyatt's personal collection of his poems, some written (and occasionally corrected or revised) in his own hand. In 1557 a large selection of Wyatt's poems, together with poems of Surrey and others, was printed by Richard Tottel, with the title *Songs and Sonnets* (commonly known now as Tottel's *Miscellany*). The collection went through eight editions – the last in 1587 – and was immensely popular and influential, the main route by which the lyric poetry of the first half of the century reached a general readership in the second. (The book is mentioned in Shakespeare: "I had rather than forty shillings I had my Book of Songs and Sonnets here": *Merry Wives of Windsor* 1.1.198–9.) Tottel printed texts of Wyatt's poems that had often been altered from their earlier manuscript form; many of these alterations are in the direction of metrical regularity, but some are merely inept. Tottel's version of "They flee from me that sometime did me seek" is given below by way of example; the coarsening of the final couplet itself helps measure the restraint of Wyatt's conclusion.

On Wyatt's translations from the Psalms, see below.

*Editions*: *Collected Poems of Sir Thomas Wyatt*, ed. Kenneth Muir and Patricia Thomson (Liverpool University Press, 1969), provides an old-spelling text; the modern-spelling edition of R. A. Rebholz – Sir Thomas Wyatt, *The Complete Poems* (Harmondsworth: Penguin, 1978) – is also important and in some particulars more reliable.

What vaileth truth, or by it to take pain?
To strive by steadfastess for to attain
To be just and true and flee from doubleness,
Sithens all alike, where ruleth craftiness,
Rewarded is both false and plain?                    5
Soonest he speedeth that most can feign;
True meaning heart is had in disdain.
Against deceit and doubleness
    What vaileth truth?

Deceived is he by crafty train                        10
That meaneth no guile and doth remain
Within the trap, without redress,
But for to love, lo, such a mistress
Whose cruelty nothing can refrain.
    What vaileth truth?

A rondeau; when the poem appears in Tottel, it is rewritten as a sonnet.

1 *vaileth* avails. *truth* In addition to the dominant modern sense, the word includes the sense of "troth," truthfulness to one's word and promises.

5 *plain* honest.
6 *speedeth* succeeds.
13 *But for* except.

The long love that in my thought doth harbor
And in mine heart doth keep his residence
Into my face presseth with bold pretense,
And therein campeth, spreading his banner.
She that me learneth to love and suffer              5
And will that my trust and lust's negligence
Be reined by reason, shame, and reverence
With his hardiness taketh displeasure.
Wherewithal unto the heart's forest he fleeth,
Leaving his enterprise with pain and cry,            10
And there him hideth and not appeareth.
What may I do when my master feareth,
But in the field with him to live and die?
For good is the life ending faithfully.

A translation of Petrarch, *Canzoniere* 140; Surrey's translation of the same poem is given below.

1 *long love* Petrarch has "love."
5 *learneth* teaches.
6 *trust* confidence.

8 *hardiness* boldness.
9 *heart's forest* Petrarch has "heart."
12–14 In Petrarch: "What can I do, when my lord is afraid, except stay with him until the last hour? For he makes a good end who dies loving well."

Whoso list to hunt, I know where is an hind,
But as for me, alas, I may no more;
The vain travail hath wearied me so sore,
I am of them that farthest cometh behind.
Yet may I by no means my wearied mind                    5
Draw from the deer, but as she fleeth afore,
Fainting I follow. I leave off therefore,
Since in a net I seek to hold the wind.
Who list her hunt, I put him out of doubt,
As well as I may spend his time in vain;                 10
And graven with diamonds in letters plain
There is written her fair neck round about,
*Noli me tangere*, for Caesar's I am,
And wild for to hold, though I seem tame.

Adapted from Petrarch, *Canzoniere* 190. The original alludes to a story of how deer belonging to Julius Caesar had been found three centuries after his death with collars inscribed "Noli me tangere, Caesaris sum" (Do not touch me, I am Caesar's). Wyatt changes numerous details, and uses nothing from Petrarch's last tercet, in which the sight of the deer becomes a disappearing vision. The topic becomes a popular one in Petrarchan sonneteering; for an important variation, see Spenser, *Amoretti* 67.

13 *Noli me tangere* Petrarch gives the inscription in Italian; the part that Wyatt gives in Latin is also the command of Christ to Mary Magdalene after his resurrection (John 20.17).

Each man me telleth I change most my device;
And, on my faith, methink it good reason
To change propose like after the season,
For in every case to keep still one guise
Is meet for them that would be taken wise,               5
And I am not of such manner condition,
But treated after a diverse fashion,
And thereupon my diverseness doth rise.
But you that blame this diverseness most,
Change you no more, but still after one rate             10
Treat ye me well, and keep ye in the same state;
And while with me doth dwell this wearied ghost,
My word nor I shall not be variable,
But always one, your own, both firm and stable.

1 *change most my device* change my behavior most often.      5 *taken* considered.
3 *propose* intent.   *like after the season* the way the seasons do.

If amorous faith, an heart unfeigned,
A sweet languor, a great lovely desire,
If honest will kindled in gentle fire,
If long error in a blind maze chained,
If in my visage each thought depainted,                  5
Or else in my sparkling voice lower or higher
Which now fear, now shame woefully doth tire,
If a pale color which love hath stained,
If to have another than myself more dear,
If wailing or sighing continually,                       10

A translation of Petrarch, *Canzoniere* 224; Wyatt returns to the same original in "If waker care, if sudden pale color," below.

2 *lovely* loving.
4 *error* wandering.
6 *sparkling* crackling (in Petrarch, *voci interrote*).

With sorrowful anger feeding busily,
If burning afar off and freezing near
Are cause that by love myself I destroy,
Yours is the fault and mine the great annoy.


Farewell, Love, and all thy laws forever;
Thy baited hooks shall tangle me no more.
Senec and Plato call me from thy lore,
To perfect wealth my wit for to endeavor.
In blind error when I did persever,                              5
Thy sharp repulse that pricketh aye so sore
Hath taught me to set in trifles no store,
And scape forth, since liberty is liever.
Therefore, farewell. Go trouble younger hearts,
And in me claim no more authority;                             10
With idle youth go use thy property
And thereon spend thy many brittle darts.
For hitherto though I have lost all my time,
Me lusteth no longer rotten boughs to climb.

3   *Senec* Seneca, the Roman philosopher and tragedian.      8   *liever* preferable.
4   *wealth* well-being.   *my wit for to endeavor* to direct my wit.      11   *use thy property* do what you do best.

It may be good, like it who list,
But I do doubt. Who can me blame?
For oft, assured, yet have I missed,
And now again I fear the same.
The windy words, the eyes' quaint game                        5
Of sudden change maketh me aghast;
For dread to fall, I stand not fast.

Alas, I tread an endless maze
That seeketh to accord two contraries,
And hope still and nothing haze,                              10
Imprisonèd in liberties,
As one unheard and still that cries.
Always thirsty, and yet nothing I taste;
For dread to fall, I stand not fast.

Assured, I doubt I be not sure;                               15
And should I trust to such surety
That oft hath put the proof in ure
And never hath found it trusty?
Nay, sir, in faith it were great folly,
And yet my life thus I do waste;                              20
For dread to fall, I stand not fast.

3   *missed* failed.
6   *aghast* afraid.
10  *haze* The Egerton manuscript reads "hase," which could    conjectures that "hase" is an otherwise unattested abbreviation
be "has," though "I has" would be anomalous. Rebholz            for "hazard," a possibility which fits well with the meaning
                                                               and the rhyme scheme.
                                                               17   *put the proof in ure* tested the outcome.

I find no peace, and all my war is done;
I fear and hope, I burn and freeze like ice;

A translation of Petrarch, *Canzoniere* 134.

I fly above the wind, yet can I not arise,
And nought I have, and all the world I seize on.
That looseth nor locketh holdeth me in prison, 5
And holdeth me not, yet can I scape no wise,
Nor letteth me live nor die at my device,
And yet of death it giveth me occasion.
Without eyen I see, and without tongue I plain;
I desire to perish, and yet I ask health; 10
I love an other, and thus I hate myself;
I feed me in sorrow, and laugh in all my pain;
Likewise displeaseth me both death and life,
And my delight is causer of this strife.

5 *that looseth nor locketh* that which neither releases nor
locks [me] up.
7 *at my device* as I choose.
9 *eyen* eyes.

11 *thus* Not in Petrarch.
14 Petrarch's conclusion is less paradoxical: "In this state
am I, Lady, on account of you."

My galley, chargèd with forgetfulness,
Thorough sharp seas in winter nights doth pass
Tween rock and rock; and eke mine enemy, alas,
That is my lord, steereth with cruelness;
And every oar a thought in readiness, 5
As though that death were light in such a case.
An endless wind doth tear the sail apace
Of forcèd sighs and trusty fearfulness.
A rain of tears, a cloud of dark disdain
Hath done the wearied cords great hinderance, 10
Wreathèd with error and eke with ignorance.
The stars be hid that led me to this pain,
Drownèd is reason that should me comfort,
And I remain despairing of the port.

A translation of Petrarch, *Canzoniere* 189.

1 *chargèd* freighted.
5–6 And every oar is a thought ready to act as if death were
a matter of no importance.

8 *trusty* hopeful.
12 *that led me to this pain* Not in Petrarch.
13 *reason* Petrarch has "reason and art." *comfort* The Egerton
manuscript reads "confort," which could be a mistake for
"consort."

Madam, withouten many words
Once I am sure ye will or no;
And if ye will, then leave your bourds
And use your wit and show it so.

And with a beck ye shall me call, 5
And if of one that burneth alway
Ye have any pity at all,
Answer him fair with yea or nay.

If it be yea, I shall be fain;
If it be nay, friends as before. 10
Ye shall another man obtain,
And I mine own and yours no more.

A translation of a popular Italian madrigal by Dragonetto
Bonifacio.

3 *bourds* jokes.
5 *beck* beckoning gesture.
9 *I shall be fain* The original has "I will write Yes in rhyme."

# Answer

Of few words, sir, you seem to be;
And where I doubted what I would do,
Your quick request hath causèd me
Quickly to tell you what you shall trust to.

For he that will be called with a beck                                        5
Makes hasty suit on light desire,
Is ever ready to the check,
And burneth in no wasting fire.

Therefore, whether you be leve or loath,
And whether it grieve you light or sore,                                       10
I am at a point, I have made an oath:
Content you with nay, for you get no more.

A reply to the preceding poem, which it follows (with this
heading) in the Egerton manuscript; the handwriting is differ-
ent, and aside from its appearance in the manuscript there is
no evidence that it was composed by Wyatt. There are several
Italian replies to the original madrigal, but not in this spirit.

4  *shall trust to* can expect.
9  *leve* willing.
10  *grieve* The Egerton manuscript reads "give."
11  *at a point* resolved.

Ye old mule, that think yourself so fair,
Leave off with craft your beauty to repair,
For it is true, without any fable,
No man setteth more by riding in your saddle;
Too much travail so do your train appair,                                      5
    Ye old mule!
With false savors though you deceive the air,
Whoso taste you shall well perceive your lair
Savoreth somewhat of a kipper's stable,
    Ye old mule!                                                               10
Ye must now serve to market and to fair,
All for the burden, for panniers a pair;
For since gray hairs been powdered in your sable,
The thing ye seek for you must yourself enable
To purchase it by payment and by prayer,                                       15
    Ye old mule!

A rondeau; the refrain in l. 6 is uncharacteristic of the form
and could be a mistake.

4  *setteth more by* puts a high value on.
5  *do your train appair* does damage to your gait.

7  *savor* perfume.
9  *kipper* colt (with the derogatory overtone of "coltish").
12  *All for* despite. *panniers* large baskets carried like
saddlebags.

They flee from me that sometime did me seek,
With naked foot stalking in my chamber.
I have seen them gentle, tame, and meek
That now are wild and do not remember
That sometime they put themself in danger                                      5

5  *danger* Partly in the older sense of "power" – they entered
my dominion – though the modern sense is strong as well.

To take bread at my hand; and now they range,
Busily seeking with a continual change.

Thankèd be fortune, it hath been otherwise
Twenty times better; but once in special,
In thin array after a pleasant guise,                    10
When her loose gown from her shoulders did fall,
And she me caught in her arms long and small,
Therewithal sweetly did me kiss,
And softly said, Dear heart, how like you this?

It was no dream; I lay broad waking.                     15
But all is turned thorough my gentleness
Into a strange fashion of forsaking;
And I have leave to go of her goodness,
And she also to use newfangleness.
But since that I so kindely am served,                   20
I would fain know what she hath deserved.

10   *guise* fashion.
19   *newfangleness* The term is as old as Chaucer.

20   *kindely* Both in the dominant modern sense of the term, and "in accord with kind," i.e., with nature in general and women's nature in particular.

## The lover showeth how he is forsaken of such as he sometime enjoyed

They flee from me that sometime did me seek,
With naked foot stalking within my chamber.
Once have I seen them gentle, tame, and meek
That now are wild and do not once remember
That sometime they have put themselves in danger         5
To take bread at my hand, and now they range,
Busily seeking in continual change.

Thankèd be fortune, it hath been otherwise
Twenty times better; but once especial,
In thin array after a pleasant guise,                    10
When her loose gown did from her shoulders fall,
And she me caught in her arms long and small,
And therewithal so sweetly did me kiss,
And softly said, Dear heart, how like you this?

It was no dream, for I lay broad awaking.                15
But all is turned now through my gentleness
Into a bitter fashion of forsaking;
And I have leave to go of her goodness,
And she also to use newfangleness.
But since that I unkindly so am served,                  20
How like you this? What hath she now deserved?

The preceding poem as revised for Tottel.

There was never nothing more me pained
Nor nothing more me moved
As when my sweetheart her complained
That ever she me loved.
      Alas, the while!                                  5

With piteous look she said and sighed,
Alas, what aileth me
To love and set my wealth so light
On him that loveth not me?
     Alas, the while!                     10

Was I not well void of all pain
When that nothing me grieved?
And now with sorrows I must complain
And cannot be relieved?
     Alas, the while!                     15

My restful nights and joyful days
Since I began to love
Be take from me; all thing decays,
Yet can I not remove.
     Alas, the while!                     20

She wept and wrung her hands withal,
The tears fell in my neck;
She turned her face and let it fall,
Scarcely therewith could speak.
     Alas, the while!                     25

Her pains tormented me so sore
That comfort had I none,
But cursed my fortune more and more
To see her sob and groan.
     Alas, the while!                     30

8   *wealth* well-being.                 19   *remove* go elsewhere.

Who hath heard of such cruelty before?
That when my plaint remembered her my woe
That causèd it, she, cruel more and more,
Wishèd each stitch as she did sit and sew
Had pricked mine heart, for to increase my sore!      5
And, as I think, she thought it had been so;
For as she thought, This is his heart indeed,
She prickèd hard and made herself to bleed.

A strambotto, an Italian verse form made popular by Aquilano    2   *remembered her* reminded her of.
Serafino (1466–1500). For the conceit, see Skelton, *Philip
Sparrow* 210–36.

If Fancy would favor
As my deserving shall,
My love, my paramour,
Should love me best of all.

But if I cannot attain                     5
The grace that I desire,

1   *Fancy* Erotic desire, but also fantasy (as in l. 26, and in
various places in manuscripts other than the Egerton).

Then may I well complain
My service and my hire.

Fancy doth know how
To further my true heart                                    10
If Fancy might avow
With Faith to take part.

But Fancy is so frail
And flitting still so fast,
That Faith may not prevail                                  15
To help me first nor last.

For Fancy at his lust
Doth rule all but by guess;
Whereto should I then trust
In truth or steadfastness?                                  20

Yet gladly would I please
The fancy of her heart,
That may me only ease
And cure my careful smart.

Therefore, my lady dear,                                    25
Set once your fantasy
To make some hope appear,
Of steadfastness' remedy.

For if he be my friend
And undertake my woe,                                       30
My grief is at an end
If he continue so.

Else Fancy doth not right,
As I deserve and shall
To have you day and night                                   35
To love me best of all.

---

**24**   *careful* full of care.
**28**   *steadfastness' remedy* The reading of the Egerton manuscript, which would presumably mean "remedy for (my) steadfastness." Another manuscript reads "steadfast remedy" – i.e., any remedy that is reliable – and most editors accept that reading.
**29**   *he* Fancy, once again personified. Another manuscript here and in l. 32 reads "ye," i.e., the woman herself.

---

Sometime I fled the fire that me brent
By sea, by land, by water, and by wind;
And now I follow the coals that be quent
From Dover to Calais against my mind.
Lo, how desire is both sprung and spent,                    5
And he may see that whilom was so blind,
And all his labor now he laugh to scorn,
Meshed in the briars that erst was all to-torn.

---

A strambotto. Anne Boleyn and Henry VIII visited Calais in October 1532, shortly before their marriage. It is reasonable to assume that Wyatt would have been in their retinue, and doing so makes excellent sense of this poem.

**1**   *brent* burned.
**2**   *By sea, by land* Wyatt's revision of the original reading in the Egerton manuscript, "By hills and dales."
**3**   *quent* quenched.
**5**   *sprung* aroused.

My lute, awake! Perform the last
Labor that thou and I shall waste,
And end that I have now begun;
For when this song is sung and past,
My lute, be still, for I have done.                                    5

As to be heard where ear is none,
As lead to grave in marble stone,
My song may pierce her heart as soon.
Should we then sigh, or sing, or moan?
No, no, my lute, for I have done.                                      10

The rocks do not so cruelly
Repulse the waves continually
As she my suit and affection,
So that I am past remedy,
Whereby my lute and I have done.                                       15

Proud of the spoil that thou hast got
Of simple hearts thorough Love's shot,
By whom, unkind, thou hast them won,
Think not he hath his bow forgot,
Although my lute and I have done.                                      20

Vengeance shall fall on thy disdain
That makest but game on earnest pain.
Think not alone under the sun
Unquit to cause thy lover's plain,
Although my lute and I have done.                                      25

May chance thee lie withered and old
The winter nights that are so cold,
Plaining in vain unto the moon;
Thy wishes then dare not be told.
Care then who list, for I have done.                                   30

And then may chance thee to repent
The time that thou hast lost and spent
To cause thy lovers sigh and swoon;
Then shalt thou know beauty but lent,
And wish and want as I have done.                                      35

Now cease, my lute. This is the last
Labor that thou and I shall waste,
And ended is what we begun;
Now is this song both sung and past;
My lute, be still, for I have done.                                    40

7  *grave* engrave.                              24  Unavenged for causing your lover to complain.
23  *Think not alone* do not think yourself the only one.

To cause accord or to agree
Two contraries in one degree
And in one point, as seemeth me,

To all men's wit it cannot be;
    It is impossible. 5

Of heat and cold when I complain
And say that heat doth cause my pain,
When cold doth shake me every vein,
And both at once, I say again
    It is impossible. 10

That man that hath his heart away,
If life liveth there as men do say,
That he heartless should last one day,
Alive and not to turn to clay,
    It is impossible. 15

Twixt life and death, say what who saith,
There liveth no life that draweth breath;
They join so near, and eke i' faith
To seek for life by wish of death,
    It is impossible. 20

Yet love that all thing doth subdue,
Whose power there may no life eschew,
Hath wrought in me that I may rue
These miracles to be so true
    That are impossible. 25

11 *that hath his heart away* whose heart has left his body
(i.e., to be with his beloved).

Unstable dream, according to the place,
Be steadfast once, or else at least be true.
By tasted sweetness make me not to rue
The sudden loss of thy false feignèd grace.
By good respect in such a dangerous case 5
Thou broughtst not her into this tossing mew,
But madest my sprite live, my care to renew,
My body in tempest her succor to embrace.
The body dead, the sprite had his desire;
Painless was the one, the other in delight. 10
Why then, alas, did it not keep it right,
Returning to leap into the fire,
And where it was at wish it could not remain?
Such mocks of dreams, they turn to deadly pain.

Compare (among others) the anonymous "In a goodly night, as in my bed I lay," above, and, at the other end of the century, John Donne's "The Dream."

1 *according to the place* appropriate to the place where it takes place (the speaker's mind or his bed).
2 *true* The dream would be true either if the woman were in fact present in the bedroom, or if she were not present in the dream.

5 *By good respect* with proper consideration.
6 *mew* cage. The version of the poem in Tottel's miscellany changes this to "seas."
9 With the sexually frustrated body being "dead" in sleep and no longer "in tempest," the spirit is free to enjoy the absent woman in dreams.
11 *it* the spirit.
13 *at wish* just as it wished.

You that in love find luck and abundance
And live in lust and joyful jollity,
Arise for shame! Do away your sluggardy!
Arise, I say, do May some observance!
Let me in bed lie dreaming in mischance;                                5
Let me remember the haps most unhappy
That me betide in May most commonly,
As one whom Love list little to advance.
Sephame said true that my nativity
Mischancèd was with the ruler of the May.                              10
He guessed; I prove of that the verity.
In May my wealth and eke my life I say
Have stood so oft in such perplexity.
Rejoice! Let me dream of your felicity.

4   One of several echoes of Chaucer in this sonnet: "rys up, and let us daunce, / And lat us don to May som observaunce" (*Troilus and Criseyde* 2.111–12; Pandarus to Criseyde).

7   *May* Wyatt found himself in prison in May 1534 and May 1536; Anne Boleyn was executed in May 1536.
9   *Sephame* Edward Sephame, a court astrologer.

If waker care, if sudden pale color,
If many sighs with little speech to plain,
Now joy, now woe, if they my cheer distain,
For hope of small if much to fear therefore,
To haste, to slack my pace less or more                                5
Be sign of love, then do I love again.
If thou ask whom, sure since I did refrain
Brunet that set my wealth in such a roar,
The unfeignèd cheer of Phyllis hath the place
That Brunet had; she hath and ever shall.                              10
She from myself now hath me in her grace;
She hath in hand my wit, my will, and all.
My heart alone well worthy she doth stay,
Without whose help scant do I live a day.

Lines 1–6 imitate the structure of Petrarch, *Canzoniere* 224, a sonnet which Wyatt also translated in its entirety ("If amorous faith, an heart unfeigned," above).

1   *waker* unsleeping.
2   If lamenting with many sighs and few words.
3   *my cheer distain* color my face.
4   If being in great anxiety over the prospect of a small reward.
7   *refrain* draw back from.

8   Wyatt altered this line in the Egerton manuscript; it originally read "Her that did set our country in a roar," almost certainly a reference to Anne Boleyn. "Brunet" (i.e., brunette, though the French adjective does not appear to have been in general use in English until the eighteenth century) in the revised line sustains this identification, though more discreetly. *wealth* well-being.
9   *Phyllis* If the reference here, like that to Anne Boleyn, is autobiographical, it is probably to Elizabeth Darrell, though there is no obvious appropriateness to the name "Phyllis."
13   *stay* support.

Tagus, farewell, that westward with thy streams
Turns up the grains of gold already tried,
With spur and sail for I go seek the Thames
Gainward the sun that showeth her wealthy pride,

A strambotto on Wyatt's departure from Spain in June 1539.

1   *Tagus* The river that flows west into Lisbon; its sands were said to look like gold.
4   *Gainward* facing (i.e., eastward, into the rising sun).

And to the town which Brutus sought by dreams 5
Like bended moon doth lend her lusty side.
My king, my country, alone for whom I live,
Of mighty love the wings for this me give.

5 *Brutus* The descendant of Aeneas who was said to have
settled Britain; according to Geoffrey of Monmouth, he
received his instructions in a dream from the goddess Diana.


Mine own John Poins, since ye delight to know
    The cause why that homeward I me draw,
    And flee the press of courts whereso they go,
Rather than to live thrall under the awe
    Of lordly looks, wrapped within my cloak, 5
    To will and lust learning to set a law,
It is not for because I scorn or mock
    The power of them to whom fortune hath lent
    Charge over us, of right to strike the stroke;
But true it is that I have always meant 10
    Less to esteem them than the common sort,
    Of outward things that judge in their intent
Without regard what doth inward resort.
    I grant sometime that of glory the fire
    Doth touch my heart; me list not to report 15
Blame by honor and honor to desire.
    But how may I this honor now attain
    That cannot dye the color black a liar?
My Poins, I cannot frame my tongue to feign,
    To cloak the truth for praise, without desert, 20
    Of them that list all vice for to retain.
I cannot honor them that sets their part
    With Venus and Bacchus all their life long,
    Nor hold my peace of them although I smart.
I cannot crouch nor kneel to do such wrong 25
    To worship them like God on earth alone
    That are as wolves these silly lambs among.
I cannot with my words complain and moan
    And suffer nought, nor smart without complaint,
    Nor turn the word that from my mouth is gone. 30
I cannot speak and look like a saint,
    Use wiles for wit and make deceit a pleasure,

One of three satiric verse epistles that Wyatt wrote on a
model provided by the Italian poet Luigi Alamanni (1495–
1556); all of them are in *terza rima*, the form that Alamanni
uses, and this one is closely based on a specific poem of
Alamanni's, "Io vi dirò poiché d'udir vi cale." Wyatt treats
the original in much the way in which Alexander Pope will
later treat the satires and epistles of Horace, with some pas-
sages close to literal translation, others changing details to fit
Wyatt's own situation, and occasional additions of entirely
new matter. Alamanni writes to Tommaso Sertini from Pro-
vence, where he is in exile from his native Florence; Wyatt
writes to John Poins (a friend at court of whom little is
known) from his father's estate in Kent, probably during his
enforced leisure there after his imprisonment in 1536.

11 *than the common sort* than most people do.
15–16 *me list not to report / Blame by honor and honor to
desire* I am not disposed to satirize honor while at the same
time desiring it for myself.
20 *praise, without desert* undeserved praise.
23 *Venus and Bacchus* sex and drink.
25 *to do such wrong* Modern editorial adjustment of several
manuscript readings, e.g. "nor to do so great a wrong."
27 *silly* defenseless.
30 *turn* take back.

And call craft counsel, for profit still to paint.
I cannot wrest the law to fill the coffer,
 With innocent blood to feed myself fat,       35
 And do most hurt where most help I offer.
I am not he that can allow the state
 Of high Caesar and damn Cato to die,
 That with his death did scape out of the gate
From Caesar's hands, if Livy do not lie,        40
 And would not live where liberty was lost,
 So did his heart the commonweal apply.
I am not he such eloquence to boast
 To make the crow singing as the swan,
 Nor call the lion of coward beasts the most     45
That cannot take a mouse as the cat can;
 And he that dieth for hunger of the gold,
 Call him Alexander; and say that Pan
Passeth Apollo in music manifold;
 Praise *Sir Thopas* for a noble tale        50
 And scorn the story that the Knight told;
Praise him for counsel that is drunk of ale;
 Grin when he laugheth that beareth all the sway,
 Frown when he frowneth and groan when he is pale;
On others' lust to hang both night and day.     55
 None of these points would ever frame in me.
 My wit is nought, I cannot learn the way;
And much the less of things that greater be,
 That asken help of colors of device
 To join the mean with each extremity,       60
With the nearest virtue to cloak alway the vice,
 And, as to purpose likewise it shall fall,
 To press the virtue that it may not rise;
As drunkenness good fellowship to call;
 The friendly foe with his double face,       65
 Say he is gentle and courteous therewithal;
And say that Favel hath a goodly grace
 In eloquence; and cruelty to name
 Zeal of justice and change in time and place;
And he that suffereth offense without blame,    70
 Call him pitiful, and him true and plain
 That raileth reckless to everyman's shame;
Say he is rude that cannot lie and feign,
 The lecher a lover, and tyranny
 To be the right of a prince's reign.        75

---

**33**  *paint* give a cosmetic appearance to things.

**38**  *Cato* Cato the Younger (95–46 BC), who fought in the civil war against Julius Caesar, and committed suicide when his cause was lost. Cato replaces Alamanni's reference to Marcus Brutus and the other conspirators who later assassinated Caesar.

**40**  *Livy* Titus Livius, author of an immense history of Rome from its founding to his own time in the reign of Augustus; the part dealing with Cato's death (book 114) survives only in summary.

**42**  *apply* devote itself to.

**45**  Nor call the most cowardly of beasts "lion."

**50**  *Sir Thopas* A burlesque romance in Chaucer's *Canterbury Tales*: contrasted in the next line with *The Knight's Tale*, the first story in the collection.

**53**  *beareth all the sway* has the most authority.

**67**  *Favel* duplicity (often personified under this name in satirical literature).

**69**  *change in time and place* The argument that seemingly severe law enforcement is justified by changing circumstances.

**71**  *pitiful* merciful. "Pitiful" in the sense of "contemptible" is not clearly attested until late in the sixteenth century; the sense here is probably "use the epithet 'merciful' for someone who observes wrongdoing without denouncing it."

I cannot, I; no, no, it will not be.
　　This is the cause that I could never yet
　　Hang on their sleeves that weigh, as thou mayst see,
A chip of chance more than a pound of wit.
　　This maketh me at home to hunt and hawk,　　　　　　　　80
　　And in foul weather at my book to sit,
In frost and snow then with my bow to stalk.
　　No man doth mark whereso I ride or go;
　　In lusty leas at liberty I walk,
And of these news I feel nor weal nor woe,　　　　　　　　85
　　Save that a clog doth hang yet at my heal.
　　No force for that, for it is ordered so
That I may leap both hedge and dike full well.
　　I am not now in France to judge the wine,
　　With savory sauce the delicates to feel;　　　　　　　　90
Nor yet in Spain, where one must him incline,
　　Rather than be, outwardly to seem.
　　I meddle not with wits that be so fine,
Nor Flander's cheer letteth not my sight to deem
　　Of black and white, nor taketh my wit away　　　　　　95
　　With beastliness they, beasts, do so esteem;
Nor I am not where Christ is given in prey
　　For money, poison, and treason at Rome,
　　A common practice usèd night and day.
But here I am in Kent and Christendom,　　　　　　　　100
　　Among the Muses where I read and rhyme;
　　Where if thou list, my Poins, for to come,
Thou shalt be judge how I do spend my time.

84　*leas* pastures.

85　*news* novelties　*weal* happiness.

86　*clog* A block tied to a human or animal to prevent escape: in this case, the order that restricted Wyatt to his father's estate. Lines 86–8 correspond to nothing in Alamanni, who insists on the voluntary nature of his retirement to Provence.

87　*No force for that* No problem there.

90　*feel* taste.

94　*letteth* prevents.

100　*Kent and Christendom* Alamanni locates himself merely "in Provence."

My mother's maids, when they did sew and spin,
　　They sang sometime a song of the field mouse,
　　That, for because her livelihood was but thin,
Would needs go seek her townish sister's house.
　　She thought herself endurèd too much pain,　　　　　　5
　　The stormy blasts her cave so sore did souse,
That when the furrows swimmèd with the rain
　　She must lie cold and wet in sorry plight.
　　And worse than that, bare meat there did remain
To comfort her when she her house had dight:　　　　　　10
　　Sometime a barleycorn, sometime a bean,
　　For which she labored hard both day and night

The fable of the city mouse and the country mouse goes back to Aesop and was available to Wyatt in a number of literary versions, but his telling of it is not tied to any specific source. Other versions begin with the visit of the city mouse to the country, where she bad-mouths the rustic life and praises the city, and end with the successful flight of the country mouse after her encounter with the cat. Wyatt's city mouse is already wary and embattled, and under few illusions about urban existence, and his country mouse never makes it to the door when trying to escape.

6　*souse* drench.

In harvest time whilst she might go and glean.
 And when her store was stroyèd with the flood,
 Then wellaway! for she undone was clean.                          15
Then was she fain to take instead of food
 Sleep, if she might, her hunger to beguile.
 My sister, quod she, hath a living good,
And hence from me she dwelleth not a mile.
 In cold and storm she lieth warm and dry                         20
 In bed of down; the dirt doth not defile
Her tender foot. She laboreth not as I;
 Richly she feedeth, and at the rich man's cost,
 And for her meat she needs not crave nor cry.
By sea, by land, of delicates the most                            25
 Her cater seeks, and spareth for no peril.
 She feedeth on boiled bacon-meat and roast,
And hath thereof neither charge nor travail;
 And when she list, the liquor of the grape
 Doth glad her heart, till that her belly swell.                  30
And at this journey she maketh but a jape,
 So forth she goeth, trusting of all this wealth
 With her sister her part so for to shape
That, if she might keep herself in health,
 To live a lady while her life doth last.                         35
 And to the door now is she come by stealth,
And with her foot anon she scrapeth full fast.
 The other for fear durst not well scarce appear,
 Of every noise so was the wretch aghast.
At last she askèd softly who was there,                           40
 And, in her language as well as she could,
 Peep, quod the other, sister I am here.
Peace, quod the town mouse, why speakest thou so loud?
 And by the hand she took her fair and well.
 Welcome, quod she, my sister, by the rood.                       45
She feasted her, that joy it was to tell
 The fare they had. They drank the wine so clear;
 And, as to purpose now and then it fell,
She cheerèd her with, How sister, what cheer?
 Amids this joy befell a sorry chance,                            50
 That, wellaway, the stranger bought full dear
The fare she had; for, as she looked askance,
 Under a stool she spied two steaming eyes
 In a round head with sharp ears. In France
Was never mouse so feared, for though the unwise                  55
 Had not yseen such a beast before,
 Yet had nature taught her after her guise
To know her foe and dread him evermore.
 The towny mouse fled; she knew whither to go.
 The other had no shift, but wondrous sore                        60
Feared of her life; at home she wished her tho.
 And to the door, alas, as she did skip,

| | |
|---|---|
| **26** *cater* caterer. | **55** *feared* afraid. |
| **31** *maketh but a jape* thinks no more serious than a joke. | **57** *after her guise* by instinct. |
| **45** *rood* cross. | **60** *shift* plan. |
| **53** *steaming* glowing. | **61** *of* for. |

The heaven it would, lo, and eke her chance was so,
At the threshold her silly foot did trip,
 And ere she might recover it again,     65
 The traitor cat had caught her by the hip,
And made her there against her will remain,
 That had forgotten her poor surety and rest
 For seeming wealth wherein she thought to reign.
Alas, my Poins, how men do seek the best     70
 And find the worst by error as they stray!
 And no marvel, when sight is so oppressed,
And blind the guide; anon out of the way
 Goeth guide and all in seeking quiet life.
 O wretched minds, there is no gold that may    75
Grant that ye seek, no war, no peace, no strife.
 No, no, although thy head were hooped with gold,
 Sergeant with mace, halberd, sword, nor knife
Cannot repulse the care that follow should.
 Each kind of life hath with him his disease.    80
 Live in delight even as thy lust would,
And thou shalt find when lust doth most thee please
 It irketh straight, and by itself doth fade.
 A small thing it is that may thy mind appease.
None of ye all there is that is so mad     85
 To seek grapes upon brambles or briars,
 Nor none, I trow, that hath his wit so bad
To set his hay for conies over rivers,
 Ne ye set not a dragnet for a hare;
 And yet the thing that most is your desire    90
Ye do misseek with more travail and care.
 Make plain thine heart, that it be not knotted
 With hope or dread, and see thy will be bare
From all affects whom vice hath ever spotted.
 Thyself content with that is thee assigned,    95
 And use it well that is to thee allotted.
Then seek no more out of thyself to find
 The thing that thou hast sought so long before,
 For thou shalt feel it sitting in thy mind.
Mad if ye list to continue your sore,     100
 Let present pass and gape on time to come
 And deep yourself in travail more and more.
Henceforth, my Poins, this shall be all and some;
 These wretched fools shall have nought else of me.
 But to the great God and to his high doom    105
None other pain pray I for them to be
 But, when the rage doth lead them from the right,
 That, looking backward, virtue they may see
Even as she is, so goodly fair and bright;
 And whilst they clasp their lusts in arms across,   110
 Grant them, good Lord, as thou mayst of thy might,
To fret inward for losing such a loss.

---

63 *The heaven it would* heaven willed it.   88 *set his hay for conies* cast his net for rabbits.
70 *Poins* See note to the previous poem.   105 *doom* judgment
83 *irketh* wearies.

# V. Innocentia
# Veritas Viat Fides

*Circumdederunt me inimici mei*

Who list his wealth and ease retain,
Himself let him unknown contain;
Press not too fast in at that gate
Where the return stands by disdain,
And sure, *circa regna tonat.*                    5

The high mountains are blasted oft,
When the low valley is mild and soft.
Fortune with health stands at debate,
The fall is grievous from aloft,
And sure, *circa regna tonat.*                    10

These bloody days have broken my heart;
My lust, my youth did then depart,
And blind desire of estate.
Who hastes to climb seeks to revert;
Of truth, *circa regna tonat.*                    15

The bell tower showed me such sight
That in my head sticks day and night.
There did I learn out of a grate,
For all favor, glory, or might,
That yet *circa regna tonat.*                     20

By proof, I say, there did I learn
Wit helpeth not defense to earn
Of innocence to plead or prate.
Bear low, therefore, give God the stern,
For sure, *circa regna tonat.*                    25

The poem's heading surrounds Wyatt's name ("Viat") with the Latin words for innocence, truth, and faith, and concludes with a slightly altered quotation from the Vulgate Bible (Psalm 16.9): "my enemies have surrounded me." The poem is credibly thought to concern Wyatt's imprisonment in 1536 in the Tower of London, where he would have been able from his cell to witness the beheading of Anne Boleyn; that would be the "sight . . . out of a grate" in the fourth stanza.

**4** *stands by disdain* exposes you to disdain.

**5** *circa regna tonat* It thunders about kingdoms (Seneca, *Hippolytus* 1140; the poem's first two stanzas paraphrase ll. 1123–40).
**13** *estate* high rank in society.
**14** *revert* go back down.
**22** *to earn* The manuscript reads "to yerne," which could also mean "too yerne," i.e., "too vigorously"; in either case the sense of ll. 22–3 is a little unclear.
**24** *stern* steering gear (helm and rudder).

It was my choice, it was no chance
That brought my heart in other's hold,
Whereby it hath had sufferance
Longer, perdy, than reason would.
Since I it bound where it was free,                5
Methinks, ywis, of right it should
        Accepted be.

**3** *sufferance* suffering.

Accepted be without refuse,
Unless that Fortune hath the power
All right of love for to abuse,                                    10
For, as they say, one happy hour
May more prevail than right or might.
If Fortune then list for to lower,
          What vaileth right?

What vaileth right if this be true?                               15
Then trust to chance and go by guess;
Then whoso loveth may well go sue
Uncertain Hope for his redress.
Yet some would say assuredly
Thou mayst appeal for thy release                                 20
          To Fantasy.

To Fantasy pertains to choose;
All this I know, for Fantasy
First unto love did me induce.
But yet I know as steadfastly                                     25
That if love have no faster knot,
So nice a choice slips suddenly.
          It lasteth not.

It lasteth not that stands by change.
Fancy doth change, Fortune is frail;                              30
Both these to please, the way is strange.
Therefore methinks, best to prevail,
There is no way that is so just
As Truth to lead, though t'other fail,
          And thereto trust.                                      35

27   *nice* delicate.                    29   *stands by* depends on.


Blame not my lute, for he must sound
Of this or that as liketh me;
For lack of wit the lute is bound
To give such tunes as pleaseth me.
Though my songs be somewhat strange                               5
And speaks such words as touch thy change,
          Blame not my lute.

My lute, alas, doth not offend,
Though that perforce he must agree
To sound such tunes as I intend                                   10
To sing to them that heareth me.
Then, though my songs be somewhat plain
And toucheth some that use to feign,
          Blame not my lute.

My lute and strings may not deny,                                 15
But as I strike they must obey.
Break not them then so wrongfully,
But wreak thyself some wiser way;

And though the songs which I indite
Do quit thy change with rightful spite,         20
    Blame not my lute.

Spite asketh spite and changing change,
And falsèd faith must needs be known;
The fault so great, the case so strange,
Of right it must abroad be blown.         25
Then since that by thine own desert
My songs do tell how true thou art,
    Blame not my lute.

Blame but thyself that hast misdone
And well deservèd to have blame;         30
Change thou thy way so evil begun,
And then my lute shall sound that same.
But if till then my fingers play
By thy desert their wonted way,
    Blame not my lute.         35

Farewell, unknown, for though thou break
My strings in spite with great disdain,
Yet have I found out for thy sake
Strings for to string my lute again;
And if perchance this foolish rhyme         40
Do make thee blush at any time,
    Blame not my lute.

20    *quit* requite.            34    *By* in accord with.

What should I say,
Since faith is dead
And truth away
From you is fled?
Should I be led         5
With doubleness?
Nay, nay, mistress!

I promised you,
And you promised me
To be as true         10
As I would be;
But since I see
Your double heart,
Farewell, my part.

Thought for to take         15
It is not my mind,
But to forsake
One so unkind;

14    *my part* The part of your duplicitous heart that is de-
voted to me.
15    *Thought* The manuscript source reads "though." The
sense for ll. 15–18 as emended is "I do not intend to think
about it any more but simply just to leave someone who has
been cruel."
18    This line is missing in the manuscript source; the read-
ing given here is conjectural.

And as I find,
So will I trust.                                                                    20
Farewell, unjust!

Can ye say nay
But that you said
That I alway
Should be obeyed?                                                              25
And thus betrayed
Ere that I wist?
Farewell, unkissed!

Tangled I was in love's snare,
Oppressed with pain, torment with care,
Of grief right sure, of joy full bare,
Clean in despair by cruelty;
But ha, ha, ha, full well is me,                                             5
For I am now at liberty.

The woeful days so full of pain,
The weary night all spent in vain,
The labor lost for so small gain,
To write them all it will not be;                                          10
But ha, ha, ha, full well is me,
For I am now at liberty.

Everything that fair doth show,
When proof is made, it proveth not so
But turneth mirth to bitter woe,
Which in this case full well I see;                                       15
But ha, ha, ha, full well is me,
For I am now at liberty.

Too great desire was my guide,
And wanton will went by my side;                                   20
Hope rulèd still and made me bide
Of love's craft the extremity.
But ha, ha, ha, full well is me,
For I am now at liberty.

With feignèd words which were but wind          25
To long delays I was assigned,
Her wily looks my wits did blind;
Thus as she would, I did agree.
But ha, ha, ha, full well is me,
For I am now at liberty.                                                    30

Was never bird tangled in lime
That brake away in better time

---

5  *ha, ha, ha* The poem's refrain mimics that of a poem of
Serafino's: "Ha ha ha! men rido tanto / Ch'io son vivo e son
di fuore" (But ha, ha, ha! I am laughing so much because I
am alive and on the outside).

21  *bide* tolerate.
31  *lime* Bird-lime, a sticky substance spread on twigs to
catch small birds.

Than I that rotten boughs did climb
And had no hurt, but scapèd free.
Now ha, ha, ha, full well is me,                                    35
For I am now at liberty.


The pillar perished is whereto I leant,
The strongest stay of mine unquiet mind.
The like of it no man again can find,
From east to west still seeking though he went,
To mine unhap, for hap away hath rent                              5
Of all my joy the very bark and rind;
And I (alas) by chance am thus assigned
Dearly to mourn till death do it relent.
But since that thus it is by destiny,
What can I more but have a woeful heart,                           10
My pen in plaint, my voice in woeful cry,
My mind in woe, my body full of smart,
And I myself myself always to hate
Till dreadful death do ease my doleful state?

An adaptation of Petrarch, *Canzoniere* 269, which laments the death of both Laura and Petrarch's patron Giovanni Colonna.

1   *pillar* Punning on the two names, Petrarch's poem begins, "Broken are the high column and the green laurel"; among other changes, Wyatt keeps only the reference to the column. The English poem is traditionally taken to refer to the fall and execution of Wyatt's patron Cromwell in July 1540.

2   *unquiet mind* Wyatt's translation of Plutarch's *On Tranquillity of Mind* (written for Catherine of Aragon and published ca. 1528) is entitled *Quiet of Mind*.
8   *relent* ease.
13–14   Petrarch's poem concludes: "O our life that is so beautiful to see, how easily it loses in one morning what has been acquired with great difficulty over many years!"
14   *ease* The reading in Tottel; the manuscript has "cause."


Stand whoso list upon the slipper top
Of court's estates and let me hear rejoice,
And use me quiet without let or stop,
Unknown in court that hath such brackish joys.
In hidden place so let my days forth pass                         5
That when my years be done, withouten noise
I may die aged after the common trace.
For him death gripeth right hard by the crop
That is much known of other, and of himself, alas,
Doth die unknown, dazed, with dreadful face.                      10

A translation of Seneca, *Thyestes* 391–403. Other poets have translated the passage as a poem in its own right, including Andrew Marvell ("Climb at court for me that will") and Abraham Cowley ("Upon the slippery top of human state").

1   *slipper* slippery.

3   *use me quiet* allow me to live quietly   *let* hindrance.
7   *after the common trace* in the common way. In Seneca, "as an old plebeian."
8   *crop* throat. In Seneca, "death lies heavy on him."
9–10   It is clear from the Latin (*ignotus moritur sibi*) that "of himself" goes with "unknown," in the sense of "to himself."

Lucks, my fair falcon, and your fellows all,
How well pleasant it were your liberty!
Ye not forsake me that fair might ye befall;
But they that sometime liked my company,
Like lice away from dead bodies they crawl.           5
Lo, what a proof in light adversity!
But ye, my birds, I swear by all your bells,
Ye be my friends, and so be but few else.

A strambotto, probably written in connection with the fall of Cromwell, possibly during Wyatt's own imprisonment in early 1541.

1   *Lucks* The falcon's name puns the English "luck" with the Latin *lux* (light).

Sighs are my food, drink are my tears;
Clinking of fetters such music would crave.
Stink and close air away my life wears.
Innocency is all the hope I have.
Rain, wind, or weather I judge by mine ears.          5
Malice assaulted that righteousness should have:
Sure I am, Brian, this wound shall heal again,
But yet, alas, the scar shall still remain.

A strambotto, apparently written in prison in 1541; cited by Surrey, "My Radcliffe, when thy reckless youth offends," below.

2   *such music* Probably referring to the sighs and tears in l. 1; otherwise the line is obscure.

7–8   Plutarch, *How to Tell a Flatterer* 65D.
7   *Brian* Sir Francis Brian (d. 1550), a cousin of Anne Boleyn and friend of Wyatt's; he had a reputation both for dissoluteness and as a collector of proverbs.

# Thomas Vaux, Baron Vaux (1510–1556)

Educated at Cambridge, and attendant at the court of Henry VIII from an early age, Vaux authored a handful of poems that survived in manuscripts and printed anthologies of the second half of the century; both the poems given here were printed in Tottel. The first is there attributed to Surrey; among its descendants is Shakespeare's Sonnet 129. The second is best known as the song that the gravedigger in *Hamlet* attempts to sing. Critical old-spelling texts of both poems may be found in *Tottel's Miscellany*, ed. Hyder Edward Rollins, 2nd edn (Cambridge, MA: Harvard University Press, 1965).

Brittle beauty that nature made so frail,
Whereof the gift is small, and short the season,
Flowering today, tomorrow apt to fail,
Tickle treasure abhorrèd of reason,
Dangerous to deal with, vain, of none avail,　　　　　　5
Costly in keeping, past not worth two peason,
Slipper in sliding as is an eel's tail,
Hard to attain, once gotten not geason,
Jewel of jeopardy that peril doth assail,
False and untrue, enticèd oft to treason,　　　　　　10
Enemy to youth – that most may I bewail.
Ah, bitter sweet, infecting as the poison,
Thou farest as fruit that with the frost is taken,
Today ready ripe, tomorrow all to-shaken.

4　*tickle* unreliable.
6　*peason* peas.

7　*Slipper* slippery.
8　*geason* extraordinary.


I loathe that I did love
In youth that I thought sweet;
As time requires for my behove,
Methinks they are not meet.

My lusts, they do me leave,　　　　　　5
My fancies all be fled,
And tract of time begins to weave
Gray hairs upon my head.

For age with stealing steps
Hath clawed me with his crutch;　　　　　　10
And lusty life, away she leaps
As there had been none such.

My Muse doth not delight
Me as she did before;
My hand and pen are not in plight　　　　　　15
As they have been of yore.

3　*behove* benefit.
7　*tract* passage.
10　*crutch* The reading of the manuscripts, consistent with the personification of "Age"; the text in Tottel reads "cowche" in the first edition and "crowch" thereafter. Shakespeare's gravedigger sings "Hath clawed me in his clutch," and editors often accept his emendation.
11　*life* Two manuscripts read "youth."
15　*in plight* fit.

For reason me denies
This youthly idle rhyme,
And day by day to me she cries,
Leave off these toys in time.                        20

The wrinkles in my brow,
The furrows in my face
Say limping age will hedge him now
Where youth must give him place.

The harbinger of death,                              25
To me I see him ride:
The cough, the cold, the gasping breath
Doth bid me to provide

A pick-ax and a spade,
And eke a shrouding sheet,                           30
A house of clay for to be made
For such a guest most meet.

Methinks I hear the clerk
That knolls the careful knell
And bids me leave my woeful work                     35
Ere nature me compel.

My keepers knit the knot
That youth did laugh to scorn,
Of me that clean shall be forgot
As I had not been born.                              40

Thus must I youth give up,
Whose badge I long did wear;
To them I yield the wanton cup
That better may it bear.

Lo, here the barèd skull                             45
By whose bald sign I know
That stooping age away shall pull
Which youthful years did sow.

For beauty with her band
These crooked cares hath wrought,                    50
And shippèd me into the land
From which I first was brought.

And ye that bide behind,
Have ye none other trust;
As ye of clay were cast by kind,                     55
So shall ye waste to dust.

55 *kind* nature.

# Henry Howard, Earl of Surrey (1517–1547)

Surrey's social rank is unique in sixteenth-century English literature, exceeding even Sidney's; no other writer of comparable importance moved in such high circles. His earldom was strictly speaking a courtesy title, granted when his father became Duke of Norfolk in 1524, but as eldest son he would have been in line for the dukedom, the highest rank below royalty itself. (His own son would inherit the title.) He grew up in close companionship with Henry Fitzroy, Duke of Richmond, the king's illegitimate son; in one of the poems below ("So cruel prison, how could betide, alas") he remembers their time together in a neo-chivalric golden glow. He was closely related to two of Henry VIII's queens, Anne Boleyn and Catherine Howard; he attended the trial of the former and the execution of the latter. A fiery sense of entitlement led to behavior that, despite his rank, landed him in prison more than once, and also involved him in dangerous political maneuvering within the paranoid world of the king's last days. An alteration in his coat of arms was interpreted, probably correctly, as implying claims of royal descent in connection with the succession; he was tried for treason and beheaded nine days before the king's own death.

He wrote two famous elegies on Wyatt. We are not sure how close the two were, but Surrey continued the older man's program of crafting English versions of important Continental literary modes. Surrey appears to have created what comes to be known as the English (or Shakespearean) sonnet (three independent quatrains followed by a couplet); he is also the inventor of blank verse, which he used for his translation of two books of Vergil's *Aeneid*, probably in imitation of the Italian *versi sciolti*. Surrey's Petrarchan imitations are smoother than Wyatt's, and, for better or worse, a more accurate anticipation of the fashionable Petrarchism of the 1590s; in "The soot season that bud and bloom forth brings," the lover's distress is shrunk even beyond what it is in Petrarch to a final unemphatic phrase, as if it were itself merely part of the spring landscape. Surrey's poems (which precede Wyatt's in Tottel) served to popularize a kind of soft-focus melancholy that was developed into a general theory of Surrey's own life (see the note on the first poem below). There is nevertheless plenty of evidence of the aristocratic fierceness to which his life records testify. "London, hast thou accusèd me" is an uncompromising jeremiad against his social inferiors, "Although I had a check" a proud and witty exercise in erotic aggression.

*Edition*: There is no satisfactory modern edition of Surrey's poetry; the closest thing is Surrey, *Poems*, ed. Emrys Jones (Oxford: Clarendon Press, 1964), which gives freshly edited old-spelling texts of almost the entire corpus.

From Tuscan came my lady's worthy race;
Fair Florence was sometime her ancient seat.
The western isle (whose pleasant shore doth face
Wild Camber's cliffs) did give her lively heat.
Fostered she was with milk of Irish breast,     5
Her sire an earl, her dame of princes' blood;
From tender years in Britain she doth rest
With a king's child, where she tastes ghostly food.
Hunsdon did first present her to mine eyen;
Bright is her hue, and Geraldine she hight.     10
Hampton me taught to wish her first for mine,

"Geraldine" (l. 10) is Elizabeth Fitzgerald, born in Ireland ca. 1528 and brought to England in 1533. Her grandfather was Earl of Kildare, whose family claimed descent from the Geraldi of Florence; her mother was Elizabeth Grey, a first cousin to Henry VIII. In 1538 she probably entered the service of Princess Elizabeth ("a king's child"), and Surrey could have encountered her at any of the numerous residences of Henry's moveable court. In 1542 she was married to Sir Anthony Browne, Master of the Horse; the best guess is that Surrey's poem was written as a graceful compliment on the occasion of her betrothal in 1541. Another theory, evidenced by nothing other than the poem itself, was developed by Thomas Nashe in *The Unfortunate Traveller* (1594), where Geraldine is the long-term object of Surrey's Petrarchan passion (and subject of his other love poems), for whom he enters the lists at Florence to defend her beauty. The legend was taken up by Michael Drayton in *England's Heroical Epistles* (1598–9), and had adherents as late as the nineteenth century.

4   *Camber* Wales (Cambria).

8   *tastes ghostly food* receives spiritual instruction.

9   *eyen* eyes.

And Windsor, alas! doth chase me from her sight.
Beauty of kind, her virtues from above,
Happy is he that may obtain her love.

13   *Beauty of kind* beauty from nature.

Love that doth reign and live within my thought
And built his seat within my captive breast,
Clad in the arms wherein with me he fought
Oft in my face he doth his banner rest.
But she that taught me love and suffer pain,                    5
My doubtful hope and eke my hot desire
With shamefast cloak to shadow and refrain,
Her smiling face converteth straight to ire;
And coward Love then to the heart apace
Taketh his flight, where he doth lurk and plain,                10
His purpose lost, and dare not show his face.
For my lord's guilt thus faultless bide I pain,
Yet from my lord shall not my foot remove.
Sweet is the death that taketh end by love.

A translation of Petrarch, *Canzoniere* 140, which Wyatt also     7   *refrain* rein in.
translated (see above).

The soot season that bud and bloom forth brings
With green hath clad the hill and eke the vale.
The nightingale with feathers new she sings,
The turtle to her make hath told her tale.
Summer is come, for every spray now springs;                    5
The hart hath hung his old head on the pale;
The buck in brake his winter coat he flings;
The fishes float with new-repairèd scale;
The adder all her slough away she slings;
The swift swallow pursueth the flies small;                     10
The busy bee her honey now she mings.
Winter is worn, that was the flowers' bale,
And thus I see among these pleasant things
Each care decays, and yet my sorrow springs.

An imitation of Petrarch, *Canzoniere* 310, though with sig-       1   *soot* sweet.
nificant changes of detail and emphasis; the Italian poem          4   *turtle* turtledove.   *make* mate.
devotes eight lines to the joys of spring and six lines to the     6   *pale* fence.
unhappiness of the speaker.                                        9   *slough* cast-off skin.
                                                                   11   *mings* remembers.

Alas, so all things now do hold their peace,
Heaven and earth disturbed in nothing.
The beasts, the air, the birds their song do cease;
The nightes char the stars about doth bring.

An adaptation of Petrarch, *Canzoniere* 164.                        4   *char* chariot.

Calm is the sea, the waves work less and less.    5
So am not I, whom love, alas, doth wring,
Bringing before my face the great increase
Of my desires, whereat I weep and sing
In joy and woe, as in a doubtful ease.
For my sweet thoughts sometime do pleasure bring,    10
But by and by the cause of my disease
Gives me a pang that inwardly doth sting
When that I think what grief it is again
To live and lack the thing should rid my pain.

11    *by and by* immediately.

Set me whereas the sun doth parch the green,
Or where his beams may not dissolve the ice,
In temperate heat where he is felt and seen,
With proud people, in presence sad and wise;
Set me in base or yet in high degree,    5
In the long night or in the shortest day,
In clear weather or where mists thickest be,
In lusty youth or when my hairs be gray;
Set me in earth, in heaven, or yet in hell,
In hill, in dale, or in the foaming flood,    10
Thrall or at large, alive whereso I dwell,
Sick or in health, in ill fame or in good:
Yours will I be, and with that only thought
Comfort myself when that my hap is nought.

A version of Petrarch, *Canzoniere* 145, which in turn looks to    13–14    Petrarch's poem ends: "still I shall be what I have
Horace, *Odes* 1.22 ("Integer vitae").    been, shall live as I have lived, continuing my trilustral [fifteen
years'] sighing."

4    *sad* serious.

In Cyprus' springs (whereas dame Venus dwelt)
A well so hot that whoso tastes the same,
Were he of stone, as thawèd ice should melt
And kindled find his breast with secret flame:
Whose moist poison dissolvèd hath my hate.    5
This creeping fire my cold limbs so oppressed
That in the heart that harbored freedom late
Endless despair long thralldom hath impressed.
One eke so cold in frozen snow is found,
Whose chilling venom of repugnant kind    10
The fervent heat doth quench of Cupid's wound
And with the spot of change infects the mind,
Whereof my dear hath tasted to my pain;
My service thus is grown into disdain.

Similar twin fountains figure in the plot of Ariosto's *Orlando*    12    *spot* stain.
*Furioso*; their contrasting operation is described there at 1.78.

Such wayward ways hath Love that most part in discord
Our wills do stand, whereby our hearts but seldom doth accord.
Deceit is his delight, and to beguile and mock
The simple hearts which he doth strike with froward divers stroke.
He causeth hearts to rage with golden burning dart,     5
And doth allay with leaden cold again the t'other's heart.
Hot gleams of burning fire and easy sparks of flame
In balance of unequal weight he pondereth by aim.
From easy ford where I might wade and pass full well
He me withdraws and doth me drive into the dark deep well,     10
And me withholds where I am called and offered place,
And will that still my mortal foe I do beseech of grace.
He lets me to pursue a conquest well near won,
To follow where my pains were spilt ere that my suit begun.
Lo, by these rules I know how soon a heart can turn     15
From war to peace, from truce to strife, and so again return.
I know how to convert my will in other's lust,
Of little stuff unto myself to weave a web of trust,
And how to hide my harm with soft dissembled cheer
When in my face the painted thoughts would outwardly appear.     20
I know how that the blood forsakes the face for dread,
And how by shame it stains again the cheeks with flaming red.
I know under the green the serpent how he lurks;
The hammer of the restless forge, I know eke how it works.
I know and can by rote the tale that I would tell,     25
But oft the words come forth awry of him that loveth well.
I know in heat and cold the lover how he shakes,
In singing how he can complain, in sleeping how he wakes,
To languish without ache, sickless for to consume,
A thousand things for to devise resolving all in fume.     30
And though he like to see his lady's face full sore,
Such pleasure as delights his eye doth not his health restore.
I know to seek the track of my desirèd foe,
And fear to find that I do seek; but chiefly this I know
That lovers must transform into the thing beloved,     35
And live, alas (who could believe?), with sprite for life removed.
I know in hearty sighs and laughters of the spleen
At once to change my state, my will, and eke my color clean.
I know how to deceive myself withouten help,
And how the lion chastised is by beating of the whelp.     40
In standing near my fire I know how that I freeze;
Far off, to burn; in both to waste, and so my life to leese.
I know how love doth rage upon the yielden mind,

---

In poulter's measure, a meter first seen in Wyatt, used by Surrey for a number of poems. The bulk of this poem (ll. 15ff) takes its rhetorical structure and many of its details from Petrarch, *Triumph of Love* 3.151–87.

6 *allay with leaden cold* remove passion with an arrow of cold lead.
8 *pondereth* weighs. *aim* guess.
13 *lets me to pursue* keeps me from pursuing.
14 *spilt* wasted.

18 *trust* hope.
25 *can by rote* know by heart.
29 *sickless for to consume* to waste away without being ill.
30 To devise a thousand ways of turning everything into smoke.
40 A lion was supposed to be trainable by being made to watch a puppy being punished in its presence. The Howard coat of arms contained a lion.
42 *leese* lose.
43 *yielden* submissive.

How small a net may take and mash a heart of gentle kind;
With seldom tasted sweet to season heaps of gall,                45
Revivèd with a glinse of grace old sorrows to let fall.
The hidden trains I know, and secret snares of love,
How soon a look may print a thought that never will remove.
That slipper state I know, those sudden turns from wealth,
That doubtful hope, that certain woe, and sure despair of health.   50

46   *glinse* glimpse.   *let fall* abate.          49   *slipper* slippery.   *wealth* well-being.
47   *trains* devices.

Although I had a check,
To give the mate is hard;
For I have found a neck
To keep my men in guard.

And you that hardy are                5
To give so great assay
Unto a man of war
To drive his men away:

I read you, take good heed,
And mark this foolish verse,           10
For I will so provide
That I will have your fers.

And when your fers is had
And all your war is done,
Then shall yourself be glad            15
To end that you begun.

For if by chance I win
Your person in the field,
Too late then come you in
Yourself to me to yield.               20

For I will use my power
As captain full of might,
And such I will devour
As use to show me spite.

And for because you gave              25
Me check in such degree,
This vantage, lo, I have:
Now check, and guard to thee.

Defend it, if thou may;
Stand stiff in thine estate.           30
For sure I will assay
If I can give the mate.

3   *neck* chess move to cover a check.          12   *fers* queen.
9   *read* advise.

When Windsor walls sustained my wearied arm,
My hand my chin to ease my restless head,
Each pleasant plot revested green with warm,
The blossomed boughs with lusty vere yspread,
The flowered meads, the wedded birds so late          5
Mine eyes discovered. Then did to mind resort
The jolly woes, the hateless short debate,
The rake-hell life that longs to love's disport.
Wherewith, alas! mine heavy charge of care,
Heaped in my breast, brake forth against my will,          10
And smoky sighs that overcast the air;
My vapored eyes such dreary tears distill,
The tender spring to quicken where they fall,
And I half-bent to throw me down withal.

In 1537 Surrey was confined to Windsor Castle for striking Sir Edward Seymour in court.

3   *revested* clothed.

4   *vere* springtime.
5   *the wedded birds so late* the birds so recently married.
8   *longs* belongs.

So cruel prison, how could betide, alas,
As proud Windsor, where I in lust and joy
With a king's son my childish years did pass
In greater feast than Priam's sons of Troy?

Where each sweet place returns a taste full sour:          5
The large green courts where we were wont to hove,
With eyes cast up unto the maidens' tower,
And easy sighs, such as folk draw in love.

The stately sales, the ladies bright of hue,
The dances short, long tales of great delight,          10
With words and looks that tigers could but rue,
Where each of us did plead the other's right.

The palm-play where, despoilèd for the game,
With dazèd eyes oft we by gleams of love
Have missed the ball and got sight of our dame          15
To bait her eyes which kept the leads above.

The graveled ground, with sleeves tied on the helm,
On foaming horse, with swords and friendly hearts,
With cheer, as though the one should overwhelm,
Where we have fought and chasèd oft with darts.          20

With silver drops the meads yet spread for ruth,
In active games of nimbleness and strength

On the same occasion as the previous poem.

1   *how could betide* how could it happen.
2   *lust* pleasure.
3   *a king's son* Henry Fitzroy, Duke of Richmond (1519–36), bastard son to Henry VIII; he married Surrey's sister in 1533.
6   *hove* linger.
9   *sales* halls.

11   *that tigers could but rue* could make even tigers feel pity.
13   *palm-play* A game like tennis, in which the hand was used rather than a racket. *despoilèd* undressed.
16   *which kept the leads above* who were on the roof.
17   *sleeves tied on the helm* Pieces of clothing were often displayed on a contestant's helmet in jousting, as a coded declaration of loyalty.
19   With cheer at the prospect of winning (?).
21   *ruth* compassion.

Where we did strain, trailèd by swarms of youth,
Our tender limbs that yet shot up in length.

The secret groves which oft we made resound                          25
Of pleasant plaint and of our ladies' praise,
Recording soft what grace each one had found,
What hope of speed, what dread of long delays.

The wild forest, the clothèd holts with green,
With reins avaled and swift ybreathèd horse,                         30
With cry of hounds and merry blasts between,
Where we did chase the fearful hart *à force*.

The void walls eke that harbored us each night,
Wherewith, alas, revive within my breast
The sweet accord, such sleeps as yet delight,                        35
The pleasant dreams, the quiet bed of rest,

The secret thoughts imparted with such trust,
The wanton talk, the divers change of play,
The friendship sworn, each promise kept so just,
Wherewith we passed the winter nights away.                          40

And with this thought the blood forsakes my face,
The tears berain my cheeks of deadly hue;
The which as soon as sobbing sighs, alas,
Upsuppèd have, thus I my plaint renew:

O place of bliss, renewer of my woes,                                45
Give me account where is my noble fere,
Whom in thy walls thou didst each night enclose,
To other lief, but unto me most dear.

Each stone, alas, that doth my sorrow rue
Returns thereto a hollow sound of plaint;                            50
Thus I, alone, where all my freedom grew,
In prison pine with bondage and restraint.

And with remembrance of the greater grief,
To banish the less I find my chief relief.

| | |
|---|---|
| 28   *speed* success. | 44   *Upsuppèd* drunk up. |
| 29   *holts* woods. | 46   *fere* companion. |
| 30   *avaled* slackened.   *ybreathèd* exercised. | 48   *to other lief* dear to others. |
| 32   *à force* to hunt it down with dogs (rather than shoot it). | |

The Assyrians' king, in peace with foul desire
And filthy lusts that stained his regal heart,
In war that should set princely hearts afire
Vanquished did yield for want of martial art.

Tradition makes this poem a coded portrait of Henry VIII.

1   *The Assyrians' king* Sardanapalus, a degenerate Persian monarch who under siege burned his treasure and then threw himself into the fire; his story comes down through Greek literature and he cannot be clearly identified with any historical figure.

The dint of swords from kisses seemèd strange,                    5
And harder than his lady's side his targe,
From glutton feasts to soldier's fare a change,
His helmet far above a garland's charge;
Who scace the name of manhood did retain,
Drenchèd in sloth and womanish delight,                          10
Feeble of sprite, unpatient of pain,
When he had lost his honor and his right,
Proud time of wealth, in storms appalled with dread,
Murdered himself to show some manful deed.

---

5  *dint* blow.  *strange* different.              8  *charge* weight.
6  *targe* shield.                                  9  *scace* scarce.

---

London, hast thou accusèd me
  Of breech of laws, the root of strife?
  Within whose breast did boil to see
(So fervent hot) thy dissolute life,
  That even the hate of sins that grow            5
  Within thy wicked walls so rife
For to break forth did convert so
  That terror could it not repress.
  The which, by words since preachers know
What hope is left for to redress,                  10
  By unknown means it likèd me
  My hidden burden to express,
Whereby it might appear to thee
  That secret sin hath secret spite.
  From justice' rod no fault is free,             15
But that all such as works unright
  In most quiet are next ill rest.
  In secret silence of the night
This made me, with a reckless breast,
  To wake thy sluggards with my bow,              20
  A figure of the Lord's behest
Whose scourge for sin the scriptures show:
  That, as the fearful thunder clap
  By sudden flame at hand we know,
Of pebble stones the soundless rap                25
  The dreadful plague might make thee see
  Of God's wrath that doth thee enwrap;
That Pride might know, from conscience free,
  How lofty works may her defend;
  And Envy find, as he hath sought,               30
  How other seek him to offend;

---

Occasioned by Surrey's brief imprisonment in 1543 for carousing in the City of London during Lent; he and others (including Thomas Wyatt, the son of the poet) had been roaming the streets at night in a "lewd and unseemly manner" and broken several windows in Cheapside with "stone bows." The poem replies to those charges with a stance of reformist zeal, echoing both Old Testament prophecy and Petrarch's denunciation of the papal court at Avignon.

Except for ll. 29–40, which catalogue the seven deadly sins, the poem is in *terza rima*, the rhyme scheme Wyatt chose for his satires and his translations from the Psalms.

7  *convert* convert me (into a reformer). Emendation to "covet" has been suggested.
17  *next* nearest to.
20  *with my bow* As in Jeremiah 50.9, 14, 29.

And Wrath taste of each cruel thought
The just shap hire in the end;
And idle Sloth, that never wrought,
To heaven his spirit lift may begin;                                           35
And greedy Lucre live in dread
To see what hate ill-got goods win;
The lechers, ye that lusts do feed,
Perceive what secrecy is in sin;
And gluttons' hearts for sorrow bleed,                                         40
Awakèd when their fault they find.
In loathsome vice each drunken wight
To stir to God, this was my mind.
Thy windows had done me no spite,
But proud people that dread no fall,                                           45
Clothèd with falsehood and unright
Bred in the closures of thy wall;
But wrested to wrath in fervent zeal,
Thou hast to strife my secret call.
Endurèd hearts no warning feel:                                                50
O shameless whore! Is dread then gone
By such thy foes as meant thy weal?
O member of false Babylon!
The shop of craft! The den of ire!
Thy dreadful doom draws fast upon;                                             55
Thy martyrs' blood by sword and fire
In heaven and earth for justice call.
The Lord shall hear their just desire,
The flame of wrath shall on thee fall.
With famine and pest lamentably                                                60
Stricken shall be thy lechers all;
Thy proud towers and turrets high,
Enemies to God, beat stone from stone;
Thine idols burnt that wrought iniquity.
When none thy ruin shall bemoan,                                              65
But render unto the right wise Lord
That hath so judgèd Babylon
Immortal praise with one accord.

33  *just shap hire* justly assigned payment ("shap" =       50  *Endurèd* hardened.
"shaped").                                                                 52  *By such* from such of.
34  *wrought* worked.                                          60  *pest* pestilence.

Divers thy death do diversely bemoan.
Some that in presence of that lively head
Lurked, whose breasts envy with hate had sown,
Yield Caesar's tears upon Pompeius' head.
Some that watchèd with the murderer's knife                                    5
With eager thrust to drink thy guiltless blood,
Whose practice brake by happy end of life,

On the death of Wyatt (October 1542).                         4  Julius Caesar wept when presented with the head of
                                                               Pompey the Great, his enemy in the Roman civil war.
1  *Divers* various people.                                    7  Whose plotting was ended by the Wyatt's timely death.

Weep envious tears to hear thy fame so good.
But I that knew what harbored in that head,
What virtues rare were tempered in that breast,                    10
Honor the place that such a jewel bred,
And kiss the ground whereas thy corse doth rest
With vapored eyes; from whence such streams avale
As Pyramus did on Thisbe's breast bewail.

12  *corse* corpse.

13  *vapored* tearful.  *avale* descend.

14  Thisbe committed suicide when she thought her lover
Pyramus was dead; he killed himself in turn when he found
what she had done.

Wyatt resteth here, that quick could never rest;
Whose heavenly gifts increasèd by disdain
And virtue sank the deeper in his breast,
Such profit he of envy could obtain.

A head where wisdom mysteries did frame,                          5
Whose hammers beat still in that lively brain
As on a stith, where some work of fame
Was daily wrought to turn to Britain's gain.

A visage stern and mild, where both did grow
Vice to contemn, in virtues to rejoice;                           10
Amid great storms whom grace assurèd so
To live upright and smile at Fortune's choice.

A hand that taught what might be said in rhyme,
That reft Chaucer the glory of his wit;
A mark the which, unperfited for time,                            15
Some may approach, but never none shall hit.

A tongue that served in foreign realms his king;
Whose courteous talk to virtue did inflame
Each noble heart; a worthy guide to bring
Our English youth by travail unto fame.                           20

An eye whose judgment no affect could blind,
Friends to allure and foes to reconcile;
Whose piercing look did represent a mind
With virtue fraught, reposèd, void of guile.

A heart where dread yet never so impressed                        25
To hide the thought that might the truth avance;
In neither fortune lift nor so repressed
To swell in wealth nor yield unto mischance.

On the death of Wyatt; published as part of a small book,
ca. 1545.

1  *quick* alive.

5  *mysteries* hidden knowledge.

7  *stith* anvil.

15  *unperfited for time* unfinished for lack of time.

26  *avance* advance.

27  In neither good fortune nor bad.

28  *swell in wealth* be confident in well-being.

A valiant corpse where force and beauty met,
Happy, alas too happy but for foes,                                    30
Livèd and ran the race that nature set,
Of manhood's shape where she the mold did lose.

But to the heavens that simple soul is fled,
Which left with such as covet Christ to know
Witness of faith that never shall be dead;                             35
Sent for our wealth, but not receivèd so.

Thus for our guilt this jewel have we lost.
The earth his bones, the heaven possess his ghost.

29   *corpse* body (living or dead).

35   *Witness of faith* Probably a reference to Wyatt's translation of the Penitential Psalms.
36   *wealth* well being.

O happy dames that may embrace
The fruit of your delight,
Help to bewail the woeful case
And eke the heavy plight
Of me, that wonted to rejoice                                          5
The fortune of my pleasant choice.
Good ladies, help to fill my mourning voice.

In ship fraught with rememberance
Of thoughts and pleasures past,
He sails that hath in governance                                       10
My life while it will last;
With scalding sighs for lack of gale
Furthering his hope that is his sail
Toward me, the sweet port of his avale.

Alas! how oft in dreams I see                                          15
Those eyes that were my food,
Which sometime so delighted me
That yet they do me good;
Wherewith I wake with his return,
Whose absent flame did make me burn.                                   20
But when I find the lack, Lord, how I mourn!

When other lovers, in arms across,
Rejoice their chief delight,
Drownèd in tears to mourn my loss
I stand the bitter night                                               25
In my window, where I may see
Before the winds how the clouds flee.
Lo, what a mariner love hath made me!

The speaker here is apparently Surrey's wife, Lady Frances Vere, from whom he was unwillingly separated while in military service in France in the mid-1540s; he wrote one other poem in her voice.

8–14   This stanza plays with some common Petrarchan metaphors comparing a frustrated lover's state to that of a ship at sea; see Wyatt's "My galley chargèd with forgetfulness" above.
14   *avale* Probably a rare use of this word as a noun, meaning in this case "disembarkation," though with a pun on "avail," i.e., "help" – which may indeed be the primary sense.
22   *in arms across* embracing.

And in green waves when the salt flood
Doth rise by rage of wind, 30
A thousand fancies in that mood
Assail my restless mind.
Alas, now drencheth my sweet foe
That with the spoil of my heart did go
And left me; but, alas, why did he so? 35

And when the seas wax calm again
To chase fro me annoy,
My doubtful hope doth cause me plain;
So dread cuts off my joy.
Thus is my wealth mingled with woe, 40
And of each thought a doubt doth grow:
Now he comes, will he come? Alas, no, no.

33   *drencheth* drowns.

My Radcliffe, when thy reckless youth offends,
Receive thy scourge by others' chastisement;
For such calling, when it works none amends,
Then plagues are sent without advertisement.
Yet Solomon said the wrongèd shall recure; 5
But Wyatt said true, the scar doth aye endure.

1   *Radcliffe* Apparently Thomas Radcliffe, Earl of Essex; no particular occasion for this poem is known.
4   *advertisement* warning.
5   *Solomon said* Ecclesiasticus 27.21.
6   *Wyatt said* See "Sighs are my food, drink are my tears," above.

# Anne Askew (1521–1546)

The daughter of a Lincolnshire knight, Askew married one Thomas Kyme in 1538, but quarreled with him over her strong Protestant convictions and came to London in the tense last years of Henry VIII's reign. She may have briefly been in the service of Catherine Parr, Henry's last queen, whose own Protestant allegiances were well known and in some circles suspect. Askew was arrested in 1545, released, and the next year arrested again, interrogated, and tortured over supposedly seditious religious opinions; she was so broken by the process that she had to be carried in a chair to Smithfield for burning at the stake. Transcripts of her interrogation and the ballad given here were soon published in Germany, and she became one of the Protestant martyrs remembered in Elizabeth's reign by John Foxe in his *Acts and Monuments*.

## The ballad which Anne Askew made and sang when she was in Newgate

Like as the armèd knight
Appointed to the field,
With this world will I fight,
And faith shall be my shield.

Faith is that weapon strong                               5
Which will not fail at need;
My foes therefore among
Therewith will I proceed.

As it is had in strength
And force of Christes way,                                10
It will prevail at length,
Though all the devils say nay.

Faith in the fathers old
Obtainèd righteousness,
Which makes me very bold                                  15
To fear no world's distress.

I now rejoice in heart,
And hope bid me do so,
For Christ will take my part
And ease me of my woe.                                    20

Thou sayst, Lord, whoso knock,
To them wilt thou attend;
Undo therefore the lock
And thy strong power send.

More enemies now I have                                   25
Than hairs upon my head;
Let them not me deprave,
But fight thou in my stead.

2 *Appointed to* equipped for.
21 *Thou sayst* Matthew 7.7.

27 *deprave* corrupt.

On thee my care I cast
For all their cruel spite;                                    30
I set not by their haste,
For thou art my delight.

I am not she that list
My anchor to let fall
For every drizzling mist,                                     35
My ship substantial.

Not oft use I to write
In prose nor yet in rhyme,
Yet will I show one sight
That I saw in my time.                                        40

I saw a royal throne
Where Justice should have sit,
But in her stead was one
Of moody cruel wit.

Absorbed was righteousness                                    45
As of the raging flood;
Satan in his excess
Sucked up the guiltless blood.

Then thought I, Jesus Lord,
When thou shalt judge us all,                                 50
Hard is it to record
On these men what will fall.

Yet, Lord, I thee desire
For that they do to me,
Let them not taste the hire                                   55
Of their iniquity.

31  *set not by* have no regard for.          51  Painful is it to think.
45  *Absorbed* swallowed up.                   55  *hire* wages.
46  *As of* as if by.

# Psalm 130

Recognition that the biblical psalms were a species of lyric poetry gave them a special place in the larger project of bringing the sacred texts into the vernaculars; below are six different versions of a single psalm.

The importance of congregational singing for Protestant worship prompted translations, mostly in ballad meter or poulter's measure, that could be readily set to music. In mid-century Thomas Sternhold's versions of a number of psalms in this style became the nucleus around which a complete collection by various hands assembled itself. Much of the work of rounding it out fell to William Whittingham (1524?–1579), who provided the version of Psalm 130 given here and also worked on the Geneva Bible. *The Whole Book of Psalms*, first published in 1562, became the most widely reprinted book of poetry of its time, with over 600 editions before it went out of print in the early nineteenth century. There was a fair amount of mockery of it in literary circles; Philip Sidney set out to provide an alternative, and rendered the first forty-three psalms into a strikingly sophisticated run of metrical patterns. After his death, his sister, the Countess of Pembroke, finished the project in an even more vigorous and inventive style, though the result remained in manuscript until the nineteenth century. Sir John Harington (1561–1612; godson to Queen Elizabeth and translator of *Orlando Furioso*) also worked on a complete psalter of verse paraphrases, which he sent to King James near the end of his life.

Translators of individual psalms sometimes take expansive liberties; the first sonnet sequence in English is Anne Vaughan Lock's twenty-six-poem "meditation of a penitent sinner upon the 51 Psalm," published with her translation of four of Calvin's sermons (1560). Gascoigne's dilation on Psalm 130 was intended to be an entry in *The Hundred Sundry Flowers*, to follow "Gascoigne's Good Night"; omitted by mistake, it was printed in *The Posies*. A prose introduction and a prefatory sonnet describe the circumstance (a sudden rainstorm during a ride from Chelmsford to London) which inspired it. The so-called Penitential Psalms (6, 32, 38, 51, 102, 130, 143) constituted a privileged unit; they were understood to be David's very personal expressions of anguish in connection with his love for Bathsheba. In 1534 the Italian writer Pietro Aretino published a prose paraphrase of them with prose narrative links of his own; Wyatt recast this whole project in English verse, with the psalms themselves in *terza rima*. Harington began his verse psalter by translating the Penitential Psalms as a unit in the 1590s; the translation of Psalm 130 given here is from this early group (transcribed, as it happens, into the same Egerton manuscript that contains Wyatt's). Their text may be found in Steven W. May, *The Elizabethan Courtier Poets: The Poems and their Contexts* (Columbia, MO: University of Missouri Press, 1991), pp. 331–7.

## Sir Thomas Wyatt

From depth of sin and from a deep despair,
   From depth of death, from depth of heartes sorrow,
   From this deep cave of darkness' deep repair
Thee have I called, O Lord, to be my borrow.
   Thou in my voice, O Lord, perceive and hear       5
   My heart, my hope, my plaint, my overthrow,
My will to rise, and let by grant appear
   That to my voice thine ears do well intend.
   No place so far that to thee is not near,
No depth so deep that thou ne mayst extend       10
   Thine ear thereto; hear then my woeful plaint.
   For, Lord, if thou do observe what men offend
And put thy native mercy in restraint,
   If just exaction demand recompense,
   Who may endure, O Lord? Who shall not faint       15

3  *repair* resort.
4  *borrow* ransom.

8  *intend* listen.

At such account? Dread, and not reverence,
   Should so reign large. But thou seeks rather love,
   For in thy hand is mercy's residence,
By hope whereof thou dost our heartes move.
   I in thee, Lord, have set my confidence;            20
   My soul such trust doth evermore approve.
Thy holy word of eterne excellence,
   Thy mercy's promise that is alway just
   Have been my stay, my pillar, and pretense;
My soul in God hath more desirous trust            25
   Than hath the watchman looking for the day,
   By the relief to quench of sleep the thrust.
Let Israel trust unto the Lord alway,
   For grace and favor arn his property;
   Plenteous ransom shall come with him, I say,       30
And shall redeem all our iniquity.

**24**  *stay* support.  *pretense* claim.              **29**  *arn* are.

## The Geneva Bible

Out of the deep places have I called unto thee, O Lord.
Lord, hear my voice; let thine ears attend to the voice of my prayers.
If thou, O Lord, straitly markest iniquities, O Lord, who shall stand?
But mercy is with thee, that thou mayst be feared.
I have waited on the Lord; my soul hath waited, and I have trusted in his word.    5
My soul waiteth on the Lord more than the morning watch watcheth for the morning.
Let Israel wait on the Lord, for with the Lord is mercy, and with him is great redemption.
And he shall redeem Israel from all his iniquities.

## William Whittingham, from *The Whole Book of Psalms*

Lord, to thee I make my moan
When dangers me oppress;
I call, I sigh, plain and groan,
Trusting to find release.

Hear now, O Lord, my request,            5
For it is full due time,
And let thine ears aye be prest
Unto this prayer mine.

O Lord, our God, if thou weigh
Our sins and them peruse,            10
Who shall then escape and say,
I can myself excuse?

But Lord, thou art merciful,
And turnest to us thy grace,

**8**  *prest* ready.

That we, with hearts most careful,                      15
Should fear before thy face.

In God I put my whole trust,
My soul waiteth on his will,
For his promise is most just,
And I hope therein still.                                20

My soul to God hath regard,
Wishing for him alway,
More than they that watch and ward
To see the dawning day.

Let Israel then boldly                                   25
In the Lord put his trust;
He is that God of mercy,
That his deliver must.

For he it is that must save
Israel from his sin,
And all such as surely have                              30
Their confidence in him.

23    *ward* stand guard.

## George Gascoigne

From depth of dole wherein my soul doth dwell,
From heavy heart which harbors in my breast,
From troubled sprite which seldom taketh rest,
From hope of heaven, from dread of darksome hell,
O gracious God, to thee I cry and yell.                  5
My God, my Lord, my lovely Lord alone,
To thee I call, to thee I make my moan;
And thou (good God), vouchsafe in gree to take
This woeful plaint
Wherein I faint.                                         10
O hear me then for thy great mercy's sake.

O bend thine ears attentively to hear,
O turn thine eyes, behold me how I wail;
O harken, Lord, give ear for mine avail,
O mark in mind the burdens that I bear.                  15
See how I sink in sorrows everywhere,
Behold and see what dolors I endure,
Give ear and mark what plaints I put in ure.
Bend willing ear, and pity therewithal
My wailing voice,                                        20
Which hath no choice
But evermore upon thy name to call.

8    *in gree* with goodwill.                18    *put in ure* give expression to.

If thou, good Lord, shouldst take thy rod in hand,
If thou regard what sins are daily done,
If thou take hold where we our works begun,                    25
If thou decree in judgment for to stand
And be extreme to see our scuses scanned,
If thou take note of everything amiss
And write in rolls how frail our nature is,
O glorious God, O King, O Prince of Power,                     30
What mortal wight
May then have light
To feel thy frown if thou have list to lower?

But thou art good, and hast of mercy store.
Thou not delightst to see a sinner fall;                       35
Thou harkenst first, before we come to call.
Thine ears are set wide open evermore;
Before we knock, thou comest to the door.
Thou art more prest to hear a sinner cry
Than he is quick to climb to thee on high.                     40
Thy mighty name be praisèd then alway;
Let faith and fear
True witness bear
How fast they stand which on thy mercy stay.

I look for thee (my lovely Lord) therefore;                    45
For thee I wait, for thee I tarry still.
Mine eyes do long to gaze on thee my fill;
For thee I watch, for thee I pry and pore.
My soul for thee attendeth evermore,
My soul doth thirst to take of thee a taste,                   50
My soul desires with thee for to be placed,
And to thy word (which can no man deceive)
Mine only trust,
My love and lust
In confidence continually shall cleave.                        55

Before the break or dawning of the day,
Before the light be seen in lofty skies,
Before the sun appear in pleasant wise,
Before the watch (before the watch, I say),
Before the ward that waits therefore alway,                    60
My soul, my sense, my secret thought, my sprite,
My will, my wish, my joy, and my delight
Unto the Lord that sits in heaven on high
With hasty wing
From me doth fling                                             65
And striveth still unto the Lord to fly.

O Israel, O household of the Lord,
O Abraham's brats, O brood of blessèd seed,

27  And not compromise in judging our excuses.
33  *have list to lower* be inclined to look harshly.
39  *prest* ready.

44  *stay* rely.

68  *brats* Not invariably a term of contempt in sixteenth-
century usage.

O chosen sheep that love the Lord indeed,
O hungry hearts, feed still upon his word,                    70
And put your trust in him with one accord.
For he hath mercy evermore at hand,
His fountains flow, his springs do never stand,
And plenteously he loveth to redeem
Such sinners all                                              75
As on him call
And faithfully his mercies most esteem.

He will redeem our deadly drooping state,
He will bring home the sheep that go astray,
He will help them that hope in him alway,                    80
He will appease our discord and debate,
He will soon save though we repent us late,
He will be ours if we continue his,
He will bring bale to joy and perfect bliss,
He will redeem the flock of his elect                        85
From all that is
Or was amiss
Since Abraham's heirs did first his laws reject.


# Mary Herbert, Countess of Pembroke

From depth of grief
Where drowned I lie,
Lord, for relief
To thee I cry:
My earnest vehement crying, praying                          5
Grant quick attentive hearing, weighing.

O Lord, if thou
Offenses mark,
Who shall not bow
To bear the cark?                                            10
But with thy justice mercy dwelleth,
Whereby thy worship more excelleth.

On thee my soul,
On thee, O Lord,
Dependeth whole,                                             15
And on thy word;
Though sore with blot of sin defaced,
Yet surest hope hath firmly placed.

Who longest watch,
Who soonest rise                                             20
Can nothing match
The early eyes:
The greedy eyes my soul erecteth
While God's true promise it expecteth.

10    *cark* burden.

Then Israel                                          25
On God attend;
Attend him well
Who, still thy friend,
In kindness hath thee dear esteemed
And often, often erst redeemed.                      30

Now, as before,
Unchangèd he
Will thee restore,
Thy state will free:
All wickedness from Jacob driving,                   35
Forgetting follies, faults forgiving.

## Sir John Harington

From horror huge of dark despair and deep
My soul hath cried, with seas of sin surrounded.
O, hear the voice that in thine ear hath sounded;
Both hear and heed, and seem not, Lord, asleep.
If thou of sins a register do keep,                  5
All flesh and blood forever were confounded;
But thou, O Lord, hast grace and mercy store,
Which makes us fear thee much but love thee more.

Then thou, my soul, abide in expectation,
For on his word I set my rest and stay,              10
As they that watch by night expect the day.
O Israel, be this thy consolation;
His mercies rich thy ransom dear can pay.
His grace is great, then fear we no damnation;
Then, Israel, trust in God, for only he              15
Redeems thee from thy sins and sets thee free.

6  *confounded* ruined.                    10  *stay* support.

# Elizabeth I (1533–1603)

Elizabeth's literary activity was intermittent but continued through almost her entire life; in the 1590s she was producing translations of Boethius, Horace, and Plutarch (in the last case rendering prose as verse). We have a dozen or so original poems by her, some of them written in quite specific response to events. "The doubt of future foes exiles my present joy" survives in several manuscripts, and was also printed by George Puttenham in *The Art of English Poesy* (1589) as an example of "the Gorgeous." Its context is the flight of the Mary Stuart to England in 1568 and the perceived threat of Catholic subversion that came with it. *On Monsieur's Departure*, a startlingly ardent piece of female Petrarchism, is connected to the end in 1582 of Elizabeth's marriage negotiations with François, duc d'Alençon – her

last serious prospect for marriage. The record of their courtship suggests some genuine feeling, or at least playfulness (she called him her "frog"), but the whole matter was politically fraught, and in the end impossibly so. The poem survives only in seventeenth-century manuscripts, but is widely accepted as genuine. For another poem of hers, see the exchange between her and Walter Ralegh given below.

*Editions*: Modernized texts of Elizabeth's poems may be found in *The Poems of Queen Elizabeth I*, ed. Leicester Bradner (Providence, RI: Brown University Press, 1964), and *Elizabeth I: The Collected Works*, ed. Leah S. Marcus, Janel Mueller, and Mary Beth Rose (Chicago: University of Chicago Press, 2000), though neither edition is complete.

The doubt of future foes exiles my present joy,
And wit me warns to shun such snares as threaten mine annoy;
For falsehood now doth flow and subjects' faith doth ebb,
Which should not be if reason ruled or wisdom weaved the web.
But clouds of joys untried do cloak aspiring minds,　　　　　　5
Which turns to rain of late repent by changèd course of winds.
The top of hope suppressed, the root upreared shall be,
And fruitless all their grafted guile, as shortly ye shall see.
The dazzled eyes with pride, which great ambition blinds,
Shall be unseeled by worthy wights, whose foresight falsehood finds.　　10
The daughter of debate, that discord aye doth sow,
Shall reap no gain, where former rule still peace hath taught to know.
No foreign banished wight shall anchor in this port;
Our realm brooks not seditious sects, let them elsewhere resort.
My rusty sword through rest shall first his edge employ　　　　　15
To poll their tops that seek such change or gape for future joy.

1　*doubt* One manuscript reads "dread."
2　*threaten mine annoy* threaten to harm me.
5　*joys* Puttenham reads "toys."
6　*rain of late repent* One manuscript reads "rage of late report."
7　One manuscript reads, "The top of hope supposed the root of rue shall be."

10　*unseeled* unsewn (a term from falconry).
14　*brooks not seditious sects* Puttenham reads "it brooks no stranger's force."
16　*poll their tops* cut off their heads. *future* One manuscript reads "lawless."

# On Monsieur's Departure

I grieve, and dare not show my discontent;
I love, and yet am forced to seem to hate;
I do, yet dare not say I ever meant;
I seem stark mute, but inwardly do prate.
I am, and not; I freeze and yet am burned,                    5
Since from myself another self I turned.

My care is like my shadow in the sun:
Follows me flying, flies when I pursue it,
Stands, and lies by me, doth what I have done.
His too familiar care doth make me rue it.                    10
No means I find to rid him from my breast,
Till by the end of things it be suppressed.

Some gentler passion slide into my mind,
For I am soft, and made of melting snow;
Or be more cruel, Love, and so be kind.                       15
Let me or float or sink, be high or low,
Or let me live with some more sweet content,
Or die, and so forget what love e'er meant.

5 One manuscript reads "I am and am not, freeze and yet am burned."

6 *another* One source reads "my other."

12 *things* One manuscript reads "living."

13 *gentler* One manuscript reads "greater."

# Isabella Whitney (fl. 1567–1573)

Isabella Whitney's publication of two volumes of original verse, in 1567 and 1573, qualifies her for the title of the first professional woman poet in English. Almost nothing else is known about her. She was probably the sister of Geoffrey Whitney of Cheshire (ca. 1546–ca. 1601), known for a book of emblems published in 1586. The poem below is the lead poem from Whitney's first volume. The title page implies that it is an actual letter "written in meter by a young gentlewoman" to a deceitful fiancé, though its literary genesis is straightforwardly from Ovid's *Heroides*.

Ovid's sequence of verse epistles, primarily from wronged women to the men who have betrayed them, was also published in 1567 in its first English translation (by George Turberville); most of the women mentioned in Whitney's poem have letters written for them by Ovid. Whitney's poem stands out against its classical precedents for the resignation and good wishes to which it comes toward the end, though the briefly tilted reasoning of ll. 45–6 shows a flash of something else: if your new love is not perfect for you in every way, I hope she dies before you marry her.

## To her Unconstant Lover

As close as you your wedding kept, yet now the truth I hear,
Which you (yer now) might me have told; what need you nay to swear?
You know I always wished you well, so will I during life;
But sith you shall a husband be, God send you a good wife.
And this (whereso you shall become) full boldly may you boast:      5
That once you had as true a love as dwelt in any coast,
Whose constantness had never quailed if you had not begun;
And yet it is not so far past but might again be won,
If you so would – yea, and not change so long as life should last.
But if that needs you marry must, then farewell, hope is past.      10
And if you cannot be content to lead a single life
(Although the same right quiet be), then take me to your wife.
So shall the promises be kept that you so firmly made.
Now choose whether ye will be true, or be of Sinon's trade,
Whose trade if that you long shall use, it shall your kindred stain.      15
Example take by many a one whose falsehood now is plain:
As by Aeneas first of all, who did poor Dido leave,
Causing the Queen by his untruth with sword her heart to cleave.
Also I find that Theseus did his faithful love forsake,
Stealing away within the night before she did awake.      20
Jason that came of noble race two ladies did beguile;
I muse how he durst show his face to them that knew his wile.
For when he by Medea's art had got the fleece of gold,
And also had of her that time all kind of things he would,
He took his ship and fled away, regarding not the vows      25

1   *close* secret.
2   *yer* ere, before.
14   *Sinon* The man commissioned by the Greeks to deceive the Trojans into taking the Trojan horse into their city.
15   *your kindred stain* disgrace your family.
17   *Aeneas* Hero of Vergil's *Aeneid*, who in obedience to his imperial destiny abandoned Dido, queen of Carthage, who was in love with him.
19   *Theseus* Ariadne, daughter of the king of Crete, fell in love with him and helped him kill the Minotaur; she fled

with him, but he abandoned her while she slept on the island of Naxos.
21   *Jason* Leader of the expedition to bring the golden fleece from Colchis on the Black Sea. On the voyage out he stopped at the island of Lemnos and fathered two children on Queen Hypsipyle before deserting her. In Colchis he was loved by Medea, daughter of the king of Colchis, who gave him her magical aid; back in Greece, he married her, but eventually deserted her for the daughter of the king of Corinth. Both Hypsipyle and Medea have letters in the *Heroides*.

That he did make so faithfully unto his loving spouse.
How durst he trust the surging seas, knowing himself forsworn?
Why did he scape safe to the land before the ship was torn?
I think King Aeolus stayed the winds, and Neptune ruled the sea;
Then might he boldly pass the waves, no perils could him slay.　　　　30
But if his falsehood had to them been manifest before,
They would have rent the ship as soon as he had gone from shore.
Now may you hear how falseness is made manifest in time,
Although they that commit the same think it a venial crime,
For they for their unfaithfulness did get perpetual fame.　　　　35
Fame? Wherefore did I term it so? I should have called it shame.
Let Theseus be, let Jason pass, let Paris also scape
That brought destruction unto Troy all through the Grecian rape,
And unto me a Troilus be; if not, you may compare
With any of these persons that above expressèd are.　　　　40
But if I cannot please your mind, for wants that rest in me,
Wed whom you list, I am content your refuse for to be.
It shall suffice me, simple soul, of thee to be forsaken;
And it may chance, although not yet, you wish you had me taken.
But rather than you should have cause to wish this through your wife,　　　　45
I wish to her, ere you her have, no more but loss of life.
For she that shall so happy be of thee to be elect,
I wish her virtues to be such, she need not be suspect.
I rather wish her Helen's face than one of Helen's trade,
With chasteness of Penelope, the which did never fade;　　　　50
A Lucrece for her constancy, and Thisbe for her truth.
If such thou have, then Peto be: not Paris, that were ruth.
Perchance ye will think this thing rare in one woman to find;
Save Helen's beauty, all the rest the gods have me assigned.
These words I do not speak thinking from thy new love to turn thee.　　　　55
Thou knowst by proof what I deserve; I need not to inform thee.
But let that pass. Would God I had Cassandra's gift me lent;
Then either thy ill chance or mine my foresight might prevent.
But all in vain for this I seek; wishes may not attain it.
Therefore may hap to me what shall, and I cannot refrain it.　　　　60
Wherefore, I pray, God be my guide and also thee defend
No worser than I wish myself, until thy life shall end.
Which life, I pray, God may again King Nestor's life renew,
And after that your soul may rest amongst the heavenly crew.
Thereto I wish King Xerxes' wealth, or else King Croesus' gold,　　　　65

---

**29** *Aeolus* god of the winds.
**37** *Paris* His abduction of Helen caused the Trojan war.
**41** *wants* defects.
**51** *Lucrece* Lucretia, the virtuous Roman wife famous for committing suicide rather than live after being raped. *Thisbe* Beloved of Pyramus, who killed himself when he thought her dead; she killed herself in turn on finding his body.
**52** *Peto* Unexplained. Conceivably William Peto (d. 1558), a prominent clergyman under Henry VIII, elected cardinal and papal legate at the very end of his life. His loyalty to Catherine of Aragon and her daughter Mary I may qualify him as an exemplar of male loyalty, though the departure

from classical examples and the citation of a Catholic priest are both odd. Alternatively, the word could be the Latin *peto*, "I urge," inserted for emphasis and slightly mishandled by the compositor: "If such thou have, then (*peto*) be not Paris – that were ruth."
**57** *Cassandra* Trojan prophetess who accurately predicted Troy's fall.
**60** *refrain* restrain.
**63** *Nestor* The aged king of Pylos and respected counsellor in the Homeric poems.
**65** *Xerxes* king of Persia, sixth century BC. *Croesus* king of Lydia, sixth century BC.

With as much rest and quietness as man may have on mold.
And when you shall this letter have, let it be kept in store;
For she that sent the same hath sworn as yet to send no more.
And now farewell, for why at large my mind is here expressed;
The which you may perceive if that you do peruse the rest.                    70

66   *mold* earth.                                        69   *for why* because.

# George Gascoigne (1534?–1577)

The son of a Bedfordshire knight, George Gascoigne probably attended Cambridge; he was admitted to Gray's Inn in 1555, and in 1558 stood in for his father at Elizabeth's coronation. From this promising start followed a seemingly endless series of misadventures. He married a wealthy widow who turned out to be already married to somebody else; a street fight and legal troubles followed before the situation was resolved in Gascoigne's favor. He attempted to set up as a gentleman farmer back in Bedfordshire, but only lost money. He became ensnarled in legal disputes with his brother and was disinherited by his mother. The likelihood of imprisonment for debt prompted him to try military service in The Netherlands; he was imprisoned by the Spaniards for four months. On his return to England he discovered that the book of his that had been published in 1573, *The Hundred Sundry Flowers*, was bringing him not fame and fortune but scandal and the threat of legal action. He reworked and rearranged the material in the book, added new poems, and republished it as *The Posies* in 1575; it offered itself as the edifying testament of a reformed prodigal. Copies of it were confiscated by the government anyway. He continued to write and publish and sue for royal patronage, and in 1575 acted before the queen during a festival at the Earl of Leicester's estate; his performance spooked Elizabeth's horse, but she stayed in the saddle. A New Year's gift to Elizabeth in 1576 included a drawing of him kneeling before her, a spear in one hand, a book in the other, a pen behind his ear, and a laurel crown hovering over his head like a leafy halo. Some modest royal employment followed but led nowhere.

This almost comically disordered life accompanied and at times provided subject matter for the most interesting literary career in England between the time of Henry VIII and the Elizabethan Golden Age of the 1580s and 1590s. It began as early as Gascoigne's stay at Gray's Inn, where he translated two prestigious Continental dramas – Ariosto's *I Suppositi* and Lodovico Dolce's *Giocasta* – and saw them performed. In the last years of his life he published *The Steel Glass* (1576, with a prefatory poem by Walter Ralegh), the first original work of blank verse in English, and *Certain Notes of Instruction* (1575), the first English poetry-writing handbook. Gascoigne's most interesting book, however, is unquestionably his *Flowers*, which included his two theatrical translations, *The Adventures of Master F.J.* (one of the premier early works of English prose fiction, with embedded poems), and "The Devices of Sundry Gentlemen," ostensibly an anthology of poems by various hands, some bearing Gascoigne's name in their title. The poetry is conspicuously clever (*Certain Notes* is insistent that a poet start with "some good and fine device, showing the quick capacity of a writer") but never heavy going, and memorably marked by a mix of high passion and downscale diction ("I seek to weigh the woolsack down with one poor pepper grain"). Some of Gascoigne's slang and occasionally baffling proverbs are unattested elsewhere and may very well have been made up on the spot. There is also a strain of sexual frankness that can enter a poem without warning, as in the famous fifth stanza of "Gascoigne's Lullaby." His dominant theme is the passage from desire to disillusion; in his greatest single poem, "Gascoigne's Woodmanship," that passage is in some detail autobiographical, a repeated stumble of ambition into failure, but also beyond that into a kind of pride and, in an unexpected and mysterious conclusion, into childlike dependence. In accord with the principle in *Certain Notes*, the telling is conducted as an explication of the conceit contained in the poem's title.

*Flowers* contains a lengthy, incomplete sequence of poems on the erotic misfortunes of "Dan Bartholomew of Bath"; the story breaks off in mid-stanza. In *The Posies* the story is rounded off, but also joined by another, somewhat more compact sequence that covers much of the same thematic ground: "The Fruit of Fetters," the story of the Green Knight. This second sequence is given here in its entirety. It is the strangest of Gascoigne's tellings of his life story, simultaneously the most oblique and the most direct. He begins with a prolonged deception as to who exactly is speaking, and webs the whole account with detailed cross-references to the Dan Bartholomew sequence and to his own war experiences. The centerpiece is a sustained, addled riff on the fortunes of a "peerless firelock piece," for which the reference is by turns literal (a valuable military firearm), symbolic (human spirit generally), and obscene. The eventual diagnosis of the Green Knight's trouble is "fancy" – desire and imagination inhabiting the same word – and "The Green Knight's Farewell to Fancy" casts the widest net of any of Gascoigne's poems of summary moral reformation (among the follies here enumerated is a failed investment in fruit-splicing); but a concluding sonnet explains how nothing is concluded.

Of the poems given here, Gascoigne claimed to have musical settings for his "Passion," his "Lullaby," his "Good Morrow," and his "Good Night," as well as for his version of Psalm 130 ("I know you will delight to hear them"). None of these settings is known to survive.

*Edition*: George Gascoigne, *A Hundreth Sundrie Flowres*, ed. G. W. Pigman III (Oxford: Clarendon Press, 2000); including material from *The Posies*.

## From *The Hundred Sundry Flowers*

I will now then present you with a sonnet written in praise of the brown beauty, which he compiled for the love of Mistress E.P. as followeth.

> The thriftless thread which pampered beauty spins
> In thralldom binds the foolish gazing eyes,
> As cruel spiders with their crafty gins
> In worthless webs do snare the simple flies.
> The garments gay, the glittering golden gite,                     5
> The ticing talk which floweth from Pallas' pools,
> The painted pale, the (too much) red made white
> Are smiling baits to fish for loving fools.
> But lo, when eld in toothless mouth appears
> And hoary hairs instead of beauty's blaze,                       10
> Then *Had I wist* doth teach repenting years
> The tickle track of crafty Cupid's maze.
> Twixt fair and foul, therefore, twixt great and small,
> A lovely nutbrown face is best of all.

> *Si fortunatus infelix.*

*which he compiled for the love of Mistress E.P.* "he" is one of the fictional "sundry gentlemen"; "E.P." has not been identified.
3   *gins* devices.
5   *gite* gown.
6   *ticing* enticing.   *Pallas' pools* Pallas is Athena, the virgin goddess of wisdom; the reference to her "pools" is possibly to her eyes but has not been paralleled elsewhere.

7   *painted pale* cosmetically enhanced pallor.
9   *eld* old age.
11   *Had I wist* Had I known; the phrase occurs in several proverbial contexts: "Had I wist comes too late," etc.
12   *tickle* unreliable.
*Si fortunatus infelix* If fortunate, unhappy.

The lover, being disdainfully abjected by a dame of high calling, who had chosen (in his place) a playfellow of baser condition, doth therefore determine to step aside, and before his departure giveth her this farewell in verse.

> Thy birth, thy beauty, nor thy brave attire
> (Disdainful dame which dost me double wrong),
> Thy high estate which sets thy heart on fire,
> Or new found choice, which cannot serve thee long,
> Shall make me dread with pen for to rehearse                     5
> Thy skittish deeds in this, my parting verse.
>
> For why thou knowest, and I myself can tell
> By many vows how thou to me wert bound,
> And how for joy thy heart did seem to swell,
> And in delight how thy desires were drowned                     10
> When of thy will the walls I did assail,
> Wherein fond fancy fought for my avail.

1   *brave* impressive to look at.

And though my mind have small delight to vaunt,
Yet must I vow my heart to thee was true;
My hand was always able for to daunt       15
Thy slanderous foes, and keep their tongues in mew.
My head (though dull) was yet of such device
As might have kept thy name always in price.

And for the rest, my body was not brave,
But able yet of substance to allay       20
The raging lust wherein thy limbs did rave,
And quench the coals which kindled thee to play.
Such one I was, and such always will be
For worthy dames: but then, I mean not thee.

For thou hast caught a proper paragon,       25
A thief, a coward, and a peacock fool;
An ass, a milksop, and a minion
Which hath none oil thy furious flames to cool.
Such one he is, a fere for thee most fit:
A wandering guest to please thy wavering wit.       30

A thief I count him, for he robs us both,
Thee of thy name, and me of my delight;
A coward is he noted where he goeth,
Since every child is matched to him in might.
And for his pride, no more but mark his plumes,       35
The which to prink he days and nights consumes.

The rest thyself in secret sort can judge;
He rides not me, thou knowest his saddle best.
And though these tricks of thine mought make me grudge
And kindle wrath in my revenging breast,       40
Yet of myself, and not to please thy mind,
I stand content my rage in rule to bind.

And far from thee now must I take my flight,
Where tongues may tell (and I not see) thy fall,
Where I may drink these drugs of thy despite       45
To purge my melancholic mind withal.
In secret so my stomach will I starve,
Wishing thee better than thou dost deserve.

*Spraeta tamen vivunt*

16  *in mew* shut up.
18  *in price* highly valued.
29  *fere* companion.
36  *prink* arrange for maximum effect.

45  *drugs* The reading in *The Posies; Flowers* has "drags."
47  *stomach* anger.
   *Spraeta tamen vivunt* Things spurned yet live.

## Gascoigne's Passion

I smile sometimes, although my grief be great,
To hear and see these lovers paint their pain,
And how they can in pleasant rhymes repeat

Retitled "The Passion of a Lover" in *The Posies*. For the erotic symptomology being referred to, see Sir Thomas Wyatt's "I find no peace, and all my war is done" (above), itself a translation from Petrarch.

The passing pangs which they in fancies fain.
But if I had such skill to frame a verse,                                    5
I could more pain than all their pangs rehearse.

Some say they find nor peace nor power to fight,
Which seemeth strange; but stranger is my state.
I dwell in dole, yet sojourn with delight,
Reposed in rest, yet wearied with debate:                                   10
For flat repulse might well appease my will
But fancy fights to try my fortune still.

Some other say they hope, yet live in dread,
They freeze, they flame, they fly aloft, they fall;
But I nor hope with hap to raise my head                                    15
Nor fear to stoop for why my gate is small,
Nor can I freeze with cold to kill my heart,
Nor yet so flame as might consume my smart.

How live I, then, which thus draw forth my days?
Or tell me how I found this fever first.                                     20
What fits I feel? What distance? What delays?
What grief? What ease? What like I best? What worst?
These things they tell which seek redress of pain,
And so will I, although I count it vain.

I live in love, even so I love to live                                      25
(O happy state, twice happy he that finds it),
But love to life this cognizance doth give,
This badge, this mark, to every man that minds it:
Love lendeth life, which (dying) cannot die,
Nor living live; and such a life lead I.                                    30

The sunny days, which glad the saddest wights,
Yet never shine to clear my misty moon;
No quiet sleep amid the moonshine nights
Can close mine eyes when I am woebegone.
Into such shades my peevish sorrow shrouds,                                  35
That sun and moon are still to me in clouds.

And feverlike I feed my fancy still
With such repast as most impairs my health,
Which fever first I caught by wanton will
When coals of kind did stir my blood by stealth,                            40
And gazing eyes in beauty put such trust
That love inflamed my liver all with lust.

My fits are like the fever ectic fits,
Which one day quakes within and burns without;
The next day heat within the bosoms sits                                    45

4   *in fancies fain* long for in their imagination (though, as almost always in Elizabethan usage, it is hard not to hear "feign" as well: these pangs are poetic figments).
9   *dole* grief.
16   Nor fear to swoop down on my prey because I cannot fly very high; "stoop" and "gate" are terms from hawking.

21   *What distance? What delays?* How long between attacks of fever?
40   *kind* nature.
43   *ectic* hectic.

And shivering cold the body goes about.
So is my heart most hot when hope is cold,
And quaketh most when I most heat behold.

Tormented thus without delays I stand,
Always in one, and evermore shall be:                                    50
In greatest grief when help is nearest hand,
And best at ease if death might make me free;
Delighting most in that which hurts my heart,
And hating change which might relieve my smart.

                    L'ENVOY

Yet you, dear dame, to whom this cure pertains,                          55
Devise betimes some drams for my disease;
A noble name shall be your greatest gains,
Whereof be sure if you will work mine ease.
And though fond fools set forth their fits as fast,
Yet grant with me that Gascoigne's passion passed.                      60

*Ever or Never*

49  *delays* interruptions.                    60  *Gascoigne's The Posies* reads "my strange."

## Gascoigne's Praise of his Mistress

The hap which Paris had as due for his desert,
Which favored Venus for her face and scorned Minerva's art,
May serve to warn the wise that they no more esteem
The glistering gloss of beauty's blaze than reason should it deem.
Dan Priam's younger son found out the fairest dame                       5
That ever trod on Trojan mold; what followed of the same?
I list not bruit her bale, let others spread it forth;
But for his part, to speak my mind, his choice was little worth.
My meaning is but this: who marks the outward show
And never gropes for grafts of grace which in the mind should grow      10
May chance upon such choice as trusty Troilus had,
And dwell in dole as Paris did when he would fain be glad.
How happy then am I, whose hap hath been to find
A mistress first that doth excel in virtues of the mind,
And yet therewith hath joined such favor and such grace                 15
As Pandar's niece, if she were here, would quickly give her place;
Within whose worthy breast Dame Bounty seeks to dwell
And saith to Beauty, Yield to me, since I do thee excel;
Between whose heavenly eyes doth right remorse appear,

1–6  Paris, son of the Trojan king Priam, judged a beauty contest among the goddesses Juno, Minerva (Athena), and Venus; for giving the prize to Venus, he was awarded Helen as a prize, an outcome which led to his death and the fall of Troy. The choice Paris faced is often interpreted as one among worldly power, intellectual and moral wisdom, and physical beauty.
6  *mold* soil.

7  *bruit* broadcast.  *bale* harm.
11  *trusty* trusting.  *Troilus* Another son of Priam, whose love affair with Cressida is the subject of a famous poem of Chaucer's; Cressida eventually becomes the mistress of a Greek warrior, and she is often cited as an example of female inconstancy.
16  *Pandar's niece* Cressida.

And pity, placèd by the same, doth much amend her cheer;                    20
Who in my dangers deep did deign to do me good,
Who did relieve my heavy heart and sought to save my blood,
Who first increased my friends and overthrew my foes,
Who loved all them that wished me well, and likèd none but those.
O ladies, give me leave; I praise her not so far,                          25
Since she doth pass you all as much as Titan stains a star.
You hold such servants dear as able are to serve;
She held me dear when I, poor soul, could no good thing deserve.
You set by them that swim in all prosperity;
She set by me whenas I was in great calamity.                              30
You best esteem the brave, and let the poorest pass;
She best esteemed my poor good will, all naked as it was.
But whither am I went? What humor guides my brain?
I seek to weigh the woolsack down with one poor pepper grain.
I seem to pen her praise that doth surpass my skill,                       35
I strive to row against the tide, I hop against the hill.
Then let these few suffice: she Helen stains for hue,
Dido for grace, Cressid for cheer, and is as Thisbe true.
Yet if you further crave to have her name displayed,
Dame Favor is my mistress' name, Dame Fortune is her maid.                 40

*Attamen ad solitum*

26  *Titan* the sun.  *stains* disgraces (by outdoing).
29  *set by* value.
31  *brave* ostentatious.
38  *Dido* queen of Carthage and lover of Aeneas in Vergil's
*Aeneid.  Thisbe* A young Babylonian girl who committed
suicide after the death of her lover Pyramus.

40  *Dame Favor* The mistress turns out to be an allegorical
figure on the model of Lady Fortune, though outranking her
socially. In context, the term "favor" inflects the general sense
of generosity or advancement bestowed by a social superior to
someone below with the specific sense of female sexual favors.
*Attamen ad solitum* Nevertheless, in the usual way.

# Gascoigne's Lullaby

Sing lullaby, as women do
Wherewith they bring their babes to rest,
And lullaby can I sing, too,
As womanly as can the best.
With lullaby they still the child;                                          5
And if I be not much beguiled,
Full many wanton babes have I
Which must be stilled with lullaby.

First, lullaby my youthful years;
It is now time to go to bed,                                               10
For crooked age and hoary hairs
Have won the haven within my head.
With lullaby, then, youth be still,
With lullaby content thy will;
Since courage quails and comes behind,                                     15
Go sleep, and so beguile thy mind.

Next, lullaby my gazing eyes,
Which wonted were to glance apace,

Retitled "The Lullaby of a Lover" in *The Posies.*

For every glass may now suffice
To show the furrows in my face.                          20
With lullaby, then, wink awhile,
With lullaby your looks beguile;
Let no fair face nor beauty bright
Entice you eft with vain delight.

And lullaby my wanton will;                              25
Let reason's rule now reign thy thought,
Since all too late I find by skill
How dear I have thy fancies bought.
With lullaby now take thine ease,
With lullaby thy doubts appease;                         30
For trust to this, if thou be still,
My body shall obey thy will.

Eke lullaby my loving boy,
My little robin, take thy rest;
Since age is cold and nothing coy,                       35
Keep close thy coin, for so is best.
With lullaby be thou content,
With lullaby thy lusts relent;
Let others pay which have moe pence,
Thou art too poor for such expense.                      40

Thus lullaby my youth, mine eyes,
My will, my ware, and all that was;
I can no moe delays devise,
But welcome pain, let pleasure pass.
With lullaby now take your leave,                        45
With lullaby your dreams deceive;
And when you rise with waking eye,
Remember Gascoigne's lullaby.

*Ever or Never*

19   *glass* mirror.
24   *eft* again.
34   *My little robin* Context makes clear that the poet is here
addressing his penis (for which there is classical precedent:
Ovid, *Amores* 3.7.65–72), but no evidence has been produced

that "robin" in this sense was established sixteenth-century
usage.
35   *coy* flirtatious.
42   *ware* merchandise; a slang term for the genitals.
48   *Gascoigne's The Posies* reads "then this."

Alexander Neville delivered him this theme, *Sat cito si sat bene*, whereupon he compiled these seven
sonnets in sequence, therein bewraying his own *Nimis cito*, and therewith his *Vix bene*, as followeth.

In haste post-haste, when first my wandering mind
Beheld the glistering court with gazing eye,
Such deep delights I seemed therein to find
As might beguile a graver guest than I.
The stately pomp of princes and their peers             5
Did seem to swim in floods of beaten gold;
The wanton world of young, delightful years

*Sat cito si sat bene* Fast enough if good enough (a saying of
Cato the Censor). *Nimis cito* Too fast.   *Vix bene* Hardly good.

Was not unlike a heaven for to behold,
Wherein did swarm (for every saint) a dame
So fair of hue, so fresh of their attire          10
As might excel Dame Cynthia for fame
Or conquer Cupid with his own desire.
These and such like were baits that blazèd still
Before mine eye to feed my greedy will.

2. Before mine eye to feed my greedy will          15
Gan muster eke mine old acquainted mates,
Who helped the dish (of vain delight) to fill
My empty mouth with dainty delicates;
And foolish boldness took the whip in hand
To lash my life into this trustless trace,          20
Till all in haste I leapt aloof from land
And hoist up sail to catch a courtly grace.
Each lingering day did seem a world of woe
Till in that hapless haven my head was brought,
Waves of wanhope so tossed me too and fro          25
In deep despair to drown my dreadful thought.
Each hour a day, each day a year did seem,
And every year a world my will did deem.

3. And every year a world my will did deem
Till lo, at last, to court now am I come,          30
A seemly swain that might the place beseem,
A gladsome guest embraced of all and some.
Not there content with common dignity,
My wandering eye in haste (yea post post-haste)
Beheld the blazing badge of bravery,          35
For want whereof I thought myself disgraced.
Then peevish pride puffed up my swelling heart
To further forth so hot an enterprise,
And comely cost began to play his part
In praising patterns of mine own device.          40
Thus was all good that might be got in haste
To prink me up, and make me higher placed.

4. To prink me up, and make me higher placed
All came too late that tarried any time.
Piles of provision pleasèd not my taste;          45
They made my heels too heavy for to climb.
Methought it best that boughs of boisterous oak
Should first be shred to make my feathers gay,
Till at the last a deadly dinting stroke
Brought down the bulk with edge-tools of decay.          50
Of every farm I then let fly a lease
To feed the purse that paid for peevishness,

---

20   *trustless trace* untrustworthy path.
25   *wanhope* hopelessness.
35   *bravery* ostentation.
42   *prink me up* show me off.
46   *Piles of provision* what had been provided for me, i.e., my inheritance.

47–8   Trees on my land were cut down to provide money to buy clothing.
47   *boisterous* massive.
48   *shred* pruned.
49   *dinting* beating.

Till rent and all were fallen in such disease
As scarce could serve to maintain cleanliness.
The bough, the body, fine, farm, lease, and land:                    55
All were too little for the merchant's hand.

5. All were too little for the merchant's hand,
And yet my bravery bigger than his book.
But when this hot account was coldly scanned,
I thought high time about me for to look;                           60
With heavy cheer I cast my head aback
To see the fountain of my furious race,
Compared my loss, my living, and my lack
In equal balance with my jolly grace,
And saw expenses grating on the ground                              65
Like lumps of lead to press my purse full oft,
When light reward and recompense were found
Fleeting like feathers in the wind aloft.
These things compared, I left the court at large.
For why? The gains doth seldom quit the charge.                     70

6. For why? The gains doth seldom quit the charge,
And so say I, by proof too dearly bought.
My haste made waste, my brave and brainsick barge
Did float too fast, to catch a thing of nought;
With leisure, measure, mean, and many moe                           75
I mought have kept a chair of quiet state,
But hasty heads cannot be settled so
Till crooked fortune give a crabbèd mate.
As busy brains must beat on tickle toys,
As rash invention breeds a raw device,                              80
So sudden falls do hinder hasty joys;
And as swift baits do fleetest fish entice,
So haste makes waste, and therefore now I say
*No haste but good* where wisdom makes the way.

7. *No haste but good* where wisdom makes the way:    85
For proof whereof, we see the silly snail,
Who sees the soldier's carcass cast away
With hot assault the castle to assail,
By line and leisure climbs the lofty wall
And wins the turret's top more cunningly                            90
Than doughty Dick, who lost his life and all
With hoisting up his head too hastily.
The swiftest bitch brings forth the blindest whelps,
The hottest fevers coldest cramps ensue,
The nakedst need hath ever latest helps.                            95
With Neville then I find this proverb true,
That *Haste makes waste*, and therefore still I say
*No haste but good* where wisdom makes the way.

    *Sic tuli*

---

**55** *body* trunk (of the oak, in addition to its limbs). *fine* a legal instrument used for transfer of land. *farm* annual payment of a fixed amount.

**65** *grating* grinding.
**79** *tickle* unreliable.
**94** *ensue* follow.
*Sic tuli* So I have borne it.

## Gascoigne's Good Morrow

You that have spent the silent night
In sleep and quiet rest
And joy to see the cheerful light
That riseth in the east,
Now clear your voice, now cheer your heart,                    5
Come help me now to sing;
Each willing wight come bear a part
To praise the heavenly king.

And you whom care in prison keeps,
Or sickness doth suppress,                                      10
Or secret sorrow breaks your sleeps,
Or dolors do distress,
Yet bear a part in doleful wise,
Yea, think it good accord
And acceptable sacrifice                                        15
Each sprite to praise the Lord.

The dreadful night with darksomeness
Had overspread the light,
And sluggish sleep with drowsiness
Had overpressed our might:                                      20
A glass wherein we may behold
Each storm that stops our breath,
Our bed the grave, our clothes like mold,
And sleep like dreadful death.

Yet as this deadly night did last                              25
But for a little space,
And heavenly day, now night is past,
Doth show his pleasant face:
So must we hope to see God's face
At last in heaven on high,                                      30
When we have changed this mortal place
For immortality.

And of such haps and heavenly joys
As then we hope to hold,
All earthly sights, all worldly toys                           35
Are tokens to behold:
The day is like the day of doom,
The sun the son of man,
The skies the heavens, the earth the tomb
Wherein we rest till then.                                      40

The rainbow bending in the sky,
Bedecked with sundry hues,
Is like the seat of God on high,
And seems to tell these news:
That as thereby he promisèd                                    45

12  *dolors* sorrows.
21  *glass* mirror.

37  *doom* judgment.
38  *the son of man* Christ.

To drown the world no more,
So by the blood which Christ hath shed
He will our health restore.

The misty clouds that fall sometime
And overcast the skies                                        50
Are like to troubles of our time,
Which do but dim our eyes;
But as such dews are dried up quite
When Phoebus shows his face,
So are such fancies put to flight                             55
Where God doth guide by grace.

The carrion crow, that loathsome beast,
Which cries against the rain,
Both for her hue and for the rest
The devil resembleth plain;                                   60
And as with guns we kill the crow
For spoiling our relief,
The devil so must we overthrow
With gunshot of belief.

The little birds which sing so sweet                          65
Are like the angels' voice,
Which render God his praises meet
And teach us to rejoice;
And as they more esteem that mirth
Than dread the night's annoy,                                 70
So must we deem our days on earth
But hell to heavenly joy.

Unto which joys for to attain,
God grant us all his grace
And send us after worldly pain                                75
In heaven to have a place,
Where we may still enjoy that light
Which never shall decay.
Lord, for thy mercy lend us might
To see that joyful day.                                       80

*Haud ictus sapio*

**54** *Phoebus* the sun.
*Haud ictus sapio* Having been struck, I am not wise. Gascoigne reverses a proverb cited by Erasmus: "Piscator ictus sapiet" (having been struck, the fisherman will be wise; *Adagia* 1.1.28).

*Ictus* is also a term for metrical stress, and it has been suggested that Gascoigne's motto also means "I do not understand prosody."

## Gascoigne's Good Night

When thou hast spent the lingering day in pleasure and delight,
Or after toil and weary way dost seek to rest at night,
Unto thy pains or pleasures past add this one labor yet:

Printing the poem this way as fourteener couplets obscures the internal rhyme: the eighth syllable of each couplet rhymes as well as the fourteenth, and the poem could be printed in four-line stanzas rhyming abab.

Ere sleep close up thine eye too fast, do not thy God forget,
But search within thy secret thoughts what deeds did thee befall,                     5
And if thou find amiss in ought, to God for mercy call.
Yea, though thou find nothing amiss which thou canst call to mind,
Yet evermore remember this: there is the more behind.
And think how well soever it be that thou hast spent the day,
It came of God, and not of thee, so to direct thy way.                                10
Thus if thou try thy daily deeds, and pleasure in this pain,
Thy life shall cleanse thy corn from weeds, and thine shall be the gain;
But if thy sinful sluggish eye will venture for to wink
Before thy wading will may try how far thy soul may sink,
Beware and wake, for else thy bed, which soft and smooth is made,                     15
May heap more harm upon thy head than blows of enemy's blade.
Thus if this pain procure thine ease, in bed as thou dost lie,
Perhaps it shall not God displease to sing thus soberly:
I see that sleep is lent me here to ease my weary bones,
As death at last shall eke appear to ease my grievous groans.                         20
My daily sports, my paunch full fed have caused my drowsy eye,
As careless life in quiet led might cause my soul to die.
The stretching arms, the yawning breath which I to bedward use
Are patterns of the pangs of death, when life will me refuse;
And of my bed each sundry part in shadows doth resemble                               25
The sundry shapes of death, whose dart shall make my flesh to tremble.
My bed itself is like the grave, my sheets the winding sheet,
My clothes the mold which I must have to cover me most meet.
The hungry fleas, which frisk so fresh, to worms I can compare,
Which greedily shall gnaw my flesh and leave the bones full bare.                     30
The waking cock that early crows to wear the night away
Puts in my mind the trump that blows before the latter day.
And as I rise up lustily when sluggish sleep is past,
So hope I to rise joyfully to judgment at the last.
Thus will I wake, thus will I sleep, thus will I hope to rise,                        35
Thus will I neither wail nor weep, but sing in godly wise.
My bones shall in this bed remain, my soul in God shall trust,
By whom I hope to rise again from death and earthly dust.

32   *latter* last.

## Gascoigne's Woodmanship

Written to the Lord Grey of Wilton upon this occasion: The said Lord Grey delighting (amongst many other good qualities) in choosing of his winter deer, and killing the same with his bow, did furnish Master Gascoigne with a crossbow *cum pertinentiis*, and vouchsafed to use his company in the said exercise, calling him one of his woodmen. Now Master Gascoigne, shooting very often, could never hit any deer, yea and oftentimes he let the herd pass by as though he had not seen them. Whereat when this noble lord took some pastime, and had often put him in remembrance of his good skill in choosing and readiness in killing of a winter deer, he thought good thus to excuse it in verse.

My worthy lord, I pray you wonder not
To see your woodman shoot so oft awry,
Nor that he stands amazèd like a sot
And lets the harmless deer (unhurt) go by.

*cum pertinentiis* with appurtenances.                    3   *sot* fool.

Or if he strike a doe which is but carrion,                              5
Laugh not, good lord, but favor such a fault.
Take well in worth, he would fain hit the barren;
But though his heart be good, his hap is nought.
And therefore now I crave your lordship's leave
To tell you plain what is the cause of this.                           10
First, if it please your honor to perceive
What makes your woodman shoot so oft amiss,
Believe me, lord, the case is nothing strange.
He shoots awry almost at every mark,
His eyes have been so usèd for to range                                15
That now, God knows, they be both dim and dark.
For proof, he bears the note of folly now
Who shot sometimes to hit philosophy.
And ask you why? Forsooth, I make avow,
Because his wanton wits went all awry.                                  20
Next that, he shot to be a man of law,
And spent some time with learnèd Littleton;
Yet in the end he provèd but a daw,
For law was dark and he had quickly done.
Then could he wish Fitzherbert such a brain                            25
As Tully had, to write the law by art,
So that with pleasure, or with little pain,
He might perhaps have caught a truant's part.
But all too late; he most misliked the thing
Which most might help to guide his arrow straight.                     30
He winkèd wrong, and so let slip the string,
Which cast him wide, for all his quaint conceit.
From thence he shot to catch a courtly grace,
And thought even there to wield the world at will;
But out, alas, he much mistook the place                               35
And shot awry at every rover still.
The blazing baits which draw the gazing eye
Unfeathered there his first affection;
No wonder then although he shot awry,
Wanting the feathers of discretion.                                    40
Yet more than them, the marks of dignity
He much mistook, and shot the wronger way,
Thinking the purse of prodigality
Had been best mean to purchase such a prey.
He thought the flattering face which fleereth still                    45
Had been full fraught with all fidelity,

---

5 *carrion* The contrast with "barren" in l. 7 suggests that the word here means "pregnant," and it is often so glossed; but no instances of this usage elsewhere have been found. It could conceivably be *ad hoc* slang, or it could be being used in the sense of "worthless."

7 *Take well in worth* Take it for what's it's worth. *The Posies* reads "will" for "well."

22 *Littleton* Sir Thomas Littleton (1422?–1481); his *Tenures*, one of the first books printed in England, was a basic law text in the sixteenth century.

23 *daw* fool.

24 *dark* hard to understand.

25 *Fitzherbert* Sir Anthony Fitzherbert (1470–1538), author of *La grand abrègement de le loi*, an attempt to systematize English common law.

26 *Tully* Marcus Tullius Cicero (106–43 BC), the famous Roman statesman, widely admired as a Latin prose stylist; Fitzherbert would have been far easier to study if he had been as good a writer.

28 *a truant's part* as much as might be learned without diligent study.

31 *winkèd wrong* sighted wrong.

32 *cast him wide* made his shot go wide. *quaint conceit* fancy notion.

45 *fleereth* smiles obsequiously.

And that such words as courtiers use at will
Could not have varied from the verity.
But when his bonnet buttonèd with gold,
His comely cape beguarded all with gay,　　　　　　　50
His bombast hose with linings manifold,
His knit silk stocks, and all his quaint array
Had picked the purse of all the Peter pence
Which might have paid for his promotion,
Then (all too late) he found that light expense　　55
Had quite quenched out the court's devotion,
So that since then the taste of misery
Hath been always full bitter in his bit.
And why? Forsooth because he shot awry,
Mistaking still the marks which others hit.　　　　60
But now behold what mark the man doth find:
He shoots to be a soldier in his age;
Mistrusting all the virtues of the mind,
He trusts the power of his personage,
As though long limbs led by a lusty heart　　　　65
Might yet suffice to make him rich again.
But Flushing frays have taught him such a part
That now he thinks the wars yield no such gain.
And sure I fear, unless your lordship deign
To train him yet into some better trade,　　　　　70
It will be long before he hit the vein
Whereby he may a richer man be made.
He cannot climb as other catchers can
To lead a charge before himself be led;
He cannot spoil the simple sackless man　　　　　75
Which is content to feed him with his bread.
He cannot pinch the painful soldier's pay
And shear him out his share in ragged sheets;
He cannot stoop to take a greedy prey
Upon his fellows groveling in the streets.　　　　80
He cannot pull the spoil from such as pill
And seem full angry at such foul offense,
Although the gain content his greedy will,
Under the cloak of contrary pretense;
And nowadays, the man that shoots not so　　　　85
May shoot amiss, even as your woodman doth.
But then you marvel why I let them go
And never shoot but say farewell, forsooth.
Alas, my lord, while I do muse hereon
And call to mind my youthful years misspent,　　90
They give me such a bone to gnaw upon

---

50　*beguarded all with gay* cheerfully embroidered.
51　*bombast hose* tights padded with cotton.
52　*stocks* stockings.
53　*Peter pence* A tax on householders payable to the papal see. It had not been imposed in England since 1534; Gascoigne uses it as slang for bribery in general.
55　*light* frivolous.
67　*Flushing* In the Low Countries, where Gascoigne saw military service.

73　*catchers* opportunists.
75　*spoil* rob. *sackless* innocent.
77–8　He cannot keep his soldiers' wages for himself and pay them in rags.
79　*stoop to* swoop down upon, like a hawk on its prey. This is the reading of *The Posies*; for "stoop" the first edition has "stop."
81　*pill* pillage.

That all my senses are in silence pent.
My mind is rapt in contemplation
Wherein my dazzled eyes only behold
The black hour of my constellation                                      95
Which framèd me so luckless on the mold.
Yet therewithal I cannot but confess
That vain presumption makes my heart to swell,
For thus I think not all the world (I guess)
Shoots bet than I: nay, some shoots not so well.                        100
In Aristotle somewhat did I learn
To guide my manners by all comeliness,
And Tully taught me somewhat to discern
Between sweet speech and barbarous rudeness.
Old Perkins, Rastell, and Dan Bracton's books                           105
Did lend me somewhat of the lawless law;
The crafty courtiers with their guileful looks
Must needs put some experience in my maw.
Yet cannot these, with many masteries moe,
Make me shoot straight at any gainful prick,                            110
Where some that never handled such a bow
Can hit the white, or touch it near the quick:
Who can nor speak nor write in pleasant wise,
Nor lead their life by Aristotle's rule,
Nor argue well on questions that arise,                                 115
Nor plead a case more than my Lord Mayor's mule.
Yet can they hit the marks that I do miss,
And win the mean which may the man maintain.
Now when my mind doth mumble upon this,
No wonder then although I pine for pain;                                120
And whiles mine eyes behold this mirror thus,
The herd goeth by, and farewell gentle does:
So that your lordship quickly may discuss
What blinds mine eyes so oft (as I suppose).
But since my Muse can to my lord rehearse                               125
What makes me miss, and why I do not shoot,
Let me imagine in this worthless verse
If right before me, at my standing's foot,
There stood a doe, and I should strike her dead,
And then she prove a carrion carcass too.                               130
What figure might I find within my head
To scuse the rage which ruled me so to do?
Some might interpret by plain paraphrase
That lack of skill or fortune led the chance,
But I must otherwise expound the case.                                  135
I say Jehovah did this doe advance
And made her bold to stand before me so
Till I had thrust mine arrow to her heart,

---

**96** *mold* earth.
**105** *Perkins* John Perkins (d. 1545), author of *Pertulis Tractatus*, an important treatise land and testamentary law. *Rastell* Either John Rastell (1475?–1536, brother-in-law to Sir Thomas More), publisher of the books of Littleton and Fitzherbert cited above, or his son William Rastell (1508?–1565), editor of a number of important sixteenth-century legal works. *Dan Bracton* Henry de Bracton (ca. 1210–68), medieval jurist whose *De legibus et consuetudinis Angliae* was published in the sixteenth century.
**110** *prick* peg marking the center of a target.
**112** *the white* circle surrounding the center of a target.
**123** *discuss* determine.
**128** *standing* hunting position.

That by the sudden of her overthrow
I might endeavor to amend my part,                                    140
And turn mine eyes that they no more behold
Such guileful marks as seem more than they be
And, though they glister outwardly like gold,
Are inwardly but brass, as men may see.
And when I see the milk hang in her teat,                             145
Methinks it sayeth, Old babe, now learn to suck,
Who in thy youth couldst never learn the feat
To hit the whites which live with all good luck.
Thus have I told, my lord (God grant, in season),
A tedious tale in rhyme, but little reason.                           150

*Haud ictus sapio*

## From *The Posies*

# The Fruit of Fetters, with the Complaint of the Green Knight and his Farewell to Fancy

Great be the griefs which bruise the boldest breasts,
And all too seld we see such burdens borne,
For cruel care (which reaveth quiet rests)
Hath oftentimes the worthiest wills forworn
And laid such weight upon a noble heart                               5
That wit and will have both given place to smart.

For proof whereof, I tell this woeful tale
(Give ear that list; I force no frolic minds);
But such as can abide to hear of bale
And rather rue the rage which Fancy finds                             10
Than scorn the pangs which may procure their pine,
Let them give ear unto these rhymes of mine.

I tear my time (ay me) in prison pent,
Wherein the flower of my consuming years
With secret grief my reason doth torment,                             15
And frets itself (perhaps) with needless fears;
For whiles I strive against the stream too fast,
My forces fail, and I must down at last.

The hasty vine for sample might me serve,
Which climbs too high about the lofty tree,                           20
But when the twist his tender joints doth carve,
Then fades he fast that sought full fresh to be;
He fades and faints before his fellows fail
Which lay full low and never hoist up sail.

Ay me, the days which I in dole consume;                              25
Alas, the nights which witness well my woe;
O wrongful world, which makst my fancy fume;

---

3   *reaveth* steals.
4   *forworn* worn out.

11   *pine* sorrow.
13   *tear* weep.

Fie, fickle Fortune, fie, thou art my foe;
Out and alas, so froward is my chance,
No days nor nights nor worlds can me advance.                    30

In reckless youth, the common plague of love
Infected me (all day) with careless mind;
Enticing dames my patience still did prove,
And bleared mine eyes till I became so blind
That, seeing not what fury brought me forth,                     35
I followed most (always) that least was worth.

In middle years, the reach of reason's rein
No sooner gan to bridle in my will,
Nor naked need no sooner gan constrain
My rash decay to break my sleeps by skill,                       40
But straight therewith hope set my heart on flame
To win again both wealth and worthy name.

And thence proceeds my most consuming grief,
For whiles the hope of mine unyolden heart
In endless toils did labor for relief,                           45
Came crabbèd Chance and marred my merry mart:
Yea, not content with one foul overthrow,
She tied me fast for tempting any moe.

She tied me fast (alas) in golden chains,
Wherein I dwell, not free nor fully thrall,                      50
Where guileful love in double doubt remains,
Nor honey sweet nor bitter yet as gall;
For every day a pattern I behold
Of scorching flame which makes my heart full cold.

And every night, the rage of restless thought                   55
Doth raise me up, my hope for to renew;
My quiet bed, which I for solace sought,
Doth irk mine ears when still the warlike crew
With sound of drums and trumpets braying shrill
Relieve their watch, yet I in thralldom still.                   60

The common joy, the cheer of company,
Twixt mirth and moan doth plunge me evermore;
For pleasant talk or music's melody
Yield no such salve unto my secret sore,
But that therewith this corsive comes me to:                     65
Why live not I at large as others do?

Lo, thus I live in spite of cruel death,
And die as fast in spite of lingering life,
Fed still with hope which doth prolong my breath,
But choked with fear and strangled still with strife,           70

---

33  *prove* test.                          46  *mart* market.
44  *unyolden* unyielded, i.e., not surrendered.   65  *corsive* corrosive.

Stark staring blind because I see too much,
Yet gazing still because I see none such.

Amid these pangs (O subtle cordial),
Those far fet sighs which most men's minds eschew
Recomfort me, and make the fury fall                                      75
Which fed the root from whence my fits renew;
They comfort me (ah, wretched doubtful clause),
They help the harm, and yet they kill the cause.

Where might I then my careful corpse convey
From company, which worketh all my woe?                                  80
How might I wink or hide mine eyes alway,
Which gaze on that whereof my grief doth grow?
How might I stop mine ears, which harken still
To every joy which can but wound my will?

How should I seem my sighs for to suppress,                              85
Which help the heart that else would swelt in sunder,
Which hurt the help that makes my torment less,
Which help and hurt (O woeful weary wonder)
One silly heart thus tossed twixt help and harm?
How should I seem such sighs in time to charm?                          90

How? How but thus: in solitary wise
To step aside and make high way to moan,
To make two fountains of my dazzled eyes,
To sigh my fill till breath and all be gone.
So sighed the knight of whom Bartello writes,                           95
All clad in green, yet banished from delights.

And since the story is both new and true,
A dreary tale much like these lots of mine,
I will assay my Muse for to renew
By rhyming out his froward fatal fine.                                  100
A doleful speech becomes a dumpish man;
So seemed by him, for thus his tale began.

74   *far fet* fetched from afar.
86   *swelt in sunder* come to pieces.
95   *Bartello* A non-existent author of "Italian riding tales" who makes a number of appearances in Gascoigne's writing; he is the fictional source for the revised version of *The Adventures of Master F.J.* in *The Posies*. His name suggests both "Bandello" (Matteo Bandello, an actual writer of *novelle*) and "bordello." In another poem in *The Posies*, Gascoigne writes that his *nom de guerre* in the Netherlands was *die groene Hopman*, the green captain.
100   *fine* end.
101   *dumpish* moody.

### THE COMPLAINT OF THE GREEN KNIGHT

Why live I, wretch (quoth he), alas and wellaway,
Or why behold my heavy eyes this gladsome sunny day?
Since never sun yet shone that could my state advance,
Why live I, wretch (alas, quoth he), in hope of better chance?
Or wherefore tells my tongue this dreary doleful tale,                  5
That every ear might hear my grief and so bemoan my bale?
Since ear was never yet that harkened to my plaint,

Why live I, wretch (alas, quoth he), my pangs in vain to paint?
Or wherefore dotes desire that doth his wish disclose
And shows the sore that seeks recure thereby to ease my woes? 10
Since yet he never found the heart where pity dwelt,
Why live I, wretch (alas, quoth he), alone in woe to swelt?
Why strive I with the stream, or hop against the hill,
Or search that never can be found, or lose my labor still?
Since destinies decreed must always be obeyed, 15
Why live I, wretch, alas (quoth he), with luck thus overlaid?
Why feeds my heart on hope? Why tire I still on trust?
Why doth my mind still muse on mirth? Why leans my life on lust?
Since hope had never hap, and trust always found treason,
Why live I, wretch, alas (quoth he), where all good luck is geason? 20
The fatal sisters three which spun my slender twine
Knew well how rotten was the yarn from whence they drew their line,
Yet have they woven the web with care so manifold
(Alas I, woeful wretch the while) as any cloth can hold.
Yea, though the threads be coarse, and such as others loathe, 25
Yet must I wrap always therein my bones and body both,
And wear it out at length, which lasteth but too long.
O weaver, weaver, work no more; thy warp hath done me wrong.
For therein have I lapped my light and lusty years
And therein hapless have I happed mine age and hoary hairs, 30
Yet never found I warmth by jetting in thy jags,
Nor never can I wear them out, although they rend like rags.
The May-moon of mine age, I mean the gallant time
When coals of kind first kindled love, and pleasure was in prime:
All bitter was the fruit which still I reapèd then, 35
And little was the gain I got, compared by other men.
Tear-thirsty were the dames to whom I sued for grace,
Some stony-stomached, other some of high disdainful race;
But all unconstant aye, and, that to think, I die.
The guerdon which Cosmana gave can witness if I lie. 40
Cosmana was the wight to whom I wishèd well,
To serve Cosmana did I seem in love to bear the bell;
Cosmana was my god, Cosmana was my joy,
Ay me, Cosmana turned my mirth to dole and dark annoy.
Revenge it, Radamanth, if I be found to lie; 45
Or if I slander her at all, condemn me then to die.
Thou knowst I honored her, no more but all too much;
Alas, thou knowst she cast me off when I deserved no grutch.
She dead (I dying yet), ay me, my tears were dried,
And teeth of time gnew out the grief which all too long I tried; 50
Yet from her ashes sprung, or from such subtle mold,

---

**12** *swelt* swelter.
**16** *overlaid* overwhelmed.
**17** *tire* feed (used of a hawk tearing at its prey). *trust* hope.
**20** *geason* scarce.
**21** *The fatal sisters three* the Fates.
**29** *lapped* wrapped.
**30** *happed* wrapped.
**31** *jetting in thy jags* strutting in your rags.

**34** *kind* nature.
**39** *that to think, I die* I die to think of it.
**42** *bear the bell* take the prize.
**45** *Radamanth* Rhadamanthys, mythical author of the Cretan law code, one of the judges of the dead in the underworld.
**48** *grutch* complaint.
**50** *gnew* gnawed. *tried* experienced.

Ferenda, she whom every eye did judge more bright than gold.
Ferenda then I saw, Ferenda I beheld,
Ferenda served I faithfully in town and eke in field.
Ferenda could not say the Green Knight was untrue,                                55
But out, alas, the Green Knight said, Ferenda changed for new.
Ferenda did her kind; then was she to be borne.
She did but wear Cosmana's clouts, which she in spite had torn;
And yet between them both they ware the threads so near
As, were they not of steel or stone, they could not hold yfere.                   60
But now, Ferenda mine, a little by thy leave:
What movèd thee to madding mood? Why didst thou me deceive?
Alas, I was all thine, thyself can say no less,
And for thy fall I bathèd oft in many a deep distress.
And yet, to do thee right, I neither blame thy race,                              65
Thy shining self, the golden gleams that glistered on thy face,
Nor yet thy fickle faith shall never bear the blame,
But I, whom kind hath framed to find a grief in every game.
The high decrees of heaven have limited my life
To linger still where Love doth lodge, yet there to starve in strife.             70
For proof, who list to know what makes me now complain,
Give ear unto the Green Knight's tale, for now begins his pain.
    When rash unbridled Youth had run his reckless race
And carried me with careless course to many a great disgrace,
Then riper, mellowed years thought good to turn their trade,                      75
And bade Repentance hold the reins to rule the brainsick jade,
So that with much to-do the bridle held him back,
And Reason made him bite on bit which had a better smack.
And for I felt myself by feebleness fordone,
And panting still for lack of breath, as one much overrun,                        80
Therefore I took advice to walk him first awhile
And so at length to set him up his travails to beguile.
Yea, when he curried was, and dusted slick and trim,
I caused both hay and provender to be allowed for him,
Whereat (alas to think) he gathered flesh so fast                                 85
That still he played his coltish pranks whenas I thought them past.
He winchèd still always, and whiskèd with his tail,
And leaping over hedge and ditch, I saw it not prevail
To pamper him so proud; wherefore I thought it best
To travail him not as I wont, yet nay to give him rest.                           90
Thus well resolvèd then, I kept him still in heart,
And found a pretty provender appointed for his part,
Which once a day, no more, he might a little taste,
And by this diet made I Youth a gentle jade at last.
And forth I might him ride an easy journeying pace;                               95
He never strave with Middle Age, but gently gave him place.

---

52 *Ferenda* The unreliable woman in the Dan Bartholomew
sequence is called Ferenda Natura, a Latin phrase which
there Gascoigne glosses as "dame Nature bears the blame",
but which is more credibly rendered "Nature must be borne";
the latter translation is visible in l. 57 below, though the full
name is not explicitly given in this sequence.
58   *clouts* clothes.
59   *they ware the threads so near* they wore their clothes so
tight (?).

60   *yfere* together.
62   *madding* maddening.
78   *smack* taste.
79   *fordone* overcome.
87   *winchèd* kicked restlessly.
88   *prevail* avail.
90   *travail* work.
91   *in heart* in good condition.

Then Middle Age stept in, and took the helm in hand
To guide my bark by better skill into some better land;
And as each noble heart is evermore most bent
To high exploits and worthy deeds where honor may be hent,                100
So mine unyolden mind by arms gan seek renown,
And sought to raise that reckless Youth had rashly tumbled down.
With sword and trusty targe then sought I for to carve
For Middle Age and Hoary Hairs, and both their turns to serve;
And in my carver's room I gan to cut such cuts                            105
And made such morsels for their mouths as well might fill their guts,
Beside some overplus, which (being kept in store)
Might serve to welcome all their friends with foison evermore.
I mean no more but this: my hand gan find such hap
As made me think that Fortune meant to play me in her lap,               110
And hope therewith had heaved my heart to be so high
That still I hoped by force of arms to climb above the sky.
I bathèd still in bliss, I led a lordly life,
My soldiers loved and feared me both, I never dreaded strife;
My board was furnished still with cates of dainty cost,                  115
My back well clad, my purse well lined, my wonted lack was lost;
My bags began to fill, my debts for to discharge,
My state so stood as sure I seemed to swim in good luck's barge.
But out and wellaway, what pleasure breeds not pain?
What sun can shine without a cloud, what thunder brings not rain?        120
Such is the life of man, such was the luck of me,
To fall so fast from highest hap, where sure I seemed to be.
Five hundred sundry suns (and more) could scarcely serve
By sweat of brows to win a room wherein my knife might carve.
One only dismal day sufficèd (with despite)                              125
To take me from my carver's place and from the table quite.
Five hundred broken sleeps had busied all my brains
To find (at last) some worthy trade that might increase my gains;
One black unlucky hour my trade hath overthrown
And marred my mart and broke my bank and all my bliss o'erblown.         130
To wrap up all in woe, I am in prison pent,
My gains possessèd by my foes, my friends against me bent,
And all the heavy haps that ever age yet bare
Assembled are within my breast to choke me up with care.
My modest middle age, which lacks of youth the lust,                     135
Can bear no such great burdens now, but throws them in the dust.
Yet in this piteous plight, behold me, lovers all,
And rue my griefs, lest you yourselves do light on such a fall.
I am that weary wretch, whom love always hath tired
And fed me with such strange conceits as never man desired.             140
For now (even now), ay me, I love and cannot choose,
So strangely yet as well may move the wisest minds to muse.
No blazing beauty bright hath set my heart on fire,
No ticing talk, no gorgeous gite tormenteth my desire;
No body finely framed, no haggard falcon's eye,                          145
No ruddy lip, no golden locks hath drawn my mind awry;

---

100  *hent* seized.                        115  *cates* culinary delicacies.
101  *unyolden* unyielded.                 130  *mart* market.
103  *targe* shield.                       144  *ticing* enticing.  *gite* gown.
108  *foison* plenty.

No teeth of shining pearl, no gallant rosy hue,
No dimpled chin, no pit in cheek presented to my view:
In fine, no such delights as lovers oft allure
Are cause why thus I do lament, or put my plaints in ure,          150
But such a strange affect as both I shame to tell
And all the world may wonder much how first therein I fell.
Yet since I have begun (quoth he) to tell my grief,
I will nought hide, although I hope to find no great relief.
And thus (quoth he) it is: amongst the sundry joys               155
Which I conceived in feats of war, and all my martial toys,
My chance was late to have a peerless firelock piece
That, to my wits, was nay the like in Turkey nor in Greece:
A piece so cleanly framed, so straight, so light, so fine,
So tempered and so polishèd as seemeth work divine;             160
A piece whose lock yet passed, for why it never failed,
And though I bent it night and day, the quickness never quailed;
A piece as well renforced as ever yet was wrought,
The bravest piece for breech and bore that ever yet was bought;
The mounture so well made, and for my pitch so fit,            165
As though I see fair pieces moe, yet few so fine as it;
A piece which shot so well, so gently and so straight,
It neither bruisèd with recule nor wrung with overweight.
In fine and to conclude, I know no fault thereby
That either might be thought in mind or well discerned with eye.   170
This piece then late I had, and therein took delight
As much as ever proper piece did please a warlike wight.
Now though it be not lost nor rendered with the rest,
Yet, being shut from sight thereof, how can I think me blest?
Or which way should I hope that such a jewel rare              175
Can pass unseen in any camp where cunning shooters are?
And therewith am I sure that, being once espied,
It never can escape their hands but that it will be tried;
And being once but proved, then farewell frost for me.
My piece, my lock, and all is lost, and I shall never see       180
The like again on earth. Now, lovers, speak your mind:
Was ever man so strangely struck, or caught in such a kind?
Was ever man so fond? Was ever man so mad?
Was ever man so woebegone, or in such cares yclad?
For restless thus I rest, the wretchedst man on live,          185
And when I think upon this piece, then still my woes revive.
Nor ever can I find good plaster for my pain,
Unless my luck might be so good to find that piece again.
To make my mourning more where I in prison pine,
I daily see a pretty piece much like that piece of mine,        190
Which helps my hurt much like unto a broken shin
That when it heals begins to itch and then rubs off the skin.

---

150   *ure* performance.
157   *piece* Modern slang senses of this term are already present
in sixteenth-century usage: "firearm" (the primary meaning
here, explored with technical specificity) but also "piece of
flesh." The usual reference of the latter is female, though
Gascoigne's development of the theme sometimes suggests
the male genitals as well ("A piece which shot so well"). See
also below on l. 37 in "The Continuance of the Author."

161   *passed* passed muster. *for why* because.
162   *quailed* lessened.
165   *mounture* support. *pitch* height.
168   *recule* recoil. *wrung* twisted.
173   *rendered* surrendered.
179   *proved* experienced. *farewell frost* so much for that.
185   *on live* alive.

Thus live I still in love, alas, and ever shall,
As well content to lose my piece as glad to find my fall:
A wonder to the world, a grief to friendly minds,                    195
A mocking stock to Momus' race and all such scornful hinds;
A love (that think I sure) whose like was never seen,
Nor never warlike wight shall be in love as I have been.
So that, in sooth (quoth he), I cannot blame the dames
Whom I in youth did most esteem; I list not foil their fames,        200
But there to lay the fault from whence it first did flow:
I say my Fortune is the root whence all these griefs did grow.
Since Fortune then (quoth he) hath turned to me her back,
Shall I go yield to mourning moan and clothe myself in black?
No, no, for noble minds can bear no thralldom so,                    205
But rather show a merry cheer when most they wade in woe.
And so will I in green my careful corpse array,
To set a brag amongst the best, as though my heart were gay.
Not green because I hope, nor green because I joy,
Not green because I can delight in any youthful toy,                 210
But green because my griefs are alway fresh and green,
Whose root is such it cannot rot, as by the fruit is seen.
Thus said, he gave a groan, as though his heart had broke,
And from the furnace of his breast sent scalding sighs like smoke;
And sighing so, he sat in solitary wise,                            215
Conveying floods of brinish tears by conduct of his eyes.
What end he had, God knoweth; Bartello writes it not,
Or if he do, my wits are short, for I have it forgot.

196  *Momus* classical Greek personification of sarcasm.  *hinds*    200  *foil* befoul.
rustic louts.                                                        216  *conduct* conduit.

THE CONTINUANCE OF THE AUTHOR, UPON THE FRUIT OF FETTERS

Thus have you heard the Green Knight make his moan,
Which well might move the hardest heart to melt.
But what he meant, that knew himself alone,
For such a cause in weary woes to swelt;
And yet, by like, some peerless piece it was                         5
That brought him so in raging storms to pass.

I have heard tell, and read it therewithal,
That near the Alps a kind of people be
Which serve with shot whereof the very ball
Is big of bulk, the piece but short to see;                          10
But yet it shoots as far, and eke as fast,
As those which are yframed of longer last.

The cause (say some) consisteth in the lock;
Some other judge, because they be so strong,
Renforcèd well, and breechèd like a brock,                           15
Stiff, straight, and stout, which, though they be not long,

4  *swelt* swelter.                                 15  *brock* A stag in its second year, when the first antlers
9  *serve with* provide.                            begin to grow; Gascoigne's next line gives the qualities he has
12  *last* model (a term from shoemaking).          in mind.

Yet spit they forth their pellets such a pace
And with such force as seems a wondrous case.

Some other think the metal maketh all,
Which tempered is both round and smooth to see;                    20
And sure methinks the bigness of the ball,
Ne yet the lock, should make it shoot so free,
But even the breech of metal good and sound,
Which makes the ball with greater force to bound.

For this we see the stiff and strongest arm                        25
Which gives a jerk and hath a cunning loose
Shoots furthest still, and doth alway most harm;
For be his flights yfeathered from the goose,
Or peacock's quills, or raven, or swan, or crow,
His shafts go swift, when others fly but slow.                     30

How so it be, the men that use to shoot
In these short guns are praisèd for the best,
And princes seek such shot for to promote
As perfectest, and better than the rest:
So that (by like) their pieces bear the sway,                      35
Else other men could shoot as far as they.

Their pieces then are callèd petronels,
And they themselves by sundry names are called:
As bandoliers, for who in mountains dwells,
In troops and bands ofttimes is stoutly stalled;                   40
Or, of the stone wherewith the lock doth strike,
Petroneliers they callèd are by like.

And so percase this peerless piece of his,
For which he mourned and made such rueful moan,
Was one of those; and therefore all his bliss                      45
Was turned to bale whenas that piece was gone,
Since martial men do set their chief delight
In arms which are both free and fair in sight.

Myself have seen some piece of such a price,
As worthy were to be esteemèd well;                                50
For this you know in any strange device
Such things as seem for goodness to excel
Are holden dear, and for great jewels deemed,
Because they be both rare and much esteemed.

But now to turn my tale from whence I came,                        55
I say his lots and mine were not unlike;
He spent his youth (as I did) out of frame,

---

**26** *loose* release (a term from archery).
**37** *petronels* Short, heavy pistols popular with horsemen. In *The Grief of Joy* (1576) Gascoigne uses "petronels" in a generic sense to refer to the women in his life, and identifies specifically "Petronella de Alquemade" and "Petronella van Sconhoven."

**40** *stalled* lodged.
**41** *of the stone* As if "petronel" were derived from "petra" (rock) – not a true etymology.
**43** *percase* perchance.
**57** *out of frame* in a disorderly way.

He came at last (like me) to trail the pike.
He pined in prison, pinched with privy pain,
And I likewise in prison still remain.                60

Yet some good fruit in fetters can I find,
As virtue rules in every kind of vice.
First, prison brings repentance to the mind
Which wandered erst in lust and lewd device;
For hardest hearts by troubles yet are taught         65
That God is good when all the world is nought.

If thou have led a careless life at large,
Without regard what liberty was worth,
And then come down to cruel jailor's charge,
Which keeps thee close and never lets thee forth,     70
Learn then this fruit in fetters by thyself,
That liberty is worth all worldly pelf.

Whose hap is such to yield himself in war,
Remember then that peace in pleasure dwells;
Whose hearts are high and know not what they are,     75
Let such but mark the jingling of their bells
When fetters fret their ankles as they go,
Since none so high but that may come as low.

To tell a truth, and therein to be short,
Prisons are plagues that fall for man's offense,      80
Which maketh some in good and godly sort
With contrite heart to grope their conscience;
Repentance then steps in and pardon craves.
These fruits (with moe) are found in darksome caves.

If thou have friends, there shalt thou know them right,   85
Since fastest friends in troubles show their faith.
If thou have foes, there shalt thou see their spite,
For all too true it is that proverb saith:
Where hedge is low, there every man treads down,
And friendship fails when Fortune list to frown.      90

Patience is found in prison (though perforce),
And temperance taught where none excess doth dwell;
Exercise calls, lest sloth should kill thy corse;
Diligence drives thy busy brains to swell
For some device which may redeem thy state.           95
These fruits I found in fetters all too late.

And with these fruits another fruit I found,
A strange conceit, and yet a trusty truth:
I found by proof there is no kind of ground
That yields a better crop to reckless youth           100
Than that same mold where fetters serve for muck
And wit still works to dig up better luck.

72 *pelf* possessions.          99 *proof* experience.

For if the seed of grace will ever grow,
Then sure such soil will serve to bear it best,
And if God's mercy therewithal do flow,                          105
Then springs it high and ruffles with the rest.
Oft hath been seen such seed in prison cast,
Which long kept close, and prospered yet at last.

But therewithal there springs a kind of tares
Which are vile weeds and must be rooted out.                      110
They choke up grace, and lap it fast in snares,
Which oftentimes do draw it deep in doubt,
And hinders plants which else would grow full high;
Yet is this weed an easy thing to spy.

Men call it fancy, sure a worthless weed;                         115
And of the same full many sorts are found.
Some fancies are which think a lawful deed
To scape away, though faith full fast be bound.
Some think by love (nay, lust in cloak of love)
From fetters fast their selves for to remove.                     120

Some be that mean by murder to prevail,
And some by fraud, as fancy rules the thought.
Sometimes such frights men's fancies do assail
That (when they see their freedom must be bought)
They vow to take a stand on Shooter's Hill                        125
Till rents come in to please their wicked will.

Some fancies hopes by lies to come on float,
As for to tell their friends and kin great tales:
What wealth they lost in coin, and many a coat,
What powder packed in coffers and in mails,                       130
What they must pay, and what their charge will be,
Wherein they mean to save themselves a fee.

Some fancies eke forecast what life to wield
When liberty shall granted be at last,
And in the air such castles gan they build                        135
That many times they fall again as fast:
For fancy hinders grace from glory's crown,
As tares and bines can pluck good grain adown.

Who list therefore by fetters fruit to have,
Take fancy first out of his privy thought,                        140
And when thou hast him, cast him in the wave
Of Lethe's lake; for sure his seed is nought.
The Green Knight, he of whom I late did tell
(Mine author saith), bade fancy thus farewell.

106   *ruffles* contends.
125   *Shooter's Hill* A hill in Greenwich; the name is obviously suggestive, but its origin is uncertain.
127   *on float* afloat.

130   *mails* bags.
138   *bines* A class of plants that twine about other plants.
142   *Lethe* The river of forgetfulness in the underworld.

### THE GREEN KNIGHT'S FAREWELL TO FANCY

Fancy (quoth he), farewell, whose badge I long did bear,
And in my hat full harebrainedly thy flowers did I wear.
Too late I find (at last) thy fruits are nothing worth,
Thy blossoms fall and fade full fast, though bravery bring them forth.
By thee I hoped always in deep delights to dwell,                    5
But since I find thy fickleness, *Fancy* (quoth he), *farewell.*

Thou mad'st me live in love, which wisdom bids me hate;
Thou blearedst mine eyes and mad'st me think that faith was mine by fate.
By thee those bitter sweets did please my taste alway,
By thee I thought that love was light, and pain was but a play.       10
I thought that beauty's blaze was meet to bear the bell,
And since I find myself deceived, *Fancy* (quoth he), *farewell.*

The gloss of gorgeous courts by thee did please mine eye;
A stately sight methought it was to see the brave go by,
To see their feathers flaunt, to mark their strange device,           15
To lie along in ladies' laps, to lisp and make it nice.
To fawn and flatter both I likèd sometimes well,
But since I see how vain it is, *Fancy* (quoth he), *farewell.*

When court had cast me off, I toilèd at the plow.
My fancy stood in strange conceits to thrive I wot not how:           20
By mills, by making malt, by sheep and eke by swine,
By duck and drake, by pig and goose, by calves and keeping kine,
By feeding bullocks fat when price at markets fell.
But since my swains eat up my gains, *Fancy* (quoth he), *farewell.*

In hunting of the deer my fancy took delight;                        25
All forests knew my folly still, the moonshine was my light.
In frosts I felt no cold, a sunburnt hue was best,
I sweat and was in temper still, my watching seemèd rest.
What dangers deep I passed, it folly were to tell;
And since I sigh to think thereon, *Fancy* (quoth he), *farewell.*    30

A fancy fed me once to write in verse and rhyme,
To wray my grief, to crave reward, to cover still my crime,
To frame a long discourse on stirring of a straw,
To rumble rhyme in raff and ruff; yet all not worth an haw
To hear it said, There goeth the *man that writes so well.*           35
But since I see what poets be, *Fancy* (quoth he), *farewell.*

At music's sacred sound my fancies eft begun.
In concords, discords, notes and clefs, in tunes of unison,
In hierarchies and strains, in rests, in rule and space,
In monochords and moving moods, in burdens under bass,               40

---

11  *bear the bell* take the prize.
14  *brave* ostentatious.
16  *lisp* Lisping carried an air of seductive refinement, though it was frequently mocked as an affectation.
20  *wot* know.

22  *kine* cattle.
24  *swains* farm workers.
32  *wray* disclose.
34  *rumble rhyme in raff and ruff* write alliterative verse.  *haw* hawthorn berry.

In descants and in chants I strainèd many a yell;
But since musicians be so mad, *Fancy* (quoth he), *farewell.*

To plant strange country fruits, to sow such seeds likewise,
To dig and delve for new-found roots where old might well suffice,
To prune the water-boughs, to pick the mossy trees                    45
(O, how it pleased my fancy once), to kneel upon my knees,
To griff a pippin-stock when sap begins to swell:
But since the gains scarce quit the cost, *Fancy* (quoth he), *farewell.*

*Fancy* (quoth he), *farewell,* which made me follow drums,
Where powdered bullets serves for sauce to every dish that comes,     50
Where treason lurks in trust, where hope all hearts beguiles,
Where mischief lieth still in wait when fortune friendly smiles,
Where one day's prison proves that all such heavens are hell;
And since I feel the fruits thereof, *Fancy* (quoth he), *farewell.*

If reason rule my thoughts, and God vouchsafe me grace,               55
Then comfort of philosophy shall make me change my race,
And fond I shall it find that Fancy sets to show,
And weakly stands that building still which lacketh grace below.
But since I must accept my fortunes as they fell,
I say God send me better speed, and *Fancy, now farewell.*           60

---

45  *water-boughs* undergrowth.
47  *griff* graft.
48  *quit* repay.

54  *since* The text in *The Posies* reads "such," breaking the
pattern of the previous stanzas for no obvious purpose.
60  *speed* success.

EPILOGISMUS

See sweet deceit that can itself beguile;
Behold self-love which walketh in a net,
And seems unseen, yet shows itself therewhile
Before such eyes as are in science set.
The Green Knight here leaves out his firelock piece,                  5
That Fancy hath not yet his last farewell.
When foxes preach, good folk beware your geese.
But holla here, my Muse too far doth mell.
Who list to mark what learnèd preacher saith
Must learn withal for to believe his lore;                           10
But what he doth, that toucheth no man's faith,
Though words with works (agreed) persuade the more.
The mounting kite oft lights on homely prey,
And wisest wits may sometimes go astray.

Finis

*Tam Marti quam Mercurio*

---

4   *science* knowledge.
8   *mell* meddle.
10  *lore* lesson.
*Tam Marti quam Mercurio* As to Mars, so to Mercury: a
motto that Gascoigne introduces in *The Posies,* and includes

in the drawing of himself that he gives to Queen Elizabeth.
It indicates a joint devotion to military service (Mars) and
literature and intellectual activity generally (Mercury, the
patron god of wits and scholars).

# Thomas Sackville, Earl of Dorset (1536–1608)

Sackville was born in Sussex, the son of a first cousin of Anne Boleyn; he apparently attended both Oxford and Cambridge, and was admitted to the Inner Temple (of which his father had been Governor). He was called to the bar, but also involved in the literary life of the Inns of Court; the neo-Senecan drama *Gorboduc*, which he co-authored with Thomas Norton, was performed at the Inner Temple in 1562, and is regularly cited as the first original tragedy in English. In 1563–6 he found it expedient to be on the Continent, and was briefly imprisoned in Rome on suspicion of spying; on return to England and the receipt of his paternal inheritance, he became a figure at court and began a very busy diplomatic career. He was named Baron Buckhurst in 1567 and Earl of Dorset in 1604.

*A Mirror for Magistrates* was an immensely popular collection of verse narratives about the misfortunes of public figures in English history (mostly kings and lords, though with a few lower figures such as Jack Cade and Jane Shore). The individual tales were written by "divers learned men whose many gifts need few praises," and collected and introduced by William Baldwin. The first edition in 1559 contained nineteen stories; in successive editions up to 1587 another fourteen were added. In 1609–10 Richard Niccols produced a further expansion and rearrangement. Sackville's contribution appeared in the edition of 1563: the Induction given here, followed by the story of the Duke of Buckingham. The Induction reads as if it could be a frame story for the whole volume, though it was not used that way. It has acquired its own fame as one of the most powerful allegorical poems in sixteenth-century English, intense and sustained at a pitch Spenser never attempts.

*Edition*: *The Mirror for Magistrates*, ed. Lily B. Campbell (Cambridge: Cambridge University Press, 1938).

## A Mirror for Magistrates: The Induction

The wrathful winter, proaching on apace,
With blustering blasts had all ybared the treen,
And old Saturnus with his frosty face
With chilling cold had pierced the tender green:
The mantles rent wherein enwrappèd been          5
The gladsome groves that now lay overthrown,
The tapets torn, and every bloom down blown.

The soil that erst so seemly was to seen
Was all despoilèd of her beauty's hue,
And soot fresh flowers (wherewith the summer's queen     10
Had clad the earth) now Boreas' blasts down blew;
And small fowls flocking in their song did rue
The winter's wrath, wherewith each thing defaced
In woeful wise bewailed the summer past.

Hawthorn had lost his motley livery,                     15
The naked twigs were shivering all for cold;
And dropping down the tears abundantly,
Each thing (methought) with weeping eye me told
The cruel season, bidding me withhold
Myself within, for I was gotten out                      20
Into the fields, whereas I walked about.

---

**2**  *treen* trees.
**3**  *Saturnus* God honored in the Saturnalia, the ancient Roman holidays at the end of the calendar year.

**7**  *tapets* tapestries.
**10**  *soot* sweet.

When, lo, the night with misty mantles spread
Gan dark the day and dim the azure skies,
And Venus in her message Hermes sped
To bloody Mars, to will him not to rise,                                   25
While she herself approached in speedy wise;
And Virgo, hiding her disdainful breast,
With Thetis now had laid her down to rest.

Whiles Scorpio, dreading Sagittarius' dart,
Whose bow, prest bent in sight, the string had slipped,     30
Down slid into the ocean flood apart;
The Bear, that in the Irish seas had dipped
His grisly feet, with speed from thence he whipped,
For Thetis, hasting from the Virgin's bed,
Pursued the Bear, that ere she came was fled.                     35

And Phaeton, now near reaching to his race,
With glistering beams, gold streaming where they bent,
Was prest to enter in his resting place.
Erythius, that in the cart first went,
Had even now attained his journey's stint,                          40
And, fast declining, hid away his head
While Titan couched him in his purple bed.

And pale Cynthia, with her borrowed light
Beginning to supply her brother's place,
Was past the noonstead six degrees in sight                       45
When sparkling stars amid the heaven's face
With twinkling light shone on the earth apace,
That while they brought about the nightes char,
The dark had dimmed the day ere I was ware.

And sorrowing I to see the summer flowers,                       50
The lively green, the lusty leas forlorn,
The sturdy trees so shattered with the showers,
The fields so fade that flourished so beforn,
It taught me well all earthly things be born
To die the death, for nought long time may last.                  55
The summer's beauty yields to winter's blast.

Then looking upward to the heaven's leams,
With nightes stars thick powdered everywhere,
Which erst so glistened with the golden streams
That cheerful Phoebus spread down from his sphere,        60
Beholding dark oppressing day so near,

24  *in her message Hermes sped* sent Hermes (Mercury) to deliver her message.
28  *Thetis* The most famous of the sea-nymphs, here used for the sea itself: the constellation Virgo has gone below the watery horizon.
30  *prest* ready.  *sight* Later editions read "fight."
32  *Bear* The constellation Ursa Major.
36  *Phaeton* Son of the sun-god Apollo, here simply the sun.

39  *Erythius* Erythraeus, one of the horses in Apollo's team.
42  *Titan* the sun.
43  *Cynthia* the moon.
45  *noonstead* position of the sun at noon.
48  *nightes char* the night's chariot.
49  *ware* aware.
51  *leas* grasslands.
53  *fade* faded.
57  *leams* rays of light.

The sudden sight reducèd to my mind
The sundry changes that in earth we find.

That musing on this worldly wealth in thought,
Which comes and goes more faster than we see 65
The flickering flame that with the fire is wrought,
My busy mind presented unto me
Such fall of peers as in this realm had be
That oft I wished some would their woes descrive
To warn the rest whom Fortune left alive. 70

And straight forth stalking with redoubled pace,
For that I saw the night drew on so fast,
In black all clad there fell before my face
A piteous wight, whom woe had all forwaste.
Forth from her eyen the crystal tears outbrast, 75
And, sighing sore, her hands she wrung and fold,
Tare all her hair, that ruth was to behold.

Her body small, forwithered and forspent,
As is the stalk that summer's drought oppressed;
Her welkèd face with woeful tears besprent, 80
Her color pale, and (as it seemed her best)
In woe and plaint reposèd was her rest;
And as the stone that drops of water wears,
So dented were her cheeks with fall of tears.

Her eyes swollen with flowing streams afloat, 85
Wherewith her looks thrown up full piteously;
Her forceless hands together oft she smote,
With doleful shrieks that echoed in the sky,
Whose plaint such sighs did straight accompany
That in my doom was never man did see 90
A wight but half so woebegone as she.

I stood aghast, beholding all her plight,
Tween dread and dolor so distrained in heart
That while my hairs upstarted with the sight,
The tears out streamed for sorrow of her smart; 95
But when I saw no end that could apart
The deadly dool which she so sore did make,
With doleful voice then thus to her I spake.

Unwrap thy woes, whatever wight thou be,
And stint betime to spill thyself with plaint. 100
Tell what thou art, and whence, for well I see
Thou canst not dure with sorrow thus attaint.

| | | | |
|---|---|---|---|
| 62 | *reducèd* recalled. | 80 | *welkèd* desiccated. *besprent* sprinkled. |
| 69 | *descrive* write down. | 90 | *doom* judgment. |
| 74 | *forwaste* wasted. | 93 | *distrained* distressed. |
| 75 | *eyen* eyes. | 96 | *apart* end. |
| 76 | *fold* folded. | 97 | *dool* lament. |
| 77 | *Tare* tore. | 100 | And immediately stop killing yourself with grief. |
| 78 | *forspent* worn out. | 102 | *attaint* afflicted. |

And with that word of sorrow, all forfaint,
She lookèd up, and, prostrate as she lay,
With piteous sound, lo, thus she gan to say.                    105

Alas, I, wretch whom thus thou seest distrained
With wasting woes that never shall aslake,
Sorrow I am, in endless torments pained
Among the furies in the infernal lake,
Where Pluto, god of hell so grisly black,                      110
Doth hold his throne, and Letheus' deadly taste
Doth reave remembrance of each thing forepast.

Whence come I am, the dreary destiny
And luckless lot for to bemoan of those
Whom Fortune in this maze of misery                            115
Of wretched chance most woeful mirrors chose,
That when thou seest how lightly they did lose
Their pomp, their power, and that they thought most sure,
Thou mayst soon deem no earthly joy may dure.

Whose rueful voice no sooner had out-brayed                    120
Those woeful words wherewith she sorrowed so,
But, Out alas, she shright, and never stayed,
Fell down, and all to-dashed herself for woe.
The cold pale dread my limbs gan overgo,
And I so sorrowed at her sorrows eft                           125
That, what with grief and fear, my wits were reft.

I stretched myself, and straight my heart revives
That dread and dolor erst did so appall.
Like him that with the fervent fever strives
When sickness seeks his castle health to scale,               130
With gathered spirits so forced I fear to avale,
And rearing her, with anguish all fordone,
My spirits returned, and then I thus begun.

O Sorrow, alas, sith Sorrow is thy name,
And that to thee this drear doth well pertain,                 135
In vain it were to seek to cease the same;
But as a man himself with sorrow slain,
So I, alas, do comfort thee in pain,
That here in sorrow art forsunk so deep
That at thy sight I can but sigh and weep.                     140

I had no sooner spoken of a sike
But that the storm so rumbled in her breast
As Aeolus could never roar the like,

103  *forfaint* weakened.
107  *aslake* slacken.
111  *Letheus* Lethe, the river of forgetfulness in the underworld.
116  *most woeful mirrors chose* chose to be most woeful mirrors.
117  *lightly* easily.
119  *dure* endure.

122  *never stayed* did not delay.
123  *to-dashed* battered.
130  *his castle health* the castle of his health.
131  *avale* yield.
141  *sike* sigh.
143  *Aeolus* god of the winds.

And showers down rainèd from her eyen so fast
That all bedreint the place, till at the last                    145
Well easèd they the dolor of her mind,
As rage of rain doth swage the stormy wind.

For forth she pacèd in her fearful tale:
Come, come (quod she), and see what I shall show.
Come hear the plaining and the bitter bale                      150
Of worthy men by Fortune overthrow.
Come thou, and see them rueing all in row.
They were but shades that erst in mind thou rolled.
Come, come with me; thine eyes shall them behold.

What could these words, but make me more aghast               155
To hear her tell whereon I mused whilere?
So was I mazed therewith, till at the last,
Musing upon her words, and what they were,
All suddenly well lessoned was my fear:
For to my mind returnèd how she telled                         160
Both what she was, and where her wone she held.

Whereby I knew that she a goddess was,
And therewithal resorted to my mind
My thought that late presented me the glass
Of brittle state, of cares that here we find,                  165
Of thousand woes to silly men assigned,
And how she now bid me come and behold
To see with eye that erst in thought I rolled.

Flat down I fell, and with all reverence
Adorèd her, perceiving now that she                            170
A goddess sent by godly providence
In earthly shape thus showed herself to me,
To wail and rue this world's uncertainty;
And while I honored thus her godhead's might,
With plaining voice these words to me she shright:             175

I shall thee guide first to the grisly lake,
And thence unto the blissful place of rest,
Where thou shalt see and hear the plaint they make
That whilom here bare swinge among the best.
This shalt thou see, but great is the unrest                   180
That thou must bide before thou canst attain
Unto the dreadful place where these remain.

And with these words as I upraisèd stood,
And gan to follow her that straight forth paced,

145  *bedreint* drenched.
147  *swage* assuage.
151  *overthrow* overthrown.
153  *rolled* noted.
157  *mazed* amazed.
159  *lessoned* informed.

160  *telled* told.
161  *wone* home.
163  *resorted* returned.
164  *glass* mirror.
179  *swinge* sway.
181  *attain* arrive.

Ere I was ware, into a desert wood                          185
We now were come, where, hand in hand embraced,
She led the way, and through the thick so traced
As, but I had been guided by her might,
It was no way for any mortal wight.

But lo, while thus amid the desert dark                     190
We passèd on with steps and pace unmeet,
A rumbling roar, confused with howl and bark
Of dogs, shook all the ground under our feet,
And struck the din within our ears so deep
As, half-distraught, unto the ground I fell,                195
Besought return, and not to visit hell.

But she, forthwith uplifting me apace,
Removed my dread, and with a steadfast mind
Bade me come on, for here was now the place,
The place where we our travail end should find.             200
Wherewith I arose, and to the place assigned
Astoined I stalk, when straight we approached near
The dreadful place that you will dread to hear.

An hideous hole, all vast, withouten shape,
Of endless depth, o'erwhelmed with ragged stone,            205
With ugly mouth and grisly jaws doth gape,
And to our sight confounds itself in one.
Here entered we, and yeding forth, anon
An horrible loathly lake we might discern
As black as pitch, that clepèd is Averne.                   210

A deadly gulf where nought but rubbish grows,
With foul black swelth in thickened lumps that lies,
Which up in the air such stinking vapors throws
That over there may fly no fowl but dies,
Choked with the pestilent savors that arise.                215
Hither we come, whence forth we still did pace,
In dreadful fear amid the dreadful place.

And first within the porch and jaws of hell
Sat deep Remorse of Conscience, all besprent
With tears; and to herself oft would she tell               220
Her wretchedness and, cursing, never stent
To sob and sigh, but ever thus lament
With thoughtful care, as she that all in vain
Would wear and waste continually in pain.

Her eyes unsteadfast, rolling here and there,               225
Whirled on each place, as place that vengeance brought,
So was her mind continually in fear,
Tossed and tormented with the tedious thought
Of those detested crimes which she had wrought:

191   *unmeet* unevenly matched.
200   *travail end* travail's end (also: travel's end).
202   *Astoined* stunned.   *stalk* walk carefully.
208   *yeding* going.
212   *swelth* filth.
221   *stent* stopped.

With dreadful cheer and looks thrown to the sky, 230
Wishing for death, and yet she could not die.

Next saw we Dread, all trembling how he shook,
With foot uncertain proffered here and there,
Benumbed of speech, and with a ghastly look
Searched every place, all pale and dead for fear, 235
His cap borne up with staring of his hair,
Stoined and amazed at his own shade for dread,
And fearing greater dangers than was need.

And next within the entry of this lake
Sat fell Revenge, gnashing her teeth for ire, 240
Devising means how she may vengeance take,
Never in rest till she have her desire,
But frets within so far forth with the fire
Of wreaking flames that now determines she
To die by death, or venged by death to be. 245

When fell Revenge with bloody foul pretense
Had showed herself as next in order set,
With trembling limbs we softly parted thence,
Till in our eyes another sight we met,
When fro my heart a sigh forthwith I fet, 250
Rueing, alas, upon the woeful plight
Of Misery, that next appeared in sight.

His face was lean, and somedeal pined away,
And eke his hands consumèd to the bone;
But what his body was, I cannot say, 255
For on his carcass raiment had he none
Save clouts and patches piecèd one by one,
With staff in hand and scrip on shoulders cast
His chief defense against the winter's blast.

His food, for most, was wild fruits of the tree, 260
Unless sometime some crumbs fell to his share,
Which in his wallet long, God wot, kept he,
As on the which full daintily would he fare.
His drink the running stream, his cup the bare
Of his palm closed, his bed the hard cold ground. 265
To this poor life was Misery ybound.

Whose wretched state when we had well beheld
With tender ruth on him and on his feres,
In thoughtful cares forth then our pace we held;
And by and by another shape appears, 270
Of greedy Care, still brushing up the briars,
His knuckles knobbed, his flesh deep dented in,
With tawèd hands and hard ytannèd skin.

236 *staring* standing on end.
253 *somedeal* somewhat.
257 *clouts* rags.
258 *scrip* bag.

264 *bare* bare skin.
268 *feres* companions.
273 *tawèd* beaten.

The morrow gray no sooner hath begun
To spread his light even peeping in our eyes,                    275
When he is up and to his work yrun;
But let the night's black misty mantles rise
And with foul dark never so much disguise
The fair bright day, yet ceaseth he no while
But hath his candles to prolong his toil.                       280

By him lay heavy Sleep, the cousin of Death,
Flat on the ground, and still as any stone,
A very corpse, save yielding forth a breath.
Small keep took he whom Fortune frownèd on,
Or whom she lifted up into the throne                           285
Of high renown, but as a living death,
So dead alive, of life he drew the breath.

The body's rest, the quiet of the heart,
The travail's ease, the still night's fere was he,
And of our life in earth the better part,                       290
Reaver of sight, and yet in whom we see
Things oft that tide, and oft that never be,
Without respect esteeming equally
King Croesus' pomp and Irus' poverty.

And next in order sad Old Age we found,                         295
His beard all hoar, his eyes hollow and blind,
With drooping cheer still poring on the ground,
As on the place where nature him assigned
To rest, when that the sisters had untwined
His vital thread, and ended with their knife                    300
The fleeting course of fast declining life.

There heard we him with broken and hollow plaint
Rue with himself his end approaching fast,
And all for nought his wretched mind torment
With sweet remembrance of his pleasures past                    305
And fresh delights of lusty youth forwaste.
Recounting which, how would he sob and shriek,
And to be young again of Jove beseek.

But and the cruel fates so fixèd be
That time forepast cannot return again,                         310
This one request of Jove yet prayèd he:
That in such withered plight and wretched pain
As eld (accompanied with his loathsome train)
Had brought on him, all were it woe and grief,
He might a while yet linger forth his life,                     315

And not so soon descend into the pit
Where Death, when he the mortal corpse hath slain,
With reckless hand in grave doth cover it,

284   *keep* care.
292   *tide* happen.
294   *Croesus* king of Lydia (d. 546 BC), legendary for his
wealth.   *Irus* an Ithacan beggar in Book 18 of the *Odyssey*.

306   *forwaste* wasted away.
309   *and* if.
313   *eld* old age.
318   *reckless* careless.

Thereafter never to enjoy again
The gladsome light, but, in the ground ylain,                    320
In depth of darkness waste and wear to nought
As he had never into the world been brought.

But who had seen him sobbing, how he stood
Unto himself and how he would bemoan
His youth forepast, as though it wrought him good            325
To talk of youth, all were his youth foregone,
He would have mused and marveled much whereon
This wretched Age should life desire so fain
And knows full well life doth but length his pain.

Crookbacked he was, toothshaken and blear-eyed,            330
Went on three feet, and sometime crept on four,
With old lamb bones that rattled by his side,
His scalp all pilled, and he with eld forlore,
His withered fist still knocking at Death's door,
Fumbling and driveling as he draws his breath:             335
For brief, the shape and messenger of Death.

And fast by him pale Malady was placed,
Sore sick in bed, her color all foregone,
Bereft of stomach, savor, and of taste,
Ne could she brook no meat but broths alone:              340
Her breath corrupt, her keepers every one
Abhorring her, her sickness past recure,
Detesting physic and all physic's cure.

But O, the doleful sight that then we see!
We turned our look, and on the other side                 345
A grisly shape of Famine mought we see,
With greedy looks, and gaping mouth that cried
And roared for meat as she should there have died,
Her body thin and bare as any bone,
Whereto was left nought but the case alone.               350

And that, alas, was gnawn on everywhere,
All full of holes, that I ne mought refrain
From tears to see how she her arms could tear
And with her teeth gnash on the bones in vain
When all for nought she fain would so sustain             355
Her starven corpse, that rather seemed a shade
Than any substance of a creature made.

Great was her force, whom stone wall could not stay,
Her tearing nails snatching at all she saw,
With gaping jaws that by no means ymay                    360
Be satisfied from hunger of her maw,
But eats herself as she that hath no law,

---

329  *length* lengthen.

330  *Crookbacked* hunchbacked.   *toothshaken* with loose teeth.

333  *pilled* bald.   *forlore* forlorn.

339  *stomach* appetite.   *savor* sense of smell.

343  *physic* medicine.

358  *stay* stop.

Gnawing, alas, her carcass all in vain,
Where you may count each sinew, bone, and vein.

On her while we thus firmly fixed our eyes                        365
That bled for ruth of such a dreary sight,
Lo, suddenly she shright in so huge wise
As made hell gates to shiver with the might;
Wherewith a dart we saw how it did light
Right on her breast, and therewithal pale Death                  370
Enthrilling it to reave her of her breath.

And by and by a dumb dead corpse we saw,
Heavy and cold, the shape of Death aright,
That daunts all earthly creatures to his law,
Against whose force in vain it is to fight:                      375
Ne peers, ne princes, nor no mortal wight,
No towns, ne realms, cities, ne strongest tower,
But all perforce must yield unto his power.

His dart anon out of the corpse he took,
And in his hand (a dreadful sight to see)                        380
With great triumph eftsoons the same he shook,
That most of all my fears affrayèd me;
His body dight with nought but bones, perdy,
The naked shape of man there saw I plain,
All save the flesh, the sinew, and the vein.                     385

Lastly stood War, in glittering arms yclad,
With visage grim, stern looks, and blackly hued.
In his right hand a naked sword he had
That to the hilts was all with blood imbrued,
And in his left (that kings and kingdoms rued)                   390
Famine and fire he held, and therewithal
He razèd towns and threw down towers and all.

Cities he sacked, and realms that whilom flowered
In honor, glory, and rule above the best
He overwhelmed, and all their fame devoured,                     395
Consumed, destroyed, wasted, and never ceased
Till he their wealth, their name, and all oppressed.
His face forhewed with wounds, and by his side
There hung his targe with gashes deep and wide.

In mids of which depainted there we found                        400
Deadly Debate, all full of snaky hair
That with a bloody fillet was ybound,
Outbreathing nought but discord everywhere;
And round about were portrayed here and there
The hugy hosts, Darius and his power,                            405
His kings, princes, his peers, and all his flower:

371   *Enthrilling* piercing.
382   *affrayèd* frightened.
389   *imbrued* stained.
397   *forhewed* cut up.

399   *targe* shield.
400   *mids* midst.
405   *Darius* Darius III, king of Persia (d. 330 BC), who lost
his kingdom and life to Alexander the Great ("great Macedo").

Whom great Macedo vanquished there in sight,
With deep slaughter, despoiling all his pride,
Pierced through his realms and daunted all his might.
Duke Hannibal beheld I there beside,        410
In Canna's field victor how he did ride,
And woeful Romans that in vain withstood
And consul Paullus covered all in blood.

Yet saw I more the fight at Trasimene
And Trebey field, and eke when Hannibal        415
And worthy Scipio last in arms were seen
Before Carthago gate, to try for all
The world's empire, to whom it should befall.
There saw I Pompey and Caesar clad in arms,
Their hosts allied and all their civil harms,        420

With conquerors' hands forbathed in their own blood
And Caesar weeping over Pompey's head.
Yet saw I Sulla and Marius where they stood,
Their great cruelty and the deep bloodshed
Of friends; Cyrus I saw and his host dead,        425
And how the Queen with great despite hath flung
His head in blood of them she overcome.

Xerxes, the Persian king, yet saw I there
With his huge host that drank the rivers dry,
Dismounted hills, and made the vales uprear;        430
His host and all yet saw I slain, perdy.
Thebes I saw, all razed how it did lie
In heaps of stones, and Tyrus put to spoil,
With walls and towers flat evened with the soil.

But Troy, alas (methought), above them all,        435
It made mine eyes in very tears consume
When I beheld the woeful weird befall
That by the wrathful will of gods was come,
And Jove's unmovèd sentence and foredoom

---

**410** *Hannibal* Carthaginian general (247–182 BC), who inflicted a great defeat on the Romans at Cannae in Apulia during the Second Punic War (216 BC).
**413** *Paullus* Lucius Aemilius Paullus, Roman consul who died at Cannae.
**414–15** *Trasimene / And Trebey field* The battles of Lake Trasimene in Etruria (217 BC) and the river Trebia near Placentia (218 BC), also victories of Hannibal over the Romans.
**416** *Scipio* Scipio Africanus Maior (236–183 BC), Roman general who ended the Second Punic War by defeating Hannibal at the battle of Zama in North Africa (202 BC).
**418** *Pompey and Caesar* Gnaeus Pompeius Magnus (106–48 BC) and Julius Caesar (100–44 BC), who waged a civil war for control of Rome and its empire (49–48 BC).
**422** *Pompey's head* Pompey was beheaded by the Egyptians to gain favor with Caesar; Caesar is said to have wept when it was presented to him.

**423** *Sulla and Marius* Lucius Cornelius Sulla (d. 78 BC) and Gaius Marius (d. 86 BC), opponents in a particularly vicious struggle for power in Rome (88–86 BC).
**425** *Cyrus* Cyrus the Great, founder of the Achaemenid Persian empire (d. 529 BC); according to Herodotus he was defeated and killed in a campaign against the Massagetae, led by Queen Tomyris, who dipped his severed head into a wineskin filled with blood.
**427** *Xerxes* King of Persia (d. 465 BC), who invaded Greece with a massive force in 480 BC; his defeat at the battle of Salamis was the end of Persian attempts to dominate the Greek world.
**430** *Dismounted* leveled.
**432** *Thebes* Greek city leveled by Alexander the Great in 336 BC.
**433** *Tyrus* Tyre, Phoenician city leveled by Alexander the Great in 332 BC.
**437** *weird* fate.

On Priam king and on his town so bent.                              440
I could not lin, but I must there lament.

And that the more sith destiny was so stern
As, force perforce, there might no force avail,
But she must fall; and by her fall we learn
That cities, towers, wealth, world, and all shall quail.           445
No manhood, might, nor nothing mought prevail,
All were there prest full many a prince and peer
And many a knight that sold his death full dear.

Not worthy Hector, worthiest of them all,
Her hope, her joy, his force is now for nought.                    450
O Troy, Troy, there is no boot but bale:
The hugy horse within thy walls is brought,
Thy turrets fall, thy knights that whilom fought
In arms amid the field are slain in bed,
Thy gods defiled, and all thy honor dead.                          455

The flames upspring, and cruelly they creep
From wall to roof, till all to cinders waste;
Some fire the houses where the wretches sleep,
Some rush in here, some run in there as fast.
In everywhere or sword or fire they taste;                         460
The walls are torn, the towers whirled to the ground.
There is no mischief but may there be found.

Cassandra yet there saw I how they haled
From Pallas' house, with sparkled tress undone,
Her wrists fast bound, and with Greeks' rout impaled;              465
And Priam eke in vain how he did run
To arms, whom Pyrrhus with despite hath done
To cruel death, and bathed him in the bain
Of his son's blood, before the altar slain.

But how can I descrive the doleful sight                           470
That in the shield so lifelike fair did shine?
Sith in this world I think was never wight
Could have set forth the half not half so fine,
I can no more but tell how there is seen
Fair Ilium fall in burning red gleeds down,                        475
And from the soil great Troy, Neptunus' town.

---

440  *Priam* king of Troy.
441  *lin* stop.
443  *force perforce* forcible resistance (on the Trojans' part) notwithstanding.
445  *quail* be ruined.
449  *Hector* Greatest of the Trojan warriors, killed before the city's fall. The picture of Troy's fall in these stanzas is closely based on Book 2 of Vergil's *Aeneid*.
451  *no boot but bale* no remedy but sorrow.
463  *Cassandra* daughter of Priam with prophetic powers.
464  *Pallas' house* the Temple of Athena. *sparkled* speckled.

465  *with Greeks' rout impaled* surrounded by a crowd of Greeks.
467  *Pyrrhus* Son of Achilles, the greatest of the Greek warriors; he came late to the Trojan war, to avenge his father's death.
468  *bain* bathwater.
469  *his son's blood* Priam took refuge with his wife and son Polites before an altar in his palace; Pyrrhus killed the son first and then the father.
475  *Ilium* Troy. *gleeds* coals.

Herefrom when scarce I could mine eyes withdraw
That filled with tears as doth the springing well,
We passèd on so far forth till we saw
Rude Acheron, a loathsome lake to tell                                 480
That boils and bubs up swelth as black as hell,
Where grisly Charon at their fixèd tide
Still ferries ghosts unto the farther side.

The agèd god no sooner Sorrow spied
But, hasting straight unto the bank apace,                             485
With hollow call unto the rout he cried
To swerve apart and give the goddess place.
Straight it was done, when to the shore we pace,
Where, hand in hand as we then linkèd fast,
Within the boat we are together placed.                               490

And forth we launch full fraughted to the brink,
When with the unwonted weight the rusty keel
Began to crack as if the same should sink.
We hoise up mast and sail, that in a while
We fet the shore, where scarcely we had while                         495
For to arrive but that we heard anon
A three-sound bark confounded all in one.

We had not long forth passed but that we saw
Black Cerberus, the hideous hound of hell,
With bristles reared, and with a three-mouthed jaw,                   500
Fordinning the air with his horrible yell
Out of the deep dark cave where he did dwell.
The goddess straight he knew, and by and by
He peased and couched while that we passèd by.

Thence come we to the horror and the hell,                            505
The large great kingdoms and the dreadful reign
Of Pluto in his throne where he did dwell,
The wide waste places and the hugy plain,
The wailings, shrieks, and sundry sorts of pain,
The sighs, the sobs, the deep and deadly groan,                       510
Earth, air, and all resounding plaint and moan.

Here puled the babes, and here the maids unwed
With folded hands their sorry chance bewailed;
Here wept the guiltless slain, and lovers dead
That slew themselves when nothing else availed.                       515
A thousand sorts of sorrows here that wailed
With sighs and tears, sobs, shrieks, and all yfere,
That (O alas) it was a hell to hear.

---

481  *bubs* bubbles.
482  *fixèd tide* appointed time.
491  *fraughted* loaded.
493  *unwonted weight* The boat usually carries ghosts, not
live people; Aeneas has the same effect (*Aeneid* 6.412–14).

494  *hoise* hoist.
495  *fet* reached.
501  *Fordinning the air* filling the air with noise.
504  *peased* became quiet.  *couched* lay down.
517  *yfere* together.

We stayed us straight, and with a rueful fear
Beheld this heavy sight, while from mine eyes                          520
The vapored tears down stillèd here and there;
And Sorrow eke, in far more woeful wise,
Took on with plaint, upheaving to the skies
Her wretched hands, that with her cry the rout
Gan all in heaps to swarm us round about.                             525

Lo, here (quoth Sorrow) princes of renown,
That whilom sat on top of Fortune's wheel,
Now laid full low, like wretches whirlèd down
Even with one frown, that stayed but with a smile.
And now behold the thing that thou erewhile                           530
Saw only in thought, and what thou now shalt hear,
Recount the same to caesar, king, and peer.

Then first came Henry, Duke of Buckingham,
His cloak of black all pilled and quite forworn,
Wringing his hands, and Fortune oft doth blame,                       535
Which of a duke hath made him now her scorn;
With ghastly looks, as one in manner lorn,
Oft spread his arms, stretched hands he joins as fast,
With rueful cheer, and vapored eyes upcast.

His cloak he rent, his manly breast he beat,                          540
His hair all torn about the place it lay;
My heart so molt to see his grief so great
As feelingly methought it dropped away.
His eyes, they whirled about withouten stay;
With stormy sighs the place did so complain                           545
As if his heart at each had burst in twain.

Thrice he began to tell his doleful tale,
And thrice the sighs did swallow up his voice,
At each of which he shriekèd so withal
As though the heavens rivèd with the noise;                           550
Till at the last, recovering his voice,
Supping the tears that all his breast berained,
On cruel Fortune weeping, thus he plained.

521   *stillèd* trickled.                          550   *rivèd* split open.
537   *lorn* lost.                                 552   *Supping* swallowing.   *berained* rained upon.
542   *molt* melted.

# Barnabe Googe (1540–1594) and
# George Turberville (1544?–1597?)

Googe was raised in Kent, attended both Oxford and Cambridge, and became a member of the Stable Inn; he entered the service of his kinsman William Cecil (later Lord Burghley and Elizabeth's chief minister), and was in Ireland in various capacities from 1574 to 1585. He published several translations, most notably one of Palingenius's *Zodiac of Life*, and in 1563 a volume of original poems. Turberville was born in Dorset, attended Oxford, and became a member of the Inns of Court. In 1568–9 he traveled to Russia as secretary to Thomas Randolph, Elizabeth's ambassador to Tsar Ivan, and wrote an uncomplimentary poem about his impressions ("the country is too cold, the people beastly be").

He published two volumes of verse (1567 and 1587). The names of the two poets are often linked as practitioners of the comparatively unadorned poetic style of the early Elizabethan period; given here are two pairs of poems where, in a manner characteristic of the period, one poet responds directly to a poem by the other. In each case, Turberville is replying in 1567 to something in Googe's collection of 1563.

*Edition*: Barnabe Googe, *Eclogues, Epitaphs, and Sonnets*, ed. Judith M. Kennedy (Toronto: University of Toronto Press, 1989); in modernized spelling. There has been no edition of Turberville's poems since the nineteenth century.

## *Oculi augent dolorem*
## Out of sight, out of mind

The oftener seen, the more I lust;
The more I lust, the more I smart;
The more I smart, the more I trust;
The more I trust, the heavier heart;
The heavy heart breeds mine unrest.     5
Thy absence, therefore, like I best.

The rarer seen, the less in mind;
The less in mind, the lesser pain;
The lesser pain, less grief I find;
The lesser grief, the greater gain;     10
The greater gain, the merrier I.
Therefore I wish thy sight to fly.

The further off, the more I joy;
The more I joy, the happier life;
The happier life, less hurts annoy;     15
The lesser hurts, pleasure most rife.
Such pleasures rife shall I obtain
When distance doth depart us twain.

*Oculi augent dolorem* Eyes heighten grief (Cicero, *Epistulae ad familiares* 6.1).

3   *trust* hope.
18   *depart* part.

## To Master Googe, his sonnet Out of sight, out of thought

The less I see, the more my teen;
The more my teen, the greater grief;
The greater grief, the lesser seen;
The lesser seen, the less relief;
The less relief, the heavier sprite          5
When P. is farthest out of sight.

The rarer seen, the rifer sobs;
The rifer sobs, the sadder heart;
The sadder heart, the greater throbs;
The greater throbs, the worser smart.          10
The worser smart proceeds of this:
That I my P. so often miss.

The nearer to, the more I smile;
The more I smile, the merrier mind;
The merrier mind doth thought exile,          15
And, thought exiled, recourse I find
Of heavenly joys. All this delight
Have I when P. is once in sight.

1    *teen* pain.

## Of Money

Give money me, take friendship whoso list,
For friends are gone come once adversity,
When money yet remaineth safe in chest,
That quickly can thee bring from misery.
Fair face show friends when riches do abound;          5
Come time of proof, farewell, they must away.
Believe me well, they are not to be found
If God but send thee once a lowering day.
Gold never starts aside, but in distress
Finds ways enough to ease thine heaviness.          10

## To Master Googe's fancy that begins, Give money me, take friendship whoso list

Friend Googe, give me the faithful friend to trust,
And take the fickle coin fro me that lust.
For friends in time of trouble and distress
With help and sound advice will soon redress
Each growing grief that gripes the pensive breast,          5
When money lies locked up in covert chest.
Thy coin will cause a thousand cares to grow,
Which if thou hadst no coin thou couldst not know.
Thy friend no care but comfort will procure;
Of him thou mayst at need thyself assure.          10
Thy money makes the thief in wait to lie,

Whose fraud thy friend and falsehood will descry.
Thou canst not keep unlocked thy careful coin
But some from thee thy money will purloin.
Thy faithful friend will never start aside, 15
But take his share of all that shall betide.
When thou art dead thy money is bereft,
But after life thy trusty friend is left.
Thy money serves another master then;
Thy faithful friend links with none other man. 20
So that, friend Googe, I deem it better, I,
To choose the friend, and let the money lie.

17 *bereft* taken away.

# Sir Edward Dyer (1543–1606)

Son of a Somerset knight, educated at Oxford, Dyer was at court by the late 1560s; by the mid-1570s he was close to Philip Sidney and Fulke Greville and a part of their literary circle. Some sixteen poems in manuscripts and printed miscellanies may be his. The most famous of them, given here, is also credibly attributed to the Earl of Oxford; it was printed with a musical setting in William Byrd's *Psalms, Sonnets, and Songs* (1588).

Dyer's poems are edited by Steven May, *The Elizabethan Courtier Poets: The Poems and their Contexts* (Columbia, MO: University of Missouri Press, 1991), pp. 287–316, though for the text of this poem, see pp. 283–4.

My mind to me a kingdom is;
Such perfect joy therein I find
That it excels all other bliss
That world affords or grows by kind.
Though much I want which most men have,     5
Yet still my mind forbids to crave.

No princely pomp, no wealthy store,
No force to win the victory,
No wily wit to salve a sore,
No shape to feed each gazing eye:     10
To none of these I yield as thrall.
For why? My mind doth serve for all.

I see how plenty suffers oft,
How hasty climbers soon do fall;
I see that those that are aloft     15
Mishap doth threaten most of all.
They get with toil, they keep with fear;
Such cares my mind could never bear.

Content I live, this is my stay.
I seek no more than may suffice;     20
I press to bear no haughty sway.
Look! What I lack, my mind supplies.
Lo, thus I triumph like a king,
Content with that my mind doth bring.

Some have too much, yet still do crave;     25
I little have, and seek no more.
They are but poor though much they have,
And I am rich with little store.
They poor, I rich; they beg, I give;
They lack, I leave; they pine, I live.     30

I laugh not at another's loss,
I grudge not at another's gain.
No worldly waves my mind can toss;

4  *by kind* naturally.
5  *want* lack.
19  *stay* support.

21  I do not strive for any arrogant position of power.
30  *leave* let go.

My state at one doth still remain.
I fear no foe nor fawning friend;                         35
I loathe not life nor dread my end.

Some weigh their pleasure by their lust,
Their wisdom by their rage of will;
Their treasure is their only trust,
And cloakèd craft their store of skill;                   40
But all the pleasure that I find
Is to maintain a quiet mind.

My wealth is health and perfect ease,
My conscience clear my chief defense;
I neither seek by bribes to please                        45
Nor by desert to breed offense.
Thus do I live, thus will I die;
Would all did so as well as I.

**46**  *by desert* by earning reward.

# Edward de Vere, Earl of Oxford (1550–1604)

Born on his father's estate in Essex, Oxford inherited his earldom at the age of 12, and was attending court by his early teens. In 1571 he married the daughter of Lord Burghley, Elizabeth's chief minister. He attended both Oxford and Cambridge and was a member of Gray's Inn; he cultivated numerous contacts with poets, and maintained a company of actors. He was famously improvident with his fortune, and erratic in his behavior. He killed a servant in 1567, and in 1579 had to be restrained from dueling with Philip Sidney after calling him a "puppy"; in 1582 he was confined to his house after a duel with another courtier. He was probably a brief convert to Catholicism. Queen Elizabeth called him her Turk, and held him in high regard until 1581, when he fathered a child on Ann Vavasour, one of Elizabeth's maids of honor; Ralegh helped engineer a partial return to favor a few years later. After the death of his wife, from whom he had been repeatedly estranged, he married another of Elizabeth's maids. He is said to have authored or co-authored dramatic scripts, but none has survived or been identified; a number of his poems appeared in printed miscellanies during his lifetime.

*Edition*: Steven May, *The Elizabethan Courtier Poets: The Poems and their Contexts* (Columbia, MO: University of Missouri Press, 1991), pp. 269–86.

> If women could be fair and yet not fond,
> Or that their love were firm, not fickle still,
> I would not marvel that they make men bond,
> By service long to purchase their good will.
> But when I see how frail those creatures are,     5
> I muse that men forget themselves so far.
>
> To mark the choice they make, and how they change,
> How oft from Phoebus they do flee to Pan,
> Unsettled still, like haggards wild they range,
> These gentle birds that fly from man to man,     10
> Who would not scorn and shake them from the fist
> And let them fly, fair fools, which way they list?
>
> Yet for disport we fawn and flatter both,
> To pass the time when nothing else can please,
> And train them to our lure with subtle oath,     15
> Till, weary of their wiles, ourselves we ease;
> And then we say, when we their fancy try,
> To play with fools, O, what a fool was I!

1 *fond* foolish, unreliable.
3 *bond* enslaved.
7 *mark* observe.

8 *Phoebus* Apollo, the god of the sun. *Pan* A lecherous rustic god, half-man, half-goat.
9 *haggards* Untamed female hawks; slang for unruly women.
17 *fancy* desire. *try* test.

> Were I a king, I could command content;
> Were I obscure, unknown should be my cares;
> And were I dead, no thought should me torment,
> Nor words, nor wrongs, nor loves, nor hopes, nor fears.
> A doubtful choice, of these things one to crave:     5
> A kingdom or a cottage or a grave.

1 *content* contentment.

5 *doubtful* uncertain, frightening.

# Edmund Spenser (1552?–1599)

Born in London to a gentleman tradesman, Spenser attended the newly founded Merchant Taylors' School and, beginning in 1569, Cambridge; earlier that year he had published, anonymously, his first poetry, some translations of Petrarch and Joachim du Bellay. Cambridge contacts provided an entry into the upper levels of Elizabethan society, beginning with a position in the household of Philip Sidney's uncle, the Earl of Leicester. In 1579 Spenser published under his own name his first major work, *The Shepherd's Calendar*, with a dedication to Sidney and a substantial scholarly (possibly parodic) commentary; the book was both in details and as a whole an allusion to Vergil's *Eclogues*, and in effect an announcement that its author was plotting for himself a poetic career on the Vergilian model. It was to be the most self-conscious such career in English poetry until Milton; Spenser appears at the time to have already begun work on his epic, whose opening lines directly place the poet in the role of a Vergil now ready for his great task.

The poetic career unfolded together with a career in public service, mostly spent in Ireland. In 1580 Spenser became secretary to Lord Grey de Wilton, the new Lord Deputy of Ireland, and stayed on after Grey's recall in a series of appointments. He secured the rank of gentleman in 1582, and in 1588 acquired the castle of Kilcolman in Munster, on an estate adjoining that of Sir Walter Ralegh. He claimed to have read parts of *The Faery Queen* to Queen Elizabeth on a trip back to England in 1589; in 1590 he published Books I–III, which pleased the monarch enough to gain him a pension of £50 a year. Over the next five years he published a range of shorter works, and in 1596 came out with a six-book version of his big poem. No new evidence of royal favor greeted it, however, and to our knowledge he wrote no more of it except for the Cantos of Mutability that appeared posthumously. In 1598 he was given the important post of Sheriff of Cork, but before the news could reach him Munster was overrun by rebels and he had to flee to London. He reportedly died destitute; the Earl of Essex bore the expense of his funeral, and he was buried next to Chaucer in Westminster Abbey.

*Editions*: *The Faerie Queene*, ed. A. C. Hamilton et al., 2nd edn. (London: Longman, 2001); *The Yale Edition of the Shorter Poems of Edmund Spenser*, ed. William A. Oram et al. (New Haven, CT: Yale University Press, 1989). A new collected edition is in preparation by Oxford University Press.

## *The Faery Queen*, Book III

Spenser's immensely ambitious poem is a complicated mixture of genres. The readiest resemblance (signaled by the division into "cantos") is to the neo-chivalric *romanzi* of Renaissance Italy, especially Ariosto's *Orlando Furioso*; for the occasion, Spenser creates a new nine-line narrative stanza (now known as the Spenserean stanza) that both recalls and outdoes the *ottava rima* of the Italian poems. Like those poems, *The Faery Queen* tells at great length a tapestry of stories about the exploits of a court of knightly heroes in service to a great leader; the stories intersect, ramify, take on an unpredictable range of tones, and almost never come to any real conclusion. There are numerous specific borrowings; the main character of Book III, Britomart, is based closely on Ariosto's Bradamante. Both characters also figure in a dynastic plot that extends into the present tense of the two poems, each of which is, among other things, the story of how two key ancestors of the poet's current monarch first met. They never do so in *The Faery Queen* as we have it (the other player, Artegall, does not even appear until Book IV), but we learn in Book III that the prophesied union will lead in time to the Tudor regime and the reign of Elizabeth; the revelation gives a teleology to the whole messy narrative. That teleology is broader and graver than that in the *romanzi*, though, and more in key with another major generic precedent, Vergil's *Aeneid* (signaled by the division into "books"; we are told that twelve of them were planned). *The Faery Queen* is, like the *Aeneid*, a self-consciously national epic with a strong sense of moral purpose, a story about the origins of a national sense of character and mission. In Spenser's case, that sense is not English but British; he avails himself of legends that make the original settlement of the British Isles a parallel endeavor to the founding of Rome – led by one Brut, like Aeneas a Trojan seeking a new homeland after the fall of his city. Prince Arthur, later to be king, is placed in this line of descent; several important digressions offer a chronicle of British history as the creation, defeat, and eventual recovery of this British ethnic identity. The one given here (III.iii.26–49) foretells the success of the Anglo-Saxons in defeating and dominating the indigenous British, but also looks forward to the time when "the Briton blood their crown again reclaim" (48.9), not in a spirit of vindictiveness but of reconciliation: "eternal union shall be made / Between the nations different afore" (49.1–2). This vision is answerable to some of the founding propaganda of the Tudor regime, which claimed Welsh descent as an important source of its legitimacy, but also reflects a seriously felt need for a new sense of national identity in the troubles of the later sixteenth century.

The fullest reaches of the poem's ambitions, however, rely on another component of its literary heritage, that of medieval allegory. The *Aeneid* and *Orlando Furioso* can be made to respond to allegorical interpretation, but allegory is an explicit part of the design and execution of *The Faery Queen*. Characters with transparently allegorical names ("Malecasta") populate the landscape of the poem; one story in Book III ends with a human being's metamorphosis into an abstraction. With the first installment in 1590 Spenser published a letter to Ralegh in which he sets forth a groundplan for the whole work as "a continued allegory or dark conceit." With its general purpose "to fashion a gentleman or noble person in virtuous and gentle discipline," the poem would analyze that discipline into "the twelve private moral virtues, as Aristotle hath devised"; each virtue would be the subject of one book, in which a particular knight would both learn and demonstrate the nature of that virtue, while the character of Prince Arthur, who would appear in each book, would represent Magnificence, the virtue which "is the perfection of all the rest, and containeth in it them all." (If the result met with favor, Spenser wrote, he would consider composing a sequel, presumably another twelve books, on "the politic virtues" demonstrated by Arthur's career after becoming king.) This schematic diagram suggests something tidier than what we encounter. It is not easy to extract a clear list of "twelve private moral virtues" from Aristotle; and, famously, the actual development of the allegory in the course of the narrative turns out to be far from simple or predictable. The body of commentary devoted to exploring the richness, subtlety, and multiplicity of its implications on various levels – moral, theological, psychological, political – has become very large.

The poem's overarching plot concerns Arthur's service to Queen Gloriana, the poem's title-character, ruler of the ambiguously defined realm of Faery, a kind of visionary double to the historical Britain in which the action also takes place; by her, Spenser writes, "I mean glory in my general intention, but in my particular I conceive the most excellent and glorious person of our

sovereign the Queen." Arthur has seen her only in a dream, but that dream has been sufficiently intense to secure his lifelong fealty (the dream is recalled in I.ix.13–15 – Gloriana's sole appearance in the poem as we have it). Books I and II are comparatively self-contained units in which the Redcross Knight, representing Holiness, and Sir Guyon, representing Temperance, undergo various trials, fail their own standards at some important point and need to be rescued by Arthur, but eventually prevail in a final episode that marks a significant triumph for their assigned virtue. Book III begins with a flurry of action whose implication is that the virtue of this book, Chastity, is a source of greater strength than either of its predecessors; but the message quickly becomes more difficult to follow. The poem's narrative begins to diversify in ways that make it more and more resemble Ariosto's; the principal knight, Britomart, is absent for much of the action as other narratives intersect hers. Only one of the stories, that of Malbecco and Hellenore – a cautionary fable about the absence of Chastity – is rounded off within Book III itself; in the 1590 edition, the story of Scudamour and Amoret was apparently brought to its conclusion, but in the 1596 edition Spenser eliminated even that sense of closure by rewriting the final stanzas (both versions are given below). The virtue of Chastity itself is refracted into three major exemplars. Two of them are twin sisters, and their pairing makes a point about the complementary forms that chastity can take; Belphoebe holds to the path of virginity, but Amoret takes the way of love and marriage (awarding the latter a dignity equal to the former was a point on which Protestant polemicists took issue with Catholicism). Britomart, the knightly embodiment of the virtue, is in a prolonged liminal state between the two possibilities: a virgin destined for a particularly momentous marriage, though one that seems as indefinitely deferred as Arthur's meeting with Gloriana. Belphoebe (along another axis an alternative figuration of Queen Elizabeth) has the simplest task, and performs it by gently but firmly, and without any evident ambivalence, resisting the desires of her adoring lover Timias. Amoret's situation is in this regard not symmetrical; though her chastity is sufficient to preserve her own virtue, it is not strong enough to free her from the peril into which she has fallen. For that she needs the special strength of Britomart, and in the revised ending of the book even that is not enough to secure her chaste union. The prospects for a chastity that opens itself to sexual love are troubled and uncertain as the book concludes.

# The Third Book of *The Faery Queen*, Containing the Legend of Britomartis, or of Chastity

## PROEM

### 1

It falls me here to write of chastity,
That fairest virtue, far above the rest;
For which what needs me fetch from Faery
Foreign ensamples, it to have expressed?
Sith it is shrinèd in my Sovereign's breast,
And formed so lively in each perfect part
That to all ladies which have it professed
Need but behold the portrait of her heart,
If portrayed it might be by any living art.

### 2

But living art may not least part express,
Nor life-resembling pencil it can paint,
All were it Zeuxis or Praxiteles;
His daedal hand would fail and greatly faint,
And her perfections with his error taint.
Ne poet's wit, that passeth painter far
In picturing the parts of beauty daint,
So hard a workmanship adventure darr,
For fear through want of words her excellence to mar.

### 3

How then shall I, apprentice of the skill
That whilom in divinest wits did reign,
Presume so high to stretch mine humble quill?
Yet now my luckless lot doth me constrain
Hereto perforce. But, O dread Sovereign,
Thus far forth pardon, sith that choicest wit
Cannot your glorious portrait figure plain,
That I in colored shows may shadow it,
And antique praises unto present persons fit.

### 4

But if in living colors and right hue
Yourself you covet to see picturèd,
Who can it do more lively or more true
Than that sweet verse, with nectar sprinkelèd,
In which a gracious servant picturèd
His Cynthia, his heaven's fairest light?
That with his melting sweetness ravishèd
And with the wonder of her beames bright
My senses lullèd are in slumber of delight.

---

**1.4** *it to have expressed* in order to give an illustration.

**2.3** *Zeuxis* classical Greek painter, fourth century BC, famous for his portrayals of women. *Praxiteles* classical Greek sculptor, third century BC.

**2.4** *daedal* skillful (worthy of the mythic inventor Daedalus).

**2.6** *daint* dainty.

**2.8** *darr* dare.

**4.5** *gracious servant* Sir Walter Ralegh, who wrote about Elizabeth under the name of Cynthia. A translation of the story of Ralegh and Elizabeth into "colored shows" occurs in Canto V below as the story of Timias and Belphoebe.

5

But let that same delicious poet lend
A little leave unto a rustic Muse
To sing his mistress' praise, and let him mend
If ought amiss her liking may abuse;
Ne let his fairest Cynthia refuse
In mirrors more than one herself to see,
But either Gloriana let her choose,
Or in Belphoebe fashionèd to be:
In the one her rule, in the other her rare chastity.

CANTO I

*Guyon encountereth Britomart,*
  *fair Florimell is chased;*
*Duessa's trains and Malecasta's*
  *champions are defaced.*

1

The famous Briton prince and Faery knight,
After long ways and perilous pains endured,
Having their weary limbs to perfect plight
Restored, and sorry wounds right well recured,
Of the fair Alma greatly were procured
To make there longer sojourn and abode;
But when thereto they might not be allured
From seeking praise and deeds of arms abroad,
They courteous congé took, and forth together yode.

2

But the captived Acrasia he sent,
Because of travel long, a nigher way,
With a strong guard all rescue to prevent
And her to Faery court safe to convey,
That her for witness of his hard assay
Unto his Faery Queen he might present;
But he himself betook another way,
To make more trial of his hardiment
And seek adventures as he with Prince Arthur went.

3

Long so they travellèd through wasteful ways
Where dangers dwelt and perils most did won,
To hunt for glory and renowmèd praise;
Full many countries did they overrun
From the uprising to the setting sun,

0.4  *defaced* defeated.
1.1  *Briton prince and Faery knight* Prince Arthur and
Sir Guyon, who make common cause in Book II. Guyon is
the main character in that book, and represents the virtue
of Temperance.
1.3  *plight* condition.
1.5  *Alma* Her name is Latin for "soul." Her castle is one of
the main allegorical sites in Book II; Arthur and Guyon study

its structure, and Arthur defends it against attack.
1.9  *congé* formal farewell.  *yode* went.
2.1  *Acrasia* The main villainess of Book II; her name is
Greek for "intemperance." Guyon's destruction of her Bower
of Bliss is the final action of that book.
3.1  *wasteful* desolate.
3.2  *won* dwell.
3.4  *overrun* run through.

And many hard adventures did achieve,
Of all the which they honor ever won,
Seeking the weak oppressèd to relieve
And to recover right for such as wrong did grieve.

4

At last as through an open plain they yode,
They spied a knight that towards prickèd fair,
And him beside an ancient squire there rode
That seemed to couch under his shield three-square,
As if that age bade him that burden spare
And yield it those that stouter could it wield;
He, them espying, gan himself prepare
And on his arm address his goodly shield
That bore a lion passant in a golden field.

5

Which seeing, good Sir Guyon dear besought
The Prince of grace to let him run that turn.
He granted; then the Faery quickly raught
His poignant spear, and sharply gan to spurn
His foamy steed, whose fiery feet did burn
The verdant grass as he thereon did tread;
Ne did the other back his foot return,
But fiercely forward came withouten dread,
And bent his dreadful spear against the other's head.

6

They been ymet and both their points arrived,
But Guyon drove so furious and fell
That seemed both shield and plate it would have rived.
Natheless it bore his foe not from his sell,
But made him stagger as he were not well;
But Guyon self, ere well he was aware,
Nigh a spear's length behind his crupper fell,
Yet in his fall so well himself he bare
That mischievous mischance his life and limbs did spare.

7

Great shame and sorrow of that fall he took,
For never yet, sith warlike arms he bore
And shivering spear in bloody field first shook,
He found himself dishonorèd so sore.
Ah gentlest knight that ever armor bore,
Let not thee grieve dismounted to have been
And brought to ground, that never wast before,
For not thy fault, but secret power unseen:
That spear enchanted was which laid thee on the green.

---

4.1 *yode* went.
4.2 *prickèd* rode.
4.4 *couch* crouch. *three-square* having three sides of equal length.
4.8 *address* make ready.

4.9 *lion passant* A lion walking, with one forepaw raised; the heraldry matches that attributed to Brut.
5.2 *of grace* as a favor.
5.3 *raught* took.
5.4 *poignant* sharp. *spurn* spur.
6.4 *sell* saddle.

8

But weenedst thou what wight thee overthrew,
Much greater grief and shamefuller regret
For thy hard fortune then thou wouldst renew,
That of a single damsel thou wert met
On equal plain, and there so hard beset;
Even the famous Britomart it was,
Whom strange adventure did from Britain fet
To seek her lover (love far sought, alas)
Whose image she had seen in Venus' looking glass.

9

Full of disdainful wrath, he fierce uprose
For to revenge that foul, reproachful shame,
And, snatching his bright sword, began to close
With her on foot, and stoutly forward came;
Die rather would he, than endure that same.
Which when his Palmer saw, he gan to fear
His toward peril and untoward blame
Which by that new rencounter he should rear,
For death sat on the point of that enchanted spear,

10

And hasting towards him gan fair persuade
Not to provoke misfortune, nor to ween
His spear's default to mend with cruel blade;
For by his mighty science he had seen
The secret virtue of that weapon keen
That mortal puissance mote not withstand.
Nothing on earth mote always happy been;
Great hazard were it, and adventure fond,
To lose long gotten honor with one evil hand.

11

By such good means he him discounselèd
From prosecuting his revenging rage;
And eke the Prince like treaty handelèd,
His wrathful will with reason to assuage,
And laid the blame not to his carriage,
But to his starting steed that swerved aside,
And to the ill purveyance of his page
That had his furnitures not firmly tied:
So is his angry courage fairly pacified.

12

Thus reconcilement was between them knit
Through goodly temperance and affection chaste,
And either vowed with all their power and wit
To let not other's honor be defaced
Of friend or foe whoever it embased,

9.6 *Palmer* Pilgrim; a character from Book II who accompanies Guyon as an attendant and spiritual advisor.
9.8 *rear* cause.
11.3 *like treaty handelèd* made a similar entreaty.

11.5 *his carriage* the way he carried himself.
11.8 *furnitures* equipment.
11.9 *fairly* fully.
12.5 *embased* devalued.

Ne arms to bear against the other's side;
In which accord the Prince was also placed
And with that golden chain of concord tied.
So goodly all agreed, they forth yfere did ride.

### 13

O goodly usage of those antique times,
In which the sword was servant unto right;
When not for malice and contentious crimes,
But all for praise and proof of manly might
The martial brood accustomèd to fight!
Then honor was the meed of victory,
And yet the vanquishèd had no despite.
Let later age that noble use envy,
Vile rancor to avoid, and cruel surquidry.

### 14

Long they thus travellèd in friendly wise
Through countries waste and eke well edified,
Seeking adventures hard, to exercise
Their puissance, whilom full dernly tried;
At length they came into a forest wide,
Whose hideous horror and sad trembling sound
Full grisly seemed. Therein they long did ride,
Yet tract of living creatures none they found,
Save bears, lions, and bulls which roamèd them around.

### 15

All suddenly out of the thickest brush,
Upon a milk-white palfrey all alone,
A goodly lady did forby them rush,
Whose face did seem as clear as crystal stone,
And eke through fear as white as whalès bone.
Her garments all were wrought of beaten gold,
And all her steed with tinsel trappings shone,
Which fled so fast that nothing mote him hold,
And scarce them leisure gave her passing to behold.

### 16

Still as she fled, her eye she backward threw,
As fearing evil that pursued her fast;
And her fair yellow locks behind her flew,
Loosely dispersed with puff of every blast:
All as a blazing star doth far outcast
His hairy beams and flaming locks dispread,
At sight whereof the people stand aghast;
But the sage wizard tells, as he has read,
That it importunes death and doleful drearihead.

**12.9** *yfere* together.
**13.8** *envy* compete with.
**13.9** *surquidry* arrogance.
**14.4** *whilom full dernly tried* once fully tested in secret. It is possible that Spenser misunderstood the archaic word "dernly" to mean something like "painfully" or "strenuously."

**14.8** *tract* trace.
**16.5** *blazing star* comet.
**16.9** *importunes* portends.

### 17

So as they gazèd after her a while,
Lo where a grisly foster forth did rush,
Breathing out beastly lust her to defile;
His tireling jade he fiercely forth did push
Through thick and thin, both over bank and bush,
In hope her to attain by hook or crook,
That from his gory sides the blood did gush.
Large were his limbs, and terrible his look,
And in his clownish hand a sharp boar-spear he shook.

### 18

Which outrage when those gentle knights did see,
Full of great envy and fell jealousy,
They stayed not to avise who first should be,
But all spurred after fast as they mote fly
To rescue her from shameful villainy.
The Prince and Guyon equally belive
Herself pursued, in hope to win thereby
Most goodly meed, the fairest dame alive;
But after the foul foster Timias did strive.

### 19

The whiles fair Britomart, whose constant mind
Would not so lightly follow beauty's chase
Ne recked of ladies' love, did stay behind,
And them awaited there a certain space
To weet if they would turn back to that place;
But when she saw them gone, she forward went
As lay her journey, through that perilous pace
With steadfast courage and stout hardiment.
Ne evil thing she feared, ne evil thing she meant.

### 20

At last as nigh out of the wood she came,
A stately castle far away she spied,
To which her steps directly she did frame.
That castle was most goodly edified
And placed for pleasure nigh that forest side;
But fair before the gate a spacious plain,
Mantled with green, itself did spreaden wide,
On which she saw six knights that did deraign
Fierce battle against one with cruel might and main.

### 21

Mainly they all at once upon him laid
And sore beset on every side around,
That nigh he breathless grew, yet nought dismayed,

---

**17.2**  *foster* forester.
**17.4**  *tireling* tired.
**17.9**  *clownish* like that of a rustic.
**18.3**  *avise* deliberate.
**18.6**  *belive* quickly.

**18.9**  *Timias* Arthur's squire, introduced in Book I but not named until now.
**19.3**  *recked of* cared about.
**19.7**  *perilous pace* dangerous passage.
**20.8**  *deraign* derange, conduct in a disordered manner.
**21.1**  *Mainly* with main force.

Ne ever to them yielded foot of ground,
All had he lost much blood through many a wound,
But stoutly dealt his blows, and every way
To which he turnèd in his wrathful stound
Made them recoil and fly from dread decay,
That none, of all the six before, him durst assay:

### 22

Like dastard curs that having at a bay
The salvage beast embossed in weary chase,
Dare not adventure on the stubborn prey,
Ne bite before, but roam from place to place
To get a snatch when turnèd is his face.
In such distress and doubtful jeopardy
When Britomart him saw, she ran apace
Unto his rescue, and with earnest cry
Bade those same six forbear that single enemy.

### 23

But to her cry they list not lenden ear,
Ne ought the more their mighty strokes surcease,
But, gathering him round about more near,
Their direful rancor rather did increase;
Till that she, rushing through the thickest press,
Perforce disparted their compacted gyre,
And soon compelled to harken unto peace.
Tho gan she mildly of them to inquire
The cause of their dissension and outrageous ire.

### 24

Whereto that single knight did answer frame:
These six would me enforce by odds of might
To change my lief and love another dame,
That death me liefer were than such despite,
So unto wrong to yield my wrested right.
For I love one, the truest one on ground,
Ne list me change; she the Errant Damsel hight,
For whose dear sake full many a bitter stound
I have endured, and tasted many a bloody wound.

### 25

Certes (said she), then been ye six to blame
To ween your wrong by force to justify;
For knight to leave his lady were great shame
That faithful is, and better were to die.
All loss is less, and less the infamy,
Than loss of love to him that loves but one.
Ne may love be compelled by mastery,

21.7  *stound* trance.
22.2  *salvage* savage.  *embossed* exhausted.
22.6  *doubtful* full of apprehension.
23.6  *Perforce* with force.
24.2  *odds* advantage.
24.3  *lief* beloved.
24.4  *liefer* preferable.

24.6–7  These lines identify the speaker as the Redcross
Knight, the hero of Book I and representative of Holiness;
the woman he serves is Una, representative of the one true
church.
24.8  *stound* dangerous situation.
25.7  *mastery* power.

For soon as mastery comes, sweet love anon
Taketh his nimble wings and soon away is gone.

### 26

Then spake one of those six: There dwelleth here
Within this castle wall a lady fair,
Whose sovereign beauty hath no living peer,
Thereto so bounteous and so debonair
That never any mote with her compare.
She hath ordained this law, which we approve,
That every knight which doth this way repair,
In case he have no lady nor no love,
Shall do unto her service never to remove.

### 27

But if he have a lady or a love,
Then must he her forgo with foul defame,
Or else with us by dint of sword approve
That she is fairer than our fairest dame,
As did this knight, before ye hither came.
Perdy (said Britomart), the choice is hard;
But what reward had he that overcame?
He should advancèd be to high regard
(Said they) and have our lady's love for his reward.

### 28

Therefore aread, sir, if thou have a love.
Love have I sure (quoth she), but lady none;
Yet will I not fro mine own love remove,
Ne to your lady will I service done,
But wreak your wrongs wrought to this knight alone,
And prove his cause. With that her mortal spear
She mightily aventred towards one,
And down him smote ere well aware he were.
Then to the next she rode, and down the next did bear.

### 29

Ne did she stay till three on ground she laid,
That none of them himself could rear again;
The fourth was by that other knight dismayed,
All were he weary of his former pain,
That now there do but two of six remain,
Which two did yield before she did them smite.
Ah (said she then), now may ye all see plain
That truth is strong, and true love most of might,
That for his trusty servants doth so strongly fight.

### 30

Too well we see (said they) and prove too well
Our faulty weakness and your matchless might;
Forthy, fair sir, yours be the damozel,

---

26.6  *approve* enforce.
27.2  *defame* loss of reputation.
27.3  *approve* prove.

28.1  *aread* declare.
28.7  *aventred* set in its rest.
29.3  *dismayed* defeated.

Which by her own law to your lot doth light,
And we your liege men faith unto you plight.
So underneath her feet their swords they marred,
And after her besought, well as they might,
To enter in and reap the due reward.
She granted, and then in they all together fared.

### 31

Long were it to describe the goodly frame
And stately port of Castle Joyëous
(For so that castle hight by common name)
Where they were entertained with courteous
And comely glee of many gracious
Fair ladies and of many a gentle knight,
Who through a chamber long and spacious
Eftsoons them brought unto their lady's sight
That of them clepèd was the Lady of Delight.

### 32

But for to tell the sumptuous array
Of that great chamber should be labor lost;
For living wit, I ween, cannot display
The royal riches and exceeding cost
Of every pillar and of every post,
Which all of purest bullion framèd were,
And with great pearls and precious stones embossed,
That the bright glister of their beames clear
Did sparkle forth great light, and glorious did appear.

### 33

These stranger knights, through passing, forth were led
Into an inner room, whose royalty
And rich purveyance might uneath be read;
Mote prince's place beseem so decked to be.
Which stately manner whenas they did see,
The image of superfluous riotise,
Exceeding much the state of mean degree,
They greatly wondered whence so sumptuous guise
Might be maintained, and each gan diversely devise.

### 34

The walls were round about apparelèd
With costly cloths of Arras and of Tours,
In which with cunning hand was portrayèd
The love of Venus and her paramour,
The fair Adonis, turnèd to a flower:
A work of rare device and wondrous wit.
First did it show the bitter, baleful stour
Which her assayed with many a fervent fit
When first her tender heart was with his beauty smit.

---

30.6 *marred* degraded.
31.2 *port* bearing.
33.3 *purveyance* furnishings. *uneath be read* not easily be told.

33.6 *superfluous riotise* excessively riotous living.
33.9 *devise* speculate.
34.7 *stour* struggle.

### 35

Then with what sleights and sweet allurements she
Enticed the boy, as well that art she knew,
And wooèd him her paramour to be:
Now making garlands of each flower that grew,
To crown his golden locks with honor due;
Now leading him into a secret shade
From his beauperes and from bright heaven's view,
Where him to sleep she gently would persuade,
Or bathe him in a fountain by some covert glade.

### 36

And whilst he slept, she over him would spread
Her mantle, colored like the starry skies,
And her soft arm lay underneath his head,
And with ambrosial kisses bathe his eyes;
And whilst he bathed, with her two crafty spies
She secretly would search each dainty limb,
And throw into the well sweet rosemaries,
And fragrant violets, and pansies trim,
And ever with sweet nectar she did sprinkle him.

### 37

So did she steal his heedless heart away,
And joyed his love in secret unespied.
But for she saw him bent to cruel play
To hunt the salvage beast in forest wide,
Dreadful of danger that mote him betide,
She oft and oft advised him to refrain
From chase of greater beasts, whose brutish pride
Mote breed him scathe unwares: but all in vain,
For who can shun the chance that dest'ny doth ordain?

### 38

Lo, where beyond he lieth languishing,
Deadly engorèd of a great wild boar,
And by his side the goddess, groveling,
Makes for him endless moan, and evermore
With her soft garment wipes away the gore
Which stains his snowy skin with hateful hue;
But when she saw no help might him restore,
Him to a dainty flower she did transmew,
Which in that cloth was wrought as if it lively grew.

### 39

So was that chamber clad in goodly wise,
And round about it many beds were dight,
As whilom was the antique worldes guise,
Some for untimely ease, some for delight,
As pleasèd them to use that use it might;
And all was full of damsels and of squires

35.7 *beauperes* companions.
37.5 *Dreadful* fearful.
37.8 *scathe* harm.

38.1 *beyond* In the next tapestry.
38.8 *transmew* transform.

Dancing and reveling both day and night
And swimming deep in sensual desires,
And Cupid still amongst them kindled lustful fires.

### 40

And all the while sweet music did divide
Her looser notes with Lydian harmony;
And all the while sweet birds thereto applied
Their dainty lays and dulcet melody,
Aye caroling of love and jollity,
That wonder was to hear their trim consort.
Which when those knights beheld, with scornful eye
They sdeignèd such lascivious disport
And loathed the loose demeanor of that wanton sort.

### 41

Thence they were brought to that great lady's view,
Whom they found sitting on a sumptuous bed
That glistered all with gold and glorious show,
As the proud Persian queens accustomèd.
She seemed a woman of great bountihead
And of rare beauty, saving that askance
Her wanton eyes, ill signs of womanhead,
Did roll too lightly and too often glance
Without regard of grace or comely amenance.

### 42

Long work it were and needless to devise
Their goodly entertainment and great glee;
She causèd them be led in courteous wise
Into a bower, disarmèd for to be
And cheerèd well with wine and spicery.
The Redcross Knight was soon disarmèd there,
But the brave maid would not disarmèd be,
But only vented up her umbriere,
And so did let her goodly visage to appear.

### 43

As when fair Cynthia in a darksome night
Is in a noyous cloud envelopèd,
Where she may find the substance thin and light
Breaks forth her silver beams, and her bright head
Discovers to the world discomfited;
Of the poor traveler that went astray
With thousand blessings she is herièd:
Such was the beauty and the shining ray
With which fair Britomart gave light unto the day.

---

40.1–2  In reference to music, to "divide" is to create "divisions," elaborations upon a basic melodic passage; Lydian music is the classical mode associated with love and sensual pleasure.
40.8  *sdeignèd* disdained.
41.5  *bountihead* generosity.
41.7  *womanhead* womanhood.

41.9  *amenance* conduct.
42.1  *devise* describe.
42.8  *vented up her umbriere* raised her visor.
43.1  *Cynthia* the moon.
43.2  *noyous* noisome.
43.7  *herièd* praised.

### 44

And eke those six which lately with her fought
Now were disarmed, and did themselves present
Unto her view and company unsought;
For they all seemèd courteous and gent,
And all six brethren, born of one parent
Which had them trained in all civility
And goodly taught to tilt and tournament,
Now were they liege men to this lady free
And her knights' service ought, to hold of her in fee.

### 45

The first of them by name Gardante hight,
A jolly person, and of comely view;
The second war Parlante, a bold knight,
And next to him Jocante did ensue;
Basciante did himself most courteous show,
But fierce Bacchante seemed too fell and keen,
And yet in arms Noctante greater grew.
All were fair knights, and goodly well beseen,
But to fair Britomart they all but shadows been.

### 46

For she was full of amiable grace
And manly terror mixèd therewithal,
That as the one stirred up affections base,
So the other did men's rash desires appall,
And hold them back that would in error fall:
As he that hath espied a vermeil rose,
To which sharp thorns and briars the way forestall,
Dare not for dread his hardy hand expose,
But, wishing it far off, his idle wish doth lose.

### 47

Whom when the lady saw so fair a wight,
All ignorant of her contrary sex
(For she her weened a fresh and lusty knight),
She greatly gan enamorèd to wax,
And with vain thoughts her falsèd fancy vex;
Her fickle heart conceivèd hasty fire,
Like sparks of fire which fall in sclender flax,
That shortly brent into extreme desire
And ransacked all her veins with passion entire.

### 48

Eftsoons she grew to great impatience
And into terms of open outrage brust
That plain discovered her incontinence,
Ne recked she who her meaning did mistrust;

**44.7** *tilt* joust.
**44.9** *her knights' service ought* owed her knights' service.  *in fee* as a matter of feudal obligation.
**45** The knights' semi-Italian names suggest the stages of love play: glancing (Gardante), talking (Parlante), joking (Jocante), kissing (Basciante), reveling (Bacchante), and spending the night (Noctante).
**47.7** *sclender* slender.
**48.4** *mistrust* suspect.

For she was given all to fleshly lust
And pourèd forth in sensual delight,
That all regard of shame she had discussed
And meet respect of honor put to flight:
So shameless beauty soon becomes a loathly sight.

### 49

Fair ladies that to love captivèd are
And chaste desires do nourish in your mind,
Let not her fault your sweet affections mar,
Ne blot the bounty of all womankind,
Mongst thousands good one wanton dame to find:
Amongst the roses grow some wicked weeds.
For this was not to love, but lust inclined;
For love does always bring forth bounteous deeds,
And in each gentle heart desire of honor breeds.

### 50

Nought so of love this looser dame did skill,
But as a coal to kindle fleshly flame,
Giving the bridle to her wanton will,
And treading under foot her honest name:
Such love is hate, and such desire is shame.
Still did she rove at her with crafty glance
Of her false eyes, that at her heart did aim
And told her meaning in her countenance;
But Britomart dissembled it with ignorance.

### 51

Supper was shortly dight and down they sat,
Where they were servèd with all sumptuous fare,
While fruitful Ceres and Lyaeus fat
Poured out their plenty, without spite or spare.
Nought wanted there that dainty was and rare;
And aye the cups their banks did overflow,
And aye between the cups she did prepare
Way to her love, and secret darts did throw,
But Britomart would not such guileful message know.

### 52

So when they slakèd had the fervent heat
Of appetite with meats of every sort,
The lady did fair Britomart entreat
Her to disarm, and with delightful sport
To loose her warlike limbs and strong effort.
But when she mote not thereunto be won
(For she her sex under that strange purport
Did use to hide and plain appearance shun),
In plainer wise to tell her grievance she begun,

48.7 *discussed* dispelled.
50.9 *dissembled it with ignorance* pretended not to recognize it because of ignorance.

51.3 *Ceres* goddess of agriculture. *Lyaeus* Bacchus, god of wine.

### 53

And all at once discovered her desire
With sighs, and sobs, and plaints, and piteous grief,
The outward sparks of her in-burning fire;
Which spent in vain, at last she told her brief
That but if she did lend her short relief
And do her comfort, she mote algates die.
But the chaste damsel, that had never prief
Of such malengin and fine forgery,
Did easily believe her strong extremity.

### 54

Full easy was for her to have belief,
Who by self-feeling of her feeble sex
And by long trial of the inward grief
Wherewith imperious love her heart did vex
Could judge what pains do loving hearts perplex.
Who means no guile, beguilèd soonest shall,
And to fair semblance doth light faith annex;
The bird that knows not the false fowler's call
Into his hidden net full easily doth fall.

### 55

Forthy she would not in discourteous wise
Scorn the fair offer of good will professed,
For great rebuke it is love to despise
Or rudely sdeign a gentle heart's request,
But with fair countenance, as beseemèd best,
Her entertained; natheless she inly deemed
Her love too light, to woo a wandering guest:
Which she, misconstruing, thereby esteemed
That from like inward fire that outward smoke had steamed.

### 56

Therewith a while she her flit fancy fed,
Till she mote win fit time for her desire,
But yet her wound still inward fleshly bled,
And through her bones the false instillèd fire
Did spread itself and venom close inspire.
Tho were the tables taken all away,
And every knight and every gentle squire
Gan choose his dame with *basciomani* gay
With whom he meant to make his sport and courtly play.

### 57

Some fell to dance, some fell to hazardry,
Some to make love, some to make merriment
As diverse wits to diverse things apply;

53.1  *discovered* revealed.
53.7  *prief* experience.
53.8  *malengin* fraud.
55.4  *sdeign* disdain.
56.1  *flit* quickly changing.
56.8  *basciomani* Italian: *Bascio le mani*, "I kiss the hands."

57.1  *hazardry* gambling.
57.2  *make love* The reference is not to physical lovemaking in the current sense of the phrase, but simply to professing love – though in the environment of Malecasta's castle it is expected that such advances will succeed.

And all the while fair Malecasta bent
Her crafty engines to her close intent.
By this the eternal lamps, wherewith high Jove
Doth light the lower world, were half yspent,
And the moist daughters of huge Atlas strove
Into the ocean deep to drive their weary drove.

58

High time it seemèd then for every wight
Them to betake unto their kindly rest;
Eftsoons long waxen torches weren light,
Unto their bowers to guiden every guest.
Tho when the Britoness saw all the rest
Avoided quite, she gan herself despoil
And safe commit to her soft feathered nest,
Where, through long watch and late days' weary toil,
She soundly slept, and careful thoughts did quite assoil.

59

Now whenas all the world in silence deep
Yshrouded was, and every mortal wight
Was drownèd in the depth of deadly sleep,
Fair Malecasta, whose engrievèd sprite
Could find no rest in such perplexed plight,
Lightly arose out of her weary bed,
And under the black veil of guilty night,
Her with a scarlet mantle coverèd
That was with gold and ermines fair envelopèd.

60

Then panting soft, and trembling every joint,
Her fearful feet towards the bower she moved,
Where she for secret purpose did appoint
To lodge the warlike maid, unwisely loved,
And, to her bed approaching, first she proved
Whether she slept or waked; with her soft hand
She softly felt if any member moved,
And lent her wary ear to understand
If any puff of breath or sign of sense she found.

61

Which whenas none she found, with easy shift,
For fear lest her unwares she should abraid,
The embroidered quilt she lightly up did lift
And by her side herself she softly laid,
Of every finest fingers' touch afraid;
Ne any noise she made, ne word she spake,
But inly sighed. At last the royal maid

---

57.4 *Malecasta* The name means "badly chaste" in Latin.
57.5 *engines* schemes.
57.8 *the moist daughters of huge Atlas* The constellation of the Hyades, setting about midnight.
57.9 *drove* herd.

58.6 *Avoided* retired. *despoil* undress.
58.9 *careful* worrisome. *assoil* dismiss.
60.5 *proved* tested.
61.2 *abraid* wake up.

Out of her quiet slumber did awake,
And changed her weary side, the better ease to take.

### 62

Where feeling one close couchèd by her side,
She lightly leapt out of her filèd bed,
And to her weapon ran, in mind to gride
The loathèd lecher. But the dame half dead
Through sudden fear and ghastly drearihead,
Did shriek aloud, that through the house it rung,
And the whole family, therewith adread,
Rashly out of their rousèd couches sprung,
And to the troubled chamber all in arms did throng.

### 63

And those six knights, that lady's champions,
And eke the Redcross Knight ran to the stound,
Half armed and half unarmed with them at once:
Where when confusedly they came, they found
Their lady lying on the senseless ground;
On the other side they saw the warlike maid
All in her snow-white smock, with locks unbound,
Threatening the point of her avenging blade,
That with so troublous terror they were all dismayed.

### 64

About their lady first they flocked around,
Whom, having laid in comfortable couch,
Shortly they reared out of her frozen swound;
And afterwards they gan with foul reproach
To stir up strife, and troublous conteck broach.
But by ensample of the last day's loss,
None of them rashly durst to her approach,
Ne in so glorious spoil themselves emboss;
Her succored eke the champion of the bloody cross.

### 65

But one of those six knights, Gardante hight,
Drew out a deadly bow and arrow keen,
Which forth he sent with felonous despite
And fell intent against the virgin sheen;
The mortal steel stayed not till it was seen
To gore her side, yet was the wound not deep,
But lightly razèd her soft silken skin,
That drops of purple blood thereout did weep,
Which did her lily smock with stains of vermeil steep.

### 66

Wherewith enraged, she fiercely at them flew
And with her flaming sword about her laid,
That none of them foul mischief could eschew,

62.2   *filèd* defiled.
62.3   *gride* pierce.
63.2   *stound* uproar.

64.3   *swound* swoon.
64.5   *conteck* conflict.

But with her dreadful strokes were all dismayed;
Here, there, and everywhere about her swayed
Her wrathful steel, that none mote it abide,
And eke the Redcross Knight gave her good aid,
Aye joining foot to foot and side to side,
That in short space their foes they have quite terrified.

67

Tho whenas all were put to shameful flight,
The noble Britomartis her arrayed,
And her bright arms about her body dight;
For nothing would she longer there be stayed,
Where so loose life and so ungentle trade
Was used of knights and ladies seeming gent.
So early, ere the gross earth's grisy shade
Was all dispersed out of the firmament,
They took their steeds and forth upon their journey went.

**67.7** *grisy* gray.

CANTO II

*The Redcross Knight to Britomart
   describeth Artegall;
The wondrous mirror by which she
   in love with him did fall.*

1

Here have I cause in men just blame to find,
That in their proper praise too partial be,
And not indifferent to womankind,
To whom no share in arms and chivalry
They do impart, ne maken memory
Of their brave gests and prowess martial;
Scarce do they spare to one or two or three
Room in their writs, yet the same writing small
Does all their deeds deface and dims their glories all.

2

But by record of antique times I find
That women wont in wars to bear most sway
And to all great exploits themselves inclined:
Of which they still the garland bore away,
Till envious men, fearing their rule's decay,
Gan coin straight laws to curb their liberty;
Yet sith they warlike arms have laid away,
They have excelled in arts and policy,
That now we foolish men that praise gin eke to envy.

3

Of warlike puissance in ages spent
Be thou, fair Britomart, whose praise I write,
But of all wisdom be thou precedent,

**1.3** *indifferent* impartial.          **3.3** *precedent* pre-eminent example.

O sovereign Queen, whose praise I would indite,
Indite I would as duty doth excite;
But ah, my rhymes too rude and rugged are
When in so high an object they do light,
And striving fit to make, I fear do mar:
Thyself thy praises tell, and make them knowen far.

4

She, traveling with Guyon by the way,
Of sundry things fair purpose gan to find
To abridge their journey long and lingering day;
Mongst which it fell into that Faery's mind
To ask this Briton maid what uncouth wind
Brought her into those parts, and what inquest
Made her dissemble her disguisèd kind.
Fair lady she him seemed, like lady dressed,
But fairest knight alive, when armèd was her breast.

5

Thereat she, sighing softly, had no power
To speak a while, ne ready answer make,
But with heart-thrilling throbs and bitter stour,
As if she had a fever fit, did quake
And every dainty limb with horror shake;
And ever and anon the rosy red
Flashed through her face, as it had been a flake
Of lightning through bright heaven fulminèd.
At last, the passion past, she thus him answerèd.

6

Fair sir, I let you weet that from the hour
I taken was from nurse's tender pap
I have been trainèd up in warlike stour,
To tossen spear and shield, and to affrap
The warlike rider to his most mishap;
Sithence I loathèd have my life to lead,
As ladies wont, in pleasure's wanton lap,
To finger the fine needle and nice thread:
Me lever were with point of foeman's spear be dead.

7

All my delight on deeds of arms is set,
To hunt out perils and adventures hard,
By sea, by land, whereso they may be met,
Only for honor and for high regard,
Without respect of richesse or reward.
For such intent into these parts I came,
Withouten compass or withouten card,
Far fro my native soil, that is by name
The greater Britain, here to seek for praise and fame.

4.1   *Guyon* Seemingly a mistake for Redcross.
4.6   *inquest* quest.
5.3   *stour* struggle.
5.7   *flake* flash.

6.4   *affrap* strike.
7.9   *greater Britain* As distinct from Brittany, sometimes
referred to as "lesser Britain."

### 8

Fame blazèd hath that here in Faery land
Do many famous knights and ladies won,
And many strange adventures to be found,
Of which great worth and worship may be won;
Which I to prove, this voyage have begun.
But mote I weet of you, right courteous knight,
Tidings of one that hath unto me done
Late foul dishonor and reproachful spite,
The which I seek to wreak, and Artegall he hight.

### 9

The word gone out she back again would call,
As her repenting so to have missaid,
But that he it uptaking ere the fall
Her shortly answerèd: Fair martial maid,
Certes ye misavisèd been, to upbraid
A gentle knight with so unknightly blame;
For weet ye well, of all that ever played
At tilt or tourney or like warlike game,
The noble Artegall hath ever borne the name.

### 10

Forthy great wonder were it, if such shame
Should ever enter in his bounteous thought,
Or ever do that mote deserven blame:
The noble courage never weeneth ought
That may unworthy of itself be thought.
Therefore, fair damsel, be ye well aware,
Lest that too far ye have your sorrow sought:
You and your country both I wish welfare
And honor both; for each of other worthy are.

### 11

The royal maid wox inly wondrous glad
To hear her love so highly magnified,
And joyed that ever she affixèd had
Her heart on knight so goodly glorified,
However finely she it fained to hide:
The loving mother that nine months did bear,
In the dear closet of her painful side,
Her tender babe, it seeing safe appear
Doth not so much rejoice as she rejoicèd there.

### 12

But to occasion him to further talk
To feed her humor with his pleasing style,
Her list in strifeful terms with him to balk,
And thus replied: However, sir, ye file
Your courteous tongue his praises to compile,
It ill beseems a knight of gentle sort,
Such as ye have him boasted, to beguile

---

8.2   *won* dwell.                    12.3   *balk* argue.
9.9   *borne the name* maintained a (good) reputation.

A simple maid and work so heinous tort
In shame of knighthood, as I largely can report.

### 13

Let be, therefore, my vengeance to dissuade,
And read where I that faitour false may find.
Ah, but if reason fair might you persuade
To slake your wrath and mollify your mind
(Said he), perhaps ye should it better find;
For hardy thing it is, to ween by might,
That man to hard conditions to bind
Or ever hope to match in equal fight,
Whose prowess' paragon saw never living wight.

### 14

Ne soothlich is it easy for to read
Where now on earth or how he may be found;
For he ne wonneth in one certain stead,
But restless walketh all the world around,
Aye doing things that to his fame redound,
Defending ladies' cause and orphans' right
Whereso he hears that any doth confound
Them comfortless, through tyranny or might:
So is his sovereign honor raised to heaven's height.

### 15

His feeling words her feeble sense much pleased,
And softly sunk into her molten heart.
Heart that is inly hurt is greatly eased
With hope of thing that may allege his smart;
For pleasing words are like to magic art
That doth the charmèd snake in slumber lay:
Such secret ease felt gentle Britomart,
Yet list the same efforce with feigned gainsay;
So discord oft in music makes the sweeter lay,

### 16

And said, Sir knight, these idle terms forbear,
And sith it is uneath to find his haunt,
Tell me some marks by which he may appear,
If chance I him encounter paravaunt;
For, perdy, one shall other slay or daunt.
What shape, what shield, what arms, what steed, what stead,
And what so else his person most may vaunt?
All which the Redcross Knight to point ared,
And him in every part before her fashionèd.

### 17

Yet him in every part before she knew,
However list her now her knowledge feign,
Sith him whilom in Britain she did view,

12.8  *tort* harm.
13.2  *read* tell.  *faitour* impostor.
15.4  *allege* alleviate.

15.8  *efforce* oppose.
16.4  *paravaunt* in public.
16.8  *to point ared* stated precisely.

To her revealèd in a mirror plain,
Whereof did grow her first engraffèd pain;
Whose root and stalk so bitter yet did taste
That, but the fruit more sweetness did contain,
Her wretched days in dolor she mote waste,
And yield the prey of love to loathsome death at last.

### 18

By strange occasion she did him behold,
And much more strangely gan to love his sight,
As it in books hath written been of old.
In Deheubarth, that now South Wales is hight,
What time king Ryence reigned and dealèd right,
The great magician Merlin had devised,
By his deep science and hell-dreaded might,
A looking glass, right wondrously aguised,
Whose virtues through the wide world soon were solemnized.

### 19

It virtue had to show in perfect sight
Whatever thing was in the world contained
Betwixt the lowest earth and heaven's height,
So that it to the looker appertained:
Whatever foe had wrought or friend had fained
Therein discovered was, ne ought mote pass
Ne ought in secret from the same remained;
Forthy it round and hollow shapèd was,
Like to the world itself, and seemed a world of glass.

### 20

Who wonders not, that reads so wondrous work?
But who does wonder, that has read the tower
Wherein the Egyptian Phao long did lurk
From all men's view, that none might her discover,
Yet she might all men view out of her bower?
Great Ptolemy it for his leman's sake
Ybuilded all of glass by magic power,
And also it impregnable did make;
Yet when his love was false, he with a peise it brake.

### 21

Such was the glassy globe that Merlin made
And gave unto king Ryence for his guard,
That never foes his kingdom might invade
But he it knew at home before he heard
Tidings thereof, and so them still debarred.
It was a famous present for a prince
And worthy work of infinite reward,
That treasons could bewray and foes convince;
Happy this realm, had it remainèd ever since.

---

18.8  *aguised* outfitted.
20  The story of Phao and Ptolemy may be Spenser's invention. Phao's name appears again later in the poem in a list of fifty sea nymphs (IV.xi.49.5). Ptolemy is the dynastic name of the Hellenistic kings of Egypt and also the name of famous astronomer (second century AD) who was later said to have magical powers; the two appear to be conflated here.
20.6  *leman* beloved.
20.9  *peise* heavy blow.
21.8  *convince* convict.

### 22

One day it fortunèd fair Britomart
Into her father's closet to repair,
For nothing he from her reserved apart,
Being his only daughter and his heir:
Where when she had espied that mirror fair,
Herself a while therein she viewed in vain;
Tho her avising of the virtues rare
Which thereof spoken were, she gan again
Her to bethink of that mote to herself pertain.

### 23

But as it falleth, in the gentlest hearts
Imperious Love hath highest set his throne,
And tyrannizeth in the bitter smarts
Of them that to him buxom are and prone:
So thought this maid (as maidens use to done)
Whom fortune for her husband would allot,
Not that she lusted after anyone;
For she was pure from blame of sinful blot,
Yet wist her life at last must link in that same knot.

### 24

Eftsoons there was presented to her eye
A comely knight, all armed in complete wise,
Through whose bright ventail, lifted up on high,
His manly face, that did his foes agrise
And friends to terms of gentle truce entise,
Looked forth, as Phoebus' face out of the east
Betwixt two shady mountains doth arise;
Portly his person was, and much increased
Through his heroic grace and honorable gest.

### 25

His crest was covered with a couchant hound,
And all his armor seemed of antique mold,
But wondrous massy and assurèd sound,
And round about yfretted all with gold,
In which there written was with ciphers old
*Achilles' arms, which Artegall did win.*
And on his shield enveloped sevenfold
He bore a crownèd little ermelin
That decked the azure field with her fair poldered skin.

### 26

The damsel well did view his personage
And likèd well, ne further fastened not,

22.7  *avising* considering.
23.4  *buxom* tractable.
24.4  *agrise* terrify.
24.8  *Portly* imposing.
24.9  *gest* bearing.
25.1  *couchant hound* hound ready to spring.
25.6  *Achilles' arms* The armor of the greatest of the Greek warriors in the Trojan war. The creation of this armor is

described in some detail in Homer's *Iliad*; after Achilles' death it was awarded to Odysseus, but there is no canonical account of its further history. Spenser is creating a point of symmetry with the chivalric romances of Boiardo and Ariosto, where one of the warriors possesses the armor of Hector, the greatest of the Trojan warriors.

25.8  *ermelin* ermine (emblem of chastity).
25.9  *poldered* powdered, i.e., spotted.

But went her way; ne her unguilty age
Did ween, unwares, that her unlucky lot
Lay hidden in the bottom of the pot.
Of hurt unwist most danger doth redound;
But the false archer, which that arrow shot
So slyly that she did not feel the wound,
Did smile full smoothly at her weetless, woeful stound.

27

Thenceforth the feather in her lofty crest,
Ruffèd of love, gan lowly to avale,
And her proud portance and her princely gest,
With which she erst triumphèd, now did quail.
Sad, solemn, sour, and full of fancies frail
She wox, yet wist she neither how nor why;
She wist not, silly maid, what she did ail,
Yet wist she was not well at ease, perdy,
Yet thought it was not love, but some melancholy.

28

So soon as night had with her pallid hue
Defaced the beauty of the shining sky
And reft from men the world's desirèd view,
She with her nurse adown to sleep did lie.
But sleep full far away from her did fly;
Instead thereof sad sighs and sorrows deep
Kept watch and ward about her warily,
That nought she did but wail, and often steep
Her dainty couch with tears, which closely she did weep.

29

And if that any drop of slumbering rest
Did chance to still into her weary sprite
When feeble nature felt herself oppressed,
Straightway with dreams and with fantastic sight
Of dreadful things the same was put to flight,
That oft out of her bed she did astart,
As one with view of ghastly fiends affright;
Tho gan she to renew her former smart,
And think of that fair visage written in her heart.

30

One night, when she was tossed with such unrest,
Her agèd nurse, whose name was Glauce hight,
Feeling her leap out of her loathèd nest,
Betwixt her feeble arms her quickly keight,
And down again in her warm bed her dight.
Ah my dear daughter, ah my dearest dread,
What uncouth fit (said she), what evil plight
Hath thee oppressed, and with sad drearihead
Changèd thy lively cheer, and living made thee dead?

**26.9** *stound* time of trial.
**27.2** *Ruffèd* ruffled. *avale* fall.
**27.3** *portance* demeanor.

**29.2** *still* distill.
**30.4** *keight* caught.

### 31

For not of nought these sudden ghastly fears
All night afflict thy natural repose,
And all the day, whenas thine equal peers
Their fit disports with fair delight do choose,
Thou in dull corners dost thyself inclose,
Ne tastest princes' pleasures, ne dost spread
Abroad thy fresh youth's fairest flower, but lose
Both leaf and fruit, both too untimely shed,
As one in willful bale forever burièd.

### 32

The time that mortal men their weary cares
Do lay away, and all wild beasts do rest,
And every river eke his course forbears,
Then doth this wicked evil thee infest,
And rive with thousand throbs thy thrillèd breast;
Like an huge Etna of deep engulfèd grief,
Sorrow is heapèd in thy hollow chest,
Whenceforth it breaks in sighs and anguish rife,
As smoke and sulphur mingled with confusèd strife.

### 33

Ay me, how much I fear lest love it be;
But if that love it be, as sure I read
By knowen signs and passions which I see,
Be it worthy of thy race and royal seed,
Then I avow, by this most sacred head
Of my dear foster child, to ease thy grief
And win thy will. Therefore, away do dread,
For death nor danger from thy due relief
Shall me debar; tell me therefore, my liefest lief.

### 34

So having said, her twixt her armes twain
She straitly strained, and collèd tenderly,
And every trembling joint and every vein
She softly felt, and rubbèd busily
To do the frozen cold away to fly;
And her fair dewy eyes with kisses dear
She oft did bathe and oft again did dry,
And ever her importuned not to fear
To let the secret of her heart to her appear.

### 35

The damsel paused, and then thus fearfully:
Ah nurse, what needeth thee to eke my pain?
Is not enough that I alone do die,
But it must doubled be with death of twain?
For nought for me but death there doth remain.
O daughter dear (said she), despair no whit,

32.5  *thrillèd* pierced.
32.6  *Etna* an active Sicilian volcano.
33.7  *away do dread* do away with dread.

33.9  *liefest lief* dearest love.
34.2  *collèd* hugged.
35.2  *eke* increase.

For never sore but might a salve obtain:
That blinded god which hath ye blindly smit
Another arrow hath your lover's heart to hit.

### 36

But mine is not (quoth she) like others' wound;
For which no reason can find remedy.
Was never such but mote the like be found
(Said she), and though no reason may apply
Salve to your sore, yet love can higher sty
Than reason's reach, and oft hath wonders done.
But neither god of love nor god of sky
Can do (said she) that which cannot be done.
Things oft impossible (quoth she) seem ere begun.

### 37

These idle words (said she) do nought assuage
My stubborn smart, but more annoyance breed.
For no, no usual fire, no usual rage
It is, O nurse, which on my life doth feed
And sucks the blood which from my heart doth bleed.
But since thy faithful zeal lets me not hide
My crime (if crime it be), I will it read.
Nor prince nor peer it is whose love hath gride
My feeble breast of late, and launchèd this wound wide.

### 38

Nor man it is, nor other living wight,
For then some hope I might unto me draw,
But the only shade and semblant of a knight,
Whose shape or person yet I never saw,
Hath me subjected to love's cruel law:
The same one day, as me misfortune led,
I in my father's wondrous mirror saw,
And pleasèd with that seeming goodlihead,
Unwares the hidden hook with bait I swallowèd.

### 39

Sithens it hath infixèd faster hold
Within my bleeding bowels, and so sore
Now rankleth in this same frail fleshly mold,
That all mine entrails flow with poisonous gore,
And the ulcer groweth daily more and more;
Ne can my running sore find remedy,
Other than my hard fortune to deplore
And languish as the leaf fallen from the tree,
Till death make one end of my days and misery.

### 40

Daughter (said she), what need ye be dismayed,
Or why make ye such monster of your mind?
Of much more uncouth thing I was afraid,

36.5  *sty* rise.
37.8  *gride* pierced.

37.9  *launchèd* cut.
38.8  *goodlihead* beauty.

Of filthy lust contrary unto kind,
But this affection nothing strange I find;
For who with reason can you aye reprove
To love the semblant pleasing most your mind,
And yield your heart whence ye cannot remove?
No guilt in you, but in the tyranny of love.

### 41

Not so the Arabian Myrrhe did set her mind,
Nor so did Byblis spend her pining heart,
But loved their native flesh against all kind,
And to their purpose usèd wicked art;
Yet played Pasiphae a more monstrous part,
That loved a bull and learned a beast to be.
Such shameful lusts who loathes not, which depart
From course of nature and of modesty?
Sweet love such lewdness bands from his fair company.

### 42

But thine, my dear (welfare thy heart, my dear),
Though strange beginning had, yet fixèd is
On one that worthy may perhaps appear,
And certes seems bestowèd not amiss;
Joy thereof have thou, and eternal bliss.
With that, upleaning on her elbow weak,
Her alablaster breast she oft did kiss,
Which all that while she felt to pant and quake
As it an earthquake were; at last she thus bespake:

### 43

Beldam, your words do work me little ease,
For though my love be not so lewdly bent
As those ye blame, yet may it nought appease
My raging smart, ne ought my flame relent,
But rather doth my helpless grief augment.
For they, however shameful and unkind,
Yet did possess their horrible intent;
Short end of sorrows they thereby did find:
So was their fortune good, though wicked were their mind.

### 44

But wicked fortune mine, though mind be good,
Can have no end nor hope of my desire,
But feed on shadows whiles I die for food,
And like a shadow wax, whiles with entire
Affection I do languish and expire.
I, fonder than Cephisus' foolish child,

---

**40.4**  *kind* nature.

**41.1–6**  The nurse cites three familiar examples of unnatural female desire from classical antiquity. Myrrhe is Myrrha, whose incestuous desire for her own father led to the birth of Adonis; Byblis was driven to suicide by lust for her twin brother; Pasiphae (usually four syllables, though treated by Spenser here as three) committed bestiality with a handsome bull and gave birth to the Minotaur.

**41.9**  *bands* Probably a misprint for "bans," which is obviously the intended sense.

**43.1**  *Beldam* old woman (a common sixteenth-century salutation for nurses).

**43.6**  *unkind* unnatural.

**43.7**  *possess their horrible intent* achieve their horrible goal (though Byblis did not).

**44.6**  *Cephisus' foolish child* Narcissus.

Who, having viewèd in a fountain sheer
His face, was with the love thereof beguiled;
I, fonder, love a shade, the body far exiled.

### 45

Nought like (quoth she), for that same wretched boy
Was of himself the idle paramour:
Both love and lover, without hope of joy,
For which he faded to a watery flower.
But better fortune thine, and better hour,
Which lov'st the shadow of a warlike knight;
No shadow, but a body hath in power:
That body, wheresoever that it light,
May learnèd be by ciphers, or by magic might.

### 46

But if thou may with reason yet repress
The growing evil ere it strength have got
And thee abandoned wholly do possess,
Against it strongly strive, and yield thee not,
Till thou in open field adown be smot.
But if the passion master thy frail might,
So that needs love or death must be thy lot,
Then I avow to thee, by wrong or right,
To compass thy desire and find that lovèd knight.

### 47

Her cheerful words much cheered the feeble sprite
Of the sick virgin, that her down she laid
In her warm bed to sleep, if that she might,
And the old woman carefully displayed
The clothes about her round with busy aid;
So that at last a little creeping sleep
Surprised her sense. She, therewith well apayed,
The drunken lamp down in the oil did steep,
And set her by to watch, and set her by to weep.

### 48

Early the morrow next, before that day
His joyous face did to the world reveal,
They both uprose and took their ready way
Unto the church, their prayers to appeal,
With great devotion, and with little zeal;
For the fair damsel from the holy hearse
Her lovesick heart to other thoughts did steal,
And that old dame said many an idle verse,
Out of her daughter's heart fond fancies to reverse.

### 49

Returnèd home, the royal infant fell
Into her former fit, for why no power
Nor guidance of herself in her did dwell.

---

47.7 *apayed* contented.                    49.1 *infant* princess.
48.6 *hearse* ceremony.

But the agèd nurse, her calling to her bower,
Had gathered rue and savin and the flower
Of camphora, and calamint and dill,
All which she in a earthen pot did pour,
And to the brim with coltwood did it fill,
And many drops of milk and blood through it did spill.

### 50

Then taking thrice three hairs from off her head,
Them trebly braided in a threefold lace,
And round about the pot's mouth bound the thread,
And after having whisperèd a space
Certain sad words with hollow voice and bass,
She to the virgin said, thrice said she it:
Come, daughter, come, come; spit upon my face,
Spit thrice upon me, thrice upon me spit:
The uneven number for this business is most fit.

### 51

That said, her round about she from her turned,
She turnèd her contrary to the sun,
Thrice she her turned contrary, and returned,
All contrary, for she the right did shun,
And ever what she did was straight undone.
So thought she to undo her daughter's love;
But love that is in gentle breast begun
No idle charms so lightly may remove:
That well can witness, who by trial it does prove.

### 52

Ne ought it mote the noble maid avail,
Ne slake the fury of her cruel flame,
But that she still did waste, and still did wail,
That through long languor and heart-burning brame
She shortly like a pinèd ghost became
Which long hath waited by the Stygian strand.
That when old Glauce saw, for fear lest blame
Of her miscarriage should in her be found,
She wist not how to amend, nor how it to withstand.

49.8  *coltwood* probably coltsfoot.          52.4  *brame* desire.

CANTO III

*Merlin bewrays to Britomart
    the state of Artegall,
And shows the famous progeny
    which from them springen shall.*

### 1

Most sacred fire that burnest mightily
In living breasts, ykindled first above
Amongst the eternal spheres and lamping sky,

1.3  *lamping* shining.

And thence poured into men, which men call love;
Not that same which doth base affections move
In brutish minds, and filthy lust inflame,
But that sweet fit that doth true beauty love,
And chooseth virtue for his dearest dame,
Whence spring all noble deeds and never dying fame:

2

Well did antiquity a god thee deem,
That over mortal minds hast so great might
To order them as best to thee doth seem,
And all their actions to direct aright;
The fatal purpose of divine foresight
Thou dost effect in destinèd descents,
Through deep impression of thy secret might,
And stirredst up the heroës' high intents,
Which the late world admires for wondrous monuments.

3

But thy dread darts in none do triumph more,
Ne braver proof in any of thy power
Showdst thou, than in this royal maid of yore,
Making her seek an unknown paramour
From the world's end, through many a bitter stour.
From whose two loins thou afterwards did raise
Most famous fruits of matrimonial bower,
Which through the earth have spread their living praise
That fame in trump of gold eternally displays.

4

Begin then, O my dearest sacred dame,
Daughter of Phoebus and of Memory,
That dost ennoble with immortal name
The warlike worthies from antiquity
In thy great volume of Eternity:
Begin, O Clio, and recount from hence
My glorious sovereign's goodly ancestry,
Till that by due degrees and long protense
Thou have it lastly brought unto her excellence.

5

Full many ways within her troubled mind
Old Glauce cast to cure this lady's grief;
Full many ways she sought, but none could find,
Nor herbs nor charms nor counsel, that is chief
And choicest medicine for sick heart's relief.
Forthy great care she took, and greater fear,
Lest that it should her turn to foul reprief
And sore reproach, whenso her father dear
Should of his dearest daughter's hard misfortune hear.

---

**2.5** *fatal* ordained by fate.
**2.6** *descents* lineages.
**3.5** *stour* struggle.
**4.6** *Clio* Muse of history (rather than epic poetry).

**4.8** *protense* extension. This is the reading of the 1590 edition; the 1596 and later editions have "pretence."
**5.7** *reprief* reproof.

6

At last she her avised that he which made
That mirror wherein the sick damozel
So strangely viewèd her strange lover's shade,
To weet, the learnèd Merlin, well could tell
Under what coast of heaven the man did dwell,
And by what means his love might best be wrought;
For though beyond the Afric Ismaël
Or the Indian Peru he were, she thought
Him forth through infinite endeavor to have sought.

7

Forthwith themselves disguising both in strange
And base attire, that none might them bewray,
To Maridunum, that is now by change
Of name Caer-Merdin called, they took their way.
There the wise Merlin whilom wont (they say)
To make his wone, low underneath the ground,
In a deep delve far from the view of day,
That of no living wight he mote be found
Whenso he counseled with his sprites encompassed round.

8

And if thou ever happen that same way
To travel, go to see that dreadful place:
It is an hideous hollow cave (they say)
Under a rock that lies a little space
From the swift Barry, tumbling down apace
Amongst the woody hills of Dynevor.
But dare thou not, I charge, in any case
To enter into that same baleful bower,
For fear the cruel fiends should thee unwares devour.

9

But standing high aloft, low lay thine ear,
And there such ghastly noise of iron chains
And brazen cauldrons thou shalt rumbling hear,
Which thousand sprites with long enduring pains
Do toss, that it will stun thy feeble brains,
And oftentimes great groans and grievous stounds
When too huge toil and labor them constrains;
And oftentimes loud strokes and ringing sounds
From under that deep rock most horribly rebounds.

10

The cause some say is this: A little while
Before that Merlin died, he did intend
A brazen wall in compass to compile
About Carmarthen, and did it commend

---

**6.7**  *Afric Ismaël* Africa was said to be populated by the descendants of Abraham's son Ishmael.

**7.4**  *Caer-Merdin* Carmarthen ("caer" is the Welsh word for a fortified city or town).

**7.6**  *wone* dwelling.

**8.5–6**  There is some confusion here about Welsh geography; Carmarthen and Dinevor (Dinefwr) Castle are on the Towy (Tywi) river, while the Barry (Cadoxton) runs some fifty miles to the east, near Cardiff.

**9.6**  *stounds* uproars.

Unto these sprites to bring to perfect end;
During which work the Lady of the Lake,
Whom long he loved, for him in haste did send,
Who, thereby forced his workmen to forsake,
Them bound till his return their labor not to slake.

### 11

In the meantime, through that false lady's train
He was surprised and buried under bier,
Ne ever to his work returned again.
Natheless those fiends may not their work forbear,
So greatly his commandement they fear,
But there do toil and travail day and night
Until that brazen wall they up do rear:
For Merlin had in magic more insight
Then ever him before or after living wight.

### 12

For he by words could call out of the sky
Both sun and moon, and make them him obey;
The land to sea, and sea to mainland dry,
And darksome night he eke could turn to day;
Huge hosts of men he could alone dismay,
And hosts of men of meanest things could frame
Whenso him list his enemies to fray:
That to this day for terror of his fame
The fiends do quake when any him to them does name.

### 13

And sooth, men say that he was not the son
Of mortal sire or other living wight,
But wondrously begotten and begun
By false illusion of a guileful sprite
On a fair lady nun, that whilom hight
Matilda, daughter to Pubidius,
Who was the lord of Mathraval by right,
And cousin unto king Ambrosius:
Whence he enduèd was with skill so marvelous.

### 14

They, here arriving, stayed a while without,
Ne durst adventure rashly in to wend,
But of their first intent gan make new doubt
For dread of danger which it might portend;
Until the hardy maid (with love to friend)
First entering, the dreadful mage there found
Deep busièd bout work of wondrous end
And writing strange characters in the ground,
With which the stubborn fiends he to his service bound.

11.1   *train* treachery.
12.7   *fray* frighten.
13   Spenser elaborates on legendary accounts of Merlin's
supernatural parentage; the names Matilda and Pubidius are
his own doing. Mathraval (Mathrafal) was a royal house
in the early history of Wales, Ambrosius (Emrys Wledig) a
legendary Welsh king, in some accounts the brother of Uther
Pendragon, Arthur's father.

15

He nought was movèd at their entrance bold,
For of their coming well he wist afore,
Yet list them bid their business to unfold,
As if ought in this world in secret store
Were from him hidden or unknown of yore.
Then Glauce thus: Let not it thee offend
That we thus rashly through thy darksome door
Unwares have pressed; for either fatal end
Or other mighty cause us two did hither send.

16

He bade tell on, and then she thus began:
Now have three moons with borrowed brother's light
Thrice shinèd fair and thrice seemed dim and wan
Sith a sore evil which this virgin bright
Tormenteth and doth plunge in doleful plight
First rooting took; but what thing it mote be
Or whence it sprung, I cannot read aright.
But this I read, that but if remedy
Thou her afford, full shortly I her dead shall see.

17

Therewith the enchanter softly gan to smile
At her smooth speeches, weeting inly well
That she to him dissembled womanish guile,
And to her said, Beldam, by that ye tell,
More need of leechcraft hath your damozel
Than of my skill; who help may have elsewhere
In vain seeks wonders out of magic spell.
The old woman wox half blank those words to hear,
And yet was loath to let her purpose plain appear,

18

And to him said: If any leech's skill
Or other learnèd means could have redressed
This my dear daughter's deep engraffèd ill,
Certes I should be loath thee to molest;
But this sad evil which doth her infest
Doth course of natural cause far exceed,
And housèd is within her hollow breast,
That either seems some cursèd witches' deed
Or evil sprite that in her doth such torment breed.

19

The wizard could no longer bear her bourd,
But brusting forth in laughter, to her said:
Glauce, what needs this colorable word
To cloak the cause that hath itself bewrayed?
Ne ye, fair Britomartis, thus arrayed,
More hidden are than sun in cloudy veil,

17.4  *Beldam* old woman.
17.5  *leechcraft* medical attention.
19.1  *bourd* game.

19.2  *brusting* bursting.
19.3  *colorable* cosmetic.

Whom thy good fortune, having fate obeyed,
Hath hither brought for succor to appeal:
The which the powers to thee are pleasèd to reveal.

### 20

The doubtful maid, seeing herself descried,
Was all abashed, and her pure ivory
Into a clear carnation sudden dyed:
As fair Aurora, rising hastily,
Doth by her blushing tell that she did lie
All night in old Tithonus' frozen bed,
Whereof she seems ashamèd inwardly.
But her old nurse was nought disheartenèd,
But vantage made of that which Merlin had ared,

### 21

And said, Sith then thou knowest all our grief
(For what dost thou not know?), of grace I pray,
Pity our plaint, and yield us meet relief.
With that the prophet still awhile did stay,
And then his spirit thus gan forth display:
Most noble virgin, that by fatal lore
Hast learned to love, let no whit thee dismay
The hard begin that meets thee in the door,
And with sharp fits thy tender heart oppresseth sore.

### 22

For so must all things excellent begin,
And eke enrooted deep must be that tree
Whose big embodied branches shall not lin
Till they to heaven's height forth stretchèd be.
For from thy womb a famous progeny
Shall spring, out of the ancient Trojan blood,
Which shall revive the sleeping memory
Of those same antique peers, the heaven's brood,
Which Greek and Asian rivers stainèd with their blood.

### 23

Renowmèd kings and sacred emperors,
Thy fruitful offspring, shall from thee descend:
Brave captains and most mighty warriors
That shall their conquests through all lands extend
And their decayèd kingdoms shall amend.
The feeble Britons, broken with long war,
They shall uprear, and mightily defend
Against their foreign foe that comes from far,
Till universal peace compound all civil jar.

### 24

It was not, Britomart, thy wandering eye,
Glancing unwares in charmèd looking glass,

---

20.4–7  See below, Marlowe, *Ovid's Elegies* 1.13
**20.9**  *ared* divined.
**21.6**  *fatal lore* fate's teaching.

**21.8**  *begin* beginning.
**22.3**  *lin* stop.
**23.9**  *compound* settle.  *jar* disturbance.

But the straight course of heavenly destiny,
Led with eternal providence, that has
Guided thy glance, to bring his will to pass;
Ne is thy fate, ne is thy fortune ill,
To love the prowest knight that ever was.
Therefore submit thy ways unto his will,
And do by all due means thy destiny fulfill.

25

But read (said Glauce), thou magician,
What means she shall out seek, or what ways take.
How shall she know, how shall she find the man?
Or what needs her to toil, sith fates can make
Way for themselves, their purpose to partake?
Then Merlin thus: Indeed, the fates are firm,
And may not shrink, though all the world do shake;
Yet ought men's good endeavors them confirm,
And guide the heavenly causes to their constant term.

26

The man whom heavens have ordained to be
The spouse of Britomart is Artegall:
He wonneth in the land of Faery,
Yet is no Faery born, ne sib at all
To Elfs, but sprung of seed terrestrial,
And whilom by false Faeries stolen away,
Whiles yet in infant cradle he did crawl;
Ne other to himself is known this day,
But that he by an Elf was gotten of a Fay.

27

But sooth he is the son of Gorloïs,
And brother unto Cador, Cornish king,
And for his warlike feats renowmèd is
From where the day out of the sea doth spring
Until the closure of the evening.
From thence, him firmly bound with faithful band
To this his native soil thou back shalt bring,
Strongly to aid his country to withstand
The power of foreign paynims which invade thy land.

28

Great aid thereto his mighty puissance
And dreaded name shall give in that sad day,
Where also proof of thy prow valiance
Thou then shalt make, to increase thy lover's prey.

24.7  *prowest* bravest.
25.5  *partake* communicate.
25.9  *constant term* fixed goal.
26.3  *wonneth* dwells.
26.4  *sib* relation.
27.1  *Gorlois* A Cornish duke, whose wife Igerne was mother of Arthur by Uther Pendragon, so that Arthur and Artegall are half-brothers. In Book II.x.5–68, Spenser gives a catalogue of British history from the earliest days and the arrival of Brut; here he in effect resumes the story just after the point at which it had earlier broken off, and continues it until the final victory of the invading Anglo-Saxons over the native British. From here to stanza 41 he is for the most part adapting Geoffrey of Monmouth's *Historia Regum Britanniae*; the implied chronology runs from the early sixth to the late seventh centuries, though much of the action is legendary.
27.9  *paynims* pagans.

Long time ye both in arms shall bear great sway,
Till thy womb's burden thee from them do call,
And his last fate him from thee take away,
Too rathe cut off by practice criminal
Of secret foes, that him shall make in mischief fall.

29

With thee yet shall he leave, for memory
Of his late puissance, his image dead,
That, living, him in all activity
To thee shall represent. He from the head
Of his cousin Constantius without dread
Shall take the crown that was his father's right,
And therewith crown himself in the other's stead;
Then shall he issue forth with dreadful might
Against his Saxon foes in bloody field to fight.

30

Like as a lion that in drowsy cave
Hath long time slept, himself so shall he shake,
And coming forth shall spread his banner brave
Over the troubled south, that it shall make
The warlike Mercians for fear to quake;
Thrice shall he fight with them, and twice shall win,
But the third time shall fair accordance make:
And if he then with victory can lin,
He shall his days with peace bring to his earthly inn.

31

His son, hight Vortipore, shall him succeed
In kingdom, but not in felicity;
Yet shall he long time war with happy speed,
And with great honor many battles try,
But at the last to the importunity
Of froward fortune shall be forced to yield.
But his son Malgo shall full mightily
Avenge his father's loss with spear and shield,
And his proud foes discomfit in victorious field.

32

Behold the man, and tell me, Britomart,
If aye more goodly creature thou didst see;
How like a giant in each manly part
Bears he himself with portly majesty,
That one of the old Heroës seems to be.
He the six islands, comprovincial
In ancient times unto great Britainy,

28.8  *rathe* soon.
29.2  *his image dead* an image of himself after he is dead.
29.5  *Constantius* Constantine, Cador's son and Arthur's successor. According to Geoffrey of Monmouth (11.4), Constantine was killed and succeeded by his nephew Aurelius Conan; the unnamed son of Britomart and Artegall occupies Conan's role in the chronicles with some softening of the details.

30.5  *Mercians* Mercia was an early Anglo-Saxon kingdom in southern England.
31.3  *speed* success.
31.9  *discomfit* defeat.
32.4  *portly* imposing.
32.6  *six islands, comprovincial* Ireland, Iceland, Gotland, the Orkneys, Norway, and Denmark.

Shall to the same reduce, and to him call
Their sundry kings to do their homage several.

### 33

All which his son Careticus awhile
Shall well defend, and Saxons' power suppress,
Until a stranger king from unknown soil
Arriving, him with multitude oppress;
Great Gormond, having with huge mightiness
Ireland subdued and therein fixed his throne,
Like a swift otter, fell through emptiness,
Shall overswim the sea with many one
Of his Norveyses, to assist the Britons' fone.

### 34

He in his fury all shall overrun,
And holy church with faithless hands deface,
That thy sad people, utterly fordone,
Shall to the utmost mountains fly apace.
Was never so great waste in any place,
Nor so foul outrage done by living men;
For all thy cities they shall sack and race,
And the green grass that groweth, they shall bren,
That even the wild beast shall die in starvèd den.

### 35

Whiles thus thy Britons do in languor pine,
Proud Etheldred shall from the north arise,
Serving the ambitious will of Augustine,
And, passing Dee with hardy enterprise,
Shall back repulse the valiant Brockwell twice,
And Bangor with massacred martyrs fill,
But the third time shall rue his foolhardice:
For Cadwan, pitying his people's ill,
Shall stoutly him defeat, and thousand Saxons kill.

### 36

But after him, Cadwallon mightily
On his son Edwin all those wrongs shall wreak,
Ne shall avail the wicked sorcery
Of false Pellite his purposes to break,
But him shall slay, and on a gallows bleak
Shall give the enchanter his unhappy hire;
Then shall the Britons, late dismayed and weak,
From their long vassalage gin to respire,
And on their paynim foes avenge their rankled ire.

33.9 *Norveyses* Norwegians. *fone* foes.
34.7 *race* raze.
34.8 *bren* burn.
35.2 *Etheldred* Athelfrid, king of Northumbria (d. 616); the narrative here becomes more securely historical.
35.3 *Augustine* St. Augustine of Canterbury (d. ca. 605), who converted the Saxon king Athelbert to Christianity and became the first Archbishop of Canterbury.

35.4 *Dee* the River Dee in northern Wales.
35.7 *foolhardice* foolhardiness.
36.6 *hire* pay.
36.8 *respire* revive.
36.9 *paynim* pagan.

### 37

Ne shall he yet his wrath so mitigate,
Till both the sons of Edwin he have slain,
Offric and Osric, twins unfortunate,
Both slain in battle upon Laybourn plain,
Together with the king of Lothian,
Hight Adin, and the king of Orkeny,
Both joint partakers of their fatal pain;
But Penda, fearful of like destiny,
Shall yield himself his leige man, and swear fealty.

### 38

Him shall he make his fatal instrument
To afflict the other Saxons unsubdued,
He marching forth with fury insolent
Against the good king Oswald, who, endued
With heavenly power and by angels rescued,
All holding crosses in their hands on high,
Shall him defeat withouten blood imbrued;
Of which, that field for endless memory
Shall Heavenfield be called to all posterity.

### 39

Whereat Cadwallon, wroth, shall forth issue
And an huge host into Northumber lead,
With which he godly Oswald shall subdue,
And crown with martyrdom his sacred head.
Whose brother Oswin, daunted with like dread,
With price of silver shall his kingdom buy,
And Penda, seeking him adown to tread,
Shall tread adown, and do him foully die,
But shall with gifts his lord Cadwallon pacify.

### 40

Then shall Cadwallon die, and then the reign
Of Britons eke with him at once shall die;
Ne shall the good Cadwallader with pain
Or power be able it to remedy
When the full time prefixed by destiny
Shall be expired of Britons' regiment.
For heaven itself shall their success envy,
And them with plagues and murrains pestilent
Consume, till all their warlike puissance be spent.

### 41

Yet after all these sorrows and huge hills
Of dying people during eight years' space,
Cadwallader, not yielding to his ills,
From Armoric, where long in wretched case
He lived, returning to his native place,
Shall be by vision stayed from his intent:
For the heavens have decreëd to displace

37.5  *Lothian* Scotland.
38.7  *imbrued* stained.

41.4  *Armoric* Armorica, i.e., Brittany.

The Britons, for their sins' due punishment,
And to the Saxons overgive their government.

### 42

Then woe, and woe, and everlasting woe
Be to the Briton babe that shall be born
To live in thralldom of his father's foe.
Late king, now captive, late lord, now forlorn,
The world's reproach, the cruel victor's scorn,
Banished from princely bower to wasteful wood:
O who shall help me to lament and mourn
The royal seed, the antique Trojan blood,
Whose empire longer here than ever any stood?

### 43

The damsel was full deep empassionèd,
Both for his grief and for her people's sake,
Whose future woes so plain he fashionèd,
And sighing sore, at length him thus bespake:
Ah, but will heaven's fury never slake,
Nor vengeance huge relent itself at last?
Will not long misery late mercy make,
But shall their name forever be defaced,
And quite from off the earth their memory be rased?

### 44

Nay, but the term (said he) is limited
That in this thralldom Britons shall abide,
And the just revolution measurèd
That they as strangers shall be notified.
For twice four hundred years shall be supplied
Ere they to former rule restored shall be
And their importune fates all satisfied;
Yet during this their most obscurity
Their beams shall oft break forth, that men them fair may see.

### 45

For Roderick, whose surname shall be Great,
Shall of himself a brave ensample show,
That Saxon kings his friendship shall entreat;
And Howell Dha shall goodly well endue
The salvage minds with skill of just and true;
Then Griffith Conan also shall uprear
His dreaded head, and the old sparks renew
Of native courage, that his foes shall fear
Lest back again the kingdom he from them should bear.

### 46

Ne shall the Saxons selves all peaceably
Enjoy the crown which they from Britons won
First ill, and after rulèd wickedly;

42.6  *wasteful* desolate.          44.4  *notified* regarded.
43.9  *rased* erased.               44.7  *importune* troubling.
44.3  *just* exact.                 45.5  *salvage* savage.

For ere two hundred years be full outrun,
There shall a raven far from rising sun
With his wide wings upon them fiercely fly,
And bid his faithless chickens overrun
The fruitful plains, and with fell cruelty
In their avenge tread down the victors' surquidry.

47

Yet shall a third both these and thine subdue;
There shall a lion from the sea-board wood
Of Neustria come roaring, with a crew
Of hungry whelps, his battailous bold brood,
Whose claws were newly dipped in cruddy blood,
That from the Danisk tyrant's head shall rend
The usurpèd crown, as if that he were wood,
And the spoil of the country conquerèd
Amongst his young ones shall divide with bountihead.

48

Tho when the term is full accomplishèd,
There shall a spark of fire, which hath long while
Been in his ashes rakèd up and hid,
Be freshly kindled in the fruitful isle
Of Mona, where it lurkèd in exile;
Which shall break forth into bright burning flame
And reach into the house that bears the style
Of royal majesty and sovereign name:
So shall the Briton blood their crown again reclaim.

49

Thenceforth eternal union shall be made
Between the nations different afore,
And sacred peace shall lovingly persuade
The warlike minds to learn her goodly lore,
And civil arms to exercise no more;
Then shall a royal virgin reign, which shall
Stretch her white rod over the Belgic shore
And the great Castle smite so sore withal
That it shall make him shake and shortly learn to fall.

50

But yet the end is not. There Merlin stayed,
As overcomen of the spirits' power,
Or other ghastly spectacle dismayed
That secretly he saw, yet note discover;
Which sudden fit and half ecstatic stour

46.5 *raven* The battle sign of the Danish Vikings, whose raids on England began in the eighth century.
46.9 *avenge* vengeance. *surquidry* arrogance.
47.2 *lion* William the Conqueror.
47.3 *Neustria* Normandy.
47.4 *battailous* warlike.
47.5 *cruddy* clotted.
47.7 *wood* insane.
47.9 *bountihead* generosity.

48.5 *Mona* Anglesey, the last outpost of Welsh resistance to the English Crown in the thirteenth century.
48.7 *style* title.
49.7 *the Belgic shore* The Netherlands; the reference is to the English expeditionary force of 1585 in support of the Dutch rebellion against Spanish rule.
49.8 *the great Castle* Castile, i.e., Spain.
50.4 *note* could not. *discover* disclose.
50.5 *stour* struggle.

When the two fearful women saw, they grew
Greatly confusèd in behavior.
At last, the fury past, to former hue
He turned again, and cheerful looks (as erst) did show.

51

Then, when themselves they well instructed had
Of all that needed them to be inquired,
They, both conceiving hope of comfort glad,
With lighter hearts unto their home retired,
Where they in secret counsel close conspired
How to effect so hard an enterprise
And to possess the purpose they desired;
Now this, now that twixt them they did devise,
And diverse plots did frame to mask in strange disguise.

52

At last the nurse in her foolhardy wit
Conceived a bold device, and thus bespake:
Daughter, I deem that counsel aye most fit
That of the time doth due advantage take.
Ye see that good king Uther now doth make
Strong war upon the paynim brethren, hight
Octa and Oza, whom he lately brake
Beside Caer-Verulam in victorious fight,
That now all Britainy doth burn in armes bright.

53

That therefore nought our passage may impeach,
Let us in feignèd arms ourselves disguise,
And our weak hands (whom need new strength shall teach)
The dreadful spear and shield to exercise;
Ne certes, daughter, that same warlike wise
I ween would you misseem, for ye been tall
And large of limb to achieve an hard emprise,
Ne ought ye want but skill, which practice small
Will bring, and shortly make you a maid martial.

54

And sooth, it ought your courage much inflame
To hear so often, in that royal house
From whence to none inferior ye came,
Bards tell of many women valorous
Which have full many feats adventurous
Performed, in paragon of proudest men:
The bold Bunduca, whose victorious

52.5–9   Spenser here makes the present tense of his poem momentarily contemporary with the battle described in Geoffrey of Monmouth 8.23. Octa and Oza (more commonly Eosa) are sons of Hengist, one of the first of the Anglo-Saxon invaders.
52.6   *paynim* pagan.
52.8   *Caer-Verulam* The Roman city of Verulamium, now St. Albans; Spenser adds a Welsh prefix.

53.1   *impeach* impede.
53.3   *(whom need new strength shall teach)* The revised reading of the 1596 edition, replacing "(need makes good scholars) teach."
54.6   *paragon* emulation.
54.7   *Bunduca* Boudicca, a first-century British queen, leader of a nearly successful revolt against the Romans.

Exploits made Rome to quake, stout Gwendolyn,
Renowmèd Martia, and redoubted Emmilen.

### 55

And that, which more than all the rest may sway,
Late days' ensample, which these eyes beheld,
In the last field before Menevia
Which Uther with those foreign pagans held,
I saw a Saxon virgin, the which felled
Great Ulfin thrice upon the bloody plain,
And had not Carados her hand withheld
From rash revenge, she had him surely slain;
Yet Carados himself from her escaped with pain.

### 56

Ah, read (quoth Britomart) how is she hight?
Fair Angela (quoth she) men do her call,
No whit less fair than terrible in fight:
She hath the leading of a martial
And mighty people, dreaded more than all
The other Saxons, which do for her sake
And love themselves of her name Angles call.
Therefore, fair infant, her ensample make
Unto thyself, and equal courage to thee take.

### 57

Her hearty words so deep into the mind
Of the young damsel sunk, that great desire
Of warlike arms in her forthwith they tind,
And generous, stout courage did inspire,
That she resolved, unweeting to her sire,
Adventurous knighthood on herself to don,
And counseled with her nurse her maid's attire
To turn into a massy habergeon,
And bad her all things put in readiness anon.

### 58

The old woman nought that needed did omit,
But all things did conveniently purvey.
It fortunèd (so time their turn did fit)
A band of Britons riding on foray
Few days before had gotten a great prey
Of Saxon goods, amongst the which was seen
A goodly armor and full rich array
Which longed to Angela, the Saxon queen,
All fretted round with gold, and goodly well beseen.

---

**54.8** *Gwendolyn* Discarded wife of Brut's son and successor Locrine; "being beyond measure indignant," she gathered an army, killed her former husband in battle, and ruled in his stead (Geoffrey of Monmouth, 2.4–6).
**54.9** *Martia* Wife of the early British king Guithelin, and regent after his death; she is said to have crafted the code later known as Mercian law (Geoffrey of Monmouth, 3.13). *redoubted Emmilen* Not decisively identified; depending on the identification, "redoubted" could mean that she is either reverenced or feared.
**55.3** *Menevia* St. David's, on the southwest coast of Wales. The battle is recounted by Geoffrey of Monmouth (8.16), but with no mention of the Saxon virgin.
**56.8** *infant* princess.
**57.3** *tind* kindle.

### 59

The same, with all the other ornaments,
King Ryence causèd to be hangèd by
In his chief church, for endless monuments
Of his success and gladful victory;
Of which herself avising readily,
In the evening late old Glauce thither led
Fair Britomart, and that same armory
Down taking, her therein apparelèd
Well as she might, and with brave baldric garnishèd.

### 60

Beside those arms there stood a mighty spear,
Which Bladud made by magic art of yore,
And used the same in battle aye to bear;
Sith which it had been here preserved in store
For his great virtues provèd long afore:
For never wight so fast in sell could sit
But him perforce unto the ground it bore.
Both spear she took and shield, which hung by it;
Both spear and shield of great power, for her purpose fit.

### 61

Thus when she had the virgin all arrayed,
Another harness, which did hang thereby,
About herself she dight, that the young maid
She might in equal arms accompany,
And as her squire attend her carefully;
Tho to their ready steeds they clomb full light,
And through back ways, that none might them espy,
Covered with secret cloud of silent night,
Themselves they forth conveyed, and passèd forward right.

### 62

Ne rested they, till that to Faery land
They came, as Merlin them directed late,
Where, meeting with this Redcross Knight, she found
Of diverse things discourses to dilate,
But most of Artegall and his estate.
At last their ways so fell, that they mote part;
Then each to other, well affectionate,
Friendship professèd with unfeignèd heart;
The Redcross Knight diversed, but forth rode Britomart.

59.5  *avising readily* observing in good time.

60.2  *Bladud* An early British king with an interest in magic;
father of Lear (Geoffrey of Monmouth 2.10).

60.6  *sell* saddle.

62.9  *diversed* took another way.

CANTO IV

*Bold Marinell of Britomart*
*is thrown on the Rich Strand;*
*Fair Florimell of Arthur is*
*long followed, but not found.*

### 1

Where is the antique glory now become,
That whilom wont in women to appear?
Where be the brave achievements done by some?
Where be the battles, where the shield and spear
And all the conquests which them high did rear,
That matter made for famous poets' verse,
And boastful men so oft abashed to hear?
Been they all dead, and laid in doleful hearse?
Or done they only sleep, and shall again reverse?

### 2

If they be dead, then woe is me therefore;
But if they sleep, O let them soon awake,
For all too long I burn with envy sore
To hear the warlike feats which Homer spake
Of bold Penthesilee, which made a lake
Of Greekish blood so oft in Trojan plain.
But when I read how stout Deborah strake
Proud Sisera, and how Camilla hath slain
The huge Orsilochus, I swell with great disdain.

### 3

Yet these and all that else had puissance
Cannot with noble Britomart compare,
As well for glory of great valiance
As for pure chastity and virtue rare
That all her goodly deeds do well declare.
Well worthy stock, from which the branches sprung
That in late years so fair a blossom bare
As thee, O queen, the matter of my song,
Whose lineage from this lady I derive along.

### 4

Who when through speeches with the Redcross Knight
She learnèd had the estate of Artegall
And in each point herself informed aright,
A friendly league of love perpetual
She with him bound, and congé took withal.
Then he forth on his journey did proceed,
To seek adventures which mote him befall
And win him worship through his warlike deed,
Which always of his pains he made the chiefest meed.

### 5

But Britomart kept on her former course,
Ne ever doffed her arms, but all the way
Grew pensive through that amorous discourse

---

1.9   *reverse* return.

2.5   *Penthesilee* Penthesilea, an Amazon who fought on the Trojan side in the Trojan war; she arrived after the death of Hector and is not in fact mentioned by Homer.

2.7   *Deborah* A Hebrew prophetess; her role in the defeat of Sisera (another woman actually kills him) is told in Judges 4.4–21.

2.8   *Camilla* A woman fighting against the Trojans in Book 11 of the *Aeneid*.

4.5   *congé* formal farewell.

4.6–9   With these lines the Redcross Knight exits the poem as we have it.

By which the Redcross Knight did erst display
Her lover's shape and chivalrous array;
A thousand thoughts she fashioned in her mind,
And in her feigning fancy did portray
Him such as fittest she for love could find,
Wise, warlike, personable, courteous, and kind.

### 6

With such self-pleasing thoughts her wound she fed,
And thought so to beguile her grievous smart;
But so her smart was much more grievous bred,
And the deep wound more deep engored her heart,
That nought but death her dolor mote depart.
So forth she rode without repose or rest,
Searching all lands and each remotest part,
Following the guidance of her blinded guest,
Till that to the seacoast at length she her addressed.

### 7

There she alighted from her lightfoot beast,
And, sitting down upon the rocky shore,
Bade her old squire unlace her lofty crest;
Tho having viewed awhile the surges hoar
That gainst the craggy cliffs did loudly roar
And in their raging surquidry disdained
That the fast earth affronted them so sore
And their devouring covetise restrained,
Thereat she sighèd deep, and after thus complained:

### 8

Huge sea of sorrow and tempestuous grief,
Wherein my feeble bark is tossèd long
Far from the hopèd haven of relief,
Why do thy cruel billows beat so strong
And thy moist mountains each on others throng,
Threatening to swallow up my fearful life?
O do thy cruel wrath and spiteful wrong
At length allay, and stint thy stormy strife,
Which in these troubled bowels reigns and rageth rife.

### 9

For else my feeble vessel, crazed and cracked
Through thy strong buffets and outrageous blows,
Cannot endure, but needs it must be wracked
On the rough rocks or on the sandy shallows,
The whiles that love it steers and fortune rows;
Love, my lewd pilot, hath a restless mind,
And fortune boatswain no assurance knows,
But sail withouten stars gainst tide and wind:
How can they other do, sith both are bold and blind?

---

6.8    *her blinded guest* Cupid.
7.6    *surquidry* arrogance.
7.7    *fast* firmly set.

7.8    *covetise* covetousness.
9.6    *lewd* ignorant, though with some of the modern sense of
lewdness as well.

### 10

Thou god of winds that reignest in the seas,
That reignest also in the continent,
At last blow up some gentle gale of ease,
The which may bring my ship, ere it be rent,
Unto the gladsome port of her intent;
Then when I shall myself in safety see,
A table for eternal monument
Of thy great grace and my great jeopardy,
Great Neptune, I avow to hallow unto thee.

### 11

Then, sighing softly sore and inly deep,
She shut up all her plaint in privy grief;
For her great courage would not let her weep,
Till that old Glauce gan with sharp reprief
Her to restrain, and give her good relief
Through hope of those which Merlin had her told
Should of her name and nation be chief,
And fetch their being from the sacred mold
Of her immortal womb, to be in heaven enrolled.

### 12

Thus as she her recomforted, she spied
Where far away one all in armor bright
With hasty gallop towards her did ride.
Her dolor soon she ceased, and on her dight
Her helmet, to her courser mounting light;
Her former sorrow into sudden wrath,
Both cousin passions of distroubled sprite,
Converting, forth she beats the dusty path:
Love and despite at once her courage kindled hath.

### 13

As when a foggy mist hath overcast
The face of heaven and the clear air engrossed,
The world in darkness dwells, till that at last
The watery south wind from the seaboard coast
Upblowing, doth disperse the vapor loosed,
And pours itself forth in a stormy shower:
So the fair Britomart, having disclosed
Her cloudy care into a wrathful stour,
The mist of grief dissolved did into vengeance pour.

### 14

Eftsoons her goodly shield addressing fair,
That mortal spear she in her hand did take
And unto battle did herself prepare.
The knight, approaching, sternly her bespake:
Sir knight, that dost thy voyage rashly make
By this forbidden way in my despite,

10.7 *table* tablet.
11.4 *reprief* reproof.
13.2 *engrossed* thickened.

13.7 *disclosed* set loose.
13.8 *stour* storm.
14.1 *addressing fair* positioning correctly.

Ne dost by others' death ensample take,
I read thee soon retire whiles thou hast might,
Lest afterwards it be too late to take thy flight.

### 15

Ythrilled with deep disdain of his proud threat,
She shortly thus: Fly they that need to fly;
Words fearen babes. I mean not thee entreat
To pass, but maugre thee will pass or die.
Ne longer stayed for the other to reply,
But with sharp spear the rest made dearly known.
Strongly the strange knight ran, and sturdily
Struck her full on the breast, that made her down
Decline her head and touch her crupper with her crown.

### 16

But she again him in the shield did smite
With so fierce fury and great puissance,
That through his threesquare scutcheon piercing quite
And through his mailèd hauberk, by mischance
The wicked steel through his left side did glance;
Him so transfixèd she before her bore
Beyond his croup the length of all her lance,
Till sadly sousing on the sandy shore,
He tumbled on an heap and wallowed in his gore.

### 17

Like as the sacred ox, that careless stands
With gilden horns and flowery garlands crowned,
Proud of his dying honor and dear bands,
Whiles the altars fume with frankincense around,
All suddenly with mortal stroke astound
Doth groveling fall, and with his streaming gore
Distains the pillars and the holy ground
And the fair flowers that deckèd him afore:
So fell proud Marinell upon the precious shore.

### 18

The martial maid stayed not him to lament,
But forward rode, and kept her ready way
Along the strand, which as she overwent,
She saw bestrewèd all with rich array
Of pearls and precious stones of great assay,
And all the gravel mixed with golden oar;
Whereat she wondered much, but would not stay
For gold or pearls or precious stones an hour,
But them despisèd all, for all was in her power.

14.8    *read* advise.
15.1    *Ythrilled* pierced.
15.3    *fearen* frighten.
15.4    *maugre* in spite of.
16.3    *threesquare scutcheon* three-sided shield.
16.4    *mailèd hauberk* coat of chain mail.
16.7    *croup* crupper.

16.8    *sousing* falling.
17.1    *careless* without care.
17.3    *dying honor* honor derived from dying.
17.5    *astound* stunned.
17.7    *Distains* stains.
18.5    *assay* worth.

### 19

Whiles thus he lay in deadly stonishment,
Tidings hereof came to his mother's ear.
His mother was the black-browed Cymoent,
The daughter of great Nereus, which did bear
This warlike son unto an earthly peer,
The famous Dumarin, who on a day
Finding the nymph asleep in secret where
As he by chance did wander that same way,
Was taken with her love, and by her closely lay.

### 20

There he this knight of her begot, whom born
She of his father Marinell did name,
And in a rocky cave as wight forlorn
Long time she fostered up, till he became
A mighty man at arms, and mickle fame
Did get through great adventures by him done;
For never man he suffered by that same
Rich Strand to travel, whereas he did won,
But that he must do battle with the sea-nymph's son.

### 21

An hundred knights of honorable name
He had subdued, and them his vassals made,
That through all Faery land his noble fame
Now blazèd was, and fear did all invade,
That none durst passen through that perilous glade.
And to advance his name and glory more,
Her sea-god sire she dearly did persuade
To endow her son with treasure and rich store
Bove all the sons that were of earthly wombs ybore.

### 22

The god did grant his daughter's dear demand
To done his nephew in all riches flow;
Eftsoons his heapèd waves he did command
Out of their hollow bosom forth to throw
All the huge treasure which the sea below
Had in his greedy gulf devoured deep,
And him enrichèd through the overthrow
And wrecks of many wretches, which did weep
And often wail their wealth, which he from them did keep.

### 23

Shortly upon that shore there heapèd was
Exceeding riches and all precious things,
The spoil of all the world, that it did pass
The wealth of the east, and pomp of Persian kings;
Gold, amber, ivory, pearls, ouches, rings,

19.4   *Nereus* A Greek sea-god, father of fifty daughters known
as the Nereids; Spenser later (IV.xi.48–51) gives a catalogue
of their names, in which Cymoent is called Cymodoce.
19.6   *Dumarin* The name means "of the sea" in French.
19.7   *where* place.

20.5   *mickle* much.
20.8   *won* dwell.
21.7   *dearly* earnestly.
23.5   *ouches* brooches or necklaces.

And all that else was precious and dear,
The sea unto him voluntary brings,
That shortly he a great lord did appear
As was in all the land of Faery or elsewhere.

24

Thereto he was a doughty, dreaded knight,
Tried often to the scathe of many dear,
That none in equal arms him matchen might,
The which his mother seeing, gan to fear
Lest his too haughty hardiness might rear
Some hard mishap, in hazard of his life;
Forthy she oft him counseled to forbear
The bloody battle and to stir up strife,
But after all his war to rest his weary knife.

25

And for his more assurance, she inquired
One day of Proteus by his mighty spell
(For Proteus was with prophecy inspired)
Her dear son's destiny to her to tell,
And the sad end of her sweet Marinell;
Who through foresight of his eternal skill
Bade her from womankind to keep him well,
For of a woman he should have much ill:
A virgin strange and stout him should dismay or kill.

26

Forthy she gave him warning every day
The love of women not to entertain:
A lesson too, too hard for living clay,
From love in course of nature to refrain.
Yet he his mother's lore did well retain,
And ever from fair ladies' love did fly;
Yet many ladies fair did oft complain
That they for love of him would algates die.
Die whoso list for him, he was love's enemy.

27

But ah, who can deceive his destiny,
Or ween by warning to avoid his fate?
That when he sleeps in most security
And safest seems, him soonest doth amate,
And findeth due effect or soon or late.
So feeble is the power of fleshly arm.
His mother bade him women's love to hate,
For she of woman's force did fear no harm;
So weening to have armed him, she did quite disarm.

---

**24.2**  *to the scathe of many dear* at great cost to the pain of many.

**25.2**  *Proteus* A Greek sea-god primarily famous for his shape-shifting powers.

**25.9**  *dismay* overthrow.

**26.5**  *lore* teaching.

**27.4**  *amate* cast down.

### 28

This was that woman, this that deadly wound,
That Proteus prophesied should him dismay,
The which his mother vainly did expound
To be heart-wounding love, which should assay
To bring her son unto his last decay.
So tickle be the terms of mortal state
And full of subtle sophisms, which do play
With double senses and with false debate
To approve the unknown purpose of eternal fate.

### 29

Too true the famous Marinell it found,
Who through late trial on that wealthy strand
Inglorious now lies in senseless swound
Through heavy stroke of Britomartis' hand;
Which when his mother dear did understand
And heavy tidings heard whereas she played
Amongst her watery sisters by a pond,
Gathering sweet daffadillies to have made
Gay garlands, from the sun their foreheads fair to shade,

### 30

Eftsoons both flowers and garlands far away
She flung, and her fair dewy locks yrent.
To sorrow huge she turned her former play,
And gamesome mirth to grievous dreariment;
She threw herself down on the continent,
Ne word did speak, but lay as in a swoon,
Whiles all her sisters did for her lament
With yelling outcries and with shrieking soun,
And every one did tear her garland from her crown.

### 31

Soon as she up out of her deadly fit
Arose, she bade her charet to be brought,
And all her sisters that with her did sit
Bade eke at once their charets to be sought.
Tho full of bitter grief and pensive thought,
She to her wagon clomb; clomb all the rest,
And forth together went, with sorrow fraught.
The waves, obedient to their behest,
Them yielded ready passage and their rage surceased.

### 32

Great Neptune stood amazèd at their sight
Whiles on his broad, round back they softly slid,
And eke himself mourned at their mournful plight,
Yet wist not what their wailing meant, yet did
For great compassion of their sorrow bid

---

28.6  *tickle* unreliable.
28.9  *approve* achieve.
29.3  *swound* swoon.

30.5  *continent* ground.
30.8  *soun* sound.
31.2  *charet* carriage.

His mighty waters to them buxom be:
Eftsoons the roaring billows still abid,
And all the grisly monsters of the sea
Stood gaping at their gate, and wondered them to see.

### 33

A team of dolphins, rangèd in array,
Drew the smooth charet of sad Cymoent;
They were all taught by Triton to obey
To the long reins at her commandement.
As swift as swallows on the waves they went,
That their broad flaggy fins no foam did rear,
Ne bubbling roundel they behind them sent;
The rest of other fishes drawen were,
Which with their finny oars the swelling sea did shear.

### 34

Soon as they been arrived upon the brim
Of the Rich Strand, their charets they forlore,
And let their teamèd fishes softly swim
Along the margent of the foamy shore,
Lest they their fins should bruise and surbate sore
Their tender feet upon the stony ground;
And coming to the place where all in gore
And cruddy blood enwallowèd they found
The luckless Marinell, lying in deadly swound,

### 35

His mother swoonèd thrice, and the third time
Could scarce recovered be out of her pain.
Had she not been devoid of mortal slime,
She should not then have been relived again;
But soon as life recovered had the rein,
She made so piteous moan and dear wayment,
That the hard rocks could scarce from tears refrain,
And all her sister nymphs with one consent
Supplied her sobbing breaches with sad complement.

### 36

Dear image of myself (she said), that is,
The wretched son of wretched mother born,
Is this thine high advancement, O is this
The immortal name with which thee, yet unborn,
Thy grandsire Nereus promised to adorn?
Now liest thou of life and honor reft;
Now liest thou a lump of earth forlorn,
Ne of thy late life memory is left,
Ne can thy irrevocable destiny be weft.

32.6  *buxom* yielding.
32.7  *still abid* stayed still.
33.3  *Triton* son of Neptune.
33.6  *flaggy* floppy.
33.7  *roundel* circular pattern.
34.2  *forlore* abandoned.

34.5  *surbate* hurt.
34.8  *cruddy* clotted.
35.4  *relived* brought back to life.
35.6  *wayment* lamentation.
35.9  Their weeping filled up the gaps in her weeping.
36.9  *weft* waived.

37

Fond Proteus, father of false prophecies,
And they more fond, that credit to thee give,
Not this the work of woman's hand ywis,
That so deep wound through these dear members drive.
I fearèd love; but they that love do live,
But they that die do neither love nor hate.
Natheless to thee thy folly I forgive,
And to myself and to accursèd fate
The guilt I do ascribe: dear wisdom bought too late.


38

O what avails it of immortal seed
To been ybred and never born to die?
Far better I it deem to die with speed
Than waste in woe and wailful misery.
Who dies, the utmost dolor doth aby,
But who that lives, is left to wail his loss;
So life is loss and death felicity.
Sad life worse than glad death, and greater cross
To see friend's grave than, dead, the grave self to engross.


39

But if the heavens did his days envy
And my short bliss malign, yet mote they well
Thus much afford me, ere that he did die
That the dim eyes of my dear Marinell
I mote have closèd, and him bade farewell,
Sith other offices for mother meet
They would not grant.
Yet maugre them, farewell, my sweetest sweet;
Farewell, my sweetest son, sith we no more shall meet.


40

Thus when they all had sorrowèd their fill,
They softly gan to search his grisly wound;
And that they might him handle more at will,
They him disarmed, and spreading on the ground
Their watchet mantles, fringed with silver round,
They softly wiped away the jelly blood
From the orifice; which having well upbound,
They poured in sovereign balm and nectar good,
Good both for earthly medicine and for heavenly food.


41

Tho when the lily-handed Liagore
(This Liagore whilom had learnèd skill
In leech's craft, by great Apollo's lore,
Sith her whilom upon high Pindus hill
He lovèd, and at last her womb did fill

38.5  *aby* suffer.
38.9  To see a friend in the grave than to be dead and fill the
grave oneself.

40.5  *watchet* light blue.
41.3  *leech's* physician's.

With heavenly seed, whereof wise Paean sprung)
Did feel his pulse, she knew there stayèd still
Some little life his feeble sprites among;
Which to his mother told, despair she from her flung.

### 42

Tho up him taking in their tender hands,
They easily unto her charet bear;
Her team at her commandment quiet stands,
Whiles they the corse into her wagon rear
And strew with flowers the lamentable bier.
Then all the rest into their coaches climb,
And through the brackish waves their passage shear;
Upon great Neptune's neck they softly swim,
And to her watery chamber swiftly carry him.

### 43

Deep in the bottom of the sea, her bower
Is built of hollow billows heapèd high,
Like to thick clouds that threat a stormy shower,
And vaulted all within, like to the sky
In which the gods do dwell eternally;
There they him laid in easy couch well dight,
And sent in haste for Tryphon to apply
Salves to his wounds, and medicines of might:
For Tryphon of sea-gods the sovereign leech is hight.

### 44

The whiles the nymphs sit all about him round,
Lamenting his mishap and heavy plight;
And oft his mother, viewing his wide wound,
Cursèd the hand that did so deadly smite
Her dearest son, her dearest heart's delight.
But none of all those curses overtook
The warlike maid, the ensample of that might,
But fairly well she thrived, and well did brook
Her noble deeds, ne her right course for ought forsook.

### 45

Yet did false Archimage her still pursue,
To bring to pass his mischievous intent,
Now that he had her singled from the crew
Of courteous knights, the Prince and Faery gent,
Whom late in chase of beauty excellent
She left, pursuing that same foster strong;
Of whose foul outrage they, impatient
And full of fiery zeal, him followed long,
To rescue her from shame and to revenge her wrong.

---

**41.6**  *Paean* Physician to the gods in Homer; the parentage
given here is Spenser's invention.
**42.4**  *corse* body.
**43.7**  *Tryphon* Not a figure in classical mythology.
**44.8**  *fairly* very.  *brook* profit from.

**45.1**  *Archimage* Archimago, an evil magician who figures
prominently in Book I and briefly in Book II; this is the last
mention of him in the poem.
**45.4**  *gent* noble.

### 46

Through thick and thin, through mountains and through plains
Those two great champions did at once pursue
The fearful damsel with incessant pains;
Who from them fled, as lightfoot hare from view
Of hunter swift and scent of houndes true.
At last they came unto a double way,
Where, doubtful which to take her to rescue,
Themselves they did dispart, each to assay
Whether more happy were to win so goodly prey.

### 47

But Timias, the Prince's gentle squire,
That lady's love unto his lord forlent,
And with proud envy and indignant ire
After that wicked foster fiercely went.
So been they three three sundry ways ybent,
But fairest fortune to the Prince befell,
Whose chance it was, that soon he did repent,
To take that way in which that damozel
Was fled afore, afraid of him as fiend of hell.

### 48

At last of her far off he gainèd view;
Then gan he freshly prick his foamy steed,
And ever as he nigher to her drew,
So evermore he did increase his speed,
And of each turning still kept wary heed.
Aloud to her he oftentimes did call,
To do away vain doubt and needless dread;
Full mild to her he spake, and oft let fall
Many meek words, to stay and comfort her withal.

### 49

But nothing might relent her hasty flight,
So deep the deadly fear of that foul swain
Was erst impressèd in her gentle sprite;
Like as a fearful dove, which through the rain
Of the wide air her way does cut amain,
Having far off espied a tassel gent
Which after her his nimble wings doth strain,
Doubleth her haste for fear to be forhent,
And with her pinions cleaves the liquid firmament.

### 50

With no less haste, and eke with no less dread,
That fearful lady fled from him, that meant
To her no evil thought nor evil deed.
Yet former fear of being foully shent
Carried her forward with her first intent;

---

**46.2** *at once* together.
**46.8** *dispart* separate.
**46.9** *Whether more happy were* which of them would be luckier.

**47.2** *forlent* gave over.
**49.6** *tassel gent* tercel-gentle, a male falcon.
**49.8** *forhent* caught.
**50.4** *shent* harmed.

And though, oft looking backward, well she viewed
Herself freed from that foster insolent
And that it was a knight which now her sued,
Yet she no less the knight feared than that villain rude.

### 51

His uncouth shield and strange arms her dismayed,
Whose like in Faery land were seldom seen,
That fast she from him fled, no less afraid
Than of wild beasts if she had chasèd been;
Yet he her followed still with courage keen,
So long that now the golden Hesperus
Was mounted high in top of heaven sheen,
And warned his other brethren joyëous
To light their blessèd lamps in Jove's eternal house.

### 52

All suddenly dim wox the dampish air,
And grisly shadows covered heaven bright,
That now with thousand stars was deckèd fair;
Which when the Prince beheld, a loathful sight,
And that perforce for want of longer light
He mote surcease his suit, and lose the hope
Of his long labor, he gan foully wite
His wicked fortune that had turned aslope,
And cursèd night that reft from him so goodly scope.

### 53

Tho when her ways he could no more descry,
But to and fro at disaventure strayed,
Like as a ship, whose lodestar suddenly
Covered with clouds, her pilot hath dismayed;
His wearisome pursuit perforce he stayed,
And from his lofty steed dismounting low,
Did let him forage. Down himself he laid
Upon the grassy ground, to sleep a throw;
The cold earth was his couch, the hard steel his pillow.

### 54

But gentle sleep envied him any rest.
Instead thereof, sad sorrow and disdain
Of his hard hap did vex his noble breast,
And thousand fancies beat his idle brain
With their light wings, the sights of semblants vain.
Oft did he wish that lady fair mote be
His Faery Queen, for whom he did complain,
Or that his Faery Queen were such as she,
And ever hasty night he blamèd bitterly.

---

**50.8**  *sued* pursued.
**51.1**  *uncouth* unknown. The designs on shields normally carry information about the identity of their possessor, but because of its magic powers Arthur's shield is kept covered in most circumstances.
**51.6**  *Hesperus* the planet Venus as the Evening Star.
**52.6**  *suit* pursuit.

**52.7**  *wite* blame.
**52.8**  *aslope* downwards.
**52.9**  *scope* sight.
**53.2**  *at disaventure* aimlessly.
**53.8**  *a throw* awhile.
**54.2**  *disdain* indignation.

### 55

Night, thou foul mother of annoyance sad,
Sister of heavy death and nurse of woe,
Which wast begot in heaven, but for thy bad
And brutish shape thrust down to hell below,
Where by the grim flood of Cocytus slow
Thy dwelling is, in Herebus' black house
(Black Herebus, thy husband, is the foe
Of all the gods), where thou, ungracious,
Half of thy days dost lead in horror hideous.

### 56

What had the eternal Maker need of thee
The world in his continual course to keep,
That dost all things deface, ne lettest see
The beauty of his work? Indeed, in sleep
The slothful body, that doth love to steep
His lustless limbs and drown his baser mind,
Doth praise thee oft, and oft from Stygian deep
Calls thee his goddess in his error blind,
And great Dame Nature's handmaid, cheering every kind.

### 57

But well I wote that to an heavy heart
Thou art the root and nurse of bitter cares,
Breeder of new, renewer of old smarts.
Instead of rest thou lendest railing tears,
Instead of sleep thou sendest troublous fears
And dreadful visions, in the which alive
The dreary image of sad death appears;
So from the weary spirit thou dost drive
Desirèd rest, and men of happiness deprive.

### 58

Under thy mantle black there hidden lie
Light-shunning theft and traitorous intent,
Abhorrèd bloodshed and vile felony,
Shameful deceit and danger imminent,
Foul horror and eke hellish dreariment.
All these I wote in thy protection be,
And light do shun, for fear of being shent;
For light ylike is loathed of them and thee,
And all that lewdness love, do hate the light to see.

### 59

For Day discovers all dishonest ways,
And showeth each thing as it is indeed;
The praises of high God he fair displays,
And his large bounty rightly doth aread.

**55.5** *Cocytus* One of the four rivers in the classical underworld.
**55.6** *Herebus* Erebus, god of darkness; in the mythological tradition sometimes the brother and sometimes, as here, the husband of Night.

**56.5** *steep* numb.
**56.7** *Stygian* Having to do with the Styx, another of the infernal rivers.
**59.4** *aread* declare.

Day's dearest children be the blessèd seed
Which darkness shall subdue and heaven win:
Truth is his daughter; he her first did breed,
Most sacred virgin, without spot of sin.
Our life is Day, but death with darkness doth begin.

### 60

O when will Day then turn to me again,
And bring with him his long expected light?
O Titan, haste to rear thy joyous wain:
Speed thee to spread abroad thy beames bright,
And chase away this too long lingering Night,
Chase her away from whence she came to hell.
She, she it is that hath me done despite;
There let her with the damnèd spirits dwell,
And yield her room to Day, that can it govern well.

### 61

Thus did the Prince that weary night outwear
In restless anguish and unquiet pain;
And early, ere the morrow did uprear
His dewy head out of the ocean main,
He up arose, as half in great disdain,
And clomb unto his steed. So forth he went,
With heavy look and lumpish pace, that plain
In him bewrayed great grudge and maltalent;
His steed eke seemed to apply his steps to his intent.

60.3 *Titan* The sun as Helios or Hyperion, from the    61.8 *maltalent* bad temper.
generation that preceded the Olympians. *wain* chariot.

CANTO V

*Prince Arthur hears of Florimell,*
*three fosters Timias wound;*
*Belphoebe finds him almost dead,*
*and reareth out of sound.*

### 1

Wonder it is to see in diverse minds
How diversely love doth his pageants play,
And shows his power in variable kinds:
The baser wit, whose idle thoughts alway
Are wont to cleave unto the lowly clay,
It stirreth up to sensual desire,
And in lewd sloth to waste his careless day;
But in brave sprite it kindles goodly fire,
That to all high desert and honor doth aspire.

### 2

Ne suffereth it uncomely idleness
In his free thought to build her sluggish nest,

0.4 *sound* swoon.

Ne suffereth it thought of ungentleness
Ever to creep into his noble brest,
But to the highest and the worthiest
Lifteth it up, that else would lowly fall.
It lets not fall, it lets it not to rest,
It lets not scarce this Prince to breathe at all,
But to his first pursuit him forward still doth call.

### 3

Who long time wandered through the forest wide
To find some issue thence, till that at last
He met a dwarf, that seemèd terrified
With some late peril which he hardly passed,
Or other accident which him aghast;
Of whom he askèd whence he lately came
And whither now he travelèd so fast,
For sore he swat, and, running through that same
Thick forest, was bescratched, and both his feet nigh lame.

### 4

Panting for breath, and almost out of heart,
The dwarf him answered, Sir, ill mote I stay
To tell the same. I lately did depart
From Faery court, where I have many a day
Servèd a gentle lady of great sway
And high account throughout all Elfin land,
Who lately left the same, and took this way.
Her now I seek, and if ye understand
Which way she farèd hath, good sir, tell out of hand.

### 5

What mister wight (said he), and how arrayed?
Royally clad (quoth he) in cloth of gold,
As meetest may beseem a noble maid;
Her fair locks in rich circlet be enrolled.
A fairer wight did never sun behold,
And on a palfrey rides more white than snow,
Yet she herself is whiter manifold.
The surest sign, whereby ye may her know,
Is that she is the fairest wight alive, I trow.

### 6

Now certes, swain (said he), such one, I ween,
Fast flying through this forest from her foe,
A foul, ill-favored foster, I have seen;
Herself, well as I might, I rescued tho,
But could not stay, so fast she did forego,
Carried away with wings of speedy fear.
Ah dearest God (quoth he), that is great woe
And wondrous ruth to all that shall it hear.
But can ye read, Sir, how I may her find, or where?

---

3.4  *hardly passed* barely escaped.      3.8  *swat* sweated.
3.5  *aghast* frightened.                 5.1  *mister wight* kind of person.

### 7

Perdy, me lever were to weeten that
(Said he) than ransom of the richest knight,
Or all the good that ever yet I gat.
But froward fortune and too forward night
Such happiness did, maugre, to me spite,
And fro me reft both life and light at one.
But dwarf, aread what is that lady bright
That through this forest wandereth thus alone;
For of her error strange I have great ruth and moan.

### 8

That lady is (quoth he), whereso she be,
The bountiest virgin and most debonair
That ever living eye I ween did see –
Lives none this day that may with her compare
In steadfast chastity and virtue rare,
The goodly ornaments of beauty bright –
And is yclepèd Florimell the fair,
Fair Florimell, beloved of many a knight,
But she loves none but one, that Marinell is hight.

### 9

A sea-nymph's son, that Marinell is hight,
Of my dear dame is lovèd dearly well;
In other none but him she sets delight,
All her delight is set on Marinell.
But he sets nought at all by Florimell,
For ladies' love his mother long ygo
Did him, they say, forwarn through sacred spell.
But fame now flies that of a foreign foe
He is yslain, which is the ground of all our woe.

### 10

Five days there be since he (they say) was slain,
And four since Florimell the court forwent,
And vowèd never to return again,
Till him alive or dead she did invent.
Therefore, fair sir, for love of knighthood gent
And honor of true ladies, if ye may,
By your good counsel or bold hardiment
Or succor her, or me direct the way;
Do one or other good, I you most humbly pray.

### 11

So may ye gain to you full great renowm
Of all good ladies through the world so wide,
And haply in her heart find highest room
Of whom ye seek to be most magnified;

---

| | |
|---|---|
| 7.1   Indeed, I would rather know that. | 8.2   *bountiest* most virtuous. |
| 7.5   *maugre* nevertheless.   *to me spite* spitefully deny me. | 9.6   *For* against. |
| 7.7   *aread* declare. | 10.2   *forwent* left. |
| 7.9   *error* wandering. | 10.4   *invent* find. |

At least, eternal meed shall you abide.
To whom the Prince: Dwarf, comfort to thee take,
For till thou tidings learn what her betide,
I hear avow thee never to forsake.
Ill wears he arms, that nill them use for ladies' sake.

### 12

So with the dwarf he back returned again,
To seek his lady, where he mote her find;
But by the way he greatly gan complain
The want of his good squire, late left behind,
For whom he wondrous pensive grew in mind,
For doubt of danger which mote him betide.
For him he lovèd above all mankind,
Having him true and faithful ever tried,
And bold as ever squire that waited by knight's side.

### 13

Who all this while full hardly was assayed
Of deadly danger which to him betid;
For whiles his lord pursued that noble maid,
After that foster foul he fiercely rid,
To been avengèd of the shame he did
To that fair damsel. Him he chasèd long
Through the thick woods, wherein he would have hid
His shameful head from his avengement strong,
And oft him threatened death for his outrageous wrong.

### 14

Natheless the villain sped himself so well,
Whether through swiftness of his speedy beast,
Or knowledge of those woods where he did dwell,
That shortly he from danger was released,
And out of sight escapèd at the least;
Yet not escapèd from the due reward
Of his bad deeds, which daily he increased,
Ne ceasèd not, till him oppressèd hard
The heavy plague that for such lechers is prepared.

### 15

For soon as he was vanished out of sight,
His coward courage gan emboldened be,
And cast to avenge him of that foul despite
Which he had borne of his bold enemy.
Tho to his brethren came; for they were three
Ungracious children of one graceless sire,
And unto them complainèd how that he
Had usèd been of that foolhardy squire;
So them with bitter words he stirred to bloody ire.

11.9  *nill* will not.                    13.1  *assayed* assailed.
12.6  *doubt* fear.                        14.5  *least* last.
12.8  *tried* proved.

16

Forthwith themselves with their sad instruments
Of spoil and murder they gan arm belive,
And with him forth into the forest went
To wreak the wrath, which he did erst revive
In their stern breasts, on him which late did drive
Their brother to reproach and shameful flight.
For they had vowed that never he alive
Out of that forest should escape their might;
Vile rancor their rude hearts had filled with such despite.

17

Within that wood there was a covert glade,
Forby a narrow ford, to them well known,
Through which it was uneath for wight to wade;
And now by fortune it was overflown.
By that same way they knew that squire unknown
Mote algates pass; forthy themselves they set
There in await, with thick woods overgrown,
And all the while their malice they did whet
With cruel threats his passage through the ford to let.

18

It fortunèd, as they devisèd had,
The gentle squire came riding that same way,
Unweeting of their wile and treason bad,
And through the ford to passen did assay;
But that fierce foster, which late fled away,
Stoutly forth stepping on the further shore,
Him boldly bade his passage there to stay,
Till he had made amends and full restore
For all the damage which he had him done afore.

19

With that at him a quivering dart he threw,
With so fell force and villainous despite
That through his habergeon the forkhead flew,
And through the linkèd mails empiercèd quite,
But had no power in his soft flesh to bite.
That stroke the hardy squire did sore displease,
But more that him he could not come to smite;
For by no means the high bank he could seize,
But labored long in that deep ford with vain disease.

20

And still the foster with his long boar-spear
Him kept from landing at his wishèd will;
Anon one sent out of the thicket near
A cruel shaft, headed with deadly ill,
And featherèd with an unlucky quill.
The wicked steel stayed not till it did light

16.1  *sad* heavy.
16.2  *belive* quickly.
17.2  *Forby* near.

17.3  *uneath* not easy.
17.9  *let* hinder.
19.9  *disease* distress.

In his left thigh, and deeply did it thrill;
Exceeding grief that wound in him empight,
But more that with his foes he could not come to fight.

### 21

At last, through wrath and vengeance making way,
He on the bank arrived with mickle pain,
Where the third brother him did sore assay,
And drove at him with all his might and main
A forest-bill, which both his hands did strain;
But warily he did avoid the blow,
And with his spear requited him again,
That both his sides were thrillèd with the throw,
And a large stream of blood out of the wound did flow.

### 22

He, tumbling down, with gnashing teeth did bite
The bitter earth, and bade to let him in
Into the baleful house of endless night,
Where wicked ghosts do wail their former sin.
Tho gan the battle freshly to begin,
For nathemore for that spectacle bad
Did the other two their cruel vengeance blin,
But both at once on both sides him bestad,
And load upon him laid, his life for to have had.

### 23

Tho when that villain he avised, which late
Affrighted had the fairest Florimell,
Full of fierce fury and indignant hate
To him he turnèd, and with rigor fell
Smote him so rudely on the pannicle
That to the chin he cleft his head in twain.
Down on the ground his carcass groveling fell;
His sinful soul with desperate disdain
Out of her fleshly farm fled to the place of pain.

### 24

That seeing now the only last of three,
Who with that wicked shaft him wounded had,
Trembling with horror, as that did foresee
The fearful end of his avengement sad
Through which he follow should his brethren bad,
His bootless bow in feeble hand upcaught
And therewith shot an arrow at the lad,
Which faintly fluttering, scarce his helmet raught
And glancing fell to ground, but him annoyèd nought.

| | |
|---|---|
| **20.7** *thrill* pierce. | **22.7** *blin* stop. |
| **20.8** *empight* implanted. | **22.8** *bestad* beset. |
| **21.2** *mickle* much. | **23.1** *avised* saw. |
| **21.5** *forest-bill* woodman's bill-hook. | **23.5** *pannicle* brain-pan. |
| **22.6** *nathemore* never the more. | **24.8** *raught* reached. |

### 25

With that he would have fled into the wood,
But Timias him lightly overhent
Right as he entering was into the flood,
And struck at him with force so violent
That headless him into the ford he sent;
The carcass with the stream was carried down,
But the head fell backward on the continent.
So mischief fell upon the meaner's crown;
They three be dead with shame, the squire lives with renown.

### 26

He lives, but takes small joy of his renown,
For of that cruel wound he bled so sore
That from his steed he fell in deadly swoon;
Yet still the blood forth gushed in so great store
That he lay wallowed all in his own gore.
Now God thee keep, thou gentlest squire alive,
Else shall thy loving lord thee see no more,
But both of comfort him thou shalt deprive,
And eke thyself of honor which thou didst achieve.

### 27

Providence heavenly passeth living thought,
And doth for wretched men's relief make way:
For lo, great grace or fortune thither brought
Comfort to him that comfortless now lay.
In those same woods ye well remember may
How that a noble hunteress did won,
She that base Braggadocchio did affray
And made him fast out of the forest run;
Belphoebe was her name, as fair as Phoebus' sun.

### 28

She on a day, as she pursued the chase
Of some wild beast which with her arrows keen
She wounded had, the same along did trace
By tract of blood, which she had freshly seen
To have besprinkled all the grassy green;
By the great persue which she there perceived
Well hopèd she the beast engored had been,
And made more haste, the life to have bereaved:
But ah, her expectation greatly was deceived.

### 29

Shortly she came whereas that woeful squire
With blood deformèd lay in deadly swound,
In whose fair eyes, like lamps of quenchèd fire,
The crystal humor stood congealèd round;
His locks, like faded leaves fallen to the ground,

---

**25.2** *lightly overhent* quickly overtook.
**25.7** *continent* ground.
**25.8** So mischief fell on the head of him who intended to do mischief.

**27.5–9** The episode in question is narrated at II.iii.21ff.
**27.6** *won* dwell.
**28.6** *persue* blood trail.

Knotted with blood, in bunches rudely ran,
And his sweet lips, on which before that stound
The bud of youth to blossom fair began,
Spoiled of their rosy red, were woxen pale and wan.

### 30

Saw never living eye more heavy sight,
That could have made a rock of stone to rue
Or rive in twain; which when that lady bright
Besides all hope with melting eyes did view,
All suddenly abashed she changèd hue,
And with stern horror backward gan to start.
But when she better him beheld, she grew
Full of soft passion and unwonted smart:
The point of pity piercèd through her tender heart.

### 31

Meekly she bowèd down, to weet if life
Yet in his frozen members did remain,
And feeling by his pulse's beating rife
That the weak soul her seat did yet retain,
She cast to comfort him with busy pain.
His double folded neck she reared upright,
And rubbed his temples and each trembling vein;
His mailèd habergeon she did undight,
And from his head his heavy burgonet did light.

### 32

Into the woods thenceforth in haste she went,
To seek for herbs that mote him remedy,
For she of herbs had great intendiment,
Taught of the nymph which from her infancy
Her nursèd had in true nobility;
There, whether it divine tobacco were,
Or panachaea, or polygony,
She found and brought it to her patient dear,
Who all this while lay bleeding out his heart-blood near.

### 33

The sovereign weed betwixt two marbles plain
She pounded small and did in pieces bruise,
And then atween her lily handes twain
Into his wound the juice thereof did scruze;
And roundabout, as she could well it use,
The flesh therewith she suppled and did steep,
To abate all spasm, and soak the swelling bruise,
And after having searched the intuse deep,
She with her scarf did bind the wound from cold to keep.

---

**29.7** *stound* time of trial.
**31.9** *burgonet* helmet.
**32.3** *intendiment* understanding.
**32.7** *panachaea* panacea, a legendary herb with universal curative powers. *polygony* snakeweed.

**33.1–4** Belphoebe's actions copy those of Angelica, tending the wounded Medoro, in *Orlando Furioso* 19.24; the story of Timias and Belphoebe is constructed as a deliberate allusion to this episode in Ariosto.
**33.4** *scruze* squeeze.
**33.6** *suppled* softened.
**33.8** *intuse* bruise.

### 34

By this he had sweet life recured again,
And groaning inly deep, at last his eyes,
His watery eyes, drizzling like dewy rain,
He up gan lift toward the azure skies,
From whence descend all hopeless remedies;
Therewith he sighed, and turning him aside,
The goodly maid, full of divinities
And gifts of heavenly grace, he by him spied,
Her bow and gilden quiver lying him beside.

### 35

Mercy, dear Lord (said he), what grace is this
That thou hast showèd to me, sinful wight,
To send thine angel from her bower of bliss
To comfort me in my distressèd plight?
Angel or goddess do I call thee right?
What service may I do unto thee meet,
That hast from darkness me returned to light,
And with thy heavenly salves and med'cines sweet
Hast dressed my sinful wounds? I kiss thy blessèd feet.

### 36

Thereat she, blushing, said, Ah, gentle squire,
Nor goddess I, nor angel, but the maid
And daughter of a woody nymph, desire
No service but thy safety and aid;
Which if thou gain, I shall be well apaid.
We mortal wights, whose lives and fortunes be
To common accidents still open laid,
Are bound with common bond of frailty
To succor wretched wights whom we captivèd see.

### 37

By this her damsels, which the former chase
Had undertaken after her, arrived,
As did Belphoebe, in the bloody place,
And thereby deemed the beast had been deprived
Of life, whom late their lady's arrow rived.
Forthy the bloody tract they followed fast,
And everyone to run the swiftest strived;
But two of them the rest far overpassed,
And where their lady was arrivèd at the last.

### 38

Where, when they saw that goodly boy with blood
Defoulèd, and their lady dress his wound,
They wondered much, and shortly understood
How him in deadly case their lady found
And rescuèd out of the heavy stound.
Eftsoons his warlike courser, which was strayed
Far in the woods whiles that he lay in swound,

---

34.5  *hopeless* unhoped for.
34.9  *gilden* gilded.

36.3  *woody* woodland.
38.5  *stound* trance.

She made those damsels search; which being stayed,
They did him set thereon, and forth with them conveyed.

### 39

Into that forest far they thence him led,
Where was their dwelling in a pleasant glade,
With mountains round about environèd,
And mighty woods which did the valley shade
And like a stately theater it made,
Spreading itself into a spacious plain.
And in the midst a little river played
Amongst the pumy stones, which seemed to plain
With gentle murmur that his course they did restrain.

### 40

Beside the same a dainty place there lay,
Planted with myrtle trees and laurels green,
In which the birds sung many a lovely lay
Of God's high praise and of their love's sweet teen,
As it an earthly paradise had been;
In whose enclosèd shadow there was pight
A fair pavilion, scarcely to be seen,
The which was all within most richly dight,
That greatest prince's living it mote well delight.

### 41

Thither they brought that wounded squire, and laid
In easy couch his feeble limbs to rest.
He rested him a while, and then the maid
His ready wound with better salves new dressed;
Daily she dressèd him, and did the best
His grievous hurt to guarish that she might,
That shortly she his dolor hath redressed,
And his foul sore reducèd to fair plight:
It she reducèd, but himself destroyèd quite.

### 42

O fruitful physic and unfruitful pain,
That heals up one and makes another wound:
She his hurt thigh to him recured again,
But hurt his heart, the which before was sound,
Through an unwary dart which did rebound
From her fair eyes and gracious countenance.
What boots it him from death to be unbound,
To be captivèd in endless durance
Of sorrow and despair without allegeance?

### 43

Still as his wound did gather and grow whole,
So still his heart wox sore and health decayed:

39.8 *pumy* pumice.
40.4 *teen* suffering. The reading given here is that of the 1596 edition; the 1590 edition has "their sweet love's teen."
41.6 *guarish* heal.

42.1 *pain* labor.
42.8 *durance* imprisonment.
42.9 *allegeance* relief.

Madness to save a part, and lose the whole.
Still whenas he beheld the heavenly maid
Whiles daily plasters to his wound she laid,
So still his malady the more increased
The whiles her matchless beauty him dismayed.
Ah God, what other could he do at least,
But love so fair a lady that his life released?

### 44

Long while he strove in his courageous breast
With reason due the passion to subdue,
And love for to dislodge out of his nest.
Still, when her excellencies he did view,
Her sovereign bounty and celestial hue,
The same to love he strongly was constrained;
But when his mean estate he did review,
He from such hardy boldness was restrained,
And of his luckless lot and cruel love thus plained.

### 45

Unthankful wretch (said he), is this the meed
With which her sovereign mercy thou dost quite?
Thy life she savèd by her gracious deed,
But thou dost ween with villainous despite
To blot her honor and her heavenly light.
Die rather, die, than so disloyally
Deem of her high desert or seem so light.
Fair death it is, to shun more shame to die:
Die rather, die, than ever love disloyally.

### 46

But if to love disloyalty it be,
Shall I then hate her, that from deathes door
Me brought? Ah far be such reproach fro me.
What can I less do than her love therefore,
Sith I her due reward cannot restore?
Die rather, die, and dying do her serve,
Dying her serve, and living her adore.
Thy life she gave, thy life she doth deserve;
Die rather, die, than ever from her service swerve.

### 47

But foolish boy, what boots thy service base
To her, to whom the heavens do serve and sue?
Thou a mean squire, of meek and lowly place;
She heavenly born, and of celestial hue.
How then? Of all love taketh equal view,
And doth not highest God vouchsafe to take
The love and service of the basest crew?
If she will not, die meekly for her sake;
Die rather, die, then ever so fair love forsake.

43.9   *released* delivered.                          45.7   *Deem of* hope for.
45.2   *quite* requite.

### 48

Thus warrèd he long time against his will,
Till that through weakness he was forced at last
To yield himself unto the mighty ill,
Which as a victor proud gan ransack fast
His inward parts and all his entrails waste,
That neither blood in face nor life in heart
It left, but both did quite dry up and blast:
As piercing levin, which the inner part
Of everything consumes, and calcineth by art.

### 49

Which seeing, fair Belphoebe gan to fear,
Lest that his wound were inly well not healed,
Or that the wicked steel empoisoned were;
Little she weened that love he close concealed.
Yet still he wasted as the snow congealed
When the bright sun his beams thereon doth beat;
Yet never he his heart to her revealed,
But rather chose to die for sorrow great
Than with dishonorable terms her to entreat.

### 50

She, gracious lady, yet no pains did spare
To do him ease or do him remedy;
Many restoratives of virtues rare
And costly cordials she did apply
To mitigate his stubborn malady.
But that sweet cordial which can restore
A lovesick heart, she did to him envy;
To him, and to all the unworthy world forlore,
She did envy that sovereign salve in secret store.

### 51

That dainty rose, the daughter of her morn,
More dear than life she tenderèd, whose flower
The garland of her honor did adorn,
Ne suffered she the midday's scorching power
Ne the sharp northern wind thereon to shower,
But lappèd up her silken leaves most chare
Whenso the froward sky began to lower;
But soon as calmèd was the crystal air,
She did it fair dispread, and let to flourish fair.

### 52

Eternal God in his almighty power,
To make ensample of his heavenly grace,
In paradise whilom did plant this flower,
Whence he it fetched out of her native place
And did in stock of earthly flesh enrace,

---

48.8  *levin* lightning.
48.9  *calcineth* reduces to ashes.
50.7  *envy* deny.
50.8  *forlore* forsaken (i.e., by Belphoebe).

51.6  *chare* carefully.
51.9  *dispread* open up.
52.5  *enrace* implant.

That mortal men her glory should admire;
In gentle ladies' breast and bounteous race
Of womankind it fairest flower doth spire,
And beareth fruit of honor and all chaste desire.

### 53

Fair imps of beauty, whose bright shining beams
Adorn the world with like to heavenly light,
And to your wills both royalties and realms
Subdue through conquest of your wondrous might,
With this fair flower your good garlands dight
Of chastity and virtue virginal,
That shall embellish more your beauty bright
And crown your heads with heavenly coronal,
Such as the angels wear before God's tribunal.

### 54

To your fair selves a fair ensample frame
Of this fair virgin, this Belphoebe fair,
To whom in perfect love and spotless fame
Of chastity none living may compare;
Ne poisonous envy justly can impair
The praise of her fresh flowering maidenhead.
Forthy she standeth on the highest stair
Of the honorable stage of womanhead,
That ladies all may follow her ensample dead.

### 55

In so great praise of steadfast chastity
Natheless she was so courteous and kind,
Tempered with grace and goodly modesty,
That seemèd those two virtues strove to find
The higher place in her heroic mind;
So striving, each did other more augment,
And both increased the praise of womankind,
And both increased her beauty excellent:
So all did make in her a perfect complement.

52.8   *spire* sprout.
53.1   *imps* children.
54.8   *womanhead* womanhood.

54.9   *follow her ensample dead* follow her example when she
is dead.

CANTO VI

*The birth of fair Belphoebe and*
  *of Amoret is told.*
*The Garden of Adonis fraught*
  *with pleasures manifold.*

### 1

Well may I ween, fair ladies, all this while
Ye wonder how this noble damozel
So great perfections did in her compile,

1.3   *salvage* savage.

Sith that in salvage forests she did dwell,
So far from court and royal citadel,
The great schoolmistress of all courtesy;
Seemeth that such wild woods should far expel
All civil usage and gentility,
And gentle sprite deform with rude rusticity.

2

But to this fair Belphoebe in her birth
The heavens so favorable were and free,
Looking with mild aspect upon the earth
In the horoscope of her nativity,
That all the gifts of grace and chastity
On her they pourèd forth of plenteous horn;
Jove laughed on Venus from his sovereign see,
And Phoebus with fair beams did her adorn,
And all the Graces rocked her cradle being born.

3

Her birth was of the womb of morning dew,
And her conception of the joyous prime,
And all her whole creation did her show
Pure and unspotted from all loathly crime
That is ingenerate in fleshly slime.
So was this virgin born, so was she bred,
So was she trainèd up from time to time
In all chaste virtue and true bountihead
Till to her due perfection she was ripenèd.

4

Her mother was the fair Chrysogonee,
The daughter of Amphisa, who by race
A Faery was, yborn of high degree.
She bore Belphoebe, she bore in like case
Fair Amoretta in the second place;
These two were twins, and twixt them two did share
The heritage of all celestial grace,
That all the rest it seemed they robbèd bare
Of bounty and of beauty and all virtues rare.

5

It were a goodly story, to declare
By what strange accident fair Chrysogone
Conceived these infants, and how them she bare
In this wild forest wandering all alone
After she had nine months fulfilled and gone;
For not as other women's common brood
They were enwombèd in the sacred throne

2.7 *see* throne.
3.2 *prime* first hour of the day.
3.5 *ingenerate* innate.
3.8 *bountihead* generosity.
4.1 *Chrysogonee* The name means "golden-born" in Greek, and was used in connection with the myth of Danaë,

impregnated by Zeus in the guise of a shower of gold. So spelled, the name has four syllables; spelled "Chrysogone," as in the next stanza, it has three.
4.2 *Amphisa* The name is derived from the Greek *amphis*, indicating doubleness.

Of her chaste body, nor with common food,
As other women's babes, they suckèd vital blood.

6

But wondrously they were begot and bred
Through influence of the heaven's fruitful ray,
As it in antique books is mentionèd.
It was upon a summer's shiny day,
When Titan fair his beames did display:
In a fresh fountain, far from all men's view,
She bathed her breast, the boiling heat to allay;
She bathed with roses red and violets blue
And all the sweetest flowers that in the forest grew.

7

Till faint through irksome weariness, adown
Upon the grassy ground herself she laid
To sleep, the whiles a gentle slumbering swoon
Upon her fell, all naked bare displayed;
The sunbeams bright upon her body played,
Being through former bathing mollified,
And pierced into her womb, where they embayed
With so sweet sense and secret power unspied,
That in her pregnant flesh they shortly fructified.

8

Miraculous may seem to him that reads
So strange ensample of conception,
But reason teacheth that the fruitful seeds
Of all things living, through impression
Of the sunbeams in moist complexion,
Do life conceive and quickened are by kind;
So after Nilus' inundation
Infinite shapes of creatures men do find
Informèd in the mud on which the sun hath shined.

9

Great father he of generation
Is rightly called, the author of life and light;
And his fair sister for creation
Ministereth matter fit, which, tempered right
With heat and humor, breeds the living wight.
So sprung these twins in womb of Chrysogone,
Yet wist she nought thereof, but, sore affright,
Wondered to see her belly so upblown,
Which still increased till she her term had full outgone.

10

Whereof conceiving shame and foul disgrace,
Albe her guiltless conscience her cleared,
She fled into the wilderness a space,

7.7  *embayed* moistened.

8.6  *kind* nature.

8.9  *Informèd* given form.

9.3  *his fair sister* the moon.

Till that unwieldy burden she had reared,
And shunned dishonor, which as death she feared;
Where, weary of long travail, down to rest
Herself she set, and comfortably cheered.
There a sad cloud of sleep her overcast
And seizèd every sense with sorrow sore oppressed.

### 11

It fortunèd fair Venus, having lost
Her little son, the wingèd god of love,
Who for some light displeasure which him crossed
Was from her fled, as flit as airy dove,
And left her blissful bower of joy above
(So from her often he had fled away
When she for ought him sharply did reprove,
And wandered in the world in strange array,
Disguised in thousand shapes, that none might him bewray),

### 12

Him for to seek, she left her heavenly house,
The house of goodly forms and fair aspects,
Whence all the world derives the glorious
Features of beauty and all shapes select
With which high God his workmanship hath decked,
And searchèd every way through which his wings
Had borne him or his tract she mote detect;
She promised kisses sweet, and sweeter things,
Unto the man that of him tidings to her brings.

### 13

First she him sought in court, where most he used
Whilom to haunt, but there she found him not,
But many there she found which sore accused
His falsehood, and with foul, infamous blot
His cruel deeds and wicked wiles did spot;
Ladies and lords she everywhere mote hear
Complaining how with his empoisoned shot
Their woeful hearts he wounded had whilere,
And so had left them languishing twixt hope and fear.

### 14

She then the cities sought from gate to gate,
And everyone did ask, did he him see;
And everyone her answered that too late
He had him seen, and felt the cruelty
Of his sharp darts and hot artillery;
And everyone threw forth reproaches rife
Of his mischievous deeds, and said that he
Was the disturber of all civil life,
The enemy of peace, and author of all strife.

10.4 *reared* given birth to.
11.4 *flit* flitting.

13.5 *spot* blame.
14.1 *sought* searched.

### 15

Then in the country she abroad him sought,
And in the rural cottages inquired,
Where also many plaints to her were brought,
How he their heedless hearts with love had fired,
And his false venom through their veins inspired;
And eke the gentle shepherd swains, which sat
Keeping their fleecy flocks, as they were hired,
She sweetly heard complain, both how and what
Her son had to them done; yet she did smile thereat.

### 16

But when in none of all these she him got,
She gan avise where else he mote him hide;
At last she her bethought that she had not
Yet sought the salvage woods and forests wide,
In which full many lovely nymphs abide,
Mongst whom might be that he did closely lie,
Or that the love of some of them him tied;
Forthy she thither cast her course to apply,
To search the secret haunts of Diane's company.

### 17

Shortly unto the wasteful woods she came,
Whereas she found the goddess with her crew,
After late chase of their imbruèd game
Sitting beside a fountain in a rew:
Some of them washing with the liquid dew
From off their dainty limbs the dusty sweat
And soil which did deform their lively hue;
Others lay shaded from the scorching heat;
The rest upon her person gave attendance great.

### 18

She, having hung upon a bough on high
Her bow and painted quiver, had unlaced
Her silver buskins from her nimble thigh,
And her lank loins ungirt and breasts unbraced,
After her heat the breathing cold to taste;
Her golden locks, that late in tresses bright
Embraided were for hindering of her haste,
Now loose about her shoulders hung undight,
And were with sweet ambrosia all besprinkled light.

### 19

Soon as she Venus saw behind her back,
She was ashamed to be so loose surprised,
And wox half wroth against her damsels slack
That had not her thereof before avised,
But suffered her so carelessly disguised

15.5  *inspired* infused.
16.2  *avise* consider.
17.1  *wasteful* desolate.
17.3  *imbruèd* blood-stained.

17.4  *rew* row.
18.4  *lank loins* slender waist.
18.7  *for hindering of* to keep them from hindering.
19.4  *avised* advised.

Be overtaken. Soon her garments loose
Upgathering, in her bosom she comprised,
Well as she might, and to the goddess rose,
Whiles all her nymphs did like a garland her enclose.

### 20

Goodly she gan fair Cytherea greet,
And shortly askèd her what cause her brought
Into that wilderness for her unmeet
From her sweet bowers and beds with pleasures fraught;
That sudden change she strange adventure thought.
To whom, half weeping, she thus answerèd
That she her dearest son Cupido sought,
Who in his frowardness from her was fled;
That she repented sore to have him angerèd.

### 21

Thereat Diana gan to smile, in scorn
Of her vain plaint, and to her scoffing said:
Great pity sure, that ye be so forlorn
Of your gay son, that gives ye so good aid
To your disports: ill mote ye been apaid.
But she was more engrievèd, and replied:
Fair sister, ill beseems it to upbraid
A doleful heart with so disdainful pride;
The like that mine, may be your pain another tide.

### 22

As you in woods and wanton wilderness
Your glory set to chase the salvage beasts,
So my delight is all in joyfulness,
In beds, in bowers, in bankets, and in feasts;
And ill becomes you with your lofty crests
To scorn the joy that Jove is glad to seek.
We both are bound to follow heaven's behests
And tend our charges with obeisance meek;
Spare, gentle sister, with reproach my pain to eke.

### 23

And tell me if that ye my son have heard
To lurk amongst your nymphs in secret wise,
Or keep their cabins: much I am affeared
Lest he like one of them himself disguise
And turn his arrows to their exercise.
So may he long himself full easy hide,
For he is fair and fresh in face and guise
As any nymph (let not it be envied).
So saying, every nymph full narrowly she eyed.

### 24

But Phoebe therewith sore was angerèd,
And sharply said: Go, dame, go seek your boy

20.1 *Cytherea* Venus.
22.4 *bankets* banquets.

22.9 *eke* increase.
24.1 *Phoebe* Diana.

Where you him lately left, in Mars his bed.
He comes not here, we scorn his foolish joy,
Ne lend we leisure to his idle toy.
But if I catch him in this company,
By Stygian lake I vow, whose sad annoy
The gods do dread, he dearly shall aby:
I'll clip his wanton wings, that he no more shall fly.


### 25

Whom whenas Venus saw so sore displeased,
She inly sorry was, and gan relent
What she had said; so her she soon appeased
With sugared words and gentle blandishment,
Which as a fountain from her sweet lips went
And wellèd goodly forth, that in short space
She was well pleased, and forth her damsels sent
Through all the woods to search from place to place
If any tract of him or tidings they mote trace.


### 26

To search the god of love, her nymphs she sent
Throughout the wandering forest everywhere,
And after them herself eke with her went
To seek the fugitive both far and near.
So long they sought, till they arrivèd were
In that same shady covert whereas lay
Fair Chrysogone in slumbery trance whilere,
Who in her sleep (a wondrous thing to say)
Unwares had born two babes, as fair as springing day.


### 27

Unwares she them conceived, unwares she bore.
She bore withouten pain that she conceived
Withouten pleasure, ne her need implore
Lucina's aid; which when they both perceived,
They were through wonder nigh of sense bereaved,
And gazing each on other, nought bespake.
At last they both agreed, her seeming grieved
Out of her heavy swoon not to awake,
But from her loving side the tender babes to take.


### 28

Up they them took, each one a babe uptook,
And with them carried to be fosterèd.
Dame Phoebe to a nymph her babe betook
To be upbrought in perfect maidenhead,
And of herself her name Belphoebe read;
But Venus hers thence far away conveyed
To be upbrought in goodly womanhead,
And in her little love's stead, which was strayed,
Her Amoretta called, to comfort her dismayed.

---

**24.3**   When married to Vulcan, Venus engaged in a particularly notorious adulterous affair with the god of war.
**24.8**   *aby* pay.

**25.2**   *relent* soften.
**27.4**   *Lucina* Juno as the patron goddess of childbirth.
**28.7**   *womanhead* womanhood.

29

She brought her to her joyous paradise
Where most she wons when she on earth does dwell,
So fair a place as Nature can devise.
Whether in Paphos or Cytheron hill
Or it in Cnidus be, I wote not well;
But well I wote by trial, that this same
All other pleasant places doth excel,
And callèd is by her lost lover's name
The Garden of Adonis, far renowmed by fame.

30

In that same garden all the goodly flowers
Wherewith dame Nature doth her beautify
And decks the garlands of her paramours
Are fetched; there is the first seminary
Of all things that are born to live and die,
According to their kinds. Long work it were
Here to account the endless progeny
Of all the weeds that bud and blossom there;
But so much as doth need, must needs be counted here.

31

It sited was in fruitful soil of old,
And girt in with two walls on either side:
The one of iron, the other of bright gold,
That none might thorough break nor overstride.
And double gates it had, which opened wide,
By which both in and out men moten pass:
The one fair and fresh, the other old and dried.
Old Genius the porter of them was,
Old Genius, the which a double nature has.

32

He letteth in, he letteth out to wend
All that to come into the world desire;
A thousand thousand naked babes attend
About him day and night, which do require
That he with fleshly weeds would them attire.
Such as him list, such as eternal fate
Ordainèd hath, he clothes with sinful mire,
And sendeth forth to live in mortal state,
Till they again return back by the hinder gate.

**29.2** *wons* dwells.
**29.4** *Paphos* A city in Cyprus, famous for its shrine to Aphrodite. *Cytheron hill* Spenser seems to be conflating Cythera, an island off the Peloponnese on which Aphrodite is said to have been born, and Cythaeron, a mountain in Boeotia sacred to the Muses.
**29.5** *Cnidus* A Greek city in Asia Minor, the home of Praxiteles' famous statue of Aphrodite.
**29.9** *Garden of Adonis* For Adonis's story, see Ovid, *Metamorphoses* 10.298–739. Adonis was the child of the incestuous love of Myrrha and her father (see above, ii.41.1), and became a young man of extraordinary beauty. Venus fell in love with him, and when he was killed by a wild boar that he was hunting she was inconsolable; her lamentations over him were famous in classical antiquity. A popular ritual then among women re-enacted those lamentations, and involved small pots of quick-growing herbs known as "gardens of Adonis." The site of cosmic regeneration that Spenser describes under that title is his own creation.
**30.4** *seminary* seedbed.

### 33

After that they again returnèd been,
They in that garden planted be again,
And grow afresh, as they had never seen
Fleshly corruption nor mortal pain.
Some thousand years so done they there remain,
And then of him are clad with other hue,
Or sent into the changeful world again,
Till thither they return where first they grew:
So like a wheel around they run from old to new.

### 34

Nor needs there gardener to set or sow,
To plant or prune, for of their own accord
All things as they created were do grow,
And yet remember well the mighty word
Which first was spoken by the almighty Lord,
That bade them to increase and multiply;
Ne do they need with water of the ford
Or of the clouds to moisten their roots dry,
For in themselves eternal moisture they imply.

### 35

Infinite shapes of creatures there are bred,
And uncouth forms which none yet ever knew,
And every sort is in a sundry bed
Set by itself, and ranked in comely rew:
Some fit for reasonable souls to endue,
Some made for beasts, some made for birds to wear,
And all the fruitful spawn of fishes' hue
In endless ranks along enrangèd were,
That seemed the ocean could not contain them there.

### 36

Daily they grow, and daily forth are sent
Into the world, it to replenish more;
Yet is the stock not lessenèd nor spent,
But still remains in everlasting store
As it at first created was of yore.
For in the wide womb of the world there lies,
In hateful darkness and in deep horror,
An huge eternal chaos, which supplies
The substances of Nature's fruitful progenies.

### 37

All things from thence do their first being fetch,
And borrow matter whereof they are made,
Which, whenas form and feature it does catch,
Becomes a body, and doth then invade
The state of life, out of the grisly shade.
That substance is eterne, and bideth so,
Ne when the life decays and form does fade

34.9  *imply* contain.                           35.7  *hue* shape.
35.5  *endue* assume.

Doth it consume and into nothing go,
But changèd is, and often altered to and fro.

### 38

The substance is not changed nor alterèd,
But the only form and outward fashion;
For every substance is conditionèd
To change her hue, and sundry forms to don,
Meet for her temper and complexion.
For forms are variable, and decay
By course of kind, and by occasion;
And that fair flower of beauty fades away
As doth the lily fresh before the sunny ray.

### 39

Great enemy to it, and to all the rest
That in the Garden of Adonis springs,
Is wicked Time, who with his scythe addressed
Does mow the flowering herbs and goodly things,
And all their glory to the ground down flings,
Where they do wither, and are foully marred.
He flies about, and with his flaggy wings
Beats down both leaves and buds without regard,
Ne ever pity may relent his malice hard.

### 40

Yet pity often did the gods relent
To see so fair things marred and spoilèd quite;
And their great mother Venus did lament
The loss of her dear brood, her dear delight.
Her heart was pierced with pity at the sight
When walking through the garden them she spied,
Yet note she find redress for such despite,
For all that lives is subject to that law:
All things decay in time, and to their end do draw.

### 41

But were it not that Time their troubler is,
All that in this delightful garden grows
Should happy be, and have immortal bliss,
For here all plenty and all pleasure flows,
And sweet love gentle fits amongst them throws,
Without fell rancor or fond jealousy;
Frankly each paramour his leman knows,
Each bird his mate, ne any does envy
Their goodly merriment and gay felicity.

### 42

There is continual spring, and harvest there
Continual, both meeting at one time,
For both the boughs do laughing blossoms bear

---

39.3 *addressed* equipped.
39.7 *flaggy* floppy.

40.7 *note* could not.
41.7 *leman* beloved.

And with fresh colors deck the wanton prime,
And eke at once the heavy trees they climb,
Which seem to labor under their fruit's load;
The whiles the joyous birds make their pastime
Amongst the shady leaves, their sweet abode,
And their true loves without suspicion tell abroad.

### 43

Right in the middest of that paradise
There stood a stately mount, on whose round top
A gloomy grove of myrtle trees did rise,
Whose shady boughs sharp steel did never lop,
Nor wicked beasts their tender buds did crop,
But like a garland compassèd the height;
And from their fruitful sides sweet gum did drop,
That all the ground, with precious dew bedight,
Threw forth most dainty odors and most sweet delight.

### 44

And in the thickest covert of that shade
There was a pleasant arbor, not by art
But of the trees' own inclination made,
Which knitting their rank branches part to part,
With wanton ivy twine entrailed athwart,
And eglantine and caprifoil among,
Fashioned above within their inmost part,
That neither Phoebus' beams could through them throng,
Nor Aeolus' sharp blast could work them any wrong.

### 45

And all about grew every sort of flower
To which sad lovers were transformed of yore:
Fresh Hyacinthus, Phoebus' paramour;
Foolish Narciss, that likes the watery shore;
Sad Amaranthus, made a flower but late,
Sad Amaranthus, in whose purple gore
Me seems I see Amintas' wretched fate,
To whom sweet poets' verse hath given endless date.

### 46

There wont fair Venus often to enjoy
Her dear Adonis' joyous company,
And reap sweet pleasure of the wanton boy.

---

42.4 *prime* spring.
44.4 *rank* dense.
44.6 *caprifoil* honeysuckle.
44.9 *Aeolus* Greek god of the winds.
45 In the 1590 and the 1596 editions this stanza has only eight lines, as here; in the 1609 edition, a truncated line 4 is inserted: "And dearest love."
45.3 *Hyacinthus* A beautiful young man inadvertently killed by his lover Apollo; the hyacinth sprang from his blood.
45.4 Narcissus died gazing at his reflection in a pool; the flower with his name grows near water.

45.5 *Amaranthus* The name of an imaginary flower that never fades, and of several real flowers; the reference to "purple gore" suggests one of the latter, also known as love-lies-a-bleeding.
45.7 *Amintas* Often taken to be Philip Sidney; Spenser's own *Astrophel* (which likens Sidney to Adonis) was one of the many elegies which were written after Sidney's death in 1586, and to which the last lines of the stanza may refer. Alternatively, the reference may be to Thomas Watson's pastoral elegy *Amintas* (1585), in which case *poets'* should read *poet's*.

There yet, some say, in secret he does lie,
Lappèd in flowers and precious spicery,
By her hid from the world, and from the skill
Of Stygian gods, which do her love envy;
But she herself, whenever that she will,
Possesseth him, and of his sweetness takes her fill.

### 47
And sooth it seems they say: for he may not
Forever die and ever buried be
In baleful night, where all things are forgot;
Albe he subject to mortality,
Yet is eterne in mutability,
And by succession made perpetual,
Transformèd oft, and changèd diversely.
For him the father of all forms they call;
Therefore needs mote he live, that living gives to all.

### 48
There now he liveth in eternal bliss,
Joying his goddess, and of her enjoyed;
Ne feareth he henceforth that foe of his,
Which with his cruel tusk him deadly cloyed.
For that wild boar, the which him once annoyed,
She firmly hath imprisonèd for aye,
That her sweet love his malice mote avoid,
In a strong rocky cave, which is, they say,
Hewn underneath that mount, that none him loosen may.

### 49
There now he lives in everlasting joy,
With many of the gods in company
Which thither haunt, and with the wingèd boy
Sporting himself in safe felicity;
Who, when he hath with spoils and cruelty
Ransacked the world, and in the woeful hearts
Of many wretches set his triumphs high,
Thither resorts, and laying his sad darts
Aside, with fair Adonis plays his wanton parts.

### 50
And his true love, fair Psyche, with him plays,
Fair Psyche to him lately reconciled
After long troubles and unmeet upbrays,
With which his mother Venus her reviled,
And eke himself her cruelly exiled;
But now in steadfast love and happy state
She with him lives, and hath him borne a child:
Pleasure, that doth both gods and men aggrate;
Pleasure, the daughter of Cupid and Psyche late.

---

**50** The story of Cupid and Psyche, ending with the birth of their daughter Pleasure (Voluptas), is told in Apuleius, *Metamorphoses* 4.28–6.24.

**50.3** *upbrays* reproaches.
**50.8** *aggrate* gratify.

### 51

Hither great Venus brought this infant fair,
The younger daughter of Chrysogonee,
And unto Psyche with great trust and care
Committed her, yfosterèd to be,
And trainèd up in true feminity;
Who no less carefully her tenderèd
Than her own daughter Pleasure, to whom she
Made her companion, and her lessonèd
In all the lore of love and goodly womanhead.

### 52

In which when she to perfect ripeness grew,
Of grace and beauty noble paragon,
She brought her forth into the worldes view,
To be the ensample of true love alone
And lodestar of all chaste affection
To all fair ladies that do live on ground.
To Faery court she came, where many one
Admired her goodly havior, and found
His feeble heart wide launchèd with love's cruel wound.

### 53

But she to none of them her love did cast,
Save to the noble knight Sir Scudamour,
To whom her loving heart she linkèd fast
In faithful love to abide forever more,
And for his dearest sake endurèd sore,
Sore trouble of an heinous enemy,
Who her would forcèd have to have forlore
Her former love and steadfast loyalty,
As ye may elsewhere read that rueful history.

### 54

But well I ween ye first desire to learn
What end unto that fearful damozel
Which fled so fast from that same foster stern,
Whom with his brethren Timias slew, befell.
That was to weet the goodly Florimell,
Who wandering for to seek her lover dear,
Her lover dear, her dearest Marinell,
Into misfortune fell, as ye did hear,
And from Prince Arthur fled with wings of idle fear.

52.9  *launchèd* lanced.                     53.7  *forlore* forsaken.

## CANTO VII

*The witch's son loves Florimell;*
  *she flies, he fains to die.*
*Satyrane saves the Squire of Dames*
  *from Giant's tyranny.*

### 1

Like as an hind forth singled from the herd,
That hath escapèd from a ravenous beast,
Yet flies away, of her own feet affeared,
And every leaf that shaketh with the least
Murmur of wind her terror hath increased,
So fled fair Florimell from her vain fear
Long after she from peril was released;
Each shade she saw and each noise she did hear
Did seem to be the same which she escaped whilere.

### 2

All that same evening she in flying spent,
And all that night her course continuèd,
Ne did she let dull sleep once to relent
Nor weariness to slack her haste, but fled
Ever alike, as if her former dread
Were hard behind, her ready to arrest;
And her white palfrey, having conquerèd
The mastering reins out of her weary wrest,
Perforce her carrièd wherever he thought best.

### 3

So long as breath and able puissance
Did native courage unto him supply,
His pace he freshly forward did advance,
And carried her beyond all jeopardy;
But nought that wanteth rest can long aby.
He, having through incessant travel spent
His force, at last perforce adown did lie,
Ne foot could further move. The lady gent
Thereat was sudden struck with great astonishment,

### 4

And forced to alight, on foot mote algates fare,
A traveler unwonted to such way;
Need teacheth her this lesson hard and rare,
That fortune all in equal lance doth sway,
And mortal miseries doth make her play.
So long she traveled, till at length she came
To an hill's side, which did to her bewray
A little valley, subject to the same,
And covered with thick woods that quite it overcame.

### 5

Through the tops of the high trees she did descry
A little smoke, whose vapor thin and light,
Reeking aloft, uprollèd to the sky;
Which cheerful sign did send unto her sight
That in the same did won some living wight.

2.3 *relent* soften.
2.8 *wrest* grip.
3.5 *aby* abide.
4.5 And makes mortal miseries her sport.

5.3 *Reeking* steaming (without the modern sense of bad odor).
5.5 *won* dwell.

Eftsoons her steps she thereunto applied,
And came at last in weary wretched plight
Unto the place to which her hope did guide
To find some refuge there, and rest her weary side.

### 6

There in a gloomy hollow glen she found
A little cottage, built of sticks and reeds
In homely wise, and walled with sods around,
In which a witch did dwell, in loathly weeds
And willful want, all careless of her needs;
So choosing solitary to abide
Far from all neighbors, that her devilish deeds
And hellish arts from people she might hide,
And hurt far off unknown whomever she envied.

### 7

The damsel, there arriving, entered in,
Where, sitting on the floor, the hag she found,
Busy (as seemed) about some wicked gin;
Who soon as she beheld that sudden stound,
Lightly upstarted from the dusty ground,
And with fell look and hollow deadly gaze
Starèd on her awhile, as one astound,
Ne had one word to speak, for great amaze,
But showed by outward signs that dread her sense did daze.

### 8

At last, turning her fear to foolish wrath,
She asked what devil had her thither brought,
And who she was, and what unwonted path
Had guided her, unwelcomèd, unsought.
To which the damsel, full of doubtful thought,
Her mildly answered: Beldam, be not wroth
With silly virgin by adventure brought
Unto your dwelling, ignorant and loath,
That crave but room to rest, while tempest overblowth.

### 9

With that, adown out of her crystal eyen
Few trickling tears she softly forth let fall,
That like two orient pearls did purely shine
Upon her snowy cheek, and therewithal
She sighèd soft, that none so bestial
Nor salvage heart, but ruth of her sad plight
Would make to melt or piteously appall;
And that vile hag, all were her whole delight
In mischief, was much movèd at so piteous sight,

---

6.4  *weeds* clothes.
7.3  *gin* device.
7.4  *stound* astounding sight.
7.7  *astound* astounded.

8.6  *Beldam* old woman.
8.7  *silly* defenseless.
9.1  *eyen* eyes.
9.6  *salvage* savage.

10

And gan recomfort her in her rude wise,
With womanish compassion of her plaint,
Wiping the tears from her suffusèd eyes
And bidding her sit down, to rest her faint
And weary limbs awhile. She, nothing quaint
Nor sdainful of so homely fashion,
Sith brought she was now to so hard constraint,
Sat down upon the dusty ground anon,
As glad of that small rest as bird of tempest gone.

11

Tho gan she gather up her garments rent,
And her loose locks to dight in order due
With golden wreath and gorgeous ornament;
Whom such whenas the wicked hag did view,
She was astonished at her heavenly hue,
And doubted her to deem an earthly wight,
But or some goddess or of Diane's crew,
And thought her to adore with humble sprite:
To adore thing so divine as beauty were but right.

12

This wicked woman had a wicked son,
The comfort of her age and weary days,
A lazy lourd, for nothing good to done,
But stretchèd forth in idleness always,
Ne ever cast his mind to covet praise
Or ply himself to any honest trade,
But all the day before the sunny rays
He used to slug or sleep in slothful shade;
Such laziness both lewd and poor at once him made.

13

He, coming home at undertime, there found
The fairest creature that he ever saw
Sitting beside his mother on the ground;
The sight whereof did greatly him adaw,
And his base thought with terror and with awe
So inly smote that, as one which hath gazed
On the bright sun unwares doth soon withdraw
His feeble eyen, with too much brightness dazed,
So starèd he on her, and stood long while amazed.

14

Softly at last he gan his mother ask
What mister wight that was, and whence derived,
That in so strange disguisement there did mask,
And by what accident she there arrived;

10.5 *quaint* fastidious.
10.6 *sdainful* disdainful.
12.3 *lourd* lout.
12.9 *lewd* ignorant (as well as lecherous).

13.1 *undertime* An ambiguous indication of time; from the Old English *undern*, which in various contexts is used to refer to different hours of the day.
13.4 *adaw* daunt.
14.2 *mister wight* kind of person.

But she, as one nigh of her wits deprived,
With nought but ghastly looks him answerèd,
Like to a ghost that lately is revived
From Stygian shores where late it wanderèd:
So both at her, and each at other wonderèd.

15

But the fair virgin was so meek and mild
That she to them vouchsafèd to embase
Her goodly port, and to their senses vild
Her gentle speech applied, that in short space
She grew familiar in that desert place.
During which time, the churl through her so kind
And courteous use conceived affection base,
And cast to love her in his brutish mind:
No love, but brutish lust, that was so beastly tind.

16

Closely the wicked flame his bowels brent,
And shortly grew into outrageous fire,
Yet had he not the heart or hardiment
As unto her to utter his desire.
His caitiff thought durst not so high aspire,
But with soft sighs and lovely semblances
He weened that his affection entire
She should aread; many resemblances
To her he made, and many kind remembrances.

17

Oft from the forest wildings he did bring,
Whose sides empurpled were with smiling red,
And oft young birds, which he had taught to sing
His mistress' praises, sweetly carolèd;
Garlands of flowers sometimes for her fair head
He fine would dight; sometimes the squirrel wild
He brought to her in bands, as conquerèd
To be her thrall, his fellow servant vild.
All which she of him took with countenance meek and mild.

18

But past awhile, when she fit season saw
To leave that desert mansion, she cast
In secret wise herself thence to withdraw,
For fear of mischief which she did forecast
Might be by the witch or that her son compassed;
Her weary palfrey, closely as she might,
Now well recovered after long repast,
In his proud furnitures she freshly dight,
His late miswandered ways now to remeasure right.

15.2  *embase* lower.
15.3  *port* demeanor.
15.9  *tind* kindled.
16.1  *Closely* secretly.  *brent* burned.

16.8  *aread* divine.  *resemblances* displays of affection.
17.1  *wildings* wild apples.
18.8  *furnitures* harness.

### 19

And early ere the dawning day appeared
She forth issued, and on her journey went.
She went in peril, of each noise affeared,
And of each shade that did itself present,
For still she fearèd to be overhent
Of that vile hag or her uncivil son;
Who when, too late awaking, well they kent
That their fair guest was gone, they both begun
To make exceeding moan, as they had been undone.

### 20

But that lewd lover did the most lament
For her depart that ever man did hear;
He knocked his breast with desperate intent,
And scratched his face, and with his teeth did tear
His rugged flesh, and rent his ragged hair,
That his sad mother, seeing his sore plight,
Was greatly woebegone, and gan to fear
Lest his frail senses were imperished quite,
And love to frenzy turned, sith love is frantic hight.

### 21

All ways she sought him to restore to plight,
With herbs, with charms, with counsel, and with tears,
But tears, nor charms, nor herbs, nor counsel might
Assuage the fury which his entrails tears:
So strong is passion that no reason hears.
Tho when all other helps she saw to fail,
She turned herself back to her wicked lears,
And by her devilish arts thought to prevail
To bring her back again, or work her final bale.

### 22

Eftsoons out of her hidden cave she called
An hideous beast, of horrible aspect,
That could the stoutest courage have appalled:
Monstrous misshaped, and all his back was specked
With thousand spots of colors quaint elect;
Thereto so swift, that it all beasts did pass,
Like never yet did living eye detect.
But likest it to an hyena was,
That feeds on women's flesh as others feed on grass.

### 23

It forth she called, and gave it straight in charge
Through thick and thin her to pursue apace,
Ne once to stay to rest or breathe at large
Till her he had attained and brought in place,
Or quite devoured her beauty's scornful grace.
The monster swift as word that from her went

---

19.5 *overhent* overtaken.
19.7 *kent* learned.
20.8 *imperished* impaired.

21.1 *plight* health.
21.7 *lears* lore.
22.5 *quaint elect* skillfully chosen.

Went forth in haste, and did her footing trace
So sure and swiftly, through his perfect scent
And passing speed, that shortly he her overhent.

### 24

Whom when the fearful damsel nigh espied,
No need to bid her fast away to fly.
That ugly shape so sore her terrified
That it she shunned no less than dread to die,
And her flit palfrey did so well apply
His nimble feet to her conceivèd fear
That whilst his breath did strength to him supply,
From peril free he her away did bear;
But when his force gan fail, his pace gan wax arrear.

### 25

Which whenas she perceived, she was dismayed
At that same last extremity full sore,
And of her safety greatly grew afraid;
And now she gan approach to the sea shore,
As it befell, that she could fly no more,
But yield herself to spoil of greediness.
Lightly she leapèd, as a wight forlore,
From her dull horse, in desperate distress,
And to her feet betook her doubtful sikerness.

### 26

Not half so fast the wicked Myrrha fled
From dread of her revenging father's hand,
Nor half so fast to save her maidenhead
Fled fearful Daphne on the Aegean strand,
As Florimell fled from that monster yond
To reach the sea ere she of him were raught;
For in the sea to drown herself she fond
Rather than of the tyrant to be caught:
Thereto fear gave her wings, and need her courage taught.

### 27

It fortunèd (high God did so ordain)
As she arrivèd on the roaring shore
In mind to leap into the mighty main,
A little boat lay hoving her before,
In which there slept a fisher old and poor
The whiles his nets were drying on the sand;
Into the same she leapt, and with the oar
Did thrust the shallop from the floating strand:
So safety found at sea, which she found not at land.

23.9  *overhent* overtook.
24.5  *flit* swift.
24.9  *wax arrear* grow less.
25.7  *forlore* desperate.
25.9  *sikerness* safety.
26.1  *Myrrha* Mother of Adonis by her own father, whom she tricked into committing incest; when he discovered her identity, he chased after her with a sword until she was changed into a myrrh-tree.
26.4  *Daphne* First love of the god Apollo; fleeing him, she was metamorphosed into the laurel-tree.
26.6  *raught* caught.
26.7  *fond* intended.
27.4  *hoving* heaving.

28

The monster, ready on the prey to seize,
Was of his forward hope deceivèd quite,
Ne durst assay to wade the perilous seas,
But, greedily long gaping at the sight,
At last in vain was forced to turn his flight
And tell the idle tidings to his dame;
Yet to avenge his devilish despite,
He set upon her palfrey, tired, lame,
And slew him cruelly ere any rescue came.

29

And after having him embowellèd
To fill his hellish gorge, it chanced a knight
To pass that way as forth he travelèd;
It was a goodly swain, and of great might
As ever man that bloody field did fight,
But in vain shows that wont young knights bewitch
And courtly services took no delight,
But rather joyed to be than seemen sich:
For both to be and seem to him was labor lich.

30

It was to weet the good Sir Satyrane,
That ranged abroad to seek adventures wild,
As was his wont in forest and in plain;
He was all armed in rugged steel unfiled,
As in the smoky forge it was compiled,
And in his scutcheon bore a satyr's head.
He, coming present where the monster vild
Upon that milk-white palfrey's carcass fed,
Unto his rescue ran, and greedily him sped.

31

There well perceived he that it was the horse
Whereon fair Florimell was wont to ride
That of the fiend was rent without remorse.
Much fearèd he, lest ought did ill betide
To that fair maid, the flower of women's pride,
For her he dearly lovèd, and in all
His famous conquests highly magnified;
Besides her golden girdle, which did fall
From her in flight, he found, that did him sore appall.

32

Full of sad fear and doubtful agony,
Fiercely he flew upon that wicked fiend,
And with huge strokes and cruel battery
Him forced to leave his prey, for to attend

29.1 *embowellèd* disembowelled.
29.8 *sich* such.
29.9 *lich* like.

30.1 *Sir Satyrane* A satyr's son by a human mother; his history is given earlier in the poem, when he rescues Una from a crowd of satyrs (I.vi.20ff).
30.4 *unfiled* unpolished.

Himself from deadly danger to defend;
Full many wounds in his corrupted flesh
He did engrave, and muchel blood did spend,
Yet might not do him die, but aye more fresh
And fierce he still appeared the more he did him thresh.

### 33

He wist not how him to despoil of life,
Ne how to win the wishèd victory,
Sith him he saw still stronger grow through strife,
And himself weaker through infirmity;
Greatly he grew enraged, and furiously
Hurling his sword away, he lightly leapt
Upon the beast, that with great cruelty
Roarèd and ragèd to be underkept:
Yet he perforce him held, and strokes upon him heaped.

### 34

As he that strives to stop a sudden flood
And in strong banks his violence enclose
Forceth it swell above his wonted mood
And largely overflow the fruitful plain,
That all the country seems to be a main
And the rich furrows float, all quite fordone;
The woeful husbandman doth loud complain
To see his whole year's labor lost so soon,
For which to God he made so many an idle boon.

### 35

So him he held, and did through might amate:
So long he held him, and him beat so long
That at the last his fierceness gan abate,
And meekly stoop unto the victor strong;
Who, to avenge the implacable wrong
Which he supposèd done to Florimell,
Sought by all means his dolor to prolong,
Sith dint of steel his carcass could not quell,
His maker with her charms had framèd him so well.

### 36

The golden riband which that virgin wore
About her sclender waist he took in hand,
And with it bound the beast, that loud did roar
For great despite of that unwonted band,
Yet darèd not his victor to withstand,
But trembled like a lamb fled from the prey,
And all the way him followed on the strand,
As he had long been learnèd to obey;
Yet never learnèd he such service till that day.

32.7   *muchel* much.
32.9   *thresh* thrash.
34.5   *main* sea.

34.9   *boon* prayer.
35.1   *amate* beat down.
36.2   *sclender* slender.

### 37

Thus as he led the beast along the way,
He spied far off a mighty giantess
Fast flying on a courser dappled gray
From a bold knight, that with great hardiness
Her hard pursued, and sought for to suppress;
She bore before her lap a doleful squire
Lying athwart her horse in great distress,
Fast bounden hand and foot with cords of wire,
Whom she did mean to make the thrall of her desire.

### 38

Which whenas Satyrane beheld, in haste
He left his captive beast at liberty,
And crossed the nearest way, by which he cast
Her to encounter ere she passèd by.
But she the way shunned nathemore forthy,
But forward galloped fast; which when he spied,
His mighty spear he couchèd warily
And at her ran. She, having him descried,
Herself to fight addressed, and threw her load aside.

### 39

Like as a goshawk that in foot doth bear
A trembling culver, having spied on height
An eagle that with plumy wings doth shear
The subtle air, stooping with all his might,
The quarry throws to ground with fell despite
And to the battle doth herself prepare,
So ran the giantess unto the fight:
Her fiery eyes with furious sparks did stare,
And with blasphemous bans high God in pieces tear.

### 40

She caught in hand an huge great iron mace,
Wherewith she many had of life deprived,
But ere the stroke could seize his aimèd place,
His spear amids her sun-broad shield arrived;
Yet nathemore the steel asunder rived,
All were the beam in bigness like a mast,
Ne her out of the steadfast saddle drived,
But, glancing on the tempered metal, brast
In thousand shivers, and so forth beside her passed.

### 41

Her steed did stagger with that puissant stroke;
But she no more was movèd with that might
Than it had lighted on an agèd oak,
Or on the marble pillar that is pight
Upon the top of Mount Olympus' height
For the brave youthly champions to assay

38.3 *cast* aimed.
39.4 *stooping* diving on its prey.
39.9 *bans* curses.

41.4–9 The description here is of an Olympic chariot race incongruously run on the top of Mount Olympus: a conflation that can be found in other Renaissance texts as well.

With burning charet wheels it nigh to smite:
But who that smites it mars his joyous play,
And is the spectacle of ruinous decay.

### 42

Yet therewith sore enraged, with stern regard
Her dreadful weapon she to him addressed,
Which on his helmet martellèd so hard
That made him low incline his lofty crest
And bowed his battered visor to his breast.
Wherewith he was so stunned, that he note ride,
But reelèd to and fro from east to west;
Which when his cruel enemy espied,
She lightly unto him adjoinèd side to side,

### 43

And on his collar laying puissant hand,
Out of his wavering seat him plucked perforce,
Perforce him plucked, unable to withstand
Or help himself, and laying thwart her horse
In loathly wise like to a carrion corse,
She bore him fast away. Which when the knight
That her pursuèd saw, with great remorse
He near was touchèd in his noble sprite,
And gan increase his speed as she increased her flight.

### 44

Whom whenas nigh approaching she espied,
She threw away her burden angrily,
For she list not the battle to abide,
But made herself more light, away to fly;
Yet her the hardy knight pursued so nigh
That almost in the back he oft her strake.
But still when him at hand she did espy,
She turned and semblance of fair fight did make;
But when he stayed, to flight again she did her take.

### 45

By this the good Sir Satyrane gan wake
Out of his dream that did him long entrance,
And, seeing none in place, he gan to make
Exceeding moan, and cursed that cruel chance
Which reft from him so fair a chevisance;
At length he spied whereas that woeful squire
Whom he had rescuèd from captivance
Of his strong foe, lay tumbled in the mire,
Unable to arise, or foot or hand to styre.

### 46

To whom approaching, well he mote perceive
In that foul plight a comely personage

41.7  *charet* chariot.
42.3  *martellèd* hammered.
42.6  *note* could not.

45.5  *chevisance* enterprise.
45.7  *captivance* captivity.
45.9  *styre* direct.

And lovely face, made fit for to deceive
Frail lady's heart with love's consuming rage,
Now in the blossom of his freshest age.
He reared him up, and loosed his iron bands,
And after gan inquire his parentage,
And how he fell into that giant's hands,
And who that was which chasèd her along the lands.

### 47

Then, trembling yet through fear, the squire bespake:
That giantess Argante is behight,
A daughter of the Titans which did make
War against heaven, and heapèd hills on height
To scale the skies and put Jove from his right;
Her sire Typhoeus was, who, mad through mirth
And drunk with blood of men slain by his might,
Through incest her of his own mother Earth
Whilom begot, being but half twin of that birth.

### 48

For at that birth another babe she bore,
To weet, the mighty Ollyphant, that wrought
Great wreak to many errant knights of yore,
And many hath to foul confusion brought.
These twins, men say (a thing far passing thought),
Whiles in their mother's womb enclosed they were,
Ere they into the lightsome world were brought,
In fleshly lust were mingled both yfere,
And in that monstrous wise did to the world appear.

### 49

So lived they ever after in like sin,
Gainst nature's law and good behavior;
But greatest shame was to that maiden twin,
Who, not content so foully to devour
Her native flesh and stain her brother's bower,
Did wallow in all other fleshly mire,
And suffered beasts her body to deflower:
So hot she burnèd in that lustful fire,
Yet all that might not slake her sensual desire.

### 50

But over all the country she did range,
To seek young men to quench her flaming thrust
And feed her fancy with delightful change.
Whomso she fittest finds to serve her lust,

**47.2–9** Argante and her twin brother are Spenser's invention, but he inserts them into the classical myth of the giants, mortal but superhuman creatures, children of Earth (Gê or Gaia), who attempted to storm Olympus and overturn the newly established reign of Jupiter.

**48.2** *Ollyphant* The name comes from Chaucer's burlesque *Tale of Sir Thopas* (*Canterbury Tales* 7.807), a work which also supplies some key elements of Prince Arthur's quest for Gloriana.

**48.3** *wreak* harm.

**48.4** The reading of the 1596 edition; the 1590 edition continues the Chaucerian allusion: "Till him Childe Thopas to confusion brought."

**48.8** *yfere* together.

**50.2** *thrust* thirst.

Through her main strength, in which she most doth trust,
She with her brings into a secret isle,
Where in eternal bondage die he must
Or be the vassal of her pleasures vile
And in all shameful sort himself with her defile.

### 51

Me, silly wretch, she so at vantage caught,
After she long in wait for me did lie,
And meant unto her prison to have brought,
Her loathsome pleasure there to satisfy;
That thousand deaths me lever were to die
Than break the vow that to fair Columbell
I plighted have, and yet keep steadfastly.
As for my name, it mistreth not to tell;
Call me the Squire of Dames, that me beseemeth well.

### 52

But that bold knight whom ye pursuing saw
That giantess is not such as she seemed,
But a fair virgin that in martial law
And deeds of arms above all dames is deemed,
And above many knights is eke esteemed
For her great worth. She Palladine is hight:
She you from death, you me from dread redeemed.
Ne any may that monster match in fight
But she, or such as she, that is so chaste a wight.

### 53

Her well beseems that quest (quoth Satyrane).
But read, thou Squire of Dames, what vow is this
Which thou upon thyself hast lately ta'en?
That shall I you recount (quoth he), ywis,
So be ye pleased to pardon all amiss.
That gentle lady whom I love and serve,
After long suit and weary services,
Did ask me how I could her love deserve,
And how she might be sure that I would never swerve.

### 54

I glad by any means her grace to gain,
Bade her command my life to save or spill.
Eftsoons she bade me with incessant pain
To wander through the world abroad at will,
And everywhere where with my power or skill
I might do service unto gentle dames,
That I the same should faithfully fulfill,
And at the twelve months' end should bring their names
And pledges, as the spoils of my victorious games.

---

51.1 *silly* pitiful.
51.5 *me lever were* I would prefer.
51.8 *mistreth not* is not necessary.
52.6 *Palladine* The character does not appear again in the poem. Her name conflates Charlemagne's twelve senior knights, known as his paladins, with Pallas Athena, the virgin goddess of wisdom.
54.2 *spill* destroy.

### 55

So well I to fair ladies service did,
And found such favor in their loving hearts
That ere the year his course had compassèd,
Three hundred pledges for my good deserts
And thrice three hundred thanks for my good parts
I with me brought, and did to her present;
Which when she saw, more bent to eke my smarts
Than to reward my trusty true intent,
She gan for me devise a grievous punishment:

### 56

To weet, that I my travel should resume,
And with like labor walk the world around,
Ne ever to her presence should presume
Till I so many other dames had found,
The which, for all the suit I could propound,
Would me refuse their pledges to afford,
But did abide forever chaste and sound.
Ah gentle squire (quoth he), tell at one word,
How many foundst thou such to put in thy record?

### 57

Indeed, sir knight (said he), one word may tell
All that I ever found so wisely staid;
For only three they were disposed so well,
And yet three years I now abroad have strayed
To find them out. Mote I (then laughing said
The knight) inquire of thee, what were those three,
The which thy proffered courtesy denayed?
Or ill they seemèd sure avised to be,
Or brutishly brought up, that ne'er did fashions see.

### 58

The first which then refusèd me (said he)
Certes was but a common courtesan,
Yet flat refused to have ado with me
Because I could not give her many a jane.
(Thereat full heartily laughed Satyrane.)
The second was an holy nun to choose,
Which would not let me be her chapelain,
Because she knew, she said, I would disclose
Her counsel, if she should her trust in me repose.

### 59

The third a damsel was of low degree,
Whom I in country cottage found by chance;
Full little weenèd I that chastity
Had lodging in so mean a maintenance,
Yet was she fair, and in her countenance

---

55.7 *eke my smarts* increase my sufferings.
57.2 *staid* steadfast.
57.7 *denayed* refused.
58.4 *jane* a small Genoese silver coin.

58.6 *to choose* by choice.
58.7 *chapelain* chaplain.
59.4 *so mean a maintenance* such a low level of subsistence.

Dwelt simple truth in seemly fashion.
Long thus I wooed her with due observance,
In hope unto my pleasure to have won,
But was as far at last as when I first begun.

### 60

Save her, I never any woman found
That chastity did for itself embrace,
But were for other causes firm and sound:
Either for want of handsome time and place,
Or else for fear of shame and foul disgrace.
Thus am I hopeless ever to attain
My lady's love in such a desperate case,
But all my days am like to waste in vain,
Seeking to match the chaste with the unchaste ladies' train.

### 61

Perdy (said Satyrane), thou Squire of Dames,
Great labor fondly hast thou hent in hand,
To get small thanks, and therewith many blames,
That may amongst Alcides' labors stand.
Thence back returning to the former land
Where late he left the beast he overcame,
He found him not; for he had broke his band,
And was returned again unto his dame,
To tell what tidings of fair Florimell became.

61.2 *hent* taken.                                      61.4 *Alcides* Hercules.

### CANTO VIII

*The witch creates a snowy lady
    like to Florimell,
Who, wronged by carl, by Proteus saved,
    is sought by Paridell.*

### 1

So oft as I this history record,
My heart doth melt with mere compassion
To think how causeless of her own accord
This gentle damsel whom I write upon
Should plungèd be in such affliction,
Without all hope of comfort or relief,
That, sure I ween, the hardest heart of stone
Would hardly find to aggravate her grief;
For misery craves rather mercy than reprief.

### 2

But that accursèd hag, her hostess late,
Had so enrankled her malicious heart

0.3 *carl* churl.                    1.3 *causeless of her own accord* innocently or inadvertently.
1.2 *mere* pure.                    1.9 *reprief* reproof.

That she desired the abridgment of her fate
Or long enlargement of her painful smart.
Now when the beast, which by her wicked art
Late forth she sent, she back returning spied
Tied with her broken girdle, it a part
Of her rich spoils whom he had erst destroyed
She weened, and wondrous gladness to her heart applied,

3

And with it running hastily to her son,
Thought with that sight him much to have relived;
Who thereby deeming sure the thing as done,
His former grief with fury fresh revived
Much more than erst, and would have algates rived
The heart out of his breast: for sith her dead
He surely dempt, himself he thought deprived
Quite of all hope wherewith he long had fed
His foolish malady, and long time had misled.

4

With thought whereof, exceeding mad he grew,
And in his rage his mother would have slain,
Had she not fled into a secret mew,
Where she was wont her sprites to entertain,
The masters of her art; there was she fain
To call them all in order to her aid,
And them conjure upon eternal pain
To counsel her, so carefully dismayed,
How she might heal her son whose senses were decayed.

5

By their advice and her own wicked wit
She there devised a wondrous work to frame,
Whose like on earth was never framèd yet,
That even Nature self envied the same
And grudged to see the counterfeit should shame
The thing itself. In hand she boldly took
To make another like the former dame,
Another Florimell, in shape and look
So lively and so like, that many it mistook.

6

The substance whereof she the body made
Was purest snow, in massy mold congealed,
Which she had gathered in a shady glade
Of the Riphaean hills, to her revealed
By errant sprites, but from all men concealed;
The same she tempered with fine mercury
And virgin wax that never yet was sealed,
And mingled them with perfect vermily,
That like a lively sanguine it seemed to the eye.

**2.3** *the abridgment of her fate* the shortening of her life.
**3.2** *relived* revived.
**3.7** *dempt* deemed.
**4.8** *carefully* with care or worry.

**6.4** *Riphaean hills* A fabled mountain range in the far north, sometimes identified with an actual range in Scythia.
**6.8** *vermily* vermilion.
**6.9** *sanguine* blood-red.

### 7

Instead of eyes, two burning lamps she set
In silver sockets, shining like the skies,
And a quick moving spirit did aret
To stir and roll them like a woman's eyes.
Instead of yellow locks, she did devise
With golden wire to weave her curlèd head,
Yet golden wire was not so yellow thrice
As Florimell's fair hair; and in the stead
Of life, she put a sprite to rule the carcass dead.

### 8

A wicked sprite, yfraught with fawning guile
And fair resemblance above all the rest,
Which with the Prince of Darkness fell somewhile
From heaven's bliss and everlasting rest;
Him needed not instruct which way were best
Himself to fashion likest Florimell,
Ne how to speak, ne how to use his gest,
For he in counterfeisance did excel,
And all the wiles of women's wits knew passing well.

### 9

Him shapèd thus, she decked in garments gay
Which Florimell had left behind her late,
That whoso then her saw would surely say
It was herself, whom it did imitate,
Or fairer than herself, if ought algate
Might fairer be. And then she forth her brought
Unto her son that lay in feeble state;
Who, seeing her, gan straight upstart, and thought
She was the lady self whom he so long had sought.

### 10

Tho fast her clipping twixt his armes twain,
Extremely joyèd in so happy sight,
And soon forgot his former sickly pain;
But she, the more to seem such as she hight,
Coyly rebutted his embracement light,
Yet still with gentle countenance retained
Enough to hold a fool in vain delight.
Him long she so with shadows entertained,
As her creatress had in charge to her ordained.

### 11

Till on a day, as he disposèd was
To walk the woods with that his idol fair,
Her to disport and idle time to pass
In the open freshness of the gentle air,
A knight that way there chancèd to repair.
Yet knight he was not, but a boastful swain

---

7.3   *aret* entrust.
8.7   *gest* bearing.

8.8   *counterfeisance* counterfeiting.
10.1   *clipping* embracing.

That deeds of arms had ever in despair:
Proud Braggadocchio, that in vaunting vain
His glory did repose and credit did maintain.

### 12

He, seeing with that churl so fair a wight,
Deckèd with many a costly ornament,
Much marvelèd thereat, as well he might,
And thought that match a foul disparagement.
His bloody spear eftsoons he boldly bent
Against the silly clown, who, dead through fear,
Fell straight to ground in great astonishment.
Villain (said he), this lady is my dear.
Die if thou it gainsay; I will away her bare.

### 13

The fearful churl durst not gainsay nor do,
But trembling stood, and yielded him the prey;
Who, finding little leisure her to woo,
On Trompart's steed her mounted without stay,
And without rescue led her quite away.
Proud man himself then Braggadocchio deemed,
And next to none, after that happy day,
Being possessèd of that spoil, which seemed
The fairest wight on ground, and most of men esteemed.

### 14

But when he saw himself free from pursuit,
He gan make gentle purpose to his dame,
With terms of love and lewdness dissolute,
For he could well his glozing speeches frame
To such vain uses that him best became;
But she thereto would lend but light regard,
As seeming sorry that she ever came
Into his power that usèd her so hard
To reave her honor, which she more than life preferred.

### 15

Thus as they two of kindness treated long,
There them by chance encountered on the way
An armèd knight upon a courser strong,
Whose trampling feet upon the hollow lay
Seemèd to thunder, and did nigh affray
That capon's courage; yet he lookèd grim,
And feigned to cheer his lady in dismay,
Who seemed for fear to quake in every limb,
And her to save from outrage meekly prayèd him.

---

11.8  *Braggadocchio* "Great Braggart"; the name is Spenser's
invention, on analogy with other Italian words. The character
first appears in II.iii, where he makes an abortive assault on
Belphoebe.

12.6  *silly clown* hapless rustic.

13.4  *Trompart* Braggadocchio's attendant.

14.4  *glozing* flattering.

15.4  *lay* pasture.

15.6  *capon* castrated chicken.

16

Fiercely that stranger forward came, and nigh
Approaching, with bold words and bitter threat
Bade that same boaster, as he mote on high,
To leave to him that lady for escheat,
Or bide him battle without further treat.
That challenge did too peremptory seem,
And filled his senses with abashment great;
Yet, seeing nigh him jeopardy extreme,
He it dissembled well, and light seemed to esteem,

17

Saying, Thou foolish knight, that weenst with words
To steal away that I with blows have won,
And brought through points of many perilous swords;
But if thee list to see thy courser run
Or prove thyself, this sad encounter shun
And seek else without hazard of thy head.
At those proud words that other knight begun
To wax exceeding wroth, and him ared
To turn his steed about, or sure he should be dead.

18

Sith then (said Braggadocchio) needs thou wilt
Thy days abridge through proof of puissance,
Turn we our steeds, that both in equal tilt
May meet again, and each take happy chance.
This said, they both a furlong's mountenance
Retired their steeds, to run in even race;
But Braggadocchio, with his bloody lance
Once having turned, no more returned his face,
But left his love to loss, and fled himself apace.

19

The knight, him seeing fly, had no regard
Him to pursue, but to the lady rode,
And having her from Trompart lightly reared,
Upon his courser set the lovely load,
And with her fled away without abode.
Well weenèd he that fairest Florimell
It was with whom in company he yode,
And so herself did always to him tell:
So made him think himself in heaven, that was in hell.

20

But Florimell herself was far away,
Driven to great distress by Fortune strange,
And taught the careful mariner to play,
Sith late mischance had her compelled to change
The land for sea, at random there to range;

16.3  *as he mote on high* as loudly as he could.
16.4  *escheat* forfeit.
16.5  *treat* discussion.
17.8  *ared* advised.

18.4  *happy chance* the chance of fortune.
18.5  *mountenance* amount.
19.5  *abode* delay.
19.7  *yode* went.

Yet there that cruel queen avengeress,
Not satisfied so far her to estrange
From courtly bliss and wonted happiness,
Did heap on her new waves of weary wretchedness.

### 21

For being fled into the fisher's boat
For refuge from the monster's cruelty,
Long so she on the mighty main did float,
And with the tide drove forward carelessly,
For the air was mild, and clearèd was the sky,
And all his winds Dan Aeolus did keep
From stirring up their stormy enmity,
As pitying to see her wail and weep;
But all the while the fisher did securely sleep.

### 22

At last when, drunk with drowsiness, he woke
And saw his drover drive along the stream,
He was dismayed, and thrice his breast he struck
For marvel of that accident extreme;
But when he saw that blazing beauty's beam
Which with rare light his boat did beautify,
He marveled more, and thought he yet did dream,
Not well awaked, or that some ecstasy
Assotted had his sense, or dazèd was his eye.

### 23

But when her well avising, he perceived
To be no vision, nor fantastic sight,
Great comfort of her presence he conceived,
And felt in his old courage new delight
To gin awake, and stir his frozen sprite,
Tho rudely asked her how she thither came.
Ah (said she) father, I note read aright
What hard misfortune brought me to the same;
Yet am I glad that here I now in safety am.

### 24

But thou, good man, sith far in sea we be,
And the great waters gin apace to swell,
That now no more we can the mainland see,
Have care, I pray, to guide the cock-boat well,
Lest worse on sea than us on land befell.
Thereat the old man did nought but fondly grin,
And said his boat the way could wisely tell;
But his deceitful eyes did never lin
To look on her fair face and mark her snowy skin.

20.6 *that cruel queen avengeress* Fortune.
21.6 *Dan Aeolus* An English form of honorific address is here attached to the name of the Greek god of the winds: Master Aeolus.
22.2 *drover* fishing boat.

22.9 *Assotted* beguiled.
23.1 *avising* considering.
23.7 *note read* cannot tell.
24.4 *cock-boat* small boat, usually one tied behind a ship.
24.8 *lin* cease.

25

The sight whereof in his congealèd flesh
Infixed such secret sting of greedy lust
That the dry withered stock it gan refresh,
And kindled heat that soon in flame forth brust:
The driest wood is soonest burnt to dust.
Rudely to her he leapt, and his rough hand
Where ill became him rashly would have thrust,
But she with angry scorn him did withstand,
And shamefully reprovèd for his rudeness fond.

26

But he, that never good nor manners knew,
Her sharp rebuke full little did esteem;
Hard is to teach an old horse amble true.
The inward smoke that did before but steam
Broke into open fire and rage extreme,
And now he strength gan add unto his will,
Forcing to do that did him foul misseem;
Beastly he threw her down, ne cared to spill
Her garments gay with scales of fish, that all did fill.

27

The silly virgin strove him to withstand
All that she might, and him in vain reviled;
She struggled strongly both with foot and hand
To save her honor from that villain vild,
And cried to heaven, from human help exiled.
O ye brave knights that boast this lady's love,
Where be ye now, when she is nigh defiled
Of filthy wretch? Well may she you reprove
Of falsehood or of sloth, when most it may behove.

28

But if that thou, Sir Satyrane, didst weet,
Or thou, Sir Peridure, her sorry state,
How soon would ye assemble many a fleet
To fetch from sea that ye at land lost late.
Towers, cities, kingdoms ye would ruinate
In your avengement and dispiteous rage,
Ne ought your burning fury mote abate;
But if Sir Calidore could it presage,
No living creature could his cruelty assuage.

29

But sith that none of all her knights is nigh,
See how the heavens of voluntary grace
And sovereign favor towards chastity
Do succor send to her distressèd case:

26.8   *cared to spill* cared if he soiled.
27.1   *silly* defenseless.
28.2   *Peridure* The name of an Arthurian knight in Geoffrey of Monmouth (9.12); his connection with Florimell is unexplained.

28.8   *Calidore* To appear later in the poem as the main knight in Book VI, where he represents Courtesy.

So much high God doth innocence embrace.
It fortunèd, whilst thus she stiffly strove
And the wide sea importunèd long space
With shrilling shrieks, Proteus abroad did rove,
Along the foamy waves driving his finny drove.

### 30

Proteus is shepherd of the seas of yore,
And hath the charge of Neptune's mighty herd;
An agèd sire with head all frory hoar
And sprinkled frost upon this dewy beard;
Who, when those pitiful outcries he heard
Through all the seas so ruefully resound,
His charet swift in haste he thither steered,
Which with a team of scaly phocas bound
Was drawn upon the waves, that foamèd him around.

### 31

And coming to that fisher's wandering boat,
That went at will, withouten card or sail,
He therein saw that irksome sight, which smote
Deep indignation and compassion frail
Into his heart at once; straight did he hale
The greedy villain from his hopèd prey,
Of which he now did very little fail,
And with his staff that drives his herd astray
Him beat so sore that life and sense did much dismay.

### 32

The whiles the piteous lady up did rise,
Ruffled and foully rayed with filthy soil,
And blubbered face with tears of her fair eyes.
Her heart nigh broken was with weary toil
To save herself from that outrageous spoil;
But when she lookèd up, to weet what wight
Had her from so infamous fact assoiled,
For shame, but more for fear of his grim sight,
Down in her lap she hid her face, and loudly shright.

### 33

Herself not savèd yet from danger dread
She thought, but changed from one to other fear;
Like as a fearful partridge that is fled
From the sharp hawk which her attachèd near,
And falls to ground to seek for succor there,
Whereas the hungry spaniels she does spy,
With greedy jaws her ready for to tear:

29.8 *shrilling* piercing. *Proteus* See above, iv.25–8. Spenser here characterizes him much more fully along classical lines, with an eye to the *Odyssey* (4.349ff) and Vergil's *Georgics* (4.387ff).
29.9 *drove* herd.
30.3 *frory hoar* frosty white.
30.7 *charet* chariot.
30.8 *phocas* seals.

31.2 *card* compass.
31.4 *frail* tender.
31.8 *astray* along.
32.2 *rayed* arrayed.
32.5 *spoil* assault.
32.7 *assoiled* released.
32.9 *shright* shrieked.
33.4 *attachèd near* nearly caught.

In such distress and sad perplexity
Was Florimell when Proteus she did see thereby.

### 34

But he endeavorèd with speeches mild
Her to recomfort and accourage bold,
Bidding her fear no more her foeman vild,
Nor doubt himself; and who he was, her told.
Yet all that could not from affright her hold,
Ne to recomfort her at all prevailed;
For her faint heart was with the frozen cold
Benumbed so inly that her wits nigh failed,
And all her senses with abashment quite were quailed.

### 35

Her up betwixt his rugged hands he reared,
And with his frory lips full softly kissed,
Whiles the cold icicles from his rough beard
Droppèd adown upon her ivory breast;
Yet he himself so busily addressed
That her out of astonishment he wrought,
And out of that same fisher's filthy nest
Removing her, into his charet brought,
And there with many gentle terms her fair besought.

### 36

But that old lecher, which with bold assault
That beauty durst presume to violate,
He cast to punish for his heinous fault.
Then took he him, yet trembling sith of late,
And tied behind his charet, to aggrate
The virgin whom he had abused so sore;
So dragged him through the waves in scornful state,
And after cast him up upon the shore,
But Florimell with him unto his bower he bore.

### 37

His bower is in the bottom of the main,
Under a mighty rock, gainst which do rave
The roaring billows in their proud disdain,
That with the angry working of the wave
Therein is eaten out an hollow cave,
That seems rough mason's hand with engines keen
Had long while laborèd it to engrave;
There was his wone, ne living wight was seen,
Save one old nymph hight Panope to keep it clean.

### 38

Thither he brought the sorry Florimell,
And entertainèd her the best he might,
And Panope her entertained eke well,

35.2 *frory* frosty.
35.5 *himself so busily addressed* worked so vigorously.
36.5 *aggrate* gratify.

37.8 *wone* dwelling.
37.9 *Panope* A name later included in Spenser's list of the fifty Nereids (IV.xi.49.8).

As an immortal mote a mortal wight,
To win her liking unto his delight.
With flattering words he sweetly wooèd her,
And offerèd fair gifts to allure her sight,
But she both offers and the offerer
Despised, and all the fawning of the flatterer.

### 39

Daily he tempted her with this or that,
And never suffered her to be at rest;
But evermore she him refusèd flat,
And all his feignèd kindness did detest,
So firmly had she sealèd up her breast.
Sometimes he boasted that a god he hight,
But she a mortal creature lovèd best;
Then he would make himself a mortal wight,
But then she said she loved none but a Faery knight.

### 40

Then like a Faery knight himself he dressed,
For every shape on him he could endue;
Then like a king he was to her expressed,
And offered kingdoms unto her in view
To be his leman and his lady true.
But when all this he nothing saw prevail,
With harder means he cast her to subdue,
And with sharp threats her often did assail,
So thinking for to make her stubborn courage quail.

### 41

To dreadful shapes he did himself transform,
Now like a giant, now like to a fiend,
Then like a centaur, then like to a storm
Raging within the waves; thereby he weened
Her will to win unto his wishèd end.
But when with fear nor favor nor with all
He else could do he saw himself esteemed,
Down in a dungeon deep he let her fall,
And threatened there to make her his eternal thrall.

### 42

Eternal thralldom was to her more lief
Than loss of chastity or change of love;
Die had she rather in tormenting grief
Than any should of falseness her reprove,
Or looseness, that she lightly did remove.
Most virtuous virgin, glory be thy meed,
And crown of heavenly praise with saints above,
Where most sweet hymns of this thy famous deed
Are still amongst them sung, that far my rhymes exceed.

40.2 *endue* assume.
40.5 *leman* beloved.

40.6 *prevail* avail.
42.1 *lief* desirable.

43

Fit song of angels carolèd to be:
But yet what so my feeble Muse can frame
Shall be to advance thy goodly chastity,
And to enroll thy memorable name
In the heart of every honorable dame,
That they thy virtuous deeds may imitate
And be partakers of thy endless fame.
It irks me leave thee in this woeful state
To tell of Satyrane, where I him left of late.

44

Who, having ended with that Squire of Dames
A long discourse of his adventures vain,
The which himself, then ladies more defames,
And finding not the hyena to be slain,
With that same squire returnèd back again
To his first way. And as they forward went,
They spied a knight fair pricking on the plain,
As if he were on some adventure bent,
And in his port appearèd manly hardiment.

45

Sir Satyrane him towards did address,
To weet what wight he was, and what his quest;
And coming nigh, eftsoons he gan to guess,
Both by the burning heart which on his breast
He bare, and by the colors in his crest,
That Paridell it was. Tho to him yode,
And him saluting, as beseemèd best,
Gan first inquire of tidings far abroad,
And afterwards on what adventure now he rode.

46

Who thereto answering, said: The tidings bad,
Which now in Faery court all men do tell,
Which turnèd hath great mirth to mourning sad,
Is the late ruin of proud Marinell
And sudden parture of fair Florimell
To find him forth; and after her are gone
All the brave knights that done in arms excel,
To safeguard her, ywandered all alone.
Amongst the rest my lot (unworthy) is to be one.

47

Ah gentle knight (said then Sir Satyrane),
Thy labor all is lost, I greatly dread,
That hast a thankless service on thee ta'en,
And offerest sacrifice unto the dead;
For dead, I surely doubt, thou mayst aread

44.7  *pricking* riding.
44.9  *port* demeanor.
45.6  *yode* went.

46.5  *parture* departure.
47.5  *aread* think.

Henceforth forever Florimell to be,
That all the noble Knights of Maidenhead
Which her adored may sore repent with me,
And all fair ladies may forever sorry be.

### 48

Which words when Paridell had heard, his hue
Gan greatly change, and seemed dismayed to be;
Then said, Fair sir, how may I ween it true
That ye do tell in such uncertainty?
Or speak ye of report, or did ye see
Just cause of dread, that makes ye doubt so sore?
For perdy, else how mote it ever be
That ever hand should dare for to engore
Her noble blood? The heavens such cruelty abhor.

### 49

These eyes did see that they will ever rue
To have seen (quoth he), whenas a monstrous beast
The palfrey whereon she did travel slew,
And of his bowels made his bloody feast;
Which speaking token showeth at the least
Her certain loss, if not her sure decay.
Besides, that more suspicion increased,
I found her golden girdle cast astray,
Distained with dirt and blood, as relic of the prey.

### 50

Ay me (said Paridell), the signs be sad,
And but God turn the same to good soothsay,
That lady's safety is sore to be drad;
Yet will I not forsake my forward way
Till trial do more certain truth bewray.
Fair sir (quoth he), well may it you succeed,
Ne long shall Satyrane behind you stay,
But to the rest which in this quest proceed
My labor add, and be partaker of their speed.

### 51

Ye noble knights (said then the Squire of Dames),
Well may ye speed in so praiseworthy pain;
But sith the sun now gins to slake his beams
In dewy vapors of the western main
And loose the team out of his weary wain,
Mote not mislike you also to abate
Your zealous haste, till morrow next again
Both light of heaven and strength of men relate?
Which if ye please, to yonder castle turn your gait.

**47.7** *Knights of Maidenhead* A distinguished knightly order
in Faeryland (described at I.vii.46), analogous to the English
Knights of the Garter.
**48.8** *engore* stain itself with.

**50.2** *soothsay* omen.
**51.5** *wain* wagon.
**51.8** *relate* restore.

### 52

That counsel pleasèd well; so all yfere
Forth marchèd to a castle them before,
Where soon arriving, they restrainèd were
Of ready entrance, which ought evermore
To errant knights be common. Wondrous sore
Thereat displeased they were, till that young squire
Gan them inform the cause why that same door
Was shut to all which lodging did desire:
The which to let you weet will further time require.

52.1    *yfere* together.

## CANTO IX

*Malbecco will no strange knights host
    for peevish jealousy.
Paridell jousts with Britomart;
    both show their ancestry.*

### 1

Redoubted knights and honorable dames,
To whom I level all my labor's end,
Right sore I fear lest with unworthy blames
This odious argument my rhymes should shend,
Or ought your goodly patience offend,
Whiles of a wanton lady I do write,
Which with her loose incontinence doth blend
The shining glory of your sovereign light,
And knighthood foul defacèd by a faithless knight.

### 2

But never let the ensample of the bad
Offend the good, for good by paragon
Of evil may more notably be read,
As white seems fairer matched with black at one,
Ne all are shamèd by the fault of one;
For lo, in heaven, whereas all goodness is,
Amongst the angels a whole legion
Of wicked sprites did fall from happy bliss.
What wonder then if one of women all did miss?

### 3

Then listen, lordings, if ye list to weet
The cause why Satyrane and Paridell
Mote not be entertained, as seemèd  meet,
Into that castle (as that squire does tell).
Therein a cankered, crabbèd carl does dwell
That has no skill of court nor courtesy,
Ne cares what men say of him ill or well;

1.4    *shend* shame.
1.7    *blend* pollute.
2.2    *paragon* comparison.

2.4    *at one* together.
2.9    *miss* misbehave.
3.5    *carl* churl.

For all his days he drowns in privity,
Yet has full large to live, and spend at liberty.

4

But all his mind is set on mucky pelf,
To hoard up heaps of evil gotten mass,
For which he others wrongs, and wrecks himself.
Yet is he linkèd to a lovely lass,
Whose beauty doth her bounty far surpass,
The which to him both far unequal years
And also far unlike conditions has;
For she does joy to play amongst her peers,
And to be free from hard restraint and jealous fears.

5

But he is old, and witherèd like hay,
Unfit fair ladies' service to supply;
The privy guilt whereof makes him alway
Suspect her truth, and keep continual spy
Upon her with his other blinkèd eye,
Ne suffereth he resort of living wight
Approach to her, ne keep her company,
But in close bower her mews from all men's sight,
Deprived of kindly joy and natural delight.

6

Malbecco he, and Hellenore she hight,
Unfitly yoked together in one team:
That is the cause why never any knight
Is suffered here to enter, but he seem
Such as no doubt of him he need misdeem.
Thereat Sir Satyrane gan smile, and say:
Extremely mad the man I surely deem,
That weens with watch and hard restraint to stay
A woman's will which is disposed to go astray.

7

In vain he fears that which he cannot shun;
For who wotes not that woman's subtleties
Can guilen Argus, when she list misdone?
It is not iron bands, nor hundred eyes,
Nor brazen walls, nor many wakeful spies
That can withhold her willful wandering feet;
But fast good will with gentle courtesies
And timely service to her pleasures meet
May her perhaps contain, that else would algates fleet.

8

Then is he not more mad (said Paridell)
That hath himself unto such service sold,

---

3.8 *privity* privacy.
4.1 *mucky pelf* filthy lucre.
4.5 *bounty* virtue.
5.3 *privy* secret.
5.5 *blinkèd* afflicted with a blink (the first eye is blind; see 27.6 below).

6.5 *misdeem* suspect.
7.3 *guilen* fool. *Argus* A creature with a hundred eyes, charged by Juno to watch over Io, one of her husband's prospective conquests.

In doleful thralldom all his days to dwell?
For sure a fool I do him firmly hold
That loves his fetters, though they were of gold.
But why do we devise of others' ill,
Whiles thus we suffer this same dotard old
To keep us out, in scorn of his own will,
And rather do not ransack all, and himself kill?

### 9

Nay, let us first (said Satyrane) entreat
The man by gentle means to let us in,
And afterwards affray with cruel threat,
Ere that we to efforce it do begin;
Then if all fail, we will by force it win,
And eke reward the wretch for his mesprise,
As may be worthy of his heinous sin.
That counsel pleased; then Paridell did rise,
And to the castle gate approached in quiet wise.

### 10

Whereat soft knocking, entrance he desired.
The good man self, which then the porter played,
Him answerèd that all were now retired
Unto their rest, and all the keys conveyed
Unto their master, who in bed was laid,
That none him durst awake out of his dream;
And therefore them of patience gently prayed.
Then Paridell began to change his theme,
And threatened him with force and punishment extreme.

### 11

But all in vain; for nought mote him relent,
And now so long before the wicket fast
They waited, that the night was forward spent,
And the fair welkin, foully overcast,
Gan blowen up a bitter stormy blast,
With shower and hail so horrible and dread
That this fair many were compelled at last
To fly for succor to a little shed,
The which beside the gate for swine was orderèd.

### 12

It fortunèd, soon after they were gone,
Another knight, whom tempest thither brought,
Came to that castle, and with earnest moan,
Like as the rest, late entrance dear besought;
But like so as the rest, he prayed for nought,
For flatly he of entrance was refused.
Sorely thereat he was displeased, and thought
How to avenge himself so sore abused,
And evermore the carl of courtesy accused.

9.4  *efforce* gain by force.
9.6  *mesprise* scorn.

11.1  *relent* soften.
11.2  *wicket fast* locked gate.

### 13

But to avoid the intolerable stour,
He was compelled to seek some refuge near,
And to that shed, to shroud him from the shower,
He came, which full of guests he found whilere,
So as he was not let to enter there;
Whereat he gan to wax exceeding wroth,
And swore that he would lodge with them yfere,
Or them dislodge, all were they lief or loath,
And so defied them each, and so defied them both.

### 14

Both were full loath to leave that needful tent,
And both full loath in darkness to debate;
Yet both full lief him lodging to have lent,
And both full lief his boasting to abate.
But chiefly Paridell his heart did grate
To hear him threaten so despitefully,
As if he did a dog to kennel rate
That durst not bark; and rather had he die
Than, when he was defied, in coward corner lie.

### 15

Tho hastily remounting to his steed,
He forth issued: like as a boisterous wind,
Which in the earth's hollow caves hath long been hid
And shut up fast within her prisons blind,
Makes the huge element against her kind
To move and tremble as it were aghast,
Until that it an issue forth may find;
Then forth it breaks, and with his furious blast
Confounds both land and seas, and skies doth overcast.

### 16

Their steel-head spears they strongly couched, and met
Together with impetuous rage and force,
That with the terror of their fierce affret
They rudely drove to ground both man and horse,
That each awhile lay like a senseless corse.
But Paridell, sore bruisèd with the blow,
Could not arise the counterchange to scorse
Till that young squire him rearèd from below;
Then drew he his bright sword, and gan about him throw.

### 17

But Satyrane, forth stepping, did them stay
And with fair treaty pacified their ire;
Then when they were accorded from the fray,
Against that castle's lord they gan conspire,
To heap on him due vengeance for his hire.

13.1  *stour* storm.
13.7  *yfere* together.
13.8  *all were they lief or loath* whether they were willing or not.
14.7  *rate* scold.
15.5  *kind* nature.

16.3  *affret* quick assault.
16.5  *corse* corpse.
16.7  *the counterchange to scorse* to repay the exchange, i.e., to trade blows.
17.5  *hire* payment.

They been agreed, and to the gates they go
To burn the same with unquenchable fire,
And that uncourteous carl, their common foe,
To do foul death to die, or wrap in grievous woe.

### 18

Malbecco, seeing them resolved indeed
To flame the gates, and hearing them to call
For fire in earnest, ran with fearful speed,
And, to them calling from the castle wall,
Besought them humbly him to bear withal,
As ignorant of servants' bad abuse
And slack attendance unto strangers' call.
The knights were willing all things to excuse,
Though nought believed, and entrance late did not refuse.

### 19

They been ybrought into a comely bower,
And served of all things that mote needful be,
Yet secretly their host did on them lower,
And welcomed more for fear than charity;
But they dissembled what they did not see,
And welcomèd themselves. Each gan undight
Their garments wet, and weary armor free,
To dry themselves by Vulcan's flaming light,
And eke their lately bruisèd parts to bring in plight.

### 20

And eke that stranger knight amongst the rest
Was for like need enforced to disarray;
Tho whenas veilèd was her lofty crest,
Her golden locks, that were in trammels gay
Upbounden, did themselves adown display,
And raught unto her heels: like sunny beams
That in a cloud their light did long time stay,
Their vapor vaded, show their golden gleams,
And through the perceant air shoot forth their azure streams.

### 21

She also doffed her heavy habergeon,
Which the fair feature of her limbs did hide,
And her well plighted frock, which she did won
To tuck about her short when she did ride,
She low let fall, that flowed from her lank side
Down to her foot, with careless modesty.
Then of them all she plainly was espied
To be a woman wight, unwist to be:
The fairest woman wight that ever eye did see.

---

19.5  But they pretended not to notice what was not being
offered to them.
19.9  *plight* health.
20.2  *disarray* undress.
20.4  *trammels* braids.
20.6  *raught* reached.

20.8  *vaded* vanished.
20.9  *perceant* piercing.
21.3  *plighted* pleated.  *did won* was accustomed.
21.5  *lank* thin.
21.6  *careless* casual.
21.8  *unwist to be* not recognized as such.

22

Like as Minerva, being late returned
From slaughter of the giants conquerèd
(Where proud Encelade, whose wide nostrils burned
With breathèd flames like to a furnace red,
Transfixèd with the spear, down tumbled dead
From top of Haemus, by him heapèd high),
Hath loosed her helmet from her lofty head,
And her Gorgonian shield gins to untie
From her left arm, to rest in glorious victory.

23

Which whenas they beheld, they smitten were
With great amazement of so wondrous sight,
And each on other, and they all on her
Stood gazing, as if sudden great affright
Had them surprised. At last avising right
Her goodly personage and glorious hue,
Which they so much mistook, they took delight
In their first error, and yet still anew
With wonder of her beauty fed their hungry view.

24

Yet note their hungry view be satisfied,
But, seeing still, the more desired to see,
And ever firmly fixèd did abide
In contemplation of divinity.
But most they marveled at her chivalry
And noble prowess, which they had approved,
That much they fained to know who she mote be;
Yet none of all them her thereof amoved,
Yet everyone her liked, and everyone her loved.

25

And Paridell, though partly discontent
With his late fall and foul indignity,
Yet was soon won his malice to relent
Through gracious regard of her fair eye
And knightly worth, which he too late did try,
And trièd did adore. Supper was dight;
Then they Malbecco prayed of courtesy
That of his lady they might have the sight
And company at meat, to do them more delight.

26

But he to shift their curious request
Gan causen why she could not come in place:

22.1   *Minerva* Virgin goddess of wisdom; the 1590 text has
"Bellona," the goddess of war.
22.3   *Encelade* One of the rebellious giants defeated by the
Olympians; Athena (Minerva) is said to have thrown the
island of Sicily on top of him.
22.6   *Haemus* A mountain in northern Thrace, the site of
Jupiter's victory over another giant, Typhoeus, whom Spenser
makes the father of the giantess Argante (see above, vii.47.6).

22.8   *Gorgonian shield* Athena's aegis, with the decapitated
head of Medusa attached to it.
23.5   *avising* perceiving.
24.1   *note* could not.
24.6   *approved* experienced.
24.8   *amoved* bestirred.
26.1   *shift* evade.
26.2   *causen* give reasons.

Her crazèd health, her late recourse to rest,
And humid evening, ill for sick folk's case.
But none of these excuses could take place,
Ne would they eat till she in presence came.
She came in presence with right comely grace,
And fairly them saluted, as became,
And showed herself in all a gentle, courteous dame.

### 27

They sat to meat, and Satyrane his chance
Was her before, and Paridell beside.
But he himself sat looking still askance
Gainst Britomart, and ever closely eyed
Sir Satyrane, that glances might not glide;
But his blind eye, that sided Paridell,
All his demeanor from his sight did hide:
On her fair face so did he feed his fill
And sent close messages of love to her at will.

### 28

And ever and anon, when none was ware,
With speaking looks that close embassage bore
He roved at her, and told his secret care;
For all that art he learnèd had of yore,
Ne was she ignorant of that lewd lore,
But in his eye his meaning wisely read,
And with the like him answered evermore.
She sent at him one fiery dart whose head
Empoisoned was with privy lust and jealous dread.

### 29

He from that deadly throw made no defense,
But to the wound his weak heart opened wide;
The wicked engine through false influence
Passed through his eyes, and secretly did glide
Into his heart, which it did sorely gride.
But nothing new to him was that same pain,
Ne pain at all; for he so oft had tried
The power thereof, and loved so oft in vain,
That thing of course he counted love to entertain.

### 30

Thenceforth to her he sought to intimate
His inward grief by means to him well known.
Now Bacchus' fruit out of the silver plate
He on the table dashed, as overthrown
Or of the fruitful liquor overflown,
And by the dancing bubbles did divine

26.3   *crazèd* broken.
26.5   *take place* find acceptance.
26.8   *saluted* kissed.   *as became* as was fitting.
28.2   *close embassage* secret embassy.
28.3   *roved* shot.

29.5   *gride* pierce.
29.7   *tried* experienced.
29.9   *thing of course he counted* he considered it a matter of course.
30.3   *Bacchus' fruit* wine.

Or therein write to let his love be shown;
Which well she read out of the learnèd line,
A sacrament profane in mystery of wine.

### 31

And whenso of his hand the pledge she raught,
The guilty cup she feignèd to mistake,
And in her lap did shed her idle draught,
Showing desire her inward flame to slake.
By such close signs they secret way did make
Unto their wills, and one-eye's watch escape;
Two eyes him needeth for to watch and wake
Who lovers will deceive. Thus was the ape
By their fair handling put into Malbecco's cape.

### 32

Now when of meats and drinks they had their fill,
Purpose was movèd by that gentle dame
Unto those knights adventurous to tell
Of deeds of arms which unto them became,
And everyone his kindred, and his name.
Then Paridell, in whom a kindly pride
Of gracious speech and skill his words to frame
Abounded, being glad of so fit tide
Him to commend to her, thus spake, of all well eyed.

### 33

Troy, that art now nought but an idle name
And in thine ashes buried low dost lie,
Though whilom far much greater than thy fame,
Before that angry gods and cruel sky
Upon thee heaped a direful destiny,
What boots it boast thy glorious descent
And fetch from heaven thy great genealogy,
Sith all thy worthy praises being blent,
Their offspring hath embased and later glory shent?

### 34

Most famous worthy of the world, by whom
That war was kindled which did Troy inflame
And stately towers of Ilion whilom
Brought unto baleful ruin, was by name
Sir Paris, far renowmed through noble fame,
Who through great prowess and bold hardiness
From Lacedaemon fetched the fairest dame
That ever Greece did boast or knight possess,
Whom Venus to him gave for meed of worthiness.

---

31.8–9 They made a fool of Malbecco (a monkey is now wearing his clothes).
32.8 *tide* opportunity.
33.9 *embased* debased. *shent* shamed.

33–51 Paridell's narrative, running from the beginning of the Trojan war to the arrival of Brut and his people in Britain, gives the beginning of the saga of British history sketched in II.x.5–68 and III.iii.27–50.
34.7 *Lacedaemon* Sparta, Helen's birthplace.

35

Fair Helen, flower of beauty excellent
And garland of the mighty conquerors,
That madest many ladies dear lament
The heavy loss of their brave paramours,
Which they far off beheld from Trojan towers,
And saw the fields of fair Scamander strown
With carcasses of noble warriors,
Whose fruitless lives were under furrow sown,
And Xanthus' sandy banks with blood all overflown.

36

From him my lineage I derive aright,
Who long before the ten years' siege of Troy,
Whiles yet on Ida he a shepherd hight,
On fair Oenone got a lovely boy,
Whom for remembrance of her passèd joy
She of his father Parius did name;
Who, after Greeks did Priam's realm destroy,
Gathered the Trojan relics saved from flame,
And with them sailing thence, to the isle of Paros came.

37

That was by him called Paros which before
Hight Nausa; there he many years did reign,
And built Nausicle by the Pontic shore,
The which he dying left next in remain
To Paridas his son.
From whom I, Paridell, by kin descend,
But for fair ladies' love and glory's gain
My native soil have left, my days to spend
In suing deeds of arms, my life's and labor's end.

38

Whenas the noble Britomart heard tell
Of Trojan wars and Priam's city sacked,
The rueful story of Sir Paridell,
She was empassioned at that piteous act
With zealous envy of Greeks' cruel fact
Against that nation, from whose race of old
She heard that she was lineally extract:
For noble Britons sprung from Trojans bold,
And Troynovant was built of old Troy's ashes cold.

39

Then, sighing soft awhile, at last she thus:
O lamentable fall of famous town,
Which reigned so many years victorious

35.6 *Scamander* In Homer, the river flowing past Troy; Spenser takes it as the name of the plain before the city.
35.9 *Xanthus* In Homer, an older name for the Scamander.
36.1–6 Paris's union with Oenone is attested in classical mythology, as is a son of that union; but the son was not named after his father, and had no further known history.
36.9 *Paros* One of the Cyclatic islands; the history given of it in the next stanza is Spenser's invention.
37.9 *suing* pursuing.
38.9 *Troynovant* London.

And of all Asie bore the sovereign crown,
In one sad night consumed and thrown down!
What stony heart that hears thy hapless fate
Is not empierced with deep compassion,
And makes ensample of man's wretched state,
That flowers so fresh at morn, and fades at evening late?

### 40

Behold, sir, how your pitiful complaint
Hath found another partner of your pain,
For nothing may impress so dear constraint
As country's cause and common foe's disdain.
But if it should not grieve you back again
To turn your course, I would to hear desire
What to Aeneas fell, sith that men sayn
He was not in the city's woeful fire
Consumed, but did himself to safety retire.

### 41

Anchises' son, begot of Venus fair
(Said he), out of the flames for safeguard fled,
And with a remnant did to sea repair,
Where he through fatal error long was led
Full many years, and weetless wanderèd
From shore to shore amongst the Lybic sands
Ere rest he found. Much there he sufferèd,
And many perils passed in foreign lands
To save his people sad from victor's vengeful hands.

### 42

At last in Latium he did arrive,
Where he with cruel war was entertained
Of the inland folk, which sought him back to drive,
Till he with old Latinus was constrained
To contract wedlock (so the fates ordained):
Wedlock contract in blood, and eke in blood
Accomplishèd, that many dear complained.
The rival slain, the victor through the flood
Escapèd hardly, hardly praised his wedlock good.

### 43

Yet after all he victor did survive,
And with Latinus did the kingdom part;
But after, when both nations gan to strive
Into their names the title to convert,
His son Iülus did from thence depart
With all the warlike youth of Trojans' blood,
And in Long Alba placed his throne apart,

---

**40.7** *Aeneas* The Trojan warrior, mentioned briefly by Homer, who becomes the hero of Vergil's *Aeneid*; the next two stanzas summarize the story of Vergil's poem.
**41.6** *Lybic* north African.
**42.1** *Latium* The area in central Italy around the future site of Rome.

**42.4** *Latinus* Legendary Italian king whose daughter Lavinia was married to Aeneas as part of their alliance; Aeneas's misgivings about his marriage are Paridell's contribution to the story.
**43.2** *part* divide.
**43.4** To gain sole sovereignty.
**43.7** *Long Alba* Alba Longa, another city in Latium.

Where fair it flourishèd and long time stood
Till Romulus, renewing it, to Rome removed.

### 44

There there (said Britomart) afresh appeared
The glory of the later world to spring,
And Troy again out of her dust was reared
To sit in second seat of sovereign king,
Of all the world under her governing.
But a third kingdom yet is to arise
Out of the Trojans' scatterèd offspring,
That in all glory and great enterprise
Both first and second Troy shall dare to equalize.

### 45

It Troynovant is hight, that with the waves
Of wealthy Thamis washèd is along,
Upon whose stubborn neck, whereat he raves
With roaring rage, and sore himself does throng,
That all men fear to tempt his billows strong,
She fastened hath her foot, which stands so high
That it a wonder of the world is sung
In foreign lands, and all which passen by,
Beholding it from far, do think it threats the sky.

### 46

The Trojan Brut did first that city found,
And Highgate made the mere thereof by west,
And Overt Gate by north: that is the bound
Toward the land; two rivers bound the rest.
So huge a scope at first him seemèd best
To be the compass of his kingdom's seat;
So huge a mind could not in lesser rest,
Ne in small meres contain his glory great,
That Albion had conquered first by warlike feat.

### 47

Ah fairest lady knight (said Paridell),
Pardon I pray my heedless oversight,
Who had forgot that whilom I heard tell
From agèd Mnemon, for my wits been light.
Indeed he said (if I remember right)
That of the antique Trojan stock there grew
Another plant, that raught to wondrous height,
And far abroad his mighty branches threw
Into the utmost angle of the world he knew.

---

**45** A reference to London Bridge and the dramatic effect on it of tidal currents.
**46.2** *mere* boundary.
**46.3** *Overt Gate* Unidentified.
**46.4** *two rivers* One is obviously the Thames; the other has not been decisively identified.

**46.9** *Albion* Britain.
**47.4** *Mnemon* The name means "reminding" or "remembering" in Greek.
**47.9** *utmost angle of the world* A commonly supposed etymology for "England."

### 48

For that same Brut, whom much he did advance
In all his speech, was Sylvius his son,
Whom having slain through luckless arrow's glance,
He fled for fear of that he had misdone,
Or else for shame, so foul reproach to shun,
And with him led to sea an youthly train,
Where weary wandering they long time did won
And many fortunes proved in the ocean main
And great adventures found, that now were long to sayn.

### 49

At last by fatal course they driven were
Into an island spacious and broad,
The furthest north that did to them appear;
Which, after rest, they seeking far abroad
Found it the fittest soil for their abode,
Fruitful of all things fit for living food,
But wholly waste, and void of people's trod,
Save an huge nation of the giants' brood
That fed on living flesh, and drunk men's vital blood.

### 50

Whom he through weary wars and labors long
Subdued with loss of many Britons bold;
In which the great Goëmagot of strong
Corineus and Coulin of Debon old
Were overthrown and laid on the earth full cold,
Which quakèd under their so hideous mass:
A famous history to be enrolled
In everlasting monuments of brass,
That all the antique worthies' merits far did pass.

### 51

His work great Troynovant, his work is eke
Fair Lincoln, both renowmèd far away,
That who from east to west will endlong seek
Cannot two fairer cities find this day,
Except Cleopolis: so heard I say
Old Mnemon. Therefore, sir, I greet you well,
Your country kin, and you entirely pray
Of pardon for the strife which late befell
Betwixt us both unknown. So ended Paridell.

### 52

But all the while that he these speeches spent,
Upon his lips hung fair dame Hellenore

**48.2**   *Sylvius his son* Sylvius's son. Sylvius was a grandson of Aeneas; the story here follows Geoffrey of Monmouth, 1.3.
**48.7**   *won* dwell.
**49.7**   *trod* tracks.
**50.3–5**   For the victory of Corineus over the giant Gogmagog (Goëmagot), see Geoffrey of Monmouth, 1.16; the victory of Debon over Coulin, otherwise unattested, is described by Spenser earlier in the poem (II.x.11).
**51.1–2**   Brut's founding of Lincoln appears to be Spenser's invention.
**51.5**   *Cleopolis* "City of Glory" in Greek; Gloriana's city.
**51.7**   *country kin* fellow countryman.

With vigilant regard and due attent,
Fashioning worlds of fancies evermore
In her frail wit, that now her quite forlore,
The whiles unwares away her wondering eye
And greedy ears her weak heart from her bore;
Which he perceiving, ever privily
In speaking many false belgardes at her let fly.


### 53

So long these knights discoursèd diversely
Of strange affairs and noble hardiment
Which they had passed with mickle jeopardy,
That now the humid night was farforth spent
And heavenly lamps were halfendeal ybrent;
Which the old man seeing well, who too long thought
Every discourse and every argument,
Which by the hours he measurèd, besought
Them go to rest. So all unto their bowers were brought.

**52.3** *attent* attention.
**52.5** *forlore* forsook.
**52.9** *belgardes* loving looks (from the Italian *bel guardo*).

**53.3** *mickle* much.
**53.5** *halfendeal* halfway. *ybrent* burned out.


### CANTO X

*Paridell rapeth Hellenore;*
*Malbecco her pursues,*
*Finds amongst satyrs, whence with him*
*to turn she doth refuse.*


### 1

The morrow next, so soon as Phoebus' lamp
Bewrayèd had the world with early light
And fresh Aurora had the shady damp
Out of the goodly heaven amovèd quite,
Fair Britomart and that same Faery knight
Uprose, forth on their journey for to wend;
But Paridell complained that his late fight
With Britomart so sore did him offend
That ride he could not, till his hurts he did amend.


### 2

So forth they fared, but he behind them stayed,
Maugre his host, who grudgèd grievously
To house a guest that would be needs obeyed,
And of his own him left not liberty;
Might wanting measure moveth surquidry.
Two things he fearèd, but the third was death:
That fierce young man's unruly mastery,

**0.1** *rapeth* abducts.
**0.4** *turn* return.

**2.2** *Maugre* despite.
**2.5** *surquidry* arrogance.

His money, which he loved as living breath,
And his fair wife, whom honest long he kept uneath.

### 3

But patience perforce he must aby
What fortune and his fate on him will lay;
Fond is the fear that finds no remedy.
Yet warily he watcheth every way
By which he feareth evil happen may,
So the evil thinks by watching to prevent;
Ne doth he suffer her nor night nor day
Out of his sight herself once to absent.
So doth he punish her and eke himself torment.

### 4

But Paridell kept better watch than he,
A fit occasion for his turn to find.
False love, why do men say thou canst not see
And in their foolish fancy feign thee blind,
That with thy charms the sharpest sight dost bind
And to thy will abuse? Thou walkest free,
And seest every secret of the mind;
Thou seest all, yet none at all sees thee.
All that is by the working of thy deity.

### 5

So perfect in that art was Paridell
That he Malbecco's halfen eye did wile,
His halfen eye he wilèd wondrous well,
And Hellenore's both eyes did eke beguile,
Both eyes and heart at once, during the while
That he there sojournèd his wounds to heal;
That Cupid self, it seeing, close did smile
To weet how he her love away did steal,
And bade that none their joyous treason should reveal.

### 6

The learnèd lover lost no time nor tide
That least avantage mote to him afford,
Yet bore so fair a sail that none espied
His secret drift, till he her laid aboard.
Whenso in open place and common board
He fortuned her to meet, with common speech
He courted her, yet bated every word,
That his ungentle host note him appeach
Of vile ungentleness or hospitage's breach.

---

2.9  *honest* chaste.  *uneath* with difficulty.
3.1  *aby* endure.
3.3  *Fond* foolish.
5.2  *halfen eye* The "blinkèd eye," the one with half its function.  *wile* deceive.
6.1  *tide* opportunity.

6.4  *laid aboard* Nautical terminology for bringing a ship alongside another to begin battle.
6.5  *board* meal.
6.7  *bated* restrained.
6.8  *note* could not.  *appeach* accuse.
6.9  *hospitage* hospitality.

### 7

But when apart (if ever her apart)
He found, then his false engines fast he plied
And all the slights unbosomed in his heart:
He sighed, he sobbed, he swooned, he perdy died
And cast himself on ground her fast beside;
Tho when again he him bethought to live,
He wept and wailed and false laments belied,
Saying, but if she mercy would him give,
Then he mote algates die, yet did his death forgive.

### 8

And otherwhiles with amorous delights
And pleasing toys he would her entertain,
Now singing sweetly to surprise her sprites,
Now making lays of love and lovers' pain,
Brawls, ballads, virelays, and verses vain;
Oft purposes, oft riddles he devised,
And thousands like which flowèd in his brain,
With which he fed her fancy and enticed
To take to his new love, and leave her old despised.

### 9

And everywhere he might, and everywhile
He did her service dutiful and sued
At hand with humble pride and pleasing guile,
So closely yet that none but she it viewed,
Who well perceivèd all, and all endued.
Thus finely did he his false nets dispread
With which he many weak hearts had subdued
Of yore, and many had ylike misled;
What wonder then, if she were likewise carrièd?

### 10

No fort so fensible, no walls so strong,
But that continual battery will rive,
Or daily siege through dispurveyance long
And lack of rescues will to parley drive;
And piece that unto parley ear will give
Will shortly yield itself, and will be made
The vassal of the victor's will belive.
That stratagem had oftentimes assayed
This crafty paramour, and now it plain displayed.

### 11

For through his trains he her entrappèd hath,
That she her love and heart hath wholly sold

7.2    *engines* schemes.
7.9    *did his death forgive* pardoned her for causing his death.
8.5    *Brawls* Dances, sometimes called French brawls and particularly associated with courtship and seduction. Spenser's spelling here is "bransles," displaying the term's French derivation, but the modern spelling represents what appears to be the Elizabethan pronunciation.    *virelays* Poems in a verse form of French derivation.

8.6    *purposes* a game of questions and answers.
9.5    *endued* absorbed.
10.3    *dispurveyance* lack of provisions.
10.5    *piece* stronghold.
10.7    *belive* quickly.
11.1    *trains* tricks.

To him, without regard of gain or scathe,
Or care of credit or of husband old,
Whom she hath vowed to dub a fair cuckold.
Nought wants but time and place, which shortly she
Devisèd hath, and to her lover told.
It pleasèd well. So well they both agree;
So ready ripe to ill, ill women's counsels be.

### 12

Dark was the evening, fit for lover's stealth,
When chanced Malbecco busy be elsewhere;
She to his closet went, where all his wealth
Lay hid. Thereof she countless sums did rear,
The which she meant away with her to bear;
The rest she fired for sport, or for despite,
As Helen, when she saw aloft appear
The Trojan flames and reach to heaven's height,
Did clap her hands and joyèd at that doleful sight.

### 13

This second Helen, fair Dame Hellenore,
The whiles her husband ran with sorry haste
To quench the flames which she had tind before,
Laughed at his foolish labor spent in waste,
And ran into her lover's arms right fast;
Where straight embracèd, she to him did cry
And call aloud for help ere help were past:
For lo, that guest would bear her forcibly,
And meant to ravish her, that rather had to die.

### 14

The wretched man, hearing her call for aid,
And ready seeing him with her to fly,
In his disquiet mind was much dismayed;
But when again he backward cast his eye
And saw the wicked fire so furiously
Consume his heart and scorch his idol's face,
He was therewith distressèd diversely,
Ne wist he how to turn, nor to what place:
Was never wretched man in such a woeful case.

### 15

Aye when to him she cried, to her he turned
And left the fire: love money overcame.
But when he markèd how his money burned,
He left his wife: money did love disclaim.
Both was he loath to lose his lovèd dame,
And loath to leave his liefest pelf behind;
Yet sith he note save both, he saved that same
Which was the dearest to his dunghill mind,
The god of his desire, the joy of misers blind.

---

11.3   *scathe* harm.
11.4   *credit* fidelity.
12.6   *fired* burned.

13.3   *tind* kindled.
13.7   *past* too late.
15.6   *liefest pelf* dearest wealth.

16

Thus whilst all things in troublous uproar were,
And all men busy to suppress the flame,
The loving couple need no rescue fear,
But leisure had and liberty to frame
Their purposed flight, free from all men's reclaim;
And Night, the patroness of love-stealth fair,
Gave them safe conduct, till to end they came.
So been they gone yfere, a wanton pair
Of lovers loosely knit, where list them to repair.

17

Soon as the cruel flames yslakèd were,
Malbecco, seeing how his loss did lie,
Out of the flames which he had quenched whilere
Into huge waves of grief and jealousy
Full deep implungèd was and drownèd nigh,
Twixt inward dole and felonous despite;
He raved, he wept, he stamped, he loud did cry,
And all the passions that in man may light
Did him at once oppress, and vex his caitiff sprite.

18

Long thus he chawed the cud of inward grief,
And did consume his gall with anguish sore;
Still when he musèd on his late mischief,
Then still the smart thereof increasèd more,
And seemed more grievous than it was before.
At last when sorrow he saw booted nought,
Ne grief might not his love to him restore,
He gan devise how her he rescue mought;
Ten thousand ways he cast in his confusèd thought.

19

At last resolving, like a pilgrim poor,
To search her forth whereso she might be found,
And bearing with him treasure in close store,
The rest he leaves in ground; so takes in hand
To seek her endlong, both by sea and land.
Long he her sought, he sought her far and near,
And everywhere that he mote understand
Of knights and ladies any meetings were,
And of each one he met, he tidings did inquire.

20

But all in vain: his woman was too wise
Ever to come into his clutch again,
And he too simple ever to surprise
The jolly Paridell, for all his pain.
One day, as he forpassèd by the plain
With weary pace, he far away espied
A couple seeming well to be his twain,

16.5    *reclaim* recall.
16.8    *yfere* together.

19.5    *endlong* from one end to the other.

Which hovèd close under a forest side,
As if they lay in wait, or else themselves did hide.

### 21

Well weenèd he that those the same mote be,
And as he better did their shape avise,
Him seemèd more their manner did agree;
For the one was armèd all in warlike wise,
Whom to be Paridell he did devise,
And the other all yclad in garments light,
Discolored like to womanish disguise,
He did resemble to his lady bright:
And ever his faint heart much earnèd at the sight.

### 22

And ever fain he towards them would go,
But yet durst not for dread approachen nigh,
But stood aloof, unweeting what to do,
Till that, pricked forth with love's extremity,
That is the father of foul jealousy,
He closely nearer crept, the truth to weet;
But as he nigher drew, he easily
Might scern that it was not his sweetest sweet,
Ne yet her belamour, the partner of his sheet.

### 23

But it was scornful Braggadocchio,
That with his servant Trompart hovered there
Sith late he fled from his too earnest foe;
Whom such whenas Malbecco spièd clear,
He turnèd back, and would have fled arear,
Till Trompart, running hastily, him did stay,
And bade before his sovereign lord appear.
That was him loath, yet durst he not gainsay,
And coming him before, low louted on the lay.

### 24

The boaster at him sternly bent his brow,
As if he could have killed him with his look,
That to the ground him meekly made to bow
And awful terror deep into him struck,
That every member of his body quook.
Said he, Thou man of nought, what dost thou here,
Unfitly furnished with thy bag and book,
Where I expected one with shield and spear,
To prove some deeds of arms upon an equal peer?

### 25

The wretched man at his imperious speech
Was all abashed, and, low prostrating, said:

20.8 *hovèd* lingered.
21.2 *avise* perceive.
21.5 *devise* suppose.
21.7 *Discolored* variegated.

21.8 *resemble* liken.
21.9 *earnèd* filled with longing.
22.9 *belamour* beloved.
23.9 *louted* did obeisance. *lay* pasture.

Good sir, let not my rudeness be no breach
Unto your patience, ne be ill ypaid;
For I unwares this way by fortune strayed,
A silly pilgrim driven to distress
That seek a lady. There he sudden stayed,
And did the rest with grievous sighs suppress,
While tears stood in his eyes, few drops of bitterness.

26

What lady, man? (said Trompart) Take good heart,
And tell thy grief, if any hidden lie;
Was never better time to show thy smart
Than now, that noble succor is thee by,
That is the whole world's common remedy.
That cheerful word his weak heart much did cheer
And with vain hope his spirits faint supply,
That bold he said: O most redoubted peer,
Vouchsafe with mild regard a wretch's case to hear.

27

Then sighing sore, It is not long (said he)
Sith I enjoyed the gentlest dame alive,
Of whom a knight, no knight at all perdy,
But shame of all that do for honor strive,
By treacherous deceit did me deprive;
Through open outrage he her bore away
And with foul force unto his will did drive,
Which all good knights that arms do bear this day
Are bound for to revenge, and punish if they may.

28

And you, most noble lord, that can and dare
Redress the wrong of miserable wight,
Cannot employ your most victorious spear
In better quarrel than defense of right,
And for a lady gainst a faithless knight;
So shall your glory be advancèd much,
And all fair ladies magnify your might,
And eke myself, albe I simple such,
Your worthy pain shall well reward with guerdon rich.

29

With that out of his budget forth he drew
Great store of treasure, therewith him to tempt;
But he on it looked scornfully askew,
As much disdaining to be so misdempt,
Or a war-monger to be basely nempt,
And said: Thy offers base I greatly loathe,
And eke thy words uncourteous and unkempt;
I tread in dust thee and thy money both,
That, were it not for shame . . . So turnèd from him wroth.

---

25.6  *silly* defenseless.
28.8  *albe I simple such* although I be so humble.
29.1  *budget* wallet.

29.4  *misdempt* misjudged.
29.5  *nempt* called.

30

But Trompart, that his master's humor knew
In lofty looks to hide an humble mind,
Was inly tickled with that golden view,
And in his ear him rounded close behind.
Yet stooped he not, but lay still in the wind,
Waiting advantage on the prey to seize,
Till Trompart, lowly to the ground inclined,
Besought him his great courage to appease,
And pardon simple man that rash did him displease.

31

Big-looking like a doughty douzeper,
At last he thus: Thou clod of vilest clay,
I pardon yield, and with thy rudeness bear.
But weet henceforth, that all that golden prey,
And all that else the vain world vaunten may,
I loathe as dung, ne deem my due reward;
Fame is my meed, and glory, virtue's pay.
But minds of mortal men are muchel marred,
And moved amiss with massy muck's unmeet regard.

32

And more, I grant to thy great misery
Gracious respect: thy wife shall back be sent,
And that vile knight, whoever that he be,
Which hath thy lady reft and knighthood shent,
By Sanglamort my sword, whose deadly dent
The blood hath of so many thousands shed,
I swear, ere long shall dearly it repent;
Ne he twixt heaven and earth shall hide his head,
But soon he shall be found, and shortly done be dead.

33

The foolish man thereat wox wondrous blithe,
As if the word so spoken were half done,
And humbly thankèd him a thousand sithe,
That had from death to life him newly won.
Tho forth the boaster marching, brave begun
His stolen steed to thunder furiously,
As if he heaven and hell would overrun
And all the world confound with cruelty,
That much Malbecco joyèd in his jollity.

34

Thus long they three together travelèd,
Through many a wood and many an uncouth way,

---

**30.4** *rounded* whispered.

**30.5** *stooped* swooped (a term from falconry: the action of a hawk suddenly descending upon its prey).

**31.1** *douzeper* One of Charlemagne's twelve paladins (*les douze pairs*); a *pezzo grosso*, a big shot.

**31.7** *pay* So the 1609 edition; 1590 and 1596 read "pray" (i.e., "prey").

**32.4** *shent* shamed.

**32.5** *Sanglamort* Bloody Death (French); in a previous appearance, Trompart claims that in accord with a knightly vow Braggadocchio has forsworn the use of a sword (II.iii.12).

**33.6** *his stolen steed* Sir Guyon's horse, purloined at II.iii.4.

To seek his wife that was far wanderèd.
But those two sought nought but the present prey,
To weet, the treasure which he did bewray,
On which their eyes and hearts were wholly set,
With purpose how they might it best betray;
For sith the hour that first he did them let
The same behold, therewith their keen desires were whet.

35

It fortunèd, as they together fared,
They spied where Paridell came pricking fast
Upon the plain, the which himself prepared
To joust with that brave stranger knight a cast,
As on adventure by the way he passed.
Alone he rode, without his paragon;
For having filched her bells, he up her cast
To the wide world, and let her fly alone.
He nould be clogged. So had he servèd many one.

36

The gentle lady, loose at randon left,
The greenwood long did walk, and wander wide
At wild adventure, like a forlorn weft,
Till on a day the satyrs her espied
Straying alone withouten groom or guide;
Her up they took, and with them home her led,
With them as housewife ever to abide,
To milk their goats and make them cheese and bread,
And everyone as common good her handelèd:

37

That shortly she Malbecco has forgot,
And eke Sir Paridell, all were he dear;
Who from her went to seek another lot,
And now by fortune was arrivèd here,
Where those two guilers with Malbecco were.
Soon as the old man saw Sir Paridell,
He fainted, and was almost dead with fear,
Ne word he had to speak, his grief to tell,
But to him louted low and greeted goodly well,

38

And after askèd him for Hellenore.
I take no keep of her (said Paridell);
She wonneth in the forest there before.
So forth he rode as his adventure fell,
The whiles the boaster from his lofty sell
Feigned to alight, something amiss to mend.
But the fresh swain would not his leisure dwell,

35.2    *pricking* riding.
35.4    *cast* bout.
35.6    *paragon* partner.
35.7–8    A metaphor for falconry; bells and jesses are the restraints on a hawk, here analogous to the bonds of matrimony.

35.9    *nould* would not.    *clogged* fitted with an encumbrance.
36.3    *weft* waif (unclaimed property).
37.5    *guilers* deceivers.
38.3    *wonneth* dwells.
38.5    *sell* saddle.

But went his way; whom when he passèd kenned,
He up remounted light, and after feigned to wend.

### 39

Perdy, nay (said Malbecco), shall ye not,
But let him pass as lightly as he came;
For little good of him is to be got,
And mickle peril to be put to shame.
But let us go to seek my dearest dame,
Whom he hath left in yonder forest wild;
For of her safety in great doubt I am,
Lest salvage beasts her person have despoiled.
Then all the world is lost, and we in vain have toiled.

### 40

They all agree, and forward them addressed.
Ah, but (said crafty Trompart) weet ye well
That yonder in that wasteful wilderness
Huge monsters haunt, and many dangers dwell;
Dragons and minotaurs and fiends of hell,
And many wild woodmen, which rob and rend
All travelers. Therefore, advise ye well
Before ye enterprise that way to wend:
One may his journey bring too soon to evil end.

### 41

Malbecco stopped in great astonishment,
And with pale eyes fast fixèd on the rest
Their counsel craved in danger imminent.
Said Trompart, You that are the most oppressed
With burden of great treasure, I think best
Here for to stay in safety behind;
My lord and I will search the wide forest.
That counsel pleasèd not Malbecco's mind,
For he was much afraid himself alone to find.

### 42

Then is it best (said he) that ye do leave
Your treasure here in some security,
Either fast closèd in some hollow greave,
Or buried in the ground from jeopardy,
Till we return again in safety.
As for us two, lest doubt of us ye have,
Hence far away we will blindfolded lie,
Ne privy be unto your treasure's grave.
It pleasèd; so he did. Then they march forward brave.

### 43

Now when amid the thickest woods they were,
They heard a noise of many bagpipes shrill,
And shrieking hubbubs them approaching near,
Which all the forest did with horror fill.

---

39.4 *mickle* much.
39.8 *salvage* savage.
40.1 *them addressed* made their way.

40.3 *wasteful* desolate.
42.3 *greave* thicket.

That dreadful sound the boaster's heart did thrill
With such amazement that in haste he fled,
Ne ever lookèd back for good or ill,
And after him eke fearful Trompart sped;
The old man could not fly, but fell to ground half dead.

### 44

Yet afterwards, close creeping as he might,
He in a bush did hide his fearful head;
The jolly satyrs, full of fresh delight,
Came dancing forth, and with them nimbly led
Fair Hellenore, with garlands all bespread,
Whom their May-lady they had newly made.
She, proud of that new honor which they read,
And of their lovely fellowship full glad,
Danced lively, and her face did with a laurel shade.

### 45

The silly man that in the thicket lay
Saw all this goodly sport, and grievèd sore,
Yet durst he not against it do or say,
But did his heart with bitter thoughts engore
To see the unkindness of his Hellenore.
All day they dancèd with great lustihead,
And with their hornèd feet the green grass wore,
The whiles their goats upon the browses fed,
Till drooping Phoebus gan to hide his golden head.

### 46

Tho up they gan their merry pipes to truss,
And all their goodly herds did gather round,
But every satyr first did give a buss
To Hellenore; so busses did abound.
Now gan the humid vapor shed the ground
With pearly dew, and the earthes gloomy shade
Did dim the brightness of the welkin round,
That every bird and beast awarnèd made
To shroud themselves, whiles sleep their senses did invade.

### 47

Which when Malbecco saw, out of his bush
Upon his hands and feet he crept full light,
And like a goat amongst the goats did rush,
That through the help of his fair horns on height,
And misty damp of misconceiving night,
And eke through likeness of his goatish beard,
He did the better counterfeit aright;
So home he marched amongst the hornèd herd,
That none of all the satyrs him espied or heard.

---

45.5  *unkindness* unnatural behavior.
45.8  *browses* fresh shoots.
46.3  *buss* kiss.

46.7  *welkin* sky.
47.4  A cuckolded husband was supposed to grow horns;
usually treated as imaginary, here they are literal.

### 48

At night, when all they went to sleep, he viewed
Whereas his lovely wife amongst them lay,
Embracèd of a satyr rough and rude,
Who all the night did mind his joyous play;
Nine times he heard him come aloft ere day,
That all his heart with jealousy did swell.
But yet that night's ensample did bewray
That not for nought his wife them loved so well,
When one so oft a night did ring his matins bell.

### 49

So closely as he could, he to them crept
When weary of their sport to sleep they fell,
And to his wife, that now full soundly slept,
He whispered in her ear, and did her tell
That it was he which by her side did dwell,
And therefore prayed her wake, to hear him plain.
As one out of a dream not wakèd well,
She turned her, and returnèd back again;
Yet her for to awake he did the more constrain.

### 50

At last with irksome trouble she abraid,
And then perceiving that it was indeed
Her old Malbecco which did her upbraid
With looseness of her love and loathly deed,
She was astonished with exceeding dread,
And would have waked the satyr by her side;
But he her prayed, for mercy or for meed,
To save his life, ne let him be descried,
But harken to his lore, and all his counsel hide.

### 51

Tho gan he her persuade to leave that lewd
And loathsome life, of God and man abhorred,
And home return, where all should be renewed
With perfect peace and bands of fresh accord,
And she received again to bed and board,
As if no trespass ever had been done;
But she it all refusèd at one word,
And by no means would to his will be won,
But chose amongst the jolly satyrs still to won.

### 52

He wooèd her till dayspring he espied,
But all in vain; and then turned to the herd,
Who butted him with horns on every side
And trod down in the dirt, where his hoar beard
Was foully dight, and he of death afeared.
Early, before the heaven's fairest light
Out of the ruddy east was fully reared,

48.5  The satyr's level of performance has specific classical precedent: Catullus 32.8; Ovid, *Amores* 3.7.25–6.
49.9  *constrain* exert himself.
50.1  *abraid* awoke.
50.9  *lore* instructions.

The herds out of their folds were loosèd quite,
And he amongst the rest crept forth in sorry plight.

### 53

So soon as he the prison door did pass,
He ran as fast as both his feet could bear,
And never lookèd who behind him was,
Ne scarcely who before: like as a bear
That, creeping close amongst the hives to rear
An honeycomb, the wakeful dogs espy,
And, him assailing, sore his carcass tear,
That hardly he with life away does fly,
Ne stays, till safe himself he see from jeopardy.

### 54

Ne stayed he, till he came unto the place
Where late his treasure he entombèd had,
Where when he found it not (for Trompart base
Had it purloinèd for his master bad),
With extreme fury he became quite mad
And ran away, ran with himself away:
That whoso strangely had him seen bestad,
With upstart hair and staring eyes' dismay,
From Limbo lake him late escapèd sure would say.

### 55

High over hills and over dales he fled,
As if the wind him on his wings had borne,
Ne bank nor bush could stay him when he sped
His nimble feet, as treading still on thorn;
Grief and despite and jealousy and scorn
Did all the way him follow hard behind,
And he himself himself loathed so forlorn,
So shamefully forlorn of womankind:
That as a snake still lurkèd in his wounded mind.

### 56

Still fled he forward, looking backward still,
Ne stayed his flight nor fearful agony
Till that he came unto a rocky hill,
Over the sea suspended dreadfully,
That living creature it would terrify
To look adown, or upward to the height;
From thence he threw himself dispiteously,
All desperate of his fore-damnèd sprite,
That seemed no help for him was left in living wight.

### 57

But through long anguish and self-murdering thought
He was so wasted and forpinèd quite,

---

**53.5** *rear* take away.
**54.7** *strangely had him seen bestad* had seen him so strangely beset.

**54.9** *Limbo lake* A lake in hell; in Christian theology, Limbo is a site for the unbaptized, but Spenser's use of the term is not so specific.
**56.8** *fore-damnèd* Because he would die a suicide.
**57.2** *forpinèd* wasted away.

That all his substance was consumed to nought
And nothing left but like an airy sprite,
That on the rocks he fell so flit and light
That he thereby received no hurt at all,
But chancèd on a craggy cliff to light;
Whence he with crooked claws so long did crawl
That at the last he found a cave with entrance small.

### 58

Into the same he creeps, and thenceforth there
Resolved to build his baleful mansion,
In dreary darkness and continual fear
Of that rock's fall, which ever and anon
Threats with huge ruin him to fall upon,
That he dare never sleep, but that one eye
Still ope he keeps for that occasion;
Ne ever rests he in tranquillity,
The roaring billows beat his bower so boisterously.

### 59

Ne ever is he wont on ought to feed
But toads and frogs, his pasture poisonous,
Which in his cold complexion do breed
A filthy blood or humor rancorous,
Matter of doubt and dread suspicious,
That doth with cureless care consume the heart,
Corrupts the stomach with gall vicious,
Crosscuts the liver with internal smart,
And doth transfix the soul with death's eternal dart.

### 60

Yet can he never die, but dying lives,
And doth himself with sorrow new sustain,
That death and life at once unto him gives,
And painful pleasure turns to pleasing pain.
There dwells he ever, miserable swain,
Hateful both to himself and every wight,
Where he through privy grief and horror vain
Is woxen so deformed that he has quite
Forgot he was a man, and Jealousy is hight.

**59.2** *pasture* food.

### CANTO XI

*Britomart chaseth Ollyphant,*
  *finds Scudamour distressed:*
*Assays the House of Busirane,*
  *where Love's spoils are expressed.*

### 1

O hateful, hellish snake, what fury first
Brought thee from baleful house of Proserpine,

**0.4** *expressed* set out.          **1.2** *house of Proserpine* Hades.

Where in her bosom she thee long had nursed
And fostered up with bitter milk of tine,
Foul Jealousy, that turnest love divine
To joyless dread, and mak'st the loving heart
With hateful thoughts to languish and to pine
And feed itself with self-consuming smart?
Of all the passions in the mind, thou vilest art.

2

O let him far be banishèd away,
And in his stead let Love forever dwell,
Sweet Love, that doth his golden wings embay
In blessèd nectar, and pure pleasure's well,
Untroubled of vile fear or bitter fell.
And ye fair ladies, that your kingdoms make
In the hearts of men, them govern wisely well,
And of fair Britomart ensample take,
That was as true in love as turtle to her make.

3

Who with Sir Satyrane, as erst ye read,
Forth riding from Malbecco's hostless house,
Far off espied a young man, the which fled
From an huge giant, that with hideous
And hateful outrage long him chasèd thus.
It was that Ollyphant, the brother dear
Of that Argante vile and vicious
From whom the Squire of Dames was reft whilere:
This all as bad as she, and worse, if worse ought were.

4

For as the sister did in feminine
And filthy lust exceed all womankind,
So he surpassèd his sex masculine
In beastly use all that I ever find;
Whom whenas Britomart beheld behind
The fearful boy so greedily pursue,
She was emmovèd in her noble mind
To employ her puissance to his rescue,
And prickèd fiercely forward, where she him did view.

5

Ne was Sir Satyrane her far behind,
But with like fierceness did ensue the chase;
Whom when the giant saw, he soon resigned
His former suit, and from them fled apace.
They after both, and boldly bade him base,
And each did strive the other to outgo;
But he them both outran a wondrous space,

---

1.4   *tine* suffering.
2.3   *embay* bathe.
2.5   *fell* gall.
2.9   *turtle* turtle-dove.   *make* mate.

4.9   *prickèd* rode.
5.2   *ensue* pursue.
5.5   *bade him base* They challenged him to turn and fight, as in a children's game called "prisoner's base."

For he was long and swift as any roe,
And now made better speed, to escape his fearèd foe.


6

It was not Satyrane whom he did fear,
But Britomart, the flower of chastity;
For he the power of chaste hands might not bear,
But always did their dread encounter fly,
And now so fast his feet he did apply
That he has gotten to a forest near,
Where he is shrouded in security.
The wood they enter, and search everywhere;
They searchèd diversely, so both divided were.


7

Fair Britomart so long him followèd
That she at last came to a fountain sheer,
By which there lay a knight all wallowèd
Upon the grassy ground, and by him near
His habergeon, his helmet, and his spear.
A little off his shield was rudely thrown,
On which the wingèd boy in colors clear
Depeincted was, full easy to be known,
And he thereby, wherever it in field was shown.


8

His face upon the ground did groveling lie,
As if he had been slumbering in the shade,
That the brave maid would not, for courtesy,
Out of his quiet slumber him abraid,
Nor seem too suddenly him to invade.
Still as she stood, she heard with grievous throb
Him groan, as if his heart were pieces made,
And with most painful pangs to sigh and sob,
That pity did the virgin's heart of patience rob.


9

At last forth breaking into bitter plaints,
He said: O sovereign Lord that sitst on high
And reignst in bliss amongst thy blessèd saints,
How sufferest thou such shameful cruelty
So long unwreakèd of thine enemy?
Or hast thou, Lord, of good men's cause no heed?
Or doth thy justice sleep, and silent lie?
What booteth then the good and righteous deed,
If goodness find no grace, nor righteousness no meed?


10

If good find grace, and righteousness reward,
Why then is Amoret in caitiff band,
Sith that more bounteous creature never fared

7.8 *Depeincted* depicted.
8.4 *abraid* awake.
8.5 *invade* intrude upon.

9.5 *unwreakèd* unavenged.
10.2 *caitiff band* wretched captivity.
10.3 *bounteous* virtuous.

On foot upon the face of living land?
Or if that heavenly justice may withstand
The wrongful outrage of unrighteous men,
Why then is Busirane with wicked hand
Suffered these seven months' day in secret den
My lady and my love so cruelly to pen?

### 11

My lady and my love is cruelly penned
In doleful darkness from the view of day,
Whilst deadly torments do her chaste breast rend,
And the sharp steel doth rive her heart in tway,
All for she Scudamour will not denay.
Yet thou vile man, vile Scudamour, art sound,
Ne canst her aid, ne canst her foe dismay;
Unworthy wretch to tread upon the ground,
For whom so fair a lady feels so sore a wound.

### 12

There an huge heap of singulfs did oppress
His struggling soul, and swelling throbs impeach
His faltering tongue with pangs of dreariness,
Choking the remnant of his plaintive speech,
As if his days were come to their last reach;
Which when she heard, and saw the ghastly fit
Threatening into his life to make a breach,
Both with great ruth and terror she was smit,
Fearing lest from her cage the weary soul would flit.

### 13

Tho stooping down, she him amovèd light;
Who therewith somewhat starting, up gan look,
And seeing him behind a stranger knight,
Whereas no living creature he mistook,
With great indignance he that sight forsook,
And down again himself disdainfully
Abjecting, the earth with his fair forehead struck;
Which the bold virgin seeing, gan apply
Fit medicine to his grief, and spake thus courteously.

### 14

Ah gentle knight, whose deep conceivèd grief
Well seems to exceed the power of patience:
Yet if that heavenly grace some good relief
You send, submit you to high providence,
And ever in your noble heart prepense

10.7   *Busirane* The name is adapted from that of Busiris, in Greek legend a king of Egypt noted for his cruelty; in Christian times, he was occasionally identified with the Pharaoh of Exodus.
10.8   *seven months' day* period of seven months.
11.4   *tway* two.
11.5   *denay* deny.
11.7   *dismay* defeat.

12.1   *singulfs* sighs.
12.2   *impeach* hinder.
13.1   *amovèd light* gently roused.
13.4   Not taking her to be a mortal being: i.e., he assumes she is some kind of divine creature, and finds no comfort from that source.
14.5   *prepense* consider beforehand.

That all the sorrow in the world is less
Than virtue's might and value's confidence.
For who nill bide the burden of distress
Must not here think to live: for life is wretchedness.

### 15

Therefore, fair sir, do comfort to you take,
And freely read what wicked felon so
Hath outraged you, and thralled your gentle make.
Perhaps this hand may help to ease your woe
And wreak your sorrow on your cruel foe;
At least it fair endeavor will apply.
Those feeling words so near the quick did go
That up his head he rearèd easily,
And leaning on his elbow, these few words let fly.

### 16

What boots it plain that cannot be redressed,
And sow vain sorrow in a fruitless ear,
Sith power of hand nor skill of learnèd breast
Ne worldly price cannot redeem my dear
Out of her thralldom and continual fear?
For he, the tyrant which hath her in ward
By strong enchantments and black magic lear,
Hath in a dungeon deep her close embarred,
And many dreadful fiends hath pointed to her guard.

### 17

There he tormenteth her most terribly,
And day and night afflicts with mortal pain,
Because to yield him love she doth deny,
Once to me yold, not to be yold again,
But yet by torture he would her constrain
Love to conceive in her disdainful breast;
Till so she do, she must in dole remain,
Ne may by living means be thence released.
What boots it then to plain that cannot be redressed?

### 18

With this sad hearsal of his heavy stress
The warlike damsel was empassioned sore,
And said: Sir knight, your cause is nothing less
Than is your sorrow, certes if not more;
For nothing so much pity doth implore
As gentle ladies' helpless misery.
But yet, if please ye listen to my lore,
I will with proof of last extremity
Deliver her from thence, or with her for you die.

14.7   *value* valor.
16.1   What good does it do to lament something that cannot
be made right?
16.6   *ward* custody.

16.7   *lear* lore.
16.8   *embarred* imprisoned.
17.4   *yold* yielded.
18.8   *proof of last extremity* risking everything.

### 19

Ah, gentlest knight alive (said Scudamour),
What huge heroic magnanimity
Dwells in thy bounteous breast? What couldst thou more
If she were thine, and thou as now am I?
O spare thy happy days, and them apply
To better boot, but let me die, that ought.
More is more loss; one is enough to die.
Life is not lost (said she) for which is bought
Endless renowm, that more than death is to be sought.

### 20

Thus she at length persuaded him to rise
And with her wend, to see what new success
Mote him befall upon new enterprise.
His arms, which he had vowed to disprofess,
She gathered up and did about him dress,
And his forwandered steed unto him got;
So forth they both yfere make their progress,
And march not past the mountenance of a shot
Till they arrived whereas their purpose they did plot.

### 21

There they, dismounting, drew their weapons bold
And stoutly came unto the castle gate;
Whereas no gate they found them to withhold,
Nor ward to wait at morn and evening late,
But in the porch, that did them sore amate,
A flaming fire, ymixed with smoldery smoke
And stinking sulphur, that with grisly hate
And dreadful horror did all entrance choke,
Enforcèd them their forward footing to revoke.

### 22

Greatly thereat was Britomart dismayed,
Ne in that stound wist how herself to bear,
For danger vain it were to have assayed
That cruel element which all things fear
Ne none can suffer to approachen near,
And, turning back to Scudamour, thus said:
What monstrous enmity provoke we here,
Foolhardy as the Earth's children, the which made
Battle against the gods? So we a god invade.

### 23

Danger without discretion to attempt
Inglorious and beastlike is; therefore, sir knight,
Aread what course of you is safest dempt,
And how we with our foe may come to fight.
This is (quoth he) the dolorous despite

---

20.7    *yfere* together.
20.8    *the mountenance of a shot* the length of a bow-shot.
21.5    *amate* daunt.
22.2    *stound* difficult situation.

22.8    *Earth's children* The giants of classical mythology; see above on vii.47.2–9.
23.3    *Aread* declare.    *dempt* deemed.

Which erst to you I plained; for neither may
This fire be quenched by any wit or might,
Ne yet by any means removed away,
So mighty be the enchantments which the same do stay.

### 24

What is there else but cease these fruitless pains,
And leave me to my former languishing?
Fair Amoret must dwell in wicked chains,
And Scudamour here die with sorrowing.
Perdy, not so (said she), for shameful thing
It were to abandon noble chevisance
For show of peril, without venturing;
Rather let try extremities of chance
Than enterprisèd praise for dread to disavance.

### 25

Therewith resolved to prove her utmost might,
Her ample shield she threw before her face
And, her sword's point directing forward right,
Assailed the flame, the which eftsoons gave place
And did itself divide with equal space,
That through she passèd: as a thunderbolt
Pierceth the yielding air, and doth displace
The soaring clouds into sad showers ymolt,
So to her yold the flames, and did their force revolt.

### 26

Whom whenas Scudamour saw past the fire
Safe and untouched, he likewise gan assay,
With greedy will and envious desire,
And bade the stubborn flames to yield him way;
But cruel Mulciber would not obey
His threatful pride, but did the more augment
His mighty rage, and with imperious sway
Him forced, maugre his fierceness, to relent
And back retire, all scorched and pitifully brent.

### 27

With huge impatience he inly swelt,
More for great sorrow that he could not pass
Than for the burning torment which he felt,
That with fell woodness he effiercèd was,
And, willfully him throwing on the grass,
Did beat and bounce his head and breast full sore;
The whiles the championess now entered has
The utmost room, and passed the foremost door:
The utmost room, abounding with all precious store.

23.6  *plained* complained of.
24.6  *chevisance* enterprise.
24.9  Than because of fear to abandon a praiseworthy endeavor already under way.
25.8  *ymolt* melted.
25.9  *revolt* turn back.
26.5  *Mulciber* Vulcan, the god of fire.

26.8  *maugre* despite.
26.9  *brent* burned.
27.1  *swelt* swelled.
27.4  *fell woodness* savage rage.  *effiercèd* made fierce.
27.6  *bounce* beat.
27.8  *utmost* outermost.

28

For roundabout the walls yclothèd were
With goodly arras of great majesty,
Woven with gold and silk so close and near
That the rich metal lurkèd privily,
As faining to be hid from envious eye;
Yet here and there and everywhere unwares
It showed itself, and shone unwillingly:
Like a discolored snake, whose hidden snares
Through the green grass his long bright burnished back declares.

29

And in those tapets weren fashionèd
Many fair portraits, and many a fair feat,
And all of love and all of lustihead,
As seemèd by their semblant, did entreat;
And eke all Cupid's wars they did repeat,
And cruel battles which he whilom fought
Gainst all the gods, to make his empire great,
Besides the huge massacres which he wrought
On mighty kings and caesars into thralldom brought.

30

Therein was writ how often thundering Jove
Had felt the point of his heart-piercing dart,
And, leaving heaven's kingdom, here did rove
In strange disguise, to slake his scalding smart:
Now like a ram, fair Helle to pervert;
Now like a bull, Europa to withdraw.
Ah, how the fearful lady's tender heart
Did lively seem to tremble, when she saw
The huge seas under her to obey her servant's law.

31

Soon after that, into a golden shower
Himself he changed, fair Danaë to view,
And through the roof of her strong brazen tower
Did rain into her lap an honey dew,
The whiles her foolish guard, that little knew
Of such deceit, kept the iron door fast barred,
And watched that none should enter nor issue;
Vain was the watch, and bootless all the ward,
Whenas the god to golden hue himself transferred.

28.8    *discolored* variegated.
29–46    The gallery of divine sexual behavior is based, in places quite closely, on Arachne's tapestry in Ovid's *Metamorphoses* 6.103–28; cf. the temple floor in Marlowe's *Hero and Leander* 141–56.
29.1    *tapets* tapestries.
29.4    Did treat, as appeared in their images.

30.5    *Helle* Not in classical literature one of Jupiter's conquests; she fled with her brother on a genuine winged ram to escape an angry stepmother.
30.6    *Europa* Abducted by Jupiter in the form of a bull, who swam with her on his back from Tyre to Crete.
31.2    *Danaë* Imprisoned in a tower by her father, because of an oracle about his prospective grandchild; the child of her seduction by Jupiter was Perseus, who did indeed kill his grandfather.

### 32

Then was he turned into a snowy swan,
To win fair Leda to his lovely trade.
O wondrous skill, and sweet wit of the man
That her in daffadillies sleeping made,
From scorching heat her dainty limbs to shade;
Whiles the proud bird, ruffing his feathers wide
And brushing his fair breast, did her invade,
She slept, yet twixt her eyelids closely spied
How towards her he rushed, and smilèd at his pride.

### 33

Then showed it how the Theban Semele,
Deceived of jealous Juno, did require
To see him in his sovereign majesty,
Armed with his thunderbolts and lightning fire,
Whence dearly she with death bought her desire.
But fair Alcmena better match did make,
Joying his love in likeness more entire:
Three nights in one, they say, that for her sake
He then did put, her pleasures longer to partake.

### 34

Twice was he seen in soaring eagle's shape,
And with wide wings to beat the buxom air,
Once when he with Asterië did scape,
Again whenas the Trojan boy so fair
He snatched from Ida hill and with him bare:
Wondrous delight it was there to behold
How the rude shepherds after him did stare,
Trembling through fear, lest down he fallen should,
And often to him calling to take surer hold.

### 35

In satyr's shape Antiopa he snatched,
And like a fire when he Aegina assayed;
A shepherd when Mnemosyne he catched,
And like a serpent to the Thracian maid.
Whiles thus on earth great Jove these pageants played,
The wingèd boy did thrust into his throne,
And, scoffing, thus unto his mother said:
Lo, now the heavens obey to me alone,
And take me for their Jove, whiles Jove to earth is gone.

32.2  *Leda* Wife of the king of Sparta, mother to Helen, Clytemnestra, and the Dioscuri.

33.1  *Semele* Already pregnant by Jupiter with Dionysus, she made the request described here, and was incinerated; Jupiter rescued his fetal son from the ashes.

33.6  *Alcmena* Seduced by Jupiter in the guise of her own husband; during their artificially long night together she conceived Hercules.

34.2  *buxom* yielding.

34.3  *Asterië* Asteria, who changed herself into a quail in her attempt to escape Jupiter.

34.4  *Trojan boy* Ganymede.

35.1  *Antiopa* Mother by Jupiter of Amphion and Zethus, builders of the walls of Thebes.

35.2  *Aegina* Abducted by Jupiter to the island which took her name; through the son so conceived she was great-grandmother to both Achilles and Ajax.

35.3  *Mnemosyne* Mother by Jupiter of the nine Muses.

35.4  *Thracian maid* Spenser's unexplained alteration of an obscure reference in Ovid to "Deois," i.e., Proserpina, Jupiter's own daughter; the metamorphosis into a serpent is otherwise unattested.

### 36

And thou, fair Phoebus, in thy colors bright
Wast there inwoven, and the sad distress
In which that boy thee plungèd, for despite
That thou bewray'dst his mother's wantonness
When she with Mars was meint in joyfulness.
Forthy he thrilled thee with a leaden dart
To love fair Daphne, which thee lovèd less:
Less she thee loved than was thy just desert,
Yet was thy love her death, and her death was thy smart.

### 37

So lovedst thou the lusty Hyacinct,
So lovedst thou the fair Coronis dear,
Yet both are of thy hapless hand extinct,
Yet both in flowers do live and love thee bear,
The one a paunce, the other a sweetbriar;
For grief whereof, ye mote have lively seen
The god himself rending his golden hair
And breaking quite his garland ever green,
With other signs of sorrow and impatient teen.

### 38

Both for those two, and for his own dear son,
The son of Climene, he did repent,
Who, bold to guide the charet of the sun,
Himself in thousand pieces fondly rent,
And all the world with flashing fire brent:
So like, that all the walls did seem to flame.
Yet cruel Cupid, not herewith content,
Forced him eftsoons to follow other game,
And love a shepherd's daughter for his dearest dame.

### 39

He lovèd Isse for his dearest dame,
And for her sake her cattle fed awhile,
And for her sake a cowherd vile became,
The servant of Admetus, cowherd vile,
Whiles that from heaven he sufferèd exile.
Long were to tell each other lovely fit,
Now like a lion hunting after spoil,
Now like a stag, now like a falcon flit:
All which in that fair arras was most lively writ.

36.5   *meint* joined.
36.6   *thrilled* pierced.
36.7   *Daphne* Daphne metamorphosed into the laurel-tree to escape Apollo's desire; elsewhere this change is seldom referred to as her "death."
37.1   *Hyacinct* Hyacinthus; a beautiful young man loved by Apollo, he was accidentally killed by the god while they were throwing the discus.
37.2   *Coronis* Mother by Apollo of Asclepius; Apollo killed her when she was unfaithful to him with a mortal.

37.5   *paunce* pansy (not the classical hyacinth, but of the same purple color). *sweetbriar* Spenser's contribution; the original Coronis underwent no metamorphosis.
37.9   *teen* suffering.
38.2   *son of Climene* Phaethon, killed when he tried to drive his father's chariot.
38.6   *So like* Referring to the vividness of the tapestry.
39.1–5   Spenser here grafts a well-attested story of Apollo's temporary servitude to Admetus onto Ovid's brief reference to his love for a young woman named Isse.

### 40

Next unto him was Neptune picturèd,
In his divine resemblance wondrous like:
His face was rugged, and his hoary head
Droppèd with brackish dew; his three-forked pike
He sternly shook, and therewith fierce did strike
The raging billows, that on every side
They trembling stood, and made a long, broad dike,
That his swift charet might have passage wide,
Which four great hippodames did draw in teamwise tied.

### 41

His sea-horses did seem to snort amain,
And from their nostrils blow the briny stream,
That made the sparkling waves to smoke again
And flame with gold, but the white foamy cream
Did shine with silver and shoot forth his beam.
The god himself did pensive seem and sad,
And hung adown his head as he did dream;
For privy love his breast empiercèd had,
Ne ought but dear Bisaltis aye could make him glad.

### 42

He lovèd eke Iphimedia dear,
And Aeolus' fair daughter, Arne hight,
For whom he turned himself into a steer
And fed on fodder to beguile her sight.
Also to win Deucalion's daughter bright,
He turned himself into a dolphin fair;
And like a wingèd horse he took his flight
To snaky-lock Medusa to repair,
On whom he got fair Pegasus that flitteth in the air.

### 43

Next Saturn was (but who would ever ween
That sullen Saturn ever weened to love?
Yet love is sullen and Saturnlike seen,
As he did for Erigone it prove),
That to a centaur did himself transmove.
So proved it eke that gracious god of wine
When for to compass Philyra's hard love
He turned himself into a fruitful vine,
And into her fair bosom made his grapes decline.

**40.9** *hippodames* Also mentioned at II.ix.50.8; apparently a playful variation on "hippotames" (hippopotami).
**41.9** *Bisaltis* Theophane, daughter of Bisaltes; she and Neptune coupled as a ewe and a ram, and she gave birth to the ram on which Helle fled (see 30.5 above).
**42.1** *Iphimedia* Mother by Neptune of two sons, the Aloadae, who grew to gigantic size and made war against Olympus.
**42.2** *Arne* More commonly known as Melanippe; her child by Neptune, named after her own father, was Aeolus, god of the winds.

**42.5** *Deucalion's daughter bright* Melantho?.
**42.7** *a wingèd horse* In Ovid just a winged creature (*volucrem*), presumably a bird.
**43** The stories of Philyra and Erigone have been reversed here. The former, seduced by Saturn in the guise of a stallion, gave birth to the centaur Chiron; the latter was the mother of a son by Bacchus.

### 44

Long were to tell the amorous assays
And gentle pangs with which he makèd meek
The mighty Mars, to learn his wanton plays;
How oft for Venus, and how often eke
For many other nymphs he sore did shriek
With womanish tears and with unwarlike smarts,
Privily moistening his horrid cheek.
There was he painted full of burning darts,
And many wide wounds launchèd through his inner parts.

### 45

Ne did he spare (so cruel was the elf )
His own dear mother (ah, why should he so?),
Ne did he spare sometime to prick himself,
That he might taste the sweet, consuming woe
Which he had wrought to many others moe.
But to declare the mournful tragedies
And spoils wherewith he all the ground did strow,
More eath to number with how many eyes
High heaven beholds sad lovers' nightly thieveries.

### 46

Kings, queens, lords, ladies, knights, and damsels gent
Were heaped together with the vulgar sort,
And mingled with the rascal rabblement,
Without respect of person or of port,
To show Dan Cupid's power and great effort;
And roundabout a border was entrailed
Of broken bows and arrows shivered short,
And a long bloody river through them railed,
So lively and so like that living sense it failed.

### 47

And at the upper end of that fair room
There was an altar built of precious stone,
Of passing value and of great renowm,
On which there stood an image all alone
Of massy gold, which with his own light shone;
And wings it had with sundry colors dight,
More sundry colors than the proud pavone
Bears in his boasted fan, or Iris bright
When her discolored bow she spreads through heaven bright.

### 48

Blindfold he was, and in his cruel fist
A mortal bow and arrows keen did hold,
With which he shot at randon, when him list,

46.4  *port* social rank.
46.5  *Dan* Master.
46.6  *entrailed* intertwined.
46.8  *railed* gushed.

46.9  *failed* deceived.
47.7  *pavone* peacock.
47.8  *Iris* goddess of the rainbow.

Some headed with sad lead, some with pure gold
(Ah, man beware how thou those darts behold);
A wounded dragon under him did lie,
Whose hideous tail his left foot did enfold,
And with a shaft was shot through either eye,
That no man forth might draw, ne no man remedy.

### 49

And underneath his feet was written thus:
*Unto the victor of the gods this be.*
And all the people in that ample house
Did to that image bow their humble knee,
And oft committed foul idolatry.
That wondrous sight fair Britomart amazed,
Ne seeing could her wonder satisfy,
But ever more and more upon it gazed,
The whiles the passing brightness her frail senses dazed.

### 50

Tho as she backward cast her busy eye
To search each secret of that goodly stead,
Over the door thus written she did spy:
*Be bold.* She oft and oft it over read,
Yet could not find what sense it figurèd;
But what so were therein or writ or meant,
She was no whit thereby discouragèd
From prosecuting of her first intent,
But forward with bold steps into the next room went.

### 51

Much fairer than the former was that room,
And richlier by many parts arrayed,
For not with arras made in painful loom,
But with pure gold it all was overlaid,
Wrought with wild antics, which their follies played
In the rich metal as they living were:
A thousand monstrous forms therein were made,
Such as false love doth oft upon him wear,
For love in thousand monstrous forms doth oft appear.

### 52

And all about, the glistering walls were hung
With warlike spoils and with victorious preys
Of mighty conquerors and captains strong,
Which were whilom captivèd in their days
To cruel love, and wrought their own decays;
Their swords and spears were broke, and hauberks rent,
And their proud garlands of triumphant bays
Troden in dust with fury insolent,
To show the victor's might and merciless intent.

---

48.4 See Ovid, *Metamorphoses* 1.468–71; the gold arrows kindle desire, the lead ones aversion, and often work together.

52.2 *preys* prizes.

### 53

The warlike maid, beholding earnestly
The goodly ordinance of this rich place,
Did greatly wonder, ne could satisfy
Her greedy eyes with gazing a long space;
But more she marveled that no footing's trace
Nor wight appeared, but wasteful emptiness
And solemn silence over all that place.
Strange thing it seemed, that none was to possess
So rich purveyance, ne them keep with carefulness.

### 54

And as she looked about, she did behold
How over that same door was likewise writ
*Be bold, be bold*, and everywhere *Be bold*,
That much she mused, yet could not construe it
By any riddling skill or common wit.
At last she spied at that room's upper end
Another iron door, on which was writ
*Be not too bold*: whereto though she did bend
Her earnest mind, yet wist not what it might intend.

### 55

Thus she there waited until eventide,
Yet living creature none she saw appear;
And now sad shadows gan the world to hide
From mortal view, and wrap in darkness drear,
Yet nould she doff her weary arms, for fear
Of secret danger, ne let sleep oppress
Her heavy eyes with nature's burden dear,
But drew herself aside in sickerness,
And her well-pointed weapons did about her dress.

53.6  *wasteful* desolate.
53.9  *purveyance* furnishings.
55.5  *nould* would not.

55.8  *sickerness* safety.
55.9  *dress* prepare.

## CANTO XII

*The Masque of Cupid and the enchanted*
  *chamber are displayed;*
*Whence Britomart redeems fair*
  *Amoret, through charms decayed.*

### 1

Tho when as cheerless night ycovered had
Fair heaven with an universal cloud,
That every wight dismayed with darkness sad
In silence and in sleep themselves did shroud,
She heard a shrilling trumpet sound aloud,
Sign of nigh battle or got victory;
Nought therewith daunted was her courage proud,
But rather stirred to cruel enmity,
Expecting ever when some foe she might descry.

2

With that, an hideous storm of wind arose,
With dreadful thunder and lightning atwixt,
And an earthquake, as if it straight would loose
The world's foundations from his center fixed.
A direful stench of smoke and sulphur mixed
Ensued, whose noyance filled the fearful stead
From the fourth hour of night until the sixth;
Yet the bold Britoness was nought ydread,
Though much emmoved, but steadfast still perseverèd.

3

All suddenly a stormy whirlwind blew
Throughout the house that clappèd every door,
With which that iron wicket open flew
As it with mighty levers had been tore;
And forth issued, as on the ready floor
Of some theater, a grave personage
That in his hand a branch of laurel bore.
With comely havior and countenance sage,
Yclad in costly garments, fit for tragic stage.

4

Proceeding to the midst, he still did stand,
As if in mind he somewhat had to say,
And, to the vulgar beckoning with his hand
In sign of silence, as to hear a play,
By lively actions he gan bewray
Some argument of matter passionèd;
Which done, he back retirèd soft away,
And passing by, his name discoverèd:
Ease, on his robe in golden letter cypherèd.

5

The noble maid, still standing, all this viewed,
And marveled at his strange intendiment.
With that, a joyous fellowship issued
Of minstrels, making goodly merriment,
With wanton bards and rhymers impudent,
All which together sung full cheerfully
A lay of love's delight, with sweet consent;
After whom marched a jolly company
In manner of a masque, enrangèd orderly.

6

The whiles a most delicious harmony
In full strange notes was sweetly heard to sound,
That the rare sweetness of the melody
The feeble senses wholly did confound,
And the frail soul in deep delight nigh drowned;
And when it ceased, shrill trumpets loud did bray,

3.2 *clappèd* slammed.
4.3 *vulgar* crowd.
4.6 *passionèd* passionate.

4.8 *discoverèd* revealed.
4.9 *cypherèd* written.
5.2 *intendiment* intent.

That their report did far away rebound,
And when they ceased, it gan again to play,
The whiles the masquers marchèd forth in trim array.

### 7

The first was Fancy, like a lovely boy,
Of rare aspect and beauty without peer,
Matchable either to that imp of Troy
Whom Jove did love and chose his cup to bear,
Or that same dainty lad which was so dear
To great Alcides, that whenas he died
He wailèd womanlike with many a tear,
And every wood and every valley wide
He filled with Hylas' name; the nymphs eke Hylas cried.

### 8

His garment neither was of silk nor say,
But painted plumes, in goodly order dight,
Like as the sunburnt Indians do array
Their tawny bodies in their proudest plight;
As those same plumes, so seemed he vain and light,
That by his gait might easily appear,
For still he fared as dancing in delight,
And in his hand a windy fan did bear,
That in the idle air he moved still here and there.

### 9

And him beside marched amorous Desire,
Who seemed of riper years than the other swain,
Yet was that other swain this elder's sire,
And gave him being, common to them twain.
His garment was disguisèd very vain,
And his embroidered bonnet sat awry;
Twixt both his hands few sparks he close did strain,
Which still he blew and kindled busily,
That soon they life conceived and forth in flames did fly.

### 10

Next after him went Doubt, who was yclad
In a discolored coat of strange disguise,
That at his back a broad capuccio had,
And sleeves dependent, Albanese-wise.
He looked askew with his mistrustful eyes,
And nicely trod, as thorns lay in his way
Or that the floor to shrink he did avise,
And on a broken reed he still did stay
His feeble steps, which shrunk when hard thereon he lay.

---

7.3   *imp* child   *that imp of Troy* Ganymede.
7.5   *that same dainty lad* Hylas, a beautiful young boy who accompanied Hercules (Alcides) on the voyage of the *Argo*; his disappearance led Hercules to abandon the voyage.
8.1   *say* A fine-textured cloth, often a blend of wool and silk.
8.4   *plight* clothing.
9.7   *strain* clasp.

10.2   *discolored* variegated.   *disguise* fashion.
10.3   *capuccio* hood like that of a Capuchin monk.
10.4   *dependent, Albanese-wise* hanging down in a Scottish fashion.
10.6   *nicely* carefully.
10.7   *shrink* give way.   *avise* perceive.
10.8   *stay* support.

## 11

With him went Danger, clothed in ragged weed
Made of bear's skin, that him more dreadful made;
Yet his own face was dreadful, ne did need
Strange horror to deform his grisly shade.
A net in the one hand, and a rusty blade
In the other was: this Mischief, that Mishap.
With the one his foes he threatened to invade,
With the other he his friends meant to enwrap;
For whom he could not kill, he practiced to entrap.

## 12

Next him was Fear, all armed from top to toe,
Yet thought himself not safe enough thereby,
But feared each shadow moving to and fro;
And his own arms when glittering he did spy
Or clashing heard, he fast away did fly,
As ashes pale of hue, and wingy-heeled,
And evermore on Danger fixed his eye,
Gainst whom he always bent a brazen shield,
Which his right hand unarmèd fearfully did wield.

## 13

With him went Hope in rank, a handsome maid,
Of cheerful look and lovely to behold.
In silken samite she was light arrayed,
And her fair locks were woven up in gold;
She alway smiled, and in her hand did hold
An holy water sprinkle dipped in dew,
With which she sprinkled favors manifold
On whom she list, and did great liking show:
Great liking unto many, but true love to few.

## 14

And after them Dissemblance and Suspect
Marched in one rank, yet an unequal pair,
For she was gentle and of mild aspect,
Courteous to all and seeming debonair,
Goodly adornèd and exceeding fair,
Yet was that all but painted and purloined,
And her bright brows were decked with borrowed hair;
Her deeds were forgèd, and her words false coined,
And always in her hand two clews of silk she twined.

## 15

But he was foul, ill favorèd, and grim,
Under his eyebrows looking still askance,
And ever as Dissemblance laughed on him,

11.1 *Danger* The word is personified here in its dominant modern sense of peril, but it also has a history in erotic literature as a term for the cold aloofness of a desirable woman. *weed* clothing.
11.4 *Strange* added from the outside. *shade* image.
11.7 *invade* assault.

13.3 *samite* a precious silk fabric, sometimes interwoven with gold.
13.6 *sprinkle* aspergillum.
14.1 *Suspect* suspicion.
14.9 *clews* balls.

He lowered on her with dangerous eye-glance,
Showing his nature in his countenance;
His rolling eyes did never rest in place,
But walked each where, for fear of hid mischance,
Holding a lattice still before his face,
Through which he still did peep, as forward he did pace.

### 16

Next him went Grief and Fury matched yfere:
Grief all in sable sorrowfully clad,
Down hanging his dull head with heavy cheer,
Yet inly being more than seeming sad;
A pair of pincers in his hand he had,
With which he pinchèd people to the heart,
That from thenceforth a wretched life they lad,
In willful languor and consuming smart,
Dying each day with inward wounds of dolor's dart.

### 17

But Fury was full ill apparelèd
In rags, that naked nigh she did appear,
With ghastly looks and dreadful drearihead,
For from her back her garments she did tear,
And from her head oft rent her snarlèd hair;
In her right hand a firebrand she did toss
About her head, still roaming here and there,
As a dismayèd deer in chase embossed,
Forgetful of his safety, hath his right way lost.

### 18

After them went Displeasure and Pleasance:
He looking lumpish and full sullen sad,
And hanging down his heavy countenance,
She cheerful, fresh, and full of joyance glad,
As if no sorrow she ne felt ne drad,
That evil matchèd pair they seemed to be.
An angry wasp the one in a vial had,
The other in hers an honey-lady bee;
Thus marchèd these six couples forth in fair degree.

### 19

After all these there marched a most fair dame,
Led of two grisy villains, the one Despite,
The other clepèd Cruelty by name;
She, doleful lady, like a dreary sprite
Called by strong charms out of eternal night,
Had death's own image figured in her face,
Full of sad signs fearful to living sight,
Yet in that horror showed a seemly grace,
And with her feeble feet did move a comely pace.

16.1  *yfere* together.
17.8  *embossed* exhausted.

19.2  *grisy* grisly.

### 20

Her breast all naked as net ivory,
Without adorn of gold or silver bright
Wherewith the craftsman wonts it beautify,
Of her due honor was despoilèd quite,
And a wide wound therein (O rueful sight)
Entrenchèd deep with knife accursèd keen,
Yet freshly bleeding forth her fainting sprite
(The work of cruel hand), was to be seen,
That dyed in sanguine red her skin all snowy clean.

### 21

At that wide orifice her trembling heart
Was drawn forth, and in silver basin laid,
Quite through transfixèd with a deadly dart,
And in her blood yet steaming fresh embayed;
And those two villains, which her steps upstayed
When her weak feet could scarcely her sustain
And fading vital powers gan to fade,
Her forward still with torture did constrain,
And evermore increasèd her consuming pain.

### 22

Next after her the wingèd god himself
Came riding on a lion ravenous,
Taught to obey the manege of that elf,
That man and beast with power imperious
Subdueth to his kingdom tyrannous.
His blindfold eyes he bade awhile unbind,
That his proud spoil of that same dolorous
Fair dame he might behold in perfect kind;
Which seen, he much rejoicèd in his cruel mind.

### 23

Of which full proud, himself uprearing high,
He lookèd round about with stern disdain,
And did survey his goodly company;
And marshalling the evil ordered train,
With that the darts which his right hand did strain
Full dreadfully he shook that all did quake,
And clapped on high his colored wingès twain
That all his many it afraid did make.
Tho blinding him again, his way he forth did take.

### 24

Behind him was Reproach, Repentance, Shame:
Reproach the first, Shame next, Repent behind.
Repentance feeble, sorrowful, and lame;
Reproach despiteful, careless, and unkind;
Shame most ill favored, bestial, and blind.
Shame lowered, Repentance sighed, Reproach did scold;
Reproach sharp stings, Repentance whips entwined,

20.1 *net* pure.
21.4 *embayed* steeped.

22.3 *manege* horsemanship.

Shame burning brand-irons in her hand did hold:
All three to each unlike, yet all made in one mold.

### 25

And after them, a rude confusèd rout
Of persons flocked, whose names is hard to read:
Amongst them was stern Strife and Anger stout,
Unquiet Care and fond Unthriftihead,
Lewd Loss of Time and Sorrow seeming dead,
Inconstant Change and false Disloyalty,
Consuming Riotise and guilty Dread
Of heavenly vengeance, faint Infirmity,
Vile Poverty, and lastly Death with infamy.

### 26

There were full many moe like maladies,
Whose names and natures I note readen well,
So many moe as there be fantasies
In wavering women's wit that none can tell,
Or pains in love, or punishments in hell;
All which disguisèd marched in masquing wise
About the chamber with that damozel,
And then returnèd, having marchèd thrice,
Into the inner room from whence they first did rise.

### 27

So soon as they were in, the door straightway
Fast lockèd, driven with that stormy blast
Which first it opened, and bore all away.
Then the brave maid, which all this while was placed
In secret shade and saw both first and last,
Issuèd forth, and went unto the door
To enter in, but found it lockèd fast;
In vain she thought with rigorous uproar
For to efforce, when charms had closèd it afore.

### 28

Where force might not avail, there sleights and art
She cast to use, both fit for hard emprise;
Forthy from that same room not to depart
Till morrow next she did her self avise,
When that same masque again should forth arise.
The morrow next appeared with joyous cheer,
Calling men to their daily exercise;
Then she, as morrow fresh, herself did rear
Out of her secret stand, that day for to outwear.

### 29

All that day she outwore in wandering
And gazing on that chamber's ornament,

---

25.4  *fond Unthriftihead* foolish prodigality.
25.7  *Riotise* riotousness.
26.6  *masquing wise* in the manner of a masque.
27.8  *rigorous uproar* stern violence.

27.9  *efforce* succeed with force.
28.2  *emprise* enterprise.
28.4  *avise* advise.

Till that again the second evening
Her covered with her sable vestiment,
Wherewith the world's fair beauty she hath blent;
Then when the second watch was almost past,
That brazen door flew open, and in went
Bold Britomart, as she had late forecast,
Neither of idle shows nor of false charms aghast.

### 30

So soon as she was entered, round about
She cast her eyes to see what was become
Of all those persons which she saw without;
But lo, they straight were vanished all and some,
Ne living wight she saw in all that room,
Save that same woeful lady, both whose hands
Were bounden fast, that did her ill become,
And her small waist girt round with iron bands
Unto a brazen pillar, by the which she stands.

### 31

And her before the vile enchanter sate,
Figuring strange characters of his art;
With living blood he those characters wrate,
Dreadfully dropping from her dying heart,
Seeming transfixèd with a cruel dart,
And all perforce to make her him to love.
Ah, who can love the worker of her smart?
A thousand charms he formerly did prove,
Yet thousand charms could not her steadfast heart remove.

### 32

Soon as that virgin knight he saw in place,
His wicked books in haste he overthrew,
Not caring his long labors to deface,
And, fiercely running to that lady true,
A murderous knife out of his pocket drew,
The which he thought for villainous despite
In her tormented body to imbrue;
But the stout damsel, to him leaping light,
His cursèd hand withheld, and masterèd his might.

### 33

From her to whom his fury first he meant
The wicked weapon rashly he did wrest,
And, turning to herself his fell intent,
Unwares it struck into her snowy chest,
That little drops empurpled her fair breast.
Exceeding wroth therewith the virgin grew,
Albe the wound were nothing deep impressed,
And fiercely forth her mortal blade she drew,
To give him the reward for such vile outrage due.

**29.5**  *blent* hidden.
**31.8**  *prove* try.
**31.9**  *remove* change.

**32.3**  Not caring if he loses all his work.
**32.7**  *imbrue* stain.

### 34

So mightily she smote him, that to ground
He fell half dead; next stroke him should have slain,
Had not the lady which by him stood bound
Dernly unto her callèd to abstain
From doing him to die. For else her pain
Should be remediless, sith none but he
Which wrought it could the same recure again.
Therewith she stayed her hand, loath stayed to be,
For life she him envied, and longed revenge to see,

### 35

And to him said, Thou wicked man, whose meed
For so huge mischief and vile villainy
Is death, or if that ought do death exceed,
Be sure that nought may save thee from to die
But if that thou this dame do presently
Restore unto her health and former state;
This do and live, else die undoubtedly.
He, glad of life that looked for death but late,
Did yield himself right willing to prolong his date,

### 36

And rising up, gan straight to overlook
Those cursèd leaves, his charms back to reverse.
Full dreadful things out of that baleful book
He read, and measured many a sad verse,
That horror gan the virgin's heart to pierce,
And her fair locks up starèd stiff on end,
Hearing him those same bloody lines rehearse;
And all the while he read, she did extend
Her sword high over him, if ought he did offend.

### 37

Anon she gan perceive the house to quake
And all the doors to rattle round about;
Yet all that did not her dismayèd make
Nor slack her threatful hand for danger's doubt,
But still with steadfast eye and courage stout
Abode, to weet what end would come of all.
At last that mighty chain which round about
Her tender waist was wound adown gan fall,
And that great brazen pillar broke in pieces small.

### 38

The cruel steel which thrilled her dying heart
Fell softly forth, as of his own accord,
And the wide wound which lately did dispart
Her bleeding breasts and riven bowels gored
Was closèd up, as it had not been bored,
And every part to safety full sound,

34.4  *Dernly* urgently or secretly.
36.6  *starèd* stood.
37.4  *for danger's doubt* for fear of danger.

37.6  *Abode* abided.
38.1  *thrilled* pierced.
38.3  *dispart* divide.

As she were never hurt, was soon restored;
Tho when she felt herself to be unbound
And perfect whole, prostrate she fell unto the ground.

### 39

Before fair Britomart she fell prostrate,
Saying, Ah, noble knight, what worthy meed
Can wretched lady, quit from woeful state,
Yield you in lieu of this your gracious deed?
Your virtue self her own reward shall breed,
Even immortal praise and glory wide,
Which I, your vassal, by your prowess freed,
Shall through the world make to be notified,
And goodly well advance that goodly well was tried.

### 40

But Britomart, uprearing her from ground,
Said, Gentle dame, reward enough I ween
For many labors more then I have found:
This, that in safety now I have you seen,
And mean of your deliverance have been.
Henceforth, fair lady, comfort to you take,
And put away remembrance of late teen;
Instead thereof, know that your loving make
Hath no less grief endurèd for your gentle sake.

### 41

She much was cheered to hear him mentionèd,
Whom of all living wights she lovèd best.
Then laid the noble championess strong hand
Upon the enchanter which had her distressed
So sore, and with foul outrages oppressed;
With that great chain wherewith not long ago
He bound that piteous lady prisoner, now released,
Himself she bound, more worthy to be so,
And captive with her led to wretchedness and woe.

### 42

Returning back, those goodly rooms, which erst
She saw so rich and royally arrayed,
Now vanished utterly and clean subversed
She found, and all their glory quite decayed,
That sight of such a change her much dismayed.
Thence forth descending to that perilous porch,
Those dreadful flames she also found delayed,
And quenchèd quite, like a consumèd torch,
That erst all enterers wont so cruelly to scorch.

38.9 *whole* The readiest primary sense is that Amoret
is returned to perfect health and bodily integrity, though
another is intimated by the spelling "hole" which is used in
the original editions.
39.5 *Your virtue self* your virtue herself.

40.7 *teen* suffering.
40.8 *make* mate.
42.3 *subversed* demolished.
42.7 *delayed* extinguished.

### 43

More easy issue now than entrance late
She found; for now that feignèd dreadful flame
Which choked the porch of that enchanted gate
And passage barred to all that thither came
Was vanished quite, as it were not the same,
And gave her leave at pleasure forth to pass.
The enchanter self, which all that fraud did frame
To have efforced the love of that fair lass,
Seeing his work now wasted, deep engrievèd was.

### 44

But when the victoress arrivèd there
Where late she left the pensive Scudamour
With her own trusty squire, both full of fear,
Neither of them she found where she them lore.
Thereat her noble heart was stonished sore,
But most fair Amoret, whose gentle sprite
Now gan to feed on hope which she before
Conceivèd had to see her own dear knight,
Being thereof beguiled was filled with new affright.

### 45

But he, sad man, when he had long in dread
Awaited there for Britomart's return,
Yet saw her not nor sign of her good speed,
His expectation to despair did turn,
Misdeeming sure that her those flames did burn,
And therefore gan advise with her old squire,
Who her dear nursling's loss no less did mourn,
Thence to depart for further aid to inquire;
Where let them wend at will, whilst here I do respire.

44.4  *lore* left.
44.9  *beguiled* deceived.

45.3  *speed* success.
45.9  *respire* take a breath.

ALTERNATE ENDING FOR CANTO XII FROM THE 1590 EDITION

### 43

At last she came unto the place where late
She left Sir Scudamour in great distress,
Twixt dolor and despite half desperate
Of his love's succor, of his own redress,
And of the hardy Britomart's success.
There on the cold earth him now thrown she found,
In willful anguish and dread heaviness,
And to him called; whose voice's knowen sound
Soon as he heard, himself he rearèd light from ground.

### 44

There did he see that most on earth him joyed,
His dearest love, the comfort of his days,
Whose too long absence him had sore annoyed
And wearièd his life with dull delays.

Straight he upstarted from the loathèd lays
And to her ran with hasty eagerness,
Like as a deer that greedily embays
In the cool soil, after long thirstiness
Which he in chase endurèd hath, now nigh breathless.

### 45

Lightly he clipped her twixt his armes twain
And straitly did embrace her body bright:
Her body, late the prison of sad pain,
Now the sweet lodge of love and dear delight.
But she, fair lady, overcomen quite
Of huge affection, did in pleasure melt,
And in sweet ravishment poured out her sprite;
No word they spake, nor earthly thing they felt,
But like two senseless stocks in long embracement dwelt.

### 46

Had ye them seen, ye would have surely thought
That they had been that fair Hermaphrodite
Which that rich Roman of white marble wrought
And in his costly bath caused to be site;
So seemed those two, as grown together quite,
That Britomart, half envying their bliss,
Was much empassioned in her gentle sprite,
And to herself oft wished like happiness:
In vain she wished that fate nould let her yet possess.

### 47

Thus do those lovers with sweet countervail
Each other of love's bitter fruit despoil.
But now my team begins to faint and fail,
All woxen weary of their journal toil;
Therefore I will their sweaty yokes assoil
At this same furrow's end, till a new day.
And ye fair swains, after your long turmoil
Now cease your work, and at your pleasure play;
Now cease your work, tomorrow is an holy day.

44.5   *lays* grasslands.
44.7   *embays* plunges.
44.8   *soil* pond.
45.1   *clipped* embraced.
45.2   *straitly* tightly.
45.9   *stocks* blocks of wood.
46.2–4   Hermaphroditus was a beautiful young man desired by the nymph Salmacis; she assaulted him with such intensity while he was swimming that the two of them were fused into a single being with the attributes of both sexes. The result appears to have been a popular subject in classical art, but no particular source for Spenser's rich Roman has been traced.
46.4   *site* placed.
46.9   *nould* would not.
47.1   *countervail* reciprocity.
47.4   *journal* daily.
47.5   *assoil* loosen.

# Two Cantos of Mutability: Which, both for form and matter, appear to be parcel of some following book of *The Faery Queen*, under the legend of Constancy

The Mutability Cantos appear mysteriously, with the above heading, at the end of the 1609 edition of *The Faery Queen*; they treat of what seems to be a self-contained episode, with no reference to the Knight of Constancy whose story would presumably provide the framework for Book VII. The allegory concerns the challenge that the spirit of Mutability herself presents to the rule of the Olympian gods; Jupiter is unable to best her on his own, and must submit to a trial judged by an intriguingly androgynous Nature. Within Spenser's moral universe the outcome would not seem to be in doubt, and Nature does finally rule against Mutability; but for most of it Mutability has the floor, and her defeat is abrupt and somewhat cryptic. In a tailpiece from Canto VIII the poet confesses himself dazed by her case, seems deeply weary from the struggle against her, and ends with a prayer for divine revelation. In the abstracted form in which we have them, the Mutability Cantos have seemed to many a summary statement about Spenser's poem as a whole and a final gesture of resignation at its unfinishability.

## CANTO VI

*Proud Change (not pleased in mortal things
    beneath the Moon to reign)
Pretends as well of gods as men
    to be the sovereign.*

### 1

What man that sees the ever-whirling wheel
Of change, the which all mortal things doth sway,
But that thereby doth find and plainly feel
How Mutability in them doth play
Her cruel sports, to many men's decay?
Which that to all may better yet appear,
I will rehearse that whilom I heard say,
How she at first herself began to rear
Gainst all the gods, and the empire sought from them to bear.

### 2

But first, here falleth fittest to unfold
Her antique race and lineage ancient,
As I have found it registered of old
In Faery land mongst records permanent;
She was, to weet, a daughter by descent
Of those old Titans that did whilom strive
With Saturn's son for heaven's regiment:
Whom though high Jove of kingdom did deprive,
Yet many of their stem long after did survive.

### 3

And many of them afterwards obtained
Great power of Jove, and high authority:
As Hecate, in whose almighty hand

---

2.6   *Titans* The Titans (including Saturn) were gods of the generation preceding the Olympians, who (led by Jupiter, Saturn's son) made war against them in order to gain power in heaven; the Titans survived to pose an ongoing threat against Olympian rule. Later versions often mingle their story with that of the later revolt of the giants, children of the same mother; see above, III.vii.47.

3.3   *Hecate* A goddess with power over various kinds of human success, and supposedly the inventor of sorcery; in the Renaissance her name is often used for the queen of the witches.

He placed all rule and principality,
To be by her disposèd diversely
To gods and men, as she them list divide;
And dread Bellona, that doth sound on high
Wars and alarums unto nations wide,
That makes both heaven and earth to tremble at her pride.

4

So likewise did this Titaness aspire
Rule and dominion to herself to gain,
That as a goddess men might her admire
And heavenly honors yield, as to them twain.
And first on earth she sought it to obtain,
Where she such proof and sad examples showed
Of her great power, to many one's great pain,
That not men only (whom she soon subdued)
But eke all other creatures her bad doings rued.

5

For she the face of earthly things so changed
That all which Nature had established first
In good estate, and in meet order ranged,
She did pervert, and all their statutes burst;
And all the world's fair frame (which none yet durst
Of gods or men to alter or misguide)
She altered quite, and made them all accursed
That God had blessed, and did at first provide
In that still happy state forever to abide.

6

Ne she the laws of Nature only brake,
But eke of justice and of policy,
And wrong of right and bad of good did make,
And death for life exchangèd foolishly;
Since which, all living wights have learned to die,
And all this world is woxen daily worse.
O piteous work of Mutability!
By which we all are subject to that curse,
And death instead of life have suckèd from our nurse.

7

And now, when all the earth she thus had brought
To her behest and thrallèd to her might,
She gan to cast in her ambitious thought
To attempt the empire of the heaven's height
And Jove himself to shoulder from his right.
And first she passed the region of the air
And of the fire, whose substance thin and slight
Made no resistance, ne could her contrair,
But ready passage to her pleasure did prepare.

3.7 *Bellona* Roman goddess of war; not linked with the Titans in classical mythology.
6.2 *policy* wise government.

7.6–7 *the region of the air / And of the fire* Above the lower atmosphere, the earth was supposed to be surrounded by a layer of fire.

8

Thence to the circle of the Moon she clamb,
Where Cynthia reigns in everlasting glory,
To whose bright shining palace straight she came,
All fairly decked with heaven's goodly story;
Whose silver gates (by which there sat an hoary
Old agèd sire, with hourglass in hand,
Hight Time) she entered, were he lief or sorry,
Ne stayed till she the highest stage had scanned,
Where Cynthia did sit, that never still did stand.

9

Her sitting on an ivory throne she found,
Drawn of two steeds, the one black, the other white,
Environed with ten thousand stars around
That duly her attended day and night,
And by her side there ran her page, that hight
Vesper, whom we the evening star intend,
That with his torch, still twinkling like twilight,
Her lightened all the way where she should wend,
And joy to weary wandering travelers did lend;

10

That when the hardy Titaness beheld
The goodly building of her palace bright,
Made of the heaven's substance, and upheld
With thousand crystal pillars of huge height,
She gan to burn in her ambitious sprite
And to envy her that in such glory reigned.
Eftsoons she cast by force and tortious might
Her to displace, and to herself to have gained
The kingdom of the night, and waters by her wained.

11

Boldly she bid the goddess down descend
And let herself into that ivory throne:
For she herself more worthy thereof weened
And better able it to guide alone,
Whether to men, whose fall she did bemoan,
Or unto gods, whose state she did malign,
Or to the infernal powers her need give loan
Of her fair light and bounty most benign,
Herself of all that rule she deemèd most condign.

12

But she that had to her that sovereign seat
By highest Jove assigned, therein to bear
Night's burning lamp, regarded not her threat,
Ne yielded ought for favor or for fear,
But, with stern countenance and disdainful cheer
Bending her hornèd brows, did put her back,

8.2  *Cynthia* goddess of the moon.
8.4  *heaven's goodly story* the constellations.
8.7  *lief* willing.
8.8  *scanned* climbed.

9.6  *intend* call.
10.7  *tortious* wrongful.
10.9  *wained* transported (referring to the action of the tides).
11.6  *malign* begrudge.

And boldly blaming her for coming there,
Bade her at once from heaven's coast to pack
Or at her peril bide the wrathful thunder's wrack.

### 13

Yet nathemore the Giantess forbare,
But boldly pressing on, raught forth her hand
To pluck her down perforce from off her chair,
And therewith lifting up her golden wand,
Threatened to strike her if she did withstand;
Whereat the stars which round about her blazed
And eke the Moon's bright wagon still did stand,
All being with so bold attempt amazed,
And on her uncouth habit and stern look still gazed.

### 14

Meanwhile, the lower world, which nothing knew
Of all that chancèd here, was darkened quite,
And eke the heavens and all the heavenly crew
Of happy wights, now unpurveyed of light,
Were much afraid, and wondered at that sight,
Fearing lest Chaos broken had his chain
And brought again on them eternal night;
But chiefly Mercury, that next doth reign,
Ran forth in haste unto the king of gods to plain.

### 15

All ran together with a great outcry
To Jove's fair palace, fixed in heaven's height,
And, beating at his gates full earnestly,
Gan call to him aloud with all their might,
To know what meant that sudden lack of light.
The father of the gods, when this he heard,
Was troubled much at their so strange affright,
Doubting lest Typhon were again upreared,
Or other his old foes, that once him sorely feared.

### 16

Eftsoons the son of Maia forth he sent
Down to the circle of the Moon, to know
The cause of this so strange astonishment,
And why she did her wonted course forslow,
And if that any were on earth below
That did with charms or magic her molest,
Him to attach and down to hell to throw;
But if from heaven it were, then to arrest
The author, and him bring before his presence prest.

13.1  *nathemore* never the more.
13.2  *raught* reached.
14  A likely allusion to the lunar eclipse of 14 April 1595, total for over an hour and a half.
14.4  *unpurveyed* unsupplied.
14.8  *that next doth reign* In the Ptolemaic system, the orbit of Mercury is next beyond that of the moon.

15.8  *Typhon* Typhoeus; see III.vii.47.6 above.
15.9  *feared* frightened.
16.1  *son of Maia* Mercury.
16.4  *forslow* slow down.
16.7  *attach* seize.
16.9  *prest* quickly.

### 17

The winged-foot god so fast his plumes did beat,
That soon he came whereas the Titaness
Was striving with fair Cynthia for her seat;
At whose strange sight and haughty hardiness
He wondered much, and fearèd her no less.
Yet laying fear aside to do his charge,
At last he bade her (with bold steadfastness)
Cease to molest the Moon to walk at large,
Or come before high Jove, her doings to discharge.

### 18

And therewithal he on her shoulder laid
His snaky-wreathèd mace, whose awful power
Doth make both gods and hellish fiends afraid;
Whereat the Titaness did sternly lower,
And stoutly answered that in evil hour
He from his Jove such message to her brought,
To bid her leave fair Cynthia's silver bower,
Sith she his Jove and him esteemèd nought,
No more than Cynthia's self, but all their kingdoms sought.

### 19

The heaven's herald stayed not to reply,
But passed away, his doings to relate
Unto his lord, who now in the highest sky
Was placèd in his principal estate,
With all the gods about him congregate;
To whom when Hermes had his message told,
It did them all exceedingly amate,
Save Jove, who, changing nought his countenance bold,
Did unto them at length these speeches wise unfold:

### 20

Harken to me awhile, ye heavenly powers.
Ye may remember since the Earth's cursèd seed
Sought to assail the heaven's eternal towers,
And to us all exceeding fear did breed;
But how we then defeated all their deed
Ye all do know, and them destroyèd quite,
Yet not so quite but that there did succeed
An offspring of their blood, which did alight
Upon the fruitful earth, which doth us yet despite.

### 21

Of that bad seed is this bold woman bred,
That now with bold presumption doth aspire
To thrust fair Phoebe from her silver bed,
And eke ourselves from heaven's high empire,
If that her might were match to her desire;
Wherefore it now behooves us to advise

---

**18.2**  *His snaky-wreathèd mace* The caduceus, Mercury's
traditional staff.
**19.7**  *amate* intimidate.

**21.3**  *Phoebe* Cynthia.
**21.9**  *Aread* declare.

What way is best to drive her to retire:
Whether by open force or counsel wise
Aread, ye sons of god, as best ye can devise.

### 22

So having said, he ceased; and with his brow
(His black eyebrow, whose doomful, dreaded beck
Is wont to wield the world unto his vow,
And even the highest powers of heaven to check)
Made sign to them in their degrees to speak;
Who straight gan cast their counsel grave and wise.
Meanwhile, the Earth's daughter, though she nought did reck
Of Hermes' message, yet gan now advise
What course were best to take in this hot bold emprise.

### 23

Eftsoons she thus resolved: that whilst the gods
(After return of Hermes' embassy)
Were troubled and amongst themselves at odds,
Before they could new counsels re-ally
To set upon them in that ecstasy,
And take what fortune time and place would lend.
So forth she rose, and through the purest sky
To Jove's high palace straight cast to ascend
To prosecute her plot; good onset bodes good end.

### 24

She, there arriving, boldly in did pass,
Where all the gods she found in counsel close,
All quite unarmed, as then their manner was.
At sight of her they sudden all arose
In great amaze, ne wist what way to choose;
But Jove, all fearless, forced them to aby,
And in his sovereign throne gan straight dispose
Himself more full of grace and majesty
That mote encheer his friends, and foes mote terrify.

### 25

That when the haughty Titaness beheld,
All were she fraught with pride and impudence,
Yet with the sight thereof was almost quelled,
And, inly quaking, seemed as reft of sense
And void of speech in that dread audience,
Until that Jove himself herself bespake:
Speak, thou frail woman, speak with confidence:
Whence art thou, and what dost thou here now make?
What idle errand hast thou, earth's mansion to forsake?

### 26

She, half confusèd with his great command,
Yet gathering spirit of her nature's pride,

22.2  *beck* nod.
22.3  *vow* wish.
22.7  *nought did reck* took no account.
22.9  *emprise* enterprise.

23.4  *re-ally* rally.
23.5  *ecstasy* distraction.
24.6  *aby* stay.

Him boldly answered thus to his demand:
I am a daughter, by the mother's side,
Of her that is grandmother magnified
Of all the gods, great Earth, great Chaos' child;
But by the father's (be it not envied)
I greater am in blood (whereon I build)
Than all the gods, though wrongfully from heaven exiled.

### 27

For Titan (as ye all acknowledge must)
Was Saturn's elder brother by birthright,
Both sons of Uranus; but by unjust
And guileful means, through Corybantes' sleight,
The younger thrust the elder from his right.
Since which, thou Jove injuriously hast held
The heaven's rule from Titan's sons by might,
And them to hellish dungeons down hast felled:
Witness, ye heavens, the truth of all that I have telled.

### 28

Whilst she thus spake, the gods that gave good ear
To her bold words, and markèd well her grace,
Being of stature tall as any there
Of all the gods, and beautiful of face
As any of the goddesses in place,
Stood all astonied, like a sort of steers
Mongst whom some beast of strange and foreign race
Unwares is chanced, far straying from his peers.
So did their ghastly gaze bewray their hidden fears,

### 29

Till, having paused awhile, Jove thus bespake:
Will never mortal thoughts cease to aspire
In this bold sort to heaven claim to make,
And touch celestial seats with earthly mire?
I would have thought that bold Procrustes' hire,
Or Typhon's fall, or proud Ixion's pain,
Or great Prometheus, tasting of our ire,
Would have sufficed the rest for to restrain,
And warned all men by their example to refrain.

### 30

But now, this off-scum of that cursèd fry
Dare to renew the like bold enterprise
And challenge the heritage of this our sky;

---

**27** Mutability's story here is significantly different from versions of the same events in classical antiquity; Titan, elder brother of Saturn (Cronus), is a new creation, apparently the invention of the Renaissance mythographer Natalis Comes.

**27.4** *Corybantes* Devotees of the goddess Cybele, herself often identified with Ops (Rhea), the mother of Jupiter; in the version of the story alluded to here, their noisemaking masked the cries of the infant Jupiter and allowed his mother to save him from being eaten by his father Saturn.

**29.5** *Procrustes* A sadistic brigand, killed by Theseus. *hire* payment.

**29.6** *Typhon* A rebellious giant, buried under Etna by Jupiter (see above 15.8, and III.vii.47). *Ixion* Would-be seducer of Juno, sent to Tartarus by Jupiter.

**29.7** *Prometheus* Titan who, in defiance of Olympian order, gave fire to the human race; Jupiter had him bound to a rock in the Caucasus and tortured.

**30.1** *fry* offspring (i.e., the Titans).

Whom what should hinder but that we likewise
Should handle as the rest of her allies
And thunder-drive to hell? With that, he shook
His nectar-dewèd locks, with which the skies
And all the world beneath for terror quook,
And eft his burning levin-brand in hand he took.

### 31

But when he lookèd on her lovely face,
In which fair beams of beauty did appear
That could the greatest wrath soon turn to grace
(Such sway doth beauty even in heaven bear),
He stayed his hand; and having changed his cheer,
He thus again in milder wise began:
But ah! if gods should strive with flesh yfere,
Then shortly should the progeny of man
Be rooted out, if Jove should do still what he can.

### 32

But thee, fair Titan's child, I rather ween
Through some vain error or inducement light
To see that mortal eyes have never seen,
Or through ensample of thy sister's might,
Bellona, whose great glory thou dost spite,
Since thou hast seen her dreadful power below
Mongst wretched men (dismayed with her affright)
To bandy crowns and kingdoms to bestow;
And sure thy worth no less than hers doth seem to show.

### 33

But wote thou this, thou hardy Titaness,
That not the worth of any living wight
May challenge ought in heaven's interess,
Much less the title of old Titan's right;
For we, by conquest of our sovereign might
And by eternal doom of fate's decree,
Have won the empire of the heavens bright,
Which to ourselves we hold, and to whom we
Shall worthy deem partakers of our bliss to be.

### 34

Then cease thy idle claim, thou foolish girl,
And seek by grace and goodness to obtain
That place from which by folly Titan fell;
Thereto thou mayst perhaps, if thou so fain,
Have Jove thy gracious lord and sovereign.
So having said, she thus to him replied:
Cease, Saturn's son, to seek by proffers vain
Of idle hopes to allure me to thy side
For to betray my right before I have it tried.

---

**30.9** *levin-brand* lightning-bolt.   **32.7** *her affright* fear of her.
**31.7** *yfere* together.   **33.3** *interess* legal right.
**32.5** *spite* envy.

### 35

But thee, O Jove, no equal judge I deem
Of my desert, or of my dueful right,
That in thine own behalf mayst partial seem;
But to the highest him, that is behight
Father of gods and men by equal might,
To weet, the god of Nature, I appeal.
Thereat Jove waxèd wroth, and in his spite
Did inly grudge, yet did it well conceal,
And bade Dan Phoebus' scribe her appellation seal.

### 36

Eftsoons the time and place appointed were
Where all, both heavenly powers and earthly wights
Before great Nature's presence should appear,
For trial of their titles and best rights:
That was, to weet, upon the highest heights
Of Arlo Hill (who knows not Arlo Hill?),
That is the highest head (in all men's sights)
Of my old father Mole, whom shepherd's quill
Renowmèd hath with hymns fit for a rural skill.

### 37

And were it not ill fitting for this file
To sing of hills and woods mongst wars and knights,
I would abate the sternness of my style
Mongst these stern sounds to mingle soft delights,
And tell how Arlo through Diana's spites
(Being of old the best and fairest hill
That was in all this holy island's heights)
Was made the most unpleasant and most ill.
Meanwhile, O Clio, lend Calliope thy quill.

### 38

Whilom, when Ireland flourishèd in fame
Of wealths and goodness far above the rest
Of all that bear the British island's name,
The gods then used (for pleasure and for rest)
Oft to resort thereto, when seemed them best;
But none of all therein more pleasure found
Than Cynthia, that is sovereign queen professed
Of woods and forests, which therein abound,
Sprinkled with wholesome waters, more than most on ground.

### 39

But mongst them all, as fittest for her game,
Either for chase of beasts with hound or bow,
Or for to shroud in shade from Phoebus' flame,

---

35.9 *Dan Phoebus' scribe* Mercury ("Dan" a modest honorific: "Master Phoebus").
36.6 *Arlo Hill* Galtymore, the highest peak in the Galtys mountains near Spenser's estate at Kilcolman.
36.8–9 *Mole, whom shepherd's quill / Renowmèd hath* Mole appears to be Spenser's name for the Ballyhoura and Galtys

ranges in general; he had written of "old father Mole" in his *Colin Clout's Come Home Again* (dated 1591, published 1595).
37.1 *file* thread (i.e., narrative thread).
37.9 Clio is the Muse of history, Calliope the Muse of epic.
38.7 *Cynthia* Diana, the virgin goddess of the hunt.

Or bathe in fountains that do freshly flow
Or from high hills or from the dales below,
She chose this Arlo, where she did resort
With all her nymphs enrangèd on a row,
With whom the woody gods did oft consort;
For with the nymphs the satyrs love to play and sport.

### 40

Amongst the which there was a nymph that hight
Molanna, daughter of old father Mole
And sister unto Mulla, fair and bright,
Unto whose bed false Bregog whilom stole,
That shepherd Colin dearly did condole
And made her luckless loves well known to be.
But this Molanna, were she not so shoal,
Were no less fair and beautiful than she;
Yet as she is, a fairer flood may no man see.

### 41

For first she springs out of two marble rocks,
On which a grove of oaks high mounted grows,
That as a garland seems to deck the locks
Of some fair bride, brought forth with pompous shows
Out of her bower, that many flowers strows;
So through the flowery dales she tumbling down
Through many woods and shady coverts flows
(That on each side her silver channel crown)
Till to the plain she come, whose valleys she doth drown.

### 42

In her sweet streams Diana usèd oft
(After her sweaty chase and toilsome play)
To bathe herself, and after on the soft
And downy grass her dainty limbs to lay
In covert shade, where none behold her may,
For much she hated sight of living eye.
Foolish god Faunus, though full many a day
He saw her clad, yet longèd foolishly
To see her naked mongst her nymphs in privity.

### 43

No way he found to compass his desire
But to corrupt Molanna, this her maid,
Her to discover for some secret hire;
So her with flattering words he first assayed,
And after, pleasing gifts for her purveyed,
Queen-apples and red cherries from the tree,
With which he her allurèd and betrayed
To tell what time he might her lady see
When she herself did bathe, that he might secret be.

**40.2**  *Molanna* The River Behanagh.
**40.3–5**  In *Colin Clout's Come Home Again* the story of the Mulla and her treacherous lover is effectively identical with the course of the Awbeg and Bregog rivers.

**40.5**  *condole* lament.
**40.6**  *shoal* shallow.
**41.4**  *pompous* ceremonious.
**43.7**  *betrayed* led astray.

**44**

Thereto he promised, if she would him pleasure
With this small boon, to quit her with a better:
To weet, that whereas she had out of measure
Long loved the Fanchin, who by nought did set her,
That he would undertake for this to get her
To be his love, and of him likèd well;
Besides all which, he vowed to be her debtor
For many moe good turns than he would tell,
The least of which this little pleasure should excel.

**45**

This simple maid did yield to him anon,
And eft him placèd where he close might view
That never any saw, save only one;
Who, for his hire to so foolhardy due,
Was of his hounds devoured in hunter's hue.
Tho, as her manner was on sunny day,
Diana with her nymphs about her drew
To this sweet spring, where, doffing her array,
She bathed her lovely limbs, for Jove a likely prey.

**46**

There Faunus saw that pleasèd much his eye
And made his heart to tickle in his breast,
That, for great joy of somewhat he did spy,
He could him not contain in silent rest,
But, breaking forth in laughter, loud professed
His foolish thought. A foolish Faun indeed,
That couldst not hold thyself so hidden blest,
But wouldest needs thine own conceit aread;
Babblers unworthy been of so divine a meed.

**47**

The goddess, all abashèd with that noise,
In haste forth started from the guilty brook,
And, running straight whereas she heard his voice,
Enclosed the bush about, and there him took,
Like the dared lark: not daring up to look
On her whose sight before so much he sought.
Thence, forth they drew him by the horns, and shook
Nigh all to pieces, that they left him nought;
And then into the open light they forth him brought.

**48**

Like as a housewife that with busy care
Thinks of her dairy to make wondrous gain,
Finding whereas some wicked beast unware
That breaks into her dair'house, there doth drain
Her creaming pans and frustrate all her pain,

---

**44.2**  *quit* requite.
**44.4**  *Fanchin* The River Funsheon, which joins the Behanagh.
**45.3**  *one* The hunter Actaeon, who according to Ovid came upon Diana by accident (*Metamorphoses* 3.137–252).

**45.5**  *hue* shape.
**46.8**  *aread* make known.
**47.5**  *dared* dazzled. Larks were hunted by fixing their attention with some bright object while the fowler readied the nets.

Hath in some snare or gin set close behind
Entrappèd him, and caught into her train,
Then thinks what punishment were best assigned,
And thousand deaths deviseth in her vengeful mind:

### 49

So did Diana and her maidens all
Use silly Faunus, now within their bail.
They mock and scorn him, and him foul miscall;
Some by the nose him plucked, some by the tail,
And by his goatish beard some did him hale.
Yet he (poor soul) with patience all did bear,
For nought against their wills might countervail,
Ne ought he said, whatever he did hear,
But, hanging down his head, did like a mome appear.

### 50

At length, when they had flouted him their fill,
They gan to cast what penance him to give.
Some would have gelt him, but that same would spill
The wood-gods' breed, which must forever live;
Others would through the river him have drive
And duckèd deep, but that seemed penance light;
But most agreed and did this sentence give,
Him in deer's skin to clad, and in that plight
To hunt him with their hounds, himself save how he might.

### 51

But Cynthia's self, more angry than the rest,
Thought not enough to punish him in sport
And of her shame to make a gamesome jest,
But gan examine him in straiter sort,
Which of her nymphs or other close consort
Him thither brought, and her to him betrayed.
He, much affeared, to her confessèd short
That twas Molanna which her so bewrayed;
Then all at once their hands upon Molanna laid.

### 52

But him (according as they had decreed)
With a deer's skin they covered, and then chased
With all their hounds that after him did speed;
But he more speedy from them fled more fast
Than any deer: so sore him dread aghast.
They after followed all with shrill outcry,
Shouting as they the heavens would have brast,
That all the woods and dales where he did fly
Did ring again, and loud re-echo to the sky.

**48.6** *gin* device.
**48.7** *train* snare.
**49.2** *bail* custody.
**49.3** *miscall* insult.
**49.5** *hale* pull.

**49.9** *mome* dolt.
**50.3** *gelt* gelded. *spill* destroy.
**50.5** *drive* driven.
**52.5** *dread* dreaded.

### 53

So they him followed till they weary were,
When, back returning to Molanna again,
They by commandment of Diana there
Her whelmed with stones. Yet Faunus (for her pain)
Of her belovèd Fanchin did obtain
That her he would receive unto his bed.
So now her waves pass through a pleasant plain,
Till with the Fanchin she herself do wed,
And (both combined) themselves in one fair river spread.

### 54

Natheless, Diana, full of indignation,
Thenceforth abandoned her delicious brook,
In whose sweet stream, before that bad occasion,
So much delight to bathe her limbs she took;
Ne only her, but also quite forsook
All those fair forests about Arlo hid
And all that mountain which doth overlook
The richest champian that may else be rid
And the fair Shure, in which are thousand salmons bred.

### 55

Them all, and all that she so dear did weigh,
Thenceforth she left; and, parting from the place,
Thereon an heavy hapless curse did lay,
To weet, that wolves where she was wont to space
Should harbored be, and all those woods deface,
And thieves should rob and spoil that coast around.
Since which, those woods and all that goodly chase
Doth to this day with wolves and thieves abound;
Which too too true that land's indwellers since have found.

54.8  *champian* plain.                    54.9  *Shure* the River Suir.

## CANTO VII

*Pealing from Jove to Nature's bar,*
*   bold Alteration pleads*
*Large evidence; but Nature soon*
*   her righteous doom areads.*

### 1

Ah! whither dost thou now, thou greater Muse,
Me from these woods and pleasing forests bring,
And my frail spirit (that doth oft refuse
This too high flight, unfit for her weak wing)
Lift up aloft, to tell of heaven's king
(Thy sovereign sire), his fortunate success
And victory in bigger notes to sing,
Which he obtained against that Titaness,
That him of heaven's empire sought to dispossess?

0.1  *Pealing* appealing.                    0.4  *doom* judgment.    *areads* declares.

### 2

Yet sith I needs must follow thy behest,
Do thou my weaker wit with skill inspire,
Fit for this turn, and in my feeble breast
Kindle fresh sparks of that immortal fire
Which learnèd minds inflameth with desire
Of heavenly things; for who but thou alone,
That art yborn of heaven and heavenly sire,
Can tell things done in heaven so long ygone,
So far past memory of man that may be known.

### 3

Now, at the time that was before agreed,
The gods assembled all on Arlo hill,
As well those that are sprung of heavenly seed
As those that all the other world do fill
And rule both sea and land unto their will.
Only the infernal powers might not appear:
As well for horror of their countenance ill
As for the unruly fiends which they did fear;
Yet Pluto and Proserpina were present there.

### 4

And thither also came all other creatures,
Whatever life or motion do retain,
According to their sundry kinds of features,
That Arlo scarcely could them all contain,
So full they fillèd every hill and plain;
And had not Nature's sergeant (that is, Order)
Them well disposèd by his busy pain
And rangèd far abroad in every border,
They would have causèd much confusion and disorder.

### 5

Then forth issued (great goddess) great dame Nature,
With goodly port and gracious majesty,
Being far greater and more tall of stature
Than any of the gods or powers on high;
Yet certes, by her face and physnomy,
Whether she man or woman inly were,
That could not any creature well descry,
For with a veil that wimpled everywhere
Her head and face was hid, that mote to none appear.

### 6

That some do say was so by skill devised
To hide the terror of her uncouth hue
From mortal eyes that should be sore agrised,
For that her face did like a lion show,
That eye of wight could not endure to view;

---

3.9 *Pluto and Proserpina* god of the underworld and his queen.
5.2 *port* demeanor.
5.5 *physnomy* physiognomy.

5.8 *wimpled* covered.
6.2 *uncouth hue* strange shape.
6.3 *agrised* frightened.

But others tell that it so beauteous was
And round about such beams of splendor threw,
That it the sun a thousand times did pass,
Ne could be seen but like an image in a glass.

7

That well may seemen true; for well I ween
That this same day, when she on Arlo sat,
Her garment was so bright and wondrous sheen
That my frail wit cannot devise to what
It to compare, nor find like stuff to that:
As those three sacred saints, though else most wise,
Yet on Mount Tabor quite their wits forgat
When they their glorious Lord in strange disguise
Transfigured saw, his garments so did daze their eyes.

8

In a fair plain upon an equal hill
She placèd was in a pavilion:
Not such as craftsmen by their idle skill
Are wont for princes' state to fashion,
But the earth herself of her own motion
Out of her fruitful bosom made to grow
Most dainty trees that, shooting up anon,
Did seem to bow their blooming heads full low
For homage unto her, and like a throne did show.

9

So hard it is for any living wight
All her array and vestiments to tell,
That old Dan Geoffrey (in whose gentle sprite
The pure wellhead of poesy did dwell)
In his *Fowls' Parley* durst not with it mell,
But it transferred to Alan, who he thought
Had in his *Plaint of Kind's* described it well;
Which who will read set forth so as it ought,
Go seek he out that Alan where he may be sought.

10

And all the earth far underneath her feet
Was dight with flowers, that voluntary grew
Out of the ground and sent forth odors sweet:
Ten thousand mores of sundry scent and hue,
That might delight the smell or please the view,
The which the nymphs from all the brooks thereby
Had gathered, which they at her footstool threw,
That richer seemed than any tapestry
That princes' bowers adorn with painted imagery.

---

7.3   *sheen* shiny.
7.6   *three sacred saints* Peter, James, and John, at the Transfiguration; see Matthew 17.1–9, Mark 9.2–9.
8.1   *equal* level-topped.
9.3   *Dan Geoffrey* Chaucer.

9.5   *Fowls' Parley* Chaucer's *Parlement of Foulys*, in which Nature presides as an allegorical figure.   *mell* meddle.
9.6   *Alan* Alanus de Insulis, to whose lengthy description of Nature in his *De planctu Naturae* Chaucer refers his readers.
10.4   *mores* plants.

### 11

And Mole himself, to honor her the more,
Did deck himself in freshest fair attire,
And his high head, that seemeth always hoar
With hardened frosts of former winters' ire,
He with an oaken garland now did tire,
As if the love of some new nymph late seen
Had in him kindled youthful fresh desire
And made him change his gray attire to green.
Ah, gentle Mole! such joyance hath thee well beseen.

### 12

Was never so great joyance since the day
That all the gods whilom assembled were
On Haemus hill in their divine array
To celebrate the solemn bridal cheer
Twixt Peleus and Dame Thetis pointed there;
Where Phoebus' self, that god of poets hight,
They say did sing the spousal hymn full clear,
That all the gods were ravished with delight
Of his celestial song and music's wondrous might.

### 13

This great grandmother of all creatures bred,
Great Nature, ever young yet full of eld,
Still moving, yet unmovèd from her stead,
Unseen of any, yet of all beheld,
Thus sitting in her throne as I have telled:
Before her came Dame Mutability,
And being low before her presence felled,
With meek obeisance and humility,
Thus gan her plaintif plea with words to amplify:

### 14

To thee, O greatest goddess, only great,
An humble suppliant, lo, I lowly fly,
Seeking for right, which I of thee entreat,
Who right to all dost deal indifferently,
Damning all wrong and tortious injury
Which any of thy creatures do to other
(Oppressing them with power, unequally),
Sith of them all thou art the equal mother,
And knittest each to each as brother unto brother.

### 15

To thee, therefore, of this same Jove I plain,
And of his fellow gods that feign to be,
That challenge to themselves the whole world's reign,

---

11.5 *tire* attire.
11.9 *hath thee well beseen* looks good on you.
12.3 *Haemus* A mountain in Thrace, according to Ovid a mortal of that name transformed because of impiety (*Metamorphoses* 6.87–9). According to various classical sources, the event in question took place on Mount Pelion.

12.5 *Peleus and Dame Thetis* A mortal hero and a sea-nymph, who became the parents of Achilles. *pointed* appointed.
13.2 *eld* old age.
13.7 *felled* fallen.
14.5 *tortious* wrongful.
14.7 *unequally* unfairly.
15.3 *challenge* claim.

Of which, the greatest part is due to me,
And heaven itself by heritage in fee;
For heaven and earth I both alike do deem,
Sith heaven and earth are both alike to thee,
And gods no more than men thou dost esteem,
For even the gods to thee as men to gods do seem.

### 16

Then weigh, O sovereign goddess, by what right
These gods do claim the world's whole sovereignty,
And that is only due unto thy might
Arrogate to themselves ambitiously;
As for the gods' own principality,
Which Jove usurps unjustly, that to be
My heritage Jove's self cannot deny,
From my great grandsire Titan unto me
Derived by due descent, as is well known to thee.

### 17

Yet maugre Jove and all his gods beside,
I do possess the world's most regiment,
As, if ye please it into parts divide
And every part's inholders to convent,
Shall to your eyes appear incontinent.
And first, the Earth (great mother of us all),
That only seems unmoved and permanent
And unto Mutability not thrall,
Yet is she changed in part, and eke in general.

### 18

For all that from her springs and is ybred,
However fair it flourish for a time,
Yet see we soon decay and, being dead,
To turn again unto their earthly slime;
Yet out of their decay and mortal crime
We daily see new creatures to arise,
And of their winter spring another prime,
Unlike in form and changed by strange disguise:
So turn they still about, and change in restless wise.

### 19

As for her tenants, that is, man and beasts,
The beasts we daily see massacred die
As thralls and vassals unto men's behests,
And men themselves do change continually
From youth to eld, from wealth to poverty,
From good to bad, from bad to worst of all.
Ne do their bodies only flit and fly,
But eke their minds (which they immortal call)
Still change and vary thoughts, as new occasions fall.

15.5   *fee* absolute and rightful possession.
17.1   *maugre* despite.
17.2   *most regiment* largest kingdom.

17.4   *inholders* inhabitants.   *convent* assemble.
17.5   *incontinent* immediately.
18.7   *prime* spring.

### 20

Ne is the water in more constant case,
Whether those same on high or these below.
For the ocean moveth still from place to place,
And every river still doth ebb and flow,
Ne any lake that seems most still and slow
Ne pool so small that can his smoothness hold
When any wind doth under heaven blow;
With which the clouds are also tossed and rolled,
Now like great hills, and straight like sluices them unfold.

### 21

So likewise are all watery living wights
Still tossed and turnèd with continual change,
Never abiding in their steadfast plights.
The fish, still floating, do at randon range
And never rest, but evermore exchange
Their dwelling places as the streams them carry;
Ne have the watery fowls a certain grange
Wherein to rest, ne in one stead do tarry,
But flitting still do fly and still their places vary.

### 22

Next is the air, which who feels not by sense
(For of all sense it is the middle mean)
To flit still and, with subtle influence
Of his thin spirit, all creatures to maintain
In state of life? O weak life! that does lean
On thing so tickle as the unsteady air,
Which every hour is changed and altered clean
With every blast that bloweth foul or fair;
The fair doth it prolong, the foul doth it impair.

### 23

Therein the changes infinite behold
Which to her creatures every minute chance:
Now boiling hot, straight freezing deadly cold,
Now fair sunshine that makes all skip and dance,
Straight bitter storms and baleful countenance
That makes them all to shiver and to shake.
Rain, hail, and snow do pay them sad penance,
And dreadful thunderclaps (that make them quake)
With flames and flashing lights that thousand changes make.

### 24

Last is the fire, which, though it live forever
Ne can be quenchèd quite, yet every day
We see his parts, so soon as they do sever,
To lose their heat and shortly to decay:
So makes himself his own consuming prey.
Ne any living creatures doth he breed,
But all that are of others bred doth slay,

---

**20.2** *those same on high* As in Genesis 1.7: "the waters which were above the firmament."
**21.7** *grange* home base.

**22.2** *the middle mean* the intervening medium (between the object and the sense organ).
**22.6** *tickle* unstable.

And with their death his cruel life doth feed,
Nought leaving but their barren ashes, without seed.

25

Thus, all these four (the which the groundwork be
Of all the world, and of all living wights)
To thousand sorts of change we subject see,
Yet are they changed (by other wondrous sleights)
Into themselves, and lose their native mights:
The fire to air, and the air to water sheer,
And water into earth; yet water fights
With fire, and air with earth approaching near,
Yet all are in one body, and as one appear.

26

So in them all reigns Mutability,
However these that gods themselves do call
Of them do claim the rule and sovereignty:
As Vesta of the fire ethereal,
Vulcan of this with us so usual,
Ops of the earth, and Juno of the air,
Neptune of seas, and nymphs of rivers all.
For all those rivers to me subject are,
And all the rest, which they usurp, be all my share.

27

Which to approven true as I have told,
Vouchsafe, O goddess, to thy presence call
The rest which do the world in being hold
As times and seasons of the year that fall.
Of all the which demand in general,
Or judge thyself by verdit of thine eye,
Whether to me they are not subject all.
Nature did yield thereto, and by and by
Bade Order call them all before her majesty.

28

So forth issued the seasons of the year.
First, lusty Spring, all dight in leaves of flowers
That freshly budded and new blooms did bear
(In which a thousand birds had built their bowers,
That sweetly sung to call forth paramours);
And in his hand a javelin he did bear,
And on his head (as fit for warlike stours)
A gilt engraven morion he did wear,
That as some did him love, so others did him fear.

29

Then came the jolly Summer, being dight
In a thin silken cassock colored green,

---

26.4   *Vesta* Roman goddess of the hearth. Her temple in
Rome contained an eternal flame, which supposedly had the
same quality as the refined fire of the sublunary sphere.
26.6   *Ops* Rhea in Greek mythology; a Titaness, Saturn's
consort, herself a child of the primordial Earth.

27.6   *verdit* verdict.
28.7   *stours* struggles.
28.8   *morion* helmet with no visor.

That was unlinèd all, to be more light,
And on his head a garland well beseen
He wore, from which, as he had chafèd been,
The sweat did drop; and in his hand he bore
A bow and shafts, as he in forest green
Had hunted late the libbard or the boar,
And now would bathe his limbs, with labor heated sore.

30

Then came the Autumn, all in yellow clad,
As though he joyèd in his plenteous store,
Laden with fruits that made him laugh, full glad
That he had banished hunger, which to-fore
Had by the belly oft him pinchèd sore.
Upon his head a wreath that was enrolled
With ears of corn of every sort he bore,
And in his hand a sickle he did hold,
To reap the ripened fruits the which the earth had yold.

31

Lastly came Winter, clothèd all in frieze,
Chattering his teeth for cold that did him chill,
Whilst on his hoary beard his breath did freeze
And the dull drops that from his purpled bill,
As from a limbeck, did adown distill.
In his right hand a tippèd staff he held,
With which his feeble steps he stayèd still;
For he was faint with cold and weak with eld,
That scarce his loosèd limbs he able was to weld.

32

These, marching softly, thus in order went,
And after them the months all riding came.
First, sturdy March, with brows full sternly bent
And armèd strongly, rode upon a ram,
The same which over Hellespontus swam;
Yet in his hand a spade he also hent,
And in a bag all sorts of seeds ysame,
Which on the earth he strowèd as he went,
And filled her womb with fruitful hope of nourishment.

33

Next came fresh April, full of lustihead,
And wanton as a kid whose horn new buds;
Upon a bull he rode, the same which led
Europa floating through the Argolic floods.

29.8  *libbard* leopard.
30.9  *yold* yielded.
31.1  *frieze* coarse woollen cloth, with a nap on one side.
31.4  *bill* nose.
31.9  *weld* wield.
32.3  *First, sturdy March* Until 1753, the legal year in England began on Lady Day, 25 March.

32.4–5  Each month is linked to a zodiacal sign, in this case Aries. On this particular ram, see the note on III.xi.30.5 above; during her flight, Helle fell to her death in the strait that came to bear her name.
32.6  *hent* held.
32.7  *ysame* together.
33.3–4  The constellation is Taurus; on the myth, see above on III.xi.30.6.

His horns were gilden all with golden studs
And garnishèd with garlands goodly dight
Of all the fairest flowers and freshest buds
Which the earth brings forth, and wet he seemed in sight
With waves, through which he waded for his love's delight.

### 34

Then came fair May, the fairest maid on ground,
Decked all with dainties of her season's pride,
And throwing flowers out of her lap around;
Upon two brethren's shoulders she did ride,
The twins of Leda, which on either side
Supported her like to their sovereign queen.
Lord! how all creatures laughed when her they spied,
And leapt and danced as they had ravished been!
And Cupid self about her fluttered all in green.

### 35

And after her came jolly June, arrayed
All in green leaves, as he a player were;
Yet in his time he wrought as well as played,
That by his plough-irons mote right well appear.
Upon a crab he rode, that did him bear
With crooked crawling steps an uncouth pace,
And backward yode, as bargemen wont to fare,
Bending their force contrary to their face,
Like that ungracious crew which feigns demurest grace.

### 36

Then came hot July, boiling like to fire,
That all his garments he had cast away.
Upon a lion raging yet with ire
He boldly rode, and made him to obey;
It was the beast that whilom did foray
The Nemean forest, till the Amphytrionide
Him slew, and with his hide did him array.
Behind his back a scythe, and by his side
Under his belt he bore a sickle circling wide.

### 37

The sixth was August, being rich arrayed
In garment all of gold down to the ground;
Yet rode he not, but led a lovely maid
Forth by the lily hand, the which was crowned
With ears of corn, and full her hand was found.
That was the righteous virgin which of old
Lived here on earth, and plenty made abound;

34.4–6  The constellation is Gemini; the twins are Castor and Pollux, sons to Leda and brothers to Helen.

35.2  *player* actor (playing in this case the stock role of the wild man of nature).

35.5  *crab* Cancer.

35.7  *yode* went.

35.9  Like those who pretend to the height of courtesy by not turning their back to you while they move away.

36.3  *lion* Leo.

36.5  *foray* ravage.

36.6  *Amphytrionide* The son of Amphytrion, i.e., Hercules; killing the lion of Nemea was the first of his twelve labors.

37.3  *a lovely maid* Virgo.

37.6  *righteous virgin* Astraea, goddess of justice, who left the Earth during the Iron Age, the last of the celestials to do so.

But after wrong was loved and justice sold,
She left the unrighteous world and was to heaven extolled.

### 38

Next him September marchèd eke on foot,
Yet was he heavy laden with the spoil
Of harvest's riches, which he made his boot,
And him enriched with bounty of the soil.
In his one hand, as fit for harvest's toil,
He held a knife-hook, and in the other hand
A pair of weights, with which he did assoil
Both more and less, where it in doubt did stand,
And equal gave to each, as justice duly scanned.

### 39

Then came October, full of merry glee,
For yet his noll was totty of the must
Which he was treading in the wine-vat's sea,
And of the joyous oil whose gentle gust
Made him so frolic and so full of lust.
Upon a dreadful scorpion he did ride,
The same which by Diana's doom unjust
Slew great Orion; and eke by his side
He had a ploughing-share and colter ready tied.

### 40

Next was November, he full gross and fat
As fed with lard, and that right well might seem;
For he had been a-fatting hogs of late,
That yet his brows with sweat did reek and steam,
And yet the season was full sharp and breme.
In planting eke he took no small delight;
Whereon he rode not easy was to deem,
For it a dreadful centaur was in sight,
The seed of Saturn and fair Naïs, Chiron hight.

### 41

And after him came next the chill December;
Yet he through merry feasting which he made
And great bonfires did not the cold remember,
His Savior's birth his mind so much did glad.
Upon a shaggy-bearded goat he rode,
The same wherewith Dan Jove in tender years,
They say, was nourished by the Idaean maid;

38.3 *boot* booty.
38.7 *A pair of weights* Libra. *assoil* resolve.
38.9 *scanned* measured.
39.2 *noll* head. *totty* unstable. *must* wine at an early stage.
39.4 *gust* taste.
39.6 *scorpion* Scorpio.
39.7–8 Diana's reason for ordering the scorpion to kill the hunter Orion varies from source to source; Spenser's "unjust" suggests he has in mind the version in which Orion prompts her anger by boasting of his ability to kill any beast. In other tellings, she is avenging attempted rape.

40.5 *breme* stormy.
40.8 *centaur* Sagittarius.
40.9 *Naïs* A generic term for a Naiad or nymph of any kind, here used by Spenser as a proper name. In classical literature, the centaur Chiron is sometimes said to be the son of Saturn and Philyra; see above on III.xi.43.
41.5 *goat* Capricorn.
41.6–7 As an infant Jupiter was raised secretly on Mount Ida in Crete, and nursed either by the nymph Amalthaea or by a she-goat of the same name.

And in his hand a broad deep bowl he bears,
Of which he freely drinks an health to all his peers.

### 42

Then came old January, wrappèd well
In many weeds to keep the cold away;
Yet did he quake and quiver like to quell
And blow his nails to warm them if he may,
For they were numbed with holding all the day
An hatchet keen, with which he fellèd wood
And from the trees did lop the needless spray.
Upon an huge great earth-pot stean he stood,
From whose wide mouth there flowèd forth the Roman flood.

### 43

And lastly came cold February, sitting
In an old wagon, for he could not ride,
Drawn of two fishes for the season fitting,
Which through the flood before did softly slide
And swim away; yet had he by his side
His plough and harness, fit to till the ground,
And tools to prune the trees before the pride
Of hasting prime did make them burgeon round.
So passed the twelve months forth and their due places found.

### 44

And after these there came the Day and Night,
Riding together, both with equal pace,
The one on a palfrey black, the other white.
But Night had covered her uncomely face
With a black veil, and held in hand a mace,
On top whereof the moon and stars were pight,
And sleep and darkness round about did trace;
But Day did bear upon his scepter's height
The goodly sun, encompassed all with beames bright.

### 45

Then came the Hours, fair daughters of high Jove
And timely Night, the which were all endued
With wondrous beauty fit to kindle love;
But they were virgins all, and love eschewed,
That might forslack the charge to them foreshowed
By mighty Jove, who did them porters make
Of heaven's gate (whence all the gods issued),
Which they did daily watch and nightly wake
By even turns, ne ever did their charge forsake.

### 46

And after all came Life, and lastly Death:
Death with most grim and grisly visage seen,
Yet is he nought but parting of the breath,
Ne ought to see, but like a shade to ween,
Unbodièd, unsouled, unheard, unseen.

---

42.3   *like to quell* as if he were dying.
42.8   *stean* jar. Its presence equates January with Aquarius.
42.9   *the Roman flood* the Tiber.

45.5   *forslack* cause them to neglect.   *foreshowed* foretold.
45.8   *wake* guard.

But Life was like a fair young lusty boy,
Such as they feign Dan Cupid to have been,
Full of delightful health and lively joy,
Decked all with flowers, and wings of gold fit to employ.

### 47

When these were past, thus gan the Titaness:
Lo, mighty mother, now be judge and say
Whether in all thy creatures, more or less,
Change doth not reign and bear the greatest sway;
For who sees not that Time on all doth prey?
But times do change and move continually,
So nothing here long standeth in one stay.
Wherefore this lower world who can deny
But to be subject still to Mutability?

### 48

Then thus gan Jove: Right true it is that these
And all things else that under heaven dwell
Are changed of Time, who doth them all disseize
Of being; but who is it (to me tell)
That Time himself doth move and still compel
To keep his course? Is not that namely we
Which pour that virtue from our heavenly cell
That moves them all, and makes them changèd be?
So them we gods do rule, and in them also thee.

### 49

To whom thus Mutability: The things
Which we see not how they are moved and swayed
You may attribute to yourselves as kings,
And say they by your secret power are made;
But what we see not, who shall us persuade?
But were they so, as ye them feign to be,
Moved by your might and ordered by your aid,
Yet what if I can prove that even ye
Yourselves are likewise changed, and subject unto me?

### 50

And first, concerning her that is the first,
Even you, fair Cynthia, whom so much ye make
Jove's dearest darling, she was bred and nursed
On Cynthus hill, whence she her name did take:
Then is she mortal born, how so ye crake.
Besides, her face and countenance every day
We changèd see, and sundry forms partake,

---

48.3 *disseize* dispossess.

50.2 *Cynthia* Diana in her role as goddess of the moon; in the argument that follows, the gods are equated with the heavenly objects named after them or associated with them. In the case of the planets, Mutability's claims have mainly to do with the discrepancy between their observed movements – which sixteenth-century astronomy measured with new accuracy – and the expectations of a geocentric model with circular orbits. Johannes Kepler's demonstration that the empirical data correspond perfectly to a heliocentric model with elliptical orbits appeared in print in the same year as the Mutability Cantos.

50.4 *Cynthus hill* On the island of Delos, birthplace of Diana and Apollo.

50.5 *crake* brag.

Now horned, now round, now bright, now brown and gray,
So that *as changeful as the Moon* men use to say.

### 51

Next, Mercury, who though he less appear
To change his hue, and always seem as one,
Yet he his course doth alter every year,
And is of late far out of order gone.
So Venus eke, that goodly paragon,
Though fair all night, yet is she dark all day;
And Phoebus' self, who lightsome is alone,
Yet is he oft eclipsèd by the way,
And fills the darkened world with terror and dismay.

### 52

Now Mars, that valiant man, is changèd most,
For he sometimes so far runs out of square,
That he his way doth seem quite to have lost
And clean without his usual sphere to fare,
That even these star-gazers stonished are
At sight thereof, and damn their lying books;
So likewise, grim Sir Saturn oft doth spare
His stern aspect, and calm his crabbèd looks.
So many turning cranks these have, so many crooks.

### 53

But you, Dan Jove, that only constant are,
And king of all the rest, as ye do claim,
Are you not subject eke to this misfare?
Then let me ask you this withouten blame:
Where were ye born? Some say in Crete by name,
Others in Thebes, and others otherwhere;
But wheresoever they comment the same,
They all consent that ye begotten were
And born here in this world, ne other can appear.

### 54

Then are ye mortal born, and thrall to me,
Unless the kingdom of the sky ye make
Immortal and unchangeable to be.
Besides, that power and virtue, which ye spake
That ye here work, doth many changes take,
And your own natures change; for each of you
That virtue have, or this or that to make,
Is checked and changèd from his nature true
By others' opposition or obliquid view.

### 55

Besides, the sundry motions of your spheres,
So sundry ways and fashions as clerks feign,

51.7  *Phoebus' self* the sun.
52.4  *without* outside.
52.9  *turning cranks* winding paths.
53.3  *misfare* misdirection.
53.7  *comment* contrive.

54.6–9  An argument from astrology: the influence of a particular planet on earthly events is affected by the position of other planets, whether they are directly opposite in the sky ("opposition") or at some oblique angle ("obliquid" – the word appears to be Spenser's own coinage).

Some in short space, and some in longer years:
What is the same but alteration plain?
Only the starry sky doth still remain,
Yet do the stars and signs therein still move,
And even itself is moved, as wizards sayen.
But all that moveth doth mutation love;
Therefore both you and them to me I subject prove.

### 56

Then, since within this wide great Universe
Nothing doth firm and permanent appear,
But all things tossed and turnèd by transverse,
What then should let, but I aloft should rear
My trophy, and from all the triumph bear?
Now judge then (O thou greatest goddess true!)
According as thyself dost see and hear,
And unto me addoom that is my due;
That is the rule of all, all being ruled by you.

### 57

So having ended, silence long ensued,
Ne Nature to or fro spake for a space,
But with firm eyes affixed the ground still viewed.
Meanwhile, all creatures, looking in her face,
Expecting the end of this so doubtful case,
Did hang in long suspense what would ensue,
To whether side should fall the sovereign place.
At length, she, looking up with cheerful view,
The silence brake, and gave her doom in speeches few.

### 58

I well consider all that ye have said,
And find that all things steadfastness do hate
And changèd be; yet being rightly weighed,
They are not changèd from their first estate,
But by their change their being do dilate,
And turning to themselves at length again,
Do work their own perfection so by fate;
Then over them change doth not rule and reign,
But they reign over change, and do their states maintain.

### 59

Cease therefore, daughter, further to aspire,
And thee content thus to be ruled by me,
For thy decay thou seekst by thy desire;
But time shall come that all shall changèd be,
And from thenceforth none no more change shall see.
So was the Titaness put down and whist,
And Jove confirmed in his imperial see.
Then was that whole assembly quite dismissed,
And Nature's self did vanish, whither no man wist.

56.4  *let* prevent.
56.8  *addoom* award.

59.6  *whist* silenced.
59.7  *see* throne.

THE VIII CANTO, UNPERFIT

1

When I bethink me on that speech whilere
Of Mutability, and well it weigh,
Me seems that, though she all unworthy were
Of the heavens' rule, yet very sooth to say
In all things else she bears the greatest sway,
Which makes me loathe this state of life so tickle,
And love of things so vain to cast away;
Whose flowering pride, so fading and so fickle,
Short Time shall soon cut down with his consuming sickle.

2

Then gin I think on that which Nature said,
Of that same time when no more change shall be,
But steadfast rest of all things firmly stayed
Upon the pillars of Eternity,
That is contrair to Mutability;
For all that moveth doth in change delight,
But thenceforth all shall rest eternally
With Him that is the God of Sabaoth hight:
O that great Sabaoth God, grant me that Sabaoth's sight.

**0.0** *unperfit* unfinished.
**1.6** *tickle* unstable.
**2.8** *God of Sabaoth* The Lord of Hosts; the Hebrew word ( *çbha'oth* in stricter transliteration) occurs in this connection in English biblical translations and other religious texts in the sixteenth century. Context suggests that Spenser also associates it with Sabbath, in the sense of a final time of rest.

# From *Amoretti*

Spenser's sequence of eighty-nine sonnets, followed by four "anacreontics" and a lengthy *Epithalamion*, was published in 1595. All but one of the sonnets are written in a rhyme scheme of Spenser's own devising, in which the rhymes of the three quatrains are linked in a kind of daisy chain. The whole volume deals with Spenser's marriage the previous year to his second wife, Elizabeth Boyle; the *Epithalamion* – an august genre put to unprecedented first-person use – presents in elaborately crafted detail the actions of the wedding-day, 11 June. The *Amoretti* concerns the course of an ultimately successful courtship. It utilizes many of the conventions of Petrarchan sonneteering, but does so in the context of an un-Petrarchan storyline, leading to a happy ending. At times the man's frustration at the woman's apparent unattainability can be as angry as it is anywhere in the tradition (10, 56), but from the start this anger is accompanied by an awareness that the difficulty in wooing her is part of the point (6). Her consent comes shortly after the New Year in March, about two-thirds of the way through the sequence; it is announced by the extravagant sensuality of a kiss (64) and a skillful turn on one of the best-established tropes of Petrarchan hopelessness (67).

6

Be nought dismayed that her unmovèd mind
Doth still persist in her rebellious pride;
Such love, not like to lusts of baser kind,
The harder won, the firmer will abide.
The dureful oak whose sap is not yet dried          5
Is long ere it conceive the kindling fire;
But when it once doth burn, it doth divide
Great heat, and makes his flames to heaven aspire.

So hard it is to kindle new desire
In gentle breast that shall endure forever;   10
Deep is the wound that dints the parts entire
With chaste affects that nought but death can sever.
Then think not long in taking little pain
To knit the knot that ever shall remain.

5   *dureful* durable.
7   *divide* dispense.

11   *dints* strikes (so as to leave a mark).

## 10

Unrighteous Lord of Love, what law is this,
That me thou makest thus tormented be,
The whiles she lordeth in licentious bliss
Of her free will, scorning both thee and me?
See how the tyranness doth joy to see   5
The huge massacres which her eyes do make,
And humbled hearts brings captives unto thee,
That thou of them mayst mighty vengeance take.
But her proud heart do thou a little shake,
And that high look, with which she doth control   10
All this world's pride, bow to a baser make,
And all her faults in thy black book enroll:
That I may laugh at her in equal sort,
As she doth laugh at me and makes my pain her sport.

3   *licentious* unrestrained.

11   *baser make* less worthy mate.

## 35

My hungry eyes, through greedy covetise
Still to behold the object of their pain,
With no contentment can themselves suffice,
But having, pine, and having not, complain.
For lacking it, they cannot life sustain,   5
And having it, they gaze on it the more,
In their amazement like Narcissus vain,
Whose eyes him starved: so plenty makes me poor.
Yet are mine eyes so fillèd with the store
Of that fair sight, that nothing else they brook,   10
But loathe the things which they did like before,
And can no more endure on them to look.
All this world's glory seemeth vain to me,
And all their shows but shadows, saving she.

1   *covetise* covetousness.
2   *Still* constantly.
6   *having* This sonnet is repeated almost verbatim as no. 83 in the sequence, with the alteration of this word to "seeing."

8   *so plenty makes me poor* Translating a phrase from Ovid's telling of the Narcissus story: *inopem me copia fecit* (*Metamorphoses* 3.466).
10   *brook* tolerate.
14   *saving she* except for her.

### 37

What guile is this, that those her golden tresses
She doth attire under a net of gold,
And with sly skill so cunningly them dresses
That which is gold or hair may scarce be told?
Is it that men's frail eyes which gaze too bold          5
She may entangle in that golden snare
And, being caught, may craftily enfold
Their weaker hearts, which are not well aware?
Take heed therefore, mine eyes, how ye do stare
Henceforth too rashly on that guileful net,             10
In which if ever ye entrappèd are,
Out of her bands ye by no means shall get.
Fondness it were for any, being free,
To covet fetters, though they golden be.

13  *Fondness* foolishness.

### 45

Leave, lady, in your glass of crystal clean
Your goodly self for evermore to view,
And in my self, my inward self I mean,
Most lively like behold your semblant true.
Within my heart, though hardly it can show          5
Thing so divine to view of earthly eye,
The fair idea of your celestial hue
And every part remains immortally;
And were it not that through your cruelty
With sorrow dimmèd and deformed it were,          10
The goodly image of your physnomy
Clearer than crystal would therein appear.
But if your self in me ye plain will see,
Remove the cause by which your fair beams darkened be.

1  *Leave* cease.  *glass* mirror.
4  *lively like* lifelike.

7  *hue* shape (as well as color).
11  *physnomy* physiognomy.

### 56

Fair ye be sure, but cruel and unkind,
As is a tiger that with greediness
Hunts after blood, when he by chance doth find
A feeble beast, doth felly him oppress.
Fair be ye sure, but proud and pitiless,          5
As is a storm that all things doth prostrate,
Finding a tree alone all comfortless,
Beats on it strongly, it to ruinate.
Fair be ye sure, but hard and obstinate,
As is a rock amidst the raging floods,             10
Gainst which a ship of succor desolate
Doth suffer wreck both of herself and goods.
That ship, that tree, and that same beast am I,
Whom ye do wreck, do ruin, and destroy.

4  *felly* cruelly.                    11  *of succor desolate* without hope of help.

### 64

Coming to kiss her lips (such grace I found),
Me seemed I smelt a garden of sweet flowers
That dainty odors from them threw around
For damsels fit to deck their lovers' bowers.
Her lips did smell like unto gillyflowers,                    5
Her ruddy cheeks like unto roses red,
Her snowy brows like budded bellamours,
Her lovely eyes like pinks but newly spread,
Her goodly bosom like a strawberry bed,
Her neck like to a bunch of columbines,                    10
Her breast like lilies ere their leaves be shed,
Her nipples like young blossomed jessamines.
Such fragrant flowers do give most odorous smell,
But her sweet odor did them all excel.

5  *gillyflowers* a variety of pinks.          12  *jessamines* jasmines.
7  *bellamours* Unidentified.

### 67

Like as a huntsman after weary chase,
Seeing the game from him escaped away,
Sits down to rest him in some shady place,
With panting hounds beguilèd of their prey:
So after long pursuit and vain assay,                    5
When I all weary had the chase forsook,
The gentle deer returned the self-same way,
Thinking to quench her thirst at the next brook.
There she, beholding me with milder look,
Sought not to fly, but fearless still did bide,            10
Till I in hand her yet half trembling took,
And with her own good will her firmly tied.
Strange thing me seemed to see a beast so wild
So goodly won, with her own will beguiled.

For the Petrarchan original on which this poem rings a          5  *assay* attempt.
significant change, see Wyatt, "Whoso list to hunt."          14  *beguiled* entrapped through some sort of charm.
4  *beguilèd* cheated.

### 68

Most glorious Lord of Life, that on this day
Didst make thy triumph over death and sin,
And, having harrowed hell, didst bring away
Captivity thence captive us to win:
This joyous day, dear Lord, with joy begin,                    5
And grant that we for whom thou didest die,
Being with thy dear blood clean washed from sin,
May live forever in felicity;
And that thy love we weighing worthily

1  *this day* Easter, which in 1594 was 31 March. Sonnet 62          3  *having harrowed hell* A medieval tradition held that
in the *Amoretti* announces the beginning of the new year,          between Good Friday and Easter Christ visited hell
which in sixteenth-century reckoning would be 25 March          and freed the souls of some of those who did not have
(see above on *Faery Queen* VII.vii.32.3).          access to his grace during their own lives.

May likewise love thee for the same again,                    10
And for thy sake that all like dear didst buy
With love may one another entertain.
So let us love, dear love, like as we ought;
Love is the lesson which the Lord us taught.


### 75

One day I wrote her name upon the strand,
But came the waves and washèd it away;
Again I wrote it with a second hand,
But came the tide and made my pains his prey.
Vain man, said she, that dost in vain assay            5
A mortal thing so to immortalize.
For I myself shall like to this decay,
And eke my name be wipèd out likewise.
Not so (quod I), let baser things devise
To die in dust, but you shall live by fame.            10
My verse your virtues rare shall eternize,
And in the heavens write your glorious name:
Where whenas death shall all the world subdue,
Our love shall live, and later life renew.

# Sir Walter Ralegh (1554?–1618)

Born into a well-established Devon family, by 1569 Ralegh was seeing military service in France (in support of the Huguenots) and embarked on one of the most spectacular public careers of his time. He attended Oxford, and became a member of the Middle Temple in 1575; in 1578 he joined his half-brother Sir Humphrey Gilbert in fitting out an expedition to North America, though it never got there. In 1580 he was given a command in the fight against the Irish rebels, and on his return to England the next year gained entrance to the court and began to rise very quickly in Elizabeth's regard; he effectively replaced the aging Earl of Leicester as her favorite, and flourished in that position for most of the decade. From 1589 on he came into competition with a new rising star, the Earl of Essex; when Elizabeth learned in 1592 that Ralegh had secretly married one of her maids of honor, Elizabeth Throckmorton, she had both of them imprisoned in the Tower of London, and after releasing them banished Ralegh from court. He only slowly returned to limited favor. Through all of this he was involved in repeated efforts to explore and colonize the New World; in 1595 he finally sailed there himself, and on his return published *The Discovery of the Large, Rich, and Beautiful Empire of Guiana*, an important piece of propaganda on behalf of English imperial ambitions. He was involved in the naval raid on Cadiz in 1596, and the expedition to the Azores in 1597. In 1603, at the accession of James I, with his pacific policy toward Spain, Ralegh's record made him an undesirable figure, and his enemies at court engineered a charge of treason; his sentence of death was stayed but not revoked, and he remained in the Tower for the next thirteen years. In 1616 he was released to lead a second expedition to Guiana; in defiance of royal instructions, his men blundered into a fight with the Spaniards, in which Ralegh's own son was killed. On his return to England Ralegh was imprisoned again, and in 1618 executed on the charges of fifteen years earlier.

Into all of this Ralegh somehow worked a literary career, which began in his Middle Temple days, when he contributed an introductory poem to George Gascoigne's *The Steel Glass* (1576), and continued through his imprisonment, when he worked on a *History of the World*, which he brought up to the second century BC. In Ireland his estate neighbored Edmund Spenser's, and he seems to have been present at the conception and gestation of *The Faery Queen*, in which he figures as the character Timias, and to which he contributed a dedicatory sonnet in 1590. Contemporaries speak highly of him as a poet, but there was no attempt to collect his poems; modern editors have pulled together from manuscripts and printed miscellanies a spotty canon of some sixty entries, with numerous uncertain attributions. The most famous of them have a witty, foursquare mordancy that sometimes comes with a countervailing message of religious faith and sometimes not; in the case of the last stanza of "Nature, that washed her hands in milk," reworked as the poem Ralegh supposedly wrote on the eve of his execution, we have it both ways. There are love poems in different keys; the most intriguing appear to concern Queen Elizabeth, and were indeed probably given to her; they offer us our most intimate look into the complicated game of courtship that took place in her inner circle. She would likely have replied in kind, and in one case we actually have that exchange.

One intriguing document is a purported section of a long poem about Ralegh and his queen entitled *The Ocean's Love to Cynthia*: what survives is said to come from Books 21 and 22. We can glimpse the outlines of the ruling conceit. Ralegh (his pronunciation of his first name came very close to "water") is the "shepherd of the ocean" (as Spenser called him), and Elizabeth (as in numerous other panegyrics) the virgin goddess of the moon, who governs the tides; she controls his movements from afar, as he travels in search of ways to do her homage. Superimposing Petrarchan love on the nascent enterprise of English imperialism, it could have been one of the definitive poems of its age. The surviving fragments, however, treat of defeat and psychic collapse, probably in connection with Ralegh's loss of favor in 1592; repetitious and unshaped, they nevertheless have the power of their dazed relentlessness. The first fragment runs to over 500 lines; the second fragment is given below. It is possible that no more of the poem was ever actually written.

*Edition*: *The Poems of Sir Walter Ralegh: A Historical Edition*, ed. Michael Rudick (Tempe, AZ: MRTS, 1999).

## A Vision upon this Conceit of the Faery Queen

Methought I saw the grave where Laura lay,
Within that temple where the vestal flame
Was wont to burn, and passing by that way
To see that buried dust of living fame,
Whose tomb fair love and fairer virtue kept,      5
All suddenly I saw the Faery Queen:
At whose approach the soul of Petrarch wept,
And from thenceforth those graces were not seen,
For they this queen attended, in whose stead
Oblivion laid him down on Laura's hearse.      10
Hereat the hardest stones were seen to bleed,
And groans of buried ghosts the heavens did pierce,
Where Homer's sprite did tremble all for grief,
And cursed the access of that celestial thief.

Printed in the 1590 edition of the first three books of *The Faery Queen*.

1 *Laura* The woman whom Petrarch celebrated in his vernacular poetry. The French poet Maurice Scève claimed to have discovered her tomb in southern France in the early sixteenth century.

Would I were changed into that golden shower
That so divinely streamèd from the skies,
To fall in drops upon the dainty flower,
Where in her bed she solitary lies.
Then would I hope such showers as richly shine      5
Would pierce more deep than these waste tears of mine.

Or would I were that plumèd swan, snow-white,
Under whose form was hidden heavenly power;
Then in that river would I most delight
Whose waves do beat against her stately bower,      10
And on those banks so tune my dying song
That her deaf ears should think my plaint too long.

Else would I were Narcissus, that sweet boy,
And she herself the fountain, crystal clear,
Who, ravished with the pride of his own joy,      15
Drenchèd his limbs with gazing over near.
So should I bring my soul to happy rest,
To end my life in that I lovèd best.

Attributed to "RA" in one manuscript; published anonymously in *The Phoenix Nest* (1593). The poem is an adaptation of a sonnet by Ronsard, "Je voudrais bien richement jaunissant." The conceit became a popular one; for a famously extreme development of it, see the sonnet by Barnabe Barnes given below.

1 *that golden shower* Jupiter seduced Danaë after entering her prison as a shower of gold.

7 *that plumèd swan* Jupiter seduced Leda in the guise of a swan.

16 *Drenchèd* drowned.

# The Advice

Many desire, but few or none deserve
To win the fort of thy most constant will.
Therefore, take heed, let fancy never swerve
But unto him that will defend thee still.
For this be sure, the fort of fame once won,       5
Farewell the rest, thy happy days are done.

Many desire, but few or none deserve
To pluck the flowers and let the leaves to fall;
Therefore take heed, let fancy never swerve
But unto him that will take leaves and all.       10
For this be sure, the flower once plucked away,
Farewell the rest, thy happy days decay.

Many desire, but few or none deserve
To cut the corn not subject to the sickle;
Therefore take heed, let fancy never swerve,       15
But constant stand, for mowers' minds are fickle.
For this be sure, the crop being once obtained,
Farewell the rest, the soil will be disdained.

Manuscripts identify the addressee as Ann Vavasour, one of Elizabeth's maids of honor, who was imprisoned in 1581 after giving birth to a child by the Earl of Oxford; she later had a son by another courtier, Sir Henry Lee.

What is our life? The play of passion,
Our mirth the music of division.
Our mothers' wombs the tiring houses be
Where we are dressed for life's short comedy.
The earth the stage, heaven the spectator is,       5
Who sits and views whosoe'er doth act amiss.
The graves which hides us from the scorching sun
Are like drawn curtains till the play is done.
Thus, playing, post we to our latest rest;
And then we die in earnest, not in jest.       10

Three manuscript copies of this poem read "tragedy" in l. 4 and do not have the final couplet. A slightly different text of the ten-line version was set to music by Orlando Gibbons in his *First Set of Madrigals and Motets* (1612).

**2** *division* variations made upon a musical line.
**3** *tiring houses* dressing rooms.
**9** *latest* last.
**10** Gibbons's text here is perhaps superior: "Only we die in earnest, that's no jest."

# The Lie

Go, soul, the body's guest,
Upon a thankless errand.
Fear not to touch the best;
The truth shall be thy warrant.

This poem was particularly popular in manuscripts, from the 1590s onward, and was printed in the anthology *A Poetical Rhapsody* in 1608. There is considerable textual variation, well beyond the examples given here, including numerous extra stanzas that appear to have been added *ad lib* as the poem circulated; one version runs to 126 lines.

Go, since I needs must die,                                                5
And give the world the lie.

Say to the Court it glows
And shines like rotten wood.
Say to the Church it shows
What's good yet doth no good.                                              10
If Court and Church reply,
Give Court and Church the lie.

Tell potentates they live
Acting but others' actions,
Not loved unless they give,                                                15
Not strong but by affections.
If potentates reply,
Give potentates the lie.

Tell men of high condition
That tend affairs of state                                                 20
Their purpose is ambition,
Their practice is but hate;
And if they once reply,
Then give them all the lie.

Tell those that brave it most,                                             25
They beg for more by spending
Who in their greatest cost
Have nothing but commending;
And if they do reply,
Give each of them the lie.                                                 30

Tell Zeal it wants devotion,
Tell Love it is but lust,
Tell Time it metes but motion,
Tell Flesh it is but dust;
And wish them not reply,                                                   35
For thou must give the lie.

Tell Age it daily wasteth,
Tell Honor how it alters,
Tell Beauty that she boasteth,
Tell Favor that she flatters;                                             40
And if they shall reply,
Give everyone the lie.

Tell Wit how much it wrangles
In tickle points of niceness,
Tell Wisdom she entangles                                                 45
Herself in others' wiseness;

6   And accuse the world of lying.

25   *brave it most* put on the best show.

33   *metes* measures. There is much variation in the manu-
scripts here; alternate readings include "it means," "it meets,"
"it is."

39   *boasteth* Several manuscripts read "blasteth," i.e.,
"withers."

44   *tickle* capricious.   *niceness* fastidiousness.

And when they do reply,
Straight give them both the lie.

Tell Physic of her boldness,
Tell Skill it is prevention,                                    50
Tell Mercy of her coldness,
Tell Law it is contention;
And as they do reply,
So give them still the lie.

Tell Fortune of her blindness,                                 55
Tell Nature of decay,
Tell Friendship of unkindness,
Tell Justice of delay;
And if they will reply,
Then give them all the lie.                                    60

Tell Arts they have no soundness,
But vary by contriving;
Tell Schools they lack profoundness,
And stand too much on striving.
If Arts and Schools reply,                                     65
Give Arts and Schools the lie.

Tell Faith it's fled the city,
Tell how the Country erreth,
Say Manhood shakes for pity,
Say virtue none preferreth;                                    70
And if they do reply,
Spare not to give the lie.

So when thou hast as I
Commanded thee done blabbing,
Although to give the lie                                       75
Deserves no less than stabbing,
Stab at thee he that will.
No stab the soul can kill.

**49** *Physic* medicine.
**50** *Skill* correct understanding. *prevention* The point is
obscure. The relevant possible senses of the word are "act-
ing ahead of time" and "acting with pre-emptive authority";
displays of knowingness are perhaps being characterized
either as scripted in advance or as arbitrarily asserted.

**62, 64** In a number of manuscripts these lines read "But
vary by esteeming" and "Stand too much on seeming" (or, in
one case, "Stand on overweening").
**70** *none preferreth* gives no one worldly advancement.

## To his love when he had obtained her

Now, Serena, be not coy,
Since we freely may enjoy
Sweet embraces, such delights

**1** *Serena* A woman with this name is a character in Book VI
of *The Faery Queen*, which appeared in 1596; with Arthur's
squire Timias, whose story elsewhere resembles Ralegh's,
she is wounded by the Blatant Beast (scandal). The name, a
rare one at the time, was perhaps poetic code in Ralegh's
circle for Elizabeth Throckmorton.

As will shorten tedious nights.
Think that beauty will not stay                           5
With you always but away,
And that tyrannizing face
That now holds such perfect grace
Will both changed and ruined be;
So frail is all things as we see,                         10
So subject unto conquering time.
Then gather flowers in their prime,
Let them not fall and perish so;
Nature her bounties did bestow
On us that we might use them, and                         15
Tis coldness not to understand
What she and youth and form persuade,
With opportunity that's made
As we could wish it. Let's then meet
Often with amorous lips, and greet                        20
Each other till our wanton kisses
In number pass the days Ulysses
Consumed in travel, and the stars
That look upon our peaceful wars
With envious luster. If this store                        25
Will not suffice, we'll number o'er
The same again, until we find
No number left to call to mind
And show our plenty. They are poor
That can count all they have and more.                    30

6   *away* go away.
17   *form* beauty.

19–30  Inspired by Catullus's poems on the kisses that he
intends for Lesbia (*Carmina* 5 and 7), with a concluding
sentiment taken from Martial (*Epigrammata* 6.34.7–8).

Our passions are most like to floods and streams:
The shallow murmur, but the deep are dumb.
So when affections yield discourse, it seems
The bottom is but shallow whence they come.
They that are rich in words must needs discover           5
That they are poor in that which makes a lover.

Wrong not, dear empress of my heart,
    The merit of true passion,
With thinking that he feels no smart
    That sues for no compassion;                          10
Since if my plaints serve not to prove
    The conquest of your beauty,
They come not from defect of love
    But from excess of duty.

For knowing that I sue to serve                           15
    A saint of such perfection
As all desire but none deserve
    A place in her affection,
I rather choose to want relief
    Than venture the revealing.                           20

When glory recommends the grief,
    Despair distrusts the healing.

Thus those desires that aim too high
    For any mortal lover,
When reason cannot make them die,        25
    Discretion will them cover.
Yet when discretion doth bereave
    The plaints that they should utter,
Then your discretion may perceive
    That silence is a suitor.        30

Silence in love bewrays more woe
    Than words, though ne'er so witty.
A beggar that is dumb, ye know,
    Deserveth double pity.
Then misconceive not (dearest heart)        35
    My true though secret passion.
He smarteth most that hides his smart,
    And sues for no compassion.

Two manuscript copies of this poem identify it as being
addressed to Queen Elizabeth. Three copies omit the metric-
ally anomalous first stanza.

# The end of the books of the Ocean's love to Cynthia, and the beginning of the 22 book, entreating of sorrow

My days' delights, my springtime joys fordone,
Which in the dawn and rising sun of youth
Had their creation and were first begun,

Do in the evening and the winter sad
Present my mind, which takes my time's account,        5
The grief remaining of the joy it had.

My times that then ran o'er themselves in these
And now run out in others' happiness
Bring unto those new joys and newborn days.

So could she not if she were not the sun        10
Which sees the birth and burial of all else,
And holds that power with which she first begun,

Leaving each withered body to be torn
By fortune and by times tempestuous,
Which by her virtue once fair fruit have borne,        15

*22 book* The numeral in the manuscript has also been read as
12.

**5**  *Present my mind* Either "figure forth my mind" or "present
themselves to my mind"; the latter would make more sense
in context, but the usage is unattested in the *OED*.

Knowing she can renew and can create
Green from the ground and flowers even out of stone,
By virtue lasting over time and date,

Leaving us only woe, which like the moss,
Having compassion of unburied bones,           20
Cleaves to mischance and unrepairèd loss,

For tender stalks . . .

    Nature, that washed her hands in milk
    And had forgot to dry them,
    Instead of earth took snow and silk,
    At Love's request to try them,
    If she a mistress could compose           5
    To please Love's fancy out of those.

    Her eyes he would should be of light,
    A violet breath, and lips of jelly;
    Her hair not black nor over bright,
    And of the softest down her belly.           10
    As for her inside, he'd have it
    Only of wantonness and wit.

    At Love's entreaty, such a one
    Nature made, but with her beauty
    She hath framed a heart of stone,           15
    So as Love, by ill destiny,
    Must die for her whom Nature gave him,
    Because her darling would not save him.

    But Time, which Nature doth despise,
    And rudely gives her Love the lie,           20
    Makes Hope a fool and Sorrow wise,
    His hands doth neither wash nor dry,
    But, being made of steel and rust,
    Turns snow and silk and milk to dust.

    The light, the belly, lips, and breath           25
    He dims, discolors, and destroys.
    With those he feeds but fills not Death,
    Which sometimes were the food of joys.
    Yea, Time doth dull each lively wit,
    And dries all wantonness with it.           30

    O cruel Time, which takes in trust
    Our youth, our joys, and all we have,
    And pays us but with age and dust,
    Who in the dark and silent grave,
    When we have wandered all our ways,          35
    Shuts up the story of our days.

Three manuscript copies of this poem consist of stanzas 1, 2,    **20**  *gives her Love the lie* accuses Love of lying.
and 4; one manuscript names the woman in it "Serena."

# The Passionate Man's Pilgrimage

Give me my scallop shell of quiet,
My staff of faith to walk upon,
My scrip of joy, immortal diet,
My bottle of salvation,
My gown of glory, hope's true gage,    5
And thus I'll take my pilgrimage.

Blood must be my body's balmer,
No other balm will there be given
Whilst my soul, like a white palmer,
Travels to the land of heaven    10
Over the silver mountains
Where spring the nectar fountains;
And there I'll kiss
The bowl of bliss,
And drink my eternal fill    15
On every milken hill.
My soul will be a-dry before,
But after it will ne'er thirst more.

And by the happy blissful way
More peaceful pilgrims I shall see    20
That have shook off their gowns of clay
And go appareled fresh, like me.
I'll bring them first
To slake their thirst,
And then to taste those nectar suckets    25
At the clear wells
Where sweetness dwells,
Drawn up by saints in crystal buckets.

And when our bottles and all we
Are filled with immortality,    30
Then the holy paths we'll travel
Strewed with rubies thick as gravel,
Ceilings of diamonds, sapphire floors,
High walls of coral, and pearl bowers.

From thence to heaven's bribeless hall    35
Where no corrupted voices brawl,
No conscience molten into gold,
Nor forged accusers bought and sold,
No cause deferred nor vain spent journey,
For there Christ is the King's Attorney,    40

The poem first appears, attributed to "one at the point of death," as an appendix to Anthony Scoloker's *Daiphantus* (1604); other evidence attests Ralegh's authorship, so the last stanza dates the poem to the time of his seemingly imminent execution in 1603. Two of the numerous sources of the text add a final couplet: "Of death and judgment, heaven and hell, / Who thinks of those [or: Who oft doth think] must needs die well."

1  *scallop shell* A traditional badge for a pilgrim.
3  *scrip* wallet.
5  *gage* A glove or cap given as a pledge.
7  *balmer* embalmer.
9  *palmer* pilgrim.
25  *suckets* succades (sweetmeats).

Who pleads for all without degrees;
And he hath angels, but no fees.

When the grand twelve million jury
Of our sins and sinful fury
Gainst our souls black verdicts give,                           45
Christ pleads his death, and then we live.
Be thou my speaker, taintless pleader,
Unblotted lawyer, true proceeder;
Thou movest salvation even for alms,
Not with a bribèd lawyer's palms.                               50

And this is my eternal plea
To him that made heaven, earth, and sea,
Seeing my flesh must die so soon
And want a head to dine next noon:
Just at the stroke when my veins start and spread,             55
Set on my soul an everlasting head.
Then am I ready like a palmer fit
To tread those blest paths which before I writ.

**42**   *angels* With a pun on the name of an English gold coin
which in its first issues had a representation of the archangel
Michael on it.

## Sir Walter Ralegh, his verses written in his Bible a little before his death

Even such is Time, which takes in trust
Our youth, our joys, and all we have,
And pays us but with age and dust,
Who in the dark and silent grave,
When we have wandered all our ways,                            5
Shuts up the story of our days;
And from which earth and grave and dust
The Lord shall raise me up, I trust.

# Sir Walter Ralegh and Elizabeth I

There is plenty of evidence that poems were common currency in Elizabeth's court, but in only a few instances can we briefly follow the conversation being conducted through them. The pair given here is an exchange between the queen and her reigning favorite during most of the 1580s. It has been plausibly conjectured that the occasion was the rise of the Earl of Essex in the queen's favor in 1587, with Fortune a code name for Essex, but there is no external evidence. Puttenham (1589) quotes from both poems; there are several manuscript sources, all but one of them incomplete. The full text of both poems was not printed until 1991; see Steven May, *The Elizabethan Courtier Poets: The Poems and their Contexts* (Columbia, MO: University of Missouri Press, 1991), pp. 318–21.

## A Sonnet

Fortune hath taken thee away, my love,
My life's joy and my soul's heaven above.
Fortune hath taken thee away, my princess,
My world's delight and my true fancy's mistress.

Fortune hath taken all away from me,          5
Fortune hath taken all by taking thee.
Dead to all joys, I only live to woe;
So Fortune now becomes my fancy's foe.

In vain, mine eyes, in vain you waste your tears;
In vain, my sighs, the smokes of mighty fears,          10
In vain you search the earth and heavens above,
In vain you search, for Fortune keeps my love.

Then will I leave my love in Fortune's hands,
Then will I leave my love in worthless bands,
And only love the sorrow due to me,          15
Sorrow, henceforth that shalt my princess be;

And only joy that Fortune, conquering kings,
Fortune that rules on earth and earthly things,
Hath ta'en my love in spite of virtue's might;
So blind a goddess did never virtue right.          20

With wisdom's eyes had but blind Fortune seen,
Then had my love my love forever been.
But love, farewell; though Fortune conquer thee,
No Fortune base shall ever alter me.

# An Answer

Ah, silly pug, wert thou so sore afraid?
Mourn not, my Wat, nor be thou so dismayed.
It passeth fickle Fortune's power and skill
To force my heart to think thee any ill.

No Fortune base, thou sayst, shall alter thee;                      5
And may so blind a wretch then conquer me?
No, no, my pug, though Fortune were not blind,
Assure thyself, she could not rule my mind.

Ne chose I thee by foolish Fortune's rede,
Ne can she make me alter with such speed;                           10
But must thou needs sour Sorrow's servant be
If, that to try, thy mistress jest with thee.

Fortune, I grant, sometimes doth conquer kings,
And rules and reigns on earth and earthly things;
But never think that Fortune can bear sway                          15
If Virtue watch and will her not obey.

Pluck up thy heart, suppress thy brackish tears,
Torment thee not, but put away thy fears.
Thy love, thy joy, she loves no worthless bands,
Much less to be in reeling Fortune's hands.                         20

Dead to all joys and living unto woe,
Slain quite by her that never gave wise man blow,
Revive again, and live without all dread;
The less afraid, the better shalt thou speed.

---

1   *pug* One of Elizabeth's pet names for Ralegh.
2   *Wat* Walter.
9   *rede* advice.
12   The line is printed here to mean "If your mistress jests with you to test her superiority to Fortune"; an alternative modernization would be "If that to try thy mistress' jest with thee," but the meaning in that case would be obscure. Two sources of the poem do not include this line; another reads "But if to try this mistress' jest with thee."
24   *speed* succeed.

# Fulke Greville, Lord Brooke (1554–1628)

Born to high-ranking gentry in Warwickshire, Greville attended Shrewsbury School, where he became close friends with Philip Sidney, and then Cambridge. By 1577 he was at court, where he became a key figure in Sidney's circle. He may well be the original of the caustic friend addressed several times in *Astrophil and Stella*; after Sidney's death, Greville served, together with the Countess of Pembroke, as Sidney's literary executor, and wrote a highly partisan biography of him. His own political career was an unusually steady one, involving a succession of significant appointments under both Elizabeth and James. He was Chancellor and Under-Treasurer of the Exchequer from 1614 to 1621; on resigning from that post, he was created Baron Brooke. He died a fairly wealthy man, stabbed by a manservant who may have been unhappy about the provision for him in his master's will.

His lyric sequence *Caelica* was work in progress for almost the entirety of Greville's adult life; a surviving manuscript shows extensive revision, at times to the point of illegibility. Some of the earlier poems are in dialogue with specific poems of Sidney's; ultimately the sequence included 109 poems, one more than the number of sonnets in *Astrophil and Stella*. The names Caelica, Cynthia, and Myra, which may or may not designate the same woman, alternate according to no obvious system; there is little sense of sustained narrative, aside from a general experience of disillusion with sexual love. Poem 84 is a decisive farewell to Cupid and all his works; religious urgency of a radical Protestant cast dominates in the last two decades of the sequence, and concludes things with an apocalyptic call for judgment. Greville's ongoing intellectual and moral seriousness do not keep some of the poems from having an extraordinary sensual charge; poems 40 and 56 are almost unparalleled renderings of the intentness and giddiness of sexual arousal. Poem 56, however, is also a dark satire on the deceitful and disabling involvement of the erotic imagination in such arousal; and the most forcefully sustained theme over the sequence as a whole is a distrust of the idolatrous powers of the human mind. Disillusion with love is also disillusion with thought.

*Caelica* was first printed in 1633; the text here generally follows that of this edition, except for poem 56, where the longer and more provocative manuscript version is given.

*Edition*: *Poems and Dramas of Fulke Greville*, ed. Geoffrey Bullough, 2 vols. (London: Oliver & Boyd, 1939).

## From *Caelica*

### 12

Cupid, thou naughty boy, when thou wert loathed,
Naked and blind, for vagabonding noted,
Thy nakedness I in my reason clothed,
Mine eyes I gave thee, so was I devoted.
Fie, wanton, fie; who would show children kindness?     5
No sooner he into mine eyes was gotten
But straight he clouds them with a seeing blindness,
Makes reason wish that reason were forgotten.
From thence to Myra's eyes the wanton strayeth,
Where, while I charge him with ungrateful measure,     10
So with fair wonders he mine eyes betrayeth
That my wounds and his wrongs become my pleasure:
Till for more spite, to Myra's heart he flyeth,
Where living to the world, to me he dieth.

---

Similar to several poems in *Astrophil and Stella*, especially sonnet 73.     **2**    *vagabonding* having no proper home or employment.

### 38

Caelica, I overnight was finely used,
Lodged in the midst of paradise, your heart.
Kind thoughts had charge I might not be refused;
Of every fruit and flower I had part.
But curious Knowledge, blown with busy flame,                    5
The sweetest fruits had down in shadows hidden,
And for it found mine eyes had seen the same,
I from my paradise was straight forbidden:
Where that cur, Rumor, runs in every place,
Barking with Care, begotten out of Fear,                        10
And glassy Honor, tender of Disgrace,
Stands Seraphin to see I come not there;
While that fine soil which all these joys did yield
By broken fence is proved a common field.

5   *blown* driven.
11   *tender* attendant.
12   *Seraphin* Greville's allusion is to Genesis 3.24, where the forbidding angels are identified as "Cherubims" in the Geneva and King James bibles.

13   *While* Greville's manuscript reaches this conjunction by successive revision that suggests a changing sense of the implied narrative: first "Till," then "Yet," and finally "While."

### 40

The nurse-life wheat, within his green husk growing,
Flatters our hope and tickles our desire,
Nature's true riches in sweet beauties showing,
Which sets all hearts with labor's love on fire.
No less fair is the wheat when golden ear                        5
Shows unto hope the joys of near enjoying;
Fair and sweet is the bud, more sweet and fair
The rose which proves that time is not destroying.
Caelica, your youth, the morning of delight,
Enamelled o'er with beauties white and red,                     10
All sense and thoughts did to belief invite
That Love and Glory there are brought to bed;
And your ripe year's love-noon (he goes no higher)
Turns all the spirits of man into desire.

1   *nurse-life* life nurturing.

13   *love-noon* Modern editorial emendation of "love none" in the original text.

### 42

Peleus, that loath was Thetis to forsake,
Had counsel from the gods to hold her fast,
Forwarned what loathsome likeness she would take,
Yet, if he held, come to herself at last.
He held; the snakes, the serpents, and the fire                 5
No monsters proved, but travails of desire.

When I beheld how Caelica's fair eyes
Did show her heart to some, her wit to me,

1   *Peleus* Father of Achilles by the sea-nymph Thetis; her shape-shifting attempts to resist his assault are narrated in Ovid, *Metamorphoses* 11.217–65. Proteus advised persistence, and she ultimately gave in.

Change, that doth prove the error is not wise,
In her mis-shape made me strange visions see;                    10
Desire held fast, till love's unconstant zone
Like Gorgon's head transformed her heart to stone.

From stone she turns again into a cloud,
Where water still had more power than the fire,
And I, poor Ixion to my Juno vowed,                              15
With thoughts to clip her, clipped my own desire;
For she was vanished, I held nothing fast
But woes to come and joys already past.

This cloud straight makes a stream, in whose smooth face,
While I the image of myself did glass,                           20
Thought-shadows I for beauty did embrace,
Till stream and all except the cold did pass;
Yet faith held fast, like foils where stones be set
To make toys dear and fools more fond to get.

Thus our desires, besides each inward throe,                     25
Must pass the outward toils of chance and fear;
Against the streams of real truths they go,
With hope alone to balance all they bear,
Spending the wealth of nature in such fashion
As good and ill luck equally breeds passion.                     30

Thus our delights, like fair shapes in a glass,
Though pleasing to our senses, cannot last.
The metal breaks, or else the visions pass;
Only our griefs in constant molds are cast.
I'll hold no more, false Caelica, live free;                     35
Seem fair to all the world, and foul to me.

**10** *mis-shape* The reading of Greville's manuscript; the 1633 edition reads "misshap," which could be read as an alternate spelling of the same word or as "mishap."
**12** *Gorgon* Medusa, the female monster whose terrifying appearance turned those who saw her into stone; she is characteristically cited in Renaissance love poetry as a symbol of the woman's petrifying effect on her male lover.

**15** *Ixion* Would-be seducer of Juno, tricked instead into intercourse with a replica made of clouds.
**16** *clip* embrace.
**23** *foils* reflective pieces of metal used to make gems shine brighter.

## 45

Absence, the noble truce
Of Cupid's war,
Where though desires want use,
They honored are.
Thou art the just protection                                     5
Of prodigal affection;
Have thou the praise.
When bankrupt Cupid braveth,
Thy mines his credit saveth
With sweet delays.                                               10

**3** *want use* are not put into action.
**8** *braveth* shows off.

Of wounds which presence makes
With beauty's shot,
Absence the anguish slakes,
But healeth not.
Absence records the stories                    15
Wherein desire glories,
Although she burn.
She cherisheth the spirits
Where constancy inherits
And passions mourn.                            20

Absence, like dainty clouds
On glorious-bright,
Nature's weak senses shrouds
From harming light.
Absence maintains the treasure                 25
Of pleasure unto pleasure,
Sparing with praise;
Absence doth nurse the fire
Which starves and feeds desire
With sweet delays.                             30

Presence to every part
Of beauty ties;
Where wonder rules the heart,
There pleasure dies.
Presence plagues mind and senses               35
With modesty's defenses;
Absence is free.
Thoughts do in absence venture
On Cupid's shadowed center:
They wink and see.                             40

But thoughts, be not so brave
With absent joy;
For you with that you have
Yourself destroy.
The absence which you glory                     45
Is that which makes you sorry
And burn in vain;
For thought is not the weapon
Wherewith thought's ease men cheapen:
Absence is pain.                               50

18  *cherisheth* nurtures.
19  *inherits* has lawful ownership.
22  *glorious-bright* the sun.

35  *Presence* Modern editorial correction of "Pleasures" in
the original sources.
49  *cheapen* purchase through bargaining.

## 56
All my senses, like beacon's flame,
Gave alarum to desire

A nocturnal erotic conceit parallel to the "Tenth Song" in
*Astrophil and Stella*, but fiercer in both its actions and its
disenchantment.

To take arms in Cynthia's name
And set all my thoughts on fire.
Fury's wit persuaded me                                        5
Happy love was hazard's heir,
Cupid did best shoot and see
In the night, where smooth is fair.
Up I start, believing well,
To see if Cynthia were awake;                                  10
Wonders I saw, who can tell?
And thus unto myself I spake:
Sweet god Cupid, where am I,
That by pale Diana's light
Such rich beauties do espy                                     15
As harm our senses with delight?
Am I borne up to the skies?
See where Jove and Venus shine,
Showing in her heavenly eyes
That desire is divine.                                         20
Look where lies the Milken Way,
Way unto that dainty throne
Where, while all the gods would play,
Vulcan thinks to dwell alone,
Shadowing it with curious art,                                 25
Nets of sullen golden hair.
Mars am I, and may not part
Till that I be taken there.
Therewithal I heard a sound,
Made of all the parts of love,                                 30
Which did sense delight and wound;
Planets with such music move.
Those joys drew desires near.
The heavens blushed, the white showed red,
Such red as in skies appear                                    35
When Sol parts from Thetis' bed.
Then unto myself I said,
Surely I Apollo am;
Yonder is the glorious maid
Which men do Aurora name,                                      40
Who, for pride she hath in me,
Blushing forth desire and fear
While she would have no man see,
Makes the world know I am there.
I resolve to play my son                                       45
And misguide my chariot fire,
All the sky to overcome
And inflame with my desire.

6   *heir* The manuscript reads "hire."
14   *Diana's light* moonlight.
24   *Vulcan* Venus's cuckolded husband.
25–48   These lines are in Greville's manuscript but not the 1633 edition.
27   *Mars* Venus's adulterous lover; her husband trapped the two of them in a net and exhibited them to the rest of the gods. *part* depart.

36   *Sol* the sun. *Thetis' bed* the sea.
40   *Aurora* goddess of the dawn.
41   *pride* Originally "joy" in Greville's manuscript.
45   *son* Phaethon, son of Apollo, who died trying to guide his father's solar chariot.

I gave reins to this conceit,
Hope went on the wheel of lust.                               50
Fancy's scales are false of weight,
Thoughts take thought that go of trust.
I stepped forth to touch the sky,
I a god by Cupid dreams;
Cynthia, who did naked lie,                                   55
Runs away like silver streams,
Leaving hollow banks behind,
Who can neither forward move
Nor, if rivers be unkind,
Turn away or leave to love.                                   60
There stand I, like Arctic pole
Where Sol passeth o'er the line,
Mourning my benighted soul
Which so loseth light divine.
There stand I like men that preach                            65
From the execution place,
At their death content to teach
All the world with their disgrace:
He that lets his Cynthia lie
Naked on a bed of play                                        70
To say prayers ere she die
Teacheth time to run away.
Let no love-desiring heart
In the stars go seek his fate;
Love is only nature's art,                                    75
Wonder hinders love and hate.
None can well behold with eyes
But what underneath him lies.

51  *Fancy* desire and imagination.                60  *leave* cease.
52  Thoughts make trouble for themselves that rely on      62  *line* equator.
expectation.

## 84

Farewell, sweet boy, complain not of my truth;
Thy mother loved thee not with more devotion.
For to thy boy's play I gave all my youth;
Young master, I did hope for your promotion.
While some sought honors, princes' thoughts observing,       5
Many wooed fame, the child of pain and anguish,
Others judged inward good a chief deserving;
I in thy wanton visions joyed to languish.
I bowed not to thy image for succession,
Nor bound thy bow to shoot reformèd kindness;                10
Thy plays of hope and fear were my confession,
The spectacles to my life was thy blindness.

4  *your promotion* your promotion of me.
9–11  These lines gesture toward some of the public issues
of sixteenth-century England: anxiety over the childless Eliza-
beth's succession, the persecution of "reformed" Christians
(i.e., Protestants) under her predecessor, and the conflicts
over religious allegiance ("confession") generally.

9  I did not worship you for the sake of begetting children to
inherit my estate.
10  *bound thy bow* strung thy bow.
12  Your blindness was the lens through which I viewed
my life.

But Cupid, now farewell. I will go play me
With thoughts that please me less, and less betray me.

## 100

In night, when colors all to black are cast,
Distinction lost or gone down with the light,
The eye, a watch to inward senses placed,
Not seeing, yet still having power of sight,
Gives vain alarums to the inward sense                    5
Where fear, stirred up with witty tyranny,
Confounds all powers, and thorough self-offense
Doth forge and raise impossibility:
Such as in thick, depriving darkness
Proper reflections of the error be,                      10
And images of self-confusedness
Which hurt imaginations only see,
And from this nothing seen tells news of devils
Which but expressions be of inward evils.

**9, 11** The rhyme words in the manuscript are "darknesses"
and "self-confusednesses."

## 109

Sion lies waste, and thy Jerusalem,
O Lord, is fallen to utter desolation;
Against thy prophets and thy holy men
The sin hath wrought a fatal combination,
Prophaned thy name, thy worship overthrown,              5
And made thee, living Lord, a God unknown.

Thy powerful laws, thy wonders of creation,
Thy word incarnate, glorious heaven, dark hell
Lie shadowed under man's degeneration,
Thy Christ still crucified for doing well;               10
Impiety, O Lord, sits on thy throne,
Which makes thee, living Light, a God unknown.

Man's superstition hath thy truths entombed,
His atheism again her pomps defaceth;
That sensual unsatiable vast womb                        15
Of thy seen church thy unseen church disgraceth.
There lives no truth with them that seem thine own,
Which makes thee, living Lord, a God unknown.

Yet unto thee, Lord (mirror of transgression),
We who for earthly idols have forsaken                   20

**1** *Sion* Zion, a holy area of Jerusalem; both names are used here symbolically for God's kingdom on earth.
**14** *her* The antecedent appears to be "truth" in the previous line; "truths" may be a mistake for "truth," or "her" a mistake for "their." The sequence of thought is clear: superstition entombed God's truths, and atheism now disfigures their tombs ("pomps").
**16** *thy seen church* the institutional church of this world. *thy unseen church* the genuine church of true believers.
**19** *mirror of transgression* God reflects back to us the image of our sinfulness.

Thy heavenly image (sinless pure impression)
And so in nets of vanity lie taken,
All desolate implore that to thine own,
Lord, thou no longer live a God unknown.

Yet, Lord, let Israel's plagues not be eternal,                    25
Nor sin forever cloud thy sacred mountains,
Nor with false flames, spiritual but infernal,
Dry up thy mercy's ever springing fountains;
Rather, sweet Jesus, fill up time and come
To yield the sin her everlasting doom.                            30

# Sir Philip Sidney (1554–1586)

The son of a knight high in Elizabeth's service and the nephew of her reigning favorite, the Earl of Leicester, Sidney was early visited by what Astrophil calls "great expectation." Born at the family estate of Penshurst in Kent, he attended Shrewsbury School (where he met Fulke Greville) and Oxford, and in 1572 embarked on a three-year tour of the Continent, where he made a strong impression on people of note as the rising star of a new generation of Englishmen. He was also in Paris during the St. Bartholomew's Day massacre in 1572, an experience which helped confirm him in a militant Protestantism. In 1577 Elizabeth gave him the mission of sounding out the princes of Germany about an anti-Catholic league; she seems not to have been happy at how aggressively he did so, and on his return he found himself without royal employment. He turned to literature, composing a first version of *Arcadia* (a prose romance with poems), *The Defense of Poesy* (also known as *An Apology for Poetry*), and the sequence given here. He continued to long for action, and in 1585 decided to accompany Sir Francis Drake on an expedition against the Spaniards. Elizabeth intervened, and gave him instead a cavalry command under Leicester in the Netherlands and appointed him Lord Governor of Flushing; it was apparently to take up those duties that he broke off an ambitious revision of his *Arcadia* and a verse translation of the book of Psalms. In September 1586 he was wounded in the thigh during a skirmish and died after lingering for almost a month. One of very few men of high rank to die in war during Elizabeth's reign, he received a great funeral at St. Paul's and was mourned in literally hundreds of verse elegies in Latin and English; one by his sister Mary, the Countess of Pembroke, is given below.

With *Astrophil and Stella* English literature has its first fully achieved Petrarchan lyric sequence, sustained with unprecedented confidence and ingenuity. Its origins are, among other things, biographical; though there is no way to know how closely the poetry fit the facts, we have decidedly more in the way of facts than for any other example of the genre. Sidney had been, in his early twenties, matched in an arranged engagement with the 13-year-old Penelope Devereux, daughter of the Earl of Essex, but nothing came of it. Seeing her again in late 1581 or early 1582, after her marriage to Robert, Lord Rich, Sidney seems to have found himself in the kind of love of which Petrarch wrote, or close enough. Astrophil ("star-lover" in Greek, to go with the Latin Stella, "star") shares half his name with Sidney, and numerous features of his life; one sonnet (65) implies that they have the same coat of arms. Three other sonnets (24, 35, 37) make no sense without knowledge of Stella's real-life married name. In the poetry, the love is eventually confessed to be mutual, though that confession is followed by a high-minded but, on Astrophil's part, half-hearted separation. In real life, Sidney in 1583 married Frances Walsingham, the daughter of Elizabeth's Secretary of State. The marriage seems to have been a happy one, though the legend that Sidney became after his death seems to have had its gravitational effect on the lives of those concerned: Penelope openly took as a lover a nobleman who had served with Sidney in The Netherlands, and her brother married Sidney's widow.

England's inaugural Petrarchan sequence is one of its least ruly. Formal experiment is conspicuous from the first sonnet, written in unconventional hexameters, as if in an attempt to naturalize the French alexandrine; there are five other hexameter sonnets in the sequence, and a steady permutation of rhyme schemes. The eleven "songs" interspersed unpredictably with the sonnets correspond to no particular precedent; they bring a change of pace and sometimes of speaker, including at one key moment a third-person narrator. Throughout, high Petrarchan melancholy and idealization mix intimately with an often comic impatience and self-rationalization; the rhythm of many of the individual sonnets is that of a clincher withheld until as late as possible, a surprise ending that can be both a cry of triumph and a pratfall. No other Petrarchan sequence in any language is as rich in narrative incident, mostly implied in the earlier stretches but increasingly explicit as the momentum gathers. Astrophil begins in distant longing, arguing with himself and with friends about the rightness of being in love with a married woman, but with sonnet 30 starts to present his case to Stella; his success in reaching new stages of intimacy with her brings things ultimately to the two decisive moments of the fourth and eighth songs. There is some possibly unintended ambiguity as to what happens between the end of the fourth song and the start of sonnet 86, but the aftermath is clear: the lover definitively denied and isolated but still incurably in love, the famous oxymorons of ice and fire, pain and joy blossoming in the sequence as never before. Astrophil's long struggle to make his Petrarchan story somehow come out differently from its predecessors ends in failure.

During his life Sidney's work circulated in various forms in manuscript. It began to reach the general public in 1590 with the publication of the unfinished later version of his *Arcadia*. *Astrophil and Stella* was first published in an unauthorized edition in 1591, with an incongruous introduction by Thomas Nashe: "here you shall find a paper stage strewed with pearl, an artificial heaven to overshadow the fair frame, and crystal walls to encounter your curious eyes, while the tragicomedy of love is performed by starlight." This edition omitted the provocative sonnet 37 as well as the eleventh song, printed songs 1–10 as a group at the end, and in general offered a fairly corrupt text; for all its defects, it was sufficient to ignite the sonnet craze of the early 1590s. The sequence was first printed in its complete form, with the songs interspersed in what has become the canonical manner, in a 1598 edition prepared by Sidney's sister and his friend Fulke Greville, together with a hybrid text of the *Arcadia* conflating both the early and later versions. The text given here for the most part follows this edition.

*Edition*: *The Poems of Sir Philip Sidney*, ed. William A. Ringler, Jr. (Oxford: Clarendon Press, 1962).

# Astrophil and Stella

## 1

Loving in truth, and fain in verse my love to show,
That she (dear she) might take some pleasure of my pain,
Pleasure might cause her read, reading might make her know,
Knowledge might pity win, and pity grace obtain,
I sought fit words to paint the blackest face of woe,                                    5
Studying inventions fine, her wits to entertain,
Oft turning others' leaves, to see if thence would flow
Some fresh and fruitful showers upon my sun-burned brain.
But words came halting forth, wanting Invention's stay;
Invention, Nature's child, fled step-dame Study's blows;                      10
And others' feet still seemed but strangers in my way.
Thus, great with child to speak, and helpless in my throes,
Biting my truand pen, beating myself for spite,
Fool, said my Muse to me, look in thy heart and write.

2   *she (dear she)* An alternative text reads "the dear she."      9   *stay* support.

## 2

Not at first sight, nor with a dribbèd shot
Love gave the wound which while I breathe will bleed;
But known worth did in mine of time proceed
Till by degrees it had full conquest got.
I saw and liked, I liked but lovèd not;                                                        5
I loved, but straight did not what Love decreed.
At length to Love's decrees I, forced, agreed,
Yet with repining at so partial lot.
Now even that footstep of lost liberty
Is gone, and now like slave-born Muscovite                                          10
I call it praise to suffer tyranny,
And now employ the remnant of my wit
To make me self believe that all is well,
While with a feeling skill I paint my hell.

1   *dribbèd shot* A shot (in archery) that falls short or wide of its mark.
3   *mine* The metaphor is from siege warfare, in which cities were subverted by mines dug underneath them and filled with explosives.

10–11 Lines remembered in different circumstances by the title character in John Webster's *The Duchess of Malfi*: "Must I like to a slave-born Russian / Account it praise to suffer tyranny?" (III.v.73–4).

3

Let dainty wits cry on the sisters nine
That, bravely masked, their fancies may be told;
Or Pindar's apes, flaunt they in phrases fine,
Enameling with pied flowers their thoughts of gold;
Or else let them in statelier glory shine,                    5
Ennobling new-found tropes with problems old,
Or with strange similes enrich each line
Of herbs or beasts which Inde or Afric hold.
For me, in sooth, no Muse but one I know,
Phrases and problems from my reach do grow,                   10
And strange things cost too dear for my poor sprites.
How then? Even thus: in Stella's face I read
What love and beauty be; then all my deed
But copying is what in her Nature writes.

1  *cry on* beg. *sisters nine* the nine Muses.
2  *bravely masked* brightly dressed.
3  *Pindar's apes* Imitators of Pindar, the extravagant Greek
choral poet of the fourth century BC.

6  *problems* Questions proposed for discussion in classical
rhetorical or philosophical contexts.
10  *from my reach* out of my reach.

4

Virtue, alas, now let me take some rest;
Thou setst a bate between my will and wit.
If vain love have my simple soul oppressed,
Leave what thou likest not, deal not thou with it.
Thy scepter use in some old Cato's breast;                    5
Churches or schools are for thy seat more fit.
I do confess, pardon a fault confessed:
My mouth too tender is for thy hard bit.
But if that needs thou wilt usurping be
The little reason that is left in me,                          10
And still the effect of thy persuasions prove,
I swear my heart such one shall show to thee
That shrines in flesh so true a deity
That, Virtue, thou thyself shalt be in love.

2  *bate* struggle.
5  *Cato* Roman statesman (23–149 BC), called "the Censor,"
famous for his moral austerity.

11  *prove* test.

5

It is most true that eyes are formed to serve
The inward light, and that the heavenly part
Ought to be king, from whose rules who do swerve,
Rebels to nature, strive for their own smart.
It is most true, what we call Cupid's dart                    5
An image is which for ourselves we carve
And, fools, adore in temple of our heart,
Till that good god make church and churchman starve;
True that true beauty virtue is indeed,
Whereof this beauty can be but a shade,                       10

9–10  Virtue is true beauty, of which physical beauty is only
a reflection.

Which elements with mortal mixture breed;
True that on earth we are but pilgrims made,
And should in soul up to our country move:
True, and yet true that I must Stella love.


6

Some lovers speak, when they their Muses entertain,
Of hopes begot by fear, of wot not what desires,
Of force of heavenly beams infusing hellish pain,
Of living deaths, dear wounds, fair storms, and freezing fires.
Some one his song in Jove and Jove's strange tales attires,          5
Bordered with bulls and swans, powdered with golden rain;
Another humbler wit to shepherd's pipe retires,
Yet hiding royal blood full oft in rural vein.
To some, a sweetest plaint a sweetest style affords,
While tears pour out his ink and sighs breathe out his words;       10
His paper, pale despair, and pain his pen doth move.
I can speak what I feel, and feel as much as they,
But think that all the map of my state I display
When trembling voice brings forth that I do Stella love.

2  *wot not* they know not.                6  The forms in which Jupiter seduced Europa, Leda, and
                                            Danaë, respectively.


7

When Nature made her chief work, Stella's eyes,
In color black why wrapped she beams so bright?
Would she in beamy black, like painter wise,
Frame dantiest luster, mixed of shades and light?
Or did she else that sober hue devise                                5
In object best to knit and strength our sight,
Lest, if no veil these brave gleams did disguise,
They sun-like should more dazzle than delight?
Or would she her miraculous power show,
That whereas black seems beauty's contrary,                         10
She even in black doth make all beauties flow?
Both so and thus: she, minding Love should be
Placed ever there, gave him this mourning weed,
To honor all their deaths who for her bleed.

6  *strength* strengthen.                  13  *weed* clothing.


8

Love, born in Greece, of late fled from his native place,
Forced by a tedious proof that Turkish hardened heart
Is no fit mark to pierce with his fine pointed dart,
And, pleased with our soft peace, stayed here his flying race;
But finding these north climes do coldly him embrace,                5
Not used to frozen clips, he strave to find some part

1–3  The Ottoman Turks in 1453 had taken Byzantium and       2  *tedious* painful.
brought the eastern (Greek) Roman Empire to its official     6  *clips* embraces.
end; in 1573 they conquered Cyprus, the reputed birthplace
of Venus.

Where with most ease and warmth he might employ his art.
At length he perched himself in Stella's joyful face,
Whose fair skin, beamy eyes like morning sun on snow
Deceived the quaking boy, who thought from so pure light                    10
Effects of lively heat must needs in nature grow.
But she, most fair, most cold, made him thence take his flight
To my close heart, where while some firebrands he did lay,
He burnt unwares his wings, and cannot fly away.

13   *close* hidden.

### 9

Queen Virtue's court, which some call Stella's face,
Prepared by Nature's choicest furniture,
Hath his front built of alablaster pure;
Gold is the covering of that stately place.
The door by which sometimes comes forth her Grace               5
Red porphyr is, which lock of pearl makes sure;
Whose porches rich (which name of cheeks endure)
Marble mixed red and white do interlace.
The windows now through which this heavenly guest
Looks over the world, and can find nothing such                 10
Which dare claim from those lights the name of best,
Of touch they are, that without touch doth touch,
Which Cupid's self from Beauty's mine did draw:
Of touch they are, and poor I am their straw.

2   *choicest* An alternative text reads "chiefest."
12–14   The exact reference in these lines is uncertain. The phrase "without touch doth touch" strongly suggests the activity of magnetism, and "straw" could be being used metaphorically for metal shavings; but a touchstone is not a magnet.

If touchstone – basanite, black like Stella's eyes – is indeed meant here, its action on actual straw could be that of static electricity; or "touch" could refer to touchwood (tinder), and the straw could be going up in flames.
13   *mine* The 1598 edition reads "mind."

### 10

Reason, in faith thou art well served, that still
Wouldst brabbling be with sense and love in me.
I rather wished thee climb the Muses' hill,
Or reach the fruit of nature's choicest tree,
Or seek heaven's course or heaven's inside to see;              5
Why shouldst thou toil our thorny soil to till?
Leave sense and those which sense's objects be;
Deal thou with powers of thoughts, leave love to will.
But thou wouldst needs fight both with love and sense
With sword of wit, giving wounds of dispraise,                  10
Till downright blows did foil thy cunning fence;
For soon as they strake thee with Stella's rays,
Reason, thou kneel'dst, and offer'dst straight to prove,
By reason good, good reason her to love.

2   *brabbling* quarreling.   *sense* the senses.
8   *will* desire.

11   *fence* defense (the context suggests specifically a defense in fencing).

### 11

In truth, O Love, with what a boyish kind
Thou dost proceed in thy most serious ways,

That when the heaven to thee his best displays,
Yet of that best thou leav'st the best behind.
For like a child, that some fair book doth find,          5
With gilded leaves or colored vellum plays,
Or at the most on some fine picture stays,
But never heeds the fruit of writer's mind:
So when thou sawst in Nature's cabinet
Stella, thou straight lookst babies in her eyes,          10
In her cheek's pit thou didst thy pitfold set,
And in her breast bo-peep or couching lies,
Playing and shining in each outward part;
But, fool, seekst not to get into her heart.

**10** *lookst babies in her eyes* A common Elizabethan figure of speech: looking into Stella's eyes, he saw tiny images of himself.

**11** *pitfold* pitfall.
**12** *bo-peep* A now-you-see-it-now-you-don't game for small children. *couching* crouching.

## 12

Cupid, because thou shin'st in Stella's eyes,
That from her locks, thy day-nets, none scapes free,
That those lips swelled, so full of thee they be,
That her sweet breath makes oft thy flames to rise,
That in her breast thy pap well sugared lies,          5
That her Grace gracious makes thy wrongs, that she
What words so e'er she speak persuades for thee,
That her clear voice lifts thy fame to the skies:
Thou countest Stella thine, like those, whose powers
Having got up a breach by fighting well,          10
Cry, Victory, this fair day all is ours!
O no, her heart is such a citadel,
So fortified with wit, stored with disdain,
That to win it is all the skill and pain.

**2** *That* because (here and in the following lines). *day-nets* Early sources for the text have several different readings here, including "dances," "dainties," and "dimness"; "day-nets" – nets for capturing birds by luring them with small mirrors – fits best with the convention of a woman's hair as a trap.

**5** *pap* baby food.
**10** *got up a breach* made a breach (in the wall of a besieged city).

## 13

Phoebus was judge between Jove, Mars, and Love,
Of those three gods whose arms the fairest were.
Jove's golden shield did eagle sables bear,
Whose talents held young Ganymede above;
But in vert field Mars bare a golden spear,          5
Which through a bleeding heart his point did shove.
Each had his crest: Mars carried Venus' glove,
Jove on his helm the thunderbolt did rear.

A male version of the contention among Juno, Athena, and Venus from which the Trojan war resulted. Two of the gods offer heraldic representations of particularly provocative love affairs: Jove's abduction of the beautiful boy Ganymede, and Mars's adulterous affair with Venus (at that point Vulcan's wife).

**3** *eagle sables* black heraldic eagles.
**4** *talents* talons.
**5** *in vert field* on a green background.

Cupid then smiles, for on his crest there lies
Stella's fair hair; her face he makes his shield,
Where roses gules are borne in silver field. 10
Phoebus drew wide the curtains of the skies
To blaze these last, and sware devoutly then
The first, thus matched, were scantly gentlemen.

11 Red roses on a silver background: a representation of
Stella's face, but also evoking the three red disks on a silver
background in the family arms of Penelope Devereux.

13 *blaze* blazon. *sware* swore.
14 *scantly* scarcely.

### 14

Alas, have I not pain enough, my friend,
Upon whose breast a fiercer gripe doth tire
Than did on him who first stale down the fire.
While Love on me doth all his quiver spend,
But with your rhubarb words you must contend 5
To grieve me worse, in saying that desire
Doth plunge my well-formed soul even in the mire
Of sinful thoughts which do in ruin end?
If that be sin which doth the manners frame,
Well stayed with truth in word and faith of deed, 10
Ready of wit and fearing nought but shame:
If that be sin which in fixed hearts doth breed
A loathing of all loose unchastity,
Then love is sin, and let me sinful be.

2 *gripe* vulture. *tire* tear.
3 *him* The Titan Prometheus, who in punishment for
giving fire to the human race was condemned to have his
liver torn out daily by an eagle.

5 *rhubarb* bitter.
10 *stayed* supported.

### 15

You that do search for every purling spring
Which from the ribs of old Parnassus flows,
And every flower, not sweet perhaps, which grows
Near thereabouts into your poesy wring;
You that do dictionary's method bring 5
Into your rhymes, running in rattling rows;
You that poor Petrarch's long deceasèd woes
With newborn sighs and denizened wit do sing:
You take wrong ways; those far-fet helps be such
As do bewray a want of inward touch, 10
And sure at length stolen goods do come to light.
But if (both for your love and skill) your name
You seek to nurse at fullest breasts of fame,
Stella behold, and then begin to indite.

2 *Parnassus* The mountain home of the Muses.
5 *dictionary's method* Choosing words by their first letter,
for purposes of alliteration (as illustrated in the next line).

8 *denizened* naturalized.
14 *indite* compose.

### 16

In nature apt to like when I did see
Beauties which were of many carats fine,

My boiling sprites did thither soon incline,
And, Love, I thought that I was full of thee;
But finding not those restless flames in me                          5
Which others said did make their souls to pine,
I thought those babes of some pin's hurt did whine,
By my soul judging what love's pain might be.
But while I thus with this young lion played,
Mine eyes (shall I say cursed or blessed?) beheld                    10
Stella: now she is named, need more be said?
In her sight I a lesson new have spelled;
I now have learned love right, and learned even so
As who by being poisoned doth poison know.

12   *spelled* learned.


### 17

His mother dear Cupid offended late,
Because that Mars, grown slacker in her love,
With pricking shot he did not throughly move
To keep the pace of their first loving state.
The boy refused for fear of Mars's hate,                             5
Who threatened stripes if he his wrath did prove;
But she in chafe him from her lap did shove,
Brake bow, brake shafts, while Cupid weeping sat,
Till that his grandam Nature, pitying it,
Of Stella's brows made him two better bows,                          10
And in her eyes of arrows infinite.
O how for joy he leaps, O how he crows!
And straight therewith like wags new got to play
Falls to shrewd turns, and I was in his way.

2   *Mars* Venus's lover during her marriage to Vulcan;   6   *stripes* whipping.   *prove* test.
see above on sonnet 13.                                     7   *chafe* a heat.
3   *pricking shot* a shot aimed at its target.   *throughly*   13   *wags* rascals.
thoroughly.                                                 14   *shrewd turns* clever tricks.


### 18

With what sharp checks I in myself am shent
When into Reason's audit I do go,
And by just counts myself a bankrout know
Of all those goods which heaven to me have lent:
Unable quite to pay even Nature's rent                               5
Which unto it by birthright I do owe,
And, which is worse, no good excuse can show,
But that my wealth I have most idly spent.
My youth doth waste, my knowledge brings forth toys,
My wit doth strive those passions to defend                          10
Which for reward spoil it with vain annoys.
I see my course to lose myself doth bend:
I see, and yet no greater sorrow take
Than that I lose no more for Stella's sake.

1   *checks* rebukes.   *shent* shamed.              3   *counts* calculations.   *bankrout* bankrupt.

19

On Cupid's bow how are my heart-strings bent,
That see my wrack, and yet embrace the same?
When most I glory, then I feel most shame;
I willing run, yet while I run repent.
My best wits still their own disgrace invent,          5
My very ink turns straight to Stella's name,
And yet my words, as them my pen doth frame,
Avise themselves that they are vainly spent.
For though she pass all things, yet what is all
That unto me, who fare like him that both          10
Looks to the skies and in a ditch doth fall?
O let me prop my mind yet in his growth,
And not in Nature, for best fruits unfit.
Scholar, saith Love, bend hitherward your wit.

8   *Avise* advise.                    12   *his* the mind's.

20

Fly, fly, my friends, I have my death wound, fly!
See there that boy, that murdering boy I say,
Who, like a thief, hid in dark bush doth lie
Till bloody bullet get him wrongful prey.
So, tyran, he no fitter place could spy          5
Nor so fair level in so secret stay,
As that sweet black which veils the heavenly eye:
There himself with his shot he close doth lay.
Poor passenger, pass now thereby I did
And stayed, pleased with the prospect of the place,          10
While that black hue from me the bad guest hid;
But straight I saw motions of lightning grace
And then descried the glistering of his dart,
But ere I could fly thence, it pierced my heart.

6   *level* take aim.

21

Your words, my friend (right healthful caustics), blame
My young mind marred, whom Love doth windlass so
That mine own writings like bad servants show
My wits, quick in vain thoughts, in virtue lame;
That Plato I read for nought but if he tame          5
Such coltish gyres; that to my birth I owe
Nobler desires, lest else that friendly foe,
Great expectation, wear a train of shame.
For since mad March great promise made of me,
If now the May of my years much decline,          10
What can be hoped my harvest time will be?
Sure you say well. Your wisdom's golden mine
Dig deep with learning's spade, now tell me this:
Hath this world ought so fair as Stella is?

2   *windlass* ensnare.          6   *gyres* gyrations. The 1598 text reads "years."

## 22

In highest way of heaven the Sun did ride,
Progressing then from fair twins' golden place,
Having no scarf of clouds before his face,
But shining forth of heat in his chief pride,
When some fair ladies, by hard promise tied,     5
On horseback met him in his furious race,
Yet each prepared with fan's well-shading grace
From that foe's wounds their tender skins to hide.
Stella alone with face unarmèd marched,
Either to do like him which open shone,     10
Or careless of the wealth because her own.
Yet were the hid and meaner beauties parched,
Her daintiest bare went free; the cause was this:
The Sun which others burned did her but kiss.

2 *fair twins' golden place* The sign of Gemini, which the sun leaves in June.

## 23

The curious wits, seeing dull pensiveness
Bewray itself in my long settled eyes,
Whence those same fumes of melancholy rise
With idle pains and missing aim do guess.
Some that know how my spring I did address     5
Deem that my Muse some fruit of knowledge plies;
Others, because the Prince my service tries,
Think that I think state errors to redress.
But harder judges judge ambition's rage,
Scourge of itself, still climbing slippery place,     10
Holds my young brain captived in golden cage.
O fools, or over-wise: alas, the race
Of all my thoughts hath neither stop nor start
But only Stella's eyes and Stella's heart.

5 *how my spring I did address* how I spent my early years (i.e., in study).

7 *the Prince my service tries* An overstatement of the case as far as Sidney's own relations with Queen Elizabeth in 1581–2 were concerned.

10 *slippery place* See Thomas Wyatt, "Stand whoso list."

## 24

Rich fools there be, whose base and filthy heart
Lies hatching still the goods wherein they flow,
And, damning their own selves to Tantal's smart,
Wealth breeding want, more blissed, more wretched grow.
Yet to those fools heaven such wit doth impart,     5
As what their hands do hold, their heads do know,
And knowing, love, and loving, lay apart
As sacred things, far from all danger's show.
But that rich fool, who by blind Fortune's lot
The richest gem of love and life enjoys     10
And can with foul abuse such beauties blot,

2 *hatching* shutting up.

3 *Tantal* Tantalus, condemned in Hades to perpetual thirst and hunger in the near presence of water and food.

Let him, deprived of sweet but unfelt joys
(Exiled for aye from those high treasures which
He knows not), grow in only folly rich.

### 25

The wisest scholar of the wight most wise
By Phoebus' doom, with sugared sentence says
That Virtue, if it once met with our eyes,
Strange flames of Love it in our souls would raise;
But for that man with pain this truth descries     5
Whiles he each thing in sense's balance weighs,
And so nor will nor can behold those skies
Which inward sun to heroic mind displays,
Virtue of late, with virtuous care to stir
Love of herself, took Stella's shape, that she     10
To mortal eyes might sweetly shine in her.
It is most true, for since I her did see,
Virtue's great beauty in that face I prove
And find the effect, for I do burn in love.

1–2   The wisest scholar (student) is Plato; Plato's teacher Socrates told the Athenian court that Apollo's oracle at Delphi had said that no man was wiser than himself (*Apology* 21A).
2   *doom* judgment.

3–4   A Platonic sentiment (*Phaedrus* 250D), as cited by Cicero *De Officiis* (1.5).
5   *for that* because.
13   *prove* experience.

### 26

Though dusty wits dare scorn astrology,
And fools can think those lamps of purest light,
Whose numbers, ways, greatness, eternity,
Promising wonders, wonder do invite,
To have for no cause birthright in the sky     5
But for to spangle the black weeds of night,
Or for some brawl which in that chamber high
They should still dance to please a gazer's sight:
For me, I do Nature unidle know,
And know great causes great effects procure,     10
And know those bodies high reign on the low;
And if these rules did fail, proof makes me sure,
Who oft fore-judge my after-following race
By only those two stars in Stella's face.

1   *dusty* earth-bound.
6   *weeds* clothes.
7   *brawl* A French dance in which dancers hold hands and move in circles.

11   *on* over.
12   *proof* experience.

### 27

Because I oft in dark, abstracted guise
Seem most alone in greatest company,
With dearth of words, or answers quite awry
To them that would make speech of speech arise,
They deem, and of their doom the rumor flies     5

5   *doom* judgment.

That poison foul of bubbling pride doth lie
So in my swelling breast that only I
Fawn on me self, and others to despise.
Yet pride I think doth not my soul possess,
Which looks too oft in his unflattering glass;                    10
But one worse fault, ambition, I confess
That makes me oft my best friends overpass,
Unseen, unheard, while thought to highest place
Bends all his powers, even unto Stella's grace.

10   *glass* mirror.

### 28

You that with allegory's curious frame
Of others' children changelings use to make,
With me those pains for God's sake do not take;
I list not dig so deep for brazen fame.
When I say *Stella*, I do mean the same                           5
Princess of Beauty for whose only sake
The reins of Love I love, though never slake,
And joy therein though nations count it shame.
I beg no subject to use eloquence
Nor in hid ways do guide philosophy;                            10
Look at my hands for no such quintessence,
But know that I in pure simplicity
Breathe out the flames which burn within my heart,
Love only reading unto me this art.

2   *changelings* Children secretly substituted for other children.        11   *quintessence* The undetectable fifth element sought by
7   *slake* slack.                                                           alchemists.

### 29

Like some weak lords, neighbored by mighty kings,
To keep themselves and their chief cities free
Do easily yield that all their coasts may be
Ready to store their camps of needful things,
So Stella's heart, finding what power Love brings,              5
To keep itself in life and liberty
Doth willing grant that in the frontiers he
Use all to help his other conquerings:
And thus her heart escapes, but thus her eyes
Serve him with shot, her lips his heralds are,                  10
Her breasts his tents, legs his triumphal car,
Her flesh his food, her skin his armor brave;
And I, but for because my prospect lies
Upon that coast, am given up for a slave.

2, 3   *their* the weak lords'.                    13   *prospect* look-out.
4   *their* the mighty kings'.

### 30

Whether the Turkish new moon minded be
To fill his horns this year on Christian coast;

1   *new moon* The Islamic crescent, on the standards of        from that quarter were expected throughout the sixteenth
the Ottoman Turks; new assaults on European Christendom        century.

How Poles' right king means without leave of host
To warm with ill-made fire cold Muscovy;
If French can yet three parts in one agree;                          5
What now the Dutch in their full diets boast;
How Holland hearts, now so good towns be lost,
Trust in the shade of pleasing Orange tree;
How Ulster likes of that same golden bit
Wherewith my father once made it half tame;                         10
If in the Scottish court be weltering yet:
These questions busy wits to me do frame.
I, cumbered with good manners, answer do,
But know not how, for still I think of you.

**3** *Poles' right king* Stephen Bathory, elective king of Poland, invaded Russia in 1580. *without leave of host* without permission of the host country.

**5** *three parts* The three main factions in France's internecine politics: the Catholics, the moderate Politiques, and the Huguenots.

**6** *Dutch* Germans (Deutsch). *diets* The Diet (parliament) of the Holy Roman Empire convened at Augsburg in 1582, for the first time since 1576.

**7–8** Several significant towns in the Low Countries fell to the Spanish in 1581–2; the hopes of the Protestant resistance focused on William of Orange.

**10** *my father* Sidney's father Sir Henry Sidney was three times Governor of Ireland, and had more success with Ulster than with the rest of the island.

**11** *weltering* political unrest. This is the reading of earlier editions; the 1598 edition reads "If in the Scotch court be no weltering yet," very probably with an eye to James's imminent accession to the English throne.

**14** *you* The first direct address to Stella in the sequence.

### 31

With how sad steps, O Moon, thou climbst the skies,
How silently, and with how wan a face.
What, may it be that even in heavenly place
That busy archer his sharp arrows tries?
Sure, if that long-with-Love-acquainted eyes                        5
Can judge of Love, thou feelst a lover's case.
I read it in thy looks; thy languished grace
To me, that feel the like, thy state descries.
Then, even of fellowship, O Moon, tell me,
Is constant love deemed there but want of wit?                      10
Are beauties there as proud as here they be?
Do they above love to be loved, and yet
Those lovers scorn whom that love doth possess?
Do they call virtue there ungratefulness?

**8** *descries* reveals.

**11** *proud* Pride is the usually cited fault of the unattainable Petrarchan mistress.

**14** Up there, do they call ungratefulness virtue?

### 32

Morpheus, the lively son of deadly sleep,
Witness of life to them that living die,
A prophet oft, and oft an history,
A poet eke, as humors fly or creep,
Since thou in me so sure a power dost keep                          5
That never I with close up sense do lie
But by thy work my Stella I descry,

**1** *Morpheus* The god of dreams.

**6** *close up* closed up.

Teaching blind eyes both how to smile and weep,
Vouchsafe of all acquaintance this to tell:
Whence hast thou ivory, rubies, pearl, and gold          10
To show her skin, lips, teeth, and head so well?
Fool, answers he, no Indes such treasures hold;
But from thy heart, while my sire charmeth thee,
Sweet Stella's image I do steal to me.

9   *of all acquaintance* for fellowship.          13   *my sire* Somnus or Hypnus, the god of sleep.


### 33

I might, unhappy word, O me, I might,
And then would not, or could not see my bliss;
Till now wrapped in a most infernal night,
I find how heavenly day, wretch, I did miss.
Heart, rent thyself, thou dost thyself but right.          5
No lovely Paris made thy Helen his,
No force, no fraud robbed thee of thy delight,
Nor Fortune of thy fortune author is;
But to myself myself did give the blow,
While too much wit (forsooth) so troubled me          10
That I respects for both our sakes must show,
And yet could not by rising morn foresee
How fair a day was near. O punished eyes,
That I had been more foolish, or more wise!

An obscure evocation of some earlier missed opportunity on          5   *rent* rend.
Astrophil's part; it may be an autobiographical reference to          6   Paris's abduction of Helen from her husband prompted
the proposed betrothal of Sidney and Penelope Devereux in          the Trojan war.
1576.


### 34

Come let me write: and to what end? To ease
A burdened heart? How can words ease, which are
The glasses of thy daily vexing care?
Oft cruel fights well pictured forth do please.
Art not ashamed to publish thy disease?          5
Nay, that may breed my fame, it is so rare.
But will not wise men think thy words fond ware?
Then be they close, and so none shall displease.
What idler thing than speak and not be heard?
What harder thing than smart and not to speak?          10
Peace, foolish wit; with wit my wit is marred.
Thus write I while I doubt to write, and wreak
My harms on ink's poor loss; perhaps some find
Stella's great powers that so confuse my mind.

3   *glasses* mirrors.          8   *close* hidden.
7   *fond ware* foolish merchandise.          12   *doubt* fear.   *wreak* avenge.


### 35

What may words say, or what may words not say,
Where truth itself must speak like flattery?

Within what bounds can one his liking stay
Where Nature doth with infinite agree?
What Nestor's counsel can my flames allay,           5
Since Reason self doth blow the coal in me?
And ah, what hope that hope should once see day
Where Cupid is sworn page to Chastity?
Honor is honored that thou dost possess
Him as thy slave, and now long needy Fame           10
Doth even grow rich, naming my Stella's name.
Wit learns in thee perfection to express;
Not thou by praise, but praise in thee is raised.
It is a praise to praise when thou art praised.

3  *stay* hold.

5  *Nestor* The aged warrior frequently sought out for counsel by his fellow Greeks during the Trojan war.

## 36

Stella, whence doth this new assault arise,
A conquered, yielden, ransacked heart to win,
Whereto long since through my long battered eyes
Whole armies of thy beauties entered in?
And there long since Love, thy lieutenant, lies,           5
My forces razed, thy banners raised within;
Of conquest do not these effects suffice,
But wilt now war upon thine own begin?
With so sweet voice, and by sweet nature so
In sweetest strength so sweetly skilled withal           10
In all sweet stratagems sweet art can show,
That not my soul, which at thy foot did fall,
Long since forced by thy beams, but stone nor tree
By sense's privilege can scape from thee.

2  *yielden* yielded. The principal early sources for the text read "yielding" or "golden."

13–14  In other circumstances stones and trees have the privilege of not responding to sensory stimulation.

## 37

My mouth doth water and my breast doth swell,
My tongue doth itch, my thoughts in labor be;
Listen then, lordings, with good ear to me,
For of my life I must a riddle tell.
Towards Aurora's court a nymph doth dwell,           5
Rich in all beauties which man's eye can see,
Beauties so far from reach of words that we
Abase her praise, saying she doth excel;
Rich in the treasure of deserved renown,
Rich in the riches of a royal heart,           10
Rich in those gifts which give the eternal crown:
Who, though most rich in these and every part
Which make the patents of true worldly bliss,
Hath no misfortune, but that Rich she is.

5  *Aurora* The goddess of the dawn; the family seat of Lord Rich was in Essex, i.e., in the direction of the dawn.

### 38

This night while Sleep begins with heavy wings
To hatch mine eyes, and that unbitted thought
Doth fall to stray, and my chief powers are brought
To leave the scepter of all subject things,
The first that straight my fancy's error brings　　　　　5
Unto my mind is Stella's image, wrought
By Love's own self, but with so curious draught
That she, methinks, not only shines but sings.
I start, look, hark, but what in closed up sense
Was held, in opened sense it flies away,　　　　　10
Leaving me nought but wailing eloquence.
I, seeing better sights in sight's decay,
Called it anew, and wooèd Sleep again;
But him, her host, that unkind guest had slain.

2　*hatch* close.　*unbitted* without a bit, i.e., unrestrained.　　7　*draught* draftsmanship.
5　*error* wandering.

### 39

Come Sleep, O Sleep, the certain knot of peace,
The baiting place of wit, the balm of woe,
The poor man's wealth, the prisoner's release,
The indifferent judge between the high and low;
With shield of proof shield me from out the press　　　　　5
Of those fierce darts Despair at me doth throw.
O make in me those civil wars to cease;
I will good tribute pay if thou do so.
Take thou of me smooth pillows, sweetest bed,
A chamber deaf to noise and blind to light,　　　　　10
A rosy garland and a weary head;
And if these things, as being thine by right,
Move not thy heavy grace, thou shalt in me,
Livelier than elsewhere, Stella's image see.

2　*baiting* resting.　　　　　14　*Livelier* more lifelike.

### 40

As good to write as for to lie and groan.
O Stella dear, how much thy power hath wrought
That hast my mind, none of the basest, brought
My still kept course, while other sleep, to moan.
Alas, if from the height of Virtue's throne　　　　　5
Thou canst vouchsafe the influence of a thought
Upon a wretch that long thy grace hath sought,
Weigh then how I by thee am overthrown,
And then think thus: although thy beauty be
Made manifest by such a victory,　　　　　10
Yet noblest conquerors do wrecks avoid.
Since then thou hast so far subduèd me
That in my heart I offer still to thee,
O do not let thy temple be destroyed.

4　*other* others.　　　　　13　*offer* make offerings.

41

Having this day my horse, my hand, my lance
Guided so well that I obtained the prize,
Both by the judgment of the English eyes
And of some sent from that sweet enemy, France –
Horsemen my skill in horsemanship advance,          5
Townfolks my strength; a daintier judge applies
His praise to sleight which from good use doth rise;
Some lucky wits impute it but to chance;
Others, because of both sides I do take
My blood from them who did excel in this,            10
Think Nature me a man of arms did make.
How far they shoot awry! The true cause is
Stella looked on, and from her heavenly face
Sent forth the beams which made so fair my race.

Sidney is known to have participated in at least three public tournaments in 1581, and one of them, the so-called Fortress of Perfect Beauty in May, was staged for important French visitors; he also performed in and may have had a hand in writing the entertainment that was part of that particular event. We have no indication that Sidney was as successful in the mock combat as Astrophil claims to have been.

5   *advance* argue for (as the reason for Astrophil's success).
6   *daintier* more precise.
7   *sleight* skill.   *use* practice.

42

O eyes which do the spheres of beauty move,
Whose beams be joys, whose joys all virtues be,
Who while they make Love conquer, conquer Love,
The schools where Venus hath learned chastity;
O eyes, where humble looks most glorious prove,     5
Only loved tyrants, just in cruelty,
Do not, O do not from poor me remove:
Keep still my zenith, ever shine on me.
For though I never see them, but straightways
My life forgets to nourish languished sprites,       10
Yet still on me, O eyes, dart down your rays;
And if from majesty of sacred lights,
Oppressing mortal sense, my death proceed,
Wracks triumphs be which Love (high set) doth breed.

7   *remove* depart.

14   Disasters which result from exalted Love are triumphs.

43

Fair eyes, sweet lips, dear heart, that foolish I
Could hope by Cupid's help on you to prey,
Since to himself he doth your gifts apply
As his main force, choice sport, and easeful stay.
For when he will see who dare him gainsay,          5
Then with those eyes he looks: lo, by and by
Each soul doth at Love's feet his weapons lay,
Glad if for her he give them leave to die.
When he will play, then in her lips he is,
Where blushing red, that Love's self them doth love,  10

4   *stay* residence.

6   *by and by* immediately.

With either lip he doth the other kiss;
But when he will for quiet's sake remove
From all the world, her heart is then his room,
Where well he knows no man to him can come.

### 44

My words I know do well set forth my mind;
My mind bemoans his sense of inward smart;
Such smart may pity claim of any heart;
Her heart, sweet heart, is of no tiger's kind:
And yet she hears, and yet no pity I find,                                      5
But more I cry, less grace she doth impart.
Alas, what cause is there so overthwart
That nobleness itself makes thus unkind?
I much do guess, yet find no truth save this,
That when the breath of my complaints doth touch                   10
Those dainty doors unto the Court of Bliss,
The heavenly nature of that place is such
That once come there, the sobs of mine annoys
Are metamorphosed straight to tunes of joys.

7   *overthwart* perverse.

### 45

Stella oft sees the very face of woe
Painted in my beclouded stormy face,
But cannot skill to pity my disgrace,
Not though thereof the cause herself she know;
Yet hearing late a fable which did show                                       5
Of lovers never known a grievous case,
Pity thereof gate in her breast such place
That, from that sea derived, tears' spring did flow.
Alas, if fancy drawn by imaged things,
Though false, yet with free scope more grace doth breed          10
Than servant's wrack, where new doubts honor brings,
Then think, my dear, that you in me do read
Of lovers' ruin some sad tragedy:
I am not I, pity the tale of me.

3   *skill* find a way.                    7   *gate* got.
4   Even though she knows that she is the cause of it.

### 46

I cursed thee oft, I pity now thy case,
Blind-hitting boy, since she that thee and me
Rules with a beck so tyrannizeth thee
That thou must want or food or dwelling place:
For she protests to banish thee her face.                                      5
Her face? O Love, a rogue thou then shouldst be,
If Love learn not alone to love and see,
Without desire to feed of further grace.
Alas, poor wag that now a scholar art

3   *beck* nod.                            6   *rogue* An able-bodied man without regular home or
5   *protests* vows.                       employment.
                                          9   *wag* rascal.

To such a schoolmistress, whose lessons new                    10
Thou needs must miss, and so thou needs must smart.
Yet dear, let me his pardon get of you
So long (though he from book miche to desire)
Till without fuel you can make hot fire.

11   *miss* fail to learn.                    13   *miche* play truant.


## 47

What, have I thus betrayed my liberty?
Can those black beams such burning marks engrave
In my free side? Or am I born a slave,
Whose neck becomes such yoke of tyranny?
Or want I sense to feel my misery,                             5
Or sprite disdain of such disdain to have,
Who for long faith, though daily help I crave,
May get no alms but scorn of beggary?
Virtue, awake! Beauty but beauty is!
I may, I must, I can, I will, I do                             10
Leave following that which it is gain to miss.
Let her do – soft, but here she comes, go to.
Unkind, I love you not: O me, that eye
Doth make my heart give to my tongue the lie.

2   *burning marks* As in the branding of slaves to establish    11   *Leave* cease.
ownership.                                                       12   *go to* go away.
8   *scorn of beggary* scorn for being a beggar.                 14   *give my tongue the lie* say that my tongue is lying.


## 48

Soul's joy, bend not those morning stars from me,
Where virtue is made strong by beauty's might,
Where love is chasteness, pain doth learn delight,
And humbleness grows one with majesty.
Whatever may ensue, O let me be                               5
Co-partner of the riches of that sight,
Let not mine eyes be hell-driven from that light:
O look, O shine, O let me die and see.
For though I oft myself of them bemoan
That through my heart their beamy darts be gone,             10
Whose cureless wounds even now most freshly bleed,
Yet since my death-wound is already got,
Dear killer, spare not thy sweet cruel shot:
A kind of grace it is to slay with speed.


## 49

I on my horse, and Love on me doth try
Our horsemanships, while by strange work I prove
A horseman to my horse, a horse to Love;
And now man's wrongs in me, poor beast, descry.
The reins wherewith my rider doth me tie                     5
Are humbled thoughts, which bit of reverence move,
Curbed in with fear, but with gilt boss above
Of hope, which makes it seem fair to the eye.
The wand is will; thou, fancy, saddle art,

Girt fast by memory; and while I spur                                    10
My horse, he spurs with sharp desire my heart.
He sits me fast, however I do stir,
And now hath made me to his hand so right
That in the manage myself takes delight.

7  *gilt boss* An ornamental gold knob on the bit.          9  *wand* whip.  *will* desire.

### 50

Stella, the fullness of my thoughts of thee
Cannot be stayed within my panting breast,
But they do swell and struggle forth of me,
Till that in words thy figure be expressed.
And yet as soon as they so formèd be                                    5
According to my lord Love's own behest,
With sad eyes I their weak proportion see
To portrait that which in this world is best:
So that I cannot choose but write my mind,
And cannot choose but put out what I write,                              10
While these poor babes their death in birth do find.
And now my pen these lines had dashèd quite,
But that they stopped his fury from the same
Because their forefront bare sweet Stella's name.

2  *stayed* restrained.

### 51

Pardon mine ears, both I and they do pray,
So may your tongue still fluently proceed
To them that do such entertainment need,
So may you still have somewhat new to say.
On silly me do not the burden lay                                       5
Of all the grave conceits your brain doth breed,
But find some Hercules to bear, instead
Of Atlas tired, your wisdom's heavenly sway.
For me, while you discourse of courtly tides,
Of cunning fishers in most troubled streams,                            10
Of straying ways when valiant error guides,
Meanwhile my heart confers with Stella's beams,
And is even irked that so sweet comedy
By such unsuited speech should hindered be.

7–8  To secure Atlas's help in stealing the apples of the
Hesperides, Hercules briefly took over the giant's task of
supporting the weight of the sky on his shoulders.

### 52

A strife is grown between Virtue and Love
While each pretends that Stella must be his;
Her eyes, her lips, her all, saith Love, do this,
Since they do wear his badge, most firmly prove.
But Virtue thus that title doth disprove:                               5
That Stella (O dear name), that Stella is
That virtuous soul, sure heir of heavenly bliss,

Not this fair outside which our hearts doth move;
And therefore, though her beauty and her grace
Be Love's indeed, in Stella's self he may                    10
By no pretense claim any manner place.
Well, Love, since this demur our suit doth stay,
Let Virtue have that Stella's self, yet thus:
That Virtue but that body grant to us.

12  *demur* Demurrer, a legal argument conceding the facts
as stated by the plaintiff but nevertheless denying that the
suit should be granted.

## 53

In martial sports I had my cunning tried
But yet to break more staves did me address,
While with the people's shouts, I must confess,
Youth, luck, and praise even filled my veins with pride,
When Cupid, having me, his slave, descried                   5
In Mars's livery, prancing in the press:
What now, Sir Fool? said he. I would no less.
Look here, I say. I looked and Stella spied,
Who hard by made a window send forth light.
My heart then quaked, then dazzled were mine eyes;           10
One hand forgat to rule, the other to fight,
Nor trumpets' sound I heard, nor friendly cries.
My foe came on and beat the air for me,
Till that her blush taught me my shame to see.

2  *staves* staffs used in tilting.
7  *I would no less* I would have you no less than *Sir* Fool.
The absence of quotation marks leaves it unclear whether
this bit of sarcasm is spoken by Love or Astrophil.

11  *forgat* forgot.
13  *beat the air for me* Astrophil's opponent answered the
call of the trumpets and charged to the middle of the lists,
only to find no one to hit.

## 54

Because I breathe not love to everyone,
Nor do not use set colors for to wear,
Nor nourish special locks of vowèd hair,
Nor give each speech a full point of a groan,
The courtly nymphs, acquainted with the moan                 5
Of them who in their lips Love's standard bear,
What he? say they of me. Now dare I swear
He cannot love; no, no, let him alone.
And think so still, so Stella know my mind.
Profess indeed I do not Cupid's art;                         10
But you fair maids at length this true shall find,
That his right badge is but worn in the heart.
Dumb swans, not chattering pies do lovers prove;
They love indeed who quake to say they love.

2  *set colors* The wearing of particular colors as a coded
statement of erotic allegiance is an established tradition
in chivalric literature, and was intermittently practiced in
aristocratic circles, particularly on self-consciously chivalric
occasions such as tilting.
4  *point* punctuation mark.
13  *pies* magpies.

## 55

Muses, I oft invoked your holy aid,
With choicest flowers my speech to engarland so
That it, despised in true but naked show,
Might win some grace in your sweet grace arrayed;
And oft whole troops of saddest words I stayed,                     5
Striving abroad a-foraging to go,
Until by your inspiring I might know
How their black banner might be best displayed.
But now I mean no more your help to try,
Nor other sugaring of my speech to prove,                          10
But on her name incessantly to cry:
For let me but name her whom I do love,
So sweet sounds straight mine ear and heart do hit
That I well find no eloquence like it.

5  *stayed* restrained.

## 56

Fie, School of Patience, fie, your lesson is
Far far too long to learn it without book.
What, a whole week without one piece of look,
And think I should not your large precepts miss?
When I might read those letters fair of bliss                      5
Which in her face teach virtue, I could brook
Somewhat thy leaden counsels, which I took
As of a friend that meant not much amiss;
But now that I, alas, do want her sight,
What, dost thou think that I can ever take                         10
In thy cold stuff a phlegmatic delight?
No, Patience, if thou wilt my good, then make
Her come and hear with patience my desire,
And then with patience bid me bear my fire.

2  *learn it without book* memorize.          9  *want* lack.
4  *miss* forget.

## 57

Woe, having made with many fights his own
Each sense of mine, each gift, each power of mind,
Grown now his slaves, he forced them out to find
The thoroughest words, fit for woe's self to groan,
Hoping that when they might find Stella alone                      5
Before she could prepare to be unkind,
Her soul, armed but with such a dainty rind,
Should soon be pierced with sharpness of the moan.
She heard my plaints, and did not only hear,
But them (so sweet is she) most sweetly sing,                      10
With that fair breast making woe's darkness clear.
A pretty case! I hopèd her to bring

4  *thoroughest* most thoroughgoing.          12  *case!* The exclamation mark is modern editorial inter-
                                              vention; the 1598 edition reads "A pretty case I hopèd her
                                              to bring."

To feel my griefs, and she with face and voice
So sweets my pains that my pains me rejoice.


58

Doubt there hath been, when with his golden chain
The orator so far men's hearts doth bind
That no pace else their guided steps can find,
But as he them more short or slack doth rein,
Whether with words this sovereignty he gain,     5
Clothed with fine tropes, with strongest reasons lined,
Or else pronouncing grace, wherewith his mind
Prints his own lively form in rudest brain.
Now judge by this: in piercing phrases late
The anatomy of all my woes I wrate;     10
Stella's sweet breath the same to me did read.
O voice, O face, maugre my speech's might
Which wooèd woe, most ravishing delight
Even those sad words even in sad me did breed.

1 *golden chain* A traditional image of the power of oratory,    7 *pronouncing grace* skillful delivery.
sometimes literalized in Renaissance illustrations.    12 *maugre* despite.


59

Dear, why make you more of a dog than me?
If he do love, I burn, I burn in love;
If he wait well, I never thence would move;
If he be fair, yet but a dog can be.
Little he is, so little worth is he;     5
He barks, my songs thine own voice oft doth prove;
Bidden, perhaps he fetcheth thee a glove,
But I, unbid, fetch even my soul to thee.
Yet while I languish, him that bosom clips,
That lap doth lap, nay, lets in spite of spite     10
This sour-breathed mate taste of those sugared lips.
Alas, if you grant only such delight
To witless things, then Love, I hope, since wit
Becomes a clog, will soon ease me of it.

4 *yet but a dog can be* he is still just a dog.    9 *clips* embraces.
6 *prove* test.    14 *clog* encumbrance.


60

When my good angel guides me to the place
Where all my good I do in Stella see,
That heaven of joys throws only down on me
Thundered disdains and lightnings of disgrace;
But when the ruggedst step of Fortune's race     5
Makes me fall from her sight, then sweetly she
With words wherein the Muses' treasures be
Shows love and pity to my absent case.
Now I, wit-beaten long by hardest fate,
So dull am that I cannot look into     10
The ground of this fierce love and lovely hate;
Then some good body tell me how I do,

Whose presence absence, absence presence is,
Blissed in my curse, and cursèd in my bliss.


### 61

Oft with true sighs, oft with uncallèd tears,
Now with slow words, now with dumb eloquence,
I Stella's eyes assayed, invade her ears,
But this at last is her sweet-breathed defense:
That who indeed infelt affection bears                    5
So captives to his saint both soul and sense
That, wholly hers, all selfness he forbears,
Then his desires he learns his life's course thence.
Now since her chaste mind hates this love in me,
With chastened mind I straight must show that she        10
Shall quickly me from what she hates remove.
O Doctor Cupid, thou for me reply,
Driven else to grant by angel's sophistry
That I love not without I leave to love.

7  *selfness* self-interest (the word appears to be Sidney's invention).
8  *learns* teaches.

12  *Doctor* Professor, hence having the knowledge of logic and rhetoric to refute the angel's "sophistry."
14  *leave* cease.


### 62

Late tired with woe, even ready for to pine,
With rage of love I called my love unkind;
She, in whose eyes love, though unfelt, doth shine,
Sweet said that I true love in her should find.
I joyed, but straight thus watered was my wine,          5
That love she did, but loved a love not blind,
Which would not let me whom she loved decline
From nobler course, fit for my birth and mind,
And therefore by her love's authority
Willed me these tempests of vain love to fly             10
And anchor fast myself on virtue's shore.
Alas, if this the only metal be
Of love, new-coined to help my beggary,
Dear, love me not, that you may love me more.


### 63

O grammar rules, O now your virtues show,
So children still read you with awful eyes,
As my young dove may in your precepts wise
Her grant to me by her own virtue know.
For late with heart most high, with eyes most low,       5
I craved the thing which ever she denies;
She, lightening love, displaying Venus' skies,
Lest once should not be heard, twice said, No, no.
Sing then, my Muse, now *Io Paean* sing!
Heavens, envy not at my high triumphing,                 10
But grammar's force with sweet success confirm:

2  *awful* respectful.
7  *lightening* flashing forth.

9  *Io Paean* A classical Greek cry of victory, used in this context by Ovid at *Ars amatoria* 2.1.

For grammar says (O this, dear Stella, weigh),
For grammar says (to grammar who says nay?)
That in one speech two negatives affirm.

12 *weigh* The 1598 edition reads "nay," which could be used in the sense of "deny."

14 A recognized rule (not without exceptions) in Latin grammar, but not regularly asserted for English until the later eighteenth century.

### FIRST SONG

Doubt you to whom my Muse these notes intendeth,
Which now my breast, o'ercharged, to music lendeth?
To you, to you all song of praise is due;
Only in you my song begins and endeth.

Who hath the eyes which marry state with pleasure?          5
Who keeps the key of Nature's chiefest treasure?
To you, to you all song of praise is due;
Only for you the heaven forgate all measure.

Who hath the lips where wit in fairness reigneth?
Who womankind at once both decks and staineth?          10
To you, to you all song of praise is due;
Only by you Cupid his crown maintaineth.

Who hath the feet whose step of sweetness planteth?
Who else for whom Fame worthy trumpets wanteth?
To you, to you all song of praise is due;          15
Only to you her scepter Venus granteth.

Who hath the breast whose milk doth passions nourish?
Whose grace is such, that when it chides doth cherish?
To you, to you all song of praise is due;
Only through you the tree of life doth flourish.          20

Who hath the hand which without stroke subdueth?
Who long-dead beauty with increase reneweth?
To you, to you all song of praise is due;
Only at you all envy hopeless rueth.

Who hath the hair which loosest, fastest tieth?          25
Who makes a man live then glad when he dieth?
To you, to you all song of praise is due;
Only of you the flatterer never lieth.

Who hath the voice which soul from senses sunders?
Whose force but yours the bolts of beauty thunders?          30

5 *state* dignity.
8 *forgate* forgot.
9 *fairness* beauty.

10 *both decks and staineth* puts in both a good and a bad light (i.e., by being a woman and by being more beautiful than all other women).
14 *wanteth* lacks.
24 *rueth* grieves.

To you, to you all song of praise is due;
Only with you not miracles are wonders.

Doubt you to whom my Muse these notes intendeth,
Which now my breast, o'ercharged, to music lendeth?
To you, to you all song of praise is due;                    35
Only in you my song begins and endeth.

32   *not miracles are wonders* wonders are not miracles (i.e.,
are natural and everyday).

### 64

No more, my dear, no more these counsels try;
O give my passions leave to run their race.
Let Fortune lay on me her worst disgrace,
Let folk o'ercharged with brain against me cry,
Let clouds bedim my face, break in mine eye,                 5
Let me no steps but of lost labor trace,
Let all the earth with scorn recount my case:
But do not will me from my love to fly.
I do not envy Aristotle's wit,
Nor do aspire to Caesar's bleeding fame,                    10
Nor ought do care though some above me sit,
Nor hope nor wish another course to frame
But that which once may win thy cruel heart.
Thou art my wit, and thou my virtue art.

### 65

Love, by sure proof I may call thee unkind
That giv'st no better ear to my just cries,
Thou whom to me such my good turns should bind
As I may well recount, but none can prize.
For when, nak'd boy, thou couldst no harbor find           5
In this old world, grown now so too, too wise,
I lodged thee in my heart, and being blind
By nature born, I gave to thee mine eyes:
Mine eyes, my light, my heart, my life, alas,
If so great services may scornèd be!                        10
Yet let this thought thy tigerish courage pass:
That I perhaps am somewhat kin to thee,
Since in thine arms, if learned fame truth hath spread,
Thou bearst the arrow, I the arrowhead.

4   *prize* reckon their value.                    14   There was an arrowhead in the Sidney family arms.

### 66

And do I see some cause a hope to feed,
Or doth the tedious burden of long woe
In weakened minds quick apprehending breed
Of every image which may comfort show?
I cannot brag of word, much less of deed,                   5
Fortune wheels still with me in one sort slow,

6   *Fortune* The 1598 edition reads "Fortunes," i.e., "For-
tune's"; "slow" would then be the verb ("move slowly").

My wealth no more, and no whit less my need,
Desire still on the stilts of fear doth go.
And yet amid all fears a hope there is,
Stolen to my heart since last fair night, nay, day: 10
Stella's eyes sent to me the beams of bliss,
Looking on me while I looked other way;
But when mine eyes back to their heaven did move,
They fled with blush, which guilty seemed of love.

### 67

Hope, art thou true, or dost thou flatter me?
Doth Stella now begin with piteous eye
The ruins of her conquest to espy?
Will she take time, before all wrackèd be?
Her eyes' speech is translated thus by thee, 5
But failst thou not in phrase so heavenly high?
Look on again, the fair text better try;
What blushing notes dost thou in margin see?
What sighs stolen out, or killed before full born?
Hast thou found such and such like arguments, 10
Or art thou else to comfort me forsworn?
Well, how so thou interpret the contents,
I am resolved thy error to maintain,
Rather than by more truth to get more pain.

4 *take time* take action while there is time.

### 68

Stella, the only planet of my light,
Light of my life, and life of my desire,
Chief good whereto my hope doth only aspire,
World of my wealth, and heaven of my delight,
Why dost thou spend the treasures of thy sprite, 5
With voice more fit to wed Amphion's lyre,
Seeking to quench in me the noble fire
Fed by thy worth and blinded by thy sight?
And all in vain, for while thy breath most sweet,
With choicest words, thy words with reasons rare, 10
Thy reasons firmly set on virtue's feet,
Labor to kill in me this killing care,
O think I then what paradise of joy
It is so fair a virtue to enjoy.

6 *Amphion's lyre* Amphion's legendary skill with the lyre was sufficient to move rocks and boulders; he used it in building the walls of Thebes.

8 *blinded* Sources other than the 1598 edition read "kindled."
14 *enjoy* A term often used for specifically sexual pleasure.

### 69

O joy, too high for my low style to show!
O bliss, fit for a nobler state than me!
Envy, put out thine eyes, lest thou do see
What oceans of delight in me do flow.
My friend, that oft saw through all masks my woe, 5
Come, come, and let me pour myself on thee.
Gone is the winter of my misery,
My spring appears, O see what here doth grow!

For Stella hath, with words where faith doth shine,
Of her high heart given me the monarchy:                                    10
I, I, O I may say that she is mine!
And though she give but thus conditionly
This realm of bliss while virtuous course I take,
No kings be crowned but they some covenants make.


### 70

My Muse may well grudge at my heavenly joy
If still I force her in sad rhymes to creep;
She oft hath drunk my tears, now hopes to enjoy
Nectar of mirth, since I Jove's cup do keep.
Sonnets be not bound prentice to annoy,                                     5
Trebles sing high as well as basses deep,
Grief but Love's winter livery is, the boy
Hath cheeks to smile as well as eyes to weep.
Come then, my Muse, show thou height of delight
In well raised notes; my pen the best it may                                10
Shall paint out joy, though but in black and white.
Cease, eager Muse; peace, pen, for my sake stay,
I give you here my hand for truth of this:
Wise silence is best music unto bliss.

4 *Nectar* The drink of the Olympian gods; Astrophil has acquired Ganymede's job. Sidney himself held the office of Royal Cupbearer.

5 Sonnets are not legally required to have unhappiness as their subject matter the way an apprentice is obligated to serve the same master for a set term.


### 71

Who will in fairest book of nature know
How virtue may best lodged in beauty be,
Let him but learn of Love to read in thee,
Stella, those fair lines which true goodness show.
There shall he find all vices' overthrow,                                   5
Not by rude force but sweetest sovereignty
Of reason, from whose light those nightbirds fly –
That inward sun in thine eyes shineth so.
And not content to be perfection's heir,
Thyself dost strive all minds that way to move                              10
Who mark in thee what is in thee most fair.
So while thy beauty draws the heart to love,
As fast thy virtue bends that love to good.
But ah, Desire still cries, Give me some food!

1–13 A compact summary of the Neoplatonic theory of Petrarchan love, whereby a beautiful and virtuous woman uses her attractiveness as means to the moral education of her admirers. In terms of overall line count (including the songs), this sonnet falls at the exact center of the sequence.


### 72

Desire, though thou my old companion art,
And oft so clings to my pure love that I
One from the other scarcely can descry
While each doth blow the fire of my heart,
Now from thy fellowship I needs must part.                                  5
Venus is taught with Dian's wings to fly;

6 *Dian* Diana, goddess of chastity.

I must no more in thy sweet passions lie,
Virtue's gold now must head my Cupid's dart.
Service and Honor, Wonder with Delight,
Fear to offend, Will worthy to appear,                    10
Care shining in mine eyes, Faith in my sprite:
These things are left me by my only dear.
But thou, Desire, because thou wouldst have all
Now banished art, but yet alas how shall?

10  *Dian* Diana, goddess of chastity.

### SECOND SONG

Have I caught my heavenly jewel
Teaching sleep most fair to be?
Now will I teach her that she,
When she wakes, is too, too cruel.

Since sweet sleep her eyes hath charmèd,              5
The two only darts of Love;
Now will I with that boy prove
Some play while he is disarmèd.

Her tongue waking still refuseth,
Giving frankly niggard No;                            10
Now will I attempt to know
What No her tongue sleeping useth.

See the hand, which waking guardeth,
Sleeping grants a free resort.
Now will I invade the fort;                           15
Cowards Love with loss rewardeth.

But, O fool, think of the danger
Of her just and high disdain!
Now will I, alas, refrain;
Love fears nothing else but anger.                    20

Yet those lips, so sweetly swelling,
Do invite a stealing kiss;
Now will I but venture this.
Who will read must first learn spelling.

O sweet kiss! But ah, she is waking,                  25
Lowering beauty chastens me;
Now will I away hence flee.
Fool, more fool for no more taking.

7  *prove* try.

### 73

Love still a boy, and oft a wanton is,
Schooled only by his mother's tender eye;
What wonder then if he his lesson miss

3  *miss* fail to learn.

When for so soft a rod dear play he try?
And yet my star, because a sugared kiss                                              5
In sport I sucked while she asleep did lie,
Doth lower, nay, chide, nay threat for only this.
Sweet, it was saucy Love, not humble I.
But no scuse serves, she makes her wrath appear
In Beauty's throne; see now who dares come near                                      10
Those scarlet judges, threatening bloody pain?
O heavenly fool, thy most kiss-worthy face
Anger invests with such a lovely grace
That Anger's self I needs must kiss again.

11   *scarlet judges* Stella's lips; High Court judges wore scarlet robes.

## 74

I never drank of Aganippe well,
Nor ever did in shade of Tempe sit,
And Muses scorn with vulgar brains to dwell –
Poor layman I, for sacred rites unfit.
Some do I hear of poets' fury tell,                                                  5
But (God wot) wot not what they mean by it;
And this I swear by blackest brook of hell,
I am no pickpurse of another's wit.
How falls it, then, that with so smooth an ease
My thoughts I speak, and what I speak doth flow                                      10
In verse, and that my verse best wits doth please?
Guess we the cause. What, is it thus? Fie, no.
Or so? Much less. How then? Sure thus it is:
My lips are sweet, inspired with Stella's kiss.

1   *Aganippe* A river-nymph, guardian of a well on Helicon, sacred to the Muses.
2   *Tempe* The narrow valley in Thessaly where Daphne was transformed into the laurel-tree.

6   *wot* knows/know.
7   *blackest brook of hell* The river Styx, by which the gods swore an unbreakable oath.
8   *pickpurse* pickpocket.

## 75

Of all the kings that ever here did reign,
Edward named fourth as first in praise I name:
Not for his fair outside nor well-lined brain,
Although less gifts imp feathers oft on fame;
Nor that he could young-wise, wise-valiant frame                                     5
His sire's revenge, joined with a kingdom's gain,
And gained by Mars, could yet mad Mars so tame
That balance weighed what sword did late obtain;
Nor that he made the Flower-de-luce so fraid,

2   *Edward named fourth* King Edward IV (1442–83); not in general highly praised by sixteenth-century chroniclers.
4   *imp* graft.

5–8   Edward avenged the death of his father, the Duke of York, by deposing King Henry VI; after a period of civil war, the latter part of Edward's reign was relatively peaceful.
9   *the Flower-de-luce* France, which Edward invaded in 1474–5.

Though strongly hedged of bloody lion's paws,          10
That witty Louis to him a tribute paid;
Nor this, nor that, nor any such small cause,
But only for this worthy knight durst prove
To lose his crown rather than fail his love.

10 *hedged* protected. *lion* Scotland, whose traditional allegiance to France had been neutralized by a truce that Edward had made.
11 *Louis* King Louis XI of France, who paid Edward a sizeable pension to return to England.

13 *prove* risk.
14 Edward in 1464 married the widow Elizabeth Grey, an unpopular choice with some of his supporters that led to rebellion and his temporary loss of the Crown in 1470–1.

## 76

She comes, and straight therewith her shining twins do move
Their rays to me, who in her tedious absence lay
Benighted in cold woe, but now appears my day,
The only light of joy, the only warmth of love.
She comes with light and warmth, which like Aurora prove     5
Of gentle force, so that mine eyes dare gladly play
With such a rosy morn, whose beams most freshly gay
Scorch not, but only do dark chilling sprites remove.
But lo, while I do speak, it groweth noon with me,
Her flamy, glistering lights increase with time and place,     10
My heart cries, Ah, it burns, mine eyes now dazzled be,
No wind, no shade can cool. What help then in my case,
But with short breath, long looks, stayed feet, and walking head
Pray that my sun go down with meeker beams to bed?

5 *Aurora* goddess of the dawn.

13 *stayed* paralyzed. *walking head* racing mind.

## 77

Those looks whose beams be joy, whose motion is delight,
That face whose lecture shows what perfect beauty is,
That presence which doth give dark hearts a living light,
That grace which Venus weeps that she herself doth miss,
That hand which without touch holds more than Atlas might,     5
Those lips which make death's pay a mean price for a kiss,
That skin whose pass-praise hue scorns this poor term of white,
Those words which do sublime the quintessence of bliss,
That voice which makes the soul plant himself in the ears,
That conversation sweet where such high comforts be     10
As, constered in true speech, the name of heaven it bears
Makes me in my best thoughts and quietest judgment see
That in no more but these I might be fully blessed:
Yet ah, my maiden Muse doth blush to tell the best.

2 *whose lecture* the reading of which.
4 *miss* fail to possess.
5 *Atlas* giant who supported the sky on his shoulders.
6 *mean* modest.

7 *pass-praise* going beyond praise.
8 *sublime* refine to a higher state.
11 *constered* construed.

## 78

O how the pleasant airs of true love be
Infected by those vapors which arise
From out that noisome gulf which gaping lies

Between the jaws of hellish jealousy:
A monster, others' harm, self-misery,                                    5
Beauty's plague, virtue's scourge, succor of lies,
Who his own joy to his own hurt applies,
And only cherish doth with injury;
Who, since he hath, by Nature's special grace,
So piercing paws as spoil when they embrace,                           10
So nimble feet as stir still, though on thorns,
So many eyes aye seeking their own woe,
So ample ears as never good news know,
Is it not evil that such a devil wants horns?

10   *spoil* injure severely.

14   *wants* lacks.   *horns* Both horns indicating his demonic nature and horns manifesting his status as a cuckolded husband.

## 79

Sweet kiss, thy sweets I fain would sweetly indite,
Which even of sweetness sweetest sweetener art:
Pleasingst consort, where each sense holds a part,
Which, coupling doves, guides Venus' chariot right;
Best charge and bravest retreat in Cupid's fight;                      5
A double key, which opens to the heart,
Most rich when most his riches it impart;
Nest of young joys, schoolmaster of delight,
Teaching the mean at once to take and give
The friendly fray where blows both wound and heal;                    10
The pretty death, while each in other live;
Poor hope's first wealth, ostage of promised weal,
Breakfast of Love – but lo, lo, where she is!
Cease we to praise, now pray we for a kiss.

1   *indite* write about.
9   *mean* means.

12   *ostage* hostage (held in security for some future act).
*weal* happiness.

## 80

Sweet swelling lip, well mayst thou swell in pride,
Since best wits think it wit thee to admire:
Nature's praise, Virtue's stall, Cupid's cold fire,
Whence words, not words but heavenly graces slide;
The new Parnassus where the Muses bide;                               5
Sweetener of music, wisdom's beautifier;
Breather of life, and fastener of desire,
Where beauty's blush in honor's grain is dyed.
Thus much my heart compelled my mouth to say,
But now, spite of my heart, my mouth will stay,                       10
Loathing all lies, doubting this flattery is;
And no spur can his resty race renew
Without how far this praise is short of you,
Sweet lip, you teach my mouth with one sweet kiss.

3   *stall* seat.

11   *resty* restive.

### 81

O kiss which dost those ruddy gems impart,
Or gems or fruits of newfound paradise,
Breathing all bliss and sweetening to the heart,
Teaching dumb lips a nobler exercise,
O kiss which souls, even souls together ties     5
By links of love and only nature's art:
How fain would I paint thee to all men's eyes,
Or of thy gifts at least shade out some part.
But she forbids; with blushing words, she says
She builds her fame on higher seated praise.     10
But my heart burns, I cannot silent be.
Then since (dear life) you fain would have me peace,
And I, mad with delight, want wit to cease,
Stop you my mouth with still, still kissing me.

8  *shade out* sketch.

12  *peace* keep my peace.

### 82

Nymph of the garden where all beauties be,
Beauties which do in excellency pass
His who till death looked in a watery glass
Or hers whom naked the Trojan boy did see;
Sweet garden nymph, which keeps the cherry tree     5
Whose fruit doth far the Hesperian taste surpass;
Most sweet-fair, most fair-sweet: do not, alas,
From coming near those cherries banish me.
For though, full of desire, empty of wit,
Admitted late by your best-gracèd grace,     10
I caught at one of them a hungry bit,
Pardon that fault, once more grant me the place,
And I do swear even by the same delight,
I will but kiss, I never more will bite.

3  Narcissus died gazing on his own beautiful image in a pond.
4  Paris (the "Trojan boy") awarded Venus the prize for beauty over Juno and Athena when she disrobed for him.

5  *cherry tree* lips.
6  *Hesperian taste* The garden of the Hesperides produced golden apples; their theft was one of Hercules' twelve labors.
11  *bit* bite.

### 83

Good brother Philip, I have borne you long;
I was content you should in favor creep
While craftily you seemed your cut to keep,
As though that fair soft hand did you great wrong.
I bare, with envy, yet I bare your song     5
When in her neck you did love ditties peep;
Nay, more fool I, oft suffered you to sleep

Stella has a pet sparrow with the same name as the bird in John Skelton's *Phillip Sparrow*; Sidney is remembering that poem, as well as a famous poem by Catullus (2) about his beloved's pet bird. Both poems deal with the provocative physical intimacy which the mistresses allow their pets, though the threat with which Astrophil ends is his own.

3  *your cut to keep* to mind your manners (as in *Philip Sparrow*, ll. 118–19).

In lilies' nest, where Love's self lies along.
What, doth high place ambitious thoughts augment?
Is sauciness reward of courtesy?                                    10
Cannot such grace your silly self content,
But you must needs with those lips billing be?
And though those lips drink nectar from that tongue,
Leave that, sir Phip, lest off your neck be wrung.


THIRD SONG

If Orpheus' voice had force to breathe such music's love
Through pores of senseless trees as it could make them move,
If stones good measure danced, the Theban walls to build
To cadence of the tunes which Amphion's lyre did yield,
More cause a like effect at leastwise bringeth;                     5
O stones, O trees, learn hearing: Stella singeth.

If love might sweeten so a boy of shepherd brood
To make a lizard dull to taste love's dainty food,
If eagle fierce could so in Grecian maid delight
As his light was her eyes, her death his endless night;            10
Earth gave that love, heaven I trow love refineth:
O beasts, O birds, look, Love, lo, Stella shineth.

The birds, beasts, stones, and trees feel this, and feeling love;
And if the trees nor stones stir not the same to prove,
Nor beasts nor birds do come unto this blessèd gaze,               15
Know that small love is quick, and great love doth amaze:
They are amazed, but you with reason armed,
O eyes, O ears of men, how are you charmed!

**1–4**  The legendary singer Orpheus was supposed to have had the power to move plants and inanimate objects with his music; Amphion (see above on 68.6) was said to have raised the walls of Thebes with the magical force of his lyre.

**7–10**  Two stories from the elder Pliny's *Natural History* about the loyalty of animals to human beings: the Arcadian Thoas was saved from robbers by a snake he had cared for (8.61), and a woman at Sestos was brought game by a pet eagle, which at her death threw itself upon her pyre (10.18).


84

Highway, since you my chief Parnassus be
And that my Muse, to some ears not unsweet,
Tempers her words to trampling horses' feet
More oft than to a chamber melody:
Now, blessèd you, bear onward blessèd me                           5
To her, where I my heart safelest shall meet;
My Muse and I must you of duty greet
With thanks and wishes, wishing thankfully.
Be you still fair, honored by public heed,
By no encroachment wronged nor time forgot,                        10
Nor blamed for blood, nor shamed for sinful deed;
And that you know I envy you no lot
Of highest wish, I wish you so much bliss:
Hundreds of years you Stella's feet may kiss.

**1**  *Parnassus* The highway is now Astrophil's chief source of poetic inspiration.

**6**  *safelest* safeliest.

85

I see the house. My heart, thyself contain;
Beware full sails drown not thy tottering barge,
Lest joy, by nature apt sprites to enlarge,
Thee to thy wrack beyond thy limits strain.
Nor do like lords whose weak, confusèd brain,                         5
Not pointing to fit folks each undercharge,
While every office themselves will discharge,
With doing all leave nothing done but pain.
But give apt servants their due place: let eyes
See beauty's total sum summed in her face,                            10
Let ears hear speech which wit to wonder ties,
Let breath suck up those sweets, let arms embrace
The globe of weal, lips love's indentures make:
Thou but of all the kingly tribute take.

6   Not delegating subsidiary tasks to the right people.    13   *weal* happiness.   *indentures* binding contracts, but also marks made by teeth.

FOURTH SONG

Only joy, now here you are,
Fit to hear and ease my care;
Let my whispering voice obtain
Sweet reward for sharpest pain.
Take me to thee, and thee to me.                                      5
No, no, no, no, my dear, let be.

Night hath closed all in her cloak,
Twinkling stars love-thoughts provoke;
Danger hence good care doth keep,
Jealousy itself doth sleep.                                           10
Take me to thee, and thee to me.
No, no, no, no, my dear, let be.

Better place no wit can find
Cupid's yoke to loose or bind;
These sweet flowers on fine bed too                                   15
Us in their best language woo.
Take me to thee, and thee to me.
No, no, no, no, my dear, let be.

This small light the moon bestows
Serves thy beams but to disclose,                                     20
So to raise my hap more high;
Fear not else, none can us spy.
Take me to thee, and thee to me.
No, no, no, no, my dear, let be.

That you heard was but a mouse;                                       25
Dumb sleep holdeth all the house.

Set to music by Henry Youll in his *Canzonets* (1608).

Yet asleep methinks they say,
Young folks, take time while you may.
Take me to thee, and thee to me.
No, no, no, no, my dear, let be.                          30

Niggard Time threats, if we miss
This large offer of our bliss,
Long stay ere he grant the same.
Sweet, then, while each thing doth frame,
Take me to thee, and thee to me.                          35
No, no, no, no, my dear, let be.

Your fair mother is a-bed,
Candles out, and curtains spread.
She thinks you do letters write;
Write, but first let me indite:                           40
Take me to thee, and thee to me.
No, no, no, no, my dear, let be.

Sweet, alas, why strive you thus?
Concord better fitteth us.
Leave to Mars the force of hands;                         45
Your power in your beauty stands.
Take me to thee, and thee to me.
No, no, no, no, my dear, let be.

Woe to me, and do you swear
Me to hate but I forbear?                                 50
Cursèd be my destines all
That brought me so high to fall.
Soon with my death I will please thee.
No, no, no, no, my dear, let be.

28   *take time* act on the opportunity (as at sonnet 67.4 above).
In the context of erotic persuasion, the phrase is in effect
a translation of Horace's often cited tag, *carpe diem* (*Odes*
1.11.8).

33   *stay* wait.
40   *indite* compose.
47   The 1598 edition reads "Take thee to me, and me to thee."

## 86

Alas, whence came this change of looks? If I
Have changed desert, let mine own conscience be
A still felt plague to self-condemning me;
Let woe gripe on my heart, shame load mine eye.
But if all faith like spotless ermine lie                 5
Safe in my soul, which only doth to thee
(As his sole object of felicity)
With wings of love in air of wonder fly,
O ease your hand, treat not so hard your slave.
In justice pains come not till faults do call;            10
Or if I needs (sweet judge) must torments have,
Use something else to chasten me withal
Than those blest eyes, where all my hopes do dwell:
No doom should make once heaven become his hell.

4   *gripe* seize.

FIFTH SONG

While favor fed my hope, delight with hope was brought,
Thought waited on delight, and speech did follow thought,
Then grew my tongue and pen records unto thy glory.
I thought all words were lost that were not spent of thee,
I thought each place was dark but where thy lights would be,            5
And all ears worse than deaf that heard not out thy story.

I said thou wert most fair, and so indeed thou art;
I said thou art most sweet, sweet poison to my heart;
I said my soul was thine (O, that I then had lied!);
I said thine eyes were stars, thy breasts the milken way,               10
Thy fingers Cupid's shafts, thy voice the angels' lay:
And all I said so well as no man it denied.

But now that hope is lost, unkindness kills delight,
Yet thought and speech do live, though metamorphosed quite,
For Rage now rules the reins which guided were by Pleasure.            15
I think now of thy faults, who late thought of thy praise,
That speech falls now to blame which did thy honor raise;
The same key open can which can lock up a treasure.

Thou, then, whom partial heavens conspired in one to frame
The proof of beauty's worth, the inheritrix of fame,                   20
The mansion seat of bliss and just excuse of lovers:
See now those feathers plucked wherewith thou flew most high,
See what clouds of reproach shall dark thy honor's sky.
Whose own fault casts him down, hardly high seat recovers.

And O, my Muse, though oft you lulled her in your lap,                 25
And then, a heavenly child, gave her ambrosian pap
And to that brain of hers your hiddenest gifts infused:
Since she, disdaining me, doth you in me disdain,
Suffer not her to laugh while both we suffer pain;
Princes in subjects wronged must deem themselves abused.              30

Your client, poor myself, shall Stella handle so?
Revenge, revenge, my Muse, defiance' trumpet blow;
Threaten what may be done, yet do more than you threaten.
Ah, my suit granted is, I feel my breast doth swell;
Now, child, a lesson new you shall begin to spell.                     35
Sweet babes must babies have, but shrewd girls must be beaten.

Think now no more to hear of warm, fine-odored snow,
Nor blushing lilies nor pearls' ruby-hidden row,
Nor of that golden sea whose waves in curls are broken,
But of thy soul, so fraught with such ungratefulness                   40
As where thou soon mightst help, most faith doth most oppress.
Ungrateful who is called, the worst of evils is spoken.

---

**4** *of* on.
**26** *ambrosian pap* celestial baby food.

**32** *defiance'* defiance's.
**36** *babies* dolls.  *shrewd* shrewish.

Yet worse than worst, I say thou art a thief, a thief!
Now, God forbid, a thief, and of worst thieves the chief:
Thieves steal for need, and steal but goods which pain recovers,          45
But thou, rich in all joys, dost rob my joys from me,
Which cannot be restored by time nor industry.
Of foes the spoil is evil, far worse of constant lovers.

Yet gentle English thieves do rob but will not slay;
Thou, English murdering thief, wilt have hearts for thy prey.             50
The name of murderer now on thy fair forehead sitteth,
And even while I do speak, my death wounds bleeding be,
Which (I protest) proceed from only cruel thee.
Who may and will not save, murder in truth committeth.

But murder, private fault, seems but a toy to thee.                       55
I lay, then, to thy charge unjustest tyranny,
If rule by force without all claim a tyran showeth;
For thou dost lord my heart who am not born thy slave,
And, which is worse, makes me most guiltless torments have.
A rightful prince by unright deeds a tyran groweth.                       60

Lo, you grow proud with this, for tyrans make folk bow.
Of foul rebellion then I do appeach thee now:
Rebel by nature's law, rebel by law of reason,
Thou sweetest subject wert born in the realm of Love,
And yet against thy prince thy force dost daily prove.                    65
No virtue merits praise once touched with blot of treason.

But valiant rebels oft in fools' mouths purchase fame.
I now then stain thy white with vagabonding shame,
Both rebel to the son and vagrant from the mother,
For, wearing Venus' badge in every part of thee,                         70
Unto Diana's train thou runaway didst flee:
Who faileth one is false, though trusty to another.

What, is not this enough? Nay, far worse cometh here:
A witch I say thou art, though thou so fair appear,
For I protest my sight never thy face enjoyeth                           75
But I in me am changed, I am alive and dead,
My feet are turned to roots, my heart becometh lead.
No witchcraft is so evil as which man's mind destroyeth.

Yet witches may repent; thou art far worse than they.
Alas, that I am forced such evil of thee to say:                         80
I say thou art a devil, though clothed in angels' shining,
For thy face tempts my soul to leave the heaven for thee
And thy words of refuse do pour even hell on me.
Who tempt and tempted plague are devils in true defining.

---

45   *pain* effort.
48   *Of foes the spoil* robbing foes.
57   *claim* right.
62   *appeach* accuse.

68   *vagabonding shame* the shame of being without proper
home or employment.
71   *Diana* goddess of chastity.
72   *trusty* faithful.
83   *refuse* refusal.

You, then, ungrateful thief, you murdering tyran you, 85
You rebel runaway, to lord and lady untrue,
You witch, you devil, alas, you still of me beloved,
You see what I can say; mend yet your froward mind,
And such skill in my Muse you reconciled shall find
That all these cruel words your praises shall be proved. 90

SIXTH SONG

O you that hear this voice,
O you that see this face,
Say whether of this choice
Deserves the former place;
Fear not to judge this bate, 5
For it is void of hate.

This side doth Beauty take,
For that doth Music speak:
Fit orators to make
The strongest judgments weak. 10
The bar to plead their right
Is only true delight.

Thus doth the voice and face
These gentle lawyers wage,
Like loving brothers' case 15
For father's heritage,
That each, while each contends,
Itself to other lends.

For Beauty beautifies
With heavenly hue and grace 20
The heavenly harmonies,
And in this faultless face
The perfect beauties be
A perfect harmony.

Music more loftly swells 25
In speeches nobly placed,
Beauty as far excels
In action aptly graced;
A friend each party draws
To countenance his cause. 30

Love more affected seems
To Beauty's lovely light,
And Wonder more esteems
Of Music's wondrous might:
But both to both so bent 35
As both in both are spent.

Set to music by William Byrd in his *Psalms, Sonnets, and Songs* (1588).

3 *whether* which.
4 *former* foremost.

11 The court before which they argue the case.
14 *wage* hire.
25 *loftly* loftily.
34 *Music's* The 1598 edition reads "Music."

Music doth witness call
The Ear, his truth to try;
Beauty brings to the hall
The judgment of the Eye:                                40
Both in their objects such
As no exceptions touch.

The Common Sense, which might
Be arbiter of this,
To be forsooth upright                                  45
To both sides partial is;
He lays on this chief praise,
Chief praise on that he lays.

Then Reason, princess high
Whose throne is in the mind,                            50
Which music can in sky
And hidden beauties find,
Say whether thou wilt crown
With limitless renown.

40   *The judgment* The 1598 edition reads "eye-judgment";
Byrd's setting has "eye witness."
42   *exceptions* legal objections.

43   *Common Sense* The inclusive faculty of sense perception,
encompassing the other five senses.
47   *this* The 1598 edition reads "this side."

## SEVENTH SONG

Whose senses in so evil consort their stepdame Nature lays
That ravishing delight in them most sweet tunes do not raise,
Or if they do delight therein, yet are so closed with wit
As with sententious lips to set a title vain on it:
O let them hear these sacred tunes, and learn in wonder's schools      5
To be, in things past bounds of wit, fools, if they be not fools.

Who have so leaden eyes as not to see sweet beauty's show,
Or, seeing, have so wooden wits as not that worth to know,
Or, knowing, have so muddy minds as not to be in love,
Or, loving, have so frothy thoughts as easily thence to move:        10
O let them see these heavenly beams, and in fair letters read
A lesson fit, both sight and skill, love and firm love to breed.

Hear then, but then with wonder hear; see, but adoring see
No mortal gifts, no earthly fruits now here descended be;
See, do you see this face? A face? Nay, image of the skies,          15
Of which the two life-giving lights are figured in her eyes.
Hear you this soul-invading voice and count it but a voice,
The very essence of their tunes when angels do rejoice?

## EIGHTH SONG

In a grove most rich of shade,
Where birds wanton music made,

In some measure the model for John Donne's "The Ecstasy."

May then young his pied weeds showing,
New perfumed with flowers fresh growing,

Astrophil and Stella sweet                                   5
Did for mutual comfort meet,
Both within themselves oppressèd,
But each in the other blessèd.

Him great harms had taught much care,
Her fair neck a foul yoke bare;                             10
But her sight his cares did banish,
In his sight her yoke did vanish.

Wept they had, alas the while,
But now tears themselves did smile,
While their eyes, by love directed,                        15
Interchangeably reflected.

Sigh they did, but now betwixt
Sighs of woe were glad sighs mixed,
With arms crossed, yet testifying
Restless rest and living dying.                            20

Their ears hungry of each word
Which the dear tongue would afford,
But their tongues restrained from walking
Till their hearts had ended talking.

But when their tongues could not speak,                    25
Love itself did silence break;
Love did set his lips asunder,
Thus to speak in love and wonder:

Stella, sovereign of my joy,
Fair triumpher of annoy,                                   30
Stella, star of heavenly fire,
Stella, lodestar of desire,

Stella, in whose shining eyes
Are the lights of Cupid's skies,
Whose beams where they once are darted,                    35
Love therewith is straight imparted,

Stella, whose voice when it speaks
Senses all asunder breaks,
Stella, whose voice when it singeth
Angels to acquaintance bringeth,                           40

Stella, in whose body is
Writ each character of bliss,
Whose face all, all beauty passeth,
Save thy mind, which yet surpasseth:

Grant, O grant – but speech, alas,                         45
Fails me, fearing on to pass.

Grant, O me, what am I saying?
But no fault there is in praying.

Grant, O dear, on knees I pray
(Knees on ground he then did stay)                    50
That not I but, since I love you,
Time and place for me may move you.

Never season was more fit,
Never room more apt for it;
Smiling air allows my reason,                         55
These birds sing, Now use the season.

This small wind which so sweet is,
See how it the leaves doth kiss,
Each tree in his best attiring,
Sense of love to love inspiring.                      60

Love makes earth the water drink,
Love to earth makes water sink;
And if dumb things be so witty,
Shall a heavenly grace want pity?

There his hands in their speech fain                  65
Would have made tongue's language plain,
But her hands, his hands repelling,
Gave repulse all grace excelling.

Then she spake; her speech was such
As not ears but heart did touch,                      70
While such wise she love denièd
As yet love she signifièd.

Astrophil, said she, my love
Cease in these effects to prove.
Now be still, yet still believe me:                   75
Thy grief more than death would grieve me.

If that any thought in me
Can taste comfort but of thee,
Let me, fed with hellish anguish,
Joyless, hopeless, endless languish.                  80

If those eyes you praisèd be
Half so dear as you to me,
Let me home return stark blinded
Of those eyes, and blinder minded.

If to secret of my heart                              85
I do any wish impart
Where thou art not foremost placèd,
Be both wish and I defacèd.

55  *allows my reason* supports my case.       88  *defaced* disfigured or destroyed.
74  *prove* test.

If more may be said, I say
All my bliss in thee I lay; 90
If thou love, my love content thee,
For all love, all faith is meant thee.

Trust me while I thee deny;
In myself the smart I try.
Tyran honor doth thus use thee; 95
Stella's self might not refuse thee.

Therefore, dear, this no more move,
Lest, though I leave not thy love,
Which too deep in me is framèd,
I should blush when thou art namèd. 100

Therewithal away she went,
Leaving him so passion rent
With what she had done and spoken
That therewith my song is broken.

94  *try* feel.                    98  *I leave not thy love* I do not cease to love you.

## NINTH SONG

Go, my flock, go get you hence;
Seek a better place of feeding,
Where you may have some defense
Fro the storms in my breast breeding
And showers from mine eyes proceeding. 5

Leave a wretch in whom all woe
Can abide to keep no measure;
Merry flock, such one forgo
Unto whom mirth is displeasure,
Only rich in mischief's treasure. 10

Yet, alas, before you go,
Hear your woeful master's story,
Which to stones I else would show;
Sorrow only then hath glory
When tis excellently sorry. 15

Stella, fiercest shepherdess,
Fiercest but yet fairest ever,
Stella, whom O heavens do bless,
Tho against me she persever,
Tho I bliss inherit never: 20

Stella hath refusèd me,
Stella who more love hath provèd
In this caitiff heart to be
Than can in good ewes be movèd
Toward lambkins best belovèd. 25

Stella hath refusèd me;
Astrophil that so well servèd
In this pleasant spring must see,
While in pride flowers be preservèd,
Himself only winter-starvèd.                                    30

Why, alas, doth she then swear
That she loveth me so dearly,
Seeing me so long to bear
Coals of love that burn so clearly,
And yet leave me helpless merely?                               35

Is that love? Forsooth, I trow,
If I saw my good dog grievèd
And a help for him did know,
My love should not be believèd
But he were by me relievèd.                                     40

No, she hates me, wellaway,
Feigning love somewhat to please me;
For she knows, if she display
All her hate, death soon would seize me
And of hideous torments ease me.                                45

Then adieu, dear flocks, adieu;
But, alas, if in your straying
Heavenly Stella meet with you,
Tell her in your piteous blaying
Her poor slave's unjust decaying.                               50

49    *blaying* bleating.


## 87

When I was forced from Stella ever dear,
Stella food of my thoughts, heart of my heart,
Stella whose eyes make all my tempests clear,
By iron laws of duty to depart,
Alas, I found that she with me did smart,                       5
I saw that tears did in her eyes appear,
I saw that sighs her sweetest lips did part,
And her sad words my saddest sense did hear.
For me, I wept to see pearls scattered so,
I sighed her sighs and wailèd for her woe,                      10
Yet swam in joy such love in her was seen.
Thus while the effect most bitter was to me,
And nothing than the cause more sweet could be,
I had been vexed if vexed I had not been.


## 88

Out, traitor Absence; darest thou counsel me
From my dear captainess to run away
Because in brave array here marcheth she
That to win me oft shows a present pay?

3    *brave array* striking clothes.                4    *present pay* quick reward.

Is faith so weak? Or is such force in thee?                                   5
When sun is hid, can stars such beams display?
Cannot heaven's food, once felt, keep stomachs free
From base desire on earthly cates to prey?
Tush, Absence, while thy mists eclipse that light,
My orphan sense flies to the inward sight                                    10
Where memory sets forth the beams of love,
That where before heart loved and eyes did see,
In heart both sight and love now coupled be:
United powers make each the stronger prove.

8   *cates* culinary delicacies.

### 89

Now that of absence the most irksome night
With darkest shade doth overcome my day,
Since Stella's eyes, wont to give me my day,
Leaving my hemisphere, leave me in night,
Each day seems long, and longs for long-stayed night,   5
The night as tedious woos the approach of day;
Tired with the dusty toils of busy day,
Languished with horrors of the silent night,
Suffering the evils both of the day and night,
While no night is more dark than is my day,              10
Nor no day hath less quiet than my night,
With such bad mixture of my night and day
That living thus in blackest winter night,
I feel the flames of hottest summer day.

### 90

Stella, think not that I by verse seek fame
Who seek, who hope, who love, who live but thee,
Thine eyes my pride, thy lips mine history:
If thou praise not, all other praise is shame.
Nor so ambitious am I as to frame                        5
A nest for my young praise in laurel tree;
In truth I swear I wish not there should be
Graved in mine epitaph a poet's name.
Ne if I would, could I just title make
That any laud to me thereof should grow                  10
Without my plumes from others' wings I take;
For nothing from my wit or will doth flow,
Since all my words thy beauty doth indite,
And Love doth hold my hand and makes me write.

10   *laud* praise.                        13   *indite* represent.

### 91

Stella, while now by honor's cruel might
I am from you, light of my life, misled,
And that fair you, my sun, thus overspread
With absence' veil, I live in sorrow's night.

4   *absence'* absence's.

If this dark place yet show, like candlelight,                                    5
Some beauty's piece as amber-colored head,
Milk hands, rose cheeks, or lips more sweet, more red,
Or seeing-jets black, but in blackness bright:
They please, I do confess, they please mine eyes,
But why? Because of you they models be,                                           10
Models such be wood-globes of glistering skies.
Dear, therefore be not jealous over me
If you hear that they seem my heart to move;
Not them, O no, but you in them I love.

8  *seeing-jets* bits of jet that can see.          11  *wood-globes of glistering skies* wooden globes with the
                                                    constellations represented on them.

### 92

Be your words made (good sir) of Indian ware
That you allow me them by so small rate?
Or do you cutted Spartans imitate,
Or do you mean my tender ears to spare,
That to my questions you so total are                                             5
When I demand of phoenix Stella's state?
You say, forsooth, you left her well of late;
O God, think you that satisfies my care?
I would know whether she did sit or walk;
How clothed, how waited on, sighed she or smiled;                                 10
Whereof, with whom, how often did she talk;
With what pastime time's journey she beguiled;
If her lips deigned to sweeten my poor name.
Say all, and all well said, still say the same.

1  *of Indian ware* Imported from the Indies, and thus exotic          3  *cutted* curt. Spartans were famously laconic.
and expensive.                                                        5  *total* summary.
2  *by so small rate* in such small quantities.

TENTH SONG

O dear life, when shall it be
That mine eyes thine eyes may see,
And in them thy mind discover,
Whether absence have had force
Thy remembrance to divorce                                                        5
From the image of thy lover?

Of if I me self find not
After parting ought forgot
Nor debarred from beauty's treasure,
Let no tongue aspire to tell                                                      10
In what high joys I shall dwell;
Only thought aims at the pleasure.

Set to music by, among others, William Byrd in his *Songs of
Sundry Natures* (1589).

Thought therefore I will send thee
To take up the place for me;
Long I will not after tarry.                                    15
There unseen thou mayst be bold
Those fair wonders to behold
Which in them my hopes do carry.

Thought, see thou no place forbear;
Enter bravely everywhere,                                       20
Seize on all to her belonging.
But if thou wouldst guarded be,
Fearing her beams, take with thee
Strength of liking, rage of longing.

Think of that most grateful time                               25
When my leaping heart will climb
In my lips to have his biding,
There those roses for to kiss
Which do breathe a sugared bliss,
Opening rubies, pearls dividing.                               30

Think of my most princely power
When I blessèd shall devour
With my greedy, lickerous senses
Beauty, music, sweetness, love,
While she doth against me prove                                35
Her strong darts, but weak defenses.

Think, think of those dallyings
When, with dovelike murmurings,
With glad moaning passèd anguish,
We change eyes, and heart for heart                            40
Each to other do depart,
Joying till joy makes us languish.

O my thought, my thoughts surcease;
Thy delights my woes increase,
My life melts with too much thinking.                          45
Think no more, but die in me
Till thou shalt revivèd be,
At her lips my nectar drinking.

33  *lickerous* eager, wanton.                39  *passèd* that has gone beyond.

## 93

O fate, O fault, O curse, child of my bliss,
What sobs can give words grace, my grief to show?
What ink is black enough to paint my woe?
Through me, wretch me, even Stella vexèd is.
Yet Truth (if caitiff's breath may call thee), this       5
Witness with me, that my foul stumbling so
From carelessness did in no manner grow,

7  *carelessness* lack of concern.

But wit confused with too much care did miss.
And do I then myself this vain scuse give?
I have (live I and know this) harmèd thee;                      10
Though worlds quit me, shall I me self forgive?
Only with pains my pains thus easèd be,
That all thy hurts in my heart's wrack I read.
I cry thy sighs, my dear, thy tears I bleed.

**8** *miss* miss the mark.                    **11** *quit* acquit.

## 94

Grief, find the words, for thou hast made my brain
So dark with misty vapors, which arise
From out thy heavy mold, that in-bent eyes
Can scarce discern the shape of mine own pain.
Do thou, then (for thou canst), do thou complain          5
For my poor soul, which now that sickness tries
Which even to sense sense of itself denies,
Though harbingers of Death lodge there his train.
Or if thy love of plaint yet mine forbears,
As of a caitiff worthy so to die,                              10
Yet wail thyself, and wail with causeful tears,
That though in wretchedness thy life doth lie,
Yet growest more wretched than thy nature bears
By being placed in such a wretch as I.

**6** *tries* experiences.         **8** *harbingers* Agents sent ahead to secure lodgings for an important personage.

## 95

Yet Sighs, dear Sighs, indeed true friends you are
That do not leave your least friend at the worst,
But as you with my breast I oft have nursed,
So grateful now you wait upon my care.
Faint coward Joy no longer tarry dare,                        5
Seeing Hope yield when this woe strake him first;
Delight protests he is not for the accursed,
Though oft himself my mate in arms he sware.
Nay, Sorrow comes with such main rage, that he
Kills his own children, Tears, finding that they             10
By love were made apt to consort with me.
Only true Sighs, you do not go away;
Thank may you have for such a thankful part,
Thank worthiest yet when you shall break my heart.

## 96

Thought, with good cause thou likest so well the night,
Since kind or chance gives both one livery:
Both sadly black, both blackly darkened be,
Night barred from sun, thou from thy own sunlight.
Silence in both displays his sullen might;                    5

**2** *kind* nature.

Slow heaviness in both holds one degree,
That full of doubts, thou of perplexity;
Thy tears express night's native moisture right.
In both a mazeful solitariness:
In night of sprites the ghastly powers do stir,        10
In thee or sprites or sprited ghastliness.
But, but (alas) night's side the odds hath far:
For that at length yet doth invite some rest;
Thou, though still tired, yet still dost it detest.

11   *sprited* causes by spirits.         12   *the odds hath far* has a great advantage.

## 97

Dian, that fain would cheer her friend, the Night,
Shows her oft at the full her fairest face,
Bringing with her those starry nymphs whose chase
From heavenly standing hits each mortal wight.
But ah, poor Night, in love with Phoebus' light,        5
And endlessly despairing of his grace,
Herself (to show no other joy hath place)
Silent and sad in mourning weeds doth dight.
Even so (alas) a lady, Dian's peer,
With choice delights and rarest company        10
Would fain drive clouds from out my heavy cheer;
But woe is me, though joy itself were she,
She could not show my blind brain ways of joy
While I despair my sun's sight to enjoy.

1   *Dian* goddess of chastity, of the moon, and of the hunt.      4   *standing* shooting position (a term from archery).
3   *chase* hunting.          5   *Phoebus* the sun.
                  8   *weeds* clothes.

## 98

Ah bed, the field where joy's peace some do see,
The field where all my thoughts to war be trained,
How is thy grace by my strange fortune stained,
How thy lee shores by my sighs stormèd be!
With sweet soft shades thou oft invitest me        5
To steal some rest, but, wretch, I am constrained
(Spurred with love's spur, though galled and shortly reined
With care's hard hand) to turn and toss in thee.
While the black horrors of the silent night
Paint woe's black face so lively to my sight,        10
That tedious leisure marks each wrinkled line;
But when Aurora leads out Phoebus' dance,
Mine eyes then only wink, for spite perchance
That worms should have their sun and I want mine.

7   *galled* The 1598 edition reads "gold."      12   *Aurora* goddess of the dawn.
11  *marks* notes. The 1598 edition reads "makes."

## 99

When far-spent night persuades each mortal eye
To whom nor art nor nature granteth light

To lay his then mark-wanting shafts of sight
Closed with their quivers in sleep's armory,
With windows ope then most my mind doth lie,                    5
Viewing the shape of darkness and delight,
Takes in that sad hue which with the inward night
Of his mazed powers keeps perfit harmony.
But when birds charm, and that sweet air which is
Morn's messenger with rose enameled skies                      10
Calls each wight to salute the flower of bliss,
In tomb of lids then buried are mine eyes,
Forced by their lord, who is ashamed to find
Such light in sense with such a darkened mind.

3  *his* its (referring to "each mortal eye").  *mark-wanting*       8  *perfit* perfect.
*shafts of sight* eye-beams that in the dark have no target at
which to shoot.

### 100

O tears, no tears, but rain from beauty's skies,
Making those lilies and those roses grow
Which aye most fair, now more than most fair show
While graceful pity beauty beautifies.
O honied sighs which from that breast do rise                  5
Whose pants do make unspilling cream to flow,
Winged with whose breath so pleasing zephyrs blow
As can refresh the hell where my soul fries.
O plaints conserved in such a sugared phrase
That eloquence itself envies your praise,                      10
While sobbed out words a perfect music give.
Such tears, sighs, plaints no sorrow is, but joy;
Or if such heavenly signs must prove annoy,
All mirth farewell, let me in sorrow live.

6  *pants* panting breath.                    9  *sugared* The 1598 edition reads "surgèd."

### 101

Stella is sick, and in that sickbed lies
Sweetness which breathes and pants as oft as she;
And Grace, sick too, such fine conclusions tries
That Sickness brags itself best graced to be.
Beauty is sick, but sick in so fair guise                      5
That in that paleness Beauty's white we see;
And Joy, which is inseparate from those eyes,
Stella now learns (strange case) to weep in thee.
Love moves thy pain, and like a faithful page,
As thy looks stir, comes up and down to make                   10
All folks prest at thy will thy pain to assuage;
Nature with care sweats for her darling's sake,
Knowing worlds pass ere she enough can find
Of such heaven-stuff to clothe so heavenly a mind.

3  *such fine conclusions tries* makes such an excellent test of its    texts other than the 1598 edition) in the next line. Some
abilities.                                                              editors have simplified the syntax by emending the first
6  *white* purity.                                                      "moves" to "moans."
9  Probably inverted word order, with "Love" the object of            11  *prest* ready.
"moves" in this line and the subject of "comes" ("runs" in

## 102

Where be those roses gone which sweetened so our eyes?
Where those red cheeks which oft with fair increase did frame
The height of honor in the kindly badge of shame?
Who hath the crimson weeds stolen from my morning skies?
How doth the color fade of those vermilion dyes          5
Which Nature self did make, and self ingrained the same?
I would know by what right this paleness overcame
That hue whose force my heart still unto thralldom ties.
Galen's adoptive sons, who by a beaten way
Their judgments hackney on, the fault on sickness lay,          10
But feeling proof makes me say they mistake it far;
It is but love which makes his paper perfit white,
To write therein more fresh the story of delight,
While beauty's reddest ink Venus for him doth stir.

3  *kindly* natural.
4  *weeds* clothes.
9  *Galen's adoptive sons* Contemporary followers of Galen, Greek author of the most influential medical treatise surviving from antiquity.

10  *hackney on* ride like an old workhorse.
11  *feeling proof* emotional experience.
12  *perfit* perfectly.

## 103

O happy Thames that didst my Stella bear,
I saw thyself, with many a smiling line,
Upon thy cheerful face joy's livery wear,
While those fair planets on thy streams did shine.
The boat for joy could not to dance forbear,          5
While wanton winds, with beauties so divine
Ravished, stayed not till in her golden hair
They did themselves (O sweetest prison) twine.
And fain those Aeol's youth there would their stay
Have made, but, forced by nature still to fly,          10
First did with puffing kiss those locks' display.
She, so disheveled, blushed; from window I
With sight thereof cried out, O fair disgrace,
Let honor self to thee grant highest place.

9  *Aeol's youth* offspring of Aeolus, god of the winds.

## 104

Envious wits, what hath been mine offense,
That with such poisonous care my looks you mark,
That to each word, nay, sigh of mine you hark,
As grudging me my sorrow's eloquence?
Ah, is it not enough that I am thence,          5
Thence, so far thence, that scarcely any spark
Of comfort dare come to this dungeon dark,
Where rigorous exile locks up all my sense?
But if I by a happy window pass,
If I but stars upon mine armor bear,          10

9  *happy window* Stella's window, or one at which she has been known to appear.

10  A coded declaration of chivalric devotion, eagerly deciphered by the witty.

Sick, thirsty, glad (though but of empty glass),
Your moral notes straight my hid meaning tear
From out my ribs, and, puffing, proves that I
Do Stella love. Fools, who doth it deny?

11    *glad (though but of empty glass)* glad, even at passing a
window at which Stella does not appear.

ELEVENTH SONG

Who is it that this dark night
Underneath my window plaineth?
It is one who, from thy sight
Being (ah) exiled, disdaineth
Every other vulgar light.                                          5

Why, alas, and are you he?
Be not yet those fancies changèd?
Dear, when you find change in me,
Though from me you be estrangèd,
Let my change to ruin be.                                          10

Well, in absence this will die;
Leave to see, and leave to wonder.
Absence sure will help, if I
Can learn how myself to sunder
From what in my heart doth lie.                                    15

But time will these thoughts remove;
Time doth work what no man knoweth.
Time doth as the subject prove,
With time still the affection groweth
In the faithful turtledove.                                        20

What if you new beauties see?
Will not they stir new affection?
I will think they pictures be
(Image like of saint's perfection),
Poorly counterfeiting thee.                                        25

But your reason's purest light
Bids you leave such minds to nourish.
Dear, do reason no such spite;
Never doth thy beauty flourish
More than in my reason's sight.                                    30

But the wrongs love bears will make
Love at length leave undertaking.
No, the more fools it do shake

Set to music by Thomas Morley in his *First Book of Airs*
(1600).

12    *Leave* cease.

18    The effect of time depends on the character of the
object in question.
27    *minds* ideas.

In a ground of so firm making,
Deeper still they drive the stake. 35

Peace, I think that some give ear;
Come no more, lest I get anger.
Bliss, I will my bliss forbear,
Fearing (sweet) you to endanger,
But my soul shall harbor there. 40

Well, be gone, be gone, I say,
Lest that Argus' eyes perceive you.
O unjustest fortune's sway
Which can make me thus to leave you,
And from louts to run away. 45

42 *Argus* Creature with multiple eyes, set by Juno to stand     43 *unjustest* The 1598 edition reads "unjust."
guard over one of Jupiter's mistresses.

## 105

Unhappy sight, and hath she vanished by
So near, in so good time, so free a place?
Dead glass, dost thou thy object so embrace
As what my heart still sees thou canst not spy?
I swear, by her I love and lack, that I 5
Was not in fault, who bent thy dazzling race
Only unto the heaven of Stella's face,
Counting but dust what in the way did lie.
But cease, mine eyes, your tears do witness well
That you guiltless thereof your nectar missed; 10
Cursed be the page from whence the bad torch fell,
Cursed be the night which did your strife resist,
Cursed be the coachman which did drive so fast
With no worse curse than absence makes me taste.

3 *Dead glass* Variously interpreted: Astrophil's eye, his tears,
a telescope, the window through which he might have caught
a glimpse of Stella.

## 106

O absent presence, Stella is not here;
False, flattering hope that with so fair a face
Bare me in hand that in this orphan place
Stella, I say my Stella should appear.
What sayst thou now? Where is that dainty cheer 5
Thou toldst mine eyes should help their famished case?
But thou art gone, now that self-felt disgrace
Doth make me most to wish thy comfort near.
But here I do store of fair ladies meet,
Who may with charm of conversation sweet 10
Make in my heavy mold new thoughts to grow;
Sure they prevail as much with me as he
That bade his friend, but then new maimed, to be
Merry with him and not think of his woe.

3 *Bare me in hand* deceived me.

### 107

Stella, since thou so right a princess art
Of all the powers which life bestows on me,
That ere by them ought undertaken be,
They first resort unto that sovereign part:
Sweet, for a while give respite to my heart,                    5
Which pants as though it still should leap to thee,
And on my thoughts give thy lieutenancy
To this great cause, which needs both use and art;
And as a queen, who from her presence sends
Whom she employs, dismiss from thee my wit,                     10
Till it have wrought what thy own will attends.
On servant's shame oft master's blame doth sit;
O let not fools in me thy works reprove,
And scorning say, See what it is to love.

11    *attends* directs.


### 108

When sorrow (using mine own fire's might)
Melts down his lead into my boiling breast,
Through that dark furnace, to my heart oppressed,
There shines a joy from thee, my only light.
But soon as thought of thee breeds my delight                   5
And my young soul flutters to thee, his nest,
Most rude despair, my daily unbidden guest,
Clips straight my wings, straight wraps me in his night,
And makes me then bow down my head and say,
Ah, what doth Phoebus' gold that wretch avail                    10
Whom iron doors do keep from use of day?
So strangely, alas, thy works in me prevail
That in my woes for thee thou art my joy,
And in my joys for thee my only annoy.

10    *Phoebus' gold* daylight.

# Anonymous

## A New Courtly Sonnet of the Lady Greensleeves

The earliest known and probably the original lyrics to a perennially popular tune, this poem was printed in *A Handful of Pleasant Delights* in 1584, though it had been registered four years earlier. The general topic is the Petrarchan one of melancholy unrequited love, but without the aristocratic refinement of the high tradition; chivalric enterprise is hinted at in the second verse ("I have both wagèd life and land"), but by the third it is clear that the real complaint is how much it has cost to keep this lady in good clothes – good enough, we hear later, for "burgess' wives." The bulk of the poem is a catalogue of what the singer has bought for her, a *blazon* of purchases. For a critical old-spelling text, see *A Handful of Pleasant Delights*, ed. Hyder Edward Rollins (Cambridge, MA: Harvard University Press, 1924).

Alas, my love, ye do me wrong
To cast me off discourteously;
And I have lovèd you so long,
Delighting in your company.

Greensleeves was all my joy,     5
Greensleeves was my delight,
Greensleeves was my heart of gold,
And who but Lady Greensleeves?

I have been ready at your hand
To grant whatever you would crave;    10
I have both wagèd life and land
Your love and good will for to have.

Greensleeves was all my joy, &c.

I bought thee kerchers to thy head
That were wrought fine and gallantly;    15
I kept thee both at board and bed,
Which cost my purse well favoredly.

Greensleeves was all my joy, &c.

I bought thee petticoats of the best,
The cloth so fine as fine might be;    20
I gave thee jewels for thy chest,
And all this cost I spent on thee.

Greensleeves was all my joy, &c.

Thy smock of silk, both fair and white,
With gold embroidered gorgeously,    25
Thy petticoat of sendal right,
And thus I bought thee gladly.

---

11 *wagèd* wagered.
14 *kerchers* kerchiefs.

17 *well favoredly* handsomely.
26 *sendal* fine silken material.

Greensleeves was all my joy, &c.

Thy girdle of gold so red,
With pearls bedeckèd sumptuously:                    30
The like no other lasses had,
And yet thou wouldst not love me.

Greensleeves was all my joy, &c.

Thy purse and eke thy gay gilt knives,
Thy pincase gallant to the eye:                      35
No better wore the burgess' wives,
And yet thou wouldst not love me.

Greensleeves was all my joy, &c.

Thy crimson stockings all of silk,
With gold all wrought above the knee,                40
Thy pumps as white as was the milk,
And yet thou wouldst not love me.

Greensleeves was all my joy, &c.

Thy gown was of the grossy green,
Thy sleeves of satin hanging by,                     45
Which made thee be our harvest queen;
And yet thou wouldst not love me.

Greensleeves was all my joy, &c.

Thy garters fringèd with the gold
And silver aglets hanging by,                        50
Which made thee blithe for to behold;
And yet thou wouldst not love me.

Greensleeves was all my joy, &c.

My gayest gelding I thee gave,
To ride wherever likèd thee;                         55
No lady ever was so brave,
And yet thou wouldst not love me.

Greensleeves was all my joy, &c.

My men were clothèd all in green,
And they did ever wait on thee;                      60
All this was gallant to be seen,
And yet thou wouldst not love me.

Greensleeves was all my joy, &c.

---

**35** *gallant* gorgeous.                    **50** *aglets* metal tags attached to lace.
**44** *grossy* dense; conceivably a misprint for "grassy."    **56** *brave* splendid.

They set thee up, they took thee down,
They served thee with humility;                              65
Thy foot might not once touch the ground,
And yet thou wouldst not love me.

Greensleeves was all my joy, &c.

For every morning when thou rose,
I sent thee dainties orderly                                 70
To cheer thy stomach from all woes,
And yet thou wouldst not love me.

Greensleeves was all my joy, &c.

Thou couldst desire no earthly thing
But still thou hadst it readily;                             75
Thy music still to play and sing,
And yet thou wouldst not love me.

Greensleeves was all my joy, &c.

And who did pay for all this gear
That thou didst spend when pleasèd thee?                     80
Even I that am rejected here,
And thou disdainst to love me.

Greensleeves was all my joy, &c.

Well, I will pray to God on high
That thou my constancy mayst see                            85
And that yet once before I die
Thou wilt vouchsafe to love me.

Greensleeves was all my joy, &c.

Greensleeves, now farewell, adieu,
God I pray to prosper thee;                                  90
For I am still thy lover true,
Come once again and love me.

Greensleeves was all my joy, &c.

70   *dainties* fine foods.   *orderly* regularly.

# Adonis

When Venus first did see
Adonis dead to be,
With woeful tattered hair
And cheeks so wan and sear,
The wingèd Loves she bade                                    5

From *Six Idyllia . . . Chosen out of the Right Famous Sicilian Poet Theocritus* (1588): a translation of a Greek poem (in anacreontics) known in the sixteenth century as Idyll 31 of Theocritus, though no longer considered his work.

The boar should straight be had;
Forthwith like birds they fly
And through the wood they hie.
The woeful beast they find,
And him with cords they bind.                    10
One with a rope before
Doth lead the captive boar;
Another on his back
Doth make his bow to crack.
The beast went wretchedly,                         15
For Venus horribly
He feared, who thus him cursed,
Of all the beasts the worst,
Didst thou this thigh so wound?
Didst thou my love confound?                       20
The beast thus spake in fear,
Venus, to thee I swear,
By thee and husband thine
And by these bands of mine
And by these hunters all,                          25
Thy husband fair and tall
I minded not to kill;
But, as an image still,
I him beheld for love,
Which made me forward shove                        30
His thigh that naked was,
Thinking to kiss, alas,
And that hath hurt me thus.
Wherefore these teeth, Venus,
Or punish or cut out;                              35
Why bear I in my snout
These needless teeth about?
If these may not suffice,
Cut off my chaps likewise!
To ruth he Venus moves,                            40
And she commands the Loves
His bands for to untie.
After, he came not nigh
The wood, but at her will
He followed Venus still;                           45
And, coming to the fire,
He burnt up his desire.

20    *confound* destroy.

26–33    The Italian poet Giambattista Marino expands on this conceit at the climax of his immensely popular poem *Adone* (1623); see 18.94–7.

39    *chaps* jaws.

47    This puzzling line translates a metrically impossible reading in the surviving Greek text. In a headnote, the translator takes it to refer to "the burning of the boar's amorous teeth."

# Robert Greene (1558–1592)

One of England's first professional writers, Greene led a life that became a moral exemplum; the poem given here is its first-person gloss. After a Cambridge education and a tour of the Continent, he left a wife and child in Lincolnshire and was in London by 1586, writing plays and publishing prose fiction and guides to the Elizabethan underworld of petty thieves and con-artists. Sporting a long, pointed red beard, he made his mark on the town and appears to have been successful enough as a writer, but died in a squalor that became famous. *A Groatsworth of Wit* appeared in the year of his death (under his own name, though some scholars think it the work of his friend Henry Chettle). It presents itself as the cautionary story of one "Roberto": "his immeasurable drinking had made him the perfect image of the dropsy, and the loathsome scourge of lust tyrannized in his bones; lying in extreme poverty, and having nothing to pay but chalk [credit], which now his host accepted not for current, this miserable man lay comfortlessly languishing, having but one groat left." At which point the pretense of authorial distance drops – "Hereafter suppose me the same Roberto . . . Greene will send you now his groatsworth of wit" – and the poem follows.

Its message of instructive repentance shares space with ongoing professional combat, including the famous attack on Shakespeare: "an upstart crow, beautified with our feathers . . . in his own conceit the only Shake-scene in a country." The point of the attack remains cryptic, but it is usually taken to involve a charge of plagiarism. Some twenty years later, one of Greene's romances, *Pandosto* (1588), became the principal source for Shakespeare's *The Winter's Tale*.

## From *A Groatsworth of Wit, Bought with a Million of Repentance*

Deceiving world, that with alluring toys
Hast made my life the subject of thy scorn,
And scornest now to lend thy fading joys
To length my life, whom friends have left forlorn,
How well are they that die ere they be born      5
And never see thy sleights, which few men shun
Till unawares they helpless are undone.

Oft have I sung of Love and of his fire,
But now I find that poet was advised
Which made full feasts increasers of desire,      10
And proves weak love was with the poor despised.
For when the life with food is not sufficed,
What thought of love, what motion of delight,
What pleasance can proceed from such a wight?

Witness my want, the murderer of my wit.      15
My ravished sense, of wonted fury reft,
Wants such conceit as should in poems fit,
Set down the sorrow wherein I am left.
But therefore have high heavens their gifts bereft,
Because so long they lent them me to use      20
And I so long their bounty did abuse.

O, that a year were granted me to live,
And for that year my former wits restored.

---

4   *length* lengthen.
9   *advised* well-informed.
12   *sufficed* satisfied.

16   *reft* deprived.
17   *Wants* lacks.

What rules of life, what counsel would I give?
How should my sin with sorrow be deplored?          25
But I must die, of every man abhorred.
Time loosely spent will not again be won;
My time is loosely spent, and I undone.

# Chidiock Tichborne (1558?–1586)

Born to a well-established and wealthy Catholic family in Hampshire, Tichborne was involved in 1586 in a plot to assassinate Elizabeth and place Mary Stuart on the throne. Sir Francis Walsingham's intelligence network knew of the plot as it developed; Tichborne was arrested along with eleven others, and executed by hanging, drawing, and quartering. Witnesses to his execution were said to be struck by his youth and beauty. On the scaffold he protested that he had been seduced by the "blind zeal and persuasion" of others, expressed gratitude for Elizabeth's safety, and cast his story as "a warning to all young gentlemen": "Here you see a company of young men (and that *generosi*,

too) playing a woeful tragedy. . . . So we young men had given us of God even all the pleasures of the world, living as it were the lusty gallants of this land, sometime in the city, sometime in the field – walking, talking, feasting, sporting. Yet one thing undid us all, as you see here the spectacle." His "Lament" was, according to one of Walsingham's agents, composed three days before his execution, and appeared in print not long after.

*Edition*: Richard S. M. Hirsch, "The Works of Chidiock Tichborne," *English Literary Renaissance*, 16 (1986), 303–18, and 17 (1987), 276–7.

## Tichborne's Lament

My prime of youth is but a frost of cares,
My feast of joy is but a dish of pain,
My crop of corn is but a field of tares,
And all my good is but vain hope of gain.
The day is gone, and yet I saw no sun;                     5
And now I live, and now my life is done.

The spring is past, and yet it hath not sprung.
The fruit is dead, and yet the leaves are green.
My youth is gone, and yet I am but young.
I saw the world, and yet I was not seen.                  10
My thread is cut, and yet it was not spun;
And now I live, and now my life is done.

I sought my death, and found it in my womb.
I looked for life, and saw it was a shade.
I trod the earth, and knew it was my tomb;                15
And now I die, and now I am but made.
The glass is full, and now the glass is run;
And now I live, and now my life is done.

Stanzas from this poem were printed with musical settings in John Mundy's *Songs and Psalms* (1594), Michael East's *Madrigals* (1604), and Richard Alison's *An Hour's Recreation in Music* (1606).

13  *my womb* The Catholic faith in which he was raised.
17  *glass* hour-glass.

# Thomas Lodge (1558?–1625)

The son of a London grocer and one-term Lord Mayor, Lodge was educated at the Merchant Taylors' School and Oxford; in 1578 he entered Lincoln's Inn, and during the 1580s and 1590s he was part of the literary scene in London. In addition to the long poem given here, he published numerous pamphlets, a sonnet sequence, two plays (one co-authored with Robert Greene), and prose romances (*Rosalind*, which appeared in 1590, became the source for Shakespeare's *As You Like It*); he sailed on expeditions to the Azores and Brazil, and found himself in prison at least once. In the late 1590s he converted to Catholicism and began a second career as a medical doctor; despite the legal difficulties connected to his conversion and the need to spend time on the Continent, he eventually established himself as a prominent London physician. His complete translation of the prose works of the Roman moralist and philosopher Seneca – the first in English – appeared in 1614.

*Scylla's Metamorphosis*, which appeared in 1589, was the first of a new genre of mythological verse romances, and set an influential pattern. The story is taken from Ovid's *Metamorphoses* (13.898–14.74), though changed in certain details and, most of all, extravagantly expanded. The expansion involves little in the way of new incident – for most of its length Lodge's narrative as such barely moves – but is rather a matter of longer speeches and, most strikingly, a great increase in personnel. The original story is one

of three characters, and ends happily for none of them. Lodge makes his main scene a court of goddesses and sea-nymphs (at which new figures keep arriving) who hear the unhappy Glaucus out and surround him with endless solicitude. Ovid's Glaucus finds no such audience, but his Renaissance descendant lives in a time when the role of the unrequited male lover is a glamorous one; complaining of his lot, he finds, charms every woman around except the refractory object of his desire. So great is their care that in due course this community rises up in group rage against the one woman who dares do wrong by him; Glaucus ends up feeling blithe and cured. The story is also framed by that of the male narrator's own encounter with Glaucus and his discovery of their common plight; by the end of the poem, he has gained a sense of literary vocation, both to tell Glaucus's story and to direct his own life to the pursuit of literary fame. Lodge's poem effects a cheerful rearrangement of the melancholy solitude of lyric Petrarchism into lush narrative fantasy.

*Edition*: There has been no comprehensive edition of Lodge's work since the nineteenth century; an old-spelling text of *Scylla's Metamorphosis* can be found in *Elizabethan Minor Epics*, ed. Elizabeth Story Donno (New York: Columbia University Press, 1963), and *Elizabethan Narrative Verse*, ed. Nigel Alexander (Cambridge, MA: Harvard University Press, 1968).

## Scylla's Metamorphosis, interlaced with the unfortunate love of Glaucus

### 1

Walking alone (all only full of grief)
Within a thicket near to Isis' flood,
Weeping my wants, and wailing scant relief,
Wringing mine arms (as one with sorrow wood),
The piteous streams, relenting at my moan,
Withdrew their tides and stayed to hear me groan.

### 2

From forth the channel, with a sorrowing cry,
The sea-god Glaucus (with his hallowed hairs
Wet in the tears of his sad mother's dye)
With piteous looks before my face appears;
For whom the nymphs a mossy coat did frame,
Embroidered with his Scylla's heavenly name.

1.4   *wood* mad.

### 3

And as I sat under a willow tree,
The lovely honor of fair Thetis' bower
Reposed his head upon my faintful knee;
And when my tears had ceased their stormy shower,
He dried my cheeks, and then bespake him so
As when he wailed I straight forgot my woe.

### 4

Infortunate, why wandereth thy content
From forth his scope, as wearied of itself?
Thy books have schooled thee from this fond repent,
And thou canst talk by proof of wavering pelf;
Unto the world such is inconstancy
As sap to tree, as apple to the eye.

### 5

Mark how the morn in roseate color shines,
And straight with clouds the sunny tract is clad;
Then see how pomp through wax and wain declines
From high to low, from better to the bad.
Take moist from sea, take color from his kind
Before the world devoid of change thou find.

### 6

With secret eye look on the earth awhile;
Regard the changes Nature forceth there.
Behold the heavens, whose course all sense beguile.
Respect thyself, and thou shalt find it clear
That, infantlike, thou art become a youth,
And, youth forspent, a wretchèd age ensueth.

### 7

In searching then the schoolmen's cunning notes
Of heaven, of earth, of flowers, of springing trees,
Of herbs, of metal, and of Thetis' floats,
Of laws and nurture kept among the bees,
Conclude and know times change by course of fate,
Then mourn no more, but moan my hapless state.

### 8

Here gan he pause, and shake his heavy head,
And fold his arms, and then unfold them straight.
Fain would he speak, but tongue was charmed by dread,
Whilst I that saw what woes did him await,
Comparing his mishaps and moan with mine,
Gan smile for joy and dry his drooping eyen.

---

3.2 *Thetis' bower* the sea.
4.1 *content* contentment.
4.2 *scope* goal.
4.3–4 Your books have taught you the folly of such lamenting, and you can talk from experience of the unreliability of possessions.

6.3 *whose course all sense beguile* whose movement defeats all attempts at understanding.
6.4 *Respect* observe.
7.3 *Thetis' floats* the ocean's waves.
8.4 *him await* wait upon him.
8.6 *eyen* eyes.

### 9

But (lo) a wonder: from the channel's glide
A sweet melodious noise of music rose
That made the stream to dance a pleasant tide;
The weeds and sallows near the bank that grows
Gan sing, as when the calmest winds accord
To greet with balmy breath the fleeting ford.

### 10

Upon the silver bosom of the stream
First gan fair Themis shake her amber locks,
Whom all the nymphs that wait on Neptune's realm
Attended from the hollow of the rocks.
In brief, while these rare paragons assemble,
The watery world to touch their teats do tremble.

### 11

Footing it featly on the grassy ground,
These damsels, circling with their brightsome fairs
The love-sick god and I, about us wound
Like stars that Ariadne's crown repairs.
Who once hath seen or pride of morn or day
Would deem all pomp within their cheeks did play.

### 12

Naïs, fair nymph, with Bacchus' ivory touch
Gan tune a passion with such sweet reports,
And every word, note, sigh, and pause was such,
And every cadence fed with such consorts
As, were the Delian harper bent to hear,
Her stately strains might tempt his curious ear.

### 13

Of love (God wot) the lovely nymph complained,
But so of love as forcèd Love to love her;
And even in Love such furious love remained
As, searching out his powerful shaft to prove her,
He found his quiver emptied of the best,
And felt the arrow sticking in his breast.

### 14

Under a poplar Themis did repose her,
And from a briar a sweetful branch did pluck,
When midst the briar, ere she could scarce suppose her,
A nightingale gan sing; but woe the luck!
The branch so near her breast, while she did quick her
To turn her head, on sudden gan to prick her.

9.1  *glide* stream.
10.2  *Themis* The goddess of law, daughter to Uranus and Gaia and second wife to Jupiter; the context suggests that Lodge may be assimilating her to her sister Tethys, wife to Oceanus.
11.1  *featly* nimbly.

11.2  *fairs* beauties.
11.4  *Ariadne's crown* The constellation Corona. *repairs* adorns.
12.5  *Delian harper* Apollo.
13.4  *prove* test.
14.5  *quick her* bestir herself.

15

Whilst smiling Clore midst her envious blushes
Gan blame her fear, and prettily said thus:
Worse pricks than these are found among these bushes,
And yet such pricks are scarcely feared of us.
Nay, soft (said Chelis), pricks do make birds sing,
But pricks in ladies' bosoms often sting.

16

Thus jest they on the nightingale's report
And on the prickle of the eglantine,
On Naïs' song, and all the whole consort
In public this sweet sentence did assign:
That while some smile, some sigh through change of time,
Some smart, some sport amidst their youthly prime.

17

Such wreaths as bound the Theban's ivory brow,
Such gay-tricked garlands plait these jolly dames.
The flowers themselves whenas the nymphs gan bow
Gan veil their crests in honor of their names,
And smiled their sweet and wooed with so much glee
As if they said, Sweet nymph, come gather me.

18

But pensive Glaucus, passionate with painings,
Amidst their revel thus began his ruth:
Nymphs, fly these groves late blasted with my plainings,
For cruel Scylla nill regard my truth,
And leave us two consorted in our groanings
To register with tears our bitter moanings.

19

The floods do fail their course to see our cross,
The fields forsake their green to hear our grief,
The rocks will weep whole springs to mark our loss,
The hills relent to store our scant relief,
The air repines, the pensive birds are heavy,
The trees to see us pained no more are leafy.

20

Ay me, the shepherds let their flocks want feeding,
And flocks to see their paly face are sorry;
The nymphs to spy the flocks and shepherds needing
Prepare their tears to hear our tragic story,
Whilst we, surprised with grief, cannot disclose them,
With sighing wish the world for to suppose them.

16.4  *sentence* meaning.
17.1  *the Theban* Hercules.
17.3  *bow* bend.

18.4  *nill* will not.
19.4  *relent* melt.  *store* reinforce.
20.2  *paly* pale.

### 21

He that hath seen the sweet Arcadian boy
Wiping the purple from his forcèd wound,
His pretty tears betokening his annoy,
His sighs, his cries, his falling on the ground,
The echoes ringing from the rocks his fall,
The trees with tears reporting of his thrall;

### 22

And Venus starting at her love-mate's cry,
Forcing her birds to haste her chariot on;
And full of grief at last with piteous eye
Seen where all pale with death he lay alone,
Whose beauty quailed as wont the lilies droop
When wasteful winter winds do make them stoop;

### 23

Her dainty hand addressed to daw her dear,
Her roseal lip allied to his pale cheek,
Her sighs, and then her looks and heavy cheer,
Her bitter threats, and then her passions meek;
How on his senseless corpse she lay a-crying,
As if the boy were then but new a-dying –

### 24

He that hath viewed Angelica the fair
Bestraught with fancy near the Caspian springs,
Renting the tresses of her golden hair;
How on her harp with piteous notes she sings
Of Roland's ruth, of Medor's false depart,
Sighing each rest from center of her heart;

### 25

How now she writes upon a beechen bough
Her Medor's name, and bedlam-like again
Calls all the heaven to witness of his vow,
And straight again begins a mournful strain;
And how in thought of her true faith forsooken
He fled her bowers, and how his league was broken;

### 26

Ay me, who marks her harp hang up again
Upon the willows watered with her tears,
And how she rues to read her Roland's pain

---

**21.1** *Arcadian boy* From the context evidently Venus's love Adonis, though he was not Arcadian.
**21.3** *annoy* pain.
**23.1** *daw* rouse.
**23.2** *roseal* rosy.
**24.1** *Angelica* The beautiful woman from east Asia who is pursued by many of the knights in *Orlando Innamorato* and *Orlando Furioso*, the popular Italian *romanzi* by, respectively, Matteo Maria Boiardo and Lodovico Ariosto; Sir John Harington's complete English translation of the latter was published in 1591. The references in the lines that follow imply either ignorance or deliberate garbling on Lodge's part: Medor (Medoro), the wounded foot soldier whom Angelica eventually marries, does not desert her; she does not come to pity the suffering that Roland (Orlando) undergoes for being in love with her; and her musical talent is never in evidence.
**24.2** *Bestraught* distraught. *fancy* desire.
**24.3** *Renting* rending.
**24.5** *depart* departure.
**24.6** *rest* musical pause.
**25.2** *bedlam-like* like a madwoman.

When but the shadow of his name appears,
Would make more plainings from his eyes to flee
Than tears distill from amber-weeping tree –

27

He that hath known the passionate mishaps
That near Olympus fair Lucina felt
Whenas her Latium love her fancy traps,
How with suspect her inward soul doth melt,
Or marked the Morn her Cephalus complaining,
May then recount the course of all our paining.

28

But tender nymphs, to you belongs no teen;
Then favor me in flying from this bower,
Whereas but care and thought of crosses been.
Leave me that lose myself through fancy's power,
Through fancy's power which, had I leave to lose it,
No fancy then should see me for to choose it.

29

When you are fled, the heaven shall lower for sorrow,
The day o'ercast shall be betime with sable,
The air from sea such streaming showers shall borrow
As earth to bear the brunt shall not be able,
And ships shall safely sail whereas beforn
The ploughman watched the reaping of his corn.

30

Go you in peace to Neptune's watery sound;
No more may Glaucus play him with so pretty,
But shun resort where solace nill be found
And plain my Scylla's pride and want of pity.
Alas, sweet nymphs, my godhead's all in vain
For why this breast includes immortal pain.

31

Scylla hath eyes, but too sweet eyes hath Scylla.
Scylla hath hands, fair hands, but coy in touching.
Scylla in wit surpasseth grave Sibylla.
Scylla hath words, but words well stored with grudging.
Scylla a saint in look, no saint in scorning:
Look saint-like, Scylla, lest I die with mourning.

32

Alas, why talk I? Sea-god, cease to mourn her,
For in her Nay my joys are ever ceasing.
Cease life or love, then shall I never blame her;

27.1–4 Lucina is the goddess of childbirth, sometimes identified with the moon-goddess Diana; the allusion is to the Moon's love for Endymion, with addled reference to the two different sites to which the story is usually assigned: Olympia (not Mount Olympus) in the Peloponnese, and Mount Latmus (misprinted or malapropized as "Latium") in Asia Minor.

27.5 Aurora, goddess of the dawn, abducted and bore a child by Cephalus, who then deserted her.
28.1 *teen* suffering.
29.2 *betime* The original text reads "bedtime."
31.3 *Sibylla* The Sibyl, the Latin prophetess who was Aeneas's guide in the underworld.

But neither love nor life may find decreasing.
A mortal wound is my immortal being,
Which passeth thought or eyes' advisèd seeing.

### 33

Herewith his faltering tongue, by sighs oppressed,
Forsook his office, and his blood resorted
To feed the heart that wholly was distressed,
Whilst pale (like Pallas' flower) my knee supported
His feeble head and arm, so full of anguish,
That they which saw his sorrows gan to languish.

### 34

Themis, the coyest of this beauteous train,
On hilly tops the wondrous moly found,
Which, dipped in balmy dew, she gan to strain,
And brought her present to recure his wound.
Clore, she gathered amaranthus flower,
And Naïs Ajax' blossom in that stour.

### 35

Some chafe his temples with their lovely hands,
Some sprinkle water on his pale wan cheeks,
Some weep, some wake, some curse affection's bands
To see so young, so fair, become so weak.
But not their piteous herbs or springs have working
To ease that heart where wanton love is lurking.

### 36

Natheless, though loath to show his holy kindness,
On everyone he spent a look for favor,
And prayed their pardon, vouching Cupid's blindness.
O fancies fond that nought but sorrows savor;
To see a lovely god leave sea-nymphs so,
Who cannot doom upon his deadly woe?

### 37

Themis, that knew that waters long restrained
Break forth with greater billows than the brooks
That sweetly float through meads with flowers distained,
With cheerful lays did raise his heavy looks,
And bade him speak and tell what him aggrieved;
For griefs disclosed (said she) are soon relieved.

### 38

And as she wished, so all the rest did woo him;
By whose incessant suits at last invited,
He thus discovered that which did undo him,
And orderly his hideous harms recited,

---

33.4   *Pallas' flower* the olive.
34.2   *moly* The magical herb that protected Odysseus from the magic of Circe.
34.5   *amaranthus flower* A mythical flower that does not fade; often identified with love-lies-a-bleeding.

34.6   *Ajax' blossom* the hyacinth.   *stour* place.
36.3   *vouching* pleading.
36.6   *doom* cast judgment.
37.3   *distained* dyed.

When first with finger's wag he gan to still them,
And thus with dreary terms of love did fill them.

### 39

Ah nymphs (quoth he), had I by reason learnt
That secret art which birds have gained by sense,
By due foresight misfortune to prevent,
Or could my wit control mine eyes' offense,
You then should smile and I should tell such stories
As woods and waves should triumph in our glories.

### 40

But Nereus' daughters, sea-born saints, attend.
Lake-breeding geese, when from the eastern clime
They list unto the western waters wend
To choose their place of rest by course of time,
Approaching Taurus' haughty toppèd hill
They charm their cackle by this wondrous skill.

### 41

The climbing mountain, neighboring air well-nigh,
Hath harbored in his rocks and desert haunts
Whole aeries of eagles, prest to fly,
That, gazing on the sun, their birthright vaunts;
Which birds of Jove with deadly feud pursue
The wandering geese whenso they press in view.

### 42

These fearful flitting troops, by nature taught,
Passing these dangerous places of pursuit,
When all the desert vales they through have sought,
With pebbles stop their beaks to make them mute,
And by this means their dangerous deaths prevent
And gain their wishèd waters of frequent.

### 43

But I, fond god (ay, god, complain thy folly),
Let birds by sense exceed my reason far.
Whilom than I who was more strong and jolly,
Who more contemned affection's wanton war?
Who less than I loved lustful Cupid's arrows,
Who now with curse and plagues poor Glaucus harrows?

### 44

How have I leapt to hear the Tritons play
A harsh retreat unto the swelling floods?
How have I kept the dolphins at a bay
Whenas I meant to charm their wanton moods?
How have the angry winds grown calm for love
Whenas these fingers did my harp-strings move?

40.1  *Nereus* father of the Nereids.
40.5  *Taurus* A mountain range in southern Asia Minor.
41.1  *neighboring air well-nigh* almost reaching to the sky.
41.3  *prest* ready.

42.6  *of frequent* which they frequent.
44.1  *Tritons* Attendants on Neptune; half-man, half-fish in
form, they used seashells as trumpets.

### 45

Was any nymph, you nymphs, was ever any
That tangled not her fingers in my tress?
Some, well I wot, and of that some full many
Wished or my fair or their desire were less;
Even Ariadne, gazing from the sky,
Became enamored of poor Glaucus' eye.

### 46

Amidst this pride of youth and beauty's treasure,
It was my chance (you floods can tell my chancing),
Fleeting along Sicilian bounds for pleasure,
To spy a nymph of such a radiant glancing
As, when I looked, a beam of subtle firing
From eye to heart incensed a deep desiring.

### 47

Ah, had the veil of reason clad mine eye,
This foe of freedom had not burnt my heart;
But birds are blest, and most accursed am I,
Who must report her glories to my smart.
The nymph I saw, and loved her, all too cruel
Scylla, fair Scylla, my fond fancy's jewel.

### 48

Her hair not trussed, but scattered on her brow,
Surpassing Hybla's honey for the view,
Or softened golden wires; I know not how
Love with a radiant beauty did pursue
My too judicial eyes in darting fire
That kindled straight in me my fond desire.

### 49

Within those snares first was my heart entrapped,
Till through those golden shrouds mine eyes did see
An ivory-shadowed front, wherein was wrapped
Those pretty bowers where Graces couchèd be;
Next which her cheeks appeared like crimson silk,
Or ruddy rose bespread on whitest milk.

### 50

Twixt which the nose in lovely tenor bends
(Too traitorous pretty for a lover's view),
Next which her lips like violets commends
By true proportion that which doth ensue;
Which, when they smile, present unto the eyes
The ocean's pride and ivory paradise.

**45.5** *Ariadne* Cretan princess, loved and abandoned by Theseus; after an unsuccessful courtship by Glaucus, she became wife to Dionysus. *from the sky* See above on 11.4.

**48.2** *Hybla* A town near Mount Etna in Sicily, famous for its honey.
**49.3** *front* forehead.
**50.4** *ensue* issue forth.

### 51

Her polished neck of milk-white snows doth shine,
As when the moon in winter night beholds them;
Her breast of alablaster clear and fine,
Whereon two rising apples fair unfolds them,
Like Cynthia's face when in her full she shineth
And blushing to her love-mate's bower declineth.

### 52

From whence in length her arms do sweetly spread
Like two rare branchy saples in the spring,
Yielding five lovely sprigs from every head,
Proportionèd alike in everything;
Which featly sprout in length like spring-born friends,
Whose pretty tops with five sweet roses ends.

### 53

But why, alas, should I that marble hide
That doth adorn the one and other flank,
From whence a mount of quickened snow doth glide?
Or else the vale that bounds this milk-white bank,
Where Venus and her sisters hide the fount
Whose lovely nectar doth all sweets surmount.

### 54

Confounded with descriptions, I must leave them.
Lovers must think, and poets must report them,
For silly wits may never well conceive them
Unless a special grace from heaven consort them.
Ay's me, these fairs attending Scylla won me;
But now (sweet nymphs) attend what hath undone me.

### 55

The lovely breast where all this beauty rested
Shrouded within a world of deep disdain,
For where I thought my fancy should be feasted
With kind affect, alas (unto my pain),
When first I wooed, the wanton straight was flying,
And gave repulse before we talked of trying.

### 56

How oft have I (too often have I done so),
In silent night when every eye was sleeping,
Drawn near her cave, in hope her love were won so,
Forcing the neighboring waters through my weeping
To wake the winds, who did afflict her dwelling
Whilst I with tears my passion was a-telling.

### 57

When midst the Caspian seas the wanton played,
I drew whole wreaths of coral from the rocks

51.5 *Cynthia* goddess of the moon.
51.6 *her love-mate* Endymion.

52.2 *saples* saplings.

53.4 *bounds* borders.

And in her lap my heavenly presents laid,
But she, unkind, rewarded me with mocks.
Such are the fruits that spring from ladies' coying,
Who smile at tears, and are entrapped with toying.

### 58

Tongue might grow weary to report my wooings,
And heart might burst to think of her denial.
May none be blamed but heaven for all these doings
That yield no helps in midst of all my trial.
Heart, tongue, thought, pen nill serve me to repent me;
Disdain herself should strive for to lament me:

### 59

*Wretched love, let me die, end my love by my death.*
*Dead, alas, still I live; fly my life, fade my love.*
*Out, alas, love abides, still I joy vital breath;*
*Death in love, love is death, woe is me that do prove.*
*Pain and woe, care and grief every day about me hovers;*
*Then but death what can quell all the plagues of hapless lovers?*

### 60

Ay's me, my moanings are like water drops
That need an age to pierce her marble heart.
I sowed true zeal, yet fruitless were my crops.
I plighted faith, yet falsehood wrought my smart.
I praised her looks, her looks despised Glaucus;
Was ever amorous sea-god scornèd thus?

### 61

A hundred swelling tides my mother spent
Upon these locks, and all her nymphs were prest
To plait them fair when to her bower I went.
He that hath seen the wandering Phoebus' crest
Touched with the crystal of Eurotas' spring
The pride of these, my bushy locks, might sing.

### 62

But short discourse beseems my bad success.
Each office of a lover I performed;
So fervently my passions did her press,
So sweet my lays, my speech so well reformed,
That (cruel) when she saw nought would beguile me,
With angry looks the nymph did thus exile me:

### 63

Pack hence, thou fondling, to the western seas,
Within some calmy river shroud thy head,
For never shall my fair thy love appease,
Since fancy from this bosom late is fled;
And if thou love me, show it in departing,
For why thy presence doth procure my smarting.

---

**57.5**  *coying* teasing.
**61.4**  *Phoebus* the sun.

**61.5**  *Eurotas* the river that flows by Sparta.
**62.5**  *beguile* divert.

### 64

This said with angry looks, away she hasted
As fast as fly the floods before the winds;
When I (poor soul), with wretched sorrows wasted,
Exclaimed on love, which wit and reason blinds,
And, banished from her bower with woeful posting,
I bent myself to seek a foreign coasting.

### 65

At last, in wandering through the greater seas,
It was my chance to pass the noted straits,
And, wearied sore in seeking after ease,
Amidst the creeks and watery cool receipts
I spied from far, by help of sunny beams,
A fruitful isle begirt with ocean streams.

### 66

Westward I fleeted, and with heedful eye
Beheld the chalky cliffs that tempt the air,
Till at the last it was my chance to spy
A pleasant entrance to the flood's repair,
Through which I pressed, and wondering there beheld
On either side a sweet and fruitful field.

### 67

Isis (the lady of that lovely stream)
Made holiday in view of my resort,
And all the nymphs of that, her watery realm,
Gan trip for joy to make me mickle sport.
But I (poor soul), with no such joys contented,
Forsook their bowers, and secretly lamented.

### 68

All solitary roam I here about;
Now on the shore, now in the stream I weep.
Fire burns within, and ghastly fear without;
No rest, no ease, no hope of any sleep.
Poor banished god, here have I still remained
Since time my Scylla hath my suits disdained.

### 69

And here consort I now with hapless men,
Yielding them comfort (though my wound be cureless).
Songs of remorse I warble now and then,
Wherein I curse fond love and fortune dureless.
Wanhope my weal, my trust but bad adventure;
Circumference is care, my heart the center.

---

65.4   *receipts* reservoirs.
66.1   *fleeted* hurried.
66.4   *repair* place of origin.
67.2   *resort* coming there.

67.4   *mickle* much.
68.6   *Since time* since the time that.
69.4   *dureless* transient.
69.5   *Wanhope* despair.   *trust* hope.   *adventure* luck.

### 70

Whilst thus he spake, fierce Ate charmed his tongue;
His senses failed, his arms were folded straight,
And now he sighs, and then his heart is stung.
Again he speaks gainst fancy's fond deceit,
And tears his tresses with his fingers fair,
And rents his robes, half mad with deep despair.

### 71

The piteous nymphs that viewed his heavy plight
And heard the sequel of his bad success
Did loose the springs of their remorseful sight
And wept so sore to see his scant redress,
That of their tears there grew a pretty brook
Whose crystal clears the clouds of pensive look.

### 72

Alas, woe's me, how oft have I bewept
So fair, so young, so lovely, and so kind,
And, whilst the god upon my bosom slept,
Beheld the scars of his afflicted mind
Imprinted in his ivory brow by care
That fruitless fancy left unto his share.

### 73

My wandering lines, bewitch not so my senses,
But, gentle Muse, direct their course aright.
Delays in tragic tales procure offenses;
Yield me such feeling words that, whilst I write,
My working lines may fill mine eyes with languish,
And they to note my moans may melt with anguish.

### 74

The woeful Glaucus thus with woes attainted,
The pensive nymphs aggrieved to see his plight,
The floods and fields with his laments acquainted,
Myself amazed to see this heavy sight,
On sudden Thetis with her train approached
And gravely thus her amorous son reproached:

### 75

My son (said she), immortal have I made thee;
Amidst my watery realms who may compare
Or match thy might? Why then should care invade thee,
That art so young, so lovely, fresh, and fair?
Alas, fond god, it merits great reproving
In states of worth to dote on foolish loving.

---

**70.1** *Ate* goddess of derangement.

**74.5** *Thetis* The most prominent of the Nereids, and the protective mother of Achilles; making her Glaucus's mother is Lodge's doing.

**75.6** *In states of worth* in those of high rank.

**76.4** *beguile* disable.

### 76

Come wend with me, and midst thy father's bower
Let us disport and frolic for awhile
In spite of Love; although he pout and lower,
Good exercise will idle lusts beguile.
Let wanton Scylla coy her where she will,
Live thou, my son, by reason's level still.

### 77

Thus said the goddess; and, although her words
Gave signs of counsel, pomp, and majesty,
Yet natheless her piteous eye affords
Some pretty witness to the standers by
That in her thoughts (for all her outward show)
She mourned to see her son amated so.

### 78

But (welladay) her words have little force.
The hapless lover, worn with working woe,
Upon the ground lay pale as any corse,
And were not tears which from his eyes did flow
And sighs that witness he enjoyed his breath,
They might have thought him citizen of Death.

### 79

Which spectacle of care made Thetis bow
And call on Glaucus, and command her son
To yield her right and her advice allow.
But (woe) the man whom fancy had undone
Nill mark her rules; nor words nor weeping tears
Can fasten counsel in the lover's ears.

### 80

The Queen of Sea, with all her nymphs, assured
That no persuasion might relieve his care,
Kneeling adown, their faltering tongues enured
To tempt fair Venus by their vowèd prayer;
The course whereof as I could bear in mind,
With sorrowing sobs they uttered in this kind:

### 81

Born of the sea, thou Paphian Queen of Love,
Mistress of sweet conspiring harmony,
Lady of Cyprus, for whose sweet behove
The shepherds praise the youth of Thessaly,
Daughter of Jove and sister to the Sun,
Assist poor Glaucus, late by love undone.

76.5  *coy her* flirt.
77.6  *amated* dismayed.
78.3  *corse* corpse.

79.3  *yield* concede.
80.3  *enured* employed.

### 82

So mayst thou bain thee in the Arcadian brooks,
And play with Vulcan's rival when thou list,
And calm his jealous anger by thy looks,
And knit thy temples with a roseate twist,
If thou thyself and thine almighty son
Assist poor Glaucus, late by love undone.

### 83

May Earth still praise thee for her kind increase,
And beasts adore thee for their fruitful wombs,
And fowls with notes thy praises never cease,
And bees admire thee for their honeycombs:
So thou thyself and thine almighty son
Assist poor Glaucus, late by love undone.

### 84

No sooner from her reverent lips were passed
Those latter lines, but, mounting in the east,
Fair Venus in her ivory coach did haste
And toward those pensive dames her course addressed.
Her doves so plied their waving wings with flight
That straight the sacred goddess came in sight.

### 85

Upon her head she bare that gorgeous crown
Wherein the poor Amyntas is a star.
Her lovely locks her bosom hang adown
(Those nets that first ensnared the god of war);
Delicious lovely shine her pretty eyes,
And on her cheeks carnation clouds arise.

### 86

The stately robe she ware upon her back
Was lily-white, wherein with colored silk
Her nymphs had blazed the young Adonis' wrack
And Leda's rape by swan as white as milk;
And on her lap her lovely son was placed,
Whose beauty all his mother's pomp defaced.

### 87

A wreath of roses hemmed his temples in,
His tress was curled and clear as beaten gold.
Haught were his looks, and lovely was his skin,
Each part as pure as heaven's eternal mold;
And on his eyes a milk-white wreath was spread,
Which longst his back with pretty plaits did shed.

---

82.1   *bain* bathe.

82.2   *Vulcan's rival* Mars; Venus had an adulterous affair with him during her marriage to Vulcan.

85.2   *Amyntas* A shepherd mentioned several times in Vergil's *Eclogues*; the name is used by the Italian poet Tasso for the main character in his pastoral drama *Aminta* (1573) and by Thomas Watson for the speaker of a sequence of laments in his neo-Latin *Amyntas* (1585), which was Englished by Abraham Fraunce (1587).

86.4   Leda gave birth to Helen and Clytemnestra after being seduced by Jupiter in the guise of a swan.

86.6   *defaced* outshown.

87.3   *Haught* lofty.

### 88

Two dainty wings of particolored plumes
Adorn his shoulders, dallying with the wind.
His left hand wields a torch that ever fumes,
And in his right his bow that fancies bind;
And on his back his quiver hangs well stored
With sundry shafts that sundry hearts have gored.

### 89

The deities arrived in place desired.
Fair Venus her to Thetis first bespake:
Princess of Sea (quoth she), as you required,
From Ceston with my son my course I take.
Frolic, fair goddess; nymphs, forsake your plaining:
My son hath power and favor yet remaining.

### 90

With that the reverend powers each other kissed,
And Cupid smiled upon the nymphs for pleasure;
So nought but Glaucus' solace there was missed,
Which to effect the nymphs withouten measure
Entreat the god, who at the last drew nigh
The place where Glaucus full of care did lie.

### 91

And from his bow a furious dart he sent
Into that wound which he had made before,
That like Achilles' sword became the taint
To cure the wound that it had carved before;
And suddenly the sea-god started up,
Revived, relieved, and free from fancy's cup.

### 92

No more of love, no more of hate he spoke,
No more he forced the sighs from out his breast.
His sudden joy his pleasing smiles provoke,
And all aloft he shakes his bushy crest,
Greeting the gods and goddesses beside,
And every nymph upon that happy tide.

### 93

Cupid and he together, hand in hand,
Approach the place of this renownèd train.
Ladies (said he), released from amorous band,
Receive my prisoner to your grace again.
Glaucus gave thanks, when Thetis, glad with bliss,
Embraced his neck and his kind cheeks did kiss.

### 94

To see the nymphs in flocks about him play,
How Naïs kempt his head and washed his brows,
How Thetis checked him with his welladay,

---

89.4 *Ceston* Lodge converts the Greek word for Venus's
girdle into a place-name.
91.3 *taint* blow.

94.2 *kempt* combed.
94.3 *checked* mocked.

How Clore told him of his amorous vows,
How Venus praised him for his faithful love,
Within my heart a sudden joy did move.

### 95

Whilst in this glee this holy troop delight,
Along the stream afar fair Scylla floated
And coyly vaunced her crest in open sight;
Whose beauties all the tides with wonder noted,
Fore whom Palemon and the Tritons danced
Whilst she her limbs upon the tide advanced.

### 96

Whose swift approach made all the godheads wonder:
Glaucus gan smile to see his lovely foe,
Rage almost rent poor Thetis' heart asunder.
Was never happy troop confusèd so
As were these deities and dainty dames
When they beheld the cause of Glaucus' blames.

### 97

Venus commends the carriage of her eye,
Naïs upbraids the dimple in her chin,
Cupid desires to touch the wanton's thigh;
Clore, she swears that every eye doth sin
That likes a nymph that so contemneth love
As no attempts her lawless heart may move.

### 98

Thetis, impatient of her wrong sustained,
With envious tears her roseate cheeks afflicted,
And thus of Scylla's former pride complained:
Cupid (said she), see her that hath inflicted
The deadly wound that harmed my lovely son,
From whom the offspring of my care begun.

### 99

O, if there dwell within thy breast, my boy,
Or grace or pity or remorse (said she),
Now bend thy bow, abate yon wanton's joy,
And let these nymphs thy rightful justice see.
The god, soon won, gan shoot, and cleft her heart
With such a shaft as caused her endless smart.

### 100

The tender nymph, attainted unawares,
Fares like the Libyan lioness that flies
The hunter's lance that wounds her in his snares;
Now gins she love, and straight on Glaucus cries,
Whilst on the shore the goddesses rejoice
And all the nymphs afflict the air with noise.

95.3   *vaunced* advanced.          100.1   *attainted* struck (a term from tilting).
96.6   *blames* injuries.

101

To shore she flits, and swift as Afric wind
Her footing glides upon the yielding grass,
And, wounded by affect, recure to find
She suddenly with sighs approached the place
Where Glaucus sat, and, weary with her harms,
Gan clasp the sea-god in her amorous arms.

102

Glaucus, my love (quoth she), look on thy lover;
Smile, gentle Glaucus, on the nymph that likes thee.
But stark as stone sat he, and list not prove her.
Ah, silly nymph, the self-same god that strikes thee
With fancy's dart, and hath thy freedom slain,
Wounds Glaucus with the arrow of disdain.

103

O, kiss no more, kind nymph, he likes no kindness.
Love sleeps in him, to flame within thy breast.
Cleared are his eyes, where thine are clad with blindness;
Freed be his thoughts, where thine must taste unrest.
Yet nill she leave, for never love will leave her,
But fruitless hopes and fatal haps deceive her.

104

Lord, how her lips do dwell upon his cheeks,
And how she looks for babies in his eyes,
And how she sighs, and swears she loves and leeks,
And how she vows, and he her vows envies.
Trust me, the envious nymphs in looking on
Were forced with tears for to assist her moan.

105

How oft with blushes would she plead for grace,
How oft with whisperings would she tempt his ears,
How oft with crystal did she wet his face,
How oft she wiped them with her amber hairs,
So oft, methought, I oft in heart desired
To see the end whereto disdain aspired.

106

Palemon with the Tritons roared for grief
To see the mistress of their joys amated;
But Glaucus scorns the nymph that waits relief,
And more she loves, the more the sea-god hated.
Such change, such chance, such suits, such storms, believe me,
Poor silly wretch, did heartily aggrieve me.

107

As when the fatal bird of augury,
Seeing a stormy dismal cloud arise

102.3  *prove* test.
104.2  *looks for babies in his eyes* stares deeply into his eyes          104.3  *leeks* likes.
(where she will see small images of herself).                             104.4  *envies* begrudges.

Within the south, foretells with piteous cry
The weeping tempest that on sudden hies,
So she, poor soul, in view of his disdain
Began to descant on her future pain.

### 108

And fixing eye upon the fatal ground,
Whole hosts of floods drew dew from out her eyes;
And when through inward grief the lass did sound,
The softened grass like billows did arise
To woo her breasts and wed her limbs so dainty,
Whom wretched love had made so weak and fainty.

### 109

Ay's me, methinks I see her Thetis' fingers
Renting her locks as she were woebegone her;
And now her lips upon his lipping lingers:
O lingering pain, where Love nill list to moan her.
Rue me that writes, for why her ruth deserves it;
Hope needs must fail, where sorrow scarce preserves it.

### 110

To make long tale were tedious to the woeful,
Woeful that read what woeful she approved.
In brief, her heart with deep despair was so full,
As since she might not win her sweet beloved.
With hideous cries, like wind borne back she fled
Unto the sea, and toward Sicilia sped.

### 111

Sweet Zephyrus upon that fatal hour
In hapless tide midst watery world was walking,
Whose milder sighs, alas, had little power
To whisper peace amongst the godheads talking;
Who all in one conclude for to pursue
The hapless nymph, to see what would ensue.

### 112

Venus herself and her fair son gan hie
Within their ivory coach drawn forth by doves
After this hapless nymph, their power to try;
The nymphs, in hope to see their vowèd loves,
Gan cut the watery bosom of the tide,
As in Caÿster Phoebus' birds do glide.

### 113

Thetis, in pomp upon a Triton's back,
Did post her straight, attended by her train;
But Glaucus, free from love by lover's wrack,
Seeing me pensive where I did remain,

---

108.3   *sound* swoon.
110.2   *approved* experienced.
110.4   *As since* because.

111.1   *Zephyrus* the west wind.
112.6   *Caÿster* The river in Asia Minor that flows by Ephesus.
        *Phoebus' birds* swans.

Upon a dolphin horsed me (as he was).
Thus on the ocean hand in hand we pass.

### 114

Our talk midway was nought but still of wonder,
Of change, of chance, of sorrow and her ending.
I wept for want; he said time brings men under,
And secret want can find but small befriending.
And as he said in that before I tried it,
I blamed my wit forewarned, yet never spied it.

### 115

What need I talk the order of my way?
Discourse was steersman while my bark did sail,
My ship conceit, and fancy was my bay.
(If these fail me, then faint, my Muse, and fail.)
Haste brought us where the hapless nymph sojourned,
Beating the weeping waves that for her mourned.

### 116

He that hath seen the northern blasts despoil
The pomp of prime, and with a whistling breath
Blast and disperse the beauties of the soil,
May think upon her pains more worse than death.
Alas, poor lass, the echoes in the rocks
Of Sicily her piteous plaining mocks.

### 117

Echo herself, when Scylla cried out, O love!
With piteous voice from out her hollow den
Returned these words, these words of sorrow (*no love*).
No love (quoth she), then fie on traitorous men,
Then fie on hope; *then fie on hope* (quoth Echo).
To every word the nymph did answer so.

### 118

For every sigh the rocks returns a sigh,
For every tear their fountains yields a drop,
Till we at last the place approachèd nigh
And heard the nymph that fed on sorrow's sop
Make woods and waves and rocks and hills admire
The wondrous force of her untamed desire.

### 119

Glaucus (quoth she) is fair, whilst Echo sings
*Glaucus is fair*. But yet he hateth Scylla,
The wretch reports; and then her arms she wrings
Whilst Echo tells her this, *he hateth Scylla*.
No hope (quoth she), *no hope* (quoth Echo then);
Then *fie on men* when she said, fie on men.

116.2 *prime* spring.

### 120

Fury and Rage, Wanhope, Despair, and Woe,
From Ditis' den by Ate sent, drew nigh.
Fury was red, with rage his eyes did glow,
Whole flakes of fire from forth his mouth did fly,
His hands and arms ybathed in blood of those
Whom fortune, sin, or fate made countries' foes.

### 121

Rage, wan and pale, upon a tiger sat,
Gnawing upon the bones of mangled men.
Nought can he view, but he repined thereat;
His locks were snakes bred forth in Stygian den.
Next whom, Despair, that deep disdainèd elf,
Delightless lived, still stabbing of herself.

### 122

Woe, all in black, within her hands did bear
The fatal torches of a funeral.
Her cheeks were wet, dispersèd was her hair,
Her voice was shrill (yet loathsome therewithal).
Wanhope (poor soul) on broken anchor sits,
Wringing his arms as robbèd of his wits.

### 123

These five at once the sorrowing nymph assail,
And captive lead her bound into the rocks,
Where, howling still, she strives for to prevail.
With no avail yet strives she, for her locks
Are changed with wonder into hideous sands,
And hard as flint become her snow-white hands.

### 124

The waters howl with fatal tunes about her,
The air doth school whenas she turns within them,
The winds and waves with puffs and billows scout her.
Waves storm, air schools, both wind and waves begin them
To make the place this mournful nymph doth weep in
A hapless haunt whereas no nymph may keep in.

### 125

The seaman wandering by that famous isle
Shuns all with fear, despairing Scylla's bower;
Nymphs, sea-gods, sirens, when they list to smile,
Forsake the haunt of Scylla in that stour.
Ah, nymphs, thought I, if every coy one felt
The like mishaps, their flinty hearts would melt.

### 126

Thetis rejoiced to see her foe depressed;
Glaucus was glad, since Scylla was enthralled;

120.2  *Ditis* god of the underworld.
124.2  *school* swarm (like a school of fish).
124.3  *scout* mock.

125.2  *despairing* fearing.
126.1  *depressed* driven down.

The nymphs gan smile to boast their Glaucus' rest.
Venus and Cupid, in their thrones installed,
At Thetis' beck to Neptune's bower repair,
Whereas they feast amidst his palace fair.

### 127

Of pure immortal nectar is their drink,
And sweet ambrosia dainties do repast them.
The Tritons sing, Palemon smiles to think
Upon the chance, and all the nymphs do haste them
To trick up mossy garlands where they won
For lovely Venus and her conquering son.

### 128

From forth the fountains of his mother's store
Glaucus let fly a dainty crystal bain
That washed the nymphs with labor tired before.
Cupid, he trips among this lovely train;
Alonely I apart did write this story
With many a sigh and heart full sad and sorry.

### 129

Glaucus, when all the goddesses took rest,
Mounted upon a dolphin full of glee,
Conveyed me friendly from this honored feast,
And by the way such sonnets sung to me
That all the dolphins neighboring of his glide
Danced with delight his reverend course beside.

### 130

At last he left me where at first he found me,
Willing me let the world and ladies know
Of Scylla's pride, and then by oath he bound me
To write no more of that whence shame doth grow,
Or tie my pen to penny-knaves' delight,
But live with fame, and so for fame to write.

L'ENVOY

### 131

*Ladies, he left me; trust me, I missay not,*
*But so he left me as he willed me tell you*
*That nymphs must yield when faithful lovers stray not,*
*Lest through contempt almighty Love compel you*
*With Scylla in the rocks to make your biding*
*A cursèd plague for women's proud back-biting.*

126.3  *rest* peace of mind.
127.5  *won* dwell.

129.4  *by* along.
130.5  *penny-knaves* cheap rascals.

# George Chapman (1559–1634)

The son of a modestly prosperous landowner in Hitchin, Chapman may have attended both Oxford and Cambridge, though in later life he praised himself as an autodidact. By 1596 he was a practicing playwright in London. Over the next two decades he was reasonably successful at it, with a run of comedies and tragedies that still command respect (though he did not escape the indignities associated with that profession: in 1605 his collaboration with Ben Jonson and John Marston, *Eastward Ho!*, landed him in jail, and not for the first time). At the same time he pursued a career as a non-dramatic poet of elite and esoteric ambitions; a volume published in 1594, *The Shadow of Night*, is the principal evidence for the existence of an occult School of Night involving Chapman, Sir Walter Ralegh, Thomas Harriot, and others (it may be the object of satire in Shakespeare's *Love's Labour's Lost*). In 1598 Chapman published a highly wrought, elaborately moralistic continuation of Marlowe's *Hero and Leander*; the same year he began publishing his verse translation of Homer's *Iliad*, the first such translation in English. The Homer project was completed in 1616 with the appearance of *The Whole Works of Homer*, accompanied with commentary by Chapman asserting his own claim to having decoded the secret knowledge at the core of the Greek poems. The project had the support of Prince Henry, who pledged £300 on its completion; but Henry died in 1612 and James did not honor his promise. A final attempt to secure aristocratic patronage involved Chapman in an inexpedient defense of James's favorite Robert Carr in connection with his marriage to the divorced Countess of Essex and the murder of Sir Thomas Overbury. In his last two decades Chapman largely disappeared from view.

Chapman is one of the most intellectually ambitious poets of English Renaissance, very self-conscious in his recondite learning and persistent in his claims for the philosophical dignity of his work. His ambitions inform a style – what he called "my far-fetched and, as it were, beyond-sea manner of writing" – that can be extraordinarily difficult to untangle into ordinary intelligibility; subjecting his verse to the discipline of modern punctuation can be a particularly vexed business. *Ovid's Banquet of Sense*, published in 1595, has been called "the most difficult poem in the English language." It purports to be an account of a momentous afternoon in the erotic life of Elizabethan England's favorite classical poet; it could be described as a fortyfold expansion of Ovid's own *Amores* 1.5 (given below in Marlowe's translation), with the man's experience of the woman's sensual attractions given slow-motion elaboration and analysis in a carefully ordered sequence of individual senses: hearing, smell, sight, taste (a kiss), and finally (as she exposes her breasts to him) touch. The telling of this is both lush and archly intellectualized; the doctrine in play seems to be precisely the commerce between the woman's body and the man's higher faculties ("The sense is given us to excite the mind"), and near the end the experience is said to be the genesis of one of Ovid's signature poems: "For thy sake I will write the Art of Love." Though the woman's acquiescence at this point seems achieved, the sense of literary mission may be the only payoff; where *Amores* 1.5 moves quickly to lovemaking, Chapman's Ovid is suddenly interrupted and flees, not enjoying love's culmination but lamenting its "defects"; a last stanza tells us that there is more to be told, but does not tell us what that is. The banquet's last course is an ambiguous frustration.

*Edition*: *The Poems of George Chapman*, ed. Phyllis Brooks Bartlett (New York: MLA, 1941).

## Ovid's Banquet of Sense

### THE ARGUMENT

Ovid, newly enamored of Julia (daughter to Octavius Augustus Caesar, after by him called Corinna), secretly conveyed himself into a garden of the Emperor's court, in an arbor whereof Corinna was bathing, playing upon her lute, and singing; which Ovid overhearing was exceedingly pleased with the sweetness of her voice, and to himself uttered the comfort he conceived in his sense of hearing.

Then the odors she used in her bath breathing a rich savor, he expresseth the joy he felt in his sense of smelling.

---

*contentation* satisfaction.                    *without her offense* without offending her.

Thus growing more deeply enamored, in great contentation with himself, he ventures to see her in the pride of her nakedness; which doing by stealth, he discovered the comfort he conceived in seeing, and the glory of her beauty.

Not yet satisfied, he useth all his art to make known his being there without her offense, or (being necessarily offended) to appease her; which done, he entreats a kiss to serve for satisfaction of his taste, which he obtains.

Then proceeds he to entreaty for the fifth sense and there is interrupted.

### NARRATIO

1

The earth from heavenly light conceivèd heat,
Which mixèd all her moist parts with her dry,
When with right beams the sun her bosom beat
And with fit food her plants did nutrify;
They (which to earth as to their mother cling
In forkèd roots), now sprinkled plenteously
With her warm breath, did hasten to the spring,
Gather their proper forces, and extrude
All power but that with which they stood indued.

2

Then did Cyrrhus fill his eyes with fire,
Whose ardor curled the foreheads of the trees
And made his green love burn in his desire,
When youth and ease (collectors of love's fees)
Enticed Corinna to a silver spring
Enchasing a round bower, which with it sees
(As with a diamant doth an ameled ring);
Into which eye most pitifully stood
Niobe, shedding tears that were her blood.

3

Stone Niobe, whose statue to this fountain
In great Augustus Caesar's grace was brought
From Sipylus, the steep Mygdonian mountain,
That statue tis, still weeps for former thought
Into this spring, Corinna's bathing place:
So cunningly to optic reason wrought
That afar off it showed a woman's face,
Heavy and weeping; but, more nearly viewed,
Nor weeping, heavy, nor a woman showed.

4

In summer only wrought her ecstasy;
And that her story might be still observed,
Octavius caused in curious imagery
Her fourteen children should at large be carved,
Their fourteen breasts with fourteen arrows gored,

**2.1** *Cyrrhus* Chapman's note: "Cyrrhus is a surname of the sun, from a town called Cyrrha, where was honored." The town was the port town for Delphi.
**2.6** *Enchasing* surrounding. *sees* Chapman's note: "By prosopopoeia he makes the fountain the eye of the round arbor, as a diamant seems to be the eye of a ring, and therefore says the arbor sees with the fountain."

**2.7** *ameled* enameled.
**2.9** *Niobe* A proud mother turned into stone by grief at the death of her children; a very common subject in classical art.
**3.3** *Sipylus* The mountain in Lydia where Niobe's metamorphosis took place.

And set by her that, for her seed so starved,
To a stone sepulcher herself deplored;
In ivory were they cut, and on each breast
In golden elements their names impressed.

### 5

Her sons were Sipylus, Agenor, Phaedimus,
Ismenus, Argus, and Damasicthen,
The seventh called like his grandsire Tantalus;
Her daughters were the fair Astiochen,
Chloris, Naeëra, and Pelopië,
Phaeta, proud Phthia, and Eugigen.
All these, apposed to violent Niobe,
Had looks so deadly sad, so lively done
As if death lived in their confusion.

### 6

Behind their mother two pyramides
Of freckled marble through the arbor viewed,
On whose sharp brows Sol and Titanides
In purple and transparent glass were hued,
Through which the sunbeams on the statues staying
Made their pale bosoms seem with blood imbrued,
Those two stern planets' rigors still bewraying.
To these dead forms came living beauty's essence,
Able to make them startle with her presence.

### 7

In a loose robe of tinsel forth she came,
Nothing but it betwixt her nakedness
And envious light. The downward–burning flame
Of her rich hair did threaten new access
Of venturous Phaëton to scorch the fields;
And thus to bathing came our poet's goddess,
Her handmaids bearing all things pleasure yields
To such a service: odors most delighted,
And purest linen which her looks had whited.

### 8

Then cast she off her robe, and stood upright.
As lightning breaks out of a laboring cloud,
Or as the morning heaven casts off the night,
Or as that heaven cast off itself and showed
Heaven's upper light, to which the brightest day
Is but a black and melancholy shroud,
Or as when Venus strived for sovereign sway
Of charmful beauty in young Troy's desire:
So stood Corinna vanishing her tire.

**4.6**  *starved* killed.
**4.7**  *deplored* mourned.
**5.7**  *apposed* set next to.
**6.3**  *Sol and Titanides* The sun and the Titan's daughter, i.e., the moon. Apollo and Diana, the deities of the sun and the moon, were the slayers of Niobe's children.
**6.6**  *imbrued* stained.
**7.1**  *tinsel* rich cloth interwoven with gold or silver.

**7.5**  *Phaëton* Apollo's son, who burned the landscape by flying too low when he attempted to drive his father's chariot.
**8.7–8**  A reference to the judgment of Paris ("young Troy") among the three goddesses Juno, Athena, and Venus; Venus's (successful) plea to be chosen the most beautiful involved displaying her naked body.
**8.9**  *vanishing her tire* making her clothes disappear.

9

A soft enflowered bank embraced the fount,
Of Chloris' ensigns an abstracted field,
Where grew melanthy, great in bees' account,
Amaracus, that precious balm doth yield,
Enamelled pansies, used at nuptials still,
Diana's arrow, Cupid's crimson shield,
Ope-morn, nightshade, and Venus' navel,
Solemn violets, hanging head as shamed,
And verdant calamint, for odor famed.

10

Sacred nepenthe, purgative of care,
And sovereign rumex that doth rancor kill,
Sya and hyacinth that furies wear,
White and red jessamines, merry, melliphil,
Fair crown-imperial, emperor of flowers,
Immortal amaranth, white aphrodil,
And cup-like twillpants, strewed in Bacchus' bowers:
These cling about this nature's naked gem
To taste her sweets, as bees do swarm on them.

11

And now she used the fount where Niobe,
Tombed in herself, poured her lost soul in tears
Upon the bosom of this Roman Phoebe;
Who, bathed and odored, her bright limbs she rears,
And drying her on that disparent round,
Her lute she takes to enamor heavenly ears
And try if with her voice's vital sound
She could warm life through those cold statues spread
And cheer the dame that wept when she was dead.

12

And thus she sung, all naked as she sat,
Laying the happy lute upon her thigh,
Not thinking any near to wonder at
The bliss of her sweet breasts' divinity.

THE SONG OF CORINNA

Tis better to contemn than love,
And to be fair than wise,
For souls are ruled by eyes,

9.2  *Chloris* Flora, goddess of flowers.
9.3  *melanthy* gith or fennel-flower.
9.4  *Amaracus* sweet marjoram. The original text reads
"Amareus," which could mean a kind of pink, though that
would make the reference to the "precious balm" puzzling.
9.6  *Diana's arrow* artemisia (?). *Cupid's crimson shield*
love-in-idleness.
9.7  *Ope-morn* bindweed. *Venus' navel* pennywort.
10.1  *nepenthe* A mythic plant, the source of a drug
supposed to cure grief.
10.2  *rumex* garden dock.

10.3  *Sya* syve, i.e., chive.
10.4  *jessamines* jasmines. *merry* black cherry. *melliphil*
honey leaf.
10.5  *crown imperial* fritillary.
10.6  *amaranth* An imaginary flower that never fades.
*aphrodil* asphodel (?).
10.7  *twillpants* tulips (?).
11.3  *Phoebe* The goddess Diana, whom Actaeon saw naked
in her bath.
11.5  *disparent* variegated.

And Jove's bird seized by Cypris' dove.
It is our grace and sport to see                                    5
Our beauty's sorcery
That makes (like destiny)
Men follow us the more we flee;
That sets wise glosses on the fool,
And turns her cheeks to books                                      10
Where Wisdom sees in looks
Derision, laughing at his school:
Who (loving) proves prophaneness holy,
Nature our fate, our wisdom folly.

### 13

While this was singing, Ovid, young in love
With her perfections, never proving yet
How merciful a mistress she would prove,
Boldly embraced the power he could not let,
And like a fiery exhalation
Followed the sun he wished might never set,
Trusting herein his constellation
Ruled by love's beams which Julia's eyes erected,
Whose beauty was the star his life directed.

### 14

And having drenched his ankles in those seas,
He needs would swim, and cared not if he drowned.
Love's feet are in his eyes; for if he please
The depth of beauty's gulfy flood to sound,
He goes upon his eyes, and up to them
At the first step he is. No shader ground
Could Ovid find, but in love's holy stream
Was past his eyes, and now did wet his ears,
For his high sovereign's silver voice he hears.

### 15

Whereat his wit assumèd fiery wings,
Soaring above the temper of his soul,
And he the purifying rapture sings
Of his ear's sense, takes full the Thespian bowl,
And it carouseth to his mistress' health,
Whose sprightful verdure did dull flesh control;
And his conceit he crowneth with the wealth
Of all the Muses in his pleasèd senses
When with the ear's delight he thus commences:

### 16

Now, Muses, come, repair your broken wings
(Plucked and prophaned by rustic ignorance)
With feathers of these notes my mistress sings,
And let quick verse her drooping head advance
From dungeons of contempt to smite the stars.

---

Song of Corinna, 4 *Jove's bird* The eagle, the form in which
the enamored Jupiter carried off Ganymede.  *Cypris* Venus.
**13.2** *proving* experiencing.
**13.4** *let* restrain.

**14.6** *shader* shadier.
**15.4** *Thespian* Related to Thespis, the traditional father of
Greek tragedy; here apparently used for poetic inspiration in
a more generalized sense.

In Julia's tunes, led forth by furious trance,
A thousand Muses come to bid you wars;
Dive to your spring, and hide you from the stroke:
All poets' furies will her tunes invoke.

### 17

Never was any sense so set on fire
With an immortal ardor as mine ears.
Her fingers to the strings doth speech inspire
And numbered laughter, that the descant bears
To her sweet voice, whose species through my sense
My spirits to their highest function rears;
To which impressed with ceaseless confluence,
It useth them as proper to her power:
Marries my soul, and makes itself her dower.

### 18

Methinks her tunes fly gilt like Attic bees
To my ears' hives with honey tried to air.
My brain is but the comb, the wax, the lees,
My soul the drone that lives by their affair.
O, so it sweets, refines, and ravisheth,
And with what sport they sting in their repair!
Rise then in swarms, and sting me thus to death,
Or turn me into swound, possess me whole,
Soul to my life and essence to my soul.

### 19

Say, gentle air, O does it not thee good
Thus to be smit with her correcting voice?
Why dance ye not, ye daughters of the wood?
Wither forever, if not now rejoice.
Rise, stones, and build a city with her notes;
And notes, infuse with your most Cynthian noise
To all the trees, sweet flowers, and crystal floats
That crown and make this cheerful garden quick,
Virtue that every touch may make such music.

### 20

O, that as man is called a little world,
The world might shrink into a little man
To hear the notes about this garden hurled,
That skill dispersed in tunes so Orphean
Might not be lost in smiting stocks and trees
That have no ears, but, grown as it began,
Spread their renowns as far as Phoebus sees
Through earth's dull veins, that she like heaven might move
In ceaseless music, and be filled with love.

---

17.4  *numbered* metrically regular.
17.5  *species* A technical term for the sensible emanation from some object: usually but not always visual.
18.2  *tried* refined.
18.8  *turn me into swound* put me in a swoon.
19.6  *Cynthian* Associated with the goddess Diana, particularly in her lunar role. On Julia's specific identification with

Diana, see above on 11.3; Chapman's complex interpretation of Diana in her various manifestations is developed in his *Shadow of the Night*.
19.7  *floats* waves.
20.4  *Orphean* worthy of the mythic poet Orpheus.
20.5  *stocks* pieces of wood.

### 21

In precious incense of her holy breath
My love doth offer hecatombs of notes
To all the gods, who now despise the death
Of oxen, heifers, wethers, swine, and goats.
A sonnet in her breathing sacrificed
Delights them more than all beasts' bellowing throats,
As much with heaven as with my hearing prized;
And as gilt atoms in the sun appear,
So greet these sounds the gristles of mine ear,


### 22

Whose pores do open wide to their regreet,
And my implanted air that air embraceth,
Which they impress. I feel their nimble feet
Tread my ear's labyrinth; their sport amazeth,
They keep such measure, play themselves and dance.
And now my soul in Cupid's furnace blazeth,
Wrought into fury with their dalliance;
And as the fire the parchèd stubble burns,
So fades my flesh and into spirit turns.


### 23

Sweet tunes, brave issue, that from Julia come,
Shook from her brain, armed like the queen of ire:
For first conceivèd in her mental womb
And nourished with her soul's discursive fire,
They grew into the power of her thought;
She gave them downy plumes from her attire,
And them to strong imagination brought;
That, to her voice; wherein most movingly
She (blessing them with kisses) lets them fly.


### 24

Who fly rejoicing, but (like noblest minds)
In giving others life themselves do die,
Not able to endure earth's rude unkinds,
Bred in my sovereign's parts too tenderly.
O, that as intellects themselves transit

21.2  *hecatombs* sacrifices in units of a hundred.

21.9  *gristles* cartilage.

22.1  *to their regreet* to greet them.

23.3  *first* Chapman's note: "In this allusion to the birth of Pallas, he shows the conceit of her sonnet, both for matter and note, and by metaphor he expresseth how she delivered her words and tunes, which was by commission of the order philosophers set down in apprehension of our knowledge and by effection of our senses. For first they affirm the species of every object propagates itself by our spirits to our common sense, that delivers it to the imaginative part; that to the cogitative; the cogitative to the passive intellect; the passive intellect to that which is called *dianoia* or *discursus*; and that delivers it up to the mind, which order he observes in her utterance." Pallas Athena ("the queen of ire") was born in full armor from the brain of Jupiter, an intellectual birth related to her role as the virgin goddess of wisdom. The analysis of the relations between sensory and mental faculties is similar to that of Aristotle in *On the Soul*; "common sense" (*aisthêsis koinê* in Aristotle) is the unified faculty to which the five individual senses transmit their data.

24.3  *unkinds* unkindnesses.

24.5  *as* Chapman's note: "The philosopher saith, *Intellectus in ipsa intelligibilia transit* [the intellect passes over into the very things that are intelligible], upon which is grounded this invention, that in the same manner his life might pass into his mistress' conceit, intending his intellectual life or soul, which by this analogy should be *Intellectus* and her conceit *Intelligibilis*." The Latin tag is a favorite of Chapman's; in the notes to his translation of the *Iliad* he calls it "my old lesson in philosophy." The philosopher appears to be Aristotle, who says something like this in his treatise *On the Soul* (3.4/429A), but no exact source for the quotation has been found.

To each intelligible quality,
My life might pass into my love's conceit,
Thus to be formed in words, her tunes, and breath,
And with her kisses, sing itself to death.

### 25

This life were wholly sweet, this only bliss;
Thus would I live to die. Thus sense were feasted,
My life that in my flesh a chaos is
Should to a golden world be thus digested;
Thus should I rule her face's monarchy,
Whose looks in several empires are invested,
Crowned now with smiles, and then with modesty;
Thus in her tune's division I should reign
For her conceit does all, in every vein.

### 26

My life then turned to that, to each note and word
Should I consort her look, which sweeter sings
Where songs of solid harmony accord,
Ruled with Love's rule, and pricked with all his stings.
Thus should I be her notes before they be,
While in her blood they sit with fiery wings,
Not vapored in her voice's stillery;
Nought are these notes her breast so sweetly frames
But motions fled out of her spirit's flames.

### 27

For as when steel and flint, together smit,
With violent action spit forth sparks of fire
And make the tender tinder burn with it,
So my love's soul doth lighten her desire
Upon her spirits in her notes' pretense,
And they convey them (for distinct attire)
To use the wardrobe of the common sense;
From whence in veils of her rich breath they fly
And feast the ear with this felicity.

### 28

Methinks they raise me from the heavy ground
And move me swimming in the yielding air,
As Zephyr's flowery blasts do toss a sound;
Upon their wings will I to heaven repair
And sing them so, gods shall descend and hear.
Ladies must be adored that are but fair,
But apt besides with art to tempt the ear
In notes of nature is a goddess' part,
Though oft men nature's notes please more than art.

25.8  *division* elaboration.
26.5  *before* Chapman's note: "This hath reference to the order of her utterance, expressed before."
26.7  *stillery* distillery.

27.5  *notes'* Chapman's note: "So is this likewise referred to the order abovesaid, for the more perspicuity." *pretense* self-display.
27.7  *common sense* See the note above on 23.3.
28.3  *Zephyr* the west wind.

### 29

But here are art and nature both confined,
Art casting nature in so deep a trance
That both seem dead because they be divined.
Buried is heaven in earthly ignorance;
Why break not men then strumpet Folly's bounds
To learn at this pure virgin utterance?
No, none but Ovid's ears can sound these sounds,
Where sing the hearts of love and poesy,
Which make my Muse so strong, she works too high.

### 30

Now in his glowing ears her tunes did sleep,
And as a silver bell, with violent blow
Of steel or iron, when his sounds most deep
Do from his sides and air's soft bosom flow,
A great while after murmurs at the stroke,
Letting the hearer's ears his hardness know,
So chid the air to be no longer broke,
And left the accents panting in his ear,
Which in this banquet his first service were.

### 31

Herewith, as Ovid something nearer drew,
Her odors, odored with her breath and breast,
Into the sensor of his savor flew,
As if the phoenix, hasting to her rest,
Had gathered all the Arabian spicery
To enbalm her body in her tomb, her nest,
And there lay burning gainst Apollo's eye,
Whose fiery air, straight piercing Ovid's brain,
Enflamed his Muse with a more odorous vein.

### 32

And thus he sung: Come, sovereign odors, come
Restore my spirits, now in love consuming;
Wax hotter, air, make them more savorsome,
My fainting life with fresh-breathed soul perfuming.
The flames of my disease are violent,
And many perish on late helps presuming,
With which hard fate must I yet stand content.
As odors put in fire most richly smell,
So men must burn in love that will excel.

### 33

And as the air is rarefied with heat,
But thick and gross with summer-killing cold,
So men in love aspire perfection's seat,
When others slaves to base desire are sold;
And if that men near Ganges lived by scent
Of flowers and trees, more I a thousandfold
May live by these pure fumes that do present

---

29.3   *divined* made divine.

My mistress' quickening and consuming breath,
Where her wish flies with power of life and death.

### 34

Methinks, as in these liberal fumes I burn,
My mistress' lips be near with kiss-entices,
And that which way soever I can turn,
She turns withal, and breathes on me her spices,
As if, too pure for search of human eye,
She flew in air disburdening Indian prizes,
And made each earthly fume to sacrifice.
With her choice breath fell Cupid blows his fire,
And after, burns himself in her desire.

### 35

Gentle and noble are their tempers framed
That can be quickened with perfumes and sounds,
And they are cripple-minded, goat-wit lamed,
That lie like fire-fit blocks, dead without wounds,
Stirred up with nought but hell-descending gain,
The soul of fools that all their souls confounds,
The art of peasants and our nobles' stain,
The bane of virtue and the bliss of sin,
Which none but fools and peasants glory in.

### 36

Sweet sounds and odors are the heavens on earth
Where virtues live of virtuous men deceased,
Which in such like receive their second birth,
By smell and hearing endlessly increased;
They were mere flesh were not with them delighted,
And every such is perished like a beast,
As all they shall that are so foggy-sprited.
Odors feed love, and love clear heaven discovers.
Lovers, wear sweets, then; sweetest minds, be lovers.

### 37

Odor in heat and dryness is concite;
Love, then, a fire, is much thereto affected,
And, as ill smells do kill his appetite,
With thankful savors it is still protected.
Love lives in spirits, and our spirits be
Nourished with odors, therefore love refected;
And air, less corpulent in quality
Than odors are, doth nourish vital spirits:
Therefore may they be proved of equal merits.

---

**34.2** *entices* enticements.
**35.4** *fire-fit blocks* pieces of wood suitable for burning.
**36.4** *and* Chapman's note: "By this allusion drawn from the effects of sounds and odors, he imitates the eternity of virtue, saying the virtues of good men live in them because they stir up pure inclinations to the like, as if infused in perfumes and sounds. Besides, he infers that such as are neither delighted with sounds (intending by sounds all utterance of knowledge, as well as musical affections) nor with odors (which properly dry the brain and delight the instruments of the soul, making them more capable of her faculties), such saith he perish without memory."
**37.1** *concite* aroused.
**37.6** *refected* refreshed.

### 38

O sovereign odors, not of force to give
Food to a thing that lives nor let it die,
But to add life to that did never live,
Nor to add life, but immortality,
Since they partake her heat that, like the fire
Stolen from the wheels of Phoebus' waggonry,
To lumps of earth can manly life inspire;
Else be these fumes the lives of sweetest dames
That (dead) attend on her for novel frames.

### 39

Rejoice, blest clime, thy air is so refined
That while she lives no hungry pestilence
Can feed her poisoned stomach with thy kind,
But as the unicorn's pregredience
To venomed pools doth purge them with his horn,
And after him the desert's residents
May safely drink, so in the wholesome morn,
After her walk, who there attends her eye
Is sure that day to taste no malady.

### 40

Thus was his course of odors sweet and slight,
Because he longed to give his sight assay;
And as in fervor of the summer's height
The sun is so ambitious in his sway
He will not let the night an hour be placed,
So in this Cupid's night (oft seen in day,
Now spread with tender clouds these odors cast)
Her sight, his sun, so wrought in his desires,
His savor vanished in his visual fires.

### 41

So vulture love on his increasing liver
And fruitful entrails eagerly did feed,
And with the goldenest arrow in his quiver
Wounds him with longings that like torrents bleeds
To see the mine of knowledge that enriched
His mind with poverty and desperate need:
A sight that with the thought of sight bewitched,
A sight taught magic his deep mystery,
Quicker in danger than Diana's eye.

### 42

Stay, therefore, Ovid, venture not. A sight
May prove thy rudeness more than show thee loving,
And make thy mistress think thou thinkst her light:

38.9  *for novel frames* in order to take on new shapes(?).
39.4  *pregredience* going first.
40.1  *slight* The original text reads "sleight," which could indeed be the word so spelled in modern usage (meaning "adroit" or "cunning"), but the point of the stanza is the brevity – short and sweet – of the olfactory course of the banquet.
41.9  *than* Chapman's note: "Allusion to the transformation of Actaeon with the sight of Diana." After seeing Diana naked, Actaeon was changed into a stag and killed by his own hounds.
42.3  *light* morally loose.

Which thought with lightest dames is nothing moving.
The slender hope of favor thou hast yet
Should make thee fear such gross conclusions proving;
Besides, the thicket Flora's hands hath set
To hide thy theft is thin and hollow-hearted,
Not meet to have so high a charge imparted.

### 43

And should it keep thy secrets, thine own eye
Would fill thy thoughts so full of lightenings
That thou must pass through more extremity;
Or stand content to burn beneath their wings,
Her honor gainst thy love in wager laid,
Thou wouldst be pricked with other senses' stings,
To taste and feel, and yet not there be stayed.
These casts he cast, and more, his wits more quick
Than can be cast by wit's arithmetic.

### 44

Forward, and back, and forward went he thus,
Like wanton Thamesis that hastes to greet
The brackish court of old Oceanus,
And as by London's bosom she doth fleet
Casts herself proudly through the bridge's twists,
Where (as she takes again her crystal feet)
She curls her silver hair like amorists,
Smooths her bright cheeks, adorns her brows with ships,
And empress-like along the coast she trips.

### 45

Till, coming near the sea, she hears him roar,
Tumbling her churlish billows in her face;
Then, more dismayed than insolent before,
Charged to rough battle for his smooth embrace,
She croucheth close within her winding banks
And creeps retreat into her peaceful palace.
Yet straight high-flowing in her female pranks,
Again she will be wanton, and again,
By no means stayed nor able to contain.

### 46

So Ovid, with his strong affections striving,
Masked in a friendly thicket near her bower,
Rubbing his temples, fainting and reviving,
Fitting his garments, praying to the hour,
Backwards and forwards went, and durst not venture
To tempt the tempest of his mistress' lower
Or let his eyes her beauty's ocean enter.
At last, with prayer he pierceth Juno's ear,
Great goddess of audacity and fear:

---

**43.8** *These casts he cast* he reckoned these possibilities.
**44.1** *Forward* Chapman's note: "A simile expressing the manner of his mind's contention in the desire of her sight and fear of her displeasure."

**44.2** *Thamesis* the Thames.
**44.4** *fleet* hurry.
**44.7** *amorists* lovers.
**46.6** *lower* frown.

47

Great goddess of audacity and fear,
Queen of Olympus, Saturn's eldest seed,
That dost the scepter over Samos bear
And rul'st all nuptial rites with power and meed:
Since thou in nature art the mean to mix
Still sulphur humors, and canst therefore speed
Such as in Cyprian sports their pleasures fix,
Venus herself, and Mars, by thee embracing,
Assist my hopes, me and my purpose gracing.

48

Make love within me not too kind, but pleasing,
Exiling aspen fear out of his forces,
My inward sight with outward seeing easing;
And if he please further to stretch his courses,
Arm me with courage to make good his charges.
Too much desire to please pleasure divorces;
Attempts, and not entreats, get ladies' larges.
Wit is with boldness prompt, with terror daunted,
And grace is sooner got of dames than granted.

49

This said, he charged the arbor with his eye,
Which pierced it through, and at her breasts reflected,
Striking him to the heart with ecstasy,
As do the sunbeams, gainst the earth prorected,
With their reverberate vigor mount in flames
And burn much more than where they were directed.
He saw the extraction of all fairest dames,
The Fair of Beauty, as whole countries come
And show their riches in a little room.

50

Here Ovid sold his freedom for a look,
And with that look was ten times more enthralled.
He blushed, looked pale, and like a fever shook,
And as a burning vapor being exhaled,
Promised by Phoebus' eye to be a star,
Heaven's walls denying to be further scaled,
The force dissolves that drew it up so far,
And then it lightens gainst his death and falls:
So Ovid's power this powerful sight appalls.

---

47.4–8  In alchemical interpretations of classical mythology, Juno was equated with mercury, which was supposed to be the ingredient that allowed certain volatile elements ("sulphur humors") to be combined into metals; Chapman is here following very closely a passage in the Italian mythographer Natalis Comes.

47.3  *Samos* Site in antiquity of a very famous temple to Hera (Juno).

47.4  *nuptial rites* Wife to the king of the gods, Juno was the patron goddess of marriage.

48.7  *larges* largess.

49.4  *prorected* The word appears to be Chapman's invention; it may mean either "reflected straight back" or "reflected at a right angle."

49.7  *extraction* extracted essence.

50.4  *a* Chapman's note: "This simile expresseth the cause and substance of those exhalations which vulgarly are called falling stars; so Homer and Vergil calls them, *stellas cadentes,* Homer comparing the descent of Pallas among the Troyans to a falling star."

50.9  So this powerful sight weakens Ovid's power.

### 51

This Beauty's Fair is an enchantment made
By nature's witchcraft, tempting men to buy
With endless shows what endlessly will fade,
Yet promise chapmen all eternity;
But like to goods ill got, a fate it hath
Brings men enriched therewith to beggary,
Unless the enricher be as rich in faith,
Enamored (like good self-love) with her own,
Seen in another: then tis heaven alone.

### 52

For sacred beauty is the fruit of sight,
The courtesy that speaks before the tongue,
The feast of souls, the glory of the light,
Envy of age and everlasting young,
Pity's commander, Cupid's richest throne,
Music entrancèd, never duly sung,
The sum and court of all proportion,
And, that I may dull speeches best afford,
All rhetoric's flowers in less than in a word.

### 53

Then in the truest wisdom can be thought,
Spite of the public axiom worldlings hold
That nothing wisdom is that getteth nought,
This all-things-nothing, since it is no gold,
Beauty enchasing love, love gracing beauty,
To such as constant sympathies enfold
To perfect riches doth a sounder duty
Than all endeavors, for by all consent
All wealth and wisdom rests in true content.

### 54

Contentment is our heaven, and all our deeds
Bend in that circle, seld or never closed,
More than the letter in the word precedes,
And to conduce that compass is reposed.
More force and art in beauty joined with love
Than thrones with wisdom; joys of them composed
Are arms more proof gainst any grief we prove
Than all their virtue-scorning misery
Or judgments graven in Stoic gravity.

### 55

But as weak color always is allowed
The proper object of a human eye,
Though light be with a far more force endowed
In stirring up the visual faculty,
This color being but of virtuous light

---

51.4   *chapmen* merchants.
53.5   *enchasing* enhancing (the way a setting enhances a jewel).
54.2   *seld* seldom.

54.3   *the letter in the word precedes* The letter C, the first letter in "content" and an unclosed circle.
54.4   And is at rest in tracing that circle.
54.7   *prove* experience.

A feeble image, and the cause doth lie
In the imperfection of a human sight,
So this for love and beauty, love's cold fire,
May serve for my praise, though it merit higher.


### 56

With this digression, we will now return
To Ovid's prospect in his fancy's storm.
He thought he saw the arbor's blossom burn,
Blazed with a fire wrought in a lady's form,
Where silver past the least and nature's vant
Did such a precious miracle perform,
She lay and seemed a flood of diamant
Bounded in flesh, as still as Vesper's hair
When not an aspen leaf is stirred with air.


### 57

She lay at length, like an immortal soul
At endless rest in blest Elysium;
And then did true felicity enrole
So fair a lady, figure of her kingdom.
Now Ovid's Muse as in her tropic shined,
And he (struck dead) was mere heaven-borne become,
So his quick verse in equal height was shrined;
Or else blame me as his submitted debtor,
That never mistress had to make me better.


### 58

Now as she lay attired in nakedness,
His eye did carve him on that feast of feasts:
Sweet fields of life which death's foot dare not press,
Flowered with the unbroken waves of my love's breasts,
Unbroke by depth of those her beauty's floods.
See where, with bent of gold curled into nests,
In her head's grove the spring-bird lameate broods;
Her body doth present those fields of peace
Where souls are feasted with the soul of ease.


### 59

To prove which paradise that nurseth these,
See, see the golden rivers that renown it:
Rich Gihon, Tigris, Phison, Euphrates.
Two from her bright Pelopian shoulders crown it,
And two out of her snowy hills do glide

---

**56.5**  *vant* boast.
**56.8**  *Vesper* Personification of the evening.
**57.1**  *lay* Chapman's note: "The amplification of this simile is taken from the blissful state of souls in Elysium, as Vergil feigns, and expresseth a regenerate beauty in all life and perfection, not intimating any rest of death; but in place of that eternal spring, he pointeth to that life of life, this beauty-clad naked lady." The Vergilian reference is to *Aeneid* 6.637ff.
**58.3**  *Sweet* Chapman's note: "He calls her body (as it were divided with her breasts) the fields of paradise, and her arms and legs the famous rivers in it."

**58.6**  *bent* grass.
**58.7**  *the spring-bird lameate broods* In the context of the next two lines, the "spring-bird" is probably the halcyon, but "lameate" remains unexplained: possibly a Latinate formation from "lamé" – a gilded bird – or a misprint for "laureate."
**59.3**  See Genesis 2.10–14; Chapman's "Phison" should be "Pishon."
**59.4**  *Pelopian shoulders* Pelops had a prosthetic shoulder made out of ivory.

That with a deluge of delights do drown it;
The highest two their precious streams divide
To ten pure floods that do the body duty,
Bounding themselves in length, but not in beauty.

### 60

These wind their courses through the painted bowers
And raise such sounds in their inflection
As ceaseless start from earth fresh sorts of flowers
And bound that book of life with every section.
In these the Muses dare not swim for drowning,
Their sweetness poisons with such blest infection
And leaves the only lookers on them swooning;
These forms so decks and color makes so shine
That gods for them would cease to be divine.

### 61

Thus, though my love be no Elysium
That cannot move from her prefixèd place,
Yet have her feet no power from thence to come,
For where she is is all Elysian grace;
And as those happy men are sure of bliss
That can perform so excellent a race
As that Olympiad where her favor is,
So she can meet them – blessing them the rather,
And give her sweets, as well as let men gather.

### 62

Ah, how should I be so most happy then
To aspire that place, or make it come to me;
To gather, or be given, the flower of women?
Elysium must with virtue gotten be,
With labors of the soul and continence,
And these can yield no joy with such as she.
She is a sweet Elysium for the sense,
And nature doth not sensual gifts infuse
But that with sense she still intends their use.

### 63

The sense is given us to excite the mind,
And that can never be by sense excited
But first the sense must her contentment find.
We therefore must procure the sense delighted,
That so the soul may use her faculty;
Mine eye then to this feast hath her invited,
That she might serve the sovereign of mine eye;
She shall bide time, and time, so feasted never,
Shall grow in strength of her renown forever.

**60.1** *These* Chapman's note: "He intends the office <of> her fingers in attiring her, touching this of their courses, in their inflection following, their playing upon an instrument."

**63.3** *find* The original text reads "mind."

64

Betwixt mine eye and object, certain lines
Move in the figure of a pyramis,
Whose chapter in mine eye's gray apple shines,
The base within my sacred object is;
On this will I inscribe in golden verse
The marvels reigning in my sovereign's bliss,
The arcs of sight, and how her arrows pierce.
This in the region of the air shall stand
In fame's brass court, and all her trump command.

65

Rich beauty that each lover labors for,
Tempting as heaps of new-coined glowing gold
(Racked of some miserable treasurer),
Draw his desires and them in chains enfold,
Urging him still to tell it and conceal it.
But beauty's treasure never can be told;
None can peculiar joy, yet all must steal it.
O Beauty, this same bloody siege of thine
Starves me that yield, and feeds me till I pine.

66

And as a taper burning in the dark
(As if it threatened every watchful eye
That viewing burns it) makes that eye his mark
And hurls gilt darts at it continually,
Or as it envied any eye but it
Should see in darkness, so my mistress' beauty
From forth her secret stand my heart doth hit,
And like the dart of Cephalus doth kill
Her perfect lover, though she mean no ill.

67

Thus, as the innocence of one betrayed
Carries an Argus with it, though unknown,
And Fate to wreak the treachery bewrayed,
Such vengeance hath my mistress' beauty shown
On me, the traitor to her modesty;
So, unassailed, I quite am overthrown,
And in my triumph bound in slavery.
O Beauty, still thy empire swims in blood,
And in thy peace, War stores himself with food.

68

O Beauty, how attractive is thy power?
For as the life's heat clings about the heart,
So all men's hungry eyes do haunt thy bower.
Reigning in Greece, Troy swum to thee in art;

64.3   *chapter* apex.
64.9   *trump* trumpet.
65.3   *Racked of* extorted by.
65.7   *peculiar* appropriate as one's own.
66.7   *stand* hunting position.

66.8   *Cephalus* Husband to Procris, who spied on him while he was hunting; thinking she was an animal in the brush, he killed her by accident.
67.2   *Argus* A creature with a hundred eyes, which never all closed at the same time.

Removed to Troy, Greece followed thee in fears.
Thou drewst each sireless sword, each childless dart,
And pulledst the towers of Troy about thine ears.
Shall I then muse that thus thou drawest me?
No, but admire I stand thus far from thee.

### 69

Herewith she rose like the autumnal star,
Fresh burnished in the lofty ocean flood,
That darts his glorious influence more far
Than any lamp of bright Olympus' brood.
She lifts her lightening arms above her head,
And stretcheth a meridian from her blood,
That slept awake in her Elysian bed;
Then knit she up, lest, loose, her glowing hair
Should scorch the center and incense the air.

### 70

Thus when her fair heart-binding hands had tied
Those liberal tresses, her high frontier part,
She shrunk in curls, and curiously plied
Into the figure of a swelling heart,
And then with jewels of device it graced.
One was a sun graven at his even's depart,
And under that a man's huge shadow placed,
Wherein was writ, in sable charactery,
*Descrescente nobilitate, crescunt obscuri.*

### 71

An other was an eye in sapphire set,
And close upon it a fresh laurel spray;
The skillful posy was *Medio caret*,
To show not eyes but means must truth display.
The third was an Apollo with his team
About a dial and a world in way;
The motto was *Teipsum et orbem*,
Graven in the dial. These exceeding rare
And other like accomplements she ware.

### 72

Not Tigris, Nilus, nor swift Euphrates,
Quoth Ovid now, can more subdue my flame.
I must through hell adventure to displease,
To taste and touch; one kiss may work the same.
If more will come, more than much more I will.

---

**69.1** *autumnal star* Sirius.
**69.6** *stretcheth a meridian* stretches her arms directly upward.
**70.5** *device* meaningful design (as on a coat of arms).
**70.7** *shadow* Chapman's note: "At the sun going down, shadows grow longest, whereupon this emblem is devised."
**70.9** With the decline of nobility, the obscure rise.
**71.3** *Medio caret* It lacks its medium. Chapman's note: "Sight is one of the three senses that hath his medium extrinsically, which now (supposed wanting) lets the sight by the close apposition of the laurel: the application whereof hath many constructions."
**71.5** *Apollo* Chapman's note: "The sun hath as much time to compass a dial [i.e., sundial] as the world, and therefore the world is placed in the dial, expressing the conceit of the impress morally, which hath a far higher intention."
**71.6** *in way* on his way.
**71.7** *Teipsum et orbem* yourself and the world.
**71.9** *accomplements* ornaments.

Each natural agent doth his action frame
To render that he works on like him still;
The fire on water working doth induce
Like quality unto his own in use.


### 73

But heaven in her a sparkling temper blew
(As love in me), and so will soon be wrought;
Good wits will bite at baits most strange and new,
And words well placed move things were never thought.
What goddess is it Ovid's wits shall dare
And he disgrace them with attempting nought?
My words shall carry spirits to ensnare,
The subtlest hearts affecting suits importune:
Best loves are lost for wit when men blame Fortune.


### 74

With this, as she was looking in her glass,
She saw therein a man's face looking on her,
Whereat she started from the frighted grass
As if some monstrous serpent had been shown her:
Rising as when (the sun in Leo's sign)
Auriga with the heavenly Goat upon her
Shows her horned forehead with her kids divine,
Whose rise kills vines, heaven's face with storms disguising;
No man is safe at sea, the haedy rising.


### 75

So straight wrapped she her body in a cloud,
And threatened tempests for her high disgrace;
Shame from a bower of roses did unshroud
And spread her crimson wings upon her face.
When running out, poor Ovid, humbly kneeling
Full in the arbor's mouth, did stay her race,
And said: Fair nymph, great goddess, have some feeling
Of Ovid's pains. But hear, and your dishonor,
Vainly surmised, shall vanish with my horror.


### 76

Traitor to ladies' modesties (said she),
What savage boldness hardened thee to this?
Or what base reckoning of my modesty?
What should I think thy fact's proud reason is?
Love (sacred madam), love exhaling me
(Wrapped in his sulphur) to this cloud of his
Made my affections his artillery,
Shot me at you, his proper citadel,
And, losing all my forces, here I fell.

---

**73.2**  *wrought* worked (into a particular shape or condition).
**74.1**  *glass* mirror.
**74.2**  *therein* Chapman's note: "Ovid standing behind her, his face was seen in the glass."

**74.5–9**  In the late summer, when the sun is in Leo, the constellation Auriga is rising, here said to bring dangerously stormy weather. Auriga is usually understood as a man driving a chariot while carrying a goat on his back; the star Capella represents the goat, and two twin stars in the constellation are known as the kids, or *haedi*.

### 77

This gloss is common, as thy rudeness strange
Not to forbear these private times (quoth she),
Whose fixèd rites none should presume to change,
Not where there is adjudged inchastity.
Our nakedness should be as much concealed
As our accomplishments desire the eye;
It is a secret not to be revealed,
But as virginity and nuptials clothed,
And to our honor all to be betrothed.

### 78

It is a want where our abundance lies,
Given a sole dower to enrich chaste Hymen's bed,
A perfect image of our purities,
And glass by which our actions should be dressed,
That tells us honor is as soon defiled
And should be kept as pure and incompressed,
But sight attainteth it; for thought, sight's child,
Begetteth sin, and nature bides defame
When light and lawless eyes bewray our shame.

### 79

Dear mistress (answered Ovid), to direct
Our actions by the straitest rule that is,
We must in matters moral quite reject
Vulgar Opinion, ever led amiss,
And let authentic Reason be our guide,
The wife of Truth and Wisdom's governess.
The nature of all actions must be weighed
And, as they then appear, breed love or loathing;
Use makes things nothing huge, and huge things nothing.

### 80

As in your sight, how can sight, simply being
A sense receiving essence to his flame
Sent from his object, give it harm by seeing,
Whose action in the seer hath his frame?
All excellence of shape is made for sight;
Else, to be like a beast were no defame.
Hid beauties lose their ends, and wrong their right;
And can kind love (where no harms kind can be)
Disgrace with seeing that is given to see?

### 81

Tis I (alas) and my heart-burning eye
Do all the harm, and feel the harm we do.
I am no basilisk, yet harmless I
Poison with sight, and mine own bosom, too.

78.2 *Hymen* god of marriage.
78.6 *incompressed* unembraced.
78.7 *attainteth* sullies.
78.8 *bides defame* awaits dishonor.

80.4 *action* Chapman's note: "Actio cernendi in homine vel animali vidente collocanda est. *Aristot.*" "The act of seeing must be assigned to a human being or animal that sees"; no specific source in Aristotle has been found.
81.3 *basilisk* A legendary reptile said to kill with its look.

So am I to myself a sorceress,
Bewitched with my conceits in her I woo;
But you unwronged and all dishonorless
No ill dares touch; affliction, sorcery
One kiss of yours can quickly remedy.

### 82

I could not times observe, as others might,
Of cold affects and watery tempers framed,
Yet well assured the wonder of your sight
Was so far off from seeing you defamed,
That ever in the fane of memory
Your love shall shine by it, in me inflamed.
Then let your power be clad in lenity;
Do not (as others would) of custom storm,
But prove your wit as pregnant as your form.

### 83

Nor is my love so sudden, since my heart
Was long love's Vulcan, with his pants' unrest:
Hammering the shafts bred this delightsome smart.
And as when Jove at once from east and west
Cast off two eagles to discern the site
Of this world center, both his birds joined breast
In Cynthian Delphos, since earth's navel hight:
So casting off my ceaseless thoughts to see
My heart's true center, all do meet in thee.

### 84

Cupid, that acts in you, suffers in me
To make himself one triumph-place of twain;
Into your tunes and odors turnèd he,
And through my senses flew into my brain,
Where rules the Prince of Sense, whose throne he takes,
And of my motions' engines framed a chain
To lead me where he list; and here he makes
Nature (my fate) enforce me, and resigns
The reins of all to you, in whom he shines.

### 85

For yielding love, then, do not hate impart,
Nor let mine eye, your careful harbinger,
That hath purveyed your chamber in my heart,
Be blamed for seeing who it lodgèd there;

**82.1**  *times observe* respect your schedule.
**82.5**  *fane* temple.
**82.7**  *lenity* leniency.
**82.8**  *of custom* in the customary way.
**83.2**  *Vulcan* the blacksmith of the gods.  *his pants' unrest* the tumult of his hard breathing.
**83.7**  *Cynthian Delphos* Apollo's oracle at Delphi; "Cynthian" usually refers to Apollo's sister Diana, but can refer to him as well. The oracle was the site of a navelstone that was claimed to be the center of the earth. The previous lines describe Jupiter's technique for determining its location; the eagles

were equally matched and released simultaneously from the far ends of the earth.
**84.5**  *Where* Chapman's note: "In cerebro est principium sentiendi, et inde nervi qui instrumenta sunt motus voluntarii oriuntur." "The beginning of sensation is in the brain, and from there arise the nerves that are the instruments of voluntary motion."
**84.8**  *my* Chapman's note: "Natura est uniuscuiusque fatum, ut *Theophrast.*" "Nature is everyone's fate." Theophrastus was Aristotle's successor at the Peripatos in Athens.
**85.3**  *purveyed* furnished.

The freer service merits greater meed.
Princes are served with unexpected cheer,
And must have things in store before they need;
Thus should fair dames be wise and confident,
Not blushing to be noted excellent.

### 86

Now, as when heaven is muffled with the vapors
His long since just divorcèd wife, the earth,
In envy breathes to mask his spurry tapers
From the unrich abundance of her birth,
When straight the western issue of the air
Beats with his flowery wings those brats of dearth
And gives Olympus leave to show his fair,
So fled the offended shadows of her cheer
And showed her pleasèd countenance full as clear.

### 87

This motion of my soul, my fantasy,
Created by three senses put in act,
Let justice nourish with thy sympathy,
Putting my other senses into fact;
If now thou grant not, now change that offense.
To suffer change doth perfect sense compact;
Change then, and suffer for the use of sense.
We live not for ourselves; the ear and eye
And every sense must serve society.

### 88

To furnish then this banquet, where the taste
Is never used, and yet the cheer divine,
The nearest mean, dear mistress, that thou hast
To bless me with, it is a kiss of thine,
Which grace shall borrow organs of my touch
To advance it to that inward taste of mine
Which makes all sense, and shall delight as much.
Then with a kiss (dear life) adorn thy feast,
And let (as banquets should) the last be best.

### 89

I see unbidden guests are boldest still,
And well you show how weak in soul you are
That let rude sense subdue your reason's skill
And feed so spoilfully on sacred fare;
In temper of such needless feasts as this,
We show more bounty still the more we spare,

---

86.3 *spurry tapers* spur-like beams of light.
87.5 *change* The original text reads "changde."
87.6 *compact* constitute. Chapman's marginal note gives a Latin version: "Alternationem pati est sentire." The idea, in not quite the same phrasing, may be found in Aristotle, *On the Soul* 2.5/416B.
88.6 *inward* Chapman's note: "He intends the common sense which is *centrum sensibus et speciebus* [the center for senses and

sensible emanations], and calls it last because it doth *sapere in effectione sensuum* [achieve knowledge in the action of the senses – where the Latin verb for 'achieve knowledge' is also the verb for 'taste']." For "sensible emanations" and the "common sense," see above on 17.5 and 23.3.
89.1 A marginal note identifies Corinna as the speaker of this stanza.
89.4 *spoilfully* rapaciously.

Chiefly where birth and state so different is.
Air too much rarefied breaks forth in fire,
And favors too far urged do end in ire.


### 90

The difference of our births (imperial dame)
Is herein noted with too trivial eyes
For your rare wits, that should your choices frame
To state of parts that most doth royalize,
Not to commend mine own, but that in yours,
Beyond your birth, are peril's sovereignties:
Which urged, your words had struck with sharper powers.
Tis for mere look-like ladies and for men
To boast of birth that still be childeren,


### 91

Running to father straight to help their needs.
True dignities and rites of reverence
Are sown in minds and reaped in lively deeds,
And only policy makes difference
Twixt states, since virtue wants due imperance.
Virtue makes honor as the soul doth sense,
And merit far exceeds inheritance;
The Graces fill Love's cup, his feasts adorning,
Who seeks your service now, the Graces scorning.


### 92

Pure love (said she) the purest grace pursues,
And there is contact, not by application
Of lips or bodies, but of bodies' virtues,
As in our elemental nation
Stars by their powers, which are their heat and light,
Do heavenly works, and that which hath probation
By virtual contact hath the noblest plight,
Both for the lasting and affinity
It hath with natural divinity.


### 93

Ovid replied: In this, thy virtual presence
(Most fair Corinna), thou canst not effuse
The true and solid parts of thy pure essence,
But dost the superficial beams produce
Of thy rich substance; which, because they flow
Rather from form than from the matter's use,
Resemblance only of thy body show
Whereof they are thy wondrous species,
And tis thy substance must my longings ease.


### 94

Speak, then, sweet air that giv'st our speech event
And teach my mistress tractability,

---

90.1  A marginal note identifies Ovid as once more the speaker.

90.4  *To state of parts* to the quality of attributes.

91.4  *policy* worldly expedience.

91.5  *imperance* ability to command.

93.8  *species* See on 17.5 above.

That art to motion most obedient;
And though thy nature swelling be and high
And occupiest so infinite a space,
Yet yieldst to words, and art condensed thereby,
Past nature pressed into a little place.
Dear sovereign, then, make air thy rule in this
And me thy worthy servant with a kiss.

### 95

Ovid (said she), I am well pleased to yield.
Bounty by virtue cannot be abused,
Nor will I coyly lift Minerva's shield
Against Minerva; honor is not bruised
With such a tender pressure as a kiss,
Nor yielding soon to words, though seldom used.
Niceness in civil favors folly is;
Long suits make never good a bad detection,
Nor yielding soon makes bad a good affection.

### 96

To some, I know (and know it for a fault),
Order and reverence are repulsed in scaling.
When pride and rudeness enter with assault,
Consents to fall are worse to get than falling;
Willing resistance takes away the will,
And too much weakness tis to come with calling.
Force in these frays is better man than skill;
Yet I like skill, and, Ovid, if a kiss
May do thee so much pleasure, here it is.

### 97

Her moving towards him made Ovid's eye
Believe the firmament was coming down
To take him quick to immortality,
And that the ambrosian kiss set on the crown.
She spake in kissing, and her breath infused
Restoring syrup to his taste in swoon,
And he imagined Hebe's hands had bruised
A banquet of the gods into his sense,
Which filled him with this furious influence.

### 98

The motion of the heavens that did beget
The golden age, and by whose harmony
Heaven is preserved, in me on work is set:
All instruments of deepest melody
Set sweet in my desires to my love's liking
With this sweet kiss in me their tunes apply,
As if the best musicians' hands were striking.

95.3  *Minerva* goddess of wisdom.
95.7  *Niceness* fastidiousness.
95.8  *detection* discovery.

97.7  *Hebe* personification of youth and cupbearer to the gods.
98.3  *on work is set* is set to work.

This kiss in me hath endless music closed,
Like Phoebus' lute on Nisus' towers imposed.

### 99

And as a pebble cast into a spring,
We see a sort of trembling circles rise,
One forming other in their issuing
Till over all the fount they circulize,
So this perpetual-motion-making kiss
Is propagate through all my faculties
And makes my breast an endless fount of bliss,
Of which, if gods could drink, their matchless fare
Would make them much more blessèd than they are.

### 100

But as when sounds do hollow bodies beat,
Air gathered there, compressed and thickenèd,
The selfsame way she came doth make retreat
And so effects the sound re-echoèd
Only in part, because she weaker is
In that redition than when first she fled:
So I, alas, faint echo of this kiss,
Only reiterate a slender part
Of that high joy it worketh in my heart.

### 101

And thus with feasting love is famished more.
Without my touch are all things turned to gold,
And till I touch I cannot joy my store;
To purchase others, I myself have sold.
Love is a wanton famine, rich in food,
But with a richer appetite controlled;
An argument in figure and in mood,
Yet hates all arguments, disputing still
For sense gainst reason with a senseless will.

### 102

Then, sacred madam, since my other senses
Have in your graces tasted such content,
Let wealth not to be spent fear no expenses,
But give thy bounty true eternizement,
Making my senses' groundwork, which is feeling,
Effect the other, endless excellent,
Their substance with flint-softening softness steeling.
Then let me feel, for know, sweet beauty's queen,
Dames may be felt as well as heard or seen.

---

98.9   *Nisus* The king of Megara, the tower of whose castle retained the sound of Apollo's lyre after it had once been placed there (Ovid, *Metamorphoses* 8.14–16).
100.1   *But* Chapman's note: "Qua ratione fiat echo." "By which means an echo may happen."
100.6   *redition* return.

101.1   Evoking Narcissus: "inopem me copia fecit," "plenty has made me poor" (*Metamorphoses* 3.466).
101.7   *in figure and in mood* The terms are part of a system for classifying the nineteen forms of recognized logical syllogisms; the phrase means "in appropriate logical order."
102.5   *feeling* Touch, which Aristotle identifies as "the primary form of sense" (*On the Soul* 2.2/413B).

## 103

For if we be allowed to serve the ear
With pleasing tunes, and to delight the eye
With gracious shows, the taste with dainty cheer,
The smell with odors, is't immodesty
To serve the senses' emperor, sweet feeling,
With those delights that fit his empery?
Shall subjects free themselves, and bind their king?
Minds taint no more with bodies' touch or tire
Than bodies nourish with the minds' desire.

## 104

The mind then clear, the body may be used,
Which perfectly your touch can spiritualize,
As by the great elixir is transfused
Copper to gold; then grant that deed of prize.
Such as transform into corrupt effects
What they receive from nature's purities
Should not wrong them that hold her due respects.
To touch your quickening side then give me leave;
The abuse of things must not the use bereave.

## 105

Herewith, even glad his arguments to hear,
Worthily willing to have lawful grounds
To make the wondrous power of heaven appear,
In nothing more than her perfections found,
Close to her navel she her mantle wrests,
Slacking it upwards, and the folds unwound,
Showing Latona's twins, her plenteous breasts,
The Sun and Cynthia in their triumph robes
Of lady-skin, more rich than both their globes.

## 106

Whereto she bade blest Ovid put his hand;
He, well acknowledging it much too base
For such an action, did a little stand,
Ennobling it with titles full of grace,
And conjures it with charge of reverend verse
To use with piety that sacred place,
And through his feeling's organ to disperse
Worth to his spirits, amply to supply
The poorness of his flesh's faculty.

## 107

And thus he said: King of the king of senses,
Engine of all the engines under heaven,
To health and life, defense of all defenses,
Bounty by which our nourishment is given,
Beauty's beautifier, kind acquaintance-maker,
Proportion's oddness that makes all things even,

---

**103.8** *tire* attire.
**104.3** *the great elixir* The philosopher's stone, the mythical
goal of alchemical research.

**105.7** *Latona's twins* Apollo and Diana.
**107.2** *Engine* The original text reads "Engines."

Wealth of the laborer, wrong's revengement-taker,
Pattern of concord, lord of exercise,
And figure of that power the world did guise:

### 108

Dear hand, most duly honorèd in this,
And therefore worthy to be well employed,
Yet know that all that honor nothing is
Compared with that which now must be enjoyed;
So think in all the pleasures these have shown
(Likened to this) thou wert but mere annoyed,
That all hands' merits in thyself alone
With this one touch have more than recompense,
And therefore feel, with fear and reverence.

### 109

See Cupid's Alps, which now thou must go over,
Where snow that thaws the sun doth ever lie;
Where thou mayst plain and feelingly discover
The worlds forepast that flowed with milk and honey;
Where (like an empress seeing nothing wanting
That may her glorious child-bed beautify)
Pleasure herself lies big with issue panting,
Ever delivered, yet with child still growing,
Full of all blessings, yet all bliss bestowing.

### 110

This said, he laid his hand upon her side,
Which made her start like sparkles from a fire,
Or like Saturnia from the ambrosian pride
Of her morn's slumber, frighted with admire
When Jove laid young Alcides to her breast:
So startled she, not with a coy retire,
But with the tender temper she was blest,
Proving her sharp, undulled with handling yet,
Which keener edge on Ovid's longings set.

### 111

And feeling still, he sighed out this effect:
Alas, why lent not heaven the soul a tongue
Nor language nor peculiar dialect
To make her high conceits as highly sung,
But that a fleshly engine must unfold
A spiritual notion? Birth from princes sprung
Peasants must nurse, free virtue wait on gold,
And a professed though flattering enemy
Must plead my honor and my liberty.

### 112

O Nature, how dost thou defame in this
Our human honors, yoking men with beasts

107.9  *guise* dress.
109.4  *forepast* of times past.
110.3  *Saturnia* Juno.

110.5  *Alcides* Hercules.
111.3  *peculiar* of its own.

And noblest minds with slaves? Thus beauty's bliss,
Love and all virtues that quick spirit feasts
Surfeit on flesh, and thou that banquetst minds,
Most bounteous mistress, of thy dull-tongued guests
Reapst not due thanks; thus rude frailty binds
What thou giv'st wings, thus joys I feel in thee
Hang on my lips and will not uttered be.

### 113

Sweet touch, the engine that Love's bow doth bend,
The sense wherewith he feels him deified,
The object whereto all his actions tend,
In all his blindness his most pleasing guide,
For thy sake I will write the Art of Love,
Since thou dost blow his fire and feed his pride,
Since in thy sphere his health and life doth move;
For thee I hate who hate society,
And such as self-love makes his slavery.

### 114

In these dog-days how this contagion smothers
The purest bloods with virtue's diet fined,
Nothing their own, unless they be some others,
Spite of themselves, are in themselves confined
And live so poor they are of all despised;
Their gifts, held down with scorn, should be divined,
And they like mummers mask, unknown, unprized.
A thousand marvels mourn in some such breast
Would make a kind and worthy patron blest.

### 115

To me (dear sovereign) thou are patroness,
And I, with that thy graces have infused,
Will make all fat and foggy brains confess
Riches may from a poor verse be deduced;
And that gold's love shall leave them groveling here
When thy perfections shall to heaven be mused,
Decked in bright verse, where angels shall appear,
The praise of virtue, love, and beauty singing,
Honor to noblesse, shame to avarice bringing.

### 116

Here Ovid, interrupted with the view
Of other dames who then the garden painted,
Shrouded himself, and did as death eschew
All note by which his love's fame might be tainted;
And as when mighty Macedon had won
The monarchy of earth, yet, when he fainted,
Grieved that no greater action could be done
And that there were no more worlds to subdue,
So love's defects love's conqueror did rue.

114.2  *fined* refined.
114.7  *mummers* actors.

115.6  *mused* carried by a Muse.
116.5  *Macedon* Alexander the Great.

### 117

But as when expert painters have displayed
To quickest life a monarch's royal hand
Holding a scepter, there is yet bewrayed
But half his fingers, when we understand
The rest not to be seen, and never blame
The painter's art, in nicest censures scanned:
So in the compass of this curious frame
Ovid well knew there was much more intended,
With whose omission none must be offended.

Intentio, animi actio.
Explicit convivium.

117.6   *in nicest censures scanned* scrutinized according to the most exacting standards.

*Intentio, animi actio* Intention is the action of the soul.
*Explicit convivium* The banquet is finished.

# Mary Herbert, Countess of Pembroke (1561–1621)

Philip Sidney's sister was born in Worcestershire, and received her title when she married Henry Herbert, Earl of Pembroke, in 1577. She was very close to her brother and became almost mortally ill at the news of his death in 1586. After recovering, she became, with Fulke Greville, her brother's literary executor, and cultivated at Wilton House in Wiltshire an important literary circle, much frequented by poets whom she favored. It was among other things the major center for neoclassical drama in the English Renaissance; the Countess herself produced a verse translation of Robert Garnier's *Marc Antoine*. With her husband's death in 1601 Wilton passed into the hands of her son William Herbert (a perennial candidate for the Young Man of Shakespeare's sonnets), and the circle dispersed.

She probably wrote "The Doleful Lay of Clorinda," an elegy on her brother published in 1595 together with Edmunds Spenser's "Astrophel." The lament given here is prefixed in manuscript to her own completion of the verse translation of the Psalms that Philip Sidney had begun; for a sample of her contribution to this translation, see the section on Psalm 130 above. A somewhat calmer version of "To the Angel Spirit" was printed in the 1623 edition of the works of Samuel Daniel; the text given here was not printed until 1823. Its emotional intensity comes with a syntax that is at times almost beyond following; in the most troubled passage, the eighth stanza, that emotion is not just grief but also tortuously formulated anger at the "owly blind" who fail to appreciate her brother's genius. These may well be reverberations off the dedication to Queen Elizabeth that accompanies this one in the manuscript.

*Edition*: *The Collected Works of Mary Sidney Herbert, Countess of Pembroke*, ed. Margaret P. Hannay, Noel J. Kinnamon, and Michael G. Brennan (Oxford: Clarendon Press, 1998).

## To the Angel Spirit of the Most Excellent Sir Philip Sidney

To thee, pure sprite, to thee alone's addressed
This coupled work, by double interest thine:
First raised by thy blest hand, and what is mine
Inspired by thee, thy secret power impressed.
So dared my Muse with thine itself combine,          5
As mortal stuff with that which is divine.
Thy lightning beams give luster to the rest,

That heaven's King may deign his own transformed,
In substance no, but superficial tire
By thee put on; to praise, not to aspire          10
To those high tones, so in themselves adorned,
Which angels sing in their celestial choir –
And all of tongues with soul and voice admire
These sacred hymns thy kingly prophet formed.

O, had that soul which honor brought to rest          15
Too soon not left and reft the world of all
What man could show which we perfection call,
This half-maimed piece had sorted with the best.
Deep wounds enlarged, long festered in their gall,
Fresh bleeding smart; not eye- but heart-tears fall.          20
Ah, memory, what needs this new arrest?

---

8  *deign* condescend to honor.
9  *tire* attire.

17  *What* that.
18  *sorted* made good company.

Yet here behold (O, wert thou to behold!)
This finished now, thy matchless Muse begun,
The rest but pieced, as left by thee undone.
Pardon (O blest soul) presumption too, too bold;      25
If love and zeal such error ill become,
Tis zealous love, love which hath never done
Nor can enough in world of words unfold.

And sith it hath no further scope to go,
Nor other purpose but to honor thee,          30
Thee in thy works where all the graces be,
As little streams with all their all do flow
To their great sea, due tribute's grateful fee,
So press my thoughts, my burdened thoughts, in me
To pay the debt of infinites I owe              35

To thy great worth, exceeding nature's store,
Wonder of men, sole born perfection's kind.
Phoenix thou wert, so rare thy fairest mind,
Heavenly adorned, earth justly might adore,
Where truthful praise in highest glory shined;      40
For there alone was praise to truth confined,
And where but there, to live for evermore?

O, when to this account, this cast-up sum,
This reckoning made, this audit of my woe,
I call my thoughts, whence so strange passions flow,      45
How works my heart, my senses stricken dumb,
That would thee more than ever heart could show?
And all too short who knew thee best doth know
There lives no wit that may thy praise become.

Truth I invoke (who scorn elsewhere to move,       50
Or here in ought my blood should partialize),
Truth, sacred Truth, thee sole to solemnize.
Those precious rites well known best minds approve;
And who but doth, hath wisdom's open eyes,
Not, owly blind, the fairest light still flies,       55
Confirm no less? At least tis sealed above,

Where thou art fixed among thy fellow lights:
My day put out, my life in darkness cast,
Thy angel's soul, with highest angels placed,
There blessèd sings, enjoying heaven delights,      60
Thy Maker's praise, as far from earthly taste
As here thy works, so worthily embraced
By all of worth, where never envy bites.

As goodly buildings to some glorious end
Cut off by fate before the Graces had          65
Each wondrous part in all their beauties clad,

---

51  *partialize* show partiality to.
54–6  The compacted sense is perhaps: And who, among those who have wisdom's open eyes, and do not, with an owl's blindness, fly the fairest light, does not confirm as much?

Yet so much done as art could not amend,
So thy rare works, to which no wit can add,
In all men's eyes which are not blindly mad
Beyond compare above all praise extend.                    70

Immortal monuments of thy fair fame,
Though not complete, nor in the reach of thought –
How on that passing piece time would have wrought
Had heaven so spared the life of life to frame
The rest? But ah, such loss, hath this world ought          75
Can equal it, or which like grievance brought?
Yet there will live thy ever-praisèd name.

To which these dearest offerings of my heart,
Dissolved to ink, while pen's impressions move
The bleeding veins of never-dying love,                     80
I render here: these wounding lines of smart,
Sad characters indeed of simple love,
Not art nor skill which abler wits do prove,
Of my full soul receive the meanest part.

Receive these hymns, these obsequies receive;              85
If any mark of thy sweet sprite appear,
Well are they born, no title else shall bear.
I can no more. Dear soul, I take my leave.
Sorrow still strives, would mount thy highest sphere,
Presuming so just cause might meet thee there.             90
O happy change, could I so take my leave!

# Robert Southwell (1561–1595)

Born to a well-to-do family in Norfolk, Southwell was raised a Catholic, and in 1576 was sent to the Continent to receive a Catholic education at Douai and elsewhere; he was ordained a priest, in the Jesuit order, in 1584. In 1586 he returned to England as a clandestine missionary; he was sheltered by several figures of note, but in 1592 he was betrayed and captured. After more than two years of imprisonment and interrogation, some of it under torture, he was convicted of treason and hanged, drawn, and quartered at Tyburn. He was canonized by the Catholic Church in 1970. Collections of Southwell's poetry were published the same year as his execution; there had been fifteen editions by 1636. Ben Jonson, himself briefly a Catholic convert, told Drummond of Hawthornden that if he had been able to write "The Burning Babe," he would have willingly burned many of his own poems.

*Edition*: *The Poems of Robert Southwell*, ed. James H. McDonald and Nancy Pollard Brown (Oxford: Clarendon Press, 1967).

## The Burning Babe

As I in hoary winter's night stood shivering in the snow,
Surprised I was with sudden heat which made my heart to glow;
And lifting up a fearful eye to view what fire was near,
A pretty babe all burning bright did in the air appear,
Who, scorchèd with excessive heat, such floods of tears did shed          5
As though his floods should quench his flames, which with his tears were fed.
Alas (quoth he), but newly born, in fiery heats I fry,
Yet none approach to warm their hearts or feel my fire but I.
My faultless breast the furnace is, the fuel wounding thorns;
Love is the fire, and sighs the smoke; the ashes, shame and scorns.          10
The fuel Justice layeth on, and Mercy blows the coals;
The metal in this furnace wrought are men's defilèd souls.
For which, as now on fire I am to work them to their good,
So will I melt into a bath to wash them in my blood.
With this he vanished out of sight, and swiftly shrunk away;          15
And straight I callèd unto mind that it was Christmas day.

# Samuel Daniel (1562–1619)

Born in Somerset and educated at Oxford, Daniel was in the 1580s briefly in the service of Sir Francis Walsingham, Elizabeth's Secretary of State and spymaster; but by the early 1590s he was established within the literary circle surrounding the Countess of Pembroke and, with the help of an impressive network of patrons, devoted himself to a productive and varied poetic career of unusually elite sanction. As early as 1601 he was publishing his collected works. In addition to the sequence given here, he is known for several plays and masques (Shakespeare seems to have taken some cues from his *Cleopatra*), the first English emblem book (a translation from Paolo Giovio), an unfinished poem on the Wars of the Roses, a verse debate on the nature and value of poetry (*Musophilus*), and a prose *Defense of Rhyme* which took public issue with Thomas Campion's polemics in favor of unrhymed quantitative verse.

Daniel's first published poems were twenty-eight sonnets unaccountably printed with the piratical first edition of Sidney's *Astrophil and Stella* in 1591. The next year Daniel incorporated twenty-three of these into a fifty-sonnet sequence (with a concluding ode) entitled *Delia*, and published it with an apologetic dedication to the Countess of Pembroke; later the same year, he published a second edition with four new poems (inserted as 27–30). It is this version which is given here; it has in places an intensity which is lessened in the detailed revisions which continued through another six editions. A phrase or two in the dedication to the countess and the geographical specificity of sonnet 52 imply some autobiographical content, but no real information has ever turned up. The literary inspiration was strong enough; no English poet was more conversant or comfortable with the close-knit international tradition that Petrarchan sonneteering had become by the late sixteenth century. Several continental visits made some of this knowledge first-hand: Daniel claimed to have met Battista Guarini in person on one of them. A number of poems in *Delia* are close adaptations – never quite translations in the strict sense – of specific poems by French or Italian Petrarchists; in several cases, the sources themselves have sources, in a lineage that reaches back to Petrarch and makes the annotation of *Delia* a modest cross-section of the whole phenomenon.

Daniel's sequence itself – in strong contrast to *Astrophil and Stella* – effaces almost any sense of narrative incident, and comes closer to some ideal of a "pure" Petrarchan sequence than any other English sequence of comparable quality and elegance. The woman's disdain for the man is decisive from the start; what plot there is is provided by the man's cycles of anguish and attempted accommodation as he explores the contours of his hopelessness. As in Petrarch, the speaker's own vocation as poet plays an important role, as does the prospect that the poems themselves will eventually vindicate him: either by humiliating the woman when she reads them in old age, or (the more frequently expressed hope) by making her beauty and the speaker's love as immortal as Laura's and Petrarch's. The latter possibility informs one of Daniel's most stirring poems (sonnet 50), but it does not close the sequence; the final poems prepare a chastened retreat into solitude and silence.

Printing the entire sequence does not do justice to a larger design here: from the first edition in 1592 onward, *Delia* is followed in Daniel's works by *The Complaint of Rosamond*, the lament of Rosamond Clifford, the wronged mistress of King Henry II. Written as if to be a new entry in *A Mirror for Magistrates*, and almost as long as the sonnet sequence that precedes it, it sets male despair for a love that never was against female misery at the harsh outcome of a successful seduction, as if these were two halves of some larger whole.

*Edition*: Samuel Daniel, *Poems and a Defence of Ryme*, ed. Arthur Colby Sprague (Cambridge, MA: Harvard University Press, 1930). Sprague bases his edition on the first (fifty-sonnet) version of 1592, but gives full information about all the other editions.

# *Delia*

## 1

Unto the boundless ocean of thy beauty
Runs this poor river, charged with streams of zeal,
Returning thee the tribute of my duty,
Which here my love, my youth, my plaints reveal.
Here I unclasp the book of my charged soul,                    5
Where I have cast the accounts of all my care;
Here have I summed my sighs, here I enroll
How they were spent for thee. Look what they are.
Look on the dear expenses of my youth,
And see how just I reckon with thine eyes;                    10
Examine well thy beauty with my truth,
And cross my cares ere greater sums arise.
Read it, sweet maid, though it be done but slightly.
Who can show all his love doth love but lightly.

**5**  *charged* burdened.                    **12**  *cross* cancel.
**6**  *cast* reckoned.

## 2

Go, wailing verse, the infants of my love,
Minerva-like brought forth without a mother.
Present the image of the cares I prove;
Witness your father's grief exceeds all other.
Sigh out a story of her cruel deeds,                    5
With interrupted accents of despair:
A monument that whosoever reads
May justly praise and blame my loveless fair.
Say her disdain hath drièd up my blood
And starvèd you, in succors still denying.                    10
Press to her eyes, importune me some good,
Waken her sleeping pity with your crying.
Knock at her hard heart, beg till you have moved her,
And tell the unkind how dearly I have loved her.

**2**  *Minerva-like* Minerva (Athena) was born full-grown from     **3**  *prove* experience.
the forehead of Jupiter.

## 3

If so it hap this offspring of my care,
These fatal anthems, sad and mournful songs,
Come to their view who like afflicted are,
Let them yet sigh their own and moan my wrongs.
But untouched hearts, with unaffected eye,                    5
Approach not to behold so great distress;
Clear-sighted, you soon note what it awry,
Whilst blinded ones mine errors never guess.
You blinded souls whom youth and errors lead,
You outcast eaglets dazzled with your sun,                    10
Ah you, and none but you my sorrows read;
You best can judge the wrongs that she hath done.
That she hath done, the motive of my pain,
Who whilst I love doth kill me with disdain.

**2**  *fatal* concerning my fate.                    **13**  *motive* cause.

### 4

These plaintive verse, the posts of my desire,
Which haste for succor to her slow regard,
Bear not report of any slender fire,
Forging a grief to win a fame's reward.
Nor are my passions limned for outward hue,        5
For that no colors can depaint my sorrows;
Delia herself and all the world may view
Best in my face how cares hath tilled deep furrows.
No bays I seek to deck my mourning brow,
O clear-eyed rector of the holy hill;        10
My humble accents crave the olive bough
Of her mild pity and relenting will.
These lines I use to unburden mine own heart;
My love affects no fame nor steems of art.

1  *posts* postmen.
9  *bays* laurels (the crown of poetic glory).

11  *olive bough* sign of peace.
14  *affects* desires.  *steems of art* praises for artistic merit.

### 5

Whilst youth and error led my wandering mind
And set my thoughts in heedless ways to range,
All unawares a goddess chaste I find,
Diana-like, to work my sudden change.
For her no sooner had my view bewrayed,        5
But, with disdain to see me in that place,
With fairest hand the sweet unkindest maid
Casts water-cold disdain upon my face;
Which turned my sport into a hart's despair,
Which still is chased, whilst I have any breath,        10
By mine own thoughts, set on me by my fair:
My thoughts like hounds pursue me to my death.
Those that I fostered of mine own accord
Are made by her to murder thus their lord.

3  *unawares* inadvertently.
4  *Diana-like* When the hunter Actaeon happened upon the virgin goddess Diana bathing, she cast water into his face and turned him into a stag, to be killed by his own hounds.

Petrarch makes significant use of the myth in his *Canzoniere* (23.147–60), and it figures widely in the poetry of his followers, with the allegory often made explicit, as Daniel does here.

### 6

Fair is my love, and cruel as she's fair;
Her brow-shades frowns, although her eyes are sunny.
Her smiles are lightning, though her pride despair,
And her disdains are gall, her favors honey.
A modest maid, decked with a blush of honor,        5
Whose feet do tread green paths of youth and love,
The wonder of all eyes that look upon her,
Sacred on earth, designed a saint above.
Chastity and Beauty, which were deadly foes,
Live reconcilèd friends within her brow;        10
And had she Pity to conjoin with those,

8  *designed* destined to be.

Then who had heard the plaints I utter now?
O had she not been fair and thus unkind,
My Muse had slept, and none had known my mind.

7

O had she not been fair and thus unkind,
Then had no finger pointed at my lightness,
The world had never known what I do find,
And clouds obscure had shaded still her brightness.
Then had no censor's eye these lines surveyed,                    5
Nor graver brows have judged my Muse so vain,
No sun my blush and error had bewrayed,
Nor yet the world had heard of such disdain.
Then had I walked with bold erected face,
No downcast look had signified my miss;                          10
But my degraded hopes, with such disgrace,
Did force me groan out griefs, and utter this.
For, being full, should not I then have spoken?
My sense, oppressed, had failed, and heart had broken.

2  *lightness* wantonness (in this sense, usually applied to a
woman).
9  *erected* upright.

10  *miss* mistake.
14  *sense* The word so used could designate either the mental and emotional faculties or the collective five senses.

8

Thou poor heart, sacrificed unto the fairest,
Hast sent the incense of thy sighs to heaven,
And still against her frowns fresh vows repairest,
And made thy passions with her beauty even.
And you, mine eyes, the agents of my heart,                     5
Told the dumb message of my hidden grief,
And oft with careful turns, with silent art,
Did treat the cruel fair to yield relief.
And you, my verse, the advocates of love,
Have followed hard the process of my case,                     10
And urged that title which doth plainly prove
My faith should win if justice might have place.
Yet, though I see that nought we do can move her,
Tis not disdain must make me cease to love her.

3  *repairest* conveys.
4  *even* equal.
7  *careful* full of care.

8  *treat* entreat.
11  *title* entitlement.

9

If this be love, to draw a weary breath,
Paint on floods, till the shore, cry to the air,
With downward looks still reading on the earth
The sad memorials of my love's despair;
If this be love, to war against my soul,                        5
Lie down to wail, rise up to sigh and grieve me,
The never-resting stone of care to roll,
Still to complain my griefs, and none relieve me;
If this be love, to clothe me with dark thoughts,

Haunting untrodden paths to wail apart,    10
My pleasure's horror, music tragic notes,
Tears in mine eyes, and sorrow at my heart;
If this be love, to live a living death,
O then love I, and draw this weary breath.

Adapted from a sonnet in Philippe Desportes's *Diane* ("Si
c'est aimer que porter bas la vue").

### 10

O then love I, and draw this weary breath
For her, the cruel fair, within whose brow
I written find the sentence of my death
In unkind letters, wrought she cares not how.
O thou that rul'st the confines of the night,    5
Laughter-loving goddess, worldly pleasure's queen,
Intenerate that heart that sets so light
The truest love that ever yet was seen,
And cause her leave to triumph in this wise
Upon the prostrate spoil of that poor heart    10
That serves a trophy to her conquering eyes
And must their glory to the world impart.
Once let her know she hath done enough to prove me,
And let her pity if she cannot love me.

**7** *Intenerate* soften.        **13** *prove* test.
**9** *cause her leave* make her cease.

### 11

Tears, vows, and prayers win the hardest heart;
Tears, vows, and prayers have I spent in vain.
Tears cannot soften flint, nor vows convert;
Prayers prevail not with a quaint disdain.
I lose my tears where I have lost my love;    5
I vow my faith where faith is not regarded;
I pray in vain a merciless to move.
So rare a faith ought better be rewarded.
Yet though I cannot win her will with tears,
Though my soul's idol scorneth all my vows,    10
Though all my prayers be to so deaf ears,
No favor though the cruel fair allows,
Yet will I weep, vow, pray to cruel she.
Flint, frost, disdain wears, melts, and yields, we see.

**4** *quaint* The word has several relevant intonations in late
sixteenth-century usage: fastidious, proud, artful. The mod-
ern "oddly old-fashioned" is probably not in play here.

### 12

My spotless love hovers with white wings
About the temple of the proudest frame,

**2** *frame* structure (commonly used for the human body in
particular).

Where blaze those lights, fairest of earthly things,
Which clear our clouded world with brightest flame.
My ambitious thoughts, confinèd in her face,                    5
Affect no honor but what she can give me.
My hopes do rest in limits of her grace;
I weigh no comfort unless she relieve me.
For she that can my heart imparadise
Holds in her fairest hand what dearest is:                      10
My fortune's wheels, the circle of her eyes,
Whose rolling grace deign once a turn of bliss.
All my life's sweet consists in her alone,
So much I love the most unloving one.

6  *Affect* desire.                          8  *weigh* value.
7  *limits* bounded territories.


### 13

Behold what hap Pygmalion had, to frame
And carve his proper grief upon a stone.
My heavy fortune is much like the same;
I work on flint, and that's the cause I moan.
For hapless, lo, even with mine own desires,                    5
I figured on the table of mine heart
The fairest form the worldes eye admires,
And so did perish by my proper art.
And still I toil to change the marble breast
Of her whose sweetest grace I do adore,                         10
Yet cannot find her breath unto my rest;
Hard is her heart, and woe is me therefore.
O happy he that joyed his stone and art;
Unhappy I to love a stony heart.

1  *Pygmalion* The sculptor who fell in love with his own       11  *unto* for the sake of.
statue, which eventually came to life (see John Marston, *The*  13  *joyed* enjoyed.
*Metamorphosis of Pygmalion's Image*).  *frame* shape.


### 14

Those amber locks are those same nets, my dear,
Wherewith my liberty thou didst surprise;
Love was the flame that firèd me so near,
The darts transpiercing were those crystal eyes.
Strong is the net, and fervent is the flame,                    5
Deep is the wound my sighs do well report;
Yet do I love, adore, and praise the same
That holds, that burns, that wounds me in this sort,
And list not seek to break, to quench, to heal
The bond, the flame, the wound that festereth so,               10
By knife, by liquor, or by salve to deal:
So much I please to perish in my woe.

A close adaptation of a sonnet from Joachim Du Bellay's    4  *darts* The reading of the text in the 1591 edition; later
*L'Olive* ("Ces cheveux d'or sont les liens, Madame").     editions read "dart."
                                                           11  *deal* contend.

Yet lest long travails be above my strength,
Good Delia, loose, quench, heal me now at length.

15

If that a loyal heart and faith unfeigned,
If a sweet languish with a chaste desire,
If hunger-starven thoughts so long retained,
Fed but with smoke, and cherished but with fire;
And if a brow with care's characters painted          5
Bewrays my love with broken words half-spoken
To her that sits in my thought's temple sainted
And lays to view my vulture-gnawn heart open;
If I have done due homage to her eyes,
And had my sighs still tending on her name;          10
If on her love my life and honor lies,
And she, the unkindest maid, still scorns the same:
Let this suffice, the world yet may see
The fault is hers, though mine the hurt must be.

An adaptation of a sonnet from Desportes's *Diane* ("Si la foi plus certaine en une âme non feinte"), which is itself closely based on Petrarch, *Canzoniere* 224; see Thomas Wyatt's translation of the latter, "If amorous faith, an heart unfeigned," above.

5 *characters* signs.

16

Happy in sleep, waking content to languish,
Embracing clouds by night, in daytime mourn,
All things I loathe save her and mine own anguish,
Pleased in my hurt, inured to live forlorn.
Nought do I crave but love, death, or my lady,          5
Hoarse with crying mercy, mercy yet my merit;
So many vows and prayers ever made I
That now at length to yield, mere pity were it.
But still the Hydra of my cares, renewing,
Revives new sorrows of her fresh disdaining.          10
Still must I go the summer winds pursuing,
Finding no end nor period of my paining,
Wail all my life, my griefs do touch so nearly;
And thus I live because I love her dearly

2 *mourn* mourning.

9 *Hydra* A mythical beast that grew multiple new heads when decapitated; eventually defeated, though not quite killed, by Hercules.

17

Since the first look that led me to this error,
To this thought's maze, to my confusion tending,
Still have I lived in grief, in hope, in terror,
The circle of my sorrows never ending,
Yet cannot leave her love that holds me hateful.          5
Her eyes exact it, though her heart disdains me.
See what reward he hath that serves the ungrateful;

5 *leave her love* stop loving her.

So true and loyal love no favor gains me.
Still must I whet my young desires abated
Upon the flint of such a heart rebelling;          10
And all in vain, her pride is so innated
She yields no place at all for pity's dwelling.
Oft have I told her that my soul did love her,
And that with tears, yet all this will not move her.

9   *abated* beaten down.          11   *innated* imbued.


### 18

Restore thy tresses to the golden ore,
Yield Cytherea's son those arks of love,
Bequeath the heavens the stars that I adore,
And to the orient do thy pearls remove.
Yield thy hands' pride unto the ivory white,          5
To Arabian odors give thy breathing sweet,
Restore thy blush unto Aurora bright,
To Thetis give the honor of thy feet.
Let Venus have thy graces her resigned,
And thy sweet voice give back unto the spheres,          10
But yet restore thy fierce and cruel mind
To Hyrcan tigers and to ruthless bears.
Yield to the marble thy hard heart again;
So shalt thou cease to plague, and I to pain.

A version of a sonnet from Du Bellay's *L'Olive* ("Rendez à l'or cette couleur, qui dore").

2   *Cytherea* Venus.   *arks of love* dimples.
3   *stars that I adore* Delia's eyes.
4   *pearls* teeth.

7   *Aurora* goddess of the dawn.
8   *Thetis* The most prominent of the Nereids, and mother to Achilles; repeatedly called "silver-footed" in Homer.
9   *her resigned* surrendered to her.
12   *Hyrcan* From Hyrcania, southeast of the Caspian Sea.


### 19

If beauty thus be clouded with a frown
That pity shines no comfort to my bliss,
And vapors of disdain so overgrown
That my life's light thus wholly darkened is,
Why should I more molest the world with cries,          5
The air with sighs, the earth below with tears,
Since I live hateful to those ruthless eyes,
Vexing with untuned moan her dainty ears?
If I have loved her dearer than my breath,
My breath that calls the heavens to witness it,          10
And still must hold her dear till after death,
And if that all this cannot move a whit,
Yet let her say that she hath done me wrong
To use me thus and know I loved so long.


### 20

Come, death, the anchor-hold of all my thoughts,
My last resort whereto my soul appealeth,
For all too long on earth my fancy dotes,
Whilst my best blood my young desires sealeth.
That heart is now the prospective of horror          5

That honored hath the cruelest fair that liveth:
The cruelest fair, that sees I languish for her,
Yet never mercy to my merit giveth.
This is her laurel and her triumph's prize,
To tread me down with foot of her disgrace,                    10
Whilst I did build my fortune in her eyes
And laid my life's rest on so fair a face.
That rest I lost, my love, my life, and all;
So high attempts to low disgraces fall.

4  *sealeth* authorizes.                    5  *prospective* scene.

### 21

These sorrowing sighs, the smokes of mine annoy,
These tears, which heat of sacred flame distills,
Are these due tributes that my faith doth pay
Unto the tyrant whose unkindness kills.
I sacrifice my youth and blooming years                    5
At her proud feet, and she respects not it;
My flower untimely is withered with my tears
And winter woes, for spring of youth unfit.
She thinks a look may recompense my care,
And so with looks prolongs my long-looked ease;                    10
As short that bliss, so is the comfort rare,
Yet must that bliss my hungry thoughts appease.
Thus she returns my hopes, so fruitless ever;
Once let her love indeed, or eye me never.

### 22

False hope prolongs my ever certain grief,
Traitors to me and faithful to my love.
A thousand times it promised me relief,
Yet never any true effect I prove.
Oft, when I find in her no truth at all,                    5
I banish her, and blame her treachery;
Yet soon again I must her back recall,
As one that dies without her company.
Thus often as I chase my hope from me,
Straightway she hastes her unto Delia's eyes;                    10
Fed with some pleasing look there shall she be
And so sent back, and thus my fortune lies.
Looks feed my hope, hope fosters me in vain;
Hopes are unsure when certain is my pain.

Adapted from a sonnet in Du Bellay's *L'Olive* ("Ce bref      4  *prove* experience.
espoir, qui ma tristesse alonge").

### 23

Look in my griefs, and blame me not to mourn,
From care to care that leads a life so bad:
The orphan of fortune, born to be her scorn,

1  *to mourn* for mourning.

Whose clouded brow doth make my days so sad.
Long are their nights whose cares do never sleep,                5
Loathsome their days whom no sun ever joyed.
Her fairest eyes do penetrate so deep
That thus I live both day and night annoyed.
But since the sweetest root doth yield thus much,
Her praise from my complaint I may not part.                    10
I love the effect for that the cause is such;
I'll praise her face, and blame her flinty heart,
Whilst that we make the world admire at us,
Her for disdain, and me for loving thus.


### 24

Oft and in vain my rebel thoughts have ventured
To stop the passage of my vanquished heart
And shut those ways my friendly foe first entered,
Hoping thereby to free my better part;
And whilst I guard these windows of this fort,                  5
Where my heart's thief to vex me made her choice,
And thither all my forces do transport,
Another passage opens at her voice.
Her voice betrays me to her hand and eye,
My freedom's tyrants conquering all by art;                     10
But ah, what glory can she get thereby
With three such powers to plague one silly heart?
Yet my soul's sovereign, since I must resign,
Reign in my thoughts: my love and life are thine.

12   *silly* hapless.


### 25

Reign in my thoughts, fair hand, sweet eye, rare voice;
Possess me whole, my heart's triumvirate.
Yet heavy heart, to make so hard a choice
Of such as spoil thy poor afflicted state.
For whilst they strive which shall be lord of all,             5
All my poor life by them is trodden down.
They all erect their trophies on my fall,
And yield me nought that gives them their renown.
When back I look, I sigh my freedom past,
And wail the state wherein I present stand,                     10
And see my fortune ever like to last,
Finding me reined with such a heavy hand.
What can I do but yield? And yield I do,
And serve all three, and yet they spoil me too.

4   *spoil* despoil.


### 26

Whilst, by her eyes pursued, my poor heart flew it
Into the sacred bosom of my dearest,
She there in that sweet sanctuary slew it,
Where it presumed his safety to be nearest.
My privilege of faith could not protect it,                    5
That was with blood and three years' witness signed;

In all which time she never could suspect it,
For well she saw my love, and how I pined.
And yet no comfort would her brow reveal me,
No lightning look which falling hopes erecteth.                     10
What boots to laws of succor to appeal me?
Ladies and tyrants never laws respecteth.
Then there I die where hoped I to have liven,
And by that hand which better might have given.

1  *flew it* A reflexive construction; "it" = "my heart."        9  *reveal me* reveal to me.
7  *suspect* distrust.

## 27

Still in the trace of my tormented thought,
My ceaseless cares must march on to my death;
Thy least regard too dearly have I bought,
Who to my comfort never deignst a breath.
Why shouldst thou stop thine ears now to my cries,                 5
Whose eyes were open ready to oppress me?
Why shutst thou not the cause whence all did rise,
Or hear me now and seek how to redress me?
Injurious Delia, yet I'll love thee still
Whilst that I breathe in sorrow of my smart.                       10
I'll tell the world that I deserved but ill,
And blame myself for to excuse thy heart.
Then judge who sins the greater of us twain:
I in my love, or thou in thy disdain.

1  *trace* part of the harness for a draught animal.

## 28

Oft do I muse whether my Delia's eyes
Are eyes or else two fair bright stars that shine;
For how could nature ever thus devise
Of earth on earth a substance so divine?
Stars sure they are, whose motions rule desires,                   5
And calm and tempest follow their aspects.
Their sweet appearing still such power inspires
That makes the world admire so strange effects.
Yet whether fixed or wandering stars are they
Whose influence rule the orb of my poor heart:                     10
Fixed sure they are, but wandering make me stray
In endless errors whence I cannot part.
Stars then, not eyes, move yet with milder view
Your sweet aspect on him that honors you.

Expanded from a madrigal of Guarini's ("Deh dimmi, Amor,      9  *wandering stars* planets.
se gli occhi di Camilla").

29

TO M.P.

Like as the spotless ermelin, distressed,
Circumpassed round with filth and loathsome mud,
Pines in her grief, imprisoned in her nest,
And cannot issue forth to seek her good:
So I, environed with a hateful want,                                        5
Look to the heavens, the heavens yield forth no grace;
I search the earth, the earth I find as scant;
I view myself, myself in woeful case.
Heaven nor earth will not, myself cannot work
A way through want to free my soul from care;                               10
But I must pine, and in my pining lurk,
Lest my sad looks bewray me how I fare.
My fortune, mantled with a cloud so obscure,
Thus shades my life so long as wants endure.

Removed from subsequent editions.
*To M.P.* The initials could be interpreted as those of Mary,
Countess of Pembroke, though there is no certainty in that
identification.

1   *ermelin* ermine (emblem of chastity).
2   *Circumpassed* encompassed.
5   *environed* surrounded.

30

My cares draw on my everlasting night;
In horror's sable clouds sets my life's sun.
My life's sweet sun, my dearest comfort's light,
Will rise no more to me, whose day is done.
I go before unto the myrtle shades                                          5
To attend the presence of my world's dear
And there prepare her flowers that never fades
And all things fit against her coming there.
If any ask me why so soon I came,
I'll hide her sin, and say it was my lot.                                   10
In life and death I'll tender her good name;
My life nor death shall never be her blot.
Although this world may seem her deed to blame,
The Elysian ghosts shall never know the same.

Removed from subsequent editions.

5   *myrtle* Venus's plant; in Vergil's underworld those who
died for love inhabit a myrtle grove (*Aeneid* 6.440–76).
14   *Elysian ghosts* spirits in the Elysian fields.

31

The star of my mishap imposed this paining,
To spend the April of my years in wailing
That never found my fortune but in waning,
With still fresh cares my present woes assailing.
Yet her I blame not, though she might have blest me,                        5
But my desire's wings so high aspiring.

6–8   Suggesting the story of Icarus, who flew too near the
sun, which melted the wax that secured his artificial wings
and plunged him to his death.

Now melted with the sun that hath possessed me,
Down do I fall from off my high desiring,
And in my fall do cry for mercy speedy.
No pitying eye looks back upon my mourning,  10
No help I find when now most favor need I.
The ocean of my tears must drown me burning,
And this my death shall christen her anew
And give the cruel fair her title due.


### 32

Raising my hopes on hills of high desire,
Thinking to scale the heaven of her heart,
My slender means presumed too high a part;
Her thunder of disdain forced me retire,
And threw me down to pain in all this fire,  5
Where, lo, I languish in so heavy smart
Because the attempt was far above my art;
Her pride brooked not poor souls should come so nigh her.
Yet I protest my high aspiring will
Was not to dispossess her of her right.  10
Her sovereignty should have remainèd still;
I only sought the bliss to have her sight.
Her sight, contented thus to see me spill,
Framed my desires fit for her eyes to kill.

12  *her sight* the sight of her.          13  *spill* die.


### 33

O, why doth Delia credit so her glass,
Gazing her beauty deigned her by the skies,
And doth not rather look on him (alas)
Whose state best shows the force of murdering eyes?
The broken tops of lofty trees declare  5
The fury of a mercy-wanting storm;
And of what force your wounding graces are,
Upon myself you best may find the form.
Then leave your glass, and gaze yourself on me;
That mirror shows what power is in your face.  10
To view your form too much may danger be;
Narcissus changed to a flower in such a case.
And you are changed, but not to a hyacinth;
I fear your eye hath turned your heart to flint.

An adaptation of a sonnet from Desportes's *Hippolyte* ("Pourquoi si follement croyez-vous à un verre"), itself based on an Italian sonnet by Antonio Tebaldeo ("A che presti, superba, a un vetro fede"). The ultimate source is Petrarch, *Canzoniere* 45, which has numerous descendants in Renaissance sonneteering; see also Spenser, *Amoretti* 45.

1  *glass* mirror.
2  *Gazing* gazing on.
8  *form* image.
12  *Narcissus* After dying while gazing upon his own image in the water, he was transformed into the flower with his name.
13  *hyacinth* The flower into which the beautiful boy Hyacinthus was transformed in another ancient myth.

### 34

I once may see when years shall wreak my wrong,
When golden hairs shall change to silver wire,
And those bright rays that kindle all this fire
Shall fail in force, their working not so strong.
Then beauty, now the burden of my song,                    5
Whose glorious blaze the world doth so admire,
Must yield up all to tyrant Time's desire;
Then fade those flowers which decked her pride so long.
When if she grieve to gaze her in her glass,
Which then presents her winter-withered hue,              10
Go you, my verse, go tell her what she was,
For what she was she best shall find in you.
Your fiery heat lets not her glory pass,
But phoenix-like shall make her live anew.

A translation of a sonnet from Desportes's *Cléonice* ("Je verray         1   *wreak* avenge.
par les ans, vengeurs de mon martire"), which is in turn       5   *burden* theme.
based on a sonnet by Torquato Tasso ("Vedrò da gli anni la
mia vendetta ancora").

### 35

Look, Delia, how we steem the half-blown rose,
The image of thy blush and summer's honor.
Whilst in her tender green she doth enclose
The pure sweet beauty Time bestows upon her –
No sooner spreads her glory in the air                     5
But straight her full-blown pride is in declining;
She then is scorned that late adorned the fair.
So clouds thy beauty after fairest shining.
No April can revive thy withered flowers
Whose blooming grace adorns thy glory now;                10
Swift speedy Time, feathered with flying hours,
Dissolves the beauty of the fairest brow.
O, let not then such riches waste in vain,
But love whilst that thou mayst be loved again.

This sonnet and the next are adapted from two stanzas in       Tasso and Spenser the seductive voice is female, luring men
Tasso's *Gerusalemme Liberata* (16.14–15); Spenser reworks    away from their heroic mission.
the same source in *The Faery Queen* (II.xii.74–5). In both

                                                              1   *steem* esteem.   *half-blown* half-opened.

### 36

But love whilst that thou mayst be loved again
Now whilst thy May hath filled thy lap with flowers;
Now whilst thy beauty bears without a stain,
Now use thy summer smiles ere winter lowers.
And whilst thou spreadst unto the rising sun                5
The fairest flower that ever saw the light,
Now joy thy time before thy sweet be done,
And, Delia, think thy morning must have night,

3   *bears* endures.                           7   *joy* enjoy.

And that thy brightness sets at length to west
When thou wilt close up that which now thou showest;          10
And think the same becomes thy fading best,
Which then shall hide it most, and cower lowest.
Men do not weigh the stalk for that it was
When once they find her flower, her glory pass.

12   *it* itself.                13   *weigh* value.

### 37

When men shall find thy flower, thy glory pass,
And thou with careful brow sitting alone
Receivèd hast this message from thy glass,
That tells the truth and says that all is gone,
Fresh shalt thou see in me the wounds thou madest,          5
Though spent thy flame, in me the heat remaining;
I that have loved thee thus before thou fadest,
My faith shall wax, when thou art in thy waning.
The world shall find this miracle in me,
That fire can burn when all the matter's spent;          10
Then what my faith hath been thyself shalt see,
And that thou wast unkind thou mayst repent.
Thou mayst repent that thou hast scorned my tears
When winter snows upon thy golden hairs.

### 38

When winter snows upon thy golden hairs
And frost of age hath nipped thy flowers near,
When dark shall seem thy day that never clears
And all lies withered that was held so dear,
Then take this picture which I here present thee,          5
Limned with a pencil not at all unworthy.
Here see the gifts that God and Nature lent thee,
Here read thyself, and what I suffered for thee.
This may remain thy lasting monument,
Which happily posterity may cherish;          10
These colors with thy fading are not spent,
These may remain when thou and I shall perish.
If they remain, then thou shalt live thereby;
They will remain, and so thou canst not die.

### 39

Thou canst not die whilst any zeal abound
In feeling hearts that can conceive these lines;
Though thou a Laura hast no Petrarch found,
In base attire yet clearly beauty shines.
And I, though born within a colder clime,          5
Do feel my inward heat as great, I know it.
He never had more faith, although more rhyme;
I love as well, though he could better show it.
But I may add one feather to thy fame,
To help her flight throughout the fairest isle;          10

2   *conceive* understand.

And if my pen could more enlarge thy name,
Then shouldst thou live in an immortal style.
For though that Laura better limnèd be,
Suffice thou shalt be loved as well as she.


## 40

O, be not grieved that these my papers should
Bewray unto the world how fair thou art,
Or that my wits have showed, the best they could,
The chastest flame that ever warmèd heart.
Think not, sweet Delia, this shall be thy shame,                    5
  My Muse should sound thy praise with mournful warble;
How many live, the glory of whose name
Shall rest in ice when thine is graved in marble?
Thou mayst in after ages live esteemed,
Unburied in these lines reserved in pureness;                       10
These shall entomb those eyes, that have redeemed
Me from the vulgar, thee from all obscureness.
Although my careful accents never moved thee,
Yet count it no disgrace that I have loved thee.


## 41

Delia, these eyes that so admireth thine
Have seen those walls, the which ambition reared
To check the world, how they entombed have lyne
Within themselves, and on them ploughs have eared.
Yet found I that no barbarous hand attained                         5
The spoil of fame deserved by virtuous men,
Whose glorious actions luckily had gained
The eternal annals of a happy pen.
Why, then, though Delia fade, let that not move her,
Though time do spoil her of the fairest veil                        10
That ever yet mortality did cover,
Which must instar the needle and the rail.
That grace, that virtue, all that served to enwoman,
Doth thee unto eternity assummon.

3  *lyne* lain.
4  *eared* ploughed.
6  *spoil* prize.
10  *spoil* rob.

12  *instar* place among the stars.  *rail* A woman's gown or neckerchief; together with "needle" (for its role in sewing), an emblem of female virtue.
13  *enwoman* make into a woman.


## 42

Fair and lovely maid, look from the shore,
See thy Leander striving in these waves,
Poor soul quite spent, whose force can do no more;
Now send forth hopes, for now calm pity saves,
And waft him to thee with those lovely eyes,                        5
A happy convoy to a holy land.
Now show thy power and where thy virtue lies;
To save thine own, stretch out the fairest hand.
Stretch out the fairest hand a pledge of peace,

2  *Leander* Young man who swam the Hellespont to be with
his love Hero; see Marlowe's *Hero and Leander*.

That hand that darts so right and never misses.                    10
I'll not revenge old wrongs, my wrath shall cease;
For that which gave me wounds, I'll give it kisses.
Once let the ocean of my cares find shore,
That thou be pleased, and I may sigh no more.


### 43

Read in my face a volume of despairs,
The wailing Iliads of my tragic woe,
Drawn with my blood and printed with my cares,
Wrought by her hand that I have honored so.
Who whilst I burn, she sings at my soul's wrack,                    5
Looking aloft from turret of her pride;
There my soul's tyrant joys her in the sack
Of her own seat whereof I made her guide.
There do these smokes that from affliction rise
Serve as an incense to a cruel dame:                               10
A sacrifice thrice grateful to her eyes
Because their power serve to exact the same.
Thus ruins she, to satisfy her will,
The temple where her name was honored still.

7–8  *the sack / Of her own seat* the pillaging of her own
residence (i.e., the poet's soul).


### 44

My Cynthia hath the waters of mine eyes,
The ready handmaids on her grace attending,
That never fall to ebb, nor ever dries,
For to their flow she never grants an ending.
The Ocean never did attend more duly                              5
Upon his sovereign's course, the night's pale Queen,
Nor paid the impost of his waves more truly
Than mine to her in truth have ever been.
Yet nought the rock of that hard heart can move,
Where beat these tears with zeal and fury driveth,               10
And yet I rather languish in her love
Than I would joy the fairest she that liveth.
I doubt to find such pleasure in my gaining
As now I taste in compass of complaining.

1  *Cynthia* The goddess of the moon, frequently a persona       7  *impost* tax.
for Queen Elizabeth (as in Walter Ralegh's *The Ocean's Love*   12  *joy* enjoy.
*to Cynthia*, to which the second quatrain may allude).         13  *doubt* do not expect.


### 45

How long shall I in mine affliction mourn,
A burden to myself, distressed in mind?
When shall my interdicted hopes return
From out despair, wherein they live confined?
When shall her troubled brow, charged with disdain,              5
Reveal the treasure which her smiles impart?
When shall my faith the happiness attain
To break the ice that hath congealed her heart?
Unto herself herself my love doth summon,

If love in her hath any power to move,                                    10
And let her tell me, as she is a woman,
Whether my faith hath not deserved her love.
I know she cannot but must needs confess it,
Yet deigns not with one simple sign to express it.

### 46

Beauty, sweet love, is like the morning dew,
Whose short refresh upon the tender green
Cheers for a time but till the sun doth show,
And straight tis gone as it had never been.
Soon doth it fade that makes the fairest flourish,      5
Short is the glory of the blushing rose:
The hue which thou so carefully dost nourish,
Yet which at length thou must be forced to lose
When thou, surcharged with burden of thy years,
Shalt bend thy wrinkles homeward to the earth,         10
When time hath made a passport for thy fears,
Dated in age the calends of our death –
But ah, no more. This hath been often told,
And women grieve to think they must be old.

**2**  *refresh* refreshment.

**12**  *calends* The first day of the month in the ancient Roman calendar, and a traditional day for settling debts.

### 47

I must not grieve my love, whose eyes would read
Lines of delight whereon her youth might smile;
Flowers have a time before they come to seed,
And she is young and now must sport the while.
Ah, sport, sweet maid, in season of these years        5
And learn to gather flowers before they wither;
And where the sweetest blossoms first appears,
Let love and youth conduct thy pleasures thither.
Lighten forth smiles to clear the clouded air,
And calm the tempest which my sighs do raise;          10
Pity and smiles do best become the fair,
Pity and smiles shall yield thee lasting praise.
I hope to say, when all my griefs are gone,
Happy the heart that sighed for such a one.

### 48

Drawn with the attractive virtue of her eyes,
My touched heart turns it to that happy coast,
My joyful north, where all my fortune lies,
The level of my hopes desirèd most.
There where my Delia, fairer than the sun,             5
Decked with her youth, whereon the world now smileth,
Joys in that honor which her beauty won,
The eternal volume which her fame compileth.
Flourish, fair Albion, glory of the north,
Neptune's darling, held between his arms,              10

**4**  *level* aim.

Divided from the world as better worth,
Kept for himself, defended from all harms.
Still let disarmèd Peace deck her and thee,
And Muse-foe Mars abroad far fostered be.

### 49

Care-charmer sleep, son of the sable night,
Brother to death, in silent darkness born,
Relieve my languish and restore the light
With dark forgetting of my cares' return.
And let the day be time enough to mourn                    5
The shipwrack of my ill-adventured youth;
Let waking eyes suffice to wail their scorn
Without the torment of the night's untruth.
Cease dreams, the imagery of our day desires,
To model forth the passions of the morrow;                10
Never let rising sun approve you liars
To add more grief to aggravate my sorrow.
Still let me sleep, embracing clouds in vain,
And never wake to feel the day's disdain.

11  *approve* prove.

### 50

Let others sing of knights and palladines
In agèd accents and untimely words,
Paint shadows in imaginary lines
Which well the reach of their high wits records;
But I must sing of thee, and those fair eyes              5
Authentic shall my verse in time to come,
When yet the unborn shall say, Lo, where she lies
Whose beauty made him speak that else was dumb.
These are the arks, the trophies I erect
That fortify thy name against old age,                    10
And these, thy sacred virtues, must protect
Against the dark and time's consuming rage.
Though the error of my youth they shall discover,
Suffice they show I lived and was thy lover.

1–2  The reference is primarily to *The Faery Queen*.
1  *palladines* The twelve highest peers serving the Emperor
Charlemagne; the popular Italian *romanzi* of Boiardo and
Ariosto, a major influence on Spenser, told of their exploits.

2  *untimely* old-fashioned.
6  *Authentic* authenticate.
13–14  Beginning with the 1601/2 edition, these lines read:
"Though the error of my youth in them appear, / Suffice
they show I lived and loved thee dear."

### 51

Like as the lute that joys or else dislikes
As is his art that plays upon the same,
So sounds my Muse according as she strikes
On my heart strings, high-tuned unto her fame.
Her touch doth cause the warble of the sound              5
Which here I yield in lamentable wise,
A wailing descant on the sweetest ground,

1  *joys* gives joy.  *dislikes* displeases.

7  *ground* the melody on which a descant is raised.

Whose due reports give honor to her eyes.
Else harsh my style, untunable my Muse;
Hoarse sounds the voice that praiseth not her name.          10
If any pleasing relish here I use,
Then judge the world her beauty gives the same.
O happy ground that makes the music such,
And blessèd hand that gives so sweet a touch.


### 52

None other fame mine unambitious Muse
Affected ever but to eternize thee;
All other honors do my hopes refuse,
Which meaner prized and momentary be.
For God forbid I should my papers blot                       5
With mercenary lines, with servile pen,
Praising virtues in them that have them not,
Basely attending on the hopes of men.
No, no, my verse respects nor Thames nor theaters,
Nor seeks it to be known unto the great;                     10
But Avon, rich in fame though poor in waters,
Shall have my song, where Delia hath her seat.
Avon shall be my Thames, and she my song;
I'll sound her name the river all along.

**2** *Affected* desired.
**11** *Avon* Because of Daniel's Somerset origins, the reference is probably to the river of this name that flows through Bath. *rich in fame, though poor in waters* In later editions, this becomes "poor in fame and poor in waters."


### 53

Unhappy pen and ill accepted papers
That intimate in vain my chaste desires,
My chaste desires, the ever-burning tapers
Enkindled by her eyes' celestial fires;
Celestial fires and unrespecting powers                      5
That deign not view the glory of your might,
In humble lines the work of careful hours,
The sacrifice I offer to her sight.
But sith she scorns her own, this rests for me:
I'll moan myself, and hide the wrong I have,                 10
And so content me that her frowns should be
To my infant style the cradle and the grave.
What though myself no honor get thereby,
Each bird sings to herself, and so will I.

**5** *unrespecting* uninterested.          **9** *rests* remains.


### 54

Lo, here the impost of a faith unfeigning
That love hath paid and her disdain extorted.
Behold the message of my just complaining
That shows the world how much my grief imported.

**1** *impost* tax.          **4** *imported* meant.

These tributary plaints fraught with desire 5
I send those eyes, the cabinets of love,
The paradise whereto my hopes aspire
From out this hell which mine afflictions prove;
Wherein I thus do live cast down from mirth,
Pensive alone, none but despair about me, 10
My joys abortive, perished at their birth,
My cares long-lived, and will not die without me.
This is my state, and Delia's heart is such;
I say no more, I fear I said too much.

8  *prove* experience.

# An Ode

Now each creature joys the other,
Passing happy days and hours;
One bird reports unto another
In the fall of silver showers,
Whilst the earth, our common mother, 5
Hath her bosom decked with flowers.

Whilst the greatest torch of heaven
With bright rays warms Flora's lap,
Making nights and days both even,
Cheering plants with fresher sap, 10
My field of flowers, quite bereaven,
Wants refresh of better hap.

Echo, daughter of the air,
Babbling guest of rocks and hills,
Knows the name of my fierce fair 15
And sounds the accents of my ills.
Each thing pities my despair,
Whilst that she her lover kills.

Whilst that she, O cruel maid,
Doth me and my love despise, 20
My life's flourish is decayed
That depended on her eyes;
But her will must be obeyed,
And well he ends for love who dies.

1  *joys* enjoys, brings joy to.
3  *reports* presents itself.
8  *Flora* goddess of flowers.
11  *bereaven* despoiled.

12  *refresh* refreshment.
21  *flourish* health.
24  Petrarch, *Canzoniere* 140.14.

# Michael Drayton (1563–1631)

Drayton claimed to have told his tutor at the age of 10, "Make me a poet, do it, if you can, / And you shall see, I'll quickly be a man." He became one of the most single-mindedly prolific English poets of his time, publishing his first collected *Poems* in 1605; in their modern edition, his works cover 2,000 pages in four volumes. Born to a yeoman family in Warwickshire, he was in service as a page by the age of 10; he received no university education, but was modestly successful pursuing aristocratic patronage – Prince Henry granted him a yearly pension of £10, though King James was a disappointment – and was also on Philip Henslowe's payroll as a collaborating playwright. His most ambitious work was the immense *Poly-Olbion* (completed in 1622), a verse survey, with prose commentary, of the topography of England. It has some claim to being the longest poem in the language.

His sonnet sequence, excerpted here, was a work in progress throughout his career. The first incarnation, a fifty-one-sonnet sequence entitled *Idea's Mirror*, appeared in 1594; for a fifty-nine-sonnet sequence published in 1599, numerous poems were removed, others revised, and new ones added, and the title changed to *Idea*. There were four more versions, culminating in the sixty-four-sonnet sequence in his 1619 *Poems*. "Idea" is Drayton's poetic name for the woman in question; there are reasons to identify her more or less with Anne Goodere, the daughter of his first patron, though there is little evidence of the biographical seriousness of that connection. *Idea's Mirror* is not as intellectualized as the title suggests, but it does have the air of Petrarchan conventionality fairly content with its self-absorption; later revisions, without entirely effacing these origins, add memorable strokes of brusqueness and impatience.

*Edition*: *The Works of Michael Drayton*, ed. J. William Hebel et al., 5 vols. (Oxford: Blackwell, 1961).

## From *Idea's Mirror*

Beauty sometime, in all her glory crowned,
Passing by that clear fountain of thine eye,
Her sunshine face there chancing to espy,
Forgot herself, and thought she had been drowned;
And thus whilst Beauty on her beauty gazed,     5
Who, then yet living, deemed she had been dying,
And yet in death some hope of life espying,
At her own rare perfections so amazed,
Twixt joy and grief, yet with a smiling frowning,
The glorious sunbeams of her eyes bright shining,     10
And she on her own destiny divining,
Threw in herself, to save herself by drowning,
The Well of Nectar, paved with pearl and gold,
Where she remains for all eyes to behold.

Included (with the heading "An allusion to Narcissus") in all editions of *Idea* except the last.　　**5** *her beauty* In *Idea* changed to "her shadow."

See, chaste Diana, where my harmless heart,
Roused from my breast, his sure and safest lair,
Nor chased by hound, nor forced by hunter's art,
Yet see how right he comes unto my fair.
See how my deer comes to thy beauty's stand,     5

Not included in *Idea*.　　**1** *Diana* The virgin goddess of the hunt. The poem alludes to the fate of Actaeon at her hands; see Samuel Daniel, *Delia* 5.
**5** *stand* Place where a hunter takes cover to wait for game.

And there stands gazing on those darting eyes,
Whilst from their rays, by Cupid's skillful hand,
Into his heart the piercing arrow flies.
See how he looks upon his bleeding wound
Whilst thus he panteth for his latest breath       10
And, looking on thee, falls upon the ground,
Smiling, as though he gloried in his death;
And, wallowing in his blood, some life yet laft,
His stone-cold lips doth kiss the blessèd shaft.

13   *laft* left.

Sweet Secrecy, what tongue can tell thy worth?
What mortal pen sufficiently can praise thee?
What curious pencil serves to limn thee forth?
What Muse hath power above thy height to raise thee?
Strong lock of kindness, closet of love's store,      5
Heart's mithridate, the soul's preservative,
O virtue which all virtues do adore,
Chief good from whom all good things we derive;
O rare effect, true bond of friendship's measure,
Conceit of angels which all wisdom teachest,      10
O richest casket of all heavenly treasure
In secret silence which such wonders preachest,
O purest mirror, wherein men may see
The lively image of divinity.

Not included in *Idea*.

6  *mithridate* An antidote against all poisons; named after Mithridates VI, king of Pontus (d. 63 BC), who was said to have achieved such an immunity.

## From *Idea*

# To the Reader of his Poems

Into these loves who but for passion looks,
At this first sight here let him lay them by
And seek elsewhere, in turning other books
Which better may his labor satisfy.
No far-fetched sigh shall ever wound my breast,      5
Love from mine eye a tear shall never wring,
Nor in *Ah-me's* my whining sonnets dressed
(A libertine) fantasticly I sing.
My verse is the true image of my mind,
Ever in motion, still desiring change;      10
And, as thus to variety inclined,
So in all humors sportively I range.
My Muse is rightly of the English strain,
Which cannot long one fashion entertain.

In all editions up to 1619.                 8  *fantasticly* in a strange and fanciful manner.

Whilst thus my pen strives to eternize thee,
Age rules my lines with wrinkles in my face,
Where, in the map of all my misery,
Is modeled out the world of my disgrace.
Whilst in despite of tyrannizing times,                    5
Medea-like, I make thee young again,
Proudly thou scornst my world-outwearing rhymes
And murderst virtue with thy coy disdain.
And though in youth my youth untimely perish
To keep thee from oblivion and the grave,              10
Ensuing ages yet my rhymes shall cherish,
Where I, entombed, my better part shall save;
And though this earthly body fade and die,
My name shall mount upon eternity.

In all editions.                              6    *Medea-like* Medea used her magic to restore the youth of
                                              Jason's father Aeson.

There's nothing grieves me but that age should haste
That in my days I may not see thee  old:
That where those two clear sparkling eyes are placed
Only two loop-holes then I might behold;
That lovely, archèd, ivory, polished brow              5
Defaced with wrinkles that I might but see;
Thy dainty hair, so curled and crispèd now,
Like grizzled moss upon some agèd tree;
Thy cheek, now flush with roses, sunk and lean;
Thy lips with age as any wafer thin;                      10
Thy pearly teeth out of thy head so clean
That, when thou feedst, thy nose shall touch thy chin.
These lines that now thou scornst, which should delight thee,
Then would I make thee read but to despite thee.

First included in the 1619 edition.

Since there's no help, come, let us kiss and part.
Nay, I have done, you get no more of me.
And I am glad, yea glad with all my heart
That thus so cleanly I myself can free.
Shake hands forever, cancel all our vows;              5
And when we meet at any time again
Be it not seen in either of our brows
That we one jot of former love retain.
Now, at the last gasp of Love's latest breath,
When his pulse failing, Passion speechless lies,        10
When Faith is kneeling by his bed of death
And Innocence is closing up his eyes,
Now if thou wouldst, when all have given him over,
From death to life thou mightst him yet recover.

First included in the 1619 edition.

# Robert Sidney, Earl of Leicester (1563–1626)

Philip Sidney's younger brother was educated at Oxford, and served with him in The Netherlands; he eventually assumed his brother's post as Governor of Flushing, and was deeply involved in the fight against the Spanish forces there. He received little advancement from Elizabeth, but found considerable favor with James, who created him successively Baron Sidney, Viscount L'Isle, and, in 1618, Earl of Leicester. His poetry went unpublished until the twentieth century.

*Edition*: *The Poems of Robert Sidney*, ed. P. J. Croft (Oxford: Clarendon Press, 1984).

You that take pleasure in your cruelty
And place your health in my infections,
You that add sorrows to afflictions
And think your wealth shines in my poverty:
Since that there is all inequality                    5
Between my wants and your perfections,
Between your scorns and my affections,
Between my bands and your sovereignty,
O, love yourself, be you yourself your care!
Joy in those acts in which your making stood.         10
Fair, lovely, good: of these made, these you are;
Pity is fair, grace lovely, mercy good.
And when sun-like you in yourself you show,
Let me the point be about which you go.

4   Changed in manuscript from "And triumphs lead in my captivity."

# Christopher Marlowe (1564–1593)

The son of a Canterbury shoemaker, Marlowe was born two months before Shakespeare and into roughly the same social station, but moved much faster. From the King's School in Canterbury he went to Cambridge. In 1587 his MA there was held up briefly because of suspicions about his attendance at the Catholic seminary at Rheims, but by then he had acquired important supporters; the university was reassured by the Privy Council that that attendance had been a matter of loyal governmental service – almost certainly as a spy. Perhaps as early as the summer of 1587, Marlowe's play *Tamburlaine the Great* was being performed in London. It revolutionized Elizabethan theater both with the bravura of its subject matter and the forcefulness of its poetic medium; its prologue announces the abandonment of rhyme and equates blank verse with "the stately tent of war" and the heroic aggression of the protagonist: "Threatening the world with high, astounding terms." A second part of *Tamburlaine* followed, and at least five other plays over the next six years. Two episodes of

brawling led to trouble with the law; in one of these a man was killed, though Marlowe himself was only briefly imprisoned. In the spring of 1593 serious accusations were made against him by the playwright Thomas Kyd and an informer named Richard Baines; surviving documents detail a range of heretical, blasphemous, and otherwise dangerous opinions that Marlowe was supposed to have held (some of them overtly homoerotic, a strain that also shows up in his writings). Marlowe was questioned by the Privy Council and instructed to report to it daily; shortly after, he was stabbed to death in Deptford during an argument with two men with whom he had been drinking and dining. His killing may have been a planned assassination, related to the charges brought against him or continuing espionage activities (or both); or it may have been the result of a drunken dispute over a bar bill.

*Edition*: *The Complete Works of Christopher Marlowe*, ed. Fredson Bowers, 2nd edn (Cambridge: Cambridge University Press, 1981).

## From *Ovid's Elegies*

Marlowe authored what appears to be the first translation of Ovid's *Amores* into English. The *Amores* had never disappeared from the educated reading list, but they never joined the *Metamorphoses* in popularity. They deal with their speaker's erotic adventures with the women of Augustan Rome: meeting them, seducing them, quarreling with them, worrying about what they are up to, and enjoying the thought of how his poems about them will make him famous. There is a principal mistress whom he calls Corinna, but there are other women as well; in several places he celebrates his programmatic promiscuity. It is usually assumed, without specific evidence, that Marlowe's translation dates from his Cambridge days; it was first published during the 1590s, in both complete and selected versions, in combination with Sir John Davies's *Epigrams*. These early editions bear no dates and are identified as having been printed in Holland;

scandal may have been expected, and indeed one edition was among the works burned in 1599 on the order of the Archbishop of Canterbury. As a collection of English love poems, they introduced into the literary world of the 1590s, under the protection of Ovid's classical prestige, an alternative to the dominant Petrarchan expectations of male frustration and single-minded devotion. They seem to have been important for the young John Donne, who wrote his own collection of "elegies" in direct imitation and kept Ovid's poems in mind when he composed some of his lyrics: the first selection below is the generic precedent for "To his Mistress Going to Bed," and the second may be sensed behind "The Sun Rising." The first selection is also reworked in the last scene of Marlowe's own *Hero and Leander*. (Both selections are from the first of Ovid's three books.)

## *Elegia 5: Corinnae concubitus*

In summer's heat and midtime of the day,
To rest my limbs upon a bed I lay.
One window shut, the other open stood,

*Corinnae concubitus* Going to bed with Corinna.

Which gave such light as twinkles in a wood,
Like twilight glimpse at setting of the sun,                     5
Or night being past and yet not day begun.
Such light to shamefast maidens must be shown,
Where they may sport and seem to be unknown.
Then came Corinna in a long loose gown,
Her white neck hid with tresses hanging down,                   10
Resembling fair Semiramis going to bed,
Or Lais of a thousand wooers sped.
I snatched her gown; being thin, the harm was small,
Yet strived she to be covered therewithal,
And striving thus as one that would be cast,                    15
Betrayed herself, and yielded at the last.
Stark naked as she stood before mine eye,
Not one wen in her body could I spy.
What arms and shoulders did I touch and see!
How apt her breasts were to be pressed my me!                   20
How smooth a belly under her waist saw I!
How large a leg, and what a lusty thigh!
To leave the rest, all liked me passing well.
I clinged her naked body; down she fell.
Judge you the rest. Being tired, she bade me kiss.             25
Jove send me more such afternoons as this.

5   *glimpse* glimmer.
11   *Semiramis* Legendary Assyrian queen, founder of the city of Babylon.

12   *Lais* Famous courtesan of Corinth, fourth century BC. *of a thousand wooers sped* successful with a thousand wooers.
18   *wen* blemish.
25   The Latin says: "Who does not know the rest? Tired, we both rested."

## Elegia 13: *Ad Auroram, ne properet*

Now o'er the sea from her old love comes she
That draws the day from heaven's cold axletree.
Aurora, whither slidest thou? Down again,
And birds for Memnon yearly shall be slain.
Now in her tender arms I sweetly bide;                          5
If ever, now well lies she by my side.
The air is cold, and sleep is sweetest now,
And birds send forth shrill notes from every bough.
Whither runst thou that men and women love not?
Hold in thy rosy horses that they move not.                     10
Ere thou rise, stars teach seamen where to sail,
But when thou comest, they of their courses fail.
Poor travellers, though tired, rise at thy sight,
And soldiers make them ready to the fight.
The painful hind by thee to field is sent;                      15
Slow oxen early in the yoke are pent.
Thou cozenst boys of sleep, and dost betray them
To pedants that with cruel lashes pay them.

*Ad Auroram, ne properet* To Aurora (goddess of the dawn), that she not hurry.

1   *old love* Tithonus, Aurora's husband. She had asked for Jupiter to make him immortal, but had neglected to ask for eternal youth, and he became aged and decrepit.
4   *Memnon* son of Aurora and Tithonus, king of Ethiopia.

Thou mak'st the surety to the lawyer run,
That with one word hath nigh himself undone.                        20
The lawyer and the client hate thy view,
Both whom thou raisest up to toil anew.
By thy means women of their rest are barred;
Thou setst their laboring hands to spin and card.
All could I bear; but that the wench should rise,                  25
Who can endure save him with whom none lies?
How oft wished I night would not give thee place,
Nor morning stars shun thy uprising face;
How oft that either wind would break thy coach,
Or steeds might fall, forced with thick clouds' approach.          30
Whither goest thou, hateful nymph? Memnon the elf
Received his coal-black color from thyself.
Say that thy love with Cephalus were not known,
Then thinkest thou thy loose life is not shown?
Would Tithon might but talk of thee awhile,                        35
Not one in heaven should be more base and vile.
Thou leav'st his bed because he's faint through age,
And early mountst thy hateful carriage.
But heldst thou in thine arms some Cephalus,
Then wouldst thou cry, Stay night, and run not thus.              40
Dost punish me because years make him wane?
I did not bid thee wed an aged swain.
The Moon sleeps with Endymion every day:
Thou art as fair as she, then kiss and play.
Jove, that thou shouldst not haste but wait his leisure,          45
Made two nights one to finish up his pleasure.
I chid no more: she blushed, and therefore heard me;
Yet lingered not the day, but morning scared me.

33  *Cephalus* An earlier lover of Aurora's, and father of one of her children.
40  *Stay night, and run not thus* Marlowe has Faustus speak a version of the original Latin phrase moments before being taken off to hell.

43  *Endymion* A young man loved by the moon goddess Selene; he was granted immortality and eternal youth through endless sleep.
45–6  When lying with Alcmena to engender Hercules, Jupiter delayed the dawn to make the night twice as long.
47  *she blushed, and therefore heard me* I could tell from her blush that she had heard me.

## Hero and Leander

A Greek poem in epic meter telling the story of Hero and Leander became one of the most widely translated classical texts in sixteenth-century Europe. The poem dates from late Roman imperial times, probably the fifth century AD, but a manuscript ascription to "Musaeus" led Renaissance scholars to assign it to the legendary colleague of Orpheus and date it at the dawn of Greek poetry, before even Homer. Marlowe at a few places copied the original quite closely, but for the most part used its narrative as a starting point for extravagant elaborations of his own, adding several new episodes to the story and intensifying the erotic tone to sometimes comic or brutal extremes. References to the eventual death of the lovers imply that Marlowe meant to tell the full story, but what he wrote ends with an intense account of their mutual loss of virginity and the fierce emotions of the next morning; the conclusion as it stands is strong enough to suggest that the poem is essentially complete, rather than abandoned by Marlowe or interrupted by his death. It was published on its own in 1598. Later that year it was printed again with an ambitious continuation by George Chapman that triples its length, adds even more to the original story, makes the general tone less erotic and more moralistic, and takes things up to a slightly altered ending in which the lovers are saved from death by an Ovidian metamorphosis into birds. Chapman also divided the whole into six "Sestyads," with Marlowe's portion constituting the first two. This is the form in which the poem became best known; the version given below is Marlowe's part alone, as given in the first edition.

On Hellespont, guilty of true love's blood,
In view and opposite two cities stood,
Sea-borderers, disjoined by Neptune's might:
The one Abydos, the other Sestos hight.
At Sestos Hero dwelt, Hero the fair, 5
Whom young Apollo courted for her hair,
And offered as a dower his burning throne
Where she should sit for men to gaze upon.
The outside of her garments were of lawn;
The lining purple silk, with gilt stars drawn; 10
Her wide sleeves green and bordered with a grove
Where Venus in her naked glory strove
To please the careless and disdainful eyes
Of proud Adonis that before her lies;
Her kirtle blue, whereon was many a stain 15
Made with the blood of wretched lovers slain.
Upon her head she ware a myrtle wreath,
From whence her veil reached to the ground beneath;
Her veil was artificial flowers and leaves,
Whose workmanship both man and beast deceives. 20
Many would praise the sweet smell as she passed,
When twas the odor which her breath forth cast;
And there for honey bees have sought in vain,
And, beat from thence, have lighted there again.
About her neck hung chains of pebble stone 25
Which, lightened by her neck, like diamonds shone.
She ware no gloves, for neither sun nor wind
Would burn or parch her hands, but to her mind
Or warm or cool them, for they took delight
To play upon those hands, they were so white. 30
Buskins of shells all silvered usèd she,
And branched with blushing coral to the knee,
Where sparrows perched, of hollow pearl and gold,
Such as the world would wonder to behold.
Those with sweet water oft her handmaid fills, 35
Which as she went would chirrup through the bills.
Some say for her the fairest Cupid pined
And looking in her face was strucken blind.
But this is true, so like was one the other,
As he imagined Hero was his mother, 40
And oftentimes into her bosom flew,
About her naked neck his bare arms threw,
And laid his childish head upon her breast,
And, with still panting rocked, there took his rest.
So lovely fair was Hero, Venus' nun, 45
As Nature wept, thinking she was undone
Because she took more from her than she left
And of such wondrous beauty her bereft.
Therefore in sign her treasure suffered wrack,
Since Hero's time hath half the world been black. 50

---

9  *lawn* sheer cotton or linen fabric.
28  *to her mind* as she wished.
44  *still* steady.

45  *Venus' nun* The phrase (which also appears in l. 319)
may have been slang for prostitute; it is so used in Stephen
Gosson's *The School of Abuse* (1587).

Amorous Leander, beautiful and young
(Whose tragedy divine Musaeus sung),
Dwelt at Abydos. Since him, dwelt there none
For whom succeeding times make greater moan.
His dangling tresses that were never shorn,                          55
Had they been cut and unto Colchis born,
Would have allured the venturous youth of Greece
To hazard more than for the Golden Fleece.
Fair Cynthia wished his arms might be her sphere;
Grief makes her pale because she moves not there.                   60
His body was as straight as Circe's wand;
Jove might have sipped out nectar from his hand.
Even as delicious meat is to the taste,
So was his neck in touching, and surpassed
The white of Pelops' shoulder. I could tell ye                      65
How smooth his breast was, and how white his belly,
And whose immortal fingers did imprint
That heavenly path, with many a curious dint,
That runs along his back, but my rude pen
Can hardly blazon forth the loves of men,                           70
Much less of powerful gods – let it suffice
That my slack Muse sings of Leander's eyes,
Those orient cheeks and lips exceeding his
That leapt into the water for a kiss
Of his own shadow, and, despising many,                             75
Died ere he could enjoy the love of any.
Had wild Hippolytus Leander seen,
Enamored of his beauty had he been.
His presence made the rudest peasant melt
That in the vast uplandish country dwelt.                           80
The barbarous Thracian soldier, moved with nought,
Was moved with him and for his favor sought.
Some swore he was a maid in man's attire,
For in his looks were all that men desire:
A pleasant similing cheek, a speaking eye,                          85
A brow for love to banquet royally.
And such as knew he was a man would say,
Leander, thou art made for amorous play;
Why art thou not in love, and loved of all?
Though thou be fair, yet be not thine own thrall.                   90
   The men of wealthy Sestos every year
(For his sake whom their goddess held so dear,
Rose-cheeked Adonis) kept a solemn feast.
Thither resorted many a wandering guest
To meet their loves; such as had none at all                        95

56–7   A fleece of gold, at Colchis on the Black Sea, was the prize sought by the Greek Argonauts in the generation before the Trojan war.

59   *Cynthia* goddess of the moon.

61   *Circe* A witch visited by Odysseus on his voyage home; with her wand she turned men into beasts.

65   *Pelops' shoulder* A shoulder of ivory. Pelops was dismembered by his father Tantalus and served as a meal for the gods; the gods recognized the deceit, brought Pelops back to life, and provided an ivory replacement for the only part that had been eaten.

68   *curious dint* exquisite indentation.

73–6   A reference to the story of Narcissus, who fell in love with his own image in the water; in the usual version, he pines away rather than drowns.

77   *wild Hippolytus* Son of Theseus and follower of Diana; famous for his vow of virginity.

80   *uplandish* rustic.

90   *thrall* slave.

Came lovers home from this great festival.
For every street like to a firmament
Glistered with breathing stars, who where they went
Frighted the melancholy earth, which deemed
Eternal heaven to burn, for so it seemed                          100
As if another Phaëthon had got
The guidance of the sun's rich chariot.
But far above the loveliest Hero shined,
And stole away the enchanted gazer's mind;
For like sea nymphs' inveigling harmony,                          105
So was her beauty to the standers by.
Nor that night-wandering pale and watery star
(When yawning dragons draw her thirling car
From Latmus mount up to the gloomy sky,
Where crowned with blazing light and majesty                      110
She proudly sits) more overrules the flood
Than she the hearts of those that near her stood.
Even as, when gaudy nymphs pursue the chase,
Wretched Ixion's shaggy-footed race,
Incensed with savage heat, gallop amain                           115
From steep pine-bearing mountains to the plain:
So ran the people forth to gaze upon her,
And all that viewed her were enamored on her.
And as in fury of a dreadful fight,
Their fellows being slain or put to flight,                       120
Poor soldiers stand with fear of death dead strucken,
So at her presence all surprised and tooken
Await the sentence of her scornful eyes;
He whom she favors lives, the other dies.
There might you see one sigh, another rage,                       125
And some (their violent passions to assuage)
Compile sharp satires; but alas, too late,
For faithful love will never turn to hate.
And many, seeing great princes were denied,
Pined as they went, and thinking on her died.                     130
   On this feast day, O cursèd day and hour,
Went Hero thorough Sestos from her tower
To Venus' temple, where unhappily,
As after chanced, they did each other spy.
So fair a church as this had Venus none;                          135
The walls were of discolored jasper stone,
Wherein was Proteus carvèd, and o'erhead
A lively vine of green sea-agate spread,
Where by one hand light-headed Bacchus hung,
And with the other wine from grapes outwrung.                     140
Of crystal shining fair the pavement was;

98   *Glistered* glittered.
101   *Phaëthon* Son of Apollo; his father allowed him to drive
the chariot of the sun, but he proved incapable of managing
its horses and scorched a large part of the earth.
107   *star* the moon.
108   *thirling* flying and spinning.
109   *Latmus mount* Mount Latmos in Greece, sacred to
Cynthia.

114   *Ixion's shaggy-footed race* The centaurs, the result of
Ixion's mating with a deceptive replica of Juno.
136   *discolored* variably colored.
137   *Proteus* A minor sea-god who could take on different
shapes.
141–56   Cf. the erotic tapestries in Spenser's House
of Busirane (*Faery Queen* III.xi.29–46), based in turn on
Arachne's tapestry in Ovid's *Metamorphoses* (6.103–28).

The town of Sestos called it Venus' glass.
There might you see the gods in sundry shapes
Committing heady riots, incest, rapes.
For know that underneath this radiant floor          145
Was Danaë's statue in a brazen tower;
Jove slyly stealing from his sister's bed
To dally with Idalian Ganymede,
And, for his love Europa, bellowing loud,
And tumbling with the rainbow in a cloud;          150
Blood-quaffing Mars heaving the iron net
Which limping Vulcan and his Cyclops set;
Love kindling fire to burn such towns as Troy;
Sylvanus weeping for the lovely boy
That now is turned into a cypress tree,          155
Under whose shade the wood-gods love to be.
And in the midst a silver altar stood;
There Hero sacrificing turtles' blood,
Veiled to the ground, veiling her eyelids close:
And modestly they opened as she rose.          160
Thence flew Love's arrow with the golden head,
And thus Leander was enamorèd.
Stone still he stood, and evermore he gazed,
Till with the fire that from his countenance blazed
Relenting Hero's gentle heart was struck.          165
Such force and virtue hath an amorous look.
    It lies not in our power to love or hate,
For will in us is overruled by fate.
When two are stripped long ere the course begin,
We wish that one should lose, the other win;          170
And one especially we do affect
Of two gold ingots like in each respect.
The reason no man knows; let it suffice
What we behold is censured by our eyes.
Where both deliberate, the love is slight;          175
Whoever loved that loved not at first sight?
    He kneeled, but unto her devoutly prayed.
Chaste Hero to herself thus softly said,
Were I the saint he worships, I would hear him,
And, as she spake those words, came somewhat near him.          180
He started up; she blushed as one ashamed,
Wherewith Leander much more was inflamed.
He touched her hand; in touching it, she trembled.
Love deeply grounded hardly is dissembled.

---

**146**  *Danaë* A mortal woman sequestered by her father; Jupiter seduced her by entering her prison as a shower of gold.
**147**  *his sister's bed* Jupiter's wife Juno was also his sister.
**148**  *Idalian Ganymede* A beautiful young boy abducted from Mount Ida by Jupiter in the form of an eagle; he became cupbearer on Olympus.
**149**  *Europa* A mortal woman abducted by Jupiter in the form of a bull.
**150**  There is no classical myth of Jupiter's seduction of the goddess of the rainbow; Marlowe offers an erotic interpretation of his cult status as Jupiter Pluvius, the god of rain.

**151–2**  When Venus committed adultery with Mars, her husband trapped the lovers in a specially made iron net and exhibited them before the other gods.
**158**  *turtles'* turtle-doves'.
**166**  *virtue* power.
**168**  *will* desire.
**174**  *censured* judged.
**176**  Cited by Shakespeare in *As You Like It*: "Dead shepherd, now I find thy saw of might: / Who ever loved that loved not at first sight?" (III.v.82–3).

These lovers parleyed by the touch of hands;                                    185
True love is mute, and oft amazèd stands.
Thus while dumb signs their yielding hearts entangled,
The air with sparks of living fire was spangled,
And Night, deep drenched in misty Acheron,
Heaved up her head, and half the world upon                                     190
Breathed darkness forth (dark night is Cupid's day).
And now begins Leander to display
Love's holy fire with words, with sighs and tears,
Which like sweet music entered Hero's ears.
And yet at every word she turned aside,                                         195
And always cut him off as he replied.
At last, like to a bold, sharp sophister,
With cheerful hope thus he accosted her:
    Fair creature, let me speak without offence.
I would my rude words had the influence                                         200
To lead thy thoughts as thy fair looks do mine;
Then shouldst thou be his prisoner who is thine.
Be not unkind and fair; misshapen stuff
Are of behavior boisterous and rough.
O shun me not, but hear me ere you go.                                          205
God knows I cannot force love, as you do.
My words shall be as spotless as my youth,
Full of simplicity and naked truth.
This sacrifice (whose sweet perfume descending
From Venus' altar to your footsteps bending)                                    210
Doth testify that you exceed her far
To whom you offer and whose nun you are.
Why should you worship her? Her you surpass
As much as sparkling diamonds flaring glass.
A diamond set in lead his worth retains;                                        215
A heavenly nymph beloved of human swains
Receives no blemish, but oft-times more grace –
Which makes me hope, although I am but base,
Base in respect of thee, divine and pure,
Dutiful service may thy love procure.                                           220
And I in duty will excel all other,
As thou in beauty dost exceed Love's mother.
Nor heaven nor thou were made to gaze upon;
As heaven preserves all things, so save thou one.
A stately builded ship, well rigged and tall,                                   225
The ocean maketh more majestical;
Why vowst thou then to live in Sestos here,
Who on Love's seas more glorious wouldst appear?
Like untuned golden strings all women are,
Which, long time lie untouched, will harshly jar.                               230
Vessels of brass oft handled brightly shine.
What difference betwixt the richest mine
And basest mold but use? For both, not used,
Are of like worth. Then treasure is abused

---

189   A marginal note in the first edition identifies this passage as "A periphrasis of night."

197   *sophister* clever philosopher; also used in the sixteenth century to indicate a second-year student at Cambridge.

231–40   Expanded from *Ovid's Elegies* 1.8.51–2: "Brass shines with use, good garments would be worn, / Houses not dwelt in are with filth forlorn."

When misers keep it; being put to loan,                          235
In time it will return us two for one.
Rich robes themselves and others do adorn;
Neither themselves nor others if not worn.
Who builds a palace and rams up the gate
Shall see it ruinous and desolate.                               240
Ah simple Hero, learn thyself to cherish;
Lone women like to empty houses perish.
Less sins the poor rich man that starves himself
In heaping up a mass of drossy pelf
Than such as you; his golden earth remains,                      245
Which after his decease some other gains.
But this fair gem, sweet in the loss alone,
When you fleet hence, can be bequeathed to none.
Or if it could, down from the enameled sky
All heaven would come to claim this legacy,                      250
And with intestine broils the world destroy
And quite confound nature's sweet harmony.
Well therefore by the gods decreed it is
We human creatures should enjoy that bliss.
One is no number; maids are nothing then                         255
Without the sweet society of men.
Wilt thou live single still? One shalt thou be,
Though never-singling Hymen couple thee.
Wild savages that drink of running springs
Think water far excels all earthly things;                       260
But they that daily taste neat wine despise it.
Virginity, albeit some highly prize it,
Compared with marriage, had you tried them both,
Differs as much as wine and water doth.
Base bullion for the stamp's sake we allow;                      265
Even so for men's impression do we you,
By which alone, our reverend fathers say,
Women receive perfection every way.
This idol which you term Virginity
Is neither essence subject to the eye,                           270
No, nor to any one exterior sense,
Nor hath it any place of residence,
Nor is't of earth or mold celestial,
Or capable of any form at all.
Of that which hath no being do not boast;                        275
Things that are not at all are never lost.
Men foolishly do call it virtuous.
What virtue is it that is born with us?
Much less can honor be ascribed thereto;
Honor is purchased by the deeds we do.                           280
Believe me, Hero, honor is not won
Until some honorable deed be done.
Seek you for chastity immortal fame,

---

239   *rams up* blocks up.
244   *drossy pelf* filthy lucre.
248   *fleet* flit.
251   *intestine broils* civil wars.

255   *One is no number* Aristotle, *Metaphysics* 14.1/1088A (though without any reference to female virginity).
258   *never-singling* never isolating.
261   *neat* undiluted.
265   We accept inferior metal as money because of its imprint.

And know that some have wronged Diana's name?
Whose name is it, if she be false or not, 285
So she be fair, but some vile tongues will blot?
But you are fair (ay me!), so wondrous fair,
So young, so gentle, and so debonair
As Greece will think, if thus you live alone,
Some one or other keeps you as his own. 290
Then Hero, hate me not nor from me fly
To follow swiftly blasting infamy.
Perhaps thy sacred priesthood makes thee loath;
Tell me, to whom mad'st thou that heedless oath?
    To Venus, answered she, and as she spake 295
Forth from those two tralucent cisterns brake
A stream of liquid pearl, which down her face
Made milk-white paths, whereon the gods might trace
To Jove's high court. He thus replied: The rites
In which Love's beauteous empress most delights 300
Are banquets, Doric music, midnight revel,
Plays, masques, and all that stern age counteth evil.
Thee as a holy idiot doth she scorn,
For thou in vowing chastity hast sworn
To rob her name and honor, and thereby 305
Commitst a sin far worse than perjury,
Even sacrilege against her deity,
Through regular and formal purity.
To expiate which sin, kiss and shake hands;
Such sacrifice as this, Venus demands. 310
    Thereat she smiled, and did deny him so
As put thereby, yet might he hope for moe –
Which makes him quickly reinforce his speech
And her in humble manner thus beseech:
    Though neither gods nor men may thee deserve, 315
Yet for her sake whom you have vowed to serve
Abandon fruitless, cold virginity,
The gentle queen of love's sole enemy.
Then shall you most resemble Venus' nun
When Venus' sweet rites are performed and done. 320
Flint-breasted Pallas joys in single life,
But Pallas and your mistress are at strife.
Love Hero then, and be not tyrannous,
But heal the heart that thou hast wounded thus,
Nor stain thy youthful years with avarice; 325
Fair fools delight to be accounted nice.
The richest corn dies, if it be not reaped;
Beauty alone is lost, too warily kept.
These arguments he used, and many more,

296  *tralucent* translucent.
298  *trace* travel.
301  *Doric music* Music in the military Spartan mode;
"Lydian" would be the term more readily associated with
erotic music.
303  *idiot* An ignorant person in general, but also specifically
a layman, someone without the knowledge possessed by the
clergy.

312  *put* repelled.
321  *Pallas* Pallas Athena, one of three virgin goddesses in
the Olympian pantheon.
323  *tyrannous* A standard characterization of the untouch-
able Petrarchan mistress.
326  *nice* fastidious, coy.

Wherewith she yielded, that was won before.                    330
Hero's looks yielded, but her words made war;
Women are won when they begin to jar.
Thus having swallowed Cupid's golden hook,
The more she strived, the deeper she was struck.
Yet evilly feigning anger, strove she still,                   335
And would be thought to grant against her will.
So, having paused a while, at last she said,
Who taught thee rhetoric to deceive a maid?
Ay me, such words as these should I abhor,
And yet I like them for the orator.                            340
    With that, Leander stooped, to have embraced her,
But from his spreading arms away she cast her,
And thus bespake him: Gentle youth, forbear
To touch the sacred garments which I wear.
Upon a rock, and underneath a hill,                            345
Far from the town (where all is whist and still,
Save that the sea, playing on yellow sand,
Sends forth a rattling murmur to the land,
Whose sound allures the golden Morpheus
In silence of the night to visit us)                           350
My turret stands, and there God knows I play
With Venus' swans and sparrows all the day.
A dwarfish beldam bears me company,
And hops about the chamber where I lie,
And spends the night (that might be better spent)              355
In vain discourse and apish merriment.
Come thither. As she spake this, her tongue tripped,
For unawares *come thither* from her slipped;
And suddenly her former color changed,
And here and there her eyes through anger ranged,              360
And like a planet moving several ways
At one self instant, she, poor soul, assays,
Loving, not to love at all, and every part
Strove to resist the motions of her heart.
And hands so pure, so innocent, nay such                       365
As might have made heaven stoop to have a touch,
Did she uphold to Venus, and again
Vowed spotless chastity, but all in vain.
Cupid beats down her prayers with his wings;
Her vows above the empty air he flings.                        370
All deep enraged, his sinewy bow he bent
And shot a shaft that burning from him went,
Wherewith she strucken, looked so dolefully
As made Love sigh to see his tyranny;
And as she wept, her tears to pearl he turned                  375
And wound them on his arm, and for her mourned.
Then towards the palace of the Destinies,
Laden with languishment and grief, he flies,
And to those stern nymphs humbly made request

332  *jar* argue.
335  *evilly* badly.
342  *cast her* cast herself.
346  *whist* quiet.

349  *Morpheus* god of sleep.
353  *beldam* old woman.
362  *At one self instant* at the same time.

Both might enjoy each other and be blest. 380
But with a ghastly, dreadful countenance,
Threatening a thousand deaths at every glance,
They answered Love, nor would vouchsafe so much
As one poor word: their hate to him was such.
  Harken a while, and I will tell you why. 385
Heaven's wingèd herald, Jove-born Mercury,
The self same day that he asleep had laid
Enchanted Argus, spied a country maid
Whose careless hair, instead of pearl to adorn it,
Glistered with dew, as one that seemed to scorn it. 390
Her breath as fragrant as the morning rose,
Her mind pure, and her tongue untaught to glose,
Yet proud she was (for lofty pride that dwells
In towered courts is oft in shepherds' cells),
And too, too well the fair vermilion knew 395
And silver tincture of her cheeks that drew
The love of every swain. On her this god
Enamored was, and with his snaky rod
Did charm her nimble feet and made her stay.
The while upon a hillock down he lay, 400
And sweetly on his pipe began to play
And with smooth speech her fancy to assay,
Till in his twining arms he locked her fast.
And then he wooed with kisses, and at last,
As shepherds do, her on the ground he laid, 405
And, tumbling in the grass, he often strayed
Beyond the bounds of shame in being bold
To eye those parts which no eye should behold,
And like an insolent, commanding lover,
Boasting his parentage, would needs discover 410
The way to new Elysium. But she,
Whose only dower was her chastity,
Having striven in vain, was now about to cry
And crave the help of shepherds that were nigh.
Herewith he stayed his fury and began 415
To give her leave to rise; away she ran.
After went Mercury, who used such cunning
As she to hear his tale left off her running
(Maids are not won by brutish force and might,
But speeches full of pleasure and delight), 420
And, knowing Hermes courted her, was glad
That she such loveliness and beauty had
As could provoke his liking, yet was mute
And neither would deny nor grant his suit.
Still vowed he love; she, wanting no excuse 425
To feed him with delays, as women use,
Or thirsting after immortality
(All women are ambitious naturally),
Imposed upon her lover such a task

---

385–484 The story here appears to be Marlowe's own improvisation.
390 *it* pearl.
392 *glose* flatter, deceive.
398 *snaky rod* the caduceus.
425 *wanting* lacking.

As he ought not perform, nor yet she ask.                          430
A draught of flowing nectar she requested,
Wherewith the king of gods and men is feasted.
He, ready to accomplish what she willed,
Stole some from Hebe (Hebe Jove's cup filled)
And gave it to his simple rustic love;                             435
Which being known (as what is hid from Jove?),
He inly stormed, and waxed more furious
Than for the fire filched by Prometheus,
And thrusts him down from heaven. He, wandering here
In mournful terms, with sad and heavy cheer                        440
Complained to Cupid; Cupid, for his sake,
To be revenged on Jove did undertake,
And those on whom heaven, earth, and hell relies –
I mean the adamantine Destinies –
He wounds with love, and forced them equally                       445
To dote upon deceitful Mercury.
They offered him the deadly fatal knife
That shears the slender threads of human life;
At his fair feathered feet the engines laid
Which the earth from ugly Chaos' den upweighed.                    450
These he regarded not, but did entreat
That Jove, usurper of his father's seat,
Might presently be banished into hell
And agèd Saturn in Olympus dwell.
They granted what he craved, and once again                        455
Saturn and Ops began their golden reign.
Murder, rape, war, lust, and treachery
Were with Jove closed in Stygian empery.
But long this blessed time continued not;
As soon as he his wishèd purpose got,                              460
He, reckless of his promise, did despise
The love of the everlasting Destinies.
They, seeing it, both Love and him abhorred,
And Jupiter unto his place restored.
And but that Learning, in despite of Fate,                         465
Will mount aloft and enter heaven gate
And to the seat of Jove itself advance,
Hermes had slept in hell with ignorance.
Yet as a punishment they added this,
That he and Poverty should always kiss.                            470
And to this day is every scholar poor;
Gross gold from them runs headlong to the boor.
Likewise the angry sisters, thus deluded,
To venge themselves on Hermes have concluded
That Midas' brood shall sit in Honor's chair,                      475

**434** *Hebe* cupbearer on Olympus before the arrival of Ganymede.
**437** *He* Jove.
**439** *him, he* Mercury.
**440** *In mournful terms* in an unhappy state.
**450** *upweighed* lifted up.
**452ff.** The reign of the god Saturn and his wife Ops, conventionally celebrated as earth's Golden Age, was ended by the rebellion of their son Jupiter, who imprisoned his father in Tartarus.
**458** *Stygian empery* the empire of Hades, beyond the river Styx.
**460** *he* Mercury.
**465** *Learning* Mercury was frequently invoked in the Renaissance as the patron god of scholars.
**475** *Midas' brood* the rich.

To which the Muses' sons are only heir;
And fruitful wits that in aspiring are
Shall, discontent, run into regions far;
And few great lords in virtuous deeds shall joy,
But be surprised with every garish toy,               480
And still enrich the lofty servile clown
Who with encroaching guile keeps learning down.
Then muse not Cupid's suit no better sped,
Seeing in their loves the Fates were injurèd.
    By this, sad Hero, with love unacquainted,        485
Viewing Leander's face, fell down and fainted.
He kissed her, and breathed life into her lips;
Wherewith, as one displeased, away she trips,
Yet, as she went, full often looked behind,
And many poor excuses did she find                490
To linger by the way, and once she stayed
And would have turned again, but was afraid
In offering parley to be counted light.
So on she goes, and in her idle flight
Her painted fan of curlèd plumes let fall,         495
Thinking to train Leander therewithal.
He, being a novice, knew not what she meant,
But stayed, and after her a letter sent:
Which joyful Hero answered in such sort
As he had hope to scale the beauteous fort       500
Wherein the liberal Graces locked their wealth;
And therefore to her tower he got by stealth.
Wide open stood the door, he need not climb;
And she herself before the pointed time
Had spread the board, with roses strewed the room,   505
And oft looked out and mused he did not come.
At last he came. O, who can tell the greeting
These greedy lovers had at their first meeting?
He asked, she gave, and nothing was denied;
Both to each other quickly were affied.         510
Look how their hands, so were their hearts united.
And what he did, she willingly requited.
(Sweet are the kisses, the embracements sweet
When like desires and affections meet;
For from the earth to heaven is Cupid raised     515
Where fancy is in equal balance peised.)
Yet she this rashness suddenly repented,
And turned aside and to herself lamented,
As if her name and honor had been wronged
By being possessed of him for whom she longed.   520
Ay, and she wished, albeit not from her heart,
That he would leave her turret and depart.
The mirthful god of amorous pleasure smiled

---

477  *in aspiring* ambitious. Some editors emend to "inaspiring," i.e., unambitious.
481  *lofty servile clown* ambitious, obsequious, ignorant person.
483  *sped* succeeded.
493  *light* shameless.

496  *train* lure.
500  *As he had hope* so as to make him hope.
504  *pointed* appointed.
505  *spread the board* set the table.
510  *affied* affianced.
516  *peised* poised.

To see how he this captive nymph beguiled;
For hitherto he did but fan the fire,                                                525
And kept it down that it might mount the higher.
Now waxed she jealous lest his love abated,
Fearing her own thoughts made her to be hated.
Therefore unto him hastily she goes,
And like light Salmacis her body throws                                          530
Upon his bosom, where with yielding eyes
She offers up herself a sacrifice
To slake his anger if he were displeased.
O what god would not therewith be appeased?
    Like Aesop's cock this jewel he enjoyed,                                     535
And as a brother with his sister toyed,
Supposing nothing else was to be done
Now he her favor and good will had won.
But know you not that creatures wanting sense
By nature have a mutual appetence,                                               540
And wanting organs to advance a step,
Moved by love's force, unto each other leap?
Much more in subjects having intellect
Some hidden influence breeds like effect.
Albeit Leander, rude in love and raw,                                            545
Long dallying with Hero, nothing saw
That might delight him more, yet he suspected
Some amorous rites or other were neglected.
Therefore unto his body hers he clung;
She, fearing on the rushes to be flung,                                          550
Strived with redoubled strength. The more she strived,
The more a gentle pleasing heat revived,
Which taught him all that elder lovers know.
And now the same gan so to scorch and glow
As in plain terms (yet cunningly) he craved it:                                 555
Love always makes those eloquent that have it.
She, with a kind of granting, put him by it;
And ever as he thought himself most nigh it,
Like to the tree of Tantalus she fled,
And, seeming lavish, saved her maidenhead.                                      560
Ne'er king more sought to keep his diadem
Than Hero this inestimable gem.
Above our life we love a steadfast friend,
Yet when a token of great worth we send,
We often kiss it, often look thereon,                                           565
And stay the messenger that would be gone.
No marvel then, though Hero would not yield
So soon to part from that she dearly held.
Jewels being lost are found again; this never.

---

527   *jealous* afraid.
530   *Salmacis* A nymph in love with the unresponsive Hermaphroditus; she assaulted him, and the gods transformed them into a single person with the attributes of both sexes; Ovid, *Metamorphoses* 4.285ff.
535   *Aesop's cock* A rooster uninterested in the jewel he finds in the barnyard.
539   *creatures wanting sense* inanimate objects.

540   *appetence* desire.
545   *rude* inexperienced.
550   *rushes* Commonly used as a floor covering.
555   *craved* asked for.  *it* No antecedent is stated.
557   *put him by it* kept him away from it.
559   *the tree of Tantalus* A tree whose fruit stays just out of reach of the famished sinner in Hades.

Tis lost but once, and once lost, lost forever.      570
   Now had the Morn espied her lover's steeds,
Whereat she starts, puts on her purple weeds,
And red for anger that he stayed so long,
All headlong throws herself the clouds among.
And now Leander, fearing to be missed,      575
Embraced her suddenly, took leave, and kissed.
Long was he taking leave, and loath to go,
And kissed again, as lovers use to do.
Sad Hero wrung him by the hand, and wept,
Saying, Let your vows and promises be kept.      580
Then, standing at the door, she turned about,
As loath to see Leander going out.
And now the sun that through the horizon peeps
As pitying these lovers, downward creeps,
So that in silence of the cloudy night,      585
Though it was morning, did he take his flight.
But what the secret trusty night concealed,
Leander's amorous habit soon revealed.
With Cupid's myrtle was his bonnet crowned;
About his arms the purple riband wound      590
Wherewith she wreathed her largely spreading hair.
Nor could the youth abstain, but he must wear
The sacred ring wherewith she was endowed
When first religious chastity she vowed:
Which made his love through Sestos to be known,      595
And thence unto Abydos sooner blown
Than he could sail, for incorporeal Fame,
Whose weight consists in nothing but her name,
Is swifter than the wind, whose tardy plumes
Are reeking water and dull earthly fumes.      600
Home when he came, he seemed not to be there
But like exilèd air thrust from his sphere,
Set in a foreign place; and straight from thence,
Alcides-like, by mighty violence,
He would have chased away the swelling main      605
That him from her unjustly did detain.
Like as the sun in a diameter
Fires and inflames objects removèd far,
And heateth kindly, shining laterally,
So beauty sweetly quickens when tis nigh,      610
But being separated and removed,
Burns where it cherished, murders where it loved.
Therefore, even as an index to a book,
So to his mind was young Leander's look.
O, none but gods have power their love to hide;      615
Affection by the countenance is descried.

---

571  *her lover's steeds* The horses pulling the chariot of the sun; in classical mythology the goddess of the dawn has a series of lovers (as in *Ovid's Elegies* 1.13 above), but the god of the sun is not among them.

572  *weeds* clothes.

576  *her* Hero.

588  *habits* style of dress.

591  *largely* widely.

600  *reeking* vaporous.

602  The reference is probably to the disposition of the elements in Ptolemaic cosmology, though it has also been suggested that "air" should be read as "heir."

604  *Alcides* Hercules.

607  *in a diameter* directly (in this case, straight down).

The light of hidden fire itself discovers,
And love that is concealed betrays poor lovers.
His secret flame apparently was seen;
Leander's father knew where he had been, 620
And for the same mildly rebuked his son,
Thinking to quench the sparkles new begun.
But love, resisted once, grows passionate,
And nothing more than counsel lovers hate.
For as a hot, proud horse highly disdains 625
To have his head controlled, but breaks the reins,
Spits forth the ringled bit, and with his hooves
Checks the submissive ground, so he that loves,
The more he is restrained, the worse he fares.
What is it now but mad Leander dares? 630
 O Hero, Hero, thus he cried full oft;
And then he got him to a rock aloft,
Where, having spied her tower, long stared he on't,
And prayed the narrow, toiling Hellespont
To part in twain that he might come and go: 635
But still the rising billows answered No.
With that he stripped him to the ivory skin,
And crying, Love, I come! leapt lively in.
Whereat the sapphire-visaged god grew proud
And made his capering Triton sound aloud, 640
Imagining that Ganymede, displeased,
Had left the heavens; therefore on him he seized.
Leander strived; the waves about him wound
And pulled him to the bottom, where the ground
Was strewed with pearl, and in low coral groves 645
Sweet-singing mermaids sported with their loves
On heaps of heavy gold, and took great pleasure
To spurn in careless sort the shipwrack treasure.
For here the stately azure palace stood
Where kingly Neptune and his train abode. 650
The lusty god embraced him, called him love,
And swore he never should return to Jove.
But when he knew it was not Ganymede –
For underwater he was almost dead –
He heaved him up and, looking on his face, 655
Beat down the bold waves with his triple mace,
Which mounted up, intending to have kissed him,
And fell in drops like tears because they missed him.
Leander, being up, began to swim,
And looking back, saw Neptune follow him. 660
Whereat aghast, the poor soul gan to cry,
O let me visit Hero ere I die!
The god put Helle's bracelet on his arm,
And swore the sea should never do him harm.

---

**619** *apparently* openly.
**627** *ringled* fitted or decorated with rings.
**628** *Checks* stamps.
**630** What is there now that mad Leander does not dare?
**639** *sapphire-visaged god* Neptune; his interest in Ganymede (and Leander) is Marlowe's invention.

**640** *Triton* Neptune's son, who blows on a conch shell.
**663** *Helle* Daughter of the Boeotian king Athamas; fleeing from him, she drowned in the body of water that was later named after her, the Hellespont.

He clapped his plump cheeks, with his tresses played, 665
And, smiling wantonly, his love bewrayed.
He watched his arms and, as they opened wide,
At every stroke betwixt them would he slide
And steal a kiss, and then run out and dance,
And, as he turned, cast many a lustful glance, 670
And threw him gaudy toys to please his eye,
And dive into the water and there pry
Upon his breast, his thighs, and every limb,
And up again and close beside him swim
And talk of love. Leander made reply, 675
You are deceived! I am no woman, I!
Thereat smiled Neptune, and then told a tale:
How that a shepherd sitting in a vale
Played with a boy so fair and kind
As for his love both earth and heaven pined, 680
That of the cooling river durst not drink,
Lest water-nymphs should pull him from the brink;
And when he sported in the fragrant lawns,
Goat-footed satyrs and up-staring fawns
Would steal him thence. Ere half his tale was done, 685
Ay me, Leander cried, the enamored sun
That now should shine on Thetis' glassy bower
Descends upon my radiant Hero's tower.
O, that these tardy arms of mine were wings!
And as he spake, upon the waves he springs. 690
Neptune was angry that he gave no ear,
And in his heart revenging malice bare.
He flung at him his mace, but as it went
He called it in, for love made him repent.
The mace, returning back, his own hand hit, 695
As meaning to be venged for darting it.
When this fresh bleeding wound Leander viewed,
His color went and came, as if he rued
The grief which Neptune felt. In gentle breasts
Relenting thoughts, remorse, and pity rests; 700
And who have hard hearts and obdurate minds
But vicious, hare-brained, and illiterate hinds?
The god, seeing him with pity to be moved,
Thereon concluded that he was beloved.
(Love is too full of faith, too credulous, 705
With folly and false hope deluding us.)
Wherefore, Leander's fancy to surprise,
To the rich ocean for gifts he flies.
Tis wisdom to give much; a gift prevails
When deep persuading oratory fails. 710
    By this Leander, being near the land,
Cast down his weary feet and felt the sand.
Breathless albeit he were, he rested not
Till to the solitary tower he got

---

**666** *bewrayed* divulged.
**679** A seventeenth-century edition fills out this metrically deficient line by reading "so lovely fair and kind."

**684** *up-staring* Seventeenth-century editions read "up-starting."
**687** *Thetis' glassy bower* the sea.
**702** *hinds* rustics.

And knocked and called: at which celestial noise                                    715
The longing heart of Hero much more joys
Than nymphs and shepherds when the timbrel rings
Or crooked dolphin when the sailor sings.
She stayed not for her robes but straight arose,
And, drunk with gladness, to the door she goes,                                     720
Where, seeing a naked man, she screeched for fear
(Such sights as this to tender maids are rare)
And ran into the dark herself to hide.
Rich jewels in the dark are soonest spied;
Unto her was he led, or rather drawn,                                               725
By those white limbs which sparkled through the lawn.
The nearer that he came, the more she fled
And, seeking refuge, slipped into her bed.
Whereon Leander sitting, thus began,
Through numbing cold all feeble, faint, and wan:                                    730
    If not for love, yet, love, for pity sake
Me in thy bed and maiden bosom take.
At least vouchsafe these arms some little room,
Who, hoping to embrace thee, cheerly swum.
This head was beat with many a churlish billow,                                     735
And therefore let it rest upon thy pillow.
Herewith affrighted Hero shrunk away,
And in her lukewarm place Leander lay:
Whose lively heat, like fire from heaven fet,
Would animate gross clay and higher set                                             740
The drooping thoughts of base declining souls
Than dreary Mars carousing nectar bowls.
His hands he cast upon her like a snare;
She, overcome with shame and sallow fear,
Like chaste Diana when Actaeon spied her,                                           745
Being suddenly betrayed, dived down to hide her.
And as her silver body downward went,
With both her hands she made the bed a tent,
And in her own mind thought herself secure,
O'ercast with dim and darksome coverture.                                           750
And now she lets him whisper in her ear,
Flatter, entreat, promise, protest, and swear.
Yet ever as he greedily assayed
To touch those dainties, she the harpy played,
And every limb did as a solider stout                                               755
Defend the fort and keep the foeman out.
For though the rising ivory mount he scaled,
Which is with azure circling lines impaled,
Much like a globe (a globe may I term this
By which love sails to regions full of bliss),                                      760

718   *crooked* curved.
726   *the lawn* Hero's sheer clothing.
734   *cheerly* gladly.
739   *fet* fetched.
742   Than carousing bowls of nectar would raise dreary (= bloodstained) Mars.
745   The reference is to the hunter Actaeon's surprising the goddess Diana in her bath, though in that story the naked woman does not dive down to hide herself but uses her divine powers to take revenge.
750   *coverture* covering.
754   *harpy* a female monster that snatches food away from her victims before they can eat.
758   *impaled* encircled.

Yet there with Sisyphus he toiled in vain,
Till gentle parley did the truce obtain.
Wherein Leander on her quivering breast
Breathless spoke something, and sighed out the rest,
Which so prevailed as he with small ado                                      765
Enclosed her in his arms, and kissed her too.
And every kiss to her was as a charm,
And to Leander as a fresh alarm,
So that the truce was broke, and she, alas
(Poor silly maiden), at his mercy was.                                       770
Love is not full of pity (as men say),
But deaf and cruel where he means to prey.
Even as a bird which in our hands we wring
Forth plungeth, and oft flutters with her wing,
She trembling strove; this strife of hers (like that                         775
Which made the world) another world begat
Of unknown joy. Treason was in her thought,
And cunningly to yield herself she sought.
Seeming not won, yet won she was at length;
In such wars women use but half their strength.                              780
Leander now, like Theban Hercules,
Entered the orchard of the Hesperides,
Whose fruit none rightly can describe but he
That pulls or shakes it from the golden tree.
    And now she wished this night were never done,                           785
And sighed to think upon the approaching sun,
For much it grieved her that the bright daylight
Should know the pleasure of this blessèd night.
And then like Mars and Erycine displayed,
Both in each others' arms chained as they laid.                              790
Again she knew not how to frame her look,
Or speak to him who in a moment took
That which so long so charily she kept,
And fain by stealth away she would have crept
And to some corner secretly have gone,                                       795
Leaving Leander in the bed alone.
But as her naked feet were whipping out,
He on the sudden clinged her so about
That mermaid-like unto the floor she slid;
One half appeared, the other half was hid.                                   800
Thus near the bed she blushing stood upright,
And from her countenance behold ye might
A kind of twilight break, which through the hair,
As from an orient cloud, glims here and there.
And round about the chamber this false morn                                  805
Brought forth the day before the day was born.

**761** *Sisyphus* A crafty and treacherous mortal, condemned in Hades to push a heavy boulder perpetually up a hill, only to have it roll back down again.

**763–74** In all editions until the nineteenth century, these lines follow l. 784. The arrangement given here seems to provide a smoother progression in the action and appears to complete the simile in ll. 773–4, and has been accepted by most editors; the original order, however, has been defended.

**770** *silly* helpless.

**781–2** One of Hercules' labors was the theft of three apples from the Garden of the Hesperides.

**789** *Erycine* Venus, so called because of her shrine on Mount Eryx; the reference is to the story alluded to in ll. 151–2.

**804** *glims* glimmers.

So Hero's ruddy cheek Hero betrayed,
And her all naked to his sight displayed,
Whence his admiring eyes more pleasure took
Than Dis on heaps of gold fixing his look.                810
By this, Apollo's golden harp began
To sound forth music to the ocean,
Which watchful Hesperus no sooner heard,
But he the day bright-bearing car prepared,
And ran before, as harbinger of light,                   815
And with his flaring beams mocked ugly Night,
Till she, o'ercome with anguish, shame, and rage,
Danged down to hell her loathsome carriage.

*Desunt nonnulla.*

810   *Dis* Roman god of wealth, usually assimilated to Pluto, god of Hades.
813   *Hesperus* the evening star.

818   *Danged* threw.
*Desunt nonnulla* Some things are missing (*sic* at the end of the first edition).

# Christopher Marlowe and Sir Walter Ralegh

Marlowe's poem and Ralegh's carefully symmetrical response were printed together in *England's Helicon* (1600); the attribution of the second to Ralegh is first made by Izaak Walton in *The Complete Angler* (1653), where both poems are reprinted. Slightly longer versions appear in Walton's second edition (1655). Donne's "The Bait" (also quoted by Walton) is inspired by the exchange. Jointly, the two poems reconfigure the classic syllogism of erotic *carpe diem* (on display in Ralegh's own "Now, Serena, be not coy"), whereby the eager seducer cites the pressure of human mortality as an incentive to present pleasure. Marlowe's shepherd makes no reference to decay and mortality, while Ralegh's nymph finds in them an argument precisely for not seizing the day.

## The Passionate Shepherd to his Love

Come live with me and be my love,
And we will all the pleasures prove
That valleys, groves, hills and fields,
Woods or steepy mountain yields.

And we will sit upon the rocks,       5
Seeing the shepherds feed their flocks,
By shallow rivers, to whose falls
Melodious birds sing madrigals.

And I will make thee beds of roses
And a thousand fragrant posies;       10
A cap of flowers, and a kirtle
Embroidered all with leaves of myrtle;

A gown made of the finest wool
Which from our pretty lambs we pull;
Fair linèd slippers for the cold,       15
With buckles of the purest gold;

A belt of straw and ivy buds,
With coral clasps and amber studs.
And if these pleasures may thee move,
Come live with me and be my love.       20

The shepherds' swains shall dance and sing
For thy delight each May morning.
If these delights thy mind may move,
Then live with me and be my love.

2 *prove* experience.

## The Nymph's Reply to the Shepherd

If all the world and love were young,
And truth in every shepherd's tongue,
These pretty pleasures might me move
To live with thee and be thy love.

Time drives the flocks from field to fold;                    5
When rivers rage and rocks grow cold
And Philomel becometh dumb,
The rest complains of cares to come.

The flowers do fade, and wanton fields
To wayward winter reckoning yields;                          10
A honey tongue, a heart of gall
Is fancy's spring but sorrow's fall.

Thy gowns, thy shoes, thy beds of roses,
Thy cap, thy kirtle, and thy posies
Soon break, soon wither, soon forgotten,                     15
In folly ripe, in reason rotten.

Thy belt of straw and ivy buds,
Thy coral clasps and amber studs,
All these in me no means can move
To come to thee and be thy love.                             20

But could youth last and love still breed,
Had joys no date, nor age no need,
Then these delights my mind might move
To live with thee and be thy love.

7   *Philomel* the nightingale.

# Thomas Nashe (1567–1601)

Born at Lowestoft and educated at Cambridge, Nashe was in London by 1588 and became a busy part of the urban literary scene; diminutive and relentlessly witty, he is sometimes thought to be the model for Moth in Shakespeare's *Love's Labor's Lost*. Most of his publications are works of satirical prose, and he involved himself in a series of public quarrels. He is possibly the "Pasquil" who made some anti-Puritan contributions to the Marprelate controversy (1588–90); his literary feud with Gabriel Harvey, indeed Nashe's right to publish under his own name, was terminated by Archbishop Whitgift in 1599 as part of a general ban on printed satire. An entry into the public theater, *The Isle of Dogs* (1597), a collaboration with Ben Jonson, gave enough offense to send Jonson and others to prison and Nashe into hiding; its text does not survive. Nashe's one extant dramatic script is *Summer's Last Will and Testament*, a masque-like entertainment written for private performance at Croydon in 1592, before the same Archbishop who later ended his literary career. Hosted by Henry VIII's jester Will Summer, the play has as its main character the allegorical figure of Summer himself, haunted by a stronger than usual sense of mortality: "Forsooth, because the plague reigns in most places in this latter end of summer, Summer must come in sick." The poem below is sung toward the play's end.

*Edition*: *The Works of Thomas Nashe*, ed. Ronald B. McKerrow, revised by F. P. Wilson, 5 vols (Oxford: Blackwell, 1958).

## From *Summer's Last Will and Testament*

Adieu, farewell, earth's bliss;
This world uncertain is.
Fond are life's lustful joys,
Death proves them all but toys;
None from his darts can fly.     5
I am sick, I must die.
Lord, have mercy on us.

Rich men, trust not in wealth;
Gold cannot buy you health.
Physic himself must fade;     10
All things to end are made.
The plague full swift goes by.
I am sick, I must die.
Lord, have mercy on us.

Beauty is but a flower     15
Which wrinkles will devour.
Brightness falls from the air,
Queens have died young and fair,
Dust hath closed Helen's eye.
I am sick, I must die.     20
Lord, have mercy on us.

---

7 A phrase from the Litany of the Saints; painted on the doors of plague victims in London.
10 *Physic* medicine.
17 This famous line occupies Stephen Dedalus in the last section of James Joyce's *A Portrait of the Artist as a Young Man*, where he misremembers it as "Darkness falls from the air." It has been argued that "air" should read "hair," which would make the line less evocative to modern ears but would in context make for a clearer sequence of thought.

Strength stoops unto the grave,
Worms feed on Hector brave;
Swords may not fight with fate.
Earth still holds ope her gate;                    25
Come, come, the bells do cry.
I am sick, I must die.
Lord, have mercy on us.

Wit, with his wantonness,
Tasteth death's bitterness.                         30
Hell's executioner
Hath no ears for to hear
What vain art can reply.
I am sick, I must die.
Lord, have mercy on us.                             35

Haste therefore each degree
To welcome destiny.
Heaven is our heritage,
Earth but a player's stage;
Mount we unto the sky.                              40
I am sick, I must die.
Lord, have mercy on us.

26   *bells* The original text reads "hells."          36   *degree* social rank.

# Sir John Davies (1569–1626)

Born in Wiltshire and educated at Oxford and the Inns of Court, Davies was called to the Bar in 1595; in the seventeenth century he served as a Member of Parliament and also held several important governmental appointments under King James, including at the very end of his life that of Lord Chief Justice. As a poet Davies was best known for two lengthy philosophical poems, *Orchestra* (1596) and *Nosce Teipsum* (1599), and for a book of epigrams published together with Marlowe's translation of *Ovid's Elegies*. The two poems given here were written in disrespectful response to the sonnet craze of the early 1590s. The first of them was attributed to "Ignoto" when it was printed with Davies's epigrams; his latest editor thinks it is his. The second is from a collection of "Gulling Sonnets" that remained in manuscript until 1873.

*Edition*: *The Poems of John Davies*, ed. Robert Krueger and Ruby Nemser (Oxford: Clarendon Press, 1975).

Faith (wench), I cannot court thy sprightly eyes
With the bass viol placed between my thighs.
I cannot lisp, nor to some fiddle sing,
Nor run upon a high-stretched minikin.
I cannot whine in puling elegies,     5
Entombing Cupid with sad obsequies.
I am not fashioned for these amorous times
To court thy beauty with lascivious rhymes.
I cannot dally, caper, dance, and sing,
Oiling my saint with supple sonneting.     10
I cannot cross my arms, or sigh, Ay me,
Ay me, forlorn – Egregious foppery!
I cannot buss thy fist, play with thy hair,
Swearing by Jove thou art most debonair.
Not I, by cock! But shall I tell thee roundly,     15
Hark in thine ear: Zounds, I can (    ) thee soundly.

4  *minikin* treble string on a string instrument.
5  *puling* whimpering.
13  *buss* kiss.

16  (   ) So printed in Davies's *Elegies*, with space for four letters.

The sacred Muse that first made Love divine
Hath made him naked and without attire,
But I will clothe him with this pen of mine,
That all the world his fashion shall admire:
His hat of hope, his band of beauty fine,     5
His cloak of craft, his doublet of desire;
Grief for a girdle shall about him twine;
His points of pride, his eyelet holes of ire,
His hose of hate, his codpiece of conceit,
His stockings of stern strife, his shirt of shame,     10
His garters of vainglory, gay and slight,
His pantofles of passions I will frame;
Pumps of presumption shall adorn his feet,
And socks of sullenness exceeding sweet.

5  *band* lippers.
6  *doublet* jacket.
8  *points* small decorative ties.

9  *hose* leggings.
12  *pantofles* slippers.

# Barnabe Barnes (1571–1609)

Born in Yorkshire, the son of an Anglican bishop, and educated at Oxford, Barnes saw military service with the Earl of Essex in Normandy in the early 1590s, and by the middle of the decade was involved in the literary feud between Thomas Nashe and Gabriel Harvey. *Parthenophil and Parthenophe* (Virgin-Lover and Virgin), a sonnet sequence with other forms mixed in, was published in 1593. Among other things, it stands out in the tradition for its unparalleled conclusion: the unwilling woman's grim defloration with the help of magic, dramatized in a triple sestina.

The sonnet given here quickly achieved its own fame; wits mocked it in print for its concluding conceit (Nashe: "if you would have any rhymes to the tune of 'stink-a-piss,' he is for you"). For the established Petrarchan topic from which it starts its flight, see Walter Ralegh, "Would I were changed into that golden shower."

*Edition*: Barnabe Barnes, *Parthenophil and Parthenophe*, ed. Victor A. Doyno (Carbondale and Edwardsville, IL: Southern Illinois University Press, 1971).

## From *Parthenophil and Parthenophe*

Jove for Europa's love took shape of bull,
And for Callisto played Diana's part;
And in a golden shower he fillèd full
The lap of Danaë with celestial art.
Would I were changed but to my mistress' gloves, 5
That those white lovely fingers I might hide;
That I might kiss those hands which mine heart loves,
Or else that chain of pearl, her neck's vain pride,
Made proud with her neck's veins; that I might fold
About that lovely neck, and her paps tickle, 10
Or her to compass like a belt of gold,
Or that sweet wine which down her throat doth trickle:
To kiss her lips, and lie next at her heart,
Run through her veins, and pass by pleasure's part.

1 *Europa* Abducted by Jupiter in the guise of a bull.
2 *Callisto* A nymph sworn to virginity, whom Jupiter approached in the guise of the virgin goddess Diana.

4 *Danaë* Confined by her father to forestall a prophecy; Jupiter entered her prison as a shower of gold and impregnated her.
11 *compass* embrace.

# John Donne (1572–1631)

The son of a successful London ironmonger, Donne attended Oxford, and possibly Cambridge; in 1591 he came to the Inns of Court. Decades later Sir Richard Baker would remember him in those days as "a great visitor of ladies, a great frequenter of plays, a great writer of conceited verses." He served in the raid against Cadiz in 1596 and the abortive expedition to the Azores in 1597. By 1598 he had obtained the valuable post of secretary to Sir Thomas Egerton, the Lord Keeper; with Egerton's patronage he served as a Member of Parliament in 1601. That year, though, he secretly married Egerton's niece, Ann More, and when the news came out in 1602 Donne was dismissed from Egerton's service and briefly imprisoned. He and his growing family lived a straitened existence for more than a decade as he vainly sought preferment; finally in 1615 he was ordained as a priest in the Church of England and began a highly successful ecclesiastical career. He became Dean of St. Paul's in 1621, and gained a reputation as one of the greatest preachers in the realm. His immense literary output covers the entirety of his adult life, up to a sermon preached a month before his own death. The selections here are from those works of his which most belong with the sixteenth century – not because they are typical of it, but because they give the poetry of that century a final, unexpected metamorphosis of striking power and complexity. Some of the poems below were unquestionably written in the seventeenth century, one perhaps as late as 1617, but they are all parts of that event.

*Editions*: The textual situation of Donne's poems is extraordinarily complicated. They circulated in manuscript form in versions that show considerable local variation; most were first published in a posthumous edition of 1633, though some not until much later. For the poems given here, critical old-spelling texts may be found in *The Elegies and the Songs and Sonnets*, ed. Helen Gardner (Oxford: Clarendon Press, 1965), and *The Satires, Epigrams and Verse Letters*, ed. W. Milgate (Oxford: Clarendon Press, 1967). Gardner's edition, however, contains some controversial editorial decisions; Theodore Redpath's edition of *The Songs and Sonets* (2nd edn, London: Methuen, 1983), with a modernized text, is also important.

## From *Satires*

Donne composed five verse satires as part of the vogue whose general scurrility led to the episcopal interdict and book-burning in 1599; they are biting enough in places, but never as reckless as much of the competition. (Alexander Pope thought two of them worth rewriting in eighteenth-century style.) Satire I is a relatively typical exercise in the genre, a portrait of a witless fashion-monger haplessly trying to work the streets of contemporary London; the poem's opening establishes that he is being viewed with the scorn possible to an educated observer steeped in the learning of the ages. There is nevertheless some unarticulated bond between that observer and the fool he seemingly dismisses in the first line, as we divine when the speaker allows himself to be lured out of his cramped study after giving us every reason to expect otherwise. The objects of his sarcasm satisfy some important appetite that his books do not. Satire III, on the choice of religion, is on an entirely different level of seriousness, and indeed not quite like anything else in sixteenth-century poetry; it is written from the stance of one for whom the choice, though urgent, was also not yet made or obvious. Donne was raised a Catholic (his mother remained so, even when living with him at St. Paul's in her old age), and though his acceptance of the Church of England seems in the long run inevitable, the decision seems to have been slow and difficult. Satire III is memorably scathing on the wrong motives for picking one's sectarian alliance – in an extended conceit, the bad reasons for liking a particular church are compared to the bad reasons men go for particular types of women – and powerfully insists on the difficulty of and need for clear-headed inquiry that refrains from knowing the answer before it starts. The hint of a solution that Donne suggests – look for the church that most resembles the earliest form of Christianity – does not conclude the poem or get much emphasis; the final topic is state power, the most formidable source of bias on the question in contemporary reality.

## I

Away, thou fondling motley humorist!
Leave me, and in this standing wooden chest,
Consorted with these few books, let me lie
In prison, and here be coffined when I die.
Here are God's conduits, grave divines, and here          5
Nature's secretary, the philosopher,
And jolly statesmen which teach how to tie
The sinews of a city's mystic body;
Here gathering chroniclers, and by them stand
Giddy fantastic poets of each land.                       10
Shall I leave all this constant company
And follow headlong, wild, uncertain thee?
First, swear by thy best love in earnest
(If thou which lov'st all canst love any best)
Thou wilt not leave me in the middle street,             15
Though some more spruce companion thou dost meet.
Not though a captain do come in thy way
Bright parcel-gilt with forty dead men's pay,
Not though a brisk, perfumed, pert courtier
Deign with a nod thy courtesy to answer,                 20
Nor come a velvet justice with a long
Great train of blue coats, twelve or fourteen strong,
Wilt thou grin or fawn on him, or prepare
A speech to court his beauteous son and heir.
For better or worse, take me or leave me;                25
To take and leave me is adultery.
O monstrous, superstitious Puritan,
Of refined manners, yet ceremonial man,
That, when thou meetst one, with inquiring eyes
Dost search and like a needy broker prize                30
The silk and gold he wears, and to that rate,
So high or low, dost raise thy formal hat;
That wilt consort none until thou have known
What lands he hath, in hope or of his own,
As though all thy companions should make thee            35
Jointures and marry thy dear company.
Why shouldst thou (that dost not only approve
But in rank itchy lust desire and love
The nakedness and bareness to enjoy
Of thy plump muddy whore or prostitute boy)              40
Hate Virtue, though she be naked and bare?
At birth and death our bodies naked are;
And till our souls be unapparelèd
Of bodies, they from bliss are banishèd.
Man's first blest state was naked, when by sin           45
He lost that, yet he was clothed but in beasts' skin;
And in this coarse attire which I now wear

---

1 *fondling* foolish. *motley* changeable. *humorist* Someone under the sway of the four bodily humors; in this case, someone susceptible to the fashions of the moment.

18 *parcel-gilt* partially gilded. *with forty dead men's pay* with the wages of forty dead men still kept on his payroll.

22 *blue coats* liveried servants.

28 *yet ceremonial man* Puritans distrusted ceremony.

30 *prize* appraise.

33 *consort* consort with.

36 *Jointures* deeds of co-ownership, often used in marriage settlements.

With God and with the Muses I confer.
   But since thou, like a contrite penitent,
Charitably warned of thy sins, dost repent 50
These vanities and giddinesses, lo,
I shut my chamber door, and come, let's go.
But sooner may a cheap whore, that hath been
Worn by as many several men in sin
As are black feathers or musk-color hose, 55
Name her child's right true father mongst all those;
Sooner may one guess who shall bear away
The Infanta of London, heir to an India;
And sooner may a gulling weather-spy
By drawing forth heaven's scheme tell certainly 60
What fashioned hats or ruffs or suits next year
Our subtle-witted antic youths will wear;
Than thou, when thou departst from me, canst show
Whither, why, when, or with whom thou wouldst go.
But how shall I be pardoned my offense 65
That thus have sinned against my conscience?
   Now we are in the street. He, first of all,
Improvidently proud, creeps to the wall,
And, so imprisoned and hemmed in by me,
Sells for a little state his liberty. 70
Yet though he cannot skip forth now to greet
Every fine silken painted fool we meet,
He them to him with amorous smiles allures,
And grins, smacks, shrugs, and such an itch endures
As prentices or schoolboys which do know 75
Of some gay sport abroad, yet dare not go.
And as fiddlers stoop lowest at highest sound,
So to the most brave stoops he nighest the ground.
But to a grave man he doth move no more
Than the wise politic horse would heretofore, 80
Or thou, O elephant or ape, wilt do
When any names the King of Spain to you.
Now leaps he upright, jogs me, and cries, Do you see
Yonder well-favored youth? Which? O, tis he
That dances so divinely. O, said I, 85
Stand still; must you dance here for company?
He drooped, we went, till one (which did excel
The Indians in drinking his tobacco well)

**55** *musk-color* dark brown.

**58** *Infanta* The daughter of a Spanish or Portuguese monarch; the term is here used to confer mock dignity on the daughter of a particularly rich London merchant. Most manuscripts and the 1633 edition read "infant," perhaps for metrical reasons, perhaps to include male heirs in the reference, perhaps to soften a perceived satirical jab at the controversial attempts of James I to arrange a marriage between his son Henry and the Infanta of Castile. For another possible bow to Spanish sensitivities, see below on ll. 81–2.

**59** *gulling weather-spy* fraudulent weather forecaster.

**60** *heaven's scheme* an astrological chart. The 1633 edition and some manuscripts read "scene" for "scheme."

**70** *a little state* a small enhancement of social rank. The pedestrian position nearer the wall, somewhat protected from the muck splashed about in the middle of the street, connoted higher standing.

**77** In playing the viol da gamba, which is held upright between the legs, a musician would bend over to play the higher notes.

**78** *brave* ostentatious.

**79** *grave* soberly dressed.

**81–2** Omitted from the 1633 edition.

**88** *drinking* smoking.

Met us. They talked. I whispered, Let us go;
'T may be you smell him not, truly I do.                              90
He hears not me, but, on the other side
A many-colored peacock having spied,
Leaves him and me. I for my lost sheep stay.
He follows, overtakes, goes on the way,
Saying, Him whom I last left, all repute                             95
For his device in handsoming a suit,
To judge of lace, pink, panes, print, cut, and pleat,
Of all the court to have the best conceit.
Our dull comedians want him, let him go;
But O, God strengthen thee, why stoopst thou so?                    100
Why? He hath traveled. Long? No, but to me
(Which understand none) he doth seem to be
Perfect French and Italian. I replied,
So is the pox. He answered not, but spied
More men of sort, of parts, of qualities.                           105
At last his love he in a window spies,
And, like light dew exhaled, he flings from me,
Violently ravished to his lechery.
Many were there, he could command no more;
He quarreled, fought, bled, and, turned out of door,               110
Directly came to me, hanging the head,
And constantly awhile must keep his bed.

96   *device* craft.  *handsoming* making handsome.
97   *pink* eyelet.  *panes* decorative strips of cloth.
98   *court* One manuscript reads "town."

104   *the pox* syphilis.
105   *sort* rank.  *parts* talents.
109   His mistress was entertaining others, and he no longer had sole command of her favors.

### III

Kind pity chokes my spleen, brave scorn forbids
Those tears to issue which swell my eyelids.
I must not laugh nor weep sins and be wise;
Can railing then cure these worn maladies?
Is not our mistress, fair Religion,                                   5
As worthy of all our soul's devotion
As Virtue was to the first blinded age?
Are not heaven's joys as valiant to assuage
Lusts as earth's honor was to them? Alas,
As we do them in means, shall they surpass                          10
Us in the end? And shall thy father's spirit
Meet blind philosophers in heaven, whose merit
Of strict life may be imputed faith, and hear
Thee, whom he taught so easy ways and near
To follow, damned? O, if thou darest, fear this;                    15
This fear great courage and high valor is.

7   *the first blinded age* classical antiquity, before the spread of Christianity.
12   *blind* For not knowing the message of Christianity.
13   *imputed faith* Imputation of faith is a key element in Lutheran theology, whereby the sinner whose own faith is inevitably deficient receives true faith and its attendant justification through Christ. Donne uses the same terminology to an unorthodox end: the strict life of the virtuous pagans of antiquity may secure their salvation while contemporary Christians are damned. For an even more scandalous application of the doctrine, see "To his Mistress Going to Bed," ll. 41–3, below.

Darest thou aid mutinous Dutch, and darest thou lay
Thee in ships' wooden sepulchers, a prey
To leaders' rage, to storms, to shot, to dearth?
Darest thou dive seas and dungeons of the earth?    20
Hast thou courageous fires to thaw the ice
Of frozen north discoveries? And thrice
Colder than salamanders, like divine
Children in the oven, fires of Spain and the line,
Whose countries limbecks to our bodies be,    25
Canst thou for gain bear? And must every he
Which cries not Goddess to thy mistress draw
Or eat thy poisonous words? Courage of straw!
O, desperate coward, wilt thou seem bold, and
To thy foes and his (who made thee to stand    30
Sentinel in his world's garrison) thus yield,
And for forbidden wars leave the appointed field?
Know thy foes. The foul Devil, whom thou
Strivest to please, for hate not love would allow,
Thee fain, his whole realm to be quit. And as    35
The world's all parts wither away and pass,
So the world's self, thy other loved foe, is
In her decrepit wane; and thou, loving this,
Dost love a withered and worn strumpet. Last,
Flesh (itself's death) and joys which flesh can taste    40
Thou lovest; and thy fair goodly soul, which doth
Give this flesh power to taste joy, thou dost loathe.
    Seek true religion. O, where? Mirreus,
Thinking her unhoused here and fled from us,
Seeks her at Rome; there, because he doth know    45
That she was there a thousand years ago,
He loves her rags so as we here obey
The state-cloth where the Prince sat yesterday.
Crants to such brave loves will not be enthralled,
But loves her only who at Geneva's called    50
Religion, plain, simple, sullen, young,
Contemptuous yet unhandsome: as among
Lecherous humors there is one that judges
No wenches wholesome but coarse country drudges.
Graius stays still at home here, and because    55
Some preachers, vile ambitious bawds, and laws

17  *mutinous Dutch* The Dutch had been in revolt against the Spanish since 1567; they received sporadic aid from the English government (Philip Sidney died on one such mission), and individual Englishmen (such as George Gascoigne) enlisted in the cause for mercenary or other reasons.

23  *Colder than salamanders* Legend had it that salamanders were unharmed by fire.

24  *Children in the oven* The three Hebrew children who emerged unhurt from the furnace into which Nebuchadnezzar had them thrown; see Daniel 3.11–30.  *the line* the equator.

25  *limbecks* alembics. The warm regions of Spain and the tropics, where Englishmen try their luck in search of glory or riches, are like alchemical devices for boiling us into vapor.

27  *draw* draw his sword (upon being challenged to a duel).

31  *Sentinel* Several manuscripts read "soldier."

34–5  The sense is unclear; some manuscripts read "rid" for "quit." The punctuation given here assumes that "thee fain" is a nominative absolute, and the meaning to be: "The foul devil, whom you strive to please, out of hate rather than love would give up his entire realm to please you."

40  *itself's death* Flesh is its own death (because its appetites lead to disease and decay).

43  *Mirreus* The name suggests *myrrheus*, "perfumed with myrrh," probably in reference to the use of incense in Catholic ceremony. The names of the other sectarians do not seem to have a comparable significance.

48  *state-cloth* canopy over a throne.

49  *brave* ostentatious.

50  *Geneva* The home base of Calvinism, with its extreme antipathy to show and ceremony.

Still new like fashions, bid him think that she
Which dwells with us is only perfect, he
Embraceth her whom his godfathers will
Tender to him, being tender, as wards still                                60
Take such wives as their guardians offer or
Pay values. Careless Phrygius doth abhor
All because all cannot be good, as one,
Knowing some women whores, dares marry none.
Graccus loves all as one, and thinks that so                               65
As women do in divers countries go
In divers habits, yet are still one kind,
So doth, so is religion; and this blind-
ness too much light breeds. But, unmovèd, thou
Of force must one, and forced but one allow,                               70
And the right. Ask thy father which is she,
Let him ask his. Though truth and falsehood be
Near twins, yet truth a little elder is;
Be busy to seek her. Believe me this,
He's not of none, nor worst, that seeks the best.                         75
To adore or scorn an image, or protest,
May all be bad. Doubt wisely. In strange way
To stand inquiring right is not to stray;
To sleep or run wrong is. On a huge hill,
Cragged and steep, Truth stands; and he that will                         80
Reach her about must and about must go,
And what the hill's suddenness resists, win so.
Yet strive so, that before age, death's twilight,
Thy soul rest, for none can work in that night.
To will implies delay; therefore, now do.                                 85
Hard deeds the body's pains, hard knowledge too
The mind's endeavors reach; and mysteries
Are, like the sun, dazzling, yet plain to all eyes.
Keep the truth which thou hast found; men do not stand
In so ill case here that God hath with his hand                           90
Signed kings blank charters to kill whom they hate,
Nor are they vicars, but hangmen to Fate.
Fool and wretch, wilt thou let thy soul be tied
To man's laws, by which she shall not be tried
At the last day? Will it then boot thee                                   95
To say a Philip or a Gregory,
A Harry or a Martin taught thee this?
Is not this excuse for mere contraries
Equally strong? Cannot both sides say so?

---

62  *Pay values* A ward who refused a properly arranged marriage had to pay a fine equal to "the value of the marriage." Under the Act of Uniformity (1559), English subjects could be fined for not attending services in the Church of England.

76  *protest* be a Protestant.

77  *In strange way* in an unfamiliar situation.

82  *suddenness* steepness.

86–7  The mind's endeavors achieve hard knowledge in the same way as the body's pains achieve hard deeds.

91  *blank charters* Financial instruments signed by noblemen with the amounts left blank, to be filled in *ad lib* by the king; here, death warrants with the names omitted.

92  *they* kings who do kill those whom they hate. *vicars* God's agents.

96–7  The individuals named are presumably King Philip II of Spain, the major agent of militant Catholicism in the late sixteenth century; Pope Gregory XIII (in office 1572–85) or XIV (1590–1); Henry VIII, who created the Church of England; and Martin Luther.

98  *mere* utter.

That thou mayst rightly obey power, her bounds know. 100
Those past, her nature and name's changed; to be
Then humble to her is idolatry.
As streams are, power is: those blest flowers that dwell
At the rough stream's calm head thrive and prove well,
But having left their roots and themselves given 105
To the stream's tyrannous rage, alas, are driven
Through mills and rocks and woods, and at last, almost
Consumed in going, in the sea are lost.
So perish souls which more choose men's unjust
Power from God claimed than God himself to trust. 110

## From *Elegies*

Donne stands out among sixteenth-century poets for his relative lack of interest in classical quotation and allusion; his *Elegies* are the distinguished exception, a sustained homage to Ovid's *Amores*, which were circulating somewhat clandestinely in the 1590s as *Ovid's Elegies*, in Christopher Marlowe's translation. Using the same verse form as Marlowe, Donne in effect adds a fourth book to that collection. Ovid's love poems, graced with the prestige of Golden Age Latinity, offered an important alternative to the powerful heritage of Petrarchism; they provided authorization to write of love that was frankly sexual, eagerly satisfied, and promiscuous on both sides, whose scene was not that of solitude or courtly refinement but the busy, populous world of a big city. Donne neglects certain strands in his model – such as Ovid's repeated references to his mission as a poet (itself part of Ovid's legacy to Petrarch) – but heightens others. Donne's satiric edge is sharper and more relentless than Ovid's: "The Perfume" is essentially a concatenation of virtuoso insults against every member of the woman's household, and does not entirely spare the woman herself. "To his Mistress Going to Bed" dilates in commanding detail on a moment of erotic compliance that Ovid handles in a few lines in *Amores* 1.5; its explicitness ("Before, behind, between, above, below") is presumably what delayed its publication for more than two decades after Donne's death, and remains startling. Other poems can be unexpectedly thoughtful about the nature of this kind of love where they might have been merely angry or flippant. In "Nature's lay idiot, I taught thee to love," the male speaker faces clearly the logic whereby the very success of his seduction of the young woman in question opens her to interest in other partners; even as he feigns outrage, he has to know that the straightforward answer to his concluding questions is Yes. "Change" makes an extraordinary attempt to accept infidelity from a woman to whom the speaker finds himself devoted; doing so is his attempt to keep her, and he almost seems not to notice that according to his own metaphor she will "never look back" if she holds to the ideal he is trying to describe.

## The Perfume

Once and but once found in thy company,
All thy supposed escapes are laid on me;
And as a thief at bar is questioned there
By all the men that have been robbed that year,
So am I (by this traitorous means surprised) 5
By thy hydroptic father catechized.
Though he had wont to search with glazèd eyes
As though he came to kill a cockatrice,
Though he have oft sworn that he would remove

2  *escapes* escapades.
3  *at bar* in court.
6  *hydroptic* Afflicted with dropsy; swollen and insatiably thirsty. Donne may be responsible for this form of the word ("hydropic" would be somewhat more correct); it appears frequently in his writing (see "A Nocturnal upon St. Lucy's Day," l. 6).
7–8  These lines are not present in the 1633 edition and some manuscripts.
8  *cockatrice* Basilisk, a legendary creature that kills with its look.

Thy beauty's beauty and food of our love,                                          10
Hope of his goods, if I with thee were seen,
Yet close and secret as our souls we've been.
Though thy immortal mother, which doth lie
Still buried in her bed yet will not die,
Take this advantage to sleep out daylight                                          15
And watch thy entries and returns all night,
And, when she takes thy hand and would seem kind,
Doth search what rings and armlets she can find,
And, kissing, notes the color of thy face,
And, fearing lest thou art swollen, doth thee embrace,                             20
And, to try if thou long, doth name strange meats,
And notes thy paleness, blushings, sighs, and sweats,
And politicly will to thee confess
The sins of her own youth's rank lustiness;
Yet love these sorceries did remove, and move                                      25
Thee to gull thine own mother for my love.
Thy little brethren, which like fairy sprites
Oft skipped into our chamber those sweet nights,
And, kissed and ingled on thy father's knee,
Were bribed next day to tell what they did see.                                    30
The grim, eight-foot-high, iron-bound serving man,
That oft names God in oaths, and only then,
He that to bar the first gate doth as wide
As the great Rhodian Colossus stride,
Which, if in hell no other pains there were,                                       35
Makes me fear hell because he must be there:
Though by thy father he were hired for this,
Could never witness any touch or kiss.
But O, too common ill, I brought with me
That which betrayed me to mine enemy:                                              40
A loud perfume, which at my entrance cried
Even at thy father's nose. So we were spied
When, like a tyran king that in his bed
Smelt gunpowder, the pale wretch shiverèd.
Had it been some bad smell, he would have thought                                  45
That his own feet or breath that smell had wrought.
But as we, in our isle imprisonèd
Where cattle only and diverse dogs are bred,
The precious unicorns strange monsters call,
So thought he good strange that had none at all.                                   50
I taught my silks their whistling to forbear;
Even my oppressed shoes dumb and speechless were.
Only thou, bitter sweet, whom I had laid
Next me, me traitorously hast betrayed,
And unsuspected hast invisibly                                                     55
At once fled unto him and stayed with me.

11   *Hope of his goods* his daughter's inheritance.
15   *sleep out* sleep through.
29   *ingled* fondled.
34   *the great Rhodian Colossus* The immense statue of
Apollo, a hundred feet tall or so, on the island of Rhodes in

Hellenistic times; Donne follows the incorrect legend that it
actually stood astride the entrance to the harbor.
50   So he who had nothing good of his own thought that
which was good something strange.
52   *oppressed* Subjected to "pressing," a punishment for
prisoners who refused to talk.

Base excrement of earth, which dost confound
Sense from distinguishing the sick from sound:
By thee the silly amorous sucks his death
By drawing in a leprous harlot's breath;                                  60
By thee the greatest stain to man's estate
Falls on us, to be called effeminate.
Though you be much loved in the prince's hall,
There things that seem exceed substantial.
Gods, when ye fumed on altars, were pleased well        65
Because you were burnt, not that they liked your smell.
You're loathsome all, being taken simply alone;
Shall we love ill things joined, and hate each one?
If you were good, your good doth soon decay;
And you are rare, that takes the good away.                     70
All my perfumes I give most willingly
To embalm thy father's corse. What? Will he die?

57  *excrement* outgrowth.
59  *silly* hapless.

67  The ingredients of perfume are individually disgusting.
72  *corse* corpse.

Nature's lay idiot, I taught thee to love,
And in that sophistry, O, thou dost prove
Too subtle. Fool, thou didst not understand
The mystic language of the eye nor hand;
Nor couldst thou judge the difference of the air            5
Of sighs and say, This lies, this sounds despair;
Nor by the eyes' water call a malady
Desperately hot, or changing feverously.
I had not taught thee then the alphabet
Of flowers, how they, devicefully being set                   10
And bound up, might with speechless secrecy
Deliver errands mutely, and mutually.
Remember since all thy words used to be
To every suitor, *Aye, if my friends agree*;
Since household charms thy husband's name to teach     15
Were all the love tricks that thy wit could reach;
And since an hour's discourse could scarce have made
One answer in thee, and that ill arrayed
In broken proverbs and torn sentences.
Thou art not by so many duties his                              20
That, from the world's common having severed thee,
Inlaid thee neither to be seen nor see,
As mine, which have with amorous delicacies
Refined thee into a blissful paradise.
Thy graces and good words my creatures be;              25
I planted knowledge and life's tree in thee,
Which, O, shall strangers taste? Must I, alas,

1  *lay idiot* "Idiot" can itself mean "layman," i.e., somebody uninitiated into the learning possessed by the clergy; the addressee is someone who was ignorant of the religion (or profession) of love until educated by the speaker.
10  *devicefully* artfully.
13  *Remember since* remember when.

19  *sentences* sententious observations.
21  *common* An open grazing area to which anyone in the district may bring his herds.
22  *Inlaid* sequestered.
26  *knowledge and life's tree* The two trees that God planted in the Garden of Eden (Genesis 2.9).

Frame and enamel plate and drink in glass?
Chafe wax for others' seals? Break a colt's force
And leave him then, being made a ready horse?                              30

**28**  Fashion and decorate vessels plated with silver and gold but myself drink out of mere glass?

**29**  *Chafe* rub into malleability (in order to receive the imprint of a seal). Donne was fond of the metaphor; see also "To his Mistress Going to Bed," l. 32, and "The Relic," ll. 29–30.

## To his Mistress Going to Bed

Come, madam, come; all rest my powers defy.
Until I labor, I in labor lie.
The foe ofttimes, having the foe in sight,
Is tired with standing, though he never fight.
Off with that girdle, like heaven's zone glittering,                       5
But a far fairer world encompassing.
Unpin that spangled breast-plate which you wear
That the eyes of busy fools may be stopped there.
Unlace yourself, for that harmonious chime
Tells me from you that now tis your bedtime.                               10
Off with that happy busk, which I envy
That still can be and still can stand so nigh.
Your gown, going off, such beauteous state reveals
As when from flowery meads the hill's shadow steals.
Off with that wiry coronet, and show                                       15
The hairy diadem which on you doth grow.
Now off with those shoes, and then softly tread
In this love's hallowed temple, this soft bed.
In such white robes heaven's angels used to be
Received by men. Thou, angel, bringst with thee                           20
A heaven like Mahomet's paradise; and though
Ill spirits walk in white, we easily know
By this these angels from an evil sprite:
Those set our hairs, but these our flesh upright.
    License my roving hands, and let them go                              25
Before, behind, between, above, below.
O my America! My new-found land!
My kingdom, safeliest when with one man manned!
My mine of precious stone, my empery,
How am I blest in thus discovering thee.                                   30
To enter in these bonds is to be free;
Then where my hand is set, my seal shall be.

Not printed until 1654 (in an anthology called *The Harmony of the Muses*), and not included in an edition of Donne's poems until 1669.

**5**  *heaven's zone* the Milky Way.

**8**  Two manuscripts read "That I may see my shrine that shines so fair."

**9**  *that harmonious chime* Possibly a chiming watch that the woman is wearing, though the wittier possibility is some noise produced by her unpinning of her "spangled breast-plate."

**11**  *busk* corset.

**17**  *softly* Many manuscripts read "safely."

**20**  *Received by* The 1669 edition reads "Revealed to."

**21**  *Mahomet's paradise* The Islamic afterlife had a reputation for being more fleshly than that promised by Christianity.

**22**  *Ill spirits walk in white* Devils can disguise themselves as angels; the 1669 text reads "All" for "Ill."

**26**  Alternative readings: "Behind, before, above, beneath, below"; "Above, behind, before, beneath, below."

**28**  *kingdom, safeliest* The 1669 text reads "kingdom's safest."

**31–2**  The metaphor is that of entering into a contractual obligation ("these bonds") by signing one's name ("my hand") and then impressing one's personal seal into heated wax. Cf. "Nature's lay idiot," l. 29, above.

Full nakedness, all joys are due to thee!
As souls unbodied, bodies unclothed must be
To taste whole joys. Gems which you women use                    35
Are like Atlanta's balls, cast in men's views
That when a fool's eye lighteth on a gem
His earthly soul may covet theirs, not them.
Like pictures or like books' gay coverings made
For laymen are all women thus arrayed;                           40
Themselves are mystic books, which only we
Whom their imputed grace will dignify
Must see revealed. Then since that I may know,
As liberally as to thy midwife show
Thyself. Cast all, yea, this white linen hence;                  45
There is no penance due to innocence.
    To teach thee, I am naked first. Why then,
What needst thou have more covering than a man?

**36** *Atlanta's balls* Atalanta, a devotee of Athena, swore to marry only the man who could beat her in a foot race; she was finally won by a suitor who distracted her by throwing down golden apples while they were running. Donne's simile gives the man's trick to the woman.

**38** *covet theirs* The 1669 text reads "court those."

**42** *imputed grace* A doctrine from Lutheran theology put to erotic use; see above on Satire III, l. 13.

**45** *white linen* The attire of either a virginal innocent or a penitent sinner.

**46** The reading of the 1669 edition and some manuscripts; other manuscripts read "There/Here is no penance, much less innocence." The difference in tone is significant. Both readings insist that the woman feel no guilt over the love-making about to happen; the former implies that the act itself is innocent, while the latter makes a sarcastic reference to her own sexual experience: she is so far past innocence that there is no point feeling guilty now.

# Change

Although thy hand and faith, and good works, too,
Have sealed thy love, which nothing should undo,
Yea though thou fall back, that apostasy
Confirm thy love. Yet much, much I fear thee.
Women are like the arts, forced unto none,                       5
Open to all searchers, unprized if unknown.
If I have caught a bird, and let him fly,
Another fowler using these means, as I,
May catch the same bird; and, as these things be,
Women are made for men, not him, nor me.                        10
Foxes and goats, all beasts change when they please;
Shall women, more hot, wily, wild than these,
Be bound to one man, and did Nature then
Idly make them apter to endure than men?
They're our clogs, not their own. If a man be                   15
Chained to a galley, yet the galley's free.
    Who hath a plough-land casts all his seed corn there,

**1** *faith, and good works, too* Hotly contested terms of sixteenth-century theological debate, applied to the religion of love; being justified through both faith and works places the woman on the Catholic side of the line.

**4** *fear* am unsure of.

**5** *forced unto* The sense is unclear; possibly "compelled to be the exclusive property of." One manuscript reads "forbid to."

**15** *clogs* Blocks tied to an animal or human to prevent escape. *not* Many manuscripts read "and"; the line in this form could be glossed, "They are our clogs, but they belong to themselves."

**17** *plough-land* A single unit of land for agriculture.

And yet allows his ground more corn should bear.
Though Danuby into the sea must flow,
The sea receives the Rhine, Volga, and Po.                               20
By nature, which gave it, this liberty
Thou lov'st, but O, canst thou love it and me?
Likeness glues love; then, if so thou do,
To make us like and love must I change, too?
More than thy hate I hate it; rather, let me                             25
Allow her change than change as oft as she,
And so not teach but force my opinion
To love not anyone nor everyone.
To live in one land is captivity,
To run all countries a wild roguery.                                     30
Waters stink soon if in one place they bide,
And in the vast sea are worse putrified;
But when they kiss one bank, and, leaving this,
Never look back, but the next bank do kiss,
Then they are purest. Change is the nursery                             35
Of music, joy, life, and eternity.

24    *like* alike.

## From *Songs and Sonnets*

There is no real precedent in English for Donne's love lyrics, either for the sustained variety of verse forms or for the comparably great variety of tone and implied occasion; and though Donne's style grows out of a general sixteenth-century aesthetic of "conceited verses," his particular way of tight, combative argumentation, demanding the relentless close attention of his reader, takes that aesthetic to a dramatically new level. At best, that argumentativeness is of a piece with the subject matter: love as battle of wits, either between the lovers themselves, or between the lovers and the world around them. Petrarchism ("whining poetry") is a recurrent point of reference, often in a spirit of brusque dismissal by a speaker whose sexual experiences and expectations are much more Ovidian; Donne writes some of the classic poems of libertine predation. They share space, however, with poems that affirm love at a Petrarchan pitch of hyperbole:

radically transformative, unshakeably enduring, with the capacity of rendering everything else irrelevant. The Petrarchan lover traditionally asserted these qualities in anguished isolation; Donne can on occasion do so himself (as in "Twickenham Garden"), but he can also make such claims for sexual love mutually felt and gratified – or at least for this unique instance, which in "The Canonization" he imagines desperate future ages remembering in prayer the way Catholics appeal to their saints. It is impossible not to link these poems to Donne's own experience with Ann More, the affirmation to set against what to outside eyes was mere disaster. The triumphant assertions of the power of mutual love find their mirror image in "A Nocturnal upon St. Lucy's Day," a comparably hyperbolic enactment of collapse and withdrawal at the loss of the loved one who made all the difference in the world.

## The Good Morrow

I wonder, by my troth, what thou and I
Did till we loved. Were we not weaned till then,
But sucked on country pleasures, childishly?

3    *country pleasures, childishly* The reading of the 1633 edition and a few manuscripts; most manuscripts read "childish pleasures, sillily" (the last word meaning "innocently" or "ignorantly"). "Country pleasures" would be rustic, unrefined pleasures, in contrast to the more sophisticated pleasures of the city, but "country" also carries rude sexual connotations, as in Hamlet's line to Ophelia: "Do you think I meant country matters?" (*Hamlet* III.ii.115).

Or snorted we in the seven sleepers' den?
Twas so. But this, all pleasures fancies be.                                            5
If ever any beauty I did see
Which I desired and got, twas but a dream of thee.

And now good morrow to our waking souls,
Which watch not one another out of fear;
For love all love of other sights controls,                                             10
And makes one little room an everywhere.
Let sea-discoverers to new worlds have gone,
Let maps to others worlds on worlds have shown.
Let us possess our world: each hath one, and is one.

My face in thine eye, thine in mine appears,                                            15
And true plain hearts do in the faces rest.
Where can we find two better hemispheres
Without sharp north, without declining west?
Whatever dies was not mixed equally.
If our two loves be one, or thou and I                                                  20
Love so alike that none do slacken, none can die.

4 *snorted* Several manuscripts read "slumbered." *seven sleepers* Seven young Christians, sealed into a cave near Ephesus during the persecutions of the third century, were said to have re-emerged unchanged two centuries later after a miraculous sleep.
5 *fancies* illusions.
10 For love controls all wish to see other things.
14 *our* The 1633 edition and a few manuscripts read "one."

17 *better* Most manuscripts read "fitter."
18 *declining west* The area where the sun goes down; our own world will never lose light and warmth.
20–1 The reading of the 1633 edition. Variant readings suggest that the lines were much worked over; in many manuscripts, the last line reads "Love just alike in all, none of these loves can die."

# Song

Go and catch a falling star,
Get with child a mandrake root,
Tell me where all past years are,
Or who cleft the Devil's foot,
Teach me to hear mermaids singing                                                       5
Or to keep off envy's stinging,
    And find
    What wind
Serves to advance an honest mind.

If thou be'est borne to strange sights,                                                  10
Things invisible go see,
Ride ten thousand days and nights
Till age snow white hairs on thee;
Thou, when thou returnst, wilt tell me
All strange wonders that befell thee,                                                    15

An anonymous musical setting of this poem survives in manuscript.

2 *mandrake root* The root of the mandrake was thought to have such a striking resemblance to the form of

the human body that it cried out when torn from the earth.
10 *be'est borne to* be enthusiastic for.
11 *go* The 1633 edition reads "to"; it became "go" in 1669.

And swear
Nowhere
Lives a woman true and fair.

If thou findst one, let me know;
Such a pilgrimage were sweet.                                    20
Yet do not, I would not go,
Though at next door we might meet.
Though she were true when you met her
And last till you write your letter,
              Yet she                                            25
              Will be
False, ere I come, to two, or three.


## Woman's Constancy

Now thou hast loved me one whole day,
Tomorrow, when thou leav'st, what wilt thou say?
Wilt thou then antedate some new-made vow?
          Or say that now
We are not just those persons which we were?                     5
Or that oaths made in reverential fear
Of Love and his wrath any may forswear?
Or, as true deaths true marriages untie,
So lovers' contracts, images of those,
Bind but till sleep, death's image, then unloose?                10
          Or, your own end to justify,
For having purposed change and falsehood, you
Can have no way but falsehood to be true?
Vain lunatic, against these scapes I could
          Dispute and conquer if I would:                        15
          Which I abstain to do,
For by tomorrow I may think so too.

3  *antedate some new-made vow* claim that some new promise      12  *purposed* intended.
of love was actually made earlier.                               14  *scapes* evasions.


## The Sun Rising

Busy old fool, unruly Sun,
          Why dost thou thus
Through windows and through curtains call on us?
Must to thy motions lovers' seasons run?
          Saucy pedantic wretch, go chide                        5
          Late schoolboys and sour prentices,
Go tell court huntsmen that the King will ride,
Call country ants to harvest offices.

For the classical antecedent of this poem, see Marlowe,         7  The line almost certainly dates the poem after the acces-
*Ovid's Elegies* 1.13 above. Ovid's assault on the dawn ends    sion of King James, who was fond of hunting and notorious
in acknowledged failure, Donne's on a confident note of         for summoning his hunting partners early in the morning.
triumph.                                                         8  *country ants* farm laborers.

Love, all alike, no season knows, nor clime,
Nor hours, days, months, which are the rags of time.                10

Thy beams so reverend and strong
        Why shouldst thou think?
I could eclipse and cloud them with a wink,
But that I would not lose her sight so long.
        If her eyes have not blinded thine,                15
        Look, and tomorrow late tell me
Whether both Indias, of spice and mine,
Be where thou leftst them, or lie here with me.
Ask for those kings whom thou sawst yesterday,
And thou shalt hear, All here in one bed lay.                20

She is all states, and all princes I.
        Nothing else is.
Princes do but play us; compared to this,
All honor's mimic, all wealth alchemy.
        Thou, Sun, art half as happy as we                25
        In that the world's contracted thus.
Thine age asks ease, and since thy duties be
To warm the world, that's done in warming us.
Shine here to us, and thou art everywhere:
This bed thy center is, these walls thy sphere.                30

9   *all alike* always the same.
17   *both Indias, of spice and mine* The East and West Indies, the former the source of the spice trade and the latter the reputed site of fabled gold and silver mines.

24   *alchemy* enticing fraud.

# The Indifferent

I can love both fair and brown;
Her whom abundance melts, and her whom want betrays;
Her who loves loneness best, and her who masques and plays;
        Her whom the country formed, and whom the town;
        Her who believes, and her who tries;                5
        Her who still weeps with spongy eyes,
And her who is dry cork and never cries.
I can love her, and her, and you, and you;
I can love any, so she be not true.

        Will no other vice content you?                10
Will it not serve your turn to do as did your mothers?
Have you old vices spent, and now would find out others?
        Or doth a fear that men are true torment you?

*Indifferent* impartial.

1–7   The theme of the first stanza, until the final turn of its argument, is the same as Ovid, *Amores* 2.4.
1   *fair and brown* light-complexioned and dark-complexioned.

2   Her whose wealth loosens her moral standards and her whose poverty makes her subject to monetary inducements.
5   Her who is trusting and her who is always testing the other person.
6   *still* constantly.
13   *fear* Some manuscripts read "shame."

O, we are not, be not you so.
Let me and do you twenty know.                                                              15
Rob me, but bind me not, and let me go.
Must I, who came to travail thorough you,
Grow your fixed subject because you are true?

Venus heard me sigh this song,
And by love's sweetest part, variety, she swore                                            20
She heard not this till now, and it should be so no more.
She went, examined, and returned ere long
And said, Alas, some two or three
Poor heretics in love there be
Which think to stablish dangerous constancy.                                               25
But I have told them, Since you will be true,
You shall be true to them who are false to you.

16   *Rob* Several manuscripts read "rack" or "wrack"; one      23   *some* Several manuscripts read "but."
reads "reach."

# The Canonization

For God's sake, hold your tongue and let me love,
Or chide my palsy, or my gout;
My five gray hairs, or ruined fortune flout.
With wealth your state, your mind with arts improve;
Take you a course, get you a place,                                                         5
Observe his Honor or his Grace,
And the King's real or his stampèd face
Contemplate. What you will, approve,
So you will let me love.

Alas, alas, who's injured by my love?                                                       10
What merchant's ships have my sighs drowned?
Who says my tears have overflowed his ground?
When did my colds a forward spring remove?
When did those heats which my veins fill
Add one man to the plaguy bill?                                                             15
Soldiers find wars, and lawyers find out still
Litigious men which quarrels move,
Though she and I do love.

Call us what you will, we are made such by love.
Call her one, me another fly.                                                               20

4   *state* social rank.
5   *Take you a course* start a career.  *place* position.
6   Pay court to a lower- or higher-ranking member of society or the church ("Grace" is the honorific for a duke or an archbishop).
7   *his stampèd face* coinage.
12   *overflowed his ground* flooded his fields.
13   *my colds* The shivering that (like sighs and tears) figured in the standard symptomology of Petrarchan love.

*a forward spring remove* Interrupt an early season of warm weather, and thus damage young crops and other vegetation.
15   *the plaguy bill* The mortality list for epidemics of the plague (which occurred both in 1603 and 1604).
17   *move* stir up.
20   *fly* The self-destructive moth of Petrarchan love poetry, attracted to the flame in the beloved's eye.

We're tapers, too, and at our own cost die;
   And we in us find the eagle and the dove.
      The phoenix riddle hath more wit
        By us: we two, being one, are it;
So to one neutral thing both sexes fit.            25
      We die and rise the same, and prove
        Mysterious by this love.

We can die by it, if not live by love;
      And if unfit for tombs or hearse
Our legend be, it will be fit for verse.         30
And if no piece of chronicle we prove,
      We'll build in sonnets pretty rooms.
      As well a well-wrought urn becomes
The greatest ashes as half-acre tombs;
      And by these hymns all shall approve     35
        Us *canonized* for love,

And thus invoke us: You, whom reverend love
      Made one another's hermitage;
You, to whom love was peace, that now is rage;
Who did the whole world's soul extract and drove     40
      Into the glasses of your eyes,
      So made such mirrors and such spies
That they did all to you epitomize,
      Countries, towns, courts: beg from above
        A pattern of your love!           45

**21** *tapers* candles. *die* Slang for sexual climax, informed by the theory that orgasm expended vital fluids and shortened one's life.

**30** *verse* The theme of immortality through poetry is extremely common in Petrarchism, but rare in Donne; for another instance, see "The Relic," ll. 20–2, below.

**31** *chronicle* written history. *prove* become.

**32** *rooms* As if literally translating the Italian *stanza*, "room."

**40** *extract* An alchemical term for distilling or subliming a pure essence. This is the reading of the manuscripts; the 1633 edition reads "contract." *drove* Several manuscripts read "draw"; one reads "have."

**41** *glasses* The glass vessels in which the extracted essence of the previous line would be stored, but also the mirrors of the next line.

**44** *Countries, towns, courts* Probably the direct objects of "drove" in l. 40, though there are other ways to parse the syntax. *beg from above* Probably still a part of the quotation that begins in l. 37; in adherence to Catholic doctrine, the future worshipers petition the future saints not to help them directly but rather to intercede on their behalf with God.

**45** *your* The reading of most of the manuscripts; the 1633 edition has "our."

## The Triple Fool

        I am two fools, I know:
     For loving, and for saying so
         In whining poetry.
But where's that wiseman that would not be I
        If she would not deny?         5
Then, as the earth's inward narrow crooked lanes
Do purge seawater's fretful salt away,
       I thought, if I could draw my pains

**6–7** A theory as to why seawater is salt and river water fresh; considered and rejected by Aristotle, endorsed by some Renaissance authorities.

Through rhyme's vexation, I could them allay.
Grief brought to numbers cannot be so fierce,                    10
For he tames it that fetters it in verse.

But when I have done so,
Some man, his art and voice to show,
Doth set and sing my pain,
And by delighting many frees again                              15
Grief, which verse did restrain.
To love and grief tribute of verse belongs,
But not of such as pleases when tis read.
Both are increasèd by such songs,
For both their triumphs so are publishèd,                       20
And I, which was two fools, do so grow three.
Who are a little wise the best fools be.

10   *numbers* metrical form.

20   *triumphs* Some manuscripts read "trials"; one reads "tortures."

# Air and Angels

Twice or thrice had I loved thee
Before I knew thy face or name.
So in a voice, so in a shapeless flame
Angels affect us oft, and worshipped be.
Still when to where thou wert I came,                            5
Some lovely glorious nothing I did see.
But since my soul, whose child love is,
Takes limbs of flesh, and else could nothing do,
More subtle than the parent is
Love must not be, but take a body, too.                          10
And therefore what thou wert, and who,
I bid love ask, and now
That it assume thy body I allow,
And fix itself in thy lip, eye, and brow.

Whilst thus to ballast love I thought                           15
And so more steadily to have gone,
With wares which would sink admiration
I saw I had love's pinnace overfraught.
Every thy hair for love to work upon
Is much too much; some fitter must be sought.                   20
For nor in nothing, nor in things
Extreme and scattering bright can love inhere.
Then, as an angel face and wings

The conceit has proved to be one of the most difficult in Donne's poetry, and the argument and tone of the poem have been much debated. The male speaker passes through two possible objects for his love – a generalized, angelic idea of a woman seemingly independent of any particular woman, and the overwhelmingly beautiful body of the poem's addressee – to settle on "thy love": I am in love with your love for me. This conclusion insists on erotic mutuality, but the way it is argued ends the poem insisting on an imbalance within that mutuality, though of exquisitely small proportions.

5   *Still when* whenever.
18   *overfraught* overloaded.

Of air, not pure as it, yet pure doth wear,
        So thy love may be my love's sphere. 25
            Just such disparity
        As is twixt air and angel's purity
Twixt women's love and men's will ever be.

**25** *sphere* The analogy is with the heavenly spheres in medieval cosmology, each inhabited by particular angelic intelligences. In "The Ecstasy" (ll. 51–2) Donne uses this metaphor to define the relationship between soul and body in a sexual context.

## Break of Day

Tis true, tis day. What though it be?
O wilt thou therefore rise from me?
Why should we rise because tis light?
Did we lie down because twas night?
Love, which in spite of darkness brought us hither,      5
Should in despite of light hold us together.

Light hath no tongue, but is all eye.
If it could speak as well as spy,
This were the worst that it could say,
That, being well, I fain would stay,      10
And that I loved my heart and honor so
That I would not from him that had them go.

Must business thee from hence remove?
O, that's the worst disease of love.
The poor, the foul, the false love can      15
Admit, but not the busied man.
He which hath business and makes love doth do
Such wrong as if a married man should woo.

One of two lyrics in the 1633 edition spoken by a woman (see also "Confined Love," below); printed by William Corkine with a musical setting in his *Second Book of Airs* (1612).

**6** *hold* The reading of some manuscripts; the 1633 edition has "keep."

**15** *foul* A few manuscripts have "fool."
**18** *as if a married man should woo* The reading of several manuscripts; the 1633 edition has "as when a married man doth woo."

## The Anniversary

All kings and all their favorites,
All glory of honors, beauties, wits,
The sun itself, which makes times as they pass,
Is elder by a year now than it was
When thou and I first one another saw.      5
All other things to their destruction draw;
    Only our love hath no decay.
This no tomorrow hath, nor yesterday;
Running, it never runs from us away,
But truly keeps his first, last, everlasting day.      10

> Two graves must hide thine and my corse;
>     If one might, death were no divorce.
> Alas, as well as other princes, we
> (Who prince enough in one another be)
> Must leave at last in death these eyes and ears,                    15
> Oft fed with true oaths and with sweet salt tears;
>     But souls where nothing dwells but love
>     (All other thoughts being inmates) then shall prove
> This or a love increasèd there above,
> When bodies to their graves, souls from their graves remove.        20
>
> And then we shall be throughly blest,
>     But we no more than all the rest.
> Here upon earth we're kings, and none but we
> Can be such kings, nor of such subjects be.
> Who is so safe as we, where none can do                             25
> Treason to us, except one of us two?
>     True and false fears let us refrain;
> Let us love nobly, and live, and add again
> Years and years unto years, till we attain
> To write threescore. This is the second of our reign.              30

11   This assertion suggests that the year-old love is still secret from the rest of the world, a circumstance that would fit with Donne's relationship to Ann More in its early stages. *corse* corpse.
18   *prove* experience.
20   *remove* depart.

21   *throughly* thoroughly.
25   *safe* The danger in which kings constantly live is a major theme in Renaissance literature.
27   *refrain* rein in.
30   *the second of our reign* This is the beginning of our second regnal year. (Threescore would be the diamond jubilee.)

## Twickenham Garden

> Blasted with sighs, and surrounded with tears,
>     Hither I come to seek the spring,
>     And at mine eyes and at mine ears
> Receive such balms as else cure everything.
>     But O, self-traitor, I do bring                                 5
> The spider love, which transubstantiates all
>     And can convert manna to gall;
> And that this place may thoroughly be thought
> True paradise, I have the serpent brought.
>
> Twere wholesomer for me that winter did                            10
>     Benight the glory of this place,
>     And that a grave frost did forbid
> These trees to laugh and mock me to my face.

Twickenham Park was the home of Lucy, Countess of Bedford (1581–1627), with whom Donne had a long friendship. Biographical information has not been helpful in understanding the relation between that friendship and the erotic torment dramatized in this poem. The popular Petrarchan template behind the poem is *Canzoniere* 310, in which the lover experiences the contrast between the joys of spring and his own misery; Surrey's "The soot season" is an influential English adaptation.

1   *surrounded* inundated.
6   *spider* Spiders were thought to extract poison from the same flowers from which bees sucked honey. *transubstantiates* The Catholic term for what happens to the host and wine when consecrated in Mass; Protestant theologians debated alternative terms.
7   *manna* The bread miraculously provided by God for the Israelites in the desert (Exodus 16.15); the more commonplace contrast to gall would be honey.

But that I may not this disgrace
Endure nor leave this garden, Love, let me                    15
    Some senseless piece of this place be;
Make me a mandrake, so I may groan here,
Or a stone fountain, weeping out my year.

Hither with crystal vials, lovers, come,
    And take my tears, which are love's wine,                 20
    And try your mistress' tears at home,
For all are false that taste not just like mine.
    Alas, hearts do not in eyes shine,
Nor can you more judge woman's thoughts by tears
    Than by her shadow what she wears.                        25
O perverse sex, where none is true but she
Who's therefore true because her truth kills me.

17   *groan* The mandrake was thought to resemble a man in shape, and to groan when pulled out of the earth. Groans as the sounds of unsatisfied love go with the tears in the next line, though "groan" is in fact the reading of only a few manuscripts; the 1633 edition and other manuscripts read "grow."

21   *try* test.
25   Than know what a woman is wearing from looking at her shadow.
27   Who stays faithful to another in order to kill me.

## Love's Growth

I scarce believe my love to be so pure
    As I had thought it was,
    Because it doth endure
Vicissitude and season, as the grass.
Methinks I lied all winter when I swore                       5
My love was infinite, if spring make it more.
But if this medicine, love, which cures all sorrow
With more, not only be no quintessence,
But mixed of all stuffs paining soul or sense,
And of the sun his working vigor borrow,                      10
Love's not so pure and abstract as they use
To say, which have no mistress but their Muse;
But as all else, being elemented too,
Love sometimes would contemplate, sometimes do.

And yet not greater, but more eminent                         15
    Love by the spring is grown,
    As, in the firmament,
Stars by the sun are not enlarged, but shown.
Gentle love deeds, as blossoms on a bough,
From love's awakened root do bud out now.                     20

Entitled "Spring" or "The Spring" in some manuscripts.

1   *pure* Not composed of different constituent elements, and therefore not subject to change.
7–8   *which cures all sorrow / With more* That is, "with more sorrow": an application of the homeopathic principle promulgated by the alchemist and medical theorist Paracelsus (1493–1541).

8   *quintessence* Imagined matter of extreme purity, separate from the four familiar elements, and according to Paracelsus a cure for all diseases.
13   *elemented* composed of constituent elements.
14   *do* As in "The Dream," l. 10, below.
18   Donne appears to be adopting the theory that starlight is reflected; "by the sun" could mean either "by means of the sun" or "near the sun." In either case, the contrast between "enlarged" and "shown" remains obscure.

If, as in water stirred more circles be
Produced by one, love such additions take,
Those, like to many spheres, but one heaven make,
For they are all concentric unto thee.
And though each spring do add to love new heat,                          25
As princes do in times of action get
New taxes, and remit them not in peace,
No winter shall abate the spring's increase.

---

23   According to the ancient theory of the cosmos as a nested set of celestial spheres.

24   *thee* The only indication that the poem has an addressee.

26   *get* levy.

## Confined Love

Some man unworthy to be possessor
Of old or new love, himself being false or weak,
  Thought his pain and shame would be lesser
If on womankind he might his anger wreak;
    And thence a law did grow                                           5
    One should but one man know.
    But are other creatures so?

Are sun, moon, or stars by law forbidden
To smile where they list or lend away their light?
  Are birds divorced or are they chidden                               10
If they leave their mate or lie abroad a-night?
    Beasts do no jointures lose
    Though they new lovers choose;
    But we are made worse than those.

Who e'er rigged fair ship to lie in harbors                            15
And not to seek new lands, or not to deal withal?
  Or built fair houses, set trees and arbors,
Only to lock up, or else to let them fall?
    Good is not good unless
    A thousand it possess,                                             20
    But doth waste with greediness.

---

One of two lyrics in the 1633 edition with a female speaker; see also "Break of Day," above.

12   *jointures* Deeds of co-ownership, commonly used in marriage settlements. In the natural world, a female can

copulate with someone new without having to return her wedding gifts.

16   *deal withal* participate in free trade.

21   *greediness* The possessiveness of a single proprietor.

## The Dream

Dear love, for nothing less than thee
Would I have broke this happy dream.
    It was a theme
For reason, much too strong for fantasy.
    Therefore thou wakedst me wisely; yet                              5
My dream thou brok'st not, but continuedst it.

Thou art so truth that thoughts of thee suffice
To make dreams truths and fables histories.
Enter these arms. For since thou thoughtst it best
Not to dream all my dream, let's do the rest. 10

     As lightning or a taper's light,
       Thine eyes, and not thy noise, waked me;
          Yet I thought thee
(For thou lov'st truth) but an angel at first sight.
       But when I saw thou sawst my heart 15
And knewst my thoughts, beyond an angel's art,
When thou knewst what I dreamt, when thou knewst when
Excess of joy would wake me, and cam'st then,
I do confess it could not choose but be
Profane to think thee anything but thee. 20

     Coming and staying showed thee thee;
       But rising makes me doubt that now
          Thou art not thou.
That love is weak where fear's as strong as he;
       Tis not all spirit, pure and brave, 25
If mixture it of fear, shame, honor have.
Perchance, as torches which must ready be
Men light and put out, so thou dealst with me:
Thou cam'st to kindle, goest to come. Then I
Will dream that hope again, but else would die. 30

7 *truth* The reading of the 1633 edition and some manuscripts; many manuscripts read "true." The use of "so" with a noun in this way is extraordinary.

8 *truths* A few manuscripts read "truth" or "true."

10 *do* A commonly used verb for sexual intercourse (as in "Love's Growth" l. 14, above); the 1633 edition and a few manuscripts read "act."

11 *taper* candle.

14 *but* Omitted in the 1633 edition and most manuscripts.

16 *beyond an angel's art* Scholastic philosophers disputed as to whether angels could read human thoughts; Donne's position here is that of Thomas Aquinas.

19 *do* The 1633 edition reads "must." *it* Some manuscripts read "I."

22 *doubt* suspect.

27 *torches which must ready be* Torches which will be needed on a particular occasion can be primed by being lit and then snuffed, to disperse any latent moisture.

29 *Then* A few manuscripts read "Thus."

# The Flea

     Mark but this flea, and mark in this
How little that which thou denyst me is.
     Me it sucked first, and now sucks thee,
And in this flea our two bloods mingled be.
     Confess it, this cannot be said 5
A sin or shame or loss of maidenhead.
     Yet this enjoys before it woo,
And, pampered, swells with one blood made of two;
And this, alas, is more than we would do.

     O stay, three lives in one flea spare, 10
Where we almost, nay, more than married are.

Flea-poems are a well-established sixteenth-century genre, in which the man observes a flea on the woman's body and envies its good fortune; Donne's development of the conceit is unique.

This flea is you and I, and this
Our marriage bed and marriage temple is.
  Though parents grudge, and you, we're met
And cloistered in these living walls of jet. 15
  Though use make thee apt to kill me,
Let not to this self-murder added be,
And sacrilege: three sins in killing three.

  Cruel and sudden, hast thou since
Purpled thy nail in blood of innocence? 20
  In what could this flea guilty be,
Except in that drop which it sucked from thee?
  Yet thou triumphst, and sayst that thou
Findst not thyself, nor me, the weaker now.
  'Tis true. Then learn how false fears be: 25
Just so much honor, when thou yieldst to me,
Will waste as this flea's death took life from thee.

16  *use* habit.  *apt to kill me* Petrarchan convention often casts the woman's refusal of her would-be lover as an act of homicide.

18  *sacrilege* Because the flea is a temple.

19  *since* since stanza 2.

## A Nocturnal upon St. Lucy's Day, Being the Shortest Day

'Tis the year's midnight, and it is the day's:
Lucy's, who scarce seven hours herself unmasks.
  The sun is spent, and now his flasks
  Send forth light squibs, no constant rays.
    The world's whole sap is sunk; 5
The general balm the hydroptic earth hath drunk
Whither, as to the bed's feet, life is shrunk,
Dead and interred. Yet all these seem to laugh,
Compared with me, who am their epitaph.

Study me, then, you who shall lovers be 10
At the next world, that is, at the next spring;
  For I am every dead thing,
  In whom Love wrought new alchemy.
    For his art did express
A quintessence even from nothingness, 15
From dull privations and lean emptiness.

It is commonly assumed that this poem concerns Donne's wife; she was seriously ill in 1611 and died in 1617, and either of those occasions could have prompted it. The argument has also been made that the poem was occasioned by a serious illness of the Countess of Bedford in 1612 (see on "Twickenham Garden," above).

*St. Lucy's Day* 13 December; under the Julian calendar, the winter solstice was 12 December. The martyrdom of St. Lucy of Syracuse involved the gouging out of her eyes, and she is the patron saint of the blind; her proper name is derived from the Latin word for light.

3  *his flasks* The stars, which in one theory stored up light from the sun; "flasks" here are powder-horns.

4  *squibs* small fireworks.

6  *hydroptic* Afflicted with dropsy; insatiably thirsty. A favored word with Donne; see "The Perfume" l. 6, above.

7  *the bed's feet* the foot of the bed.

14  *express* extract.

15  *quintessence* The refined essence, purified beyond the four ordinary elements, that was the object of alchemical extraction; the speaker defines his desolation as a hyperbolic refinement of something that begins as non-existence. The repeated point is that he is not, as he has it in l. 35, "an ordinary nothing."

He ruined me, and I am rebegot
Of absence, darkness, death: things which are not.

All others from all things draw all that's good,
Life, soul, form, spirit, whence they being have.          20
   I, by Love's limbeck, am the grave
    Of all that's nothing. Oft a flood
      Have we two wept, and so
Drowned the whole world, us two. Oft did we grow
To be two chaoses when we did show                         25
Care to ought else, and often absences
Withdrew our souls and made us carcasses.

But I am by her death (which word wrongs her)
Of the first nothing the elixir grown.
   Were I a man, that I were one                     30
    I needs must know; I should prefer,
      If I were any beast,
Some ends, some means. Yea plants, yea stones detest
And love. All, all some properties invest.
If I an ordinary nothing were,                             35
As shadow, a light and body must be here.

But I am none, nor will my sun renew.
You lovers, for whose sake the lesser sun
   At this time to the Goat is run
    To fetch new lust and give it you,               40
      Enjoy your summer all.
Since she enjoys her long night's festival,
Let me prepare towards her, and let me call
This hour her Vigil and her Eve, since this
Both the year's and the day's deep midnight is.           45

21 *limbeck* alembic (used in alchemical work).
29 *the first nothing* The non-existence which preceded God's creation of the universe. *elixir* quintessence.
34 *some properties invest* have some distinguishing characteristics.
36 *As* such as. *shadow* A commonly used term to invoke insubstantiality; the point here is that a shadow implies the existence of light and a solid body to cast that shadow.
39 *the Goat* Capricorn, which the sun entered on 12 December in the Julian calendar. The goat is a traditional figure for lust.
44 *Vigil* service on the night before a festival.

## The Bait

Come live with me and be my love,
And we will some new pleasures prove
Of golden sands and crystal brooks
With silken lines and silver hooks.

See Marlowe and Ralegh, "The Passionate Shepherd to his Love" and "The Nymph's Reply." Isaak Walton, who quotes Donne's poem in *The Complete Angler* (1633), says that Donne wrote it "to show the world that he could make soft and smooth verses when he thought them fit and worth his labor." There is a musical setting for the poem in William Corkine's *Second Book of Airs* (1612).

2 *prove* experience.

There will the river whispering run,                                5
Warmed by thine eyes more than the sun;
And there the enamored fish will stay,
Begging themselves they may betray.

When thou wilt swim in that live bath,
Each fish which every channel hath                                  10
Will amorously to thee swim,
Gladder to catch thee than thou him.

If thou to be so seen be'est loath
By sun or moon, thou darkenest both;
And if my heart have leave to see,                                  15
I need not their light, having thee.

Let others freeze with angling reeds
And cut their legs with shells and weeds,
Or treacherously poor fish beset
With strangling snare or windowy net.                               20

Let coarse bold hands from slimy nest
The bedded fish in banks outwrest,
Or curious traitors, sleave-silk flies,
Bewitch poor fish's wandering eyes.

For thee, thou needst no such deceit,                               25
For thou thyself art thine own bait.
That fish that is not catched thereby,
Alas, is wiser far than I.

8  Begging that they may betray themselves.
15  *my heart* The reading of two manuscripts; the 1633
edition and most manuscripts read "myself."

23  *sleave-silk* Silk that can be "sleaved," i.e., separated into
its component filaments for fine embroidery.

# The Apparition

When, by thy scorn, O murderess, I am dead,
        And that thou thinkst thee free
From all solicitation from me,
Then shall my ghost come to thy bed
And thee, feigned vestal, in worse arms shall see.                  5
Then thy sick taper will begin to wink,
And he whose thou art then, being tired before,
Will, if thou stir or pinch to wake him, think
        Thou callst for more
And in false sleep will from thee shrink.                           10
And then, poor aspen wretch, neglected thou

1  *dead* A commonplace in Petrarchan love poetry is that the
woman's refusal to return the man's love is a threat to his life;
the threat is sometimes imagined to be deliberate.
5  *vestal* Vestal virgin, one of the attendants of the shrine
of the virgin goddess Vesta in classical Rome, for whom
unchastity was a capital offense.

6  *taper* candle.  *wink* flicker (a traditional sign of the pres-
ence of ghosts).
11  *aspen* The leaves of aspens are famous for quivering in
the slightest breeze.

Bathed in a cold quicksilver sweat wilt lie,
    A verier ghost than I.
What I will say, I will not tell thee now,
Lest that preserve thee; and since my love is spent,           15
I had rather thou shouldst painfully repent
Than by my threatenings rest still innocent.

12 *quicksilver* A metaphor for shining beads of sweat, with a glance both at the toxicity of mercury and its use in the treatment of syphilis.

13 *verier* truer.

14 *What I will say* Something sufficiently terrifying that, were he to say it now, it would move her not to commit the crime of murder anticipated in the first line.

## A Valediction: Forbidding Mourning

As virtuous men pass mildly away
And whisper to their souls to go,
Whilst some of their sad friends do say,
The breath goes now, and some say, No,

So let us melt and make no noise,           5
No tear-floods nor sigh-tempests move;
Twere profanation of our joys
To tell the laity our love.

Moving of the earth brings harms and fears,
Men reckon what it did and meant;           10
But trepidation of the spheres,
Though greater far, is innocent.

Dull sublunary lovers' love
(Whose soul is sense) cannot admit
Absence, because it doth remove           15
Those things which elemented it;

But we, by a love so much refined
That ourselves know not what it is,
Interassurèd of the mind,
Care less eyes, lips, and hands to miss.           20

Our two souls, therefore, which are one,
Though I must go, endure not yet
A breach, but an expansion,
Like gold to airy thinness beat.

Quoted by Isaak Walton in the fourth edition of his life of Donne (1675), with the claim that the poem was given by Donne to his wife before a trip to France in 1611; that claim is uncorroborated and has been doubted.

6 *move* stir up.

11 *trepidation of the spheres* An irregular movement of the eighth or ninth celestial sphere, postulated in the medieval version of Ptolemaic astronomy to account for precession of the equinoxes and other phenomena now known to be caused by movement of the earth's axis.

12 *innocent* In the etymological sense of "causing no harm," unlike earthquakes.

13 *sublunary* Living below the sphere of the moon, i.e., earthly.

19 *Interassurèd* See on "The Ecstasy," l. 42, below; the word is likely Donne's own formation.

24 *gold to airy thinness beat* As in the creation of gold leaf; an ounce of gold can yield leaf that covers 250 square feet.

If they be two, they are two so                                        25
As stiff twin compasses are two.
Thy soul, the fixed foot, makes no show
To move, but doth if the other do;

And though it in the center sit,
Yet when the other far doth roam,                                      30
It leans and harkens after it,
And grows erect as that comes home.

Such wilt thou be to me, who must
Like the other foot obliquely run;
Thy firmness draws my circle just,                                     35
And makes me end where I begun.

**26** *compasses* A simile probably prompted by a madrigal by Giambattista Guarini ("son simile al compasso"), though a closer parallel occurs in Omar Khayyám. The transition from the previous stanza may owe something to the fact that the alchemical symbol for gold is a circle with a dot in the center. Donne's development of the simile has been much discussed; it combines two different movements: the drawing of a circle, in which one foot traces a circle while the other turns about a stationary point (ll. 27–8, 33–6), and the spreading out and closing together of the two legs before and after (ll. 29–32). The confusion may a deliberate part of the drama of the poem.

**34** *obliquely* in a curved path.

**35** *draws* The attractive reading of a few manuscripts; the 1633 edition and most manuscripts read "makes."

# The Ecstasy

Where, like a pillow on a bed,
A pregnant bank swelled up to rest
The violet's reclining head,
Sat we two, one another's best.

Our hands were firmly cemented                                         5
With a fast balm which thence did spring;
Our eye-beams twisted, and did thread
Our eyes upon one double string.

So to intergraft our hands as yet
Was all the means to make us one,                                      10
And pictures in our eyes to get
Was all our propagation.

As twixt two equal armies fate
Suspends uncertain victory,
Our souls (which to advance their state                               15
Were gone out) hung twixt her and me.

And whilst our souls negotiate there,
We like sepulchral statues lay;
All day the same our postures were,
And we said nothing all the day.                                       20

*Ecstasy* In the root sense of "standing outside," i.e., an out-of-body experience.

**7** *eye-beams* Beams which the eye was thought to send out in search of the objects of sight.

**11–12** The reflection of another person's face in one's eye at close range was known as "making babies."

If any, so by love refined
That he soul's language understood
And by good love were grown all mind,
Within convenient distance stood,

He (though he knows not which soul spake,    25
Because both meant, both spake the same)
Might thence a new concoction take,
And part far purer than he came.

This ecstasy doth unperplex
(We said) and tell us what we love.    30
We see by this it was not sex;
We see we saw not what did move.

But as all several souls contain
Mixture of things, they know not what,
Love these mixed souls doth mix again,    35
And makes both one, each this and that.

A single violet transplant,
The strength, the color, and the size
(All which before was poor and scant)
Redoubles still, and multiplies.    40

When love with one another so
Interinanimates two souls,
That abler soul which thence doth flow
Defects of loneliness controls.

We then, who are this new soul, know    45
Of what we are composed and made,
For the atomies of which we grow
Are souls, whom no change can invade.

But O, alas, so long, so far
Our bodies why do we forbear?    50
They are ours, though they are not we; we are
The intelligences, they the sphere.

We owe them thanks because they thus
Did us to us at first convey,

---

**31** *sex* Sexual differentiation, i.e., the fact that I am male and you female, though Donne's usage here comes very close to the casual modern sense, and is the earliest such usage to be identified.

**37** *transplant* Probably to be read as a verb, with the rest of the stanza understood as the consequence of that action. Contemporary texts refer to the ability of transplantation to make single flowers bloom double in their new environment, and that may be the phenomenon to which Donne is referring.

**42** *interinanimates* The reading of most manuscripts; the 1633 edition reads "interanimates." Donne is particularly fond of "inter-" combinations (e.g., "intergraft" in l. 9 here, or "interassurèd" in "A Valediction: Forbidding Mourning," l. 19, above), and the verb here is likely his own formation.

**50** *forbear* forgo.

**51–2** Our souls in our bodies are like the angelic intelligences of medieval cosmology, inhabiting and controlling the nine celestial spheres. Donne uses the same metaphor in "Air and Angels" (l. 25) for the relation between male and female love.

Yielded their forces, sense, to us,                                    55
Nor are dross to us, but allay.

On man heaven's influence works not so
But that it first imprints the air;
So soul into the soul may flow,
Though it to body first repair.                                        60

As our blood labors to beget
Spirits as like souls as it can,
Because such fingers need to knit
That subtle knot which makes us man,

So must pure lovers' souls descend                                     65
To affections and to faculties
Which sense may reach and apprehend,
Else a great prince in prison lies.

To our bodies turn we then, that so
Weak men on love revealed may look;                                    70
Love's mysteries in souls do grow,
But yet the body is his book.

And if some lover such as we
Have heard this dialogue of one,
Let him still mark us, he shall see                                     75
Small change when we are to bodies gone.

---

55  *forces, sense* The reading of most manuscripts; as punctuated here, the line would mean "yielded to us their forces, i.e., sense, as opposed to the mental forces of the soul." The 1633 edition reads "senses force"; other manuscripts read "forces, since" or "forces first."

56  *allay* alloy. Our bodies are not a useless by-product, but something that, when mixed with our souls, makes those souls stronger and more durable.

57–8  An astrological reference: in influencing human life, the stars first must make their mark on the air.

59  *So* The 1633 edition reads "for."

62  *Spirits* The term is being used here as in Renaissance physiological theory, for a substance that works in human blood to mediate between soul and body; see, for instance, Robert Burton, *The Anatomy of Melancholy* 1.1.2.2.

69  *turn* return.

76  *to bodies gone* One manuscript reads "to bodies grown," another "two bodies grown."

# Love's Deity

I long to talk with some old lover's ghost
Who died before the God of Love was born.
I cannot think that he who then loved most
Sunk so low as to love one which did scorn.
But since this god produced a destiny,                                 5
And that vice-nature, custom, lets it be,
     I must love her that loves not me.

Sure, they which made him god meant not so much,
Nor he in his young godhead practiced it;
But when an even flame two hearts did touch,                           10

---

9  *in his young godhead* during his early years as a god.          10  *even* equal.

His office was indulgently to fit
Actives to passives. Correspondency
Only his subject was: it cannot be
  Love till I love her that loves me.

But every modern god will now extend     15
His vast prerogative as far as Jove.
To rage, to lust, to write to, to commend,
All is the purlieu of the God of Love.
O, were we wakened by this tyranny
To ungod this child again, it could not be    20
  I should love her who loves not me.

Rebel, and atheist too, why murmur I
As though I felt the worst that love could do?
Love might make me leave loving, or might try
A deeper plague: to make her love me, too –   25
Which, since she loves before, I am loath to see.
Falsehood is worse than hate, and that must be
  If she whom I love should love me.

12 *Correspondency* reciprocity.      26 *loves before* already loves someone else.
17 The conventional activities of lovers tormented by
unreciprocated desire.

# Love's Diet

To what a cumbersome unwieldiness
And burdenous corpulence my love had grown
  But that I did, to make it less
  And keep it in proportion,
Give it a diet, made it feed upon      5
That which love worst endures, *discretion*.

Above one sigh a day I allowed him not,
Of which my fortune and my faults had part;
  And if sometimes by stealth he got
  A she-sigh from my mistress' heart
And thought to feast on that, I let him see   10
'Twas neither very sound, nor meant to me.

If he wrung from me a tear, I brined it so
With scorn or shame that him it nourished not.
  If he sucked hers, I let him know    15
  'Twas not a tear which he had got;
His drink was counterfeit as was his meat,
For eyes which roll towards all weep not, but sweat.

Whatever he would dictate, I writ that,
But burnt my letters. When she writ to me   20

8 In which allowance I included sighs for my own bad luck  17 *meat* The sighs of the previous stanza.
and personal failings.

And that that favor made him fat,
        I said, If any title be
Conveyed by this, ah, what doth it avail
To be the fortieth name in an entail?

Thus I reclaimed my buzzard love, to fly                    25
At what and when and how and where I choose;
        Now negligent of sport I lie
        And now as other falconers use,
I spring a mistress, swear, write, sigh, and weep,
And, the game killed or lost, go talk, and sleep.          30

---

24   *the fortieth name in an entail* the person who inherits a property if thirty-nine others die first.

25   *reclaimed* called back (a term from falconry).   *buzzard* An undistinguished variety of hawk, and slang insult for a greedy but slow-witted person.

29   *spring* rouse from hiding (as in hunting birds).

## The Funeral

Whoever comes to shroud me, do not harm
        Nor question much
That subtle wreath of hair which crowns my arm.
The mystery, the sign, you must not touch,
        For tis my outward soul,                            5
Viceroy to that which, unto heaven being gone,
        Will leave this to control
And keep these limbs, her provinces, from dissolution.

For if the sinewy thread my brain lets fall
        Through every part                                  10
Can tie those parts and make me one of all,
These hairs, which upward grew, and strength and art
        Have from a better brain,
Can better do it – except she meant that I
        By this should know my pain,                        15
As prisoners are manacled when they're condemned to die.

Whate'er she meant by it, bury it with me,
        For since I am
Love's martyr, it might breed idolatry
If into others' hands these relics came.                    20
        As twas humility
To afford to it all that a soul can do,
        So tis some bravery
That, since you would have none of me, I bury some of you.

---

9   *the sinewy thread my brain lets fall* the nervous system.

14   *except* unless.

19   *Love's martyr* The speaker will die for his idolatrous love of the woman in question (who gives him a lock of her hair but still refuses him); the Petrarchan context is not made explicit until late in the poem.

23   *bravery* bravado.

24   *have* The reading of the 1633 edition and some manuscripts; other manuscripts read "save."

# The Blossom

Little thinkst thou, poor flower,
 Whom I have watched six or seven days,
And seen thy birth, and seen what every hour
Gave to thy growth, thee to this height to raise,
And now dost laugh and triumph on this bough:      5
  Little thinkst thou
That it will freeze anon, and that I shall
Tomorrow find thee fallen, or not at all.

Little thinkst thou, poor heart
 That laborst yet to nestle thee          10
And thinkst by hovering here to get a part
In a forbidden or forbidding tree,
And hop'st her stiffness by long siege to bow:
  Little thinkst thou
That thou tomorrow, ere that sun doth wake,      15
Must with this sun and me a journey take.

But thou, which lov'st to be
 Subtle to plague thyself, wilt say,
Alas, if you must go, what's that to me?
Here lies my business, and here I will stay.       20
You go to friends whose love and means present
  Various content
To your eyes, ears, and tongue, and every part.
If then your body go, what need you a heart?

Well then, stay here; but know,         25
 When thou hast stayed and done thy most,
A naked thinking heart that makes no show
Is to a woman but a kind of ghost.
How shall she know my heart, or, having none,
  Know thee for one?          30
Practice may make her know some other part;
But, take my word, she doth not know a heart.

Meet me at London, then,
 Twenty days hence, and thou shalt see
Me fresher and more fat by being with men       35
Than if I had stayed still with her and thee.
For God's sake, if you can, be you so, too.
  I would give you
There to another friend, whom we shall find
As glad to have my body as my mind.        40

---

**12** *forbidden or forbidding* The first adjective implies that the love that the heart longs for is illicit (presumably because the woman is married), the second that she is actively resisting.
**15** *that sun* The woman who is rejecting the speaker's courtship.

**22** *content* contentment.
**23** *tongue* The reading of almost all manuscripts; the 1633 edition has "taste."
**38** *would* The 1633 edition reads "will."

# The Relic

When my grave is broke up again
Some second guest to entertain
(For graves have learned that womanhead,
To be to more than one a bed),
        And he that digs it spies                5
A bracelet of bright hair about the bone,
        Will he not let us alone
And think that there a loving couple lies,
Who hoped that this device might be a way
To make their souls, at the last busy day,         10
Meet at this grave, and make a little stay?

If this fall in a time or land
Where misdevotion doth command,
Then he that digs us up will bring
Us to the Bishop and the King               15
        To make us relics; then
Thou shalt be a Mary Magdalen, and I
        A something else thereby.
All women shall adore us, and some men;
And, since at such times miracles are sought,       20
I would have that age by this paper taught
What miracles we harmless lovers wrought.

First, we loved well and faithfully,
Yet knew not what we loved, nor why;
Difference of sex no more we knew           25
Than our guardian angels do.
        Coming and going, we
Perchance might kiss, but not between those meals;
        Our hands ne'er touched the seals
Which Nature, injured by late law, sets free.       30
These miracles we did, but now, alas,
All measure and all language I should pass
Should I tell what a miracle she was.

---

3 *womanhead* behavior characteristic of women.

9 *hoped* The reading of most manuscripts; the 1633 edition reads "thought." *a* The manuscript reading that accompanies "hoped"; the 1633 edition reads "some."

10 *the last busy day* the Resurrection.

13 *misdevotion* From the following lines, it is clear that Donne means Catholicism, whose cultivation of saints and their relics was a major object of Protestant attack.

17 *Mary Magdalen* One of Jesus's inner circle of followers; post-biblical tradition made her a reformed prostitute. The reference has led some to relate the poem to Donne's friendship with Magdalen Herbert (1558–1627), mother of the poet George Herbert.

27 *Coming and going* when greeting each other and when saying goodbye.

30 The phrasing here seems to owe something to Myrrha's defense of incest in Ovid's *Metamorphoses* (10.329–31); it resembles other passages in Donne which celebrate a supposedly golden age of sexual freedom before the advent of restrictive human laws (e.g., "Confined Love," above), though here the lovers' effortless observance of those laws is being celebrated.

# A Lecture upon the Shadow

Stand still, and I will read to thee
A lecture, love, in love's philosophy.
These three hours that we have spent
Walking here, two shadows went
Along with us, which we ourselves produced;                   5
But, now the sun is just above our head,
We do those shadows tread,
And to brave clearness all things are reduced.
So, whilst our infant loves did grow,
Disguises did, and shadows, flow                              10
From us and our care; but now tis not so.

That love hath not attained the highest degree
Which is still diligent lest others see.

Except our loves at this noon stay,
We shall new shadows make the other way.                      15
As the first were made to blind
Others, these which come behind
Will work upon ourselves, and blind our eyes.
If our loves faint, and westwardly decline,
To me thou falsely thine                                      20
And I to thee mine actions shall disguise.
The morning shadows wear away,
But these grow longer all the day;
But O, love's day is short if love decay.

Love is a growing or full constant light,                     25
And his first minute after noon is night.

First printed in 1635.

12  *highest* Several manuscripts read "least"; one reads "last."
26  *first* The 1635 edition reads "short."

# Richard Barnfield (1574–1627)

Born to landed gentry in Shropshire and educated at Oxford, Barnfield gained some entry into the Countess of Pembroke's literary circle and in 1594 published a volume called *The Affectionate Shepherd*, dedicated to Penelope Rich, Philip Sidney's Stella. The title poem is a homoerotic pastoral lament, "The Complaint of Daphnis for the Love of Ganymede." In a new collection called *Cynthia*, published the next year, Barnfield replies to unnamed critics by insisting that he was merely imitating Vergil's second eclogue, but also continues the story, with a twenty-sonnet sequence on the same subject. Most of its themes mirror those of orthodox Petrarchism, though with a sensual lushness that is striking in places; Shakespeare's sonnets to the Young Man are austere in comparison. Barnfield published another volume of poems in 1598, but by 1606 had returned to the country and seems to have abandoned any literary activity.

*Edition*: Richard Barnfield, *The Complete Poems*, ed. George Klawitter (Selinsgrove, PA: Susquehanna University Press, 1990).

## From *Cynthia*

Sweet coral lips where Nature's treasure lies,
The balm of bliss, the sovereign salve of sorrow,
The secret touch of Love's heart-burning arrow,
Come, quench my thirst, or else poor Daphnis dies.
One night I dreamed (alas, twas but a dream)    5
That I did feel the sweetness of the same;
Wherewith inspired, I young again became,
And from my heart a spring of blood did stream.
But when I waked, I found it nothing so,
Save that my limbs (methought) did wax more strong,    10
And I more lusty far, and far more young;
This gift on him rich Nature did bestow.
Then if in dreaming so I so did speed,
What should I do if I did so indeed?

13  *speed* prosper.

Thus was my love, thus was my Ganymede
(Heaven's joy, world's wonder, nature's fairest work,
In whose aspect hope and despair do lurk),
Made of pure blood in whitest snow yshed;
And for sweet Venus only formed his face,    5
And his each member delicately framed,
And last of all fair Ganymede him named,
His limbs (as their creatrix) her embrace.
But as for his pure, spotless, virtuous mind,
Because it sprung of chaste Diana's blood    10
(Goddess of maids, directress of all good),
It wholly is to chastity inclined.
And thus it is: as far as I can prove,
He loves to be beloved, but not to love.

6  *framed* designed.             13  *prove* learn through testing.
10  *Diana* The virgin goddess of the hunt.

Sighing and sadly sitting by my love,
He asked the cause of my heart's sorrowing,
Conjuring me by heaven's eternal king
To tell the cause which me so much did move.
Compelled (quoth I), to thee will I confess 5
Love is the cause, and only love it is
That doth deprive me of my heavenly bliss;
Love is the pain that doth my heart oppress.
And what is she (quoth he) whom thou dost love?
Look in this glass (quoth I), there shalt thou see 10
The perfect form of my felicity.
When, thinking that it would strange magic prove,
He opened it, and taking off the cover,
He straight perceived himself to be my lover.

10   *glass* mirror.

Cherry-lipped Adonis in his snowy shape
Might not compare with his pure ivory white,
On whose fair front a poet's pen may write,
Whose roseate red excels the crimson grape.
His love-enticing delicate soft limbs 5
Are rarely framed to entrap poor gazing eyes;
His cheeks the lily and carnation dyes
With lovely tincture which Apollo's dims.
His lips ripe strawberries in nectar wet,
His mouth a hive, his tongue a honeycomb 10
Where Muses (like bees) make their mansion,
His teeth pure pearl in blushing coral set.
O, how can such a body, sin-procuring,
Be slow to love, and quick to hate, enduring?

3   *front* forehead.
6   *rarely framed* exquisitely designed.

8   *which Apollo's dims* which makes Apollo's complexion look pale.

# John Marston (1576–1634)

The son of a lawyer, Marston attended Oxford and then joined his father at the Middle Temple, where he was intermittently in residence until 1606. In 1598 he published the two volumes of poetry from which the selections here are taken; they proved sufficiently notorious to be among the books called in and burned by episcopal order in 1599. Marston had already turned to playwrighting. His *Histriomastix* was probably first written for performance within the elite circles of the Inns of Court, though as of 1600 he was writing for the public theater, in which he was an important and controversial figure for nearly a decade (he was one of the key figures in the so-called War of the Theaters in 1599–1603). The offense given by *Eastward Ho!*, his collaboration with Ben Jonson and George Chapman, probably landed him in jail in 1605; a brief term of imprisonment in 1608 may have had a similar cause. By now done with the theater, he married the daughter of James I's chaplain, was ordained an Anglican priest, and spent most of the rest of his life as a churchman.

*Edition*: *The Poems of John Marston*, ed. Arnold Davenport (Liverpool: Liverpool University Press, 1961).

## The Metamorphosis of Pygmalion's Image

Marston's neo-Ovidian narrative is perhaps the most lubricious example of the popular genre whose pattern was set by Lodge in *Scylla's Metamorphosis*; the story of the sculptor who falls in love with his own statue is elaborated with a sexual explicitness barely hinted at in Ovid's own telling (*Metamorphoses* 10.243–97). Marston also contributes several layers of aggressive joking. The stoniness of the woman makes her a literalization of one of the dominant tropes of Petrarchan love poetry, and the physical absurdity of Pygmalion's obsession occasions virtuoso satire on the reigning clichés of male desire; but with the miraculous turn in the narrative, the poem celebrates with some gleefulness the very folly it mocks.

1

Pygmalion, whose high, love-hating mind
Disdained to yield servile affection
Or amorous suit to any woman-kind,
Knowing their wants and men's perfection:
Yet Love at length forced him to know his fate,
And love the shade whose substance he did hate.

2

For having wrought in purest ivory
So fair an image of a woman's feature,
That never yet proudest mortality
Could show so rare and beauteous a creature
(Unless my mistress' all-excelling face,
Which gives to beauty beauty's only grace),

3

He was amazèd at the wondrous rareness
Of his own workmanship's perfection.
He thought that Nature ne'er produced such fairness
In which all beauties have their mansion,
And thus admiring, was enamorèd
Of that fair image himself portrayèd.

1.4  *wants* deficiencies.

4

And naked as it stood before his eyes,
Imperious Love declares his deity.
O what alluring beauties he descries
In each part of his fair imagery!
Her nakedness each beauteous shape contains;
All beauty in her nakedness remains.

5

He thought he saw the blood run through the vein
And leap and swell with all alluring means,
Then fears he is deceived, and then again
He thinks he see'th the brightness of the beams
Which shoot from out the fairness of her eye:
At which he stands as in an ecstasy.

6

Her amber-colorèd, her shining hair
Makes him protest the sun hath spread her head
With golden beams to make her far more fair.
But when her cheeks his amorous thoughts have fed,
Then he exclaims, Such red and so pure white
Did never bless the eye of mortal sight.

7

Then views her lips: no lips did seem so fair
In his conceit, through which he thinks doth fly
So sweet a breath that doth perfume the air.
Then next her dimpled chin he doth descry,
And views, and wonders, and yet views her still.
Love's eyes in viewing never have their fill.

8

Her breasts like polished ivory appear,
Whose modest mount do bless admiring eye
And makes him wish for such a pillowbere.
Thus fond Pygmalion striveth to descry
Each beauteous part, not letting overslip
One parcel of his curious workmanship,

9

Until his eye descended so far down
That it descrièd Love's pavilion,
Where Cupid doth enjoy his only crown,
And Venus hath her chiefest mansion.
There would he wink, and winking look again;
Both eyes and thoughts would gladly there remain.

10

Whoever saw the subtle city dame
In sacred church, when her pure thoughts should pray,
Peer through her fingers, so to hide her shame,

4.4  *imagery* replica (pronounced with four syllables).    8.5  *overslip* escape.
8.3  *pillowbere* pillowcase.

When that her eye her mind would fain bewray:
So would he view, and wink, and view again;
A chaster thought could not his eyes retain.

## 11

He wondered that she blushed not when his eye
Saluted those same parts of secrecy,
Conceiting not it was imagery
That kindly yielded that large liberty.
O that my mistress were an image too,
That I might blameless her perfections view!

## 12

But when the fair proportion of her thigh
Began appear, O Ovid, would he cry,
Did e'er Corinna show such ivory
When she appeared in Venus' livery?
And thus enamored, dotes on his own art,
Which he did work to work his pleasing smart.

## 13

And fondly doting, oft he kissed her lip.
Oft would he dally with her ivory breasts.
No wanton love-trick would he overslip,
But still observed all amorous behests
Whereby he thought he might procure the love
Of his dull image, which no plaints could move.

## 14

Look how the peevish papists crouch and kneel
At some dumb idol with their offering,
As if a senseless carvèd stone could feel
The ardor of his bootless chattering;
So fond he was, and earnest in his suit
To his remorseless image, dumb and mute.

## 15

He oft doth wish his soul might part in sunder
So that one half in her had residence.
Oft he exclaims, O Beauty's only wonder,
Sweet model of delight, fair excellence,
Be gracious unto him that formèd thee;
Compassionate his true love's ardency.

## 16

She, with her silence, seems to grant his suit.
Then he, all jocund like a wanton lover,
With amorous embracements doth salute
Her slender waist, presuming to discover
The vale of Love, where Cupid doth delight
To sport and dally all the sable night.

10.4   *bewray* divulge.
11.3–4   Not realizing that it was an image of a woman, rather than a real woman, that was kind enough to allow such liberty.
12.6   *pleasing smart* enjoyable pain.
13.3   *overslip* omit.
15.6   *Compassionate* have compassion for.

17

His eyes her eyes kindly encounterèd;
His breast her breast oft joinèd close unto;
His arms' embracements oft she sufferèd;
Hands, arms, eyes, tongue, lips, and all parts did woo.
His thigh with hers, his knee played with her knee:
A happy consort when all parts agree.

18

But when he saw, poor soul, he was deceived
(Yet scarce he could believe his sense had failed),
Yet when he found all hope from him bereaved,
And saw how fondly all his thoughts had erred,
Then did he like to poor Ixion seem,
That clipped a cloud instead of heaven's queen.

19

I oft have smiled to see the foolery
Of some sweet youths, who seriously protest
That Love respects not actual luxury,
But only joys to dally, sport, and jest.
Love is a child, contented with a toy;
A busk-point or some favor stills the boy.

20

Mark my Pygmalion, whose affection's ardor
May be a mirror to posterity;
Yet viewing, touching, kissing (common favor)
Could never satiate his love's ardency.
And therefore, ladies, think that they ne'er love you
Who do not unto more than kissing move you.

21

For my Pygmalion kissed, viewed, and embraced,
And yet exclaims, Why were these women made,
O sacred gods, and with such beauties graced?
Have they not power as well to cool and shade
As for to heat men's hearts? Or is there none?
Or are they all like mine, relentless stone?

22

With that he takes her in his loving arms,
And down within a down-bed softly laid her.
Then on his knees he all his senses charms
To invocate sweet Venus for to raise her
To wishèd life, and to infuse some breath
To that which, dead, yet gave a life to death.

23

Thou sacred queen of sportive dallying
(Thus he begins), Love's only emperess,

---

18.5 *Ixion* A mortal who attempted to rape Juno; Jupiter
diverted him with a replica of Juno made of cloud, on which
Ixion engendered the Centaurs.

18.6 *clipped* embraced.

19.3 *actual luxury* full sexual enjoyment.

19.6 *busk-point* the lace tie on a woman's corset.

Whose kingdom rests in wanton revelling,
Let me beseech thee, show thy powerfulness
In changing stone to flesh. Make her relent,
And kindly yield to thy sweet blandishment.

### 24

O gracious gods, take compassion.
Instill into her some celestial fire,
That she may equalize affection,
And have a mutual love, and love's desire.
Thou knowst the force of love; then pity me,
Compassionate my true love's ardency.

### 25

Thus having said, he riseth from the floor,
As if his soul divinèd him good fortune,
Hoping his prayers to pity moved some power.
For all his thoughts did all good luck importune,
And therefore straight he strips him naked quite,
That in the bed he might have more delight.

### 26

Then thus, Sweet sheets, he says, which now do cover
The idol of my soul, the fairest one
That ever loved or had an amorous lover,
Earth's only model of perfection,
Sweet, happy sheets, deign for to take me in,
That I my hopes and longing thoughts may win.

### 27

With that his nimble limbs do kiss the sheets,
And now he bows him for to lay him down,
And now each part with her fair parts do meet.
Now doth he hope for to enjoy love's crown;
Now do they dally, kiss, embrace together
Like Leda's twins at sight of fairest weather.

### 28

Yet all's conceit, but shadow of that bliss
Which now my Muse strives sweetly to display
In this, my wondrous metamorphosis.
Deign to believe me, now I sadly say
The stony substance of his image feature
Was straight transformed into a living creature.

### 29

For when his hands her fair formed limbs had felt
And that his arms her naked waist embraced,
Each part like wax before the sun did melt;
And now, O now, he finds how he is graced

27.6 *Leda's twins* Castor and Pollux; their constellation,   28.4 *sadly* seriously.
Gemini, represents two linked bodies, and its appearance was
regarded by sailors as a forecast of good weather.

By his own work. Tut, women will relent
Whenas they find such moving blandishment.

### 30

Do but conceive a mother's passing gladness,
After that death her only son hath seized
And overwhelmed her soul with endless sadness,
When that she sees him gin for to be raised
From out his deadly swoon to life again:
Such joy Pygmalion feels in every vein.

### 31

And yet he fears he doth but dreaming find
So rich content and such celestial bliss.
Yet when he proves and finds her wondrous kind,
Yielding soft touch for touch, sweet kiss for kiss,
He's well assured no fair imagery
Could yield such pleasing, love's felicity.

### 32

O wonder not to hear me thus relate
And say to flesh transformèd was a stone!
Had I my love in such a wishèd state
As was afforded to Pygmalion,
Though flinty hard, of her you soon should see
As strange a transformation wrought by me.

### 33

And now methinks some wanton, itching ear
With lustful thoughts and ill attention
Lists to my Muse, expecting for to hear
The amorous description of that action
Which Venus seeks and ever doth require
When fitness grants a place to please desire.

### 34

Let him conceit but what himself would do
When that he had obtainèd such a favor
Of her to whom his thoughts were bound unto,
If she, in recompense of his love's labor,
Would deign to let one pair of sheets contain
The willing bodies of those loving twain.

### 35

Could he, O could he, when that each to either
Did yield kind kissing, and more kind embracing,
Could he, when that they felt and clipped together
And might enjoy the life of dallying,
Could he abstain midst such a wanton sporting
From doing that which is not fit reporting?

30.1  *passing* surpassing.                      31.3  *proves* tests.
31.2  *content* contentment.                    34.1  *conceit* imagine.

### 36

What would he do when that her softest skin
Saluted his with a delightful kiss,
When all things fit for love's sweet pleasuring
Invited him to reap a lover's bliss?
What he would do, the self same action
Was not neglected by Pygmalion.

### 37

For when he found that life had took his seat
Within the breast of his kind, beauteous love,
When that he found that warmth and wishèd heat
Which might a saint and coldest spirit move,
Then arms, eyes, hands, tongue, lips, and wanton thigh
Were willing agents in love's luxury.

### 38

Who knows not what ensues? O pardon me,
Ye gaping ears that swallow up my lines.
Expect no more. Peace, idle Poesy;
Be not obscene, though wanton in thy rhymes.
And chaster thoughts, pardon if I do trip,
Or if some loose lines from my pen do slip.

### 39

Let this suffice, that that same happy night,
So gracious were the gods of marriage,
Midst all their pleasing and long wished delight
Paphos was got: of whom in after age
Cyprus was Paphos called, and evermore
Those islanders do Venus' name adore.

38.1   Cf. Ovid, *Amores* 1.5.25: "caetera quis nescit?"

39.5   *Paphos* In turn the mother of Cinyras, founder of the city of Paphos, site of a famous temple of Aphrodite.

## From *The Scourge of Villainy*

*The Scourge of Villainy* is one of several collections of verse satires to appear in the 1590s; their popularity was sufficiently troublesome to provoke an official ban on the genre in 1599. Verse satire in the Renaissance looks to distinguished classical precedents – Horace, Persius, Juvenal – but adds a new level of roughness and unguarded spite; a false etymology that derived "satire" from "satyr" was often cited to justify the genre's general shamelessness and a frequent sense that the satirist is cheerfully guilty of the same vices that he attacks. The satire given here begins with Marston's indignant response to understandable complaints about the lasciviousness of his *Pygmalion*, and returns the favor with an extended denunciation of the erotic and other crimes of an array of fellow poets. The targets are given code names, but were almost certainly specific and meant to be recognized; except in the case of Curio (who from evidence elsewhere appears to be Sir John Davies), modern decoding has been incomplete and indecisive. The depiction of the Elizabethan literary world is nevertheless vivid: combat without quarter, righteous and scabrous at the same time, culminating in the giddy egotism of the poem's last lines. In a second edition in 1599, Marston made that final note even clearer, with a new dedication of the entire volume "to his most esteemed and best beloved self."

# Satire VI: Hem nosti'n

Curio, knowst me? Why, thou bottle-ale,
Thou barmy froth, O stay me, lest I rail
Beyond *Nil ultra*, to see this butterfly,
This windy bubble, task my balladry
With senseless censure! Curio, knowst my sprite,                    5
Yet deemst that in sad seriousness I write
Such nasty stuff as is *Pygmalion*,
Such maggot-tainted, lewd corruption?
　Ha! now he glavers with his fawning snout,
And swears he thought I meant but faintly flout          10
My fine smug rhyme. O barbarous, dropsy noll!
Thinkst thou that Genius that attends my soul
And guides my fist to scourge Magnificoes
Will deign my mind be ranked in Paphian shows?
Thinkst thou that I, which was create to whip          15
Incarnate fiends, will once vouchsafe to trip
A pavan's traverse? Or will lisp *sweet love*
Or pule *Ay me* some female soul to move?
Thinkst thou that I in melting poesy
Will pamper itching sensuality,                    20
That in the body's scum all fatally
Entombs the soul's most sacred faculty?
　Hence, thou misjudging censor! Know I wrote
Those idle rhymes to note the odious spot
And blemish that deforms the lineaments          25
Of modern poesy's habiliments.
O, that the beauties of invention,
For want of judgment's disposition,
Should all be soiled! O, that such treasury,
Such strains of well-conceited poesy,              30
Should molded be in such a shapeless form
That want of art should make such wit a scorn.
　Here's one must invoke some loose-legged dame,
Some brothel drab, to help him stanzas frame,
Or else (alas) his wits can have no vent          35
To broach conceit's industrious intent.
Another yet dares tremblingly come out,
But first he must invoke good *Colin Clout*.
　Yon's one hath yeaned a fearful prodigy,

---

*Hem nosti'n* "Ha! Do you know [me]?" (Latin).
1　*bottle-ale* frothy ale with a low alcohol content.
3　*Nil ultra* "Nothing beyond"; a Latin phrase associated with the straits of Gibraltar, as marking the bounds of the known world.
4　*task* burden.
6　*sad* grave.
9　*glavers* flatters deceitfully.
10–11　The sense is unclear; perhaps: "he swears he thought I was half-hearted just now in scorning my polished little poem."
11　*dropsy noll* head swollen with fluid.
14　*ranked* dressed. *Paphian* having to do with Venus.

17　*pavan's traverse* A movement in a stately form of dancing. The original texts read "Paunis," which makes no obvious sense; deciphering this as "Pauins" = "pavan's" is modern editorial conjecture.
18　*pule* whimper.
32　*scorn* object of scorn.
33　*invocate* invoke.
34　*drab* whore.
38　*Colin Clout* Originally the speaker of a satire of the same name by John Skelton; later adopted as a literary persona by Edmund Spenser in *The Shepherd's Calendar* and elsewhere. The reference here is to contemporary poets who feel they must begin their work with some salute to Spenser.
39　*yeaned* given birth to (usually used of sheep).

Some monstrous, misshapen balladry.                                    40
His guts are in his brains, huge jobbernowl,
Right gurnet's-head, the rest without all soul.
Another walks, is lazy, lies him down,
Thinks, reads, at length some wonted sleep doth crown
His new-fallen lids, dreams, straight, ten pound to one,                45
Out steps some fairy with quick motion
And tells him wonders of some flowery vale,
Awakes, straight rubs his eyes, and prints his tale.
   Yon's one whose strains have flown so high a pitch
That straight he flags, and tumbles in a ditch.                        50
His sprightly, hot, high-soaring poesy
Is like that dreamèd-of imagery
Whose head was gold, breast silver, brassy thigh,
Lead legs, clay feet: O fair framed poesy!
   Here's one, to get an undeserved repute                   55
Of deep, deep learning, all in fustian suit
Of ill-placed, far-fetched words attireth
His period that all sense forsweareth.
   Another makes old Homer Spenser cite,
Like my Pygmalion, where with rare delight                             60
He cries *O Ovid*. This caused my idle quill
The world's dull ears with such lewd stuff to fill
And gull with bumbast lines the witless sense
Of these odd nags, whose pate's circumference
Is filled with froth! O these same buzzing gnats                       65
That sting my sleeping brows, these Nilus rats,
Half dung, that have their life from putrid slime,
These that do praise my loose, lascivious rhyme:
For these same shades, I seriously protest
I slubbered up that chaos indigest                                     70
To fish for fools that stalk in goodly shape:
What though in velvet cloak, yet still an ape.
Capro reads, swears, scrubs, and swears again,
Now, by my soul, an admirable strain;
Strokes up his hair, cries, Passing, passing good.                     75
O, there's a line incends his lustful blood!
   Then Muto comes, with his new glass-set face,
And with his late-kissed hand my book doth grace,
Straight reads, then smiles, and lisps, Tis pretty good,
And praises that he never understood.                                  80
But room for Flaccus, he'll my satires read.
O how I trembled straight with inward dread!
But when I saw him read my fustian,

---

41   *jobbernowl* blockhead.

42   *gurnet* gurnard, a fish notable for its outsized head.

52   *imagery* image (pronounced as four syllables).

56   *fustian* A term used both for a coarse cotton-linen fabric and for bombastic rhetoric.

57   *ill-placed* The second edition changes this to "ill-paced."

58   *period* sentence.

59   Another makes old Homer cite Spenser.

60   *rare* The second edition reads "rage," i.e., "raging."

63   *bumbast* bombastic; the term refers both to cotton padding and to exaggerated rhetoric.

66   *Nilus rats* rats from the Nile, which was said to breed new life directly out of its mud.

70   *slubbered up* put together hastily. *indigest* indigested.

76   *incends* inflames.

77   *glass-set face* with an expression rehearsed in front of a mirror.

81   *Flaccus* Cognomen of the Roman poet Horace, but also Latin for "flop-eared."

And heard him swear I was a Pythian,
Yet straight recalled, and swears I did but quote                    85
Out of Xylinum to that margent's note,
I could scarce hold and keep myself concealed,
But had well-nigh myself and all revealed.
    Then straight comes Friscus, that neat gentleman,
That new discarded academian,                                       90
Who, for he could cry *Ergo* in the school,
Straightway with his huge judgment dares control
Whatsoe'er he views. That's pretty, pretty good;
That epithet hath not that sprightly blood
Which should enforce it speak; that's Persius' vein,                95
That's Juvenal's, here's Horace's crabb'd strain –
Though he ne'er read one line in Juvenal,
Or in his life his lazy eye let fall
On dusky Persius. O indignity
To my respectless, free-bred poesy!                                 100
   Hence, ye big-buzzing, little-bodied gnats,
Ye tattling echoes, huge-tongued pygmy brats!
I mean to sleep; wake not my slumbering brain
With your malignant, weak, detracting vein.
What though the sacred issue of my soul                             105
I here expose to idiots' control?
What though I bare to lewd opinion,
Lay ope to vulgar profanation
My very Genius? Yet know my poesy
Doth scorn your utmost, rank'st indignity.                          110
My pate was great with child, and here tis eased.
Vex all the world, so that thyself be pleased.

---

84  *Pythian* follower of Apollo, the god of poetry.

85–6  Flaccus has read and misconstrued a marginal note to Satire IV in Marston's *Certain Satires*: "huc usque Xylinum" means "up to this point bombast," and is not an acknowledgment of indebtedness to a non-existent author named Xylinus.

91  *Ergo* The start to the conclusion of a syllogism; the reference is to Friscus's experience in formal academic disputation.

99  *dusky* obscure, hard to understand (hence not to be read with a "lazy eye").

100  *respectless* without deference or indebtedness to others.

110  *rank'st* most rank.

# Anonymous

Those whose kind hearts sweet pity did attaint
With ruthful tears bemoaned my miseries;
Those which had heard my never-ceasing plaint
Or read my woes engraven on the trees
At last did win my lady to consort them                    5
Unto the fountain of my flowing anguish,
Where she, unkind, and they might boldly sport them,
Whilst I meanwhile in sorrow's lap did languish.
Their meaning was that she some tears should shed
Into the well in pity of my pining.                       10
She gave consent, and, putting forth her head,
Did in the well perceive her beauty shining;
Which seeing, she withdrew her head, puffed up with pride,
And would not shed a tear should I have died.

From *The Tears of Fancy* (1593), a sonnet sequence formerly
attributed to Thomas Watson (1557?–1592).

1  *attaint* affect.
5  *consort* accompany.
9  *meaning* intention.

Come away, come, sweet love,
The golden morning breaks.
All the earth, all the air
Of love and pleasure speaks.
Teach thine arms then to embrace,            5
And sweet rosy lips to kiss
And mix our souls in mutual bliss.
Eyes were made for Beauty's grace,
Viewing, ruing love-long pains
Procured by Beauty's rude disdain.            10

Come away, come, sweet love,
The golden morning wastes
While the sun from his sphere
His fiery arrows casts,
Making all the shadows fly,               15
Playing, staying in the grove
To entertain the stealth of love.
Thither, sweet love, let us hie,
Flying, dying in desire,
Winged with sweet hopes and heavenly fire.      20

Come away, come, sweet love,
Do not in vain adorn
Beauty's grace that should rise
Like to the naked morn.
Lilies on the river's side               25

Published with a musical setting in John Dowland, *First Book of Airs* (1597), and on its own in *England's Helicon* (1600). For the text, see Edward Doughtie, *Lyrics from English Airs 1596–1622* (Cambridge, MA: Harvard University Press, 1970).

And fair Cyprian flowers new blown
Desire no beauties but their own.
Ornament is nurse of pride,
Pleasure, measure love's delight.
Haste then, sweet love, our wishèd flight.                    30

26  *Cyprian* belonging to Venus.  *blown* bloomed.

Absence, hear thou my protestation
Against thy strength,
Distance and length.
Do what thou canst for alteration,
For hearts of truest mettle,                    5
Absence doth join and Time doth settle.

Who loves a mistress of such quality,
He soon hath found
Affection's ground
Beyond time, place, and all mortality.                    10
To hearts that cannot vary,
Absence is present, Time doth tarry.

My senses want their outward motions,
Which now within
Reason doth win,                    15
Redoubled in her secret notions,
Like rich men that take pleasure
In hiding, more than handling, treasure.

By Absence this good means I gain
That I can catch her                    20
Where none can watch her,
In some close corner of my brain.
There I embrace and kiss her,
And so I both enjoy and miss her.

Printed with a musical setting in Thomas Morley's *First Book of Airs* (1600), and on its own in *A Poetical Rhapsody* (1602). Formerly attributed to John Donne; there is modest manuscript evidence for attributing it to John Hoskyns (1566–1638). For the text, see *A Poetical Rhapsody 1602– 1621*, ed. Hyder Edward Rollins, 2 vols. (Cambridge, MA: Harvard University Press, 1931–2).

13  *motions* activities.
23  Manuscript versions of this line include: "There I embrace and there kiss her"; "There I embrace her and there kiss her"; "There I embrace and there I kiss her."
24  Manuscripts read "And so enjoy her and so miss her."

# Index of Titles and First Lines